The Discourse with Chinese Characteristics

An CHEN on International Economic Law

中国特色话语
陈安论国际经济法学

陈安 著

第四卷

北京大学出版社
PEKING UNIVERSITY PRESS

简目

第四卷

第五编 国际经济法热点学术问题长、短评 ……………………………… 2055

第1章 改进我国国际法教育的"他山之石"
　　　——欧美之行考察见闻 …………………………………………… 2057

第2章 从难从严训练 成果人才并出 ……………………………………… 2066

第3章 "博士"新解 …………………………………………………………… 2074

第4章 是"棒打鸳鸯"吗？
　　　——就"李爽案件"评《纽约时报》报道兼答美国法学界同行问 …… 2081

第5章 小议对外学术交流的"大忌" ……………………………………… 2111

第6章 向世界展现中国理念 ………………………………………………… 2113

第7章 朝着合作共赢方向发展 推动国际经济法理念变革 …………… 2115

第8章 建构中国特色国际法学理论 ……………………………………… 2117

第9章 "左公柳"、中国魂与新丝路
　　　——"七七事变"七十周年随笔 ………………………………… 2119

第六编 有关陈安学术论著和学术观点的书评等 ……………………… 2125

第1章 《陈安论国际经济法学》书评荟萃 ………………………………… 2127

第2章 《中国的呐喊》书评荟萃 …………………………………………… 2177

第3章 陈安早期论著书评荟萃（1981—2008） ………………………… 2408

第4章 群贤毕至，少长咸集，坐而论道，畅叙旧情 ……………………… 2436

第七编　有关陈安学术活动的报道、函件等 … 2455

第1章　媒体报道 … 2457
第2章　学界来函 … 2475
第3章　陈安学术小传及历年主要论著目录（以倒计年为序）… 2518
第4章　陈安论著、业绩获奖一览（以倒计年为序/2016—1960）… 2525

索引 … 2528

后记 … 2546

目录

第五编 国际经济法热点学术问题长、短评

第1章 改进我国国际法教育的"他山之石"
　　——欧美之行考察见闻 ······ 2057
　一、关于国际法专业人才的培养 ······ 2058
　二、关于国际法资料中心的建立 ······ 2064
　三、关于国际法专业力量的合作 ······ 2065

第2章 从难从严训练 成果人才并出 ······ 2066
　一、实行"大运动量"训练,过法学专业英语关 ······ 2067
　二、多学科交叉渗透,建立合理的知识结构 ······ 2069
　三、理论联系实际,提高实务工作能力 ······ 2070
　四、充分信赖,畀以"重担",严密组织,严格把关 ······ 2071
　五、赋予较大"成才自留权",加速形成"人才生产力" ······ 2072

第3章 "博士"新解 ······ 2074
　附录一 官员与老板:心仪博士帽 ······ 2076
　附录二 "教授"贬值为哪般 ······ 2077
　附录三 该挤挤"学术泡沫"了 ······ 2079

第4章 是"棒打鸳鸯"吗?
　　——就"李爽案件"评《纽约时报》报道兼答美国法学界同行问 ······ 2081
　一、李爽是何许人?"李爽案件"的背景如何? ······ 2082
　二、李爽触犯了什么法律?犯了什么罪? ······ 2084
　三、是打击"鸳鸯"的无情棒,还是拯救沉沦的救生圈? ······ 2087
　附录一 中国拘禁了法国男人的情妇 ······ 2092
　附录二 法国外交官说中国拘留了他的未婚妻 ······ 2094

附录三　小题大做
　　　　——评白天祥等人在所谓"李爽案件"上的喧嚷 ………………… 2094
　　附录四　The Li Shuang Case: A Wet Blanket over Romantic Love?
　　　　……………………………………………………………………… 2096
　　附录五　《纽约时报》报道英文原文 ……………………………………… 2108
第5章　小议对外学术交流的"大忌" ……………………………………… 2111
第6章　向世界展现中国理念 ………………………………………………… 2113
第7章　朝着合作共赢方向发展　推动国际经济法理念变革 …………… 2115
第8章　建构中国特色国际法学理论 ………………………………………… 2117
第9章　"左公柳"、中国魂与新丝路
　　　　——"七七事变"七十周年随笔 ………………………………… 2119

第六编　有关陈安学术论著和学术观点的书评等

第1章　《陈安论国际经济法学》书评荟萃 ………………………………… 2127
　　一、陈安：知识报国，壮心不已 …………………………………………… 2127
　　二、中国国际经济法学的基石之作
　　　　——评陈安教授的《论国际经济法学》 ………………………… 2130
　　三、试论秉持第三世界共同立场的中国特色国际经济法学派的形成及其
　　　　代表性成果 ………………………………………………………… 2132
　　四、从陈安教授辛勤探索的结晶中感悟其治学之道 …………………… 2145
　　五、中国特色国际经济法学的理念与追求
　　　　——《陈安论国际经济法学》的学术创新与特色贡献 ………… 2149
　　六、中国参与经济全球化管理的战略思考
　　　　——评《陈安论国际经济法学》的主导学术理念 ……………… 2166
第2章　《中国的呐喊》书评荟萃 …………………………………………… 2177
　　一、中国呐喊　发聋振聩 ………………………………………………… 2178
　　　　The Enlightening and Thought-provoking Voice from China …… 2180
　　二、晨起临窗坐　书香伴芳菲
　　　　——喜览《中国的呐喊：陈安论国际经济法》…………………… 2182
　　　　By the Casement at Dawn, in the Fragrance of New Book
　　　　—A Joyful Browse of *The Voice from China: An CHEN on*

International Economic Law …………………………………………… 2183

三、弘中华正气　为群弱发声 ……………………………………………… 2185
　　Spreading China's Justice, Voicing for the Global Weak ……………… 2187

四、老艄公的铿锵号子　发出时代的最强音
　　——《中国的呐喊：陈安论国际经济法》读后的点滴感悟 ………… 2190
　　The Sonorous Work Song of an Old Helmsman of International
　　　Economic Law
　　—Some Reflections and Thoughts After Reading *The Voice from
　　　China: An CHEN on International Economic Law* …………………… 2193

五、天下视野　家国情怀　公平秉守
　　——读《中国的呐喊：陈安论国际经济法》……………………………… 2198
　　Global Perspective, State Position and Equity Pursuance
　　—Introducing *The Voice from China: An CHEN on International
　　　Economic Law* ………………………………………………………… 2203

六、"提出中国方案、贡献中国智慧"的先行者
　　——评《中国的呐喊：陈安论国际经济法》……………………………… 2209
　　A Pioneer in "Providing China's Proposal and Contributing
　　　China's Wisdom"
　　—Review on *The Voice from China: An CHEN on International
　　　Economic Law* ………………………………………………………… 2213

七、追求全球正义　抵制国际霸权 ………………………………………… 2220
　　Pursuing Global Justice Resisting International Hegemony …………… 2225

八、国家主权等国际经济法宏观问题的深刻反思
　　——评《中国的呐喊：陈安论国际经济法》……………………………… 2232
　　Reflections on State Sovereignty and Other Grand Themes of
　　　International Law ……………………………………………………… 2235

九、精当透彻的论证　尽显大师的风采
　　——简评《中国的呐喊：陈安论国际经济法》…………………………… 2241
　　Precise and Thorough Analyses—Illustrating a Guru's Profound
　　　Knowledge
　　—A Brief Commentary on *The Voice from China: An CHEN on
　　　International Economic Law* ………………………………………… 2246

十、独具中国风格气派 发出华夏学术强音
——评《中国的呐喊:陈安论国际经济法》 …………………… 2254
Academic Voice with Chinese Characteristics
—A Commentary on *The Voice from China: An CHEN
on International Economic Law* …………………………… 2261

十一、把准南方国家共同脉搏的学术力作
——评《中国的呐喊:陈安论国际经济法》 …………………… 2269
A Highly Recommendable Monograph that Senses the Pulse of
the South …………………………………………………… 2270

十二、国际经济法研究的"中国立场"
——读《中国的呐喊》有感 ……………………………………… 2272
A Chinese School of Jurisprudence on International
Economic Law ……………………………………………… 2276

十三、不为浮云遮眼 兼具深邃坚定
——评《中国的呐喊:陈安论国际经济法》 …………………… 2281
Never Covered by Cloud, Insisting Profound Insight
—Comments on *The Voice from China* …………………… 2282

十四、任你风向东南西北 我自岿然从容不迫
——国际经济新秩序的重思:以陈安教授的国际经济法研究为
视角 ……………………………………………………… 2285
Disregarding Whither the Wind Blows, Keeping Firm Confidence
of His Owns
—A Revisit to Prof. Chen's Research on NIEO …………… 2290

十五、老战士新呐喊 捍卫全球公义
——评《中国的呐喊:陈安论国际经济法》 …………………… 2296
An Old Warrior's New Defense of Global Justice
—Comments on *The Voice from China* …………………… 2298

十六、二十五年实践显示了1991年陈安预言的睿智 中美国际经贸关系
需增进互补、合作和互相依存
——评《中国的呐喊》专著第十四章 …………………………… 2302
Twenty-Five Years of Experience Show the Wisdom of An Chen's
1991 Prediction of Increasing Complementarity, Cooperation and

　　　　Interdependence of Sino-American International Business Relations
　　　　——Comments on Chapter 14 of Chen's Monograph ………… 2304

十七、评陈安教授英文专著《中国的呐喊》：聚焦 ISDS 和 2015 中美 BIT
　　　谈判 ………………………………………………………………… 2307
　　　　Review on Prof. Chen's English Monograph
　　　　——Focusing on the ISDS & 2015 China-U. S. BIT Negotiation … 2312

十八、矢志不渝倡导南南联合自强与国际经济新秩序
　　　　——评陈安教授专著《中国的呐喊：陈安论国际经济法》……… 2317
　　　　A Tireless Advocate for S-S Coalition and NIEO: Comments
　　　　　on Prof. Chen's Monograph ……………………………… 2321

十九、中国呼声 理应倾听
　　　　——评陈安教授专著《中国的呐喊》…………………………… 2326
　　　　China's Voice Deserves Hearing
　　　　——Comments on Prof. Chen's *The Voice from China* …………… 2329

二十、魅力感召、法治理念与爱国情怀之和谐统一
　　　　——读陈安教授《中国的呐喊》有感 …………………………… 2333
　　　　Harmonization of Charisma, Jurisprudence and Patriotism
　　　　——The Inspiration from *The Voice from China*: *An CHEN on
　　　　International Economic Law* ……………………………… 2342

二十一、驳"中国威胁"论——史学、政治学与法学的视角
　　　　——读陈安教授《中国的呐喊》第四章 ……………………… 2355
　　　　Rebutting "China's Threat" Slander from the Perspectives of
　　　　　History, Politics and Jurisprudence
　　　　——On Chapter 4 of Professor Chen's Monograph *The
　　　　　Voice from China* ……………………………………… 2358

二十二、论国际经济法的普遍性
　　　　——评《中国的呐喊：陈安论国际经济法》…………………… 2364
　　　　On the Universality of International Economic Law
　　　　——Comments on *The Voice from China*: *An CHEN on
　　　　International Economic Law* ……………………………… 2372
　　　　国際経済法の普遍性について
　　　　——An Chen, *The Voice from China*: *An CHEN on International*

　　　　　　Economic Law，Berlin/Heidelberg：Springer，2013 を素材に
　　　　　　.. 2385

二十三、一部深邃厚重的普及读物
　　　　——评陈安教授对"中国威胁"谰言的古今剖析 2393
　　　　A Profound but Popular Reading Material
　　　　——On the Anatomy of the "China Threat" Slander
　　　　　　by Professor Chen 2397

二十四、揭露"中国威胁"论的本质：三把利匕剖示美霸谰言真相 2402
　　　　"China Threat" Slander's Ancestors & Its US Hegemony
　　　　　　Variant：Dissecting with Sharp Daggers 2404

第3章　陈安早期论著书评荟萃(1981—2008) 2408

一、立意新颖务实　分析缜密深入　理论实践交融
　　——对陈安主编《国际投资法的新发展与中国双边投资条约的
　　　　新实践》一书的评价 2408

二、内容丰富　系统完整　洵是佳作
　　——《美国对海外投资的法律保护及典型案例分析》评介 2409

三、评陈安主编的国际经济法系列专著(1987年版) 2410

四、新视角：从南北矛盾看国际经济法
　　——评陈安主编的《国际经济法总论》 2413

五、独树中华一帜　跻身国际前驱
　　——评陈安主编的《MIGA与中国》 2418

六、深入研究　科学判断
　　——《"解决投资争端国际中心"述评》简介 2419

七、国际投资争端仲裁研究的力作
　　——评《国际投资争端仲裁——"解决投资争端国际中心"机制
　　　　研究》 2421

八、俯视规则的迷宫
　　——读陈安教授主编的《国际经济法学专论》 2424

九、"问题与主义"中的"问题"
　　——读《国际经济法学专论》 2428

十、高屋建瓴 视角独到
　　——推荐《晚近十年来美国单边主义与WTO多边主义交锋的三大回合》……………………………………………………………………… 2431

十一、以史为师 力排"众议" 说理透辟
　　——推荐《南南联合自强五十年的国际经济立法反思》…… 2433

十二、紧扣学科前沿 力求与时俱进
　　——推荐《国际经济法学》(第三版)……………………………… 2434

第4章　群贤毕至,少长咸集,坐而论道,畅叙旧情 …………… 2436

一、在"中国国际经济法的研究方法暨陈安教授学术思想"研讨会上的致辞 ………………………………………………………………… 2436

二、我与陈安教授 ……………………………………………… 2438

三、诲人不倦 师道悠悠 ………………………………………… 2439

四、陈安老师与中国国际经济法事业 …………………………… 2440

五、知识报国　后学师范 ………………………………………… 2442

六、春分化雨育新人 ……………………………………………… 2444

七、八十感怀 ……………………………………………………… 2445

八、高山仰止
　　——写于陈安老师八十寿诞之际 ……………………………… 2448

九、五"严"源自一"爱" …………………………………………… 2452

第七编　有关陈安学术活动的报道、函件等

第1章　媒体报道 …………………………………………………… 2457

一、在哈佛的讲坛上
　　——访厦门大学政法学院副院长陈安 ………………………… 2457

二、他把法的目光投向世界与未来
　　——访厦门大学法律系陈安教授 ……………………………… 2459

三、适应对外开放和发展外向型经济需要,国际经济法系列专著问世
　　…………………………………………………………………… 2462

四、为对外开放铺路
　　——记厦门大学法学教授陈安 ………………………………… 2463

五、就闽台两省结拜"姊妹"一事,厦门大学法学教授发表看法 …… 2465

六、理性务实的学术交流盛会
　　——1993年两岸法学学术研讨会综述 ⋯⋯⋯⋯⋯⋯⋯⋯⋯⋯⋯⋯⋯ 2466
七、春风吹拂紫梅 白鹭振翅腾飞
　　——陈安教授谈厦门获得立法权 ⋯⋯⋯⋯⋯⋯⋯⋯⋯⋯⋯⋯⋯⋯ 2468
八、第十二届"安子介国际贸易研究奖"颁奖大会圆满结束(摘要) ⋯⋯ 2470
九、第十二届"安子介国际贸易研究奖"颁奖 ⋯⋯⋯⋯⋯⋯⋯⋯⋯⋯⋯ 2471
十、中国特色国际经济法学的探索者和开拓者
　　——陈安教授 ⋯⋯⋯⋯⋯⋯⋯⋯⋯⋯⋯⋯⋯⋯⋯⋯⋯⋯⋯⋯⋯ 2472
十一、十位厦大学者入选中国杰出社会科学家 ⋯⋯⋯⋯⋯⋯⋯⋯⋯⋯ 2474

第2章　学界来函 ⋯⋯⋯⋯⋯⋯⋯⋯⋯⋯⋯⋯⋯⋯⋯⋯⋯⋯⋯⋯⋯ 2475
　一、来函概述 ⋯⋯⋯⋯⋯⋯⋯⋯⋯⋯⋯⋯⋯⋯⋯⋯⋯⋯⋯⋯⋯⋯ 2475
　二、来函选辑 ⋯⋯⋯⋯⋯⋯⋯⋯⋯⋯⋯⋯⋯⋯⋯⋯⋯⋯⋯⋯⋯⋯ 2483

第3章　陈安学术小传及历年主要论著目录(以倒计年为序) ⋯⋯⋯ 2518
　一、陈安学术小传 ⋯⋯⋯⋯⋯⋯⋯⋯⋯⋯⋯⋯⋯⋯⋯⋯⋯⋯⋯⋯ 2518
　二、陈安历年主要论著 ⋯⋯⋯⋯⋯⋯⋯⋯⋯⋯⋯⋯⋯⋯⋯⋯⋯⋯ 2519

第4章　陈安论著、业绩获奖一览(以倒计年为序/2016—1960) ⋯ 2525
　一、国家级、省部级一等奖 ⋯⋯⋯⋯⋯⋯⋯⋯⋯⋯⋯⋯⋯⋯⋯⋯⋯ 2525
　二、国家级、省部级二等奖 ⋯⋯⋯⋯⋯⋯⋯⋯⋯⋯⋯⋯⋯⋯⋯⋯⋯ 2526
　三、国家级三等奖 ⋯⋯⋯⋯⋯⋯⋯⋯⋯⋯⋯⋯⋯⋯⋯⋯⋯⋯⋯⋯ 2527
　四、厦门大学最高荣誉奖 ⋯⋯⋯⋯⋯⋯⋯⋯⋯⋯⋯⋯⋯⋯⋯⋯⋯⋯ 2527

索引 ⋯⋯⋯⋯⋯⋯⋯⋯⋯⋯⋯⋯⋯⋯⋯⋯⋯⋯⋯⋯⋯⋯⋯⋯⋯⋯ 2528
后记 ⋯⋯⋯⋯⋯⋯⋯⋯⋯⋯⋯⋯⋯⋯⋯⋯⋯⋯⋯⋯⋯⋯⋯⋯⋯⋯ 2546

第五编
国际经济法热点学术问题长、短评

第1章　改进我国国际法教育的"他山之石"*
——欧美之行考察见闻

▶▶ 内容提要

1984年3—4月,笔者应联合国教科文组织邀请,作为中国派出的"国际法教育考察组"成员之一,出访西欧和北美五国二十个城市,对西方发达国家的法学教育进行调研、考察,并与一百多位法学界相关人士进行交流。本文是依据此次考察见闻,结合中国国情,就国际法专业人才培养等方面的问题提出的具体改进建议。如今这些建议有的已被有关部门采纳,并行之有效;有的则尚待借鉴他山之石,付诸实践,俾使中国的国际法人才培养事业与时俱进,更上层楼。

▶▶ 目　次

一、关于国际法专业人才的培养
　（一）派人员出国深造应考虑门类、品种和国别的多样化
　（二）应积极参加国际性的学术讨论会或学术团体
　（三）国际法课程的教学应注重培养学生解决实际问题的能力——大量的课前预习和活跃的课堂对话
　（四）提倡由优秀研究生主办学刊——法学拔尖人才的摇篮
　（五）注重开发利用外籍华人和港台留学生中的法学人才资源
二、关于国际法资料中心的建立
三、关于国际法专业力量的合作

---

* 本文原题为《对我国国际法教育的刍议》,发表于原国家教委主办的《国际学术动态》（内部刊物）1985年第4期"考察综述"专栏。其中部分内容曾以《欧美之行看西方法学院对学生实践能力的培养》为题,先期发表于《福建高教研究》1985年第1期。此次辑入本书,综合上述两文,对标题和若干提法稍加调整订订。

应联合国教科文组织的邀请,中国国际法教育考察组一行三人,由北大国际法研究所所长王铁崖教授率领[1],于1984年3月3日至4月21日对西欧和北美的五国进行了法学教育的考察。考察的目的是,了解和学习西方发达国家国际法教学与科研的主要经验;争取外来资助,为选送更多的青年教师与研究生出国深造而沟通渠道;同时,也向国际同行介绍中国国际法教学与科研的现状、我国在若干国际法问题上的原则立场以及我国涉外的政策法令。

考察期间,我们历经比利时的布鲁塞尔、鲁汶,瑞士的日内瓦,联邦德国的波恩、法兰克福、海德堡,加拿大的渥太华、哈利法克斯、多伦多、蒙特利尔、埃德蒙顿,美国的纽约、纽黑文、罗莱、查洛斯维尔、华盛顿特区、旧金山等二十个城市,走访了享有国际声誉的大学法学院、国际法研究所、联合国总部、联合国欧洲总部、欧洲共同体总部等重要国际组织以及议会、法院、国会图书馆、国际性大型律师事务所、国际法专业书刊出版社等,约三十个单位,先后与一百多名国际法学界的知名人士和专家、学者进行了学术交流,并就开展国际学术协作、培养人才、交流资料等进行了初步的磋商。现将访问考察过程的若干见闻和感想,结合中国国情,从国际法专业人才的培养、国际法资料中心的建立以及国际法专业力量的合作这三个方面,综合简述如下:

一、关于国际法专业人才的培养

我国法学人才短缺,国际法人才尤其缺。现有国际法专业人才的数量和质量,与发达国家相比,差距很大。为了提高我国的国际地位,大力开展国际交往活动,我们必须加速国际法专业人才的培养。借鉴有关经验,我国现有的培养方法宜在以下几方面加以改进:

(一) 派人员出国深造应考虑门类、品种和国别的多样化

目前我国选派出国深造的国际法专业人员,绝大多数集中在美国,绝大多数攻读法学硕士(L.L.M.)学位,选读的课程和选定的学位论文题目,其计划性、目的性、针对性也不够强,未必完全切合我国开展国际斗争和扩大国际交往的急需。例如,欧洲共同体是我国对外交往中的主要对象之一,有些主攻欧洲共同体法律的出国人

---

[1] 除王铁崖先生和笔者外,还有一人是西南政法学院的刘鸿惠教授。

员不是派往西欧,却送到美国去,这就不如派往比利时或联邦德国、法国这些欧洲共同体成员国学习,从而耳濡目染,获得更多感性认识和理性认识。

据了解,联邦德国基于自身利益的考虑,亟欲扩大对中国的经济、文化交流。阿登纳基金会等组织对于提供资助吸收中国留学生前往联邦德国学习法律很有积极性,所提供的资助也是比较优厚的。但国内选派的预备人选只有德语训练,缺乏基本的法学专业知识,不符合对方要求,故两年来该基金会为中国学生留下的资助名额,至今还空着。它们的要求是宁可德语差些,也要先具备基本法学知识,在联邦德国可以进行德语速成训练,进而专攻欧洲共同体法律或联邦德国法律。因此,国内有条件的法律系中,不妨自一年级起就要求部分学生修习德、法、日、俄、西班牙等语种,作为第一外语必修课,便于从中选派前往相应国家深造的人员,这是很有必要的。

在联邦德国、加拿大和美国的若干大学里,学习中国法律已成为"热门",但我国现有的法律系,却极少开设德国法、加拿大法或美国法的专门课程。这些国家的政府或投资者在与中国交往中,多半聘有熟知中国法律的本国专家或律师参加谈判或立约,而我国现有法学人员中,既掌握国际法又熟知对方国内法者几乎完全阙如。例如,近年来我国对美国经济关系中就发生过"蘑菇贸易官司"、纺织品配额纠纷、湖广铁路债券案件等,在有关讼争中,我方往往不得不花费重金聘请美国律师提供法律帮助,其不得力、不相称是可想而知的。所以,我们从现在起,应以较大的注意力,有计划地选送适量的留学生专攻中国对外交往重点对象国家的国内法。以美国为例,就是攻读 J. D. 学位而不是攻读 L. L. M. 或 S. J. D. 学位。而在攻读 L. L. M. 或 S. J. D. 学位的留学生中,也应根据我国的现实需要,在国际公法、国际私法、国际经济法(国际贸易法、国际投资法、国际货币金融法、国际税法、国际组织法等等)以及有关的重要分支专业(诸如海洋法、外层空间法、国际环境保护法、国际海事法等等)各门各类中,分别有所侧重,有所专攻。通过上述措施,使我国的国际法专业人才"品种齐全,配套成龙",有能力在各种国际场合打各种"国际官司",以维护我国权益。

此外,鉴于我国国内目前的培养力量(国际法专家、师资)严重不足,图书资料奇缺,而国际法专业训练又具有特别强的国际性,因此,即使是国内在学的国际法研究生,如能获得外国学术资助,又不增加国家负担,也宜尽量多地送往国外培养,以求迅速成才。我国目前有关"在学研究生不得出国"的现行规定,自有一定道理,但考虑到国际法专业人才的特殊情况,似乎不宜"一刀切",而宜灵活掌握或对原规定加以调整。

(二) 应积极参加国际性的学术讨论会或学术团体

享有国际声誉的联邦德国马普国际法研究所对于加强中、德国际法学术交流具有浓厚兴趣,他们主动倡议1985年春在联邦德国海德堡或中国北京举办一次国际法学术讨论会,主题是有关国际投资保护条约的理论和实践,建议中、德双方各提供五六篇学术论文,并欢迎中国青年学者届时出席会议。他们还建议把这类学术讨论会制度化,今后每两年定期举行一次。我们建议首次讨论会最好在北京举行,对方初步表示同意,并即将派专人前来北京进一步找中国国际法学会会长宦乡同志具体磋商确定。如果此种形式果真制度化,我们应有与之相应的准备。

美国国际法学会是一个国际性的学术组织,拥有许多其他国家的会员。其年会讨论的问题丰富多彩,多半是国际法学科中新出现的疑难问题或有争论的问题,事后又将有关的专题论文和讲稿汇编出版。会议期间,不但国内外国际法学者云集,而且全美经营国际法专业书刊的各家大出版商也摆出二十余个书摊,推销最新出版和即将出版的各种国际法读物专著,可谓琳琅满目。据了解,来自发展中国家的学会会员,每年只需缴纳30美元的会员费,即获免费赠阅《美国国际法杂志》(美国权威性学术杂志,一年六期,原定价为78美元)一份,还可以用40美元的订阅价获得一份《国际法学资料》(一年四册,原定价为85美元)。以上两种杂志,是当前我国各大学法律系国际法课程的重要参考读物,各校多按原订阅价付款订购,而没有人利用入会会员资格获得上述半价优待。看来这是一种可以避免的浪费,而其"思想障碍"则可能是认为"中国人不宜参加美国学会"。其实,我国国际法专业人员以个人名义参加这种实际上是国际性的学术组织作为会员,有利于维护我国的权益。适当地有组织地选派我国部分国际法学者加入这种学会,实质上有如派人出国留学、进修一样,符合鲁迅先生所提倡的"拿来主义"精神。利用会员资格和派人参加这种会议,我们可以从中了解国际法学科的最新动态。

(三) 国际法课程的教学应注重培养学生解决实际问题的能力——大量的课前预习和活跃的课堂对话

我国法律系各科目前的教学内容,大多侧重于理论体系的分析讲解,在一定程度上存在着"纯理论"的偏向,对引导学生研究与分析典型的实际案例,是不够注意的。在教学方法上,则相当普遍地采取"满堂灌"的办法。课堂上自始至终,全是主讲教员的"一言堂",学生则全神贯注,忙于记录,无暇思考,形成"课上记笔记、课后对笔记、考试背笔记、考后全忘记"的消极、被动、低效率的学习局面。可以说,这是文科教学中常见的积弊,亟待改革。

西方发达国家的教学内容和教学方法,颇可以借鉴。一般说来,他们的课堂教学主要采取两种方式:20 人以上的大班,采取以教师为主的讲授式;20 人以下的小班,采取教师指导下的讨论式。当然,根据课程的性质和教师个人的喜好,也有采用讲授式的小班。但不论采取何种方式,全都要求学生事先进行大量的预习,由教师指定阅读范围,每两节课要求事先预习 60—80 页(16 开)的图书和资料,其内容主要是典型案例及有关的原始文档。讨论式教学中,学生围绕典型案例各抒己见,教师加以引导。讲授式教学中,也有大量时间用于师生对话,即教师就预习内容和案例提问,要求学生当堂阐述自己的看法;或者由学生随时举手,经教师许可,就教师讲授内容中的疑点提出质询、问难或发表自己不同的意见。因此,教师事先也必须充分备课,以便随时对付这种"半路杀出来的程咬金"。这种以大量预习为基础,课堂上穿插大量师生对话的讲授,对师生双方都提出了更高的要求,在课堂上能充分激发学生的积极思维,利于师生思想和知识的及时交流。这样,不但课堂气氛生动活泼,而且学生学得积极主动,大大加深了对所学内容的理解,同时培养了独立思考的习惯和能力。

他们认为,教师应当了解学生心理,讲究教学艺术,鼓励学生"自我表现":在刻苦钻研的基础上,敢于探索新知识,提出新见解。青年学生精力旺盛,在课前经过刻苦钻研,往往有许多新鲜的看法、独特的观点和丰富的联想。他们在课堂上当众表述、答疑或质疑,不但可以锻炼他们的口头表达能力(这也是一种重要的基本功),而且可以使他们带着一种高涨、激动的情绪进行学习和思考,既在学习和辩难中意识到自己的智慧和力量,体验到开拓与创造的欢乐,也在同一过程中发现自己的缺陷和不足,"知不足而后学",从而获得新的提高。在课堂上让他们阐发歧议、开展争论,还可以进一步激发学生群体的思考,扩大和加深对有关问题的理解;与此同时,教师也从课堂上的辩难中,大大增强备课和讲授的广度、深度和针对性,十分有利于教学水平的提高。这种教学相长、师生互促共进的效果,是那种"台上播音员,台下打字员"的老办法所无法达到的。

西方法学院重视培养学生的实践能力,还体现在普遍开设模拟法庭课(Moot Court)、法律门诊课(Clinical Program in Legal Aid)或学生法律援助服务项目(Student Legal Aid Service)上。

模拟法庭课在许多学校法学院是一年级学生(研究生)的必修课。自第二年开始,则有"模拟法庭竞赛"选修课。它由选修学生自行结合为许多二人小组,就教师所指定的案例案情,轮流充当原告或被告的代理人(或辩护人)出庭辩论,采取淘汰赛的办法,最后胜诉者获得"竞赛冠军"称号。初赛中的法官(审判员)由毕业班学习成绩突出者担任,复赛中的法官由授课老师或聘请律师事务所有名望的律师志愿担任(义务工作,无报酬,受聘者引为一种荣誉),决赛时则请法院现职老法官裁判。最后的胜诉竞赛冠军小组取得奖品银杯或银盾后,把姓名镌刻其上,交还学校保管,以供下届竞赛之用,一如国际性球赛奖杯的颁发与收藏。学校当局往往把这种优胜银杯或银盾作为一种学习荣誉展品,放在大会客厅或公共图书馆最显眼处,陈列展览,供历届入学新生和外宾参观。

模拟法庭竞赛也常在校际进行。美国国际法学会年会则每年举办模拟国际法庭竞赛最后阶段的复赛和决赛,这是全国性的校际竞赛,奖杯命名为"杰塞普杯",争夺十分激烈。对学生来说,模拟法庭中复赛或决赛的优胜者,不唯是一项荣誉,而且是日后获得良好职业岗位的初步保证。因为各大律师事务所前来法学院征聘新人员时,毕业生在模拟法庭课中的成绩和表现,往往是主管人(雇主)决定取舍的一项重要标准。

至于法律门诊课或学生法律援助服务项目,实际上就是模拟的律师事务所。前者由有关师生联合组成,另由学校出资聘请数位开业律师兼任部分指导工作,对前来寻求法律援助的托办人(当事人)收取低廉费用或完全免费,主要目的在于训练在学学生初步学会开业律师的"基本功";后者则纯是学生自行组织的免费服务项目,为社会上无力支付律师费用的人解答法律上的疑难,提供法律援助,学生们从免费服务中获得运用课堂知识的实践锻炼,提高了独立分析和解决实际问题的能力。

目前,我国法律系一般只要求高年级学生参加司法实习,而低年级学生则很少有实习锻炼的机会。实习成绩在四年学习总成绩中所占的比重很低,毕业生中往往出现"高分低能"的现象。离校从事司法工作或经办法律事务,在相当一段时期内,往往不能适应实际工作需要,审案办案能力不强或案情分析能力欠佳,抓不住要害,或庭辩谈锋不健,说不清论点论据。这与在校期间的训练方法欠妥有密切关系。

(四)提倡由优秀研究生主办学刊——法学拔尖人才的摇篮

一般说来,西方每所法学院都有一种以上的法学学术杂志,而校办法学学术杂志一般都是由该校学习成绩最优的研究生担任主编和编委,这尤其是美国校办法学刊物的一大特点。他们的一般做法是:法学院二年级研究生可以自愿报名,要求参加该校法学刊物编辑工作,然后由刊物的主编、编委(都是高年级研究生)共同进行考核和审批。考核的主要根据是一年级的学生成绩以及当场出题测试的成绩,择其最优者参加编辑工作。头年的工作主要是查对来稿的脚注,称为"脚注编辑",要求把作者投寄的论文来稿中的所有脚注一一查对出处，弄清是否言之有据，是否符合原文原意，并对作者的引证和论证，从内容到方法，作出自己的评论，提交"论文编辑"审议。一篇法学论文，脚注一般在100—200个之间，脚注编辑每审毕一稿，等于是"被迫"认真细致地阅读了大量的原始资料和有关书刊，大大开阔了学术视野，锻炼了缜密思考的习惯，培养了一丝不苟的学风。

脚注编辑工作成绩优良者，次年（即研究生三年级）始能被编委会提升为论文编辑，担任论文编辑所经受的学术锻炼和专业知识水平的提高，较之脚注编辑，自然更胜一筹。整个编委会，全由学习成绩优异的高年级研究生组成，来稿的取舍，全由编委民主决定。若干学术精深的教授，则被编委会礼聘为刊物顾问，为专业疑难问题提供咨询意见，但并不干预编务工作。编委中大约半数逐年毕业离校，因而逐年更新一半，使更多新人获得锻炼的机会。据了解，曾经担任过校办学术刊物编委的毕业生，本身就是高才生的标志之一，一般是各家大律师事务所争相罗致的对象。因此，尽管担任编委纯是无偿的义务性社会工作，但美国诸法学院的研究生却竞相争取入选，乐此不疲。看来，法学院、法律系多办法学刊物，并由成绩优异的高年级研究生主办的方式，既有利于法学学术繁荣，也是促使青年人早日成才和培养拔尖法学人才的有效途径之一。

在世界民族之林中，中国人的智慧、勤劳和开拓精神，素来享有盛誉。"拿来主义"更是鲁迅先生所一贯倡导的信条。"他山之石，可以攻玉。"在法学人才培养的措施和方法上，我们不妨借鉴他人的经验，拓出自己的新路，使法苑新苗茁壮成长，人才辈出。

（五）注重开发利用外籍华人和港台留学生中的法学人才资源

在国外，不时可以遇到开业的外籍华人律师、法学教授以及正在法学院攻读 J. D. 或 L. L. M. 或 S. J. D. 学位的港台研究生。他们的共同点是：(1) 英文根底深厚，法学基本知识较好，对所在国的法律学有专长或较为熟悉；(2) 对我党十一届三中全会以来所厘定和贯彻的基本政策表示赞同，民族凝聚力和向心力与日俱增；(3) 有的已在国外立足，有的正在争取并有很大可能在国外就业。由于国外物质待遇远较内地优厚，而且他们对内地还存在不同程度的疑虑或误解，所以不愿长期回国工作，但不少人很想短期回国讲学、工作或居留，既为祖国法学繁荣和法制建设出点力，也便于他们自己更深入具体地学习中国法律，提高在国外执业的能力和充当中外交往中的法律桥梁。鉴于我国现有法学人才短缺，能熟练掌握外文而且熟知外国国内法的法学人才尤缺，因此，上述人才资源颇有开发利用的必要与可能。如何适应他们的业务特点和思想特点,拟订相应的政策,采取相应的措施(包括建立短期招聘的制度),是值得考虑的。

二、关于国际法资料中心的建立

在国内从事国际法教学和研究的人员,常苦于专业资料奇缺,难为无米之炊。再加上国内现有的外文图书资料分散收藏,互不通气,单位"垄断""保密"不愿外传的现象亦非绝无仅有,这些都是我国国际法学并不繁荣昌盛的重要原因。而国外有些著名的国际法研究所之所以成果累累,原因之一就在于注意资料的长期积累和广泛收集。访德期间,马普国际法研究所的图书馆人员在引导客人参观时,检索书目,发现了王铁崖教授1945年所撰写的英文小册子《论外国人与外国企业的地位》。他们为表示友好情谊,经有关领导同意,当即复印一份收藏,而将原本当面奉赠原作者。原作者此书当年出版于中国战乱时期,早已散失;此次竟在国外偶获样书,实属喜出望外。该研究所收集资料之广泛,由此可见一斑。

为尽快改变我国国际法资料奇缺的状况,似可采取以下办法:

(1) 建立一两个全国性的国际法资料中心。以我国现有的北京大学国际法研究所和武汉大学国际法研究所为基础,给以采购专业图书资料的外汇保证和自主使用权,并指定专人负责,陆续收集和统一整理目前我国各大学、研究所以及外交、外贸等实务部门所收藏的国际法外文图书资料目录,陆续印发各有关单位。同时,在资料中心配备较好的复印机,便于各地专业单位或专业人员前来复制使用。这样做,既可大量节省外汇,避免外文书刊采购上的重复和疏漏,又能大大提高外文书刊的使用效率。

(2) 有些外国法学院、研究所或学术基金会表示愿意免费赠送法学书刊,但也要求我方免费赠送公开出版的中文法学书刊资料。为此,应当给资料中心定期拨付专款,供采购中文书刊和对外邮寄交流之用。

(3) 访问联合国欧洲总部(即联合国驻日内瓦办事处)时,该部总负责官员E. Suy表示愿将私人收藏多年的全套《美国国际法杂志》(自1946年迄今,计38年,二百余册)赠送给我国大学。访美时,纽约大学的图书馆负责人表示愿将馆中收藏的多余复本图书资料,免费赠送我国大学,以便腾出藏书空间。此外,联合国总部法律事务局的负责人也有免费赠书的同类表示。对于我国国际法教学和科研来说,这些图书资料都是难得的、珍贵的,但问题是这些书刊的运费须由我方负担。这一问题亟待有关部门研究解决。

三、关于国际法专业力量的合作

西方发达国家的国际法学术机关（大学、研究所）与国家政府的涉外实务部门，往往是互相通气、联系密切的。许多学有专长的国际法教授和专家，往往同时是政府有关部门的常年顾问或谈判代表；在政府涉外部门工作多年的专家或实务人员，也经常受聘到大学讲学或到研究所从事研究工作，总结工作经验，著书立说。教授、研究员的研究成果和有关建议，常为政府涉外部门所采纳，而政府涉外部门也经常提出一些实务问题交付教授、研究员研究讨论，并拨出专款，以供征聘研究工作助手和购置图书资料等项开支。大学与独立研究所之间的分工合作和人才交流，也是常见现象。专职研究人员往往到大学兼课，讲授研究成果；而大学教授也往往是独立研究所的兼职研究员。联邦德国的马普国际法研究所、加拿大的麦吉尔比较法研究所和外层空间法研究所，其人员结构，都是如此。因此，这些研究成果累累，人才辈出，饮誉世界，颇为国际同行所称道。看来，上述这类体制，颇有利于理论与实际的结合，也有利于国际法学术的繁荣，值得师法。

结合我国的现状，下述办法似乎也是可行的：

（1）在外交部、外经贸部、司法部、最高人民法院等实务部门同各大学、研究所之间建立密切联系的体制：由前者定期向后者介绍涉外事务和涉外案件中的实况和存在的问题，布置研究的课题和任务，在不违反保密原则的前提下，尽可能提供必要的文档资料，要求大学、研究所定期写出研究报告。目前，我国国务院设有国家科委，专司自然科学方面研究任务的布置和下达，在社会科学（包括国际法学）方面，也不妨设立类似的机构，主持研究项目的布置下达和研究经费的调拨。

（2）大学和研究所可随时聘请外交部、外经贸部等实务部门在职或离休、退休的老干部和专业人员，担任兼职教员或研究人员，举办专题讲座、讲学授课或参加研究工作。

（3）现有的北大国际法研究所与武大国际法研究所，除编制以内的专职研究人员外，可以聘请外校、外单位的国际法教授、讲师作为兼职的研究人员，以加强校际、所际的互相通气和分工合作。在研究课题上，力求成龙配套，以适应国家对外交往中的各种需要，避免重复和疏漏；在图书资料上，互通信息，互通有无，避免耳目不灵不周，学术情报闭塞无知；在治学经验和研究方法上，向老前辈、老专家学习，并提倡校际交流，互相取长补短，避免"近亲繁衍"，见闻受囿，不利创新。

第 2 章　从难从严训练　成果人才并出*

>> 内容提要

培养研究生的目的是为国家输送高层次的专业人才，为了快出人才，出好人才，很有必要把出成果作为培养人才的手段。从研究生入学伊始，就从难从严出发，狠抓基本功训练，力争实现成果与人才同时并出，其基本训练方式包括：实行"大运动量"训练，敢于坚持严格要求，力排怕苦"众议"和畏难"惰性"，过法学专业英语关；多学科交叉渗透，提倡兼修相关相邻课程，建立合理的知识结构；理论联系实际，参加各类实践，提高实务工作能力；充分信赖，畀以"重担"，严密组织，严格把关；赋予新设专业较大"成才自留权"，加速形成"人才生产基地"，提高人才生产力。

>> 目　次

一、实行"大运动量"训练，过法学专业英语关
二、多学科交叉渗透，建立合理的知识结构
三、理论联系实际，提高实务工作能力
四、充分信赖，畀以"重担"，严密组织，严格把关
五、赋予较大"成才自留权"，加速形成"人才生产力"

培养研究生的目的是为国家输送高层次的专业人才，因而人们通常认为：衡量研究生培养工作的优劣，端视所出人才的质量和数量。至于**出科研成果**，则是培养**成才之后的事**，必须待以时日。我们在培养研究生过程中认识到，出人才与出成果，其先后次序并非如此截然分明。在从严训练基本功的基础上，应适时地给年轻人压担子，让他们承担一定的科研任务，早出成果，多出成果，**把出成果作为培养人才的**

---

* 本文于 1988 年由当时的厦门大学博士生刘智中根据笔者的讲话录音整理，原载于国务院学位委员会和国家教委联合主办的《学位与研究生教育》1988 年第 5 期。因篇幅所限，原文稿在该刊发表时曾有所删节，现恢复全文，辑入本书。

手段,或者说,力求创成果与出人才二者互相促进,**同时并举**。从研究生入学伊始,我们就确定了这么一条原则:从难从严出发,狠抓基本功训练,以便为创成果与出人才奠定坚实、必要的基础。

一、实行"大运动量"训练,过法学专业英语关

本专业研究生的培养目标是造就从事国际经济法律教学、科研和涉外经济法律实务的高层次专门人才。这一培养目标决定了外语基本功的重要性,甚至可以说是一切基本功的首要前提。尤其是在目前,我国实行对外开放的时间还不长,造成了对国际经济往来所适用的国际惯例不够了解,对各国的涉外经济法律知之甚少。要在较短时间内迎头赶上,了解最新学术动态和实务,及时引进最新专业知识,就必须能够熟练地阅读、准确地理解外文资料和**原始文档**。

在有限时间内练好外语基本功,不宜在听、说、读、写四方面平均花力气,而应侧重于**阅读—理解—翻译**这一主要环节。我们招收的研究生,外文底子比较好,但即使是外语专业毕业的本科生,也同样面临无法熟练阅读和准确翻译的问题。因为所接触的已不是一般的文艺读物、政论文章,而是专业性很强的国际经济法文献。法律语言的特点是准确、精练,但表达的思想又深邃复杂,对句式、语法都有很高的要求,往往一字之差,含义全变。要准确透彻地理解,就得发狠下一番苦功夫。我们在抓外语基本功训练时,主要注意两点:一是认真扎实,一丝不苟,逐词逐句地弄通弄懂;二是要广泛接触,大量阅读,准确地译成中文。具体的训练过程要环环紧扣。我们从近年出版的最新文档资料中选取国际经济法律的重要参考文献,或者让学生们根据自己的研究课题选取有关参考资料,由学生在认真阅读、深刻理解之后译成中文,并随时记下翻译过程中碰到的疑难问题,包括语言难点和学术上有争议的问题。译稿誊写三份,一份交给导师,一份留底,一份给同班研究生搞"循环校对"。一方面要在校对中发现他人译文中的错误、不妥之处,予以修改更正;另一方面要解答他人翻译过程中悬而未决的难题。这就体现和发挥了同窗的作用,相互切磋,共同提高。随后,在导师指导下进行小组讲评,发挥集体的智慧协力攻关,解决疑难。这样做,既扩大了研究生的知识面,又促使他们认真地去思考问题,发挥学习的积极主动性。

翻译、互校、讲评、答疑、讨论,每一个步骤都要求学生认真对待,实行"综合评分"。实践表明,经过这几个环节的反复训练,学生的专业外语阅读理解能力以及专

业知识水平都能在较短时间内得到明显提高。因为在阅读外文专业文献中,从似懂非懂到透彻理解,是一个飞跃;从只能意会、无法言传到克服障碍、正确地表达,又是一个飞跃;就翻译而言,从逐词逐句对译、佶屈聱牙,到修改成通顺规范的现代汉语,又是一个飞跃。我们的专业外语训练并不停留于此。由于学生接触、阅读的都是近期的外文资料,这些资料反映了国际上本专业的最新学术动态和研究成果,因而有必要予以引进、消化、吸收并介绍给国内学术界。再者,研究生的训练中还有教学实践这一环,还要进一步要求他们把从专业外文新资料中获得的知识条理化,经过融会贯通,写成讲稿,传授给同窗和本专业的本科生。因此,备课、试讲这些环节,又是一次新的飞跃。简言之,研究生的专业外语基本功的训练是与日后的教学、科研紧密联系在一起的。总的要求就是**熟练地阅读、深刻地理解、准确地翻译、流畅地表达**。要达到这一境界,需要付出艰苦的劳动。导师的职责,不仅在于从方法上给予指导,还在于严格要求,使研究生在训练过程中养成一丝不苟的、严谨的学风。

抓专业外语基本功训练,要坚持"大运动量"原则。起初,研究生对"大运动量"训练的意义认识不足,压力大些,钻研辛苦些,就颇有牢骚,用他们自己的话来说,"有时甚至会'怨声载道'"!但导师秉持"教不严,师之惰"的古训,从不"姑息"迁就,敢于力排怕苦"众议"和畏难"惰性",坚持严格训练的原则。同时,又常常援引当年周恩来总理特聘日本"狠"教练大松博文严格培训中国女排,苦练基本功,打下坚实基础,从而使她们在后来的国际大赛中连连夺取冠军的故事,对"叫苦不迭"的青年同学加以启发诱导,促使他们提高勇于吃苦的自觉性。反复引导他们思考:中国女排成功的秘诀何在?为什么能在短期内不但达到国际水平,而且夺得"五连冠"?显然,其主要经验之一就在于日常坚持大量的、严格的、单调的摸、爬、滚、打。只有在基本功训练中不怕大量流汗、不怕皮破血流,才能练出过硬的水平,赢得胜利和荣誉。总之,基本功的训练绝对不能"讲价钱,打折扣"。就这样,促使每个研究生在短短一年中,精读细译 10 万字以上的原始资料,循环校对他人 10 万字以上的译稿,之后,阅读理解能力普遍得到提高。正如俗话所说:"磨刀不误砍柴工。"他们也尝到了基本功训练的甜头。不少研究生事后反映:为写作论文或专著而收集资料时,能从浩瀚的外文专业书刊中较快地检索所需材料,略加浏览,便可决定取舍。撰写论文时,也取得了时间上的效益,因为得心应手地使用专业外语这个工具,为他们的科研提供了很大的便利。自此以后,历届研究生都心悦诚服地接受了这一整套的严格训练方案。

二、多学科交叉渗透,建立合理的知识结构

建立合理的知识结构,是每一学科都可能面临的问题。国际经济法是新兴的边缘学科,与世界经济、国际经济关系、法学都有密切的关系;同时,它虽然是一个独立的法律部门,但与国际公法、国际私法又都具有许多互相交叉渗透之处。因此,就知识结构而言,从上到下,应该包含三个层次:

第一个层次,是国际经济法这一学科的核心知识。从课程设置来说,国际经济法总论、国际贸易法、国际投资法、国际货币金融法、国际税法、国际海事法等应作为国际经济法专业的主干课程,是本专业硕士研究生必须系统学习、牢固掌握的。

第二个层次,包括一般法律基础课和国际经济法的专业基础课。一般法律基础课指法学基础理论、宪法、民法、民事诉讼法等课程,专业基础课则包括国际公法、国际私法、比较民商法、涉外经济合同法等课程。这些基础课都在不同程度上与国际经济法具有内在的联系,对本专业的学习和研究也是必不可少的。

第三个层次是政治经济学、世界经济、国际贸易、国际金融等学科的基础理论和知识。国际经济法作为一门边缘学科,植根于国际经济关系,它的产生和发展,必然受到世界经济形势的影响。要把握国际经济法的本质和规律,只有上述两个层次还不够,必须对国际经济学作一番深入的探讨。涉外经济实务方面的知识,对于本专业的学习也有很大的帮助。为了使本专业的研究生具有坚实的基础知识,我们总是鼓励他们跨系、跨学院选修并学好相邻学科的课程,打好基础,扩大知识面。我们认为,就法学法,就法论法,不利于本专业研究生建立合理的知识结构。因此,对相邻学科知识的学习和掌握,也应包括在基本功训练的范围里,而且是本专业研究生训练基本功的重要内容之一。

扩大知识面与有所专攻,如能妥善处理,二者并不矛盾,也可以同时并举。前几批招收的十余名研究生相继进入高年级后,我们就在确定学位论文选题时有意识地把他们分布在国际经济法的五个主要分支,让他们把各自的科研、学习与本专业本科生课程设置的需要结合起来,分别选定国际贸易法、国际投资法、国际货币金融法、国际税法、国际海事法等为重点学习和研究的范围。这样,在打好基础的同时又各有所长,毕业后,很快就能承担本专业本科生各门主干课程的教学工作。通过自力更生,"成龙配套"地培养了厦大国际经济法专业本科的第一代师资力量,不但在

短期内就开齐了本专业的应有课程,使教学逐步系统化,而且准备了促使本专业科研成果逐步系统化的有利条件。

三、理论联系实际,提高实务工作能力

国际经济法这门学科的实践性很强。我们利用学校地处经济特区的有利条件,结合本省市的具体情况,学术界当前争论的现实、理论问题,国家决策方面的疑难问题,进行学习和研究。厦门特区的涉外经济活动比较多,从客观条件来看,可谓"得天独厚",有利于在国际经济法的教学与科研中培养理论与实际相结合的优良学风。

厦大设有律师事务所,法律系多数教师都参加了兼职律师工作,律师事务所成了他们很好的实践基地。我们也安排研究生从在学期间起就在律师事务所实习,在兼职律师指导下,参加涉外经济法律的实务工作,如涉外经济合同的草拟、谈判,提供涉外经贸问题的法律咨询,参加涉外经贸纠纷的诉讼活动等,充分运用所学的知识,在分析和解决实际问题的过程中,深化理论知识,并不断得到提高。另外,组织高年级研究生参加经济特区的立法活动,为特区法制建设做贡献。如厦门市人大草拟厦门经济特区条例时,就请厦大法律系教师提供咨询意见,我们也安排研究生参加讨论,探讨和权衡各项有关条文规定的利弊得失,锻炼和提高他们分析实际问题的能力。我们还曾接受福建省有关领导部门的委托,组织研究生翻译校订本省为贯彻执行《国务院关于鼓励外商投资的规定》所制定的地方性法规。在为地方政府提供服务的过程中,锻炼了运用专业英语对外商宣传我国有关政策法令的实务本领。这些工作实践都为研究生日后从事涉外经济、法律工作积累了有益的经验。

近年来,随着我国进一步实行对外开放政策,许多新的法律问题也不断出现。我们获悉:我国正在考虑是否参加 1965 年制定的《华盛顿公约》,即《解决国家与他国国民之间投资争端公约》。对此,国内学术界意见不一,众说纷纭。我们认为,争论双方都有一定理由,但均从一般原则出发立论,缺乏足够的事实根据。除了应该进一步深入研究仲裁机构(ICSID)的体制以外,还应了解它设立以来是怎么运转的,处理过哪些具体的案件,处理过程中对发达国家有哪些偏袒,对发展中国家是否有过歧视等等,据以判断我国作为发展中国家是否应该参加。根据这种认识,我们组织研究生结合他们的外语基本功训练和学位论文写作,翻译了大量有关 ICSID 的基本文献,分工撰写专题研究报告,并拟将研究成果汇集成册出版,供我国有关决策部门

和立法部门参考。这项研究课题,由于紧密联系实际,切合国家急需,已得到有关部门重视。同时,对于本届研究生也是一次有益的尝试,使他们从解决现实问题出发,开展科研、集体攻关。

四、充分信赖,畀以"重担",严密组织,严格把关

经过两三年严格的基本功训练之后,研究生的视野扩大了,思维、表达、写作各方面的能力也都有了一定程度的提高,再加上年轻人特定的优势,诸如精力充沛、思维敏捷、善于接受新知识等等,因此具有较大的潜力。如果把他们组织起来,适时地给他们压担子,并加以引导,就可以成为一支具有**攻坚实力**和**开拓精神**的科研队伍。我们认为,应充分估计到这支队伍蕴藏的能量,信赖他们,热情地鼓励他们承担科研任务,**勇于"自讨苦吃",敢于超过常规负荷**,从在学期间,就把学习的心得体会、知识积累、专题研究与日后的实际工作、教学任务、科研项目结合起来,经过不断努力,力争多出成果,快出人才。

在出成果中培养人才是一个行之有效的办法,但这同样需要在导师的精心组织、悉心指导之下,才能达到预期的目标。若放任自流,就形不成一股强劲的攻坚实力,也不利于对研究生个人的培养。1985 年,我们接受了国家教委博士点基金的重点科研项目,编写一套国际经济法系列专著,包括国际贸易法、国际投资法、国际货币金融法、国际税法、国际海事法等。这在当时是一个大胆的设想,因为要对国际经济法这一学科的五个分支部门同时进行深入的研究,在短短两年内写出共约 155 万字的系列专著,成套推出,这在国内尚属初次尝试,任务是相当艰巨的,更何况我们的第一批专业师资队伍当时才刚刚建立,人员和力量显然都不足。但我们对这些年轻人的潜能作了实事求是的估量。接受任务之后,就以这批初出茅庐的硕士毕业生为骨干,同时也挑选了几名较优秀的在学研究生,组成攻关小组,既"**异想天开**",又**脚踏实地**,立足于刻苦的学习和研究,充分发挥潜力,要求他们尽可能广泛地收集国内外最新的研究成果,潜心钻研。另外,在充分估量年轻硕士生潜力的同时,也清醒地看到他们的弱点,如学术上不够成熟,不同程度地存在治学经验不足,学风不够严谨,知识面不够宽等,这些都有待于及时得到同行、前辈的指导。针对这些弱点,本专业点导师又分别**邀请**国内各有关分支学科的**知名学者**、教授(如安徽大学朱学山教授、复旦大学董世忠教授、南开大学潘同龙教授和高尔森教授、中国政法大学吴焕宁教授等)给予具体指导和**严格把关**。在审订年轻作者的书稿时,不符合要求者退

回重写，有疏漏处退回补充，错误的予以改正，累赘者予以删除。在青年硕士生勤奋笔耕、同行前辈学者严格把关之下，终于完成了国家教委下达的科研任务。1987年11月，全套五本系列专著正式出版，不但成书质量得到保证，而且使年轻人在写作过程中经受了较全面的严格锻炼。

学界人士认为，这套系列专著问世，对于国际经济法这门边缘性学科在中国的兴起，在一定程度上发挥了开拓创新的作用。它们具有两个鲜明的特点：（1）材料新：引进了国际经济法的新知识和新信息，因为它们直接取材于近期外文书刊有关国际经济法的最新学术动态和科研成果；（2）见解新：站在第三世界国家的共同立场上，从中国的实际出发，评析国际经济往来中的法律问题，提出自己的见解，为建立具有中国特色的国际经济法学体系作了添砖加瓦的努力，也得到有关部门的重视。1986年，司法部教育司教材编辑部组织编写国际经济法学科系列教材，除了本专业导师担任《国际经济法总论》《国际经济法参考资料》两本书的主编以外，还有五位青年教师应邀参加其他五本教材的编写工作。这说明他们的刻苦劳动已经得到了一定的社会承认；也说明了在严密组织、严格把关的前提下，这些**新生力量**是可以信赖的，他们将在实践中不断地得到锻炼，取得进步和提高。

五、赋予较大"成才自留权"，加速形成"人才生产力"

几年来，我们的培养工作取得了一些成绩，这与国家教委和学校领导的关心和重视是分不开的。我们希望再经过若干年的努力，利用现有的基础和有利的客观条件，把厦大国际经济法专业建设成为我国培养国际经济法高层次专门人才的主要"生产"基地之一，进入全国同类专业的前列，为国家输送更多的人才。

就目前的情况来看，我们认为首先有必要允许新兴学科的新设专业在毕业研究生的使用和分配方面适用灵活政策，拥有更多的自主权和"自留权"，对毕业研究生的使用应该相对地集中，组织他们集体攻关，相互配合，分工协作，以便在较短的期间内，迅速形成培养人才的生产力，从而源源不断地为国家输送这方面的人才。新学科与老学科、白手起家的学校与积累有余的学校应该区别对待。对新学科中的新设专业，应当像对刚开始赢利的外资、合资企业一样，允许它们享有"二年免税、三年减半纳税"的优惠待遇。在成才研究生的分配上，允许培养单位多留些人，这才有利于他们在没有外来援助的情况下，通过自力更生，加速形成生产力。对老学科、老专业来说，"防止近亲繁衍"是对的，但不能绝对化，不分青红皂白地推行于新设的专业。成才研究生的分配使用如果过于分散,就有如一架拆散的工作母机,东一个马达,西一条皮带,南一个齿轮,北一个螺丝钉,不利于更多地制造新机器,不可能建设起人才培养的生产基地。

其次,学校的物质待遇比起涉外经贸部门、政府机关、企事业单位来要相对差些,研究生的"从政热""从商热"在各个专业不同程度地存在着,而在国际经济法专业尤甚。要使研究生安心在教学、科研机构工作,还有待于各级领导部门采取合理的、切实有效的措施解决待遇差距问题,以便"稳定军心""提高士气"。此外,高职称的比例和名额限制,也直接影响到学术梯队的形成以及教学、科研人员的工作积极性。对确有才华,又经过努力取得颇佳科研成果的年轻人,应该努力创造条件,让他们上。这个问题,对于新兴学科的发展影响较大,希望能够引起有关部门和领导的重视。

第3章 "博士"新解*

>> 内容提要

"博士"应当是博学之士、博采之士与博斗之士的"综称"或"合成体"。一个合格的"博士",其学识范围应扩及本专业的中、外、古、今;应能瞄准本学科的中外最新前沿新知,消化吸收后创出新高度;应刻苦拼搏,"自讨苦吃",方能有成。

>> 目　次

附录一　官员与老板:心仪博士帽
附录二　"教授"贬值为哪般
附录三　该挤挤"学术泡沫"了

"傻博士"曾与"穷教授"并列,一度是用以嘲人或自嘲的一对"美称"。嘲的大概是其耕耘之艰辛与其收获之菲薄,反差甚大,因而感慨于分配之不公。然而,曾经"萧条"一时的"博士业",近来却出现了"考博热",而且迅猛升温。这标志着人们在体制改革深化过程中价值观念的重要改变,自属可喜。不过,据报道,也有业内人士担心在这种新气象下不无某种隐忧,"使博士教育**严格的管理体系**面临着从未有过的考验"[2]。

五六年前的这种隐忧,如今竟在某种程度上"不幸而言中"。在商品经济大潮的冲击下,在某种腐败风气的侵蚀下,一向相对"清高"甚至拥有"名牌"的某些高校,某些管理者和被管理者也放松了应有的学术自律,其教授和博士的知识"含金量"明显下滑,甚至出现了镀金冒称"足赤";刚刚入学就大量印发名片,赫然自封"J. D."或"博士",以攫取某种"效益";存心混过三年,就文凭到手,也果真有如愿以偿的。诸

---

* 本文原辑于《专家论坛:中国法学教育的改革与未来》,载《中国大学教学》2001年第4期,高等教育出版社2001年版。

[2] 参见《官员与老板:心仪博士帽》,载《人民日报》(海外版)1995年11月24日。

如此类,说轻些,是"短斤缺两",说重些,恐怕近乎掺假伪劣产品及虚假广告。对此类现象,社会正直人士已经公开质问:"教授贬值为哪般?"并且大声呐喊:"该挤挤学术泡沫了!"[3]

单就博士而言,看来问题就出在其"严格的管理体系"在某些学校日渐松弛了。在强调"依法治国"的宏观环境下,攻读法学博士学位乃是"博士热"中之一大热。追求者众,难免也面临着严格管理体系是否日渐松弛的现实问题。

说到"严格的管理",无非是把好质量关,做到"严进"和"严出",使博士之名与博士之实严格相符。这显然应是管理者与被管理者的共同追求。

从这个意义上说,似不妨对"博士"一词略作新解:它是**博学**之士、**博采**之士与**搏斗**之士的"综称"或"合成体"。

"博士"必须博学,自是题中应有之义。一个合格的博士,其学识范围自应扩及本专业的中、外、古、今。业务上的高精尖,离不开比较宽广的基础知识面和过硬的中文、外文基本功。如果博士阅读外文资料的速度只比蜗牛略快,或笔下中文错别字不断,而又自解为"雕虫小技,微不足道",则此种"大将"风度实在不敢恭维。

博学是目的,博采是手段。博采提倡瞄准本学科的中外最前沿新知,奉行"拿来主义"与"消化主义"相结合,创出新高度。有如蜜蜂,广泛采集最新鲜的"花蜜",绞尽脑汁,和以心血,酿成科学之新蜜。而不是如蜘蛛之悬空结网,貌似"体系完整",却华而不实;也并非如蚂蚁之只善搬运和堆砌,却不致力于开拓和创新。博采的前提之一,是虚怀若谷,具备"海绵"精神,善于吸收他人科学新知的涓涓滴滴,忌的是"自我感觉良好",浅尝辄止,或眼高手低,志大才疏。

"博",古通"搏",两字同音同义。故"博士"亦指其"拼搏"的必备之素志恒心和必具之治学精神。"梅花香自苦寒来","学海无涯苦作舟",所喻的都是务必刻苦拼搏和"自讨苦吃",方能有成。如此,平日"喝咖啡的时间"比别人少,却心安理得;必要时通宵达旦,废寝忘餐,也不喊累,却自得其乐,甚至自觉活得很"潇洒",这就渐臻于"博士"的化境了。

一言以蔽之,如能致力于兼具此三"博"要素,则博士之名实严格相符,并不难预期。

---

[3] 参见以上述质问和呐喊为题的两篇文章,已作为本文附录二、三。

附录一 官员与老板：心仪博士帽*

王晓晖

当几位经理漫步在中国社会科学院研究生院秋日的校园时，共青团中央书记处第一书记李克强已经在未名湖畔戴过博士帽了。

海关总署副局级官员黄胜强今年以骄人成绩叩开博士之门的时候，中国名牌三鸣养生王的总裁又报考了中国科技大学研究生院。

不知数学与养生之间有多少的距离和联系，但可以确认的是，近两年的中国"考博热"中，官员考博和老板考博已成为此间一大景观。

"考博热"来得迅猛。前十年招不满博士生的中国社会科学院近来招考比例激增到1∶5。中国科学院招收的博士再次突破了历史最高水平，今年入学的博士人数预计又很可观。国家教委去年的计划在众多方面的要求之下被打破，实际招收人数超出预定人数两千多，达到九千人以上。

计划变更的原因有多少是因为官员与老板的介入，这个数字难以统计。不过事情正像中国社科院研究生院党委副书记翁杰明所说的，戴上黑帽子的博士官居要职的事实和身居星级宾馆的老板日夜兼程备考博士的消息已成为中国"考博热"与生源多元化的重要依据。

平心静气，参与过中国政治经济生活具体运作，官员与老板重返校园去读书，这中间的动力何在呢？在政府部门供职的李先生说，我们必须先期致力于自身知识结构的完善。因为，经济给政治带来的影响无法回避，因为国家的现代化首先要求人的现代化。

按照翁杰明估计，20年后，中国的领导群体将由一批具有硕士、博士头衔的职业、半职业管理者组成，而一个健全的知识结构是他们所必需的。

至于老板对博士帽的向往则隐约折射出他们对儒商的向往。另外，在商言利，有一顶博士帽戴在公司头顶，公司的信誉即可瞬间陡增，届时，知识的力量便可以在公司的生意上以数字的形式表现出来。

其实，以考博为愚钝之举还只是昨天的事情，"傻博士"的称呼仍依稀响在耳畔，

---

* 本文原载于《人民日报》（海外版）1995年11月24日。

考博士的热潮就迅猛地来到了眼前。无论是向往健全的知识结构,还是借助博士桂冠达到实利的目的,究其根本,还是知识的力量越来越被人们认识。翁杰明说,中国的市场经济逐步有序化,靠机遇和冒险去获取超额利润不会再是一种普遍现象了。不过,也有业内人士指出"考博热"引出招博方式的多样化。据称,操作过程中各种利益的驱动使博士教育严格的管理体系面临着从未有过的考验。

附录二 "教授"贬值为哪般[*]

苗体君

近年来,"教授满街走"已成为高校的普遍现象。北京大学著名学者季羡林教授曾极而言之:"如今不管是谁,只要能在北大谋一个教书的位子,就能评上教授。"而在七八十年前,连鲁迅、梁漱溟这样的大学者也只能被聘为讲师。今天,稍有名气的大学多在拼命增加教授的数量,一些院系甚至提出"告别有讲师"的奋斗目标,广东还有大学趁合并之机一次性突击评出了四十多个博导。这不禁使人想起"大跃进"时期全民炼钢铁的那一幕。

笔者日前在南京大学档案馆查阅有关校中资料时发现,1927 年时的南京大学(时称"第四中山大学")竟没有一位教授,即使是从国外回来的诸如芝加哥大学毕业的吴有训博士、哈佛大学毕业的竺可桢博士、法国国家科学院毕业的严济慈博士,也都只被聘为副教授。而到新千年来临之际,南京大学的教授已达千余名。难怪那里的一位博导对学生说:"别称我教授,现在的教授一分钱能买好几个。"

当今社会对教授们的期望值总是很高,其实高校也并非什么理想、干净的知识殿堂。十年前毕业的优秀本科生、研究生很少有人愿意到高校当教师,因为这个职业太清贫,连不太优秀留下来做教师的,也被视作进了"鬼门关"。教师队伍的整体素质亟待提高已是不争的事实。笔者认为,现在的高校教师大致可分为两类:一类真正有本事且热心教育;另一类没什么本事,因能力不足从社会大舞台退到学校,只图混口饭吃而已。

在新中国的五十多年历史中,"文化大革命"前对教授的评审,在数量和质量上

---

[*] 本文原载于《瞭望新闻周刊》2001 年 5 月 21 日第 21 期。经征得该刊总编室杨桃源主任同意,转录于此,以飨读者。谨向该刊和本文原作者致谢。

都有所限制,教授是潜心做学问的象征,含金量大,中央教育部直接参与对教授的评审与任命。"文化大革命"结束,在恢复高校职称评审制度的开始几年还比较正规,后来随着职称评审的最终权力下放,"滥评"现象就出现了。

一些学校对教授的评审不重视学术水平和教学能力,而要按教师的工作年限排队。有些学校为了解决教师职称,竟由校领导出面编写教材及教学指导书目,再强卖给学生使用,其实有些教授们编的教材几乎都是照抄别人的,实在没有多少学术价值。

我国现行的官本位体制是导致教授贬值的一大原因。在高校仅做个专职教师还不够,想尽快提升职称不从政不行,多数人称之为"曲线提升"。有了行政职务就有了"学术",就可以凭借手中的权力占有科研经费,出版专著都可以找人代笔。

学贯中西的大学者钱仲联,可谓江苏省学术界的一块金招牌。20年前国家首次审批申报博导时,他所在的学校向北京申报了不包括他的一百余人,甚至该校的膳食科长也名列其中。北京的评审者没有找到他的名字,就通知江苏省火速上报他的材料。结果当只有钱仲联一人为博导的批文回到该校,大家都呆了。这个真实的故事很快传遍了全国学术界,当时中央评审之正规可见一斑。

这类事情同时反映了我国"不患寡而患不均"的传统观念对评聘教授工作的渗透。天津某大学的一个好友告诉我,他取得博导的成功秘诀是在学术上"团结领导和广大群众"。原来他每次撰写著作或论文,总是添上领导或一些教师的名字,如此把自己辛勤获得的成果均分,以求得大家的支持和拥护。

不能破除教授终身制是造成教授贬值的又一个原因。教授头衔多是高校教师最终的追求目标,一旦得到,他们中的不少人便要享受教授头衔带来的诸多好处,而对教学、科研不会再有多少兴趣。

眼下拉关系、送礼在职称评审时也成为时尚,最具学术说服力的博导评审都不例外。笔者今年在北京参加一个学术会时,才得知一个多年未见的好友成了博导。他的学术资本只是两篇质量一般的论文,此次荣升的关键是他占据教务处处长的职位。他私下里对我说,他们学校刚成为博士点的某专业,是花了20万元买来的。

附录三　该挤挤"学术泡沫"了*

周大平

据教育部去年底统计,在我国高校的46.3万名教师中,教授和副教授占32.4%。高级教学职称头衔的人数指标符合国家标准,而其中是否如这篇来稿中所言"教授"贬值,恐怕只有透过"学术泡沫"去洞察它的深层。

近两年有的高校扩招,实际上是把大量高考分数中等偏下的考生扩招进了学校,因为考分较高的考生不必扩招也能考入大学。面对新生质量的参差不齐,高校普遍出现了教师的结构性短缺,致使一些本科专业的教师达到满负荷授课的极限,有的基础课甚至由在校研究生讲授。这种现状使人想起两年前北京大学高教研究所的一个预言:就供给的角度说,要大规模扩大招生,必定以降低教育质量为代价。

瑞士洛桑国际管理开发研究院发表的《2000年度国际竞争力报告》表明,中国的国际竞争力已由1998年的第24位降到第31位。清华大学的一个课题组在调查两个工科系后认为,这与当前我国高等教育质量严重下滑有关,其中教师的教学质量下滑是一个关键因素。教育部一位官员也委婉地表示,这支队伍的整体素质有待提高。

尽管谁也无从知道到底有多少高校教师所拥有的教学职称与实际能力不符,然而教师教学质量下滑的现状,使我们仍有理由作出这样的推断:是那些形形色色无法定论为学术腐败的行为,导致了当今高校中一些名不副实的"教授"们在"滥竽充数"。

高校的根本任务是培养人。从经济学的角度讲,学生好比是产品,评定其质量是否合格,首先必须拥有一些基础性的标准,这与教育部所称的建立教育质量的多样化模式并不矛盾。其次必须拥有施教者个人的良好素质,如果施教者的教学职称是注了水的,他本人也就没有了"可靠度",所谓"人而无信不知其可"。原复旦大学校长杨福家院士曾举过一个同类型的例子:前些年上海有个很有名的年轻教授,后来被人发现他的许多论文都是抄别人的,于是他失去了所有的光环。

目前高校教学职称中所以存在"假冒",一个重要原因是教学质量评价机制的自

---

* 本文原载于《瞭望新闻周刊》2001年5月21日第21期。经征得该刊总编室杨桃源主任同意,转录于此,以飨读者。谨向该刊和本文原作者致谢。

我封闭,其运作的客观性和公正性完全取决于体系内主管者的道德自律。一旦这种自律失控,教学职称评定的"学术泡沫"必然发生。广东某大学去年一次性突击评出四十多个博导的事情,就被业内人士判定是一个"内行包庇同行"的典型。

我国不是没有教师职务聘任方面的规定,也不是没有强调教师教学业绩表现的政策导向,然而为什么还是对混迹在教师队伍中的"滥竽"无能为力?这的确是一个值得反思的问题。

多年来,我们的教育督导往往侧重于评价学校的各项硬件达没达标,各项投入符不符合法定的标准等,而对教师的教学效果如何,学校对师资的管理是否有利于培养人(包括对教授这样的高级职称有没有按需设岗,有没有面向社会、公开招聘,有没有平等竞争、择优录用、合同管理)等有所忽视。如果教育督导没有把"人"放在督导的核心,实际上就是在客观上为那些违反道德准则的行为网开一面。

高校的自主办学权正在逐年扩大,教学质量是教育永恒的话题。从进一步强化监管职能考虑,教育部已着手建立高校教学质量的监控体系。从未来走上社会就业考虑,苦读几年的学生最关心的莫过于高校的教学质量"能使自己学到多少东西"。而从自身的生存和竞争考虑,一些学校如果没有危机感,置学校教学质量于不顾,频频在教学职称评定上违规做手脚,终究要自食其果,被市场淘汰,只是到时候他们有何颜面面对为此付出了沉重代价的在校生们?

第 4 章　是"棒打鸳鸯"吗？

——就"李爽案件"评《纽约时报》报道兼答美国法学界同行问*

▶▶ 内容提要

1981年秋，时值中国实行对外开放基本国策之初，北京发生了一起涉及法国驻华外交官昂玛努·贝耶华(E. Bellefroid)的"绯闻"和拘留中国女青年李爽的事件。经外国媒体炒作，在国际上闹得沸沸扬扬，成为轰动一时的"外交事件"。当时，美国法学界有些人士也借题发挥，对中国的"人权"状况和法制问题议论纷纷，或误解，或指责，或抨击，或质疑，不一而足。诸如，中国政府是否尊重和保护人身自由和婚恋自由？中国对驻华外交官的身份地位和外交特权是否给予应有的尊重和足够的保护？中国政府及民众是否具有强烈的盲目排外情绪？中国当局是否乘机制造借口迫害前卫知识分子？此事在中国何以不公开审理并接受外国记者自由采访和舆论监督？当时笔者正在美国哈佛大学从事国际经济法学研究，并兼部分讲学工作，遂应邀针对由此事件引发的一系列具体问题和质疑作了一次专题演讲，依据中国当时有效的法律法规、有关的国际公约以及美国的相关法律和司法实践判例，对上述有关问题逐一作了评论和剖析。以下是此次专题演讲的基本内容。

▶▶ 目　次

一、李爽是何许人？"李爽案件"的背景如何？

---

* 本文根据1982年初笔者在哈佛大学所作的一次专题演讲整理而成，原文刊载于美国纽约法学院《国际法与比较法学刊》第3卷第1期(1982年初出版)。原文见本文附录四。文中所援引和评析的法律法规，均以1981年当时有效者为准。阅读时请注意查对和比较1981年以来有关法律法规的发展情况，以明其历史发展脉络，并获得最新信息。

二、李爽触犯了什么法律？犯了什么罪？
三、是打击"鸳鸯"的无情棒，还是拯救沉沦的救生圈？
附录一　中国拘禁了法国男人的情妇
附录二　法国外交官说中国拘留了他的未婚妻
附录三　小题大做——评白天祥等人在所谓"李爽案件"上的喧嚷
附录四　The Li Shuang Case: A Wet Blanket over Romantic Love?
附录五　《纽约时报》报道英文原文

《纽约时报》记者克利斯托弗·S.雷恩（Christopher S. Wren）写了一篇新闻特别报道，题为《中国拘禁了法国男人的情妇》[4]。1982年1月间，这篇特稿连同另一则短讯[5]，由任课的美国教授[6]加以复印，分发给哈佛大学法学院的博士研究生，供作"当代中国法律"这一热门课程的参考资料。看来，这两篇报道，特别是其中第一篇，现在已被当作研究中国现行法律制度的重要素材。

不久前，我从中华人民共和国应邀来到哈佛大学法学院。不少美国同行朋友和研究生得知我来自中国，先后向我提出了有关这一事件的许多问题。诸如李爽究竟是何许人？此案产生的背景如何？她究竟触犯了什么法，犯下了什么罪？中国政府何故干预她的婚姻自由，竟然"棒打多情鸳鸯"，不尊重基本人权？此案为什么不公开审理？面对这形形色色的诸多问题，身为来自中国的法律学人，我感到有责任也很乐意同对这一事件感兴趣的美国同行朋友们一起来展开讨论。同时，鉴于《纽约时报》的上述两篇报道有含糊不清、不正确或自相矛盾之处，我谨结合中国现行法律、法规的有关规定，提出个人看法，希望通过共同讨论，把这一事件的真相和本质尽可能弄个一清二楚、水落石出。

一、李爽是何许人？"李爽案件"的背景如何？

雷恩先生撰写的上述特别报道称：

---

[4] 原文载于《纽约时报》1981年11月13日第36版第1栏。该文中译本见附录一。

[5] 题为《法国外交官说中国拘留了他的未婚妻》，载于《纽约时报》1981年9月13日第5版第6栏。该文中译本见附录二。

[6] 即哈佛大学法学院前副院长、东亚法律研究中心主任柯恩（Jerome Cohen）教授，他是美国法学界知名的"中国通"。当时修习柯恩教授主讲的"当代中国法律"这门课的博士生，除来自美国外，还有许多来自英、法、德、日、澳等国的留学人员。

"李爽是一名年方 24 岁的前卫派美工人员,她与法国驻华大使馆一名馆员,即年已 33 岁的昂玛努·贝耶华坠入情网,并且已经订婚。此间的朋友们都说,**中国人先前曾经许诺这一对情侣可以正式结婚**……但是,本星期二,中国当局公开宣布:这位李小姐已经被判处在一所惩罚机构中接受'劳动教养'两年。""贝耶华先生已经与他的妻子分居"。

这一段报道中含有不少误解、失实和不确切之处。

根据中国的新闻报道,李爽本来是中国青年艺术剧院的一名美工人员,1981 年 1 月辞职后,成为一名无业游民和女"阿飞"。她在很长一段时间里没有正当职业,却从事各种下流活动,违反公共道德,影响了社会秩序。特别应当指出:尽管有关当局曾反复多次对她提出劝诫,但她却置若罔闻,依然我行我素,拒不改正;并且进一步发展到不顾一切后果,干脆明目张胆地搬入法国外交官贝耶华的寓所,与他同居达两个月之久,并利用贝耶华的外交官特权来庇护自己。因此,依据中国法律的有关规定,她被有关当局拘留,并由一家执法机关按照正当的执法程序处以两年劳动教养。随后,贝耶华就大喊大叫,歪曲事实真相,煽动舆论,猛烈抨击中国有关当局针对李爽不轨行为依法采取的正当的措施。

针对这些抨击,看来很有必要严格区分正当、合法的恋爱婚姻关系与不正当、不合法的男女两性关系。众所周知,中国是一个社会主义国家。国家要求具有劳动能力的每个公民都应当自食其力,并遵守公共秩序和社会道德。中华人民共和国的《宪法》明确规定,公民享有多种自由权利,诸如言论自由、出版自由、集会自由、结社自由、游行示威自由等等。但是,《宪法》从来未曾规定个人可以享有从事不道德、不合法两性腐化行为的"自由"。恰恰相反,在中国,一切不道德和不合法的两性行为都会受到公众的谴责;而情节严重者,则会受到法律的惩罚。毫无疑义,世界上一切正直的人士,包括一切理智的人权主义者和人权倡导者,都绝不会把通奸"自由"或卖淫"自由"认定为个人的正当"自由",认定为公民"人权"的一个正当组成部分。因为诸如此类的不正当、不合法的两性行为,早已被公认为违反公共道德、损害和危害民族健康。

自从粉碎"四人帮"之后,中国人民与世界各国人民的接触日益频繁。绝大多数外国人是中国人民的忠实朋友,他们致力于促进中国与其他各国的文化经济交流。但是,也确实还有极少数外国人仍然沿袭老殖民主义者居高临下、傲慢无礼的态度,仍然视独立自主的新中国如半殖民地的旧中国,仍然把新中国看作"外国冒险家的乐园",他们往往在各种外衣的掩护之下,来到中国为非作歹,恣意欺凌中国老百姓。他们认为在这里依然可以随心所欲,寻花问柳。

遗憾的是，也确有少数中国女青年为某些外国来客的财富所诱惑，不顾民族的尊严和自己的人格，向外国人出卖自己的灵魂和肉体。换言之，她们竟然从事卖淫活动，或从事变相的卖淫活动。如所周知，自1949年新中国建立以后，娼妓卖淫活动在中国一直受到严禁，并曾一度销声匿迹。但是，自1979年中国实行对外开放政策以后，娼妓卖淫活动又开始在少数城市中死灰复燃。特别可恶的是，有一些卖淫或变相卖淫活动，竟是在某些外国人的强权地位和特权豁免掩护之下，明目张胆、肆无忌惮地进行的。这显然是藐视和嘲弄了中国法律的庄严，严重地伤害了中国人民的民族自尊，并且激怒了中国民众。因为，这种丑恶现象勾起了中国民众对1949年以前遭受一百多年殖民地屈辱的痛苦回忆，他们强烈地希望在这种丑恶现象重新萌长的初期阶段就予以严厉禁止。

可以说，这就是产生"李爽案件"的部分重要背景。人们如果能在这样的背景下，结合其他各种因素来观察这次事件，就不难理解中国有关当局何以采取如此严肃认真的态度来处理此事。这种态度正是准确地反映了中国民众的共同愿望，因而获得了他们的全力支持。

诚然，也不难设想，在西方某些国家中，人们对此类现象的看法和态度也许会与中国人有很大的差异。这是因为他们的历史、文化、社会制度和道德观念迥然不同于中国民众。但是，我仍然确信，一切外国朋友定能充分理解：中国人曾经饱经忧患，饱受殖民主义者和帝国主义者强加的不胜枚举的各种苦难、蹂躏、侵害、亵渎和凌辱，因此，他们不能不时时回顾和总结过去的痛苦经历，一切外国朋友也定能充分理解和自觉自愿地充分尊重中国民众正当的、无可非议的民族感情。

二、李爽触犯了什么法律？犯了什么罪？

由于李爽是中国公民，她的违法行为发生于中国境内，因此，作为一个主权独立的国家，中国当局依据中国法律处置李爽的违法行为，并且视之为纯属内国事务，与外交无涉，这是理所当然、无可非议的。看来，有关法律选择或准据法的此项普通常识，目前已被某些人士置之脑后，因此，有必要重新强调此项常识，并把它作为评析本案的前提和基础。

我个人的初步看法是李爽的行为触犯了以下几种中国法律法规：

首先,她可能触犯了《中华人民共和国治安管理处罚条例》[7]。该条例第5条规定:"有下列扰乱公共秩序行为之一的,处十日以下拘留、二十元以下罚款或者警告",其中所列的第8种违法行为,就是"违反政府取缔娼妓的命令,卖淫或者奸宿暗娼"。作为一项十分重要的补充,该条例第30条进一步规定:"对于一贯游手好闲、不务正业、屡次违反治安管理的人,在处罚执行完毕后需要劳动教养的,可以送交劳动教养机关实行劳动教养。"

其次,她触犯了中国国务院《关于劳动教养问题的决定》[8]。该决定第1条规定,对于不务正业,有流氓行为,违反治安管理,屡教不改的人,应当加以收容实行劳动教养。1979年,国务院又公布了《关于劳动教养的补充规定》[9],其中第3条载明:"劳动教养的期限为一年至三年。必要时得延长一年。节日、星期日休息。"

雷恩先生的报道中提到,中国驻法国大使馆在1981年11月12日发表的一项声明中"并未说明李爽小姐究竟犯了什么罪"。这是不足为奇的。因为该大使馆发表的声明并不是一份裁决书或判决书,因此它无须逐一详细列出被指控的违法行为和被援引的有关法律条文。但是,1981年11月14日新华社记者发表的评论中却已经明确指出:根据中国国务院颁行的《关于劳动教养问题的决定》第1条,李爽被送去接受"劳动教养"两年。[10]

有人质疑:李爽究竟是否触犯了中国的刑法?

要回答这个问题,必须先指出以下两点:

第一,根据我在美国所看到的有关新闻报道,中国政府并未认定李爽的行为是触犯了中国刑法的犯罪行为,从而根据刑法的有关规定加以惩处;中国政府只是按照劳动教养的有关规定加以处罚。关于这一点,前面已经提到,本文的第三部分将进一步加以评析。

第二,李爽的行为是否触犯了中国的刑法,取决于法国外交官贝耶华当时的婚姻状态:在贝耶华与李爽公开同居的当时,这位男人究竟是单身未婚、已经结婚、丧

---

[7] 该案例于1957年10月22日第一届全国人民代表大会常务委员会第八十一次会议通过,同日公布施行。收辑于《中华人民共和国公安法规选编》(1950—1979),法律出版社1982年版,第73、79—80页。该条例于1986年9月5日修订,原第5条和第30条的规定合并改列为第30条,并有重要补充。1994年5月12日,该条例再次修订,其中第30条规定未作更动。2005年8月28日,第十届全国人民代表大会常务委员会第十七次会议通过《中华人民共和国治安管理处罚法》,自2006年3月1日起施行。1994年5月12日修订公布的《中华人民共和国治安管理处罚条例》同时废止。

[8] 该决定于1957年8月1日第一届全国人民代表大会常务委员会第七十八次会议批准,1957年8月3日国务院公布施行。

[9] 该规定于1979年11月29日第五届全国人民代表大会常务委员会第十二次会议批准,同日国务院公布施行。

[10] 参见新华社记者评论:《小题大做》,载《光明日报》1981年11月15日。详见本文附录三。

偶鳏居、已经离异,或是正在分居之中? 雷恩先生在报道中说"贝耶华已与他的妻子实行分居",但在同一篇报道的开头,却又说贝耶华和李爽"已经订婚",而且"中国人先前曾经许诺这一对情侣可以正式结婚"。[11] 同一篇报道中出现的这两种说法难道不是自相矛盾吗? 众所周知,"分居"是与"离婚"具有本质差异的一种婚姻状态。即使在美国的法律规定与官方文件中,前者与后者从来都是严格地加以区分的。[12] 显而易见,"离婚"意味着有关的法定婚姻关系已经死亡,而"分居"则意味着有关的法定婚姻关系仍然存活着,只不过是男女配偶双方各自分别居住而已。既然如此,贝耶华作为一个有着合法妻子的"有妇之夫",在其并未正式依法离婚之前,怎么可以合法地与另外的一个女人——李爽"订婚"? 中国人又怎能"许诺"他们两人可以合法地"正式结婚"? 由此可见,如果雷恩先生关于贝耶华与其合法妻子"分居"的报道属实,那么,贝耶华和李爽两人就犯下了重婚罪。[13]

有人辩难说:李爽并未与贝耶华正式结婚,而只不过是与贝耶华同居两个月而已,因此,她的行为并未构成重婚罪。诚然,根据1980年公布的《中华人民共和国婚姻法》的规定,一项合法的婚姻,必须由男女双方前往婚姻登记机关进行结婚登记。符合法定条件的,发给结婚证书,确立夫妻关系。[14] 但是,社会实际生活中却有不少这样的事例:男方或女方已经有一个依法登记在案的合法配偶,却又与另一个异性住在一起,他和她不是秘密地通奸,而是公开地俨然以夫妻相待,共同生活,而并不进行另一次(第二次)结婚登记。在中国的司法实践中,此类公开同居往往被认定为"事实上的重婚",并且按重婚罪处断,以便更有效地控制这种犯罪行为。这种司法实践已被总结成为一项公认的原则,并被辑入1980年出版的《法学词典》[15];中国官方主办的一家周报——《中国法制报》对这一原则也加以采纳和宣传。[16]

对照上述这类司法实践中总结出来的断案原则,可以看出,如果雷恩先生对于贝耶华当时婚姻状态所作的描述准确无误,那么,李爽进入外交人员聚居的使馆区,

---

[11] 见本文附录一。雷恩先生在1981年9月13日发表的另一篇报道中,也说到李爽是贝耶华的"未婚妻"。
[12] 例如,在美国驻华大使馆颁发的非移民签证申请书中,其第19栏就对"分居"与"离婚"作了明显的区分。
[13] 1979年7月1日通过的《中华人民共和国刑法》第180条规定:"有配偶而重婚的,或者明知他人有配偶而与之结婚的,处二年以下有期徒刑或者拘役。"(按:该法已于1997年3月14日修订,原第180条有关重婚罪的规定改为第258条。文字未作改动。)
[14] 参见1980年9月10日公布的《中华人民共和国婚姻法》第7条。(按:该法已于2001年4月28日修订,原第7条改列为第8条。文字内容稍有增补。)
[15] "重婚:已有配偶的男女未办理离婚手续又与他人结婚,或虽未登记而实际上与他人以夫妻关系相对待而共同生活。是破坏一夫一妻制的违法行为。……凡以重婚论处的,应解除其非法的重婚关系,追究其刑事。"参见《法学词典》,上海辞书出版社1980年版,第521—522页。
[16] 参见《他犯有重婚罪吗?》,载《中国法制报》1981年10月2日。文章以"本报法律顾问组"解答咨询的形式指出:"所谓重婚……是指已有配偶的男女,在其配偶没有死亡,或者其婚姻关系没有依法解除之前,又同他人登记结婚,或者虽未进行结婚登记,但与他人在事实上以夫妻关系同居生活,构成了事实婚姻。"

并在外交官住所内与贝耶华公开同居达两个月,这一行为本来就已经构成了事实上的重婚罪。

当然,还应当补充说:如果贝耶华在与李爽公开同居之前,**确实已经与他的法国妻子办妥了离婚手续**,那么,李爽的行为可以不构成事实上的重婚。不过,她与贝耶华的所作所为,就其整体而言,仍然可以被认定为**流氓阿飞和娼妓行为**。[17]

三、是打击"鸳鸯"的无情棒,还是拯救沉沦的救生圈?

雷恩先生报道说,中国"有关当局一向警告中国公民,不要和外国人厮混"。"十分明显,处罚李爽的用意在于杀鸡吓猴,儆戒其他情侣。不过,现在还弄不清楚此事是否也表明当局有意对知识界的不驯分子采取更加严厉的镇压迫害措施。"雷恩这些模棱两可、含糊其辞的评论,把中国人与外国人之间正常、合法的交往与两者之间不正常、不合法的关系混为一谈,也混淆了法律问题与政治问题的界限,并且把再就业培训曲解为镇压迫害与威胁恫吓。

众所周知,中国人民绝不会盲目排外,绝不会不分青红皂白,反对一切来自外国的事物和人员,也从来不反对中国人与外国人之间进行正常、合法的接触和交往,包括正常、合法的中外联姻结亲。这方面的事例可谓不胜枚举,无须逐一列举最近几年来已经正式结成佳偶的许多中外情侣。最能说明问题的是:在同一个北京,属于同一个法国驻华大使馆的另一名外交官克里斯琴·加依亚诺(Christian Galliano),就在1981年10月与一名中国女青年赵江愉快地结为夫妻。仅此一例,就足以说明:中国当局对于"中外合璧"型的美满姻缘,向来是成人之美和乐观其成的。关于这一项中外联姻,雷恩先生在前述那篇新闻特稿中也如实地作了报道,这是令人高兴的。遗憾的是,法国外交官贝耶华的所作所为却迥异于这另一位法国外交官加依亚诺。

---

[17] 据另外一篇报道说:1980年9月间,法国外交官贝耶华与李爽在北京一次美术展览中相遇。按贝耶华的描述,两人"一见钟情"。当时,贝耶华的妻子在法新社驻北京办事处工作。到了1981年5月,贝耶华向中国有关当局申请,要求与李爽结婚,并且出具了与法国妻子离婚的证明。但是,在此之前好几个月里,李爽仗仗洋人外交特权公开从事变相卖淫的下流放荡行为已经严重地影响了社会秩序,并激起当地群众的愤怒。由于当时李爽的流氓阿飞行为问题正在处理之中,尚悬而未决,在此种情况下,中国有关当局暂且不能批准李爽与贝耶华结婚。于是,李爽不顾有关当局的一再劝诫,明目张胆地搬入北京使馆区贝耶华居住的外交官住所,公开同居两个月,并且利用贝耶华的外交官特权庇护自己,因为中国治安人员不能随意进入使馆区外交官住所。其后,1981年9月间,在李爽离开使馆区外交官住所外出时,被中国有关当局依法拘留,接着又在1981年11月间被送交"劳动教养"。参见中国新闻社特写稿,载美国商务部:《FBIS每日报道》(中国专辑)1981年11月16日,第G2页。

贝耶华利用他所享有的外交官特权,包括司法管辖上的豁免权[18],藐视其派驻所在地东道国的法律法规,从事与其外交官身份极不相称的不轨行为。具体说来,他作为有妇之夫,却在正式离婚前就与李爽乱搞男女关系,从事两性交易,任意触犯中国法律,并且**滥用**他所享有的外交官住所不可侵犯的特权[19],以窝藏和包庇李爽。为什么说是"滥用"外交特权呢?因为,《维也纳外交关系公约》明文规定:"在不妨碍外交特权和豁免权的情况下,凡享有外交特权与豁免权的人员,均负有尊重接受国(东道国)法律规章的**义务**。这些人员并负有不干涉该国内政的**义务**。"[20]与此相关,一切使馆馆舍以及享有同等不可侵犯特权的一切外交官住所,也理所当然地"**不得充作**与本公约或一般国际法之其他规则或派遣国与接受国间有效之特别协定所规定之**使馆职务不相符合之用途**"[21]。贝耶华利用外交官住所窝藏和包庇李爽、非法同居的所作所为,显然违反了《维也纳外交关系公约》的禁止规定。

任何外交官员,如果滥用其享有的各种特权,从而严重触犯了接受国(东道国)的法律,则按照《维也纳外交关系公约》有关规定的精神,享有主权的东道国就有权根据国际公法的原则采取严肃的措施,对付该违法胡为的外交官员。诸如向社会公众披露其不光彩行为(如贝耶华之不轨行为)的有关事实,宣布他为"不受欢迎的人员"(persona non grata),要求派遣国把他召回或撤换,实质上也就是东道国有权把他驱逐出境。[22]但是,中国政府出于珍视中法两国友谊的考虑,尽力避免如此行事。中国有关当局仅仅是局限于依据本国国内法的有关规定,对本国的违法公民(李爽)加以处罚,而并未对触犯中国法律的贝耶华本人采取本来可以采取的严厉措施。

然而,贝耶华不但不领情,反而恩将仇报。他伙同他的一帮朋友,肆无忌惮地猛烈抨击中国有关当局处置李爽是所谓"镇压迫害"知识分子,"压制自由化",并且标志着"中国的改革发生变化"。诸如此类的信口雌黄、造谣中伤、捏造歪曲和大吵大

---

〔18〕 1961 年 4 月 18 日签订的《维也纳外交关系公约》第 29 条规定:"外交代表人身不得侵犯。外交代表不受任何方式之逮捕或拘禁。接受国对外交代表应特示尊重,并应采取一切适当步骤以防止其人身、自由或尊严受到任何侵犯。"第 31 条进一步规定:"外交代表对接受国之刑事管辖享有豁免权。"参见王铁崖、田如萱编:《国际法资料选编》,法律出版社 1982 年版,第 606 页。

〔19〕《维也纳外交关系公约》第 30 条第 1 款规定:"外交代表之私人寓所一如使馆馆舍,应享有同样的不可侵犯权和同等的保护。"第 22 条第 1 款进一步明确规定:"使馆馆舍不得侵犯。接受国官员非经使馆馆长许可,不得进入使馆馆舍。"参见王铁崖、田如萱编:《国际法资料选编》,法律出版社 1982 年版,第 606 页。

〔20〕《维也纳外交关系公约》第 41 条第 1 款。参见王铁崖、田如萱编:《国际法资料选编》,法律出版社 1982 年版,第 610 页。

〔21〕《维也纳外交关系公约》第 41 条第 3 款。参见王铁崖、田如萱编:《国际法资料选编》,法律出版社 1982 年版,第 610 页。

〔22〕《维也纳外交关系公约》第 9 条第 1 款规定:"接受国可以随时不必解释决策理由的条件下,通知派遣国,宣告使馆馆长或使馆任何外交职员为不受欢迎人员,或使馆任何其他职员为不能接受人员。遇此情形,派遣国应斟酌情况召回该有关人员或解除其在使馆中之职务。"参见王铁崖、田如萱编:《国际法资料选编》,法律出版社 1982 年版,第 601 页。

闹,显然都是为了混淆视听,借以为贝耶华自己那些与外交官身份极不相称的不轨行为遮羞盖丑,借以转移中外社会公众的视线和注意力。简言之,贝耶华正是竭尽全力,妄图把法律问题歪曲为所谓的"政治"问题,借以为自己的丑行涂脂抹粉;把李爽下流放荡的违法行为美化为所谓"政治自由化",并把中国有关当局依法给予李爽的正当处罚诋毁为对知识分子施加所谓政治上的"镇压迫害"。

显而易见,所有这些诽谤无非是一场烟幕。明眼人一眼就看穿这场闹剧的本质。即使有些人士暂时还不明白此事的真相,但只要不存在"先入为主"的偏见(或许雷恩先生也属此类人士),则随着时间的推移,也不难透过贝耶华所施放的烟幕,逐渐地看清此事的本来面目。

说到这里,也有必要针对李爽受到处罚所依据的"劳动教养"法律制度,简略地谈谈它的程序和性质。

许多外国朋友以为,在有关当局决定对李爽处以"劳动教养"之前,没有经过什么必要的程序,因为他们在雷恩先生的报道中没有看到有关这方面的叙述。但是,据我所知,在中国驻法国大使馆所发表的一项声明中,却已经明确指出,"中国的一家执法机关依据执法程序",决定对李爽处以两年"劳动教养"。[23] 依据1957年与1979年由中国国务院先后公布施行的《关于劳动教养问题的决定》与《关于劳动教养的补充规定》,对于需要实行劳动教养的人,应由当地民政、公安部门及有关单位提出申请,报请劳动教养管理委员会认真审查批准后,送往劳动教养机关实行劳动教养。在各省、自治区、直辖市和大中城市分别设立劳动教养管理委员会,由当地民政、公安、劳动部门的负责人组成,领导和管理各该地区的劳动教养工作。劳动教养机关的各种活动,应由当地的人民检察院实行监督。[24]

雷恩先生并没有在报道中概述中国实施"劳动教养"的程序。人们当然不应为此而苛责于他。因为,在一篇短短的特别报道中,不可能说得面面俱到,巨细无遗。况且,他也未必熟悉有关实行"劳动教养"的程序问题。即使他对此略有所知,也未必就有机会直接参加或采访李爽案件的审讯过程。

在有关审讯问题上,依据《中华人民共和国刑事诉讼法》的有关规定,作为基本原则,人民法院审判案件,一律公开进行。但是,"有关国家机密或者个人阴私的案

---

[23] 参见《中国驻巴黎大使馆澄清对李爽的劳教处罚》,载美国商务部:《FBIS每日报道》(中国专辑)1981年11月13日,第G1页。

[24] 参见《关于劳动教养问题的决定》第2条、第3条,《关于劳动教养的补充规定》第1条、第5条。

件,不公开审理"[25]。在案件涉及国家秘密或者个人隐私,如果公开审理可能对国家利益或者对公共道德和社会风气产生不良影响的情况下,中国民众和外国来客(包括外国新闻记者)都会被谢绝列席旁听审理。因为,这些人既不是利害攸关的诉讼当事人,不是证人,也不是通常被允许进入法庭的诉讼当事人的近亲、密友、法律顾问、陪审员、法官、法院职员以及与法院业务有关的其他人员。

诚然,前文已经提到,李爽案件并未作为一起刑事犯罪案件并且严格地依据刑事诉讼法的程序进行审理,但是,上述审理个人隐私案件有关规定的基本精神,显然也是适用的,因为这些基本精神本来就应当适用于像李爽这样的案件。

在这方面,有些美国朋友提出了一些重要的疑问:即使这些涉及个人隐私的案件不予公开审理只是一些例外,即使这些不公开审理的案件总数可能不多,但是,这种做法岂不是侵害了新闻出版自由?更为重要的是,此类不予公开审理的例外做法,使得法院在审理案件过程中不受社会公众的监督,这岂不是把被告置于可能遭受到不公待遇的危境?

这些问题确实很有趣也很重要,值得进一步探讨。如所周知,在这些问题上,人们向来见仁见智,意见分歧;而且就是在美国法学界,也一直聚讼纷纭。究竟应当如何看待不公开审理这一例外做法,是一项有待深入研究和剖析的课题,就此足以写出多篇学术论文。在这里,我们只需要指出一点,即在对待公开审理的问题上,美国法本身也存在着**原则**和**例外**,并且采取类似于中国法的做法。

譬如,作为一项基本原则,美国《宪法》在其第一修正案中规定:"国会不得制定……剥夺言论自由或新闻出版自由……的法律。"第六修正案中进一步规定:"在一切刑事诉讼中,被告有权要求实行快速和公开的审理。"第五修正案以及第十四修正案中反复强调:非经"正当的法律程序"(due process of law),不得剥夺任何个人的生命、自由或财产。综合这些规定,从整体上说,"新闻出版自由"和"被告公开审理权"两者都受到宪法的保护,联邦和各州当局都不得任意加以剥夺。

但是,美国的司法实践表明,"新闻出版自由"和"被告公开审理权"这两者都不是**绝对的**,两者都必须结合其他方面的权益加以综合权衡,而有些权益则可能证明:在法院审理某些案件时,不让公众和新闻界列席旁听是合情合理的。在美国的司法实践中,向来可以引据和论证各种各样的权益,足以令人信服地承认:在某些情况下,完全地或部分地拒绝社会公众和新闻记者列席旁听庭审,是合理合法的,为此目

---

[25] 参见1979年7月1日通过的《中华人民共和国刑事诉讼法》第8条、第111条第1款。该法已于1996年3月17日修订,原第8条改列为第11条,原第111条改列为第152条,同时在文字上将"国家机密"更改为"国家秘密","个人阴私"更改为"个人隐私"。

的,甚至**可以不顾被告的反对意见**。这些曾经被引据和论证的各种权益中,就含有以下几种情况:在许多强奸案件中,有必要切实保护少年受害人和出庭作证的少年目击者[26];在某类案件中,有必要防止暴露隐名代理人的身份[27];有必要防止泄漏公司的商业秘密[28];有必要对制止空中劫机的做法保密[29],等等。同时,根据这些案例所述,完全地或部分地不让社会公众和新闻记者列席旁听审理并不是没有宪法依据的。

除此之外,有些被告往往自愿放弃获得公开审理的权利,并且主动请求采取封闭式或半封闭式的审理,以便保护自己,免受新闻炒作、危言耸听、猎奇哗众之苦,并且避免可能由此造成的审理不公的结果。

两相比较,社会公众和新闻记者列席旁听法院审理的权利,其宪法依据和重要性,当然不会必然超过被告是否愿意选择公开审理的权利。因此,在上面列举的类似情况下,前一种权利往往会被后一种权利所否定。

重温这些法律规定和司法判例,人们就会获得这样的初步印象:在有关公开审理的问题上,立法机关或司法机关都应当仔细评估和全面权衡各种互相对抗的权益(competing interests),或者在每一起具体案件中,慎重考虑各种有利因素和不利因素,准确地划分原则和例外,从而在审理和断案进程中尽可能做到对社会、对国家、对涉案的个人都是公正和公平的。

最后,除了上述有关"封闭式"审理的问题之外,看来也很有必要进一步说明一下李爽所受到的处罚——"劳动教养"的性质和特点。

就其固有意义来说,"劳动教养"本来就不只是一种惩罚,而且是对被教养者实行强制性教育的一种措施。大家知道,中国是社会主义国家,中国《宪法》规定:"劳动是一切有劳动能力的公民的光荣职责";国家实行"不劳动者不得食"的原则,公民必须"遵守劳动纪律,遵守公共秩序,尊重社会公德"。[30] 根据宪法的上述基本精神,"劳动教养"制度的建立,目的在于改造那些虽有能力劳动,却游手好闲、违法乱纪、不务正业的人,通过劳动教养,把这些人员改造成为自食其力的新人,从而维护公共秩序,有利于社会主义建设。依据有关法规的明文规定,"劳动教养,是对于被劳动

---

[26] See Geise v. United States, 262 F. 2d 151, 151-157 (9th Cir. 1958), cert. denied, 361 U. S. 842 (1959).

[27] See United States ex. rel. Lloyd v. Vincent, 520 F. 2d 1272, 1272-1276 (2d Cir. 1975), cert. denied, 423 U. S. 937 (1975).

[28] See Stamicarbon v. American Cyanamid Co., 506 F. 2d 532, 532-542 (2d Cir. 1974).

[29] See United States v. Bell, 464 F. 2d 667, 667-676 (2d Cir. 1972), cert. denied, 409 U. S. 991 (1972).

[30] 参见 1978 年 3 月 5 日通过的《宪法》第 10 条、第 57 条。中国现行宪法制定于 1982 年,其后又经过 1988 年、1993 年、1999 年、2004 年以及 2018 年五次修正。1978 年《宪法》第 10 条和第 57 条的基本精神,已分别被吸收于 1982 年《宪法》的第 6、42、53 条。

教养的人实行强制性教育改造的一种措施,也是对他们安置就业的一种办法"。在实行劳动教养期间,对于被劳动教养的人,"应当按照其劳动成果发给适当的工资";同时,为了避免他们在拿到工资后即时挥霍,吃光花光,管理机构可以酌量预先扣出其一部分工资,作为其家属赡养费或者日后本人安家立业的储备金。[31]

这些规定表明,"劳动教养"迥然不同于中国刑法所规定的"劳动改造",这主要体现在两个方面:(1) 劳动改造是执行有期徒刑或无期徒刑的重要组成部分,本质上是一种刑罚;劳动教养在本质上却不是简单的处罚,它是一种强制性的教育和职业培训措施。(2) 劳动改造是不能领取工资的;而劳动教养则是有权领取适当工资的。

在中国,劳动教养制度行之已久,实践证明:在改造和拯救失足青年,使他们转变为对社会有益的劳动者过程中,劳动教养是特别有效的措施。许多国际知名的外国法官和法学家参观、访问了中国的劳动教养所,他们都肯定这种制度对社会进步能够发挥积极、有益的作用,而且其中还体现了革命人道主义的精神。

因此,任何不存偏见的人自然会得出这样的结论:中国当局对李爽个人采取的措施,既不是打击"鸳鸯"情侣的无情棒,也不是恫吓知识界不驯分子的杀威棒,而只是拯救沉沦青年的救生圈!

附录一 中国拘禁了法国男人的情妇*

〔美〕克里斯托弗·S.雷恩

(北京 1981 年 11 月 12 日电) 一个中国女人与一名法国外交官员在北京本地外国人围墙住区中同居,随后她被逮捕了。中国政府正在想方设法向西方世界证明:对这个女人进行的审判是合理合法的。

李爽是一名年方 24 岁的前卫派美工人员,她与法国驻华大使馆的一名馆员,即年已 33 岁的昂玛努·贝耶华坠入情网,并且已经订婚。此间的朋友们都说,中国人先前曾经许诺这一对情侣可以正式结婚。

但是,11 月 9 日,在李爽进入贝耶华先生的公寓同居两个月之后,她在北京三里屯外交官围墙住区的入口处被几名便衣警察逮捕带走了,当时贝耶华先生正在香港停留,随后他已返回法国。

---

[31] 参见国务院《关于劳动教养问题的决定》,小引言,第 2 条第 2 款、第 3 款。
* 原文载于《纽约时报》1981 年 11 月 13 日第 36 版第 1 栏。

此后两个月,李爽杳无音信。直到本星期二,中国当局公开宣布:这位李小姐已经被判处在一所惩罚机构中接受"劳动教养"两年。

法国官员十分恼火

此事影响广泛,涉及许多方面。因为,在宣布判处李爽劳动教养两年之际,法国外贸部长米歇尔·约伯(Michel Jobert)正在北京和官员们会谈。据报道,约伯曾为这对情侣出面干预,设法与中国的高级官员,包括邓小平先生和赵紫阳总理进行交涉。但他被告知此案纯属中国的内部事务。

据此间法国消息灵通人士说,约伯先生一怒之下,竟然取消了其日程上原定的一场新闻发布会和最后两场技术性会谈,并在当天傍晚拂袖而去,离开北京。另一位消息人士报道说,正值法国高官访问北京之际,却披露了李爽被判受罚的信息,邓小平认为这是一次"令人遗憾的偶然巧合"。

今天,中国官方的新华社发布了一份专为驻巴黎以及其他各地的中国大使馆准备的声明,针对此事提出了"北京版本"的说法。

这份声明也由中国外交部提供给在北京当地的一些西方记者。据这份声明说,"这个问题并不像某些人所说的,是什么李爽与贝耶华之间的婚姻问题,而是李爽触犯了中国法律"。

并未说明准确的罪名

这份声明并未说明李爽小姐究竟犯了什么罪。不过,有关当局一向警告中国公民,不要和外国人厮混。在北京,外国居民被指定聚居在用围墙隔开的公寓里,周围有士兵保卫。在一些公共餐馆,外国人往往被带到另外的餐厅,与其他中国顾客分隔开来。

尽管此类接触和结婚都受到阻拦,但都并非不可能实现。今天发表的声明中就提到,法国驻华大使馆中的另一名馆员克里斯琴·加依亚诺(Christian Galliano)就在上个月被许可与中国女青年赵江结为夫妻。今年早些时候,有一个加拿大人被许可与一名中国舞蹈演员结婚。

此间有些外国居民熟悉李小姐案件的有关情况,他们认为,中国的官员们一般持有清教徒般的思想观念,反对与异己分子搞男女关系,反对婚外私通行为。李爽明目张胆地搬进贝耶华的公寓和他同居,公开藐视共产党人的清规戒律,这就激怒了中国的官员们。贝耶华先生已经与他的妻子分居,她已返回法国。

此外,李爽在北京美术界一个前卫团伙中表现突出,这些美术界人员玩世不恭,政治上标新立异。十分明显,处罚李爽的用意在于杀鸡吓猴,儆戒其他情侣,不过,现在还弄不清楚此事是否也表明当局有意对知识界的不驯分子采取更加严厉的镇压迫害措施。

贝耶华目前住在法国。当地正在围绕李爽案件掀起阵阵喧嚣,新华社发表的这份声明表明这些喧嚣使中国人感到困窘。

新华社这份声明指出:"中国作为一个享有主权的国家,依据中国的法律处理李爽的犯法行为,这是完全正当的。""此举纯属中国内部事务,它同中法两国关系毫不相干。我们相信法国的朋友们一定会也一定能够理解。"

附录二　法国外交官说中国拘留了他的未婚妻*

(美联社北京 1981 年 9 月 12 日电)　一位法国外交官说,警察今天把他的中国籍未婚妻拘留了。

昂玛努·贝耶华,现年 33 岁,是法国驻华大使馆的一名馆员。他说,星期四这天他从国外回到北京,得知李爽星期三在外国人聚居的围墙住区(使馆区)外面被抓走了。他们俩就住在这个围墙区里面。

贝耶华先生称:他到公安局去解释说,李小姐住在他的公寓里是合法的,公安局拒不接见他。这位外交官说,李爽离开围墙住区,想去看望她的姐妹,就被抓走了。中国人必须持有特别通行证,或在外国人陪伴下,才能获准进入这个围墙住区。

附录三　小 题 大 做**
——评白天祥等人在所谓"李爽案件"上的喧嚷

近日来,法国一些报刊和电台、电视台就所谓"李爽案件"大做文章。法国前驻华使馆外交官埃马纽埃尔·贝勒弗鲁瓦[32](中文名叫白天祥)接二连三地对法国报纸和电台、电视台发表谈话,歪曲事实真相,攻击中国的政策。中国舆论界注意到,

---

　　* 原文载于《纽约时报》1981 年 9 月 13 日第 5 版第 6 栏。
　　** 原文载于《光明日报》1981 年 11 月 15 日。
　　〔32〕 法文原名为 Emmanuel Bellefriod,前文译为昂玛努·贝耶华,系参照商务印书馆 1973 年出版的《译音表》所列法语标准译音而改译的。——摘录者注

这样大规模的宣传攻势,是自1964年中法两国建立外交关系以来所罕见的。

所谓"李爽案件"是怎么一回事呢?原来,这个被白天祥称作是他的"未婚妻"的李爽,是中国一个女公民。今年7月起,她被白天祥利用其外交官身份窝藏在北京他的寓所达两个月之久。李爽由于触犯中国法律,9月间被拘留,最近根据国务院《关于劳动教养问题的决定》第1条,决定对她进行劳动教养两年。

这本来是中国政府挽救、教育失足青年的措施,纯属中国内部事务。它同中法两国关系毫无关系。但令人遗憾的是,白天祥和法国某些人士却小题大做,歪曲事实,搞得满城风雨。他们把事情说成是中国阻挠了白天祥和李爽的婚姻,"嘲弄了人权";还说什么"中国改变了政策""压制自由化",甚至扬言李爽案件"损害了中法两国关系"。

李爽的被决定劳教,根本不是什么"婚姻"问题。我们决不排外,也不反对中国人同外国人正常的接触。但李爽的行为表明,在中国确有极个别的人,不顾国家和民族的尊严,丧失国格与人格,从事出卖自己灵魂的活动;也确实有极个别的外国人在各种外衣掩护下,从事欺负中国人甚至是别有用心、干涉中国内政的活动。

白天祥攻击中国政府对李爽的处理"粗暴"。这位曾经担任过驻中国的外交官,对中国"劳动教养"这一改造、挽救失足青年的有成效的制度居然这样无知,是令人吃惊的。参观过中国劳教所的许多国际法学界知名人士都知道,劳动教养不是判刑,这种制度所体现的人道主义精神,使许多失足青年转变成有用之才。

尤其奇怪的是,白天祥等人攻击中国对李爽的处理是"镇压""制服"知识分子,攻击"中国改变了政策"。中国执行什么样的政策完全是中国的内政,是用不着外国人来指手画脚的。中国坚持四项原则,也坚持对外开放的方针,是前后一贯的。"中国改变政策""压制自由化"的喧嚣,完全是无的放矢,有意制造混乱。为什么白天祥硬要把处理一个犯有罪行的女青年这样一件事,说成是中国"政策的改变"呢?他这样做是不是要掩盖他的那些不合外交官身份的活动,转移人们的视线呢?

中国政府和人民十分珍视中法人民之间的友谊和中法两国之间的友好关系。中国人是照顾大局的。正是出于这样的原因,我们对于干了与外交官身份不相容的事情的白天祥本人并未采取严厉措施,也没有公布他的那些活动事实。我们希望不出现需要公布这些材料的情况。正因为这样,我们对于今年9月以来法国一些报刊、电台就所谓"李爽案件"进行的歪曲宣传,迄今未予理会。但是,令人遗憾的是,白天祥等人反而变本加厉,利用这件小事,掀起新的轩然大波,这是违背中法两国人民的意愿的。

附录四　The Li Shuang Case: A Wet Blanket over Romantic Love?*

A newspaper special report, written by Mr. Christopher S. Wren and entitled "China Jails Woman for Affair with Frenchman"[33], has been duplicated, together with another short report[34], and distributed to the students of Harvard Law School this January as reference materials for a course in Contemporary Chinese Law. It seems that both of these reports, especially the first, are now considered to be important materials for researching current Chinese law.

Since I have recently arrived at Harvard Law School from the People's Republic of China(PRC), a lot of American friends and students here put many questions to me regarding this case, such as: Who is Li Shuang? What is the background of her case? What laws did she violate, what crimes did she commit? Why did the Chinese government interfere with her freedom to marry, throwing a wet blanket over romantic love and disrespecting human rights? Confronted so often with so many questions, I feel obligated to discuss this case with any who are interested. I should like, therefore, to present my personal view of Chinese law in order that the truth and essence of this case might be as clear as possible, for the aforesaid newspaper reports contain many unclear, incorrect or self-contradictory points.

Who Is Li and What Is the Background of Her Case?

Mr. Wren's special report stated:

Li Shuang, a 24-year-old avant garde artist, fell in love with Emmanuel Bellefroid, a 33-year-old French Embassy attaché, and they became engaged. Friends here say that the couple was promised by the Chinese that they could get married... On Tuesday the authorities disclosed that Miss Li had been sentenced to two years of "re-education through labor" in a penal institution... Mr. Bellefroid was separated from his wife...

---

* This Article was first published in the New York Law School *Journal of International and Comparative Law* (U.S.A.), Vol. 3, No. 1, 1982. This article was written in January, 1982 on the basis of a speech made by the author at Harvard Law School.

[33] *N.Y. Times*, Nov. 13, 1981, at 36, Col. 1. See App. 1.

[34] French Diplomat Says China Holds His Fiancée, *N.Y. Times*, Sept. 13, 1981, at 5, Col. 6. See App. 2.

This account contains much misunderstanding, misstatement and inexactitude.

Who is Li? As Chinese reports say, she was originally an art designer for the China Youth Arts Theater. After resigning in January 1981, she became an unemployed vagrant and woman hoodlum. She had no regular employment for a long time, and instead engaged in indecent activities, offensive to public morals, thus affecting social order. It is especially necessary to point out that she refused to mend her ways in spite of the repeated admonitions of authorities. Heedless of the consequences, she moved flagrantly into Bellefroid's apartment and lived with him for two months, taking advantage of his diplomatic privileges to protect herself. As a result, in accordance with the provisions of Chinese law, she was detained and subjected to two years of rehabilitation through labor (RHTL) by a Chinese judicial organ and according to correct judicial procedure. Since then, Bellefroid has incited a large-scale outcry about this case, distorting the facts and attacking the perfectly correct actions of the Chinese authorities.

Here, a word about the strict distinction between illegal sexual relationships and lawful love and marriage may be quite necessary. As we know, first of all, the People's Republic of China is a socialist country. The state requires each citizen to live by his own work, so long as he is able to work, and to observe public order and social morals. The Constitution of the PRC confirms many kinds of freedom, such as, inter alia, freedom of speech, correspondence, the press, assembly, association, and even freedom of demonstration and freedom to strike. But it has never provided for so-called "individual freedom" for immoral and unlawful corruption of sex. Quite to the contrary, all immoral and unlawful sexual activities are condemned by the public and, if the circumstances are serious, are punishable by law. Undoubtedly, all honest and upright persons in the world, including all fair-minded humanitarians and human rights advocates should never consider "freedom" of adultery or of prostitution as a proper kind of freedom to individuals or as a proper part of human rights to citizens, because it is universally acknowledged that these activities offend public morals, and harm and endanger national health.

Second, since the smashing of the "Gang of Four", contacts between the peoples of China and other countries have increased. Most foreigners are true friends of the Chinese people. They continue to work hard to accelerate the cultural and economic exchanges between China and other countries. But a few foreigners inherit the insulting attitude of old colonialists and mistakenly consider the new China to be still the old China—a semi-colony, a paradise for the foreign adventurers—where sexual enjoyment and dissoluteness can be obtained at will. They go in for bullying the Chinese under the cover of various garbs.

Unfortunately, a few Chinese girls, dazzled by the display of wealth of some foreigners, disregard national dignity and forfeit national character and their own personality, by selling their own souls and bodies. In other words, they engage in prostitution, or prostitution in disguised form. As everyone knows, prostitution, strictly banned since 1949, has disappeared from the Chinese mainland. Its recrudescence in a very few cities, especially that which occurs under the flagrant protection of foreigner's powerful position or certain privileges of a foreigner and thus despises and mocks the sanctity of Chinese Law, seriously injures the national self-respect of the Chinese people and enrages them, because it has brought back the painful memories of the colonial humiliations that they suffered for more than one hundred years before 1949. They do wish to prohibit sternly this phenomenon in its re-sprouting stage as soon as possible.

This is an important part of the background of Li's case. If we view this case against such a background, together with other factors, we can easily understand why the Chinese authorities handled this case in such a serious manner. This strictness accurately reflects the common will of the Chinese people and meets with their full support.

Of course, it is not difficult to imagine that the same situation would probably be viewed quite differently in some Western countries because of the difference in history, culture, social system and concepts of morality. But I am sure that all foreign friends can understand that the Chinese have had to review their bitter experiences of the past, which are full of untold tribulations, tramplings, violations and insults imposed on the Chinese people by colonialists and imperialists. They must also, therefore, fully understand and willingly respect the proper national feelings of the Chinese people.

What Laws Did Li Violate and What Crime Did Li Commit?

Since Li is a citizen of China and her illegal activities occurred in China, it is entirely proper for China, a sovereign state, to handle the violation of law by Li according to Chinese law, treating it as a purely internal affair. This common sense choice of law seems to have been forgotten by many, so we must re-emphasize it as a prerequisite to analyzing this case.

My own speculation is that Li may have violated the following laws of China: First, she may have violated the Security Administration Punishment Act of PRC.[35] Article 5 provides: "A person who commits any one of the following acts disrupting public order shall be punished by detention, fine or warning." One of the acts listed in section 8 is "engaging in prostitution or having sexual relations with a woman secretly engaged in prostitution in violation of the government order repressing prostitutes"[36]. As an important addition, Article 30 further provides: "After their punishment has been completed, persons who are habitual loafers, do not engage in proper employment and repeatedly violate security administration may be sent to organs of RHTL if they require such rehabilitation."[37]

Second, she violated the Decision of the State Council of the PRC on Rehabilitation Through Labor.[38] Article 1 of this decree provides: "The following kinds of persons shall be taken in and their RHTL shall be carried out: (1) Those who do not engage in proper employment, behave like hoodlums,... violate security administration and refuse to mend their ways despite repeated admonitions."[39] In 1979, a Supplementary Regulation was promulgated, in which Article 3 added, "The time period for RHTL is from one to three years... Holidays and Sundays shall be days of rest"[40].

Mr. Wren's report said that the statement issued by the Chinese Embassy in France on November 12 last year "did not say what crime Miss Li had committed."

---

[35] Passed at the 81st Meeting of Standing Committee of the National People's Congress, Oct. 22, 1957; promulgated on the same day.

[36] The Policy and Law Research Section of the Public Security Ministry of the People's Republic of China: A Corpus of Public Security Laws and Regulations (1950-1979) 114, Mass Press, Beijing (1980) [hereinafter cited as Public Security Laws]. See also 22 *Xinhua Banyuekan* 82 (1957).

[37] Public Security Laws, art. 121.

[38] Approved at the 78th Meeting of the Standing Committee of the First Session of the NPC, Aug. 1, 1957; promulgated by the State Council, Aug. 3, 1957.

[39] Public Security Laws, art. 391. See also 17 *Xinhua Banyuekan* 195 (1957).

[40] Supplementary Regulations of the State Council on RHTL. Approved at the 12th Meeting of the Fifth Session of the NPC, Nov. 29, 1979; promulgated by the State Council on the same day. See Public Security Laws, art. 393. See also 11 *Xinhua Yuebao* 12-13 (documents ed. 1979).

Of course not. The Embassy's statement was not a written verdict or judgment, and so it did not need to list, one by one, the details of the charges and to cite the relevant laws. But the commentary issued by Xinhua reporter on November 14 last year had already clearly pointed out that Li was sent to RHTL for two years in accordance with Article 1 of the State Council's "Decision on Rehabilitation Through Labor."[41]

Then, did Li violate the current Criminal Law of the PRC? To answer this question it is necessary to point out both of the following: 1) In the light of reports that I have read, the Chinese government did not consider Li's behavior a crime violating the Criminal Law and therefore did not punish her according to that law, but disposed of this case pursuant to the Decision on RHTL. This point has been mentioned previously and will be developed further in Part Three of the present article. 2) Whether Li's activities violated the Criminal Law depends upon the marital status of Bellefroid: when he was living with Li, was he single, married, widowed, divorced, or only separated? Mr. Wren reported: "Bellefroid was separated from his wife." But at the beginning of the same report, he said that Bellefroid and Li "became engaged... [and] were promised by the Chinese that they could get married"[42]. Isn't this contradictory? As everyone knows, "separated" is a marital status substantially different from "divorced." Even in the legal provisions and official documents of the United States, the former has always been strictly distinguished from the latter.[43] It is obvious that "divorced" means the death of the legal marital relationship, while "separated" means the legal marital relationship is still alive, but that each spouse lives apart from the other. How could a husband, then, having a lawful wife, legally "become engaged" to another woman and call the latter his "fiancée"? How could they be "promised by the Chinese that they could get married" legally? Thus, if Mr. Wren's version is correct, Bellefroid and Li were

---

[41] Commentary by Xinhua reporter, A Big Fuss over a Trifle, *Guangming Daily*, Nov. 15, 1981.

[42] *N.Y. Times*, Nov. 13, 1981, at 36, Col. 1. See App. 1. The other report, published Sept. 13, 1981 also stated that Li was Bellefroid's "fiancée." See French Diplomat Says China Holds His Fiancée, *N.Y. Times*, Sept. 13, 1981, at 5, Col. 6. See App. 2.

[43] For instance, such a distinction also appears in the 19th column of the Non-immigrant Visa Application issued by the U.S. Embassy in China.

committing the crime of bigamy.[44]

One might argue that Li didn't marry Bellefroid, but merely lived together with him for two months, therefore, she didn't commit bigamy. True, according to the Marriage Law of the PRC (1980), a marriage, to be legal, must be registered at the marriage registration office and a marriage certificate must be issued.[45] But there are many cases in which a man or a woman having a legal spouse, lives with another person of the opposite sex, not only secretly committing adultery, but openly treating each other as husband and wife without a second marriage registration. In judicial practice, these cases have always been considered de facto bigamy and have been punished as bigamy, so as to control this crime more effectively. These practices have already been summed up in a generally recognized principle accepted in the recently published *The Legal Dictionary*[46] and also adopted by the authoritative weekly, *Zhongguo Fazhi Bao* (*Chinese Legal System Reports*).[47]

Contrasted with these practices, we may say that Li's openly living together with Bellefroid inside the diplomatic compound for two months (had Mr. Wren's narration about Bellefroid's marital status at that time been correct) would have already constituted a crime of bigamy in fact.

Certainly, I should add that if Bellefroid had actually gone through the formalities of divorce with his French wife before Li publicly lived together with him, Li would not have been committing bigamy in fact, but her relationship with Bellefroid, as a whole,

---

[44] Article 180 of the Criminal Law of the PRC provides: "Whoever has a spouse and commits bigamy or whoever marries another person clearly knowing the other has a spouse shall be sentenced to not more than two years of fixed-term imprisonment or to criminal detention." See *Renmin Ribao* (*People's Daily*), July 7, 1979. See also 6 *Xinhua Yuebao* 77 (documents ed. 1979).

[45] See article 7 of the Marriage Law of the PRC (1980), *Renmin Ribao*, Sept. 16, 1980. See also 9 *Xinhua Yuebao* 61 (documents ed. 1980).

[46] "Bigamy: A man or a woman who already has a spouse and does not go through formalities of divorce, marries another person via marriage registration; or although not via such a registration yet lives together with the other, factually treating each other in the relationship of husband and wife." See *The Legal Dictionary*, Shanghai Dictionaries Press, 1980, p. 521.

[47] See Did He Commit a Bigamy? *Zhongguo Fazhi Bao*, Oct. 2, 1981, at 3; Concretely to say, bigamy means that a man or a woman who already has a spouse, registeredly marries another person again before his/her spouse has died or before their marriage relationship has been legally terminated; or, although (he or she) has not yet initiated any marriage registration again, yet lives together with the other factually in the status of husband-and-wife relationship, it thus constitutes a factual marriage. Ibid.

would still have been considered hoodlumish and meretricious.[48]

A Wet Blanket, a Big Stick or a Life Buoy?

Mr. Wren reported that in China, "the authorities have warned Chinese citizens against mixing with foreigners... While she(Li) was obviously used as an example for other couples, it is uncertain whether the case represents a more significant crackdown against the intellectual nonconformity". These ambiguous comments confuse the normal, legal contacts between the Chinese and foreigners with the abnormal, illegal ones. They also confuse problems of law with those of politics, and mistake an attempt to rehabilitate for persecution and intimidation.

It is common knowledge that Chinese are never blindly xenophobic, never indiscriminately opposed to things and persons foreign, and have never objected to normal and legal contacts, including normal and legitimate marriages between Chinese and foreigners. We can cite many examples to illustrate this. There is no need to list the couples who have been married throughout the years. The recent happy marriage between another diplomat of the very same French Embassy in Beijing, Christian Galliano, and a Chinese woman, Zhao Jiang, last October, speaks sufficiently for Chinese allowance of the matrimony between the Chinese and foreigners. This marriage, I am glad to say, has been reported objectively in Mr. Wren's article.

Regrettably, Bellefroid's case was quite different from Galliano's. Taking advantage of his diplomatic privileges, including the immunity of judicial jurisdiction,[49] Bellefroid paid no heed to the statutes and codes of the host country

---

[48] Another source said, Bellefroid met Li Shuang at an art exhibition in Beijing in September 1980. As Bellefroid put it, "It was love at first sight". At the time Bellefroid's wife was working in the AFP office in Beijing. Up to May, 1981 Bellefroid applied to the Chinese authorities concerning his intention to marry Li Shuang and produced a certificate of his divorce. At the time, Li Shuang's indecent behavior for several months had already seriously interfered with social order, and had made the masses extremely angry. The departments concerned obviously could not approve the marriage of Li Shuang to Bellefroid while her hoodlum case was pending. Then, in spite of repeated admonitions, she flagrantly moved into Bellefroid's apartment and lived with him for two months, taking advantage of his diplomatic privileges to protect herself. Hence, in accordance with Chinese law, Li was detained in September 1981, and was sent to RHTL in November 1981. See Zhongguo Xinwen She, Feature, U. S. Department of Commerce: FBIS, Daily Report—China, Nov. 16, 1981, G2.

[49] Vienna Convention on Diplomatic Relations, done at Vienna April 18, 1961, 23 U. S. T. 3227, T. I. A. S. No. 7502, 500 U. N. T. S. 95 [hereinafter cited as Vienna Convention]. "The person of a diplomatic agent shall be inviolable. He shall not be liable to any form of arrest or detention." Ibid., art. 29. "A diplomatic agent shall enjoy immunity from the criminal jurisdiction of the receiving State." Ibid., art. 31. As of January 1, 1981, one hundred and forty-eight nations including the People's Republic of China, France, United Kingdom, United States and the U. S. S. R. were parties to the Convention. See Treaties in Force—A List of Treaties and Other International Agreements of the United States in Force on January 1, 1981.

to which he was accredited, and behaved in a way incompatible with his diplomatic status. Together with Li Shuang, he transgressed the above-mentioned Chinese laws and abused his diplomatic privilege of residence inviolability[50] to harbor and shield Li. Why do I say "abused"? Because the Vienna Convention on Diplomatic Relations expressly provides: "Without prejudice to their privileges and immunities, it is the duty of all persons enjoying such privileges and immunities to respect the laws and regulations of the receiving State. They also have a duty not to interfere in the internal affairs of that State."[51] And, of course, the private residence of a diplomat as well as the premises of the mission "must not be used in any manner incompatible with the functions of the mission as laid down in the present Convention or by other rules of general international law."[52]

In the event a diplomat abuses his diplomatic privileges and thereby violates the law of the receiving State, the host sovereign State is entitled, according to the principles of international law, to take harsh action against the law-violating diplomat, such as making public all facts concerning his (such as Bellefroid's) disreputable behavior, pronouncing him a persona non grata and deporting him.[53] But the Chinese government refrained from doing this out of respect for the Sino-French friendship. This is why the Chinese authorities limited themselves only to punishing a law-violating citizen of their own, in accordance with their internal law.

Bellefroid, however, requited kindness with ingratitude. He and his friends wantonly attacked China's handling of the Li Shuang case as a "cracking down" on intellectuals, "suppressing liberalization" and as an indication of "a change of policy in China". This hullabaloo of slander and fabrication, of entirely random accusations, is obviously intended to create confusion, so as to cover up Bellefroid's

---

[50] Section 1 of article 30 of Vienna Convention provides: "The private residence of a diplomatic agent shall enjoy the same inviolability and protection as the premises of the mission." Section 1 of article 22 of Vienna Convention provides in advance that: "The premises of the mission shall be inviolable. The agents of the receiving State may not enter them, except with the consent of the head of the mission."

[51] Ibid., art. 41, sec. 1.

[52] Ibid., art. 41, sec. 3.

[53] Article 9 of Vienna Convention provides: "The receiving State may at any time and without having to explain its decision, notify the sending State that the head of the mission or any member of the diplomatic staff of the mission is persona non grata or that any other member of the staff of the mission is not acceptable. In any such case, the sending State shall, as appropriate, either recall the person concerned or terminate his functions with the mission."

activities, which were extremely incompatible with his diplomatic status, and to divert public attention. In a word, Bellefroid tried hard to whitewash and prettify himself by confusing legal problems with politics: embellishing and beautifying Li's indecent law-violating behavior as so-called "political liberalization", and calumniating a proper legal punishment of Li as so-called political "cracking down" on intellectuals.

This is nothing but a smoke-screen! Those with discerning eyes can see the essence of it at first sight. Someone ignorant of the real facts, but without prejudices, perhaps even Mr. Wren, would gradually come to see the truth clearly, even through Bellefroid's smoke-screen.

I must also say a few words about the procedure and nature of the RHTL that Li has been subjected to. Many may assume that no procedure for RHTL existed before the decision was made against Li because they didn't find it in the narration of the said report. But, as the statement issued by the Chinese Embassy in France noted, Li was subjected to two years of RHTL "by a Chinese judicial organ according to judicial procedure"[54]. In accordance with the Supplementary Regulations on RHTL promulgated in 1979, when a person is to be subjected to RHTL, the matter shall be considered and approved (on the basis of a full investigation, of course) by the "Administrative Committees for Rehabilitation Through Labor". These Committees are established in the provinces, as well as the large and medium cities, and are composed of responsible persons of the civil administration, public security and labor departments. All activities of RHTL organs must be "supervised" by the people's procuracies.[55]

Certainly, no one should criticize Mr. Wren too harshly for his failure to outline the RHTL procedure in his report. We understand that it is impossible to include everything in a short special report and that he might not have been familiar with the procedure involving RHTL. Even if he were, he had not been accorded the opportunity to be present at the interrogation proceedings.

---

[54] See PRC Paris Embassy Clarifies Li's Reeducation, U. S. Department of Commerce: FBIS, Daily Report—China, Nov. 13, 1981, G1.

[55] See Supplementary Regulations of the State Council on RHTL, arts. 1, 2, and 5. Article 5 provides: "the people's procuracies shall exercise supervision over the activities of the organs of rehabilitation through labor." See also 11 *Xinhua Yuebao* 13 (documents ed. 1979).

As to the last point, according to the Criminal Procedure Law of the PRC, though all cases shall, in general, be publicly tried by people's court, those "cases involving state secrets or the shameful secrets of individuals shall not be tried and heard in public"[56]. On such occasions, i. e., in cases where the state secrets, personal reputation, or public morality and the fresh air of the community are felt to be at stake, attendance is denied to both ordinary Chinese and foreigners (including foreign newsmen and reporters). These persons are neither interested parties to the action, nor witnesses, nor are they persons who are ordinarily allowed entry into the courtroom: close relatives and friends of the actual parties, legal counsels, jurors, judges and court officers and other persons having business with the court in the case.

Indeed, Li's case was not considered a criminal one and therefore was not tried strictly according to the Criminal Procedure Law; nevertheless, it is obvious that the fundamental spirit of the aforesaid provision should be applicable since it would have been applied to a case such as Li's.

In this regard, some American friends have raised important questions: Even though those cases that are not heard and tried in public are exceptional and may be few in number, don't they nonetheless infringe upon and injure freedom of the press? And even more important, do not such exceptions pose the threat that defendants may be treated unjustly when the court's actions are not subject to public scrutiny?

These are very interesting and significant questions, worthy of further discussion. And, as people are well aware, these issues themselves are not only debatable, but have been debated in legal circles in the United States too. The exceptions to public trial are a subject that requires in-depth research and analysis, and can comprise many treatises in itself. Here we may only point out that in the United States there exist principles and exceptions with regard to public trials that

---

[56] See *Renmin Ribao*, July 8, 1979, and 6 *Xinhua Yuebao* 79, 88 (documents ed. 1979). Article 8 of the Criminal Procedure Law of the PRC provides: "the people's courts shall try and adjudicate all cases in public unless otherwise provided by this law. Defendants have a right to obtain defense, and the people's courts have a duty to guarantee that defendant's obtain defense." Article 111 of the Criminal Procedure Law of the PRC provides: "the people's courts shall try and adjudicate cases of the first instance in public. However, cases involving state secrets or the shameful secrets of individuals shall not be tried and heard in public."

are considerably similar to those of China.

For example, as a general principle, the United States Constitution provides in its First Amendment that the "Congress shall make no law abridging freedom of the press". Furthermore, the Sixth Amendment provides: "In all criminal prosecutions, the accused shall enjoy the right to a speedy and public trial"; and section 1 of the Fourteenth Amendment provides that no state shall deprive any person of life, liberty, or property without "due process of law". In short, freedom of the press and the defendant's right to a public trial both are generally protected by the Constitution against deprivation by federal and state authorities. [57]

On the other hand, however, the judicial practices of the United States show that neither freedom of the press nor the defendant's right to a public trial is absolute, but that each must be balanced against other interests that might justify closing the courtroom to the public and the press. Various state interests have been held to be sufficiently compelling to justify the total or partial exclusion of the public and the press even over the defendant's objections. Such interests have included protecting young victims and complaining witnesses in rape cases[58]; preventing the revelation of an undercover agent's identity[59]; avoiding disclosure of a corporation's trade secrets[60]; and preserving the confidentiality of anti-skyjacking procedures[61], etc. Moreover, according to these cases, total or partial exclusion of the public and the press is not without constitutional foundation.

Additionally, the defendant often prefers to waive his right to a public trial and even on his own initiative asks for a closed or partially closed one in order to protect himself from sensationalism in the press, public favor, and any possibility of an unfair trial that may result therefrom.

Surely the right of access of the public or the press to judicial proceedings is of no greater constitutional moment than the defendant's right to a public trial. Thus, the former right might similarly be overridden in circumstances like those listed above.

---

[57] See In Re Oliver, 333 U. S. 257, 272-273 (1948).
[58] See Geise v. United States, 262 F. 2d 151, 151-157 (9th Cir. 1958), cert. denied, 361 U. S. 842 (1959).
[59] See United States ex. rel. Lloyd v. Vincent, 520 F. 2d 1272, 1272-1276 (2d Cir. 1975), cert. denied, 423 U. S. 937 (1975).
[60] See Stamicarbon v. American Cyanamid Co., 506 F. 2d 532, 532-542 (2d Cir. 1974).
[61] See United States v. Bell, 464 F. 2d 667, 667-676 (2d Cir. 1972), cert. denied, 409 U. S. 991 (1972).

Reviewing these legal provisions and judicial precedents, we may get a preliminary impression that with regard to the problem of public trials, the legislature or judiciary must carefully assess and balance the different competing interests in general, or in each particular case, attentively consider the advantages and disadvantages, so as to precisely carve out the properly principled exception that will be fair and equitable for the society, the state and the individuals concerned.

Finally, in addition to the closed trial issue, it is essential to further explain the nature and features of RHTL, to which Li has been subjected.

RHTL is not a penalty in the proper sense, but rather a form of education by compulsion. As everyone knows, the PRC is a socialist state. Its Constitution provides: "Work is an honorable duty for every citizen able to work"; the state applies the socialist principle: "He who does not work, neither shall he eat." Citizens must "observe labor discipline, observe public order, respect social ethics"[62]. On the basis of this constitutional spirit, the RHTL system was established in order to reform those persons who have the capacity to work, but who loaf, violate law and discipline, and do not engage in proper employment. RHTL transforms them into new persons who support themselves by their own labor. Further, RHTL preserves public order and benefits socialist construction. In accordance with the express provisions of the relevant decree, the RHTL is "a measure of a coercive nature for carrying out the education and reform of persons receiving it. It is also a method of arranging their getting employment". Persons who receive RHTL shall "study labor and production skills and cultivate the habit of loving labor", so as to "have the conditions of getting employment". During the period of RHTL, they "shall be paid appropriate wages in accordance with the results of their labor". Moreover, consideration may be given to deducting a part of their wages in order to "provide for the maintenance expenses of their family members or to serve as a reserve fund that will enable them to have a family and an occupation"[63].

These provisions show that the RHTL quite differs from the "reform through labor" of Criminal Law in two main aspects: 1) The latter is an important part of

---

[62] Arts. 10, and 57. See *Remnin Ribao*, March 8, 1978.
[63] Public Security Laws, art. 392. See also 17 *Xinhua Banyuekan* 195 (1957).

fixed-term imprisonment, a kind of criminal punishment—penalty; and the former is not a simple penalty in its proper sense, but a coercive educational and professional training measure; 2) The latter forced labor is without any pay, whereas the former enjoys appropriate wages.

This long-held practice in China has proved that the system of RHTL is especially effective in remolding and redeeming delinquent and sinking youths into people useful to the society. Both the active, and beneficial role played by this system and the revolutionary humanitarian spirit embodied in it have been recognized by many noted international jurists and scholars who have visited RHTL centers in China.

Thus, anyone without prejudice and bias would certainly come to the conclusion that what the Chinese authorities have done to Li is neither a wet blanket over romantic love, nor a big stick on intellectual nonconformity, but a life buoy for the sinking person!

附录五 《纽约时报》报道英文原文

N.Y. Times, Nov. 13, 1981, at 36, Col. 1.

China Jails Woman for Affair with Frenchman*

By Christopher S. Wren

Special to N.Y. Times

Peking, Nov. 12—The Chinese Government has been trying to justify to the West the sentence it imposed on a Chinese woman who was arrested, after she began living with a French diplomat in a compound for foreigners here.

Li Shuang, a 24-year-old avant garde artist, fell in love with Emmanuel Bellefroid, a 33-year-old French Embassy attaché, and they became engaged. Friends here say that the couple was promised by the Chinese that they could get married.

---

* 1981 by The New York Times Company. Reprinted by permission.

But on Sept. 9, after living for two months in Mr. Bellefroid's apartment, she was seized and taken away by plainclothes policemen at the entrance to the San Li Tun diplomatic compound while Mr. Bellefroid was in Hong Kong. He has since returned to France.

On Tuesday the authorities disclosed that Miss Li, who had not been heard from for two months, had been sentenced to two years of "re-education through labor" in a penal institution.

French Official Angered

The case took on wider implications because France's Foreign Trade Minister, Michel Jobert, was meeting officials in Peking when the two-year sentence was disclosed. Mr. Jobert reportedly tried to intervene for the couple with senior officials, including Deng Xiaoping and Prime Minister Zhao Ziyang, but was told that the matter was China's internal affair.

According to French sources here, an angry Mr. Jobert canceled a news conference and the last two technical meetings on his schedule and left Peking the same evening. One source reported that Mr. Deng called it a "regrettable coincidence" that Miss Li's sentence was disclosed while the French official was visiting Peking.

Today the official New China News Agency issued a statement prepared for Chinese embassies in Paris and elsewhere giving Peking's version of the affair.

"The problem is not a problem of marriage between Li Shuang and Emmanuel Bellefroid, as someone said, but her violation of the Chinese law", according to the statement, which was also provided here by the Foreign Ministry to some Western reporters.

Exact Crime Not Specified

The statement did not say what crime Miss Li had committed. But the authorities have warned Chinese citizens against mixing with foreigners. In Peking, foreign residents are assigned to walled off, segregated apartment that are guarded by soldiers. At public restaurants, foreigners are usually steered to separate dining rooms away from other customers.

But while such contacts, and marriages, are discouraged, they are not impossible. Today's statement took note of another staff member at the French Embassy, Christian Galliano, who last month was allowed to marry a Chinese woman, Zhao Jiang. In an earlier case this year, a Canadian was allowed to marry a dancer.

Some foreign residents here familiar with Miss Li's case believe that she outraged Chinese officials, who in general hold puritanical views, by moving into Mr. Bellefroid's apartment, thereby flouting Communist strictures against fraternization and extramarital sex. Mr. Bellefroid was separated from his wife, who returned to France.

Moreover, Miss Li was prominent in an avant garde group of Peking artists who had flirted with political dissidence. While she was obviously used as an example for other couples, it is uncertain whether the case represents a more significant crackdown against the intellectual nonconformity.

The New China News Agency statement indicated that the Chinese are discomfited by the uproar that the incident has created in France, where Mr. Bellefroid is living.

"It is entirely proper for China, a sovereign state, to handle the violation of law by Li Shuang according to Chinese law," the statement said. "It has nothing to do with the relations between China and France. We are sure that our French friends will and can understand China's handling of this purely internal affair."

N.Y. Times, Sept. 13, 1981, at 5, Col. 6.

French Diplomat Says China Holds His Fiancée[*]

Peking, Sept. 12 (AP)—A French Diplomat said today that the police were holding his Chinese fiancée.

Emmanuel Bellefroid, 33 years old, an attaché at the French Embassy, said he returned from abroad Thursday and learned that Li Shuang, had been seized Wednesday outside the foreigners' compound in which they live.

Mr. Bellefroid said the police refused to see him when he went to explain that Miss Li had been in his apartment legally. She was seized as she was leaving the compound to meet her sister, the diplomat said. Chinese are allowed inside the compound only with special passes or in the company of a foreigner.

---

[*] 1981 by The New York Times Company. Reprinted by permission.

第5章　小议对外学术交流的"大忌"*

中华文明,博大精深;中外文明平等交流,源远流长。数千年来,其间充满无数互相碰撞、激荡和扬弃,更充满无数互相借鉴、渗透、吸收和交融。后者是中外文明交流的主流,促进了世界文明的繁荣绚丽,但也时时出现一些逆流,对于中外文明交流起了损害的作用,不容小觑。为了弘扬主流,抑制逆流,特以国际经济法为例,就对外学术交流中需要防止的三种"大忌",小议一番。

第一,忌闭目塞听,夜郎自大。历史上,中国有许多明君倡导向域外先进文明虚心学习,汲取精华,兼容并蓄,但也有不少昏庸颟顸的统治者惯于夜郎自大,对域外先进文明闭目塞听,视为异端邪说,一律贬斥。他们自命为"奉天承运"的"天子",并以"天朝大国"自居,在对待周边国家的态度上,存在着一定的自大与轻狂。直到鸦片战争的大炮轰开"天朝大国"的国门,才猛然醒悟:不向域外先进文明虚心学习,势必导致落后,落后必然挨打!

第二,忌囫囵吞枣,盲目附和。就人文社科而言,来自外国的思潮和理论,其中多有精神食粮,但也有不少是精神鸦片。鉴此,在国际学术交流中,我们切忌言必称希腊罗马、哈佛耶鲁、剑桥牛津,而对自己祖宗留下的深厚文明积淀和丰富思想瑰宝则"不晓得"或"忘记了"。我们既要谦虚谨慎,认真学习和吸收外来的一切有益新知,切忌闭目塞听,妄自尊大;又要对外来的种种"权威"理论,结合国情和世情,深入探讨,独立思考,加以鉴别,切忌妄自菲薄,盲目附和。为此,要刻苦学习中外历史,钻研理论,善于史论结合,摆出事实,讲清道理,有理有据地阐明自己的见解,平等而又自信地参加国际热点难点问题的讨论和争鸣,不渝不懈,追求客观真理和社会公平。

第三,忌屁股坐歪,脊梁缺钙。在国际学术交流中,身为中国人,应时刻不忘祖国,践行"知识报国,兼济天下"的使命。试剖一例,举一反三:WTO组织成立至今已经二十余年,许多事实证明,WTO法制为全球各国或地区提供了多边贸易平台,功

---

* 本文发表于《光明日报》2015年7月31日第2版"文化评析·讲好中国故事"。

不可没,值得赞扬。但WTO法并非全是"良法",其中既有"良法",也有"劣法",不应全盘肯定,更不能顶礼膜拜;WTO/DSB(WTO争端解决实体)的执法实践也非全盘"善治",其中也有偏袒强权成员和欺凌弱势成员的不公裁决,不容漠视和掩盖。

特别是,2012—2014年在WTO"稀土案"中,"被告"中国在专家组和上诉机构两审中连续败诉,举世瞩目,全国哗然。按照裁决,中国出口的稀土,虽属全球稀缺、极其珍贵的高精尖工业"维生素",但就是必须只卖"白菜价",既不许限制出口,也不许出口加税。对此蛮横裁决,众多中国学者深感"切肤之痛",依法据理,撰文揭露和批判其执法不公,努力诉诸国际公正舆论,讨回公道;也有高明专家,呼吁WTO及时纠正失误,建立判例纠错制度,亡羊补牢,以免失去公信。但是,人们也遗憾地看到,竟有一些宣讲文稿和相关出版物,三年多来在国内多个论坛反复宣讲散发,极力赞颂"WTO是模范国际法",是"良法善治的典型",甚至把《WTO协议》和《入世议定书》吹捧为"圣经"。对于上述"稀土案"中WTO的两审裁决,只津津乐道一审裁决思路是如何之"严谨缜密",二审裁决思路是如何之"技高一筹";而对于中国横遭两审裁决沉重打击之特大冤屈和深远祸害,却三缄其口,不置一词。难怪有人提出异议和质疑:此种视角和做派,是否有些"屁股坐歪,脊梁缺钙"?是否略欠赤子之心,家国情怀?

第 6 章　向世界展现中国理念*

在二战后七十多年的全球治理中,一直存在两种理念。一种理念由以美国为首的强权发达国家所主导,倾向于强权政治,由强国垄断国际话语权;另一种理念由包括中国在内的众多发展中国家所倡导,强调各国不论大小强弱,在国际事务中均应平等相待、互利共赢。

中国一贯主张确立公正合理的全球治理理念和全球治理体制。1974 年,邓小平同志在联合国大会第六届特别会议上阐述了毛泽东同志提出的"三个世界"理论,并庄严声明:中国是一个社会主义国家,也是一个发展中的国家,属于第三世界;中国坚决反对任何形式的霸权主义,自己也决不搞霸权主义。21 世纪以来,中国的综合国力持续增强,中国积极与新兴经济体和广大发展中国家合作,在国际社会形成日益强劲的新兴力量。特别是党的十八大以来,以习近平同志为总书记的党中央提出打造人类命运共同体的主张和弘扬共商共建共享的全球治理理念,并积极努力践行,突出显示了敢于和善于提出中国方案、贡献中国智慧的胆略和气魄。当前,顺应历史潮流和时代呼唤,中国正在大力倡导国家主权、民族自决、和平共处、睦邻友好、联合自强等观念,得到了世界上越来越多国家和人民的认同;积极推进"一带一路"建设、发起成立亚洲基础设施投资银行等实践,推动全球治理体制向着更加公正合理的方向发展。当今世界,各国相互依存、休戚与共。推进世界和平稳定与发展繁荣,必须构建以合作共赢为核心的新型国际关系,打造人类命运共同体。中国将为此做出自己的贡献。

中国提出的共商共建共享的全球治理理念,是中华传统文化中积极处世之道的继承、发展与创新。中国传统文化中有构建"大同世界"的理想。早在春秋战国时代,以孔子为代表的儒家先贤就针对当时社会的不公不义和战乱频仍,提出了构建美好和谐社会的理念和追求。儒家学者还提出兼善天下、四海之内皆兄弟等理念,认为人与人之间不分强弱、贫富,都可以亲如兄弟、平等相待。儒家倡导"和为贵",

---

* 本文发表于《人民日报》2016 年 6 月 5 日第 5 版。

同时强调君子应和而不同,既能与他人和睦相处,但又不苟同其错误见解。在条件不具备的时候,至少应做到独善其身;在条件具备的时候,就应勇于承担、兼善天下,参与治国平天下的大业。中国坚持奉行的和平外交政策、共商共建共享理念,均可以从上述思想理念中找到历史渊源。

中国主张和倡导的打造人类命运共同体的主张和弘扬共商共建共享的全球治理理念,符合时代潮流,符合全人类的根本利益。中国的大国外交、周边外交协调推进、丰富多彩,突出展现了全方位外交的创新活力和蓬勃生机,也证明了中国特色全球治理理念具有引领作用。当今时代国际舞台上的竞争,很大程度上是思想理念的较量。不同的全球治理理念对于国际话语权的分配和全球治理体制的确立发挥着很大的能动作用。对于中国来说,要向世界传播中国观念、阐明中国价值,就要坚持道路自信、理论自信、制度自信,并将其转化为行动自觉。一方面,苦练"内功",增强自己的综合国力,以实力增强理念的说服力;另一方面,弘扬新的全球治理理念不能单靠一己之力,而需要致力于国际合作,形成强大合力,促使现存治理秩序不断弃旧图新,走向公正合理。中国在努力宣扬"和为贵""化干戈为玉帛"等思想的同时,也应警惕一些国家破坏国际安宁与世界和平秩序的企图和行动,做好各方面周全准备,安而不忘危,治而不忘乱。

第 7 章　朝着合作共赢方向发展
　　　　推动国际经济法理念变革*

　　第二次世界大战结束后七十余年来,全球治理中有两种理念及其相应体制一直在矛盾中不断碰撞嬗变,一种是以美国为首的西方若干发达国家所主导的全球治理理念和体制,另一种是众多发展中国家参与的全球治理理念和体制。这两大理念和体制的分歧或差异在于:由谁来主导实施全球治理?如何实施全球治理?前者主张仅由少数几个发达强国来治理,垄断和操纵国际事务话语权和决策权;后者则主张世界事务应秉持合作共赢原则,由世界各国包括发展中国家平等参与治理。这两种针锋相对的治理理念对许多世界事务的解决产生了影响。与之相对应,当代全球治理体系变革也对国际经济法理念产生着影响。

　　在传统国际经济法律格局中,磋商和决策过程只在七八个最发达国家内部进行,它们定出基调或基本框架之后,交由十几个或二十几个发达国家组成的经济性组织或区域性组织协调各方利害关系,定出共同主张和一致步调,然后才提交全球性的经贸大会或国际经济组织进行讨论。这种做法,从一开始就排除、剥夺了众多发展中国家的知情权、参与权、话语权、决策权,从而使它们在磋商过程中处于弱势地位。另外,在全球性国际经济组织规章中,几个发达国家也定出不公平、不合理的表决制度,实行表决权力大小不一甚至极端悬殊的投票安排,从而使寥寥几个西方发达大国加在一起,就可以操纵全球重大经济事务的决策。有的超级大国享有的特多投票权或特大表决权,往往可以在很大程度上左右重大决策,甚至可以在一定条件下实现其独家否决的特权。西方大国在这种磋商和决策过程中,凭借其经济实力上的优势操纵世界经济贸易合作走向,甚至随时根据自己的需要,拒不遵守或完全背弃自己依国际条约应承担的义务。众多发展中国家在这种决策体制下,往往难以实现和保护自己的经济权益。这样不公平不合理的局面,在经济全球化、各国经济

---

* 本文发表于《人民日报》2016年11月7日第16版。

互相紧密依存的现实情势下,不仅会损害发展中国家的经济主权和各种经济权益,而且不利于全球经济持续健康发展。

要改变这种局面,就必须从根本上改变世界经济贸易决策权力分配不公的格局,强调一切国家应当对世界经济贸易享有平等的参与权、话语权和决策权。这就要以公正、公平、合理为原则,对当今现存的国际经济贸易规则予以分析,凡是达到公正、公平、合理标准,符合建立国际经济新秩序需要的,就可加以沿用、重申;凡是不符合这种需要,只是"口惠而实不至"的空头支票,就要积极加以改善;凡是直接与这一标准背道而驰的,就努力废弃和破除。

变革现存国际经济秩序的要求,并非单纯是一种政治口号或政治理念。它在实践中也推动了国际经济秩序和国际经济法走上吐故纳新的道路,使广大发展中国家在一定程度上逐步改变完全无权、听凭强权国家任意摆布的处境。实际上,二战结束后,国际社会中改变国际经济法制的争斗就时起时伏。比如,2001年11月开启的多哈回合谈判,就体现出新旧两种观念的较量。现存国际经济法律规范中蕴含各种不公平规则是一种客观现实。在这种情况下,如果学者还吹捧国际经济规则全都是良法、模范法,对它应俯首帖耳,是不符合正直学者应有的法律理念和法律职责的。

改变当今国际经济法律规则的制定格局任重而道远。面对当代国际社会"南弱北强"、实力分化的战略态势,发展中国家要变法图强,既不可能一蹴而就,也不能无所作为,而应动员和凝聚实力,坚持不懈建立国际经济新秩序,一步一个脚印地向前迈进。

全球治理体系变革源于国际力量对比变化,全球治理的新格局取决于国际力量的新对比。在中国的积极引领下,众多发展中国家变革全球治理体系的合理要求、呐喊和努力,其强度和力度都有较大的提升。当前,加强全球治理、推动全球治理体系变革乃是大势所趋。中国要抓住机遇、顺势而为,推动国际经济秩序朝着更加公正合理的方向发展,联合众多发展中国家以及愿意顺应历史潮流的发达国家,共同构建合作共赢的全球治理体系,为促进人类福祉做出更大贡献。

第 8 章　建构中国特色国际法学理论[*]

当代中国正走在实现中华民族伟大复兴的历史征程上。中国综合国力的持续增长，引起许多国家的关注和赞许，但也遭到西方一些国家及人士的误读。在新的历史条件下，中国日益广泛深入地融入经济全球化进程，需要承担更大的国际责任，这就相应地需要扩大在全球治理中的话语权。世界也期待中国在全球事务的治理和决策中、在实现国际公平正义方面发挥更大作用。

从法律视角看，中国扩大和增强在全球治理中的话语权，就是要在制定国际法律规范中拥有更大的参与权和决策权。不可否认，迄今通行的国际法律规范及其相应的理论学说，主要是在特定历史条件下，以美国为首的西方发达国家主持制定并主导推动的，其中含有不少蔑视国际秩序的"恶法"。这些"恶法"损害了发展中国家应有的公平合理权益。在这种情况下，中国的国际法学者理应顺应时代呼声，致力于建构具有中国特色的国际法学理论新体系，增强中国参与全球治理的话语权，追求国际公平正义。

关注国际秩序的除旧布新。 从发展中国家的视角看，当代的国际政治经济秩序既有基本公平合理、符合《联合国宪章》的部分，也存在不公平不合理的部分。相应地，现存的国际法律规范，既有基本公平合理、符合《联合国宪章》和发展中国家权益的"良法"，也存在不公平不合理、损害发展中国家权益的"恶法"。因此，国际法学研究应当对国际法律规范进行分析整理，推动破旧立新、开拓创新。创建具有中国特色的国际法学理论新体系，是时代赋予中国国际法学人的历史使命，责无旁贷。

研究治理变革的相关主张。 随着时代发展，现行全球治理体系与时代潮流不适应的地方越来越多，国际社会对全球治理体系变革的呼声越来越高。努力推动全球治理体系变革日益成为国际社会密切关注的新焦点，也理应成为中国国际法学者的关注点。推动全球治理体系变革是国际社会共同的事业，应坚持共商共建共享原则，使全球治理体系变革的相关主张转化为各方共识，形成一致行动。中国要引导

---

[*] 本文发表于《人民日报》2017 年 5 月 8 日第 15 版。

利益不同、见解相异的各方形成共识,共同推动全球治理体系变革,确实需要下很大的力气。这就需要国际法学者贡献力量,继续向国际社会阐释我们关于推动全球治理体系变革的理念,让全球各方聆听到清晰、坚定的中国话语,从而凝聚人心,共同将这种体系变革由理念变为现实。

立足中国实际。中国改革开放以来,学习引进了不少西方发达国家的国际法学理论。这些理论往往立足于那些国家各自的实际,以其国家利益为核心。因此,其中难免蕴含着维护发达国家既得权益、维护国际旧秩序的内容,不符合中国实际,在实践中可能侵犯众多发展中国家的应有权益。因此,中国学者很有必要在学习、借鉴有关国际法学新知识的基础上,密切联系中国实际,从中国的角度和人类命运共同体的立场来研究和评析当代国际法,敢于和善于开拓创新,逐步确立起以马克思主义为指导、具有中国特色的国际法学理论新体系。

学会自主鉴别。在国际学术舞台上,中国学者既要谦虚谨慎,认真学习和吸收有益的知识,切忌闭目塞听、妄自尊大;又要敢于和善于对外来的种种所谓权威理论或时髦学说加以鉴别,切忌妄自菲薄、盲目附和。应平等地参加国际热点难点问题的讨论,有理有据地阐明自己的见解,发出中国的正义之声,为全球治理贡献中国智慧。

第9章 "左公柳"、中国魂与新丝路
——"七七事变"七十周年随笔

"七七"傍晚散步，口哼童年老歌自娱，见微风轻拂道柳，浮想联翩，忆起抗日战争当年流行一时的《玉门出塞》，如今60岁以下的青壮年大众恐怕多半不知道、不会唱。此曲乃1919年五四运动闯将、北京学生领袖罗家伦[64]作词，李惟宁谱曲，不但词句优美，寥寥数语，便将伟大祖国西部边陲——辽阔新疆的美景、历史、地理高度概括，栩栩如生地尽显纸上，跳跃在流畅悦耳的音乐中，读来、唱来均朗朗上口，充满诗情画意；更重要的是，其中凝聚着浓浓的"中华魂"和强烈的家国情怀，被人们推崇为罗氏一生的最佳诗作，[65]很值得后人温故知新，大力弘扬。兹特抄录如下，并根据历史记载和个人理解，略加诠释，提供大众共享。罗家伦原词是：

> 左公柳拂玉门晓，塞上春光好！天山融雪灌田畴，大漠飞沙旋落照，沙中水草堆，好似仙人岛；过瓜田碧玉丛丛，望马群白浪滔滔。想乘槎张骞，定远班超，汉唐先烈经营早，当年是匈奴右臂，将来更是欧亚孔道，经营趁早！经营趁早！莫让碧眼儿（木展儿），射西域盘雕！

李惟宁把罗家伦词谱曲如下：

---

[64] 参见郑笛：《罗家伦情系边塞》，载《世纪》2005年第1期；张昌华：《大学校长罗家伦》，载《读书文摘》2007年第6期。另参见朱磊：《每棵左公柳都有档案》，戴岚：《为古柳创造更好生存空间》，两篇文章均载于《人民日报》2014年9月13日第10版，其电子版本见于人民网：http://nx.people.com.cn/n/2014/0913/c192150-22295544.html。

[65] 参见陈一萍：《唱起〈玉门出塞〉这首歌》，载《世纪》2005年第4期；王涛：《忆〈玉门出塞歌〉》，载《晚霞》2006年第3期。

[《玉门出塞》 罗家伦 词 李惟宁 曲 简谱及歌词：左公柳拂玉门晓，塞上春光好！天山溶雪灌田畴，大漠飞沙旋落照，沙中水草堆，好似仙人岛。过瓜田碧玉丛丛，望马群白浪滔滔，想乘槎张骞，定远班超，汉唐先烈经营早，当年是匈奴右臂，将来更是欧亚孔道，经营趁早，经营趁早，莫让碨鞬儿射西域盘雕。]

歌词作者罗家伦（1897—1969），既是五四运动时期的学生领袖和革命闯将，后来又成长为我国著名的教育家、思想家、社会活动家。他 1917 年入北京大学，颇受蔡元培校长熏陶和器重；曾与傅斯年等创办《新潮》杂志，积极投身五四新文化运动和爱国学生运动。"内惩国贼，外抗强权"的口号就是他在学运传单中率先提出的。1920 年获蔡元培选拔，赴欧美留学。1926 年回国后，历任国立清华大学、国立中央大学校长。他把"创造有机体的民族文化"作为中央大学的使命。1937 年"七七事变"后，日军大举侵华，国难当头，他主持该校西迁重庆，在日机狂轰滥炸中坚持弦歌不辍，改革办学体制，建树颇多。1943 年，国民党政府积极建设西北地区，以增强抗战能力，特派罗家伦为"监察使"，兼西北考察团长，从事陕西、甘肃、宁夏、新疆等五省国防建设的考察与设计。据此推断，这首讴歌新疆"塞上春光好"、激励抗日斗志的名曲，当系 1943 年他率团考察新疆时触景生情、弘扬中华国魂的一大杰作。

"**左公柳**"[66]是晚清重臣和著名儒将**左宗棠**在 1877 年带领数万湘军西进收复新疆时一路所植**道柳**。左宗棠当年来到西北大漠地区，深感气候干燥，了无生气，而又水土不服，遂命令部队在进军大道沿途、宜林地带和近城道旁遍栽杨树、柳树，绵延千里。其用意在于，一是巩固路基，二是防风固沙，三是暂歇戎马之足，四是利行人

---

[66] 参见秦翰才：《左文襄公在西北》，岳麓书社 1984 年版。此书是作者秦翰才先生长期研究中国晚清重臣左宗棠抗击帝国主义侵华、收复中国新疆的力作，商务印书馆 1945 年初版于重庆，1946 年再版于上海。新中国建立前后，开国大将王震率领中国人民解放军挺进新疆、解放新疆、屯垦开发新疆和保卫中国西陲（戍边）过程中，立下重大功勋，他深知当年左宗棠率军抗击帝国主义侵华、收复中国新疆的历史伟绩对后世的教育意义和启迪作用，故特建议左宗棠祖籍湖南省岳麓书社于 1984 年重印秦翰才《左文襄公在西北》一书，其提倡以史为师、弘扬中国国魂和家国情怀的深刻寓意，是不言而喻的。参见甘肃老姜：《"左公柳"与左公柳档案》，载《兰州日报》2010 年 6 月 2 日第 11 版，其电子版本见于兰州新闻网：http://rb.lzbs.com.cn/html/2010-06/02/content_55463.htm。

遮凉。凡他所到之处,都要动员军民植树造林。后来人们便将左宗棠及其部属所植造福百姓的柳树,尊称为"左公柳"。左公此举,体现了朴素的改善生态环境、民生福祉至上意识。

众所周知,自从1840年英帝国主义发动侵略中国的鸦片战争以来,西方帝国主义列强频频发动侵华战争,迫使清政府签订大量丧权辱国的不平等条约。19世纪下半期,晚清政府面临严重的内忧外患危机,当时身为陕甘总督的左宗棠,面对外寇入侵,国土沦丧,挺身而出,同朝廷投降派抗争,力排"众议",赢得朝野广泛支持,接受重任,**挂帅西征,指挥清军剿灭了在俄英列强支持下大举入侵新疆的阿古柏匪徒,并坚持斗争抗拒了沙俄的侵略,以实力为后盾与沙俄谈判,终于使大片沦陷的国土重新回到祖国怀抱,为维护祖国的统一,做出了不可磨灭的贡献。**

在这同时左宗棠挟军事胜利之威,掀起了一股新政的狂飙,扫荡着那经年累世的污泥浊水。左宗棠在西北开创的政治新风有几个鲜明特点。第一,强化国家主权,力主新疆建省。他痛斥朝中那些放弃西北的谬论,"周、秦、汉、唐之盛,奄有西北。及其衰也,先捐西北,以保东南,国势浸弱,以底灭亡"。强调一旦放弃西北,势必导致国家灭亡。从汉至清,新疆只设军事机构而无行省郡县。左公前后五次上书吁请建省,终得批准,从此西北版图归于一统。第二,反贪倡廉。清晚期的官场已成糜烂之局,贪腐成性。他严惩了几起地方官和军官贪污、吃空饷的典型,严立新规。而他自己高风亮节,以身作则,陕甘军费,每年过手1240万两白银,无一毫进入私囊。西北主政十年,没有安排一个亲朋,坚持"欲肃政风先严家风"。第三,惩治尸位素餐不作为。他最恨那些对贪污、失职、营私等事"官官相护",身居要位却怕事、躲事、不干事的懒官、庸官,常驳回其文,令其重办,"如有一字含糊,定惟该道(主官)是问!"

罗家伦歌词中"过瓜田碧玉丛丛,望马群白浪滔滔"一句,形象地描绘了新疆哈密瓜田绿色硕果累累,犹如丛丛碧玉;草原放牧的白色马群,犹如滔滔白浪。歌词中"想乘槎张骞,定远班超"一句,乃回想历史,颂扬汉代张骞、班超的历史功勋。张骞(公元前164年—公元前114年)是中国西汉时期杰出的外交家和政治家,多次出使西域。他开辟"丝绸之路"的卓越贡献,至今彪炳史册,举世敬仰。"张骞乘槎"是民间传说:汉武帝指令张骞穷溯河源,张骞乘槎(小舟)而去。经月至一处,见城郭如官府,室内有一织女,又见一丈夫(男人)牵牛饮河。后还至蜀中(四川),方知已至"牛郎、织女"二星座。[67]

班超(32—102)是东汉时期著名军事家、外交家。他在中国西域促进民族融合

---

[67] 参见周妍、任继昉:《"张骞乘槎"典故研究》,载《长春师范大学学报(人文社会科学版)》2014年第3期。

和开拓镇边长达31年之久,在担任西域都护主官期间,平定内乱,外御强敌,为保护西域的安全、"丝绸之路"的畅通,以及促进中外文化的交流做出了巨大贡献。班超以36人出西域为始,以西域五十余国全部归附而终,实现了当初"投笔从戎"的愿望,显示了他杰出的军事才能。后世尊称他为"班定远",缘于他历经数十年艰苦奋斗,贡献了自己毕生的心血,终于完成了促进民族融合、维护祖国统一的大业,被授予"定远侯"封号,实至名归。[68]

"汉唐先烈经营早"句中的"先烈"是多义词,一般指当代为革命而捐躯牺牲的烈士,此处特指汉唐历代建功立业的先驱和先贤。[69]

歌词末尾大声疾呼"经营趁早!经营趁早!莫让碧眼儿(木屐儿),射西域盘雕!",是整首歌的创作主旨和核心,也是画龙点睛之"睛",更是歌唱的最强音。其中,"碧眼儿(木屐儿)"[70]显然隐指沙俄、英国、日本等侵华夺疆的帝国主义势力;"西域盘雕"[71]则泛指中国新疆的所有资源和一切财富,绝不许帝国主义列强肆意掠夺。

罗家伦这首名曲强烈体现了"中华国魂"和"中华脊梁",却又独具一格,与当年传唱大江南北的抗日救亡歌曲,互相媲美,互相补充。如今,六七十年过去了,中华大地饱经沧桑,斗换星移,已成为和平崛起的复兴大国。国家主席习近平同志提出的"一带一路"倡议及其实践,近年来正在日益广泛地获得国际社会的普遍认同和积极参与,越来越多的周边国家和远方友邦正在参与共建共享,新的陆上"丝绸之路"和欧亚交通孔道,[72]正在大踏步地向西拓展延伸。现实表明:"中国智慧""中华国魂"和"中华脊梁",不但正在华夏代代传承发展和不断创新,而且正在引领全人类利益共同体不断走向普遍繁荣。

2017年7月7日初草,2018年3月第七稿改定

---

[68] 参见泰卫星:《班超与西域》,载《新疆大学学报(哲学·社会科学版)》1983年第1期;莫任南:《班超对中西交通的贡献》,载《湖南师院学报(哲学社会科学版)》1980年第2期;张永辉:《从班超经略西域看东汉丝绸之路上的民族政策》,载《中国民族博览》2018年第1期。

[69] 参见《现代汉语词典》(第7版),"烈士"词条,商务印书馆2016年版,第823页。

[70] "碧眼"是白种人的特征之一。"碧眼儿"是当年中国文人对西方列强侵华白种人的贬称。"木屐(ji)"是日本人过去常用的木制拖鞋。"木屐儿"是当年中国文人对侵华日本人的贬称。"莫让碧眼儿(木屐儿),射西域盘雕"一句后来被普遍修改为"莫让木屐儿射西域盘雕"。

[71] "盘雕",指大型猛禽,体型粗壮,翅及尾羽长而宽阔,扇翅较慢,常在近山区的高空盘旋翱翔,能捕食野兔、蛇、幼畜等大型动物,也嗜食鼠类。我国常见的种类有金雕和乌雕。

[72] "孔道",指交通往来必经之道路。罗家伦所撰《玉门出塞》中"将来更是欧亚孔道"一语,在当年是中国人的预见和期盼,如今在中国牵头引领和积极推动的"一带一路"国际实践中,正在加速转化为现实,为中国、为欧亚两洲和全球大众造福。

※　※　※

以下摘录秦翰才《左文襄公在西北》一书"结论"数点附在本文末尾,谅必有助于有心的读者进一步理解左宗棠当年的个人抱负、自律修身、爱国情怀、"中华国魂"和"中华脊梁"与当今中国人应有的个人抱负、自律修身、爱国情怀、"中华国魂"和"中华脊梁"之间的代代传承发展和不断砥砺创新。[73]

结束这一本书,我想不嫌重复,再把文襄公经营西北的所有成就,就以前所说,归纳为下面几点:

第一,文襄公从《天下郡国利病书》《读史方兴纪要》,研究到《新疆识略》《海国图志》,于西北险要厄塞、风土人情和西北境外情形,瞭如指掌。文襄公又从汉武帝以后的追击匈奴和羌,唐太宗以后的应付突厥、回纥和吐番,研究到清圣祖、世宗、高宗三朝的平定準、回两部和青海,同治朝杨岳斌辈在陕、甘、新用兵的情形,于他们政略和战略的得失成败,了然于胸。文襄公根据研究所得,消化了前人的良法美意,同时注意尽量避免重蹈前人的覆辙。这样,才成立了他自己的经营西北的方案,文襄公在西北的成就,就是这一种对于西北大势健全的、准确的和实际的认识在起作用。

第二,文襄公是一个忠贞的人:"可以托七尺之孤,可以寄百里之命。"所以,他既奉命西征,便自誓"与西事相终始"。文襄公是一个刚强的人:"富贵不能淫,贫贱不能移,威武不能屈。"所以,他能敢作敢为,排除了当地一般骄兵悍将,贪官污吏,土豪劣绅,乃至国外强邻所给予他种种困难。文襄公是一个谨慎的人:"临事而惧,好谋而成"。所以,虽说"每一出兵,须发为白",到底算无遗策,战无不胜;而在政治上的一切措施,经他深思熟虑的结果,也绝不搞乱子。文襄公又是一个清廉的人:"一介不取,一尘不染。"布衣蔬食,度他淡泊的生活;所以虽经费支绌万分,时闹饥荒,而仍能号召朋俦部属,收群策群力、一心一德之效。文襄公在西北的成就,是这一种吾国向来所贵重的士大夫的素养在起作用。

第三,文襄公在上海设一个采办转运局,采运枪炮弹药和机械,筹措华洋商借款,探报中外重要消息。文襄公在汉口设一个后路粮台,采运土产器材,照料新募和过境的勇丁,转运上海军需,筹措华商借款。文襄公在西北设一个总粮台和一个军需局,催收和转解各省协款,接运和分配沪鄂军需,照料新募和遣散的过境勇丁,筹措华商借款。文襄公在用兵关外时,更设帮办一织,坐镇兰州。

---

[73] 参见秦翰才:《左文襄公在西北》,岳麓书社1984年版,第282—284页。

而从老河口以上,一路还有络绎不断的运输的机构,供应的设备,防护的部队。文襄公本人先以平凉为大本营,嗣以宿州为大本营,最后以哈密为大本营,居中指挥前敌,照顾方兵。兵事一了,更跟着赶办善后,于是当大军直捣新疆南路西四城时,从上海而汉口,而西安,而兰州,而肃州,而喀什噶尔,数千万里绵绵一线,宛如常山之蛇,节节呼应,文襄公自己阐发这一个"一气卷舒"的局势说:"如琴瑟然,手与弦调,心与手调,乃能成声,此理易晓。"这好比如今所说的"工作配合"。文襄公在西北的成就,就是这一种前后方圆满的配合在起作用。

第四,当然还要说到清政府,他们能信任文襄公,给他完全的权力;撤回了景廉、袁保恒和穆图善辈和文襄公不能合作的人;容纳了刘典、周开锡、刘松山、刘锦棠、张曜、王加敏和沈应奎辈文襄公所引重的人,他们能采纳文襄公眼光远大的主张,摒弃了李鸿章辈反对的议论,拒绝和修正了英俄两国的无理的要求。文襄公的成功,也就是一种内外一致的局面在起作用。

于是吾们可采三国演义中"后人有诗赞曰"的方式,引下面一首宋伯鲁的七律来歌咏文襄公,怀念文襄公,并作为本书的尾声:

"左侯崛起中兴日,誓扫天骄扩帝仁。万里车书通绝域,三湘子弟尽功臣。凤林鱼海春风远,玉色金城柳色新。今日西陲需保障,九原谁为起斯人!"

第六编
有关陈安学术论著和学术观点的书评等

本书第六编所辑书评荟萃数十篇，并非本书作者所撰，但均是对本书作者近四十年来的学术理念和学术追求的积极呼应和同气相求，形成了对国际经济法学领域"中国特色话语"的共鸣强音，在国际论坛上对共同构建"中国特色国际经济法学理论新体系"发挥了积极的推动作用。

由《诗经·伐木》佳句"嘤其鸣矣，求其友声"衍生的古谚古训"同声相求，同气相投"，源自《易经·乾卦》的"同声相应，同气相求"，先后措辞略异，其含义基本相同，都是提倡汇合社会正能量的理念、话语，聚集形成大声的理论呐喊，加以弘扬，促其转化为造福社会的物质力量。这些古谚古训迄今已在中华大地内外广泛流传了数千年。当代中国人对这些传承数千年的精辟古谚古训和先进实践，自应赋以新的时代意义，更加自觉地积极践行。

正是秉持和自觉践行这些精辟的古谚古训，本书作者特地把国内外高端同行学者所撰数十篇书评，荟萃一起，辑入本书，以飨读者，冀能从一个侧面，证明国际经济法学领域的"中国特色话语"，确实是"友声四起，吾道不孤"[1]；同时，也殷切期待从更多的国内外学者和读者中获得"中国特色话语"更大的共鸣强音，共同参与构建"中国特色国际经济法学理论新体系"的理论长征，共同推动国际经济秩序和全球治理体系与时俱进的变革和创新。

---

[1] 孔子说："德不孤，必有邻。"（见《论语·里仁》）。这句话的意思是指凡是有道德、胸怀正气、追求正义的人，都不会感到孤单无助、孤掌难鸣、孤立无援。因为，他的四周（邻）必定有不少志同道合的人，和他价值观念相同，与他互相呼应，互相帮助，互相配合，共同为正义事业奋斗。

第1章 《陈安论国际经济法学》书评荟萃

复旦大学出版社于2008年出版《陈安论国际经济法学》(五卷本)之后,曾经邀请中国国际经济法学界知名学者撰文针对这部多卷本专著加以评论,进行"笔谈",先后收到6篇书评,相继发表于不同报刊。其中1篇同时发表于《中华读书报》和光明网(2009年8月15日),4篇发表于《西南政法大学学报》(2012年第2期),另1篇言简意赅的短评,发表于《国际经济法学刊》2009年第16卷第3期。现在把6篇全部收录于此,以存完璧,并向各位书评作者谨致衷心谢忱。

一、陈安:知识报国,壮心不已

张永彬[*]

2009年5月,新中国国际经济法学的奠基人、厦门大学法学教授陈安先生迎来了自己的80岁生日。虽然年已耄耋,先生依然壮心不已,汇集自己自改革开放以来、30年研究国际经济法学主要成果的五卷本《陈安论国际经济法学》,几乎在同时,由复旦大学出版社推出。"赶在'老年痴呆症'光临之前,多做些力所能及的'知识报国'点滴小事,汇入振兴中华的大潮,才能对此生有个起码交代。"先生如是言道。而作为中国改革开放30年来首次以独撰多卷本形式推出的当代法学家的个人研究成果合集,《陈安论国际经济法学》被认为是中国学者构建中国特色国际经济法学派的奠基之作和代表性成果,引起了中外法学界的极大关注。

老骥伏枥,志在千里

回忆往事,历历在目,51岁重返法学领域,在别人冲刺的年龄起跑,陈安称这"是

---

[*] 张永彬,复旦大学出版社法学编审、副总编辑,《陈安论国际经济法学》(五卷本)的责任编辑。本文原载于《中华读书报》2009年12月9日。

我们这一代法学工作者特殊的遭遇"。1950年7月,陈安从厦大法律系毕业后,服从组织分配,历经法院、法律系、马列主义教研室(哲学、政治经济学、政治学)、教育系、历史系等单位,多次奉命"转行",直到1978年底拨乱反正、改革开放后,1980年厦大复办法律系,陈安才奉命"归队",重操已经荒疏了27年的旧业——法律,开始关注"久违"了的国际法。这半世纪光阴流转,陈安只用"弹指之间"来形容,"前五十年,蹉跎岁月,虚掷韶华;后三十年,欣逢邓小平路线指引下的太平盛世,来日无多,产生了紧迫感:必须急起直追,才能努力'抢回'一点失去的时间"。近二十年来,陈安先生先后取得了11项国家级、省部级科研成果一等奖,7项国家级、省部级科研成果二等奖,其获奖等级之高、数量之多,在中国人文社会科学学者中是罕见的,而在上述11项一等奖成果中,8项是在他70岁退休以后取得的。

可以说,中国认真恢复法学特别是国际法的教学和研究,和中国实行改革开放基本国策几乎是同步的。对外开放首先遇到的是大量的国际经济法律问题。多年来,陈安一直注意有的放矢,针对外国媒体、政坛和法学界对中国的各种误解和非难,撰写多篇双语专论,予以澄清和批驳;通过学术论证,努力维护中国的国家尊严、国际信誉和民族自尊,他提出的著名的"6C轨迹"论获得了国际法学界的公认,这也是陈安先生依据大量史实,探索建立国际经济新秩序的规律和路径得出的初步结论。陈安先生说,总结历史,以史为师,国际弱势群体争取和维护平权地位和公平权益,舍韧性的"南南联合自强",别无他途可循。在这条路上,既不能盲目"乐观",期待"毕其功于一役";也不能盲目"悲观",遇到挫折就灰心丧志;更不能奢望只凭孤军奋斗,即可克敌制胜。

作为中国国际经济法学的奠基人之一,1993年至今,陈安先生连选连任中国国际经济法学会会长,在国际权威期刊上发表了18篇长篇英文版专题论文,其中《南南联合自强五十年的国际经济立法反思》一文被长期担任发展中国家政府间组织"南方中心"秘书长的国际知名人士Branislav Gosovic先生评价为"对第三世界思想体系的重大创新来自中国",为中国国际经济法赢得了极大声誉。

就中国的人文社会科学如何在世界学术论坛上获得自己的位置,先生自有独到见解:"在国际学术论坛上,中国人既要谦虚谨慎,认真学习和吸收有益的新知,切忌闭目塞听,妄自尊大;又要敢于对外来的种种'权威'理论,衡诸国情和世情,深入探讨,独立思考,加以鉴别,乃至质疑,切忌妄自菲薄,盲目附和。简言之,要认真刻苦地学历史,钻理论,摆事实,讲道理,有据有理地阐明自己的见解,敢于发出中华之声和弱势群体之声,平等地参加国际热点难点问题的讨论和争鸣,追求客观真理和社会公平。"

经济主权上的"攻防战"

而他自己,便是如此践行的。早在 1980 年底,陈安先生便和在美国享有"中国通"美誉的哈佛大学法学院的柯恩教授在有关征收外资的问题上有过一场针锋相对、事关国家经济主权的辩论。其时,柯恩教授来访厦门,在一场演讲中批评新中国政府不尊重私有财产,随意没收(confiscate)外国人资产;主张为了吸引外商来华投资,应当在立法中规定绝对不侵犯外国人一切财产。在场的学者回忆,陈安先生当面坦率指出,他的批评不符合中国的实际情况,并列举中国的有关法律规定逐一予以反驳,同时援引美国的相关法律和国际惯例,辨析"没收"(confiscation)与"征收"(expropriation)的区别。柯恩教授当即表示:"你的知识补充了我的不足",并邀请陈安先生前往哈佛访问和讲学。后来,以此次辩论为基础,陈安撰写了相关的中英双语论文《我国涉外经济立法中可否规定对外资绝不实行国有化》,其中有关观点被后来的修订立法所吸收。

2004 年,柯恩教授应邀来厦参加国际学术会议,老友重逢,聚叙甚欢,"但我们之间又在美国单边主义与 WTO 多边主义之间矛盾冲突问题上,各持己见,激烈争辩"。陈安先生说,可以说,他们是"不打不相识"的"诤友",在互相尊重对方的基础上,通过国际性前沿问题的学术争鸣,实行知识互补,达到共同提高。

在《陈安论国际经济法学》第一卷第一编第一篇论文《论国际经济法学科的边缘性、综合性和独立性》一文中,陈安先生对美国著名的洛文费尔德(Andreas F. Lowenfeld)教授所撰、流行全美、宣扬"美国立场"的《国际经济法》通用教材中的若干观点提出了尖锐的批评。先生回忆,那是数年前在海牙的一次国际学术会议上。"洛文费尔德教授在国际经济法学领域建树颇多,享有国际盛誉。但是,他的某些学术观点却弥漫着或残留着殖民主义、扩张主义、霸权主义气息。这是国际弱势群体发展中国家不能苟同的。作为发展中国家一员的中国,其学人固然可以而且应当从洛文费尔德教授的著作中学习国际经济法前沿知识的精华,却不能不加认真思考、鉴别和必要的剔除,以致连同其中包含的糟粕,囫囵吞下。""我认为,这既是国际弱势群体即发展中国家的学者们的权利,也是这些学者们义不容辞的职责。"陈安先生表示。

创建中国的国际经济法学派

除个人的学术努力外,陈安先生还不负国内同行所托,在志士仁人的鼎力支持下,使中国国际经济法学会获得中华人民共和国民政部批准,正式登记成为国家一级的民间学术社团。通过这个学术平台,更有效地积极开展国际经济法领域的国内外学术交流,逐渐形成和确立了"以文会友,以友辅仁,知识报国,兼济天下"的学会宗旨和共识。陈安先生初创和主编的《国际经济法学刊》,在全国同行、先进的积极参与下,定位为全国性、开放性的国际经济法领域优秀学术著述的集刊,现由北京大学出版社出版。10年来,已连续出版15卷。其学术水平和社会影响受到国内外理论界和实务界的普遍肯定和赞誉,并已入选"中文社会科学引文索引"(CSSCI)学术数据来源集刊。

"'创建中国的国际经济法学派',此议最初是1993年在中国国际经济法珠海年会期间由中国社科院法学所李泽锐教授和复旦大学法学院董世忠教授提出来的。我认为,这项创新建议符合于中国的国情,也符合于时代的需要。中国人当然不能妄自尊大,但也不必妄自菲薄。'创建中国的国际经济法学派',当然不可能一蹴而就,也不可能期待在三五年、一二十年之中由几个人完全实现。要完全实现,并获得广泛的国际认同,需要几代中国学人群体的连续努力和不懈追求。中国人应当有这种志气和抱负,从现在就起步,朝这个方向迈步前进。"先生平和地说。

笔者发现,《陈安论国际经济法学》这部五卷本专著的书名也参照国际上著名法学著作常用的"××论××法"的惯例命名,先生解释说,"以人名冠于书名,确有不少先例,诸如《奥本海国际法》(*Oppenheim's International Law*)、《戴西和莫里斯论冲突法》(*Dicey & Morris on the Conflict of Laws*)等等。我以自己的姓名冠于五卷本,主要是表示这部书中所论,均属个人学习和研究心得体会,文责自负。"因此,把此举理解为"是当代中国人排除百年来形成的民族自卑残余、努力树立应有的'跻身国际前驱'自信自强之心愿与追求,似也非绝对不可"。他俏皮地反问:"阁下以为然否?"

二、中国国际经济法学的基石之作
——评陈安教授的《论国际经济法学》

张玉卿[*]

摆在面前的五卷本《陈安论国际经济法学》是厦门大学陈安教授的力作,由复旦

---

[*] 张玉卿,中国政法大学国际法学院教授、博士生导师、中国商务部条法司前司长、WTO争端解决机构专家组指示名单成员、中国国际经济法学会副会长。本文原载于《国际经济法学刊》2009年第16卷第3期。

大学出版社出版,其内容涵盖国际经济法基本理论、国际贸易法、国际投资法、国际仲裁法以及世贸组织(WTO)法等内容。本书第二、三卷包括对一系列经典国际投资、国际仲裁或国际贸易案件的解析与评论,第四、五卷还包括陈安教授多年来在国内外英文期刊上发表的十八篇英文长篇专论文章。

探究学科的前沿问题是这套著作的一大特点。《陈安论国际经济法学》并不是一部四平八稳、面面俱到的教科书式著作,而是篇篇都在研究、探讨和论述当前国际经济法非常尖锐、极为复杂、最需要关注与解决的问题。从南北矛盾到南南合作,从国际投资到投资争端解决,从 OPIC、MIGA、ICSID 到 GATT/WTO,从美国贸易法到开展国际贸易的原则与惯例,从国际商事法律到国际仲裁,这套著作涵盖了当前中国国际经济法的前沿和热门的课题,既有广度,又有深度,值得我们认真研读。

观点鲜明、论据坚实充分是本书的另一个特点。例如,陈安教授力主建立国际经济新秩序,坚持经济主权原则、公平互利原则、全球合作原则以及有约必守原则,反对贸然拆除《华盛顿公约》赋予发展中国家的四个"安全阀",并主张公正、公平的国际仲裁与严格的监督体制。这些问题都紧扣中国国际经济法领域的实际与需要,立论务实、清晰,论述旁征博引,有理有据,落地有声,分析深入细致,条理逻辑严密,可谓持之有故,言之有理,堪称法学专业著作中的精品。

陈安教授是中国国际经济法学的创始人与领军人之一,他通过撰写和主编一系列著作建立了比较完善的中国国际经济法学学科体系,这些著作包括:《国际贸易法学》《国际投资法学》《国际金融法学》《国际税法学》《国际海事法学》以及《国际经济组织法》等。另外,他还撰写了一系列有关介评 MIGA、ICSID 以及其中与中国相关问题的专论,撰写了大量的投资与国际贸易方面的案例分析文章以及中国涉外仲裁的监督机制方面的评论与立法建议,可谓学富五车,著作等身。这些著作与专论所体现的思想充满中国特色,独具创新之见,不落窠臼,体现了陈安教授勇于开拓、治学严谨、孜孜不倦、勤于笔耕的学者风范。读陈安教授的著作,我们还会体会到他赤诚的爱国情怀,他以自己的知识和身体力行谆谆教诲后学,服务于社会实践,服务于国家的改革开放,是我们学人的典范。

我与陈安教授相识近三十年,他一直是我的良师益友。陈安教授待人谦虚诚恳,乐于助人,是一位可亲可敬的长者。为人、为学我都从他那里受益良多。

我为本套专著的出版,向陈安教授致以衷心的祝贺。

三、试论秉持第三世界共同立场的中国特色国际经济法学派的形成及其代表性成果

张永彬*

在国际上,作为一门新兴边缘学科,国际经济法学较之国际公法学、国际私法学的独立突出不免落后"晚成";而在中国,国际经济法学研究与教学的正式启动则更显姗姗来迟,其启动和发展几乎和 1978 年中国实行改革开放基本国策同步俱进。究其主要缘因,在于闭关锁国、积贫积弱之时似乎"无须"国际经济法,而对外开放首先遇到的恰是大量的国际经济法律问题。国际经济法学遂因缘际会,在改革开放后的中国应运而生,并迅速成长。随着国力的强盛,秉持第三世界共同立场的中国国际经济法学者的声音日益受到全世界的关注。这其中,不能不提到,中国国际经济法学的开拓者和奠基人之一、国际知名的中国学者、1993 年至今连选连任中国国际经济法学会会长的厦门大学法学院陈安教授及其代表性成果——五卷本《陈安论国际经济法学》。

老骥伏枥,志在千里

回首三十多年前,经济面临崩溃边缘的中国,结束了"十年浩劫",拨乱反正,开始实行改革开放的基本国策。[2] 时已 51 岁的陈安重返法学领域,"在应当冲刺的年龄才起跑"[3],陈安称"这是我们这一代法学工作者特殊的遭遇"[4]。陈安重返法学生涯于改革开放之始,他的学术生命从此与改革开放紧密相连。[5] 早在 1950 年 7 月,陈安即从厦门大学法律系毕业,嗣后,他服从组织分配,相继在地方法院、厦大法律系、厦大马列主义教研室(哲学、政治经济学、政治学)、下放农村锻炼、厦大教育系及历史系等单位工作,多次奉命"转行",直到 1980 年厦大复办法律系,陈安才奉命"归队",重操已经荒疏了 27 年的旧业——法律,再次关注"久违"了的国际法。前半

---

* 张永彬,复旦大学出版社法学编审、副总编辑,《陈安论国际经济法学》(五卷本)的责任编辑。本文原载于《西南政法大学学报》2012 年第 2 期。

〔2〕 参见《中共中央第十一届三中全会决议》(1978 年 12 月)、《中共中央关于建国以来党的若干历史问题的决议》(1981 年 6 月)。

〔3〕 杨亚男:《为对外开放铺路——记厦门大学法学教授陈安》,载《人民日报》(海外版)1992 年 7 月 7 日。

〔4〕 转引自张永彬:《陈安:知识报国,壮心不已》,载《中华读书报》2009 年 12 月 9 日。

〔5〕 参见陈安:《陈安论国际经济法学》(第五卷),复旦大学出版社 2008 年版,第 2624—2626 页。

世纪的光阴流转,他用"蹉跎岁月"来自我形容,后 30 多年则是急起直追,只为"挽回"失去的宝贵时光。正是这样的人生境遇和不懈努力,陈安先生 30 多年来先后取得 13 项国家级、省部级科研成果一等奖,8 项国家级、省部级科研成果二等奖,[6] 其获奖等级之高、数量之多,在中国人文社会科学学者中罕有其匹,而在上述 13 项一等奖成果中,10 项是在他 70 岁退休以后取得的,[7] 而最新的一项一等奖[8],更是在他 82 岁之际摘取的。新近,他又针对当代霸权主义者横加于中国的诬蔑——"中国威胁"论,撰写中英双语论文,史论结合,揭露真相,痛加挞伐,以正国际视听,引起国内外人士的高度重视。[9] 概言之,其学术生命之旺盛之长久,爱国情怀之强烈,行文笔锋之犀利,三者如此紧密融合,且均臻上乘,堪称学界一奇。

中国特色国际经济法学派的创建轨迹

回顾 30 年来以陈安为代表的中国国际经济法学者在国际经济法领域走过的历程,其轨迹清晰可寻,历历在目。

(一) 1987 年"国际经济法学系列专著"的出版,开创了中国特色国际经济法学理论体系的先河,此后 20 多年又相继推出多部高校教材、专题专著和多篇双语学术论文,使这一特色理论体系逐步走向成熟

1987 年由鹭江出版社出版、陈安教授主编的"国际经济法学系列专著",包括了《国际投资法》《国际贸易法》《国际货币金融法》《国际税法》和《国际海事法》五部著作,这是中国第一套国际经济法学系列专著。出版后次年(1988 年)即荣获福建省人民政府社科优秀成果一等奖,这也是陈安教授学术生涯中荣获的第一个省部级一等奖。

当时国内外学者对国际经济法的概念、性质、范围解释不一,尚无定论。具代表性的有两种观点:一种观点认为,国际经济法属于国际公法的范畴,是经济领域的国际公法,属于国际公法的一个分支,各国国内的涉外经济法规范,应排除在国际经济

---

[6] 参见陈安:《陈安论国际经济法学》(第五卷),复旦大学出版社 2008 年版,第 2624—2626 页。
[7] 同上。
[8] 即陈安教授发表的《论中国在建立国际经济新秩序中的战略定位》一文,2011 年获得"福建省第九届社会科学优秀成果奖"一等奖。
[9] 参见陈安:《"黄祸"论的本源、本质及其最新霸权"变种":"中国威胁"论——中国对外经济交往史的主流及其法理原则的视角》,载《现代法学》2011 年第 6 期。See also An Chen, On the Source, Essence of "Yellow Peril" Doctrine and Its Latest Hegemony "Variant"—the "China Threat" Doctrine: From the Perspective of Historical Mainstream of Sino-Foreign Economic Interactions and Their Inherent Jurisprudential Principles, *The Journal of World Investment & Trade*, Vol. 13, No. 1, 2012.

法之外。学界通常称此种观点为"狭义国际经济法学说"。另一种观点认为,国际经济法不限于、不等于经济领域的国际公法,而应综合调整国际经济关系的国内法规范和调整国际经济关系的国际法规范,成为一门新的独立的法学部门。学界通常称此种观点为"广义国际经济法学说"。1982年前后,美国纽约大学法学院洛文费尔德教授编写的一套以"国际经济法"命名的六卷本丛书,持"广义国际经济法"观点,被世界国际经济法学界认为是具有重大影响的著作。但其立足于美国的实际,以美国的利益为核心来分析美国涉外经济法以及国际经济法的各种问题,阐述和论证西方发达国家对这些问题的基本观点。

陈安教授1987年主编的上述国际经济法学系列专著,首次在中国以系列专著的形式阐述了国际经济法学是一门新的独立的边缘性法学部门,同时密切联系中国实际,注意从中国的立场来研究和评析国际交往中的有关法律问题,同时注意阐述和论证第三世界发展中国家对有关法律问题的共同立场。与洛文费尔德教授的前述六卷本丛书相比,虽然同样主张国际经济法是独立的法学部门,但却站在不同的立场上,与前者形成鲜明的对照,在国际经济法这个引人关注的国际学术舞台上,发出了中国国际经济法学者独立自主的声音。学界认为这开创了中国特色国际经济法学科体系和理论体系的先河。[10] 虽然今日来看,20多年前的研究难言完备,但依然不掩其当年初创时期的学术光芒和思辨锋芒。例如,在辑入《陈安论国际经济法学》五卷本的开宗明义第一篇《论国际经济法学科的边缘性、综合性和独立性》一文中,陈安先生早在20年前就对美国著名的洛文费尔德教授所撰、流行全美、宣扬"美国立场"的《国际经济法》通用教材中的若干观点,提出了尖锐的批评。[11] 陈安先生认为,洛文费尔德教授在国际经济法学领域建树颇多,享有国际盛誉。但是,他的某些学术观点却弥漫着或残留着殖民主义、扩张主义、霸权主义气息。这是国际弱势群体即发展中国家不能苟同的。作为发展中国家一员的中国,其学人固然可以而且应当从洛文费尔德教授的著作中学习国际经济法前沿知识的精华,却不能不加认真思考、仔细鉴别和必要剔除,以致连同其中包含的糟粕囫囵吞下。他认为,这既是国际

---

[10] 本系列专著问世后,国内多家主流媒体多次报道,给予密切关注和高度学术评价(参见林鸿禧等:《适应对外开放和发展外向型经济需要,国际经济法系列专著问世》,载《光明日报》(海外版)1988年4月26日;张安南等:《人以少胜多,书以优取胜》,载《人民日报》1988年10月26日;余劲松:《评陈安主编:国际经济法系列专著(1987年版)》,载《中国国际法年刊》,法律出版社1988年版;杨亚男:《为对外开放铺路——记厦门大学法学教授陈安》,载《人民日报》(海外版)1992年7月7日)。当时主管福建省对外经贸事务的游德馨副省长特地亲笔致函表示赞扬和鼓励——"陈安教授:感谢你赠送的五本巨作。当前全省上下议外向、想外向、干外向的形势下,外向知识何等重要又何等贫乏。这五本书可算及时雨,它大大有助于人们提高外向型知识,推动沿海开放事业发展……"

[11] 参见陈安:《论国际经济法学科的边缘性、综合性和独立性》,载陈安:《陈安论国际经济法学》(第一卷),复旦大学出版社2008年版,第13—16、33—37页。

弱势群体即发展中国家的学者们的权利,也是这些学者们义不容辞的职责。

就中国的人文社会科学如何在世界学术论坛上获得自己的位置,先生自有独到见解:"在国际学术论坛上,中国人既要谦虚谨慎,认真学习和吸收有益的新知,切忌闭目塞听,妄自尊大;又要敢于对外来的种种'权威'理论,衡诸国情和世情,深入探讨,独立思考,加以鉴别,乃至质疑,切忌妄自菲薄,盲目附和。简言之,要认真刻苦地学历史,钻理论,摆事实,讲道理,有据有理地阐明自己的见解,敢于发出中华之声和弱势群体之声,平等地参加国际热点难点问题的讨论和争鸣,追求客观真理和社会公平。"[12]

秉持这种学术理念和学术追求,陈安先生率领他的学术团队批判地学习和研究外来新鲜知识,取其精华,弃其糟粕,并在此基础上,敢于和善于不断开拓创新,相继推出《国际经济法总论》[13]《国际经济法学》《国际经济法学概论》《国际经济法学专论》(两卷本)[14]、"国际经济法学系列专著"(五卷本,北京大学出版社 1999—2001 年版)、《国际经济法学刍言》(两卷本)等教材和教学参考书,供全国不同层次和不同专业的高校学员学习之需。同时,又瞄准国际经济法学领域前沿的最新动态和热点难点问题,带领团队集体攻关,先后推出《美国对海外投资的法律保护及典型案例分析》[15]《"解决投资争端国际中心"述评》[16]《MIGA 与中国:多边投资担保机构述评》[17]《国际投资争端仲裁——"解决投资争端国际中心机制"研究》[18]《国际投资法

---

[12] 张永彬:《陈安:知识报国,壮心不已》,载《中华读书报》2009 年 12 月 9 日。
[13] 对本书的学术评价,请参见徐崇利:《新视角:从南北矛盾看国际经济法——评〈国际经济法总论〉》,载《厦门大学学报(哲社版)》1992 年第 3 期。
[14] 对本书的学术评价,请参见车丕照:《"问题与主义"中的"问题"——读〈国际经济法学专论〉》,载《政法论坛》2005 年第 1 期。
[15] 对本书的学术评价,请参见韩德培:《致力知己知彼 出色研究成果——〈美国对海外投资的法律保护及典型案例分析〉序言》,载陈安:《陈安论国际经济法学》(第五卷),复旦大学出版社 2008 年版,第 2536 页。
[16] 对本书的学术评价,请参见 1965 年"华盛顿公约"、"解决投资争端国际中心"(ICSID)在 1990 年出版的《ICSID 讯息》(ICSID News)第 7 卷第 1 期,宣告:中国正式签署参加《华盛顿公约》,同时,在"有关 ICSID 的近期最新论著"专栏中,列出世界各国近期出版的有关 ICSID 的新著六种,把陈安教授主撰写的上述专著列在首位。1990 年 8 月,ICSID 法律顾问帕拉(A. R. Parra)写信给陈安教授,称:"您论述'中心'的新书,已在本期的《ICSID 讯息》上宣布了有关的出版消息。根据本书内容目录的英文译文来判断,这肯定是一本极有有益的著作。"当时中国对外经贸部条法司对本书的出版也给予很大的鼓励和良好的评价,认为:"该书的出版无疑会推动我国学术界对于《华盛顿公约》和'解决投资争端国际中心'的理论研究,同时亦对我们研究加入该公约的工作具有积极的参考价值和借鉴作用";"您的大作,对我们的立法工作帮助很大"。参见陈安:《陈安论国际经济法学》(第五卷),复旦大学出版社 2008 年版,第八编"来函选辑"之八、九、十、十一、二十;单文华:《深入研究,科学判断——"解决投资争端国际中心"述评)简介》,载《福建日报》1995 年 3 月 31 日。
[17] 对本书的学术评价,请参见吴焕宁:《独树中华一帜,跻身国际前驱——评陈安主编:〈MIGA 与中国〉》,载《文汇读书周报》1996 年 3 月 23 日。
[18] 对本书的学术评价,请参见张乃根:《国际投资争端仲裁研究的力作——评〈国际投资争端仲裁机制(ICSID)研究〉》,载《中国图书评论》2002 年第 5 期。

的新发展与中国双边投资条约的新实践》[19]等专著。此外,他个人还针对上述热点难点问题撰写中英双语论文,[20]积极参加国际学术争鸣,有理有据地阐述独到观点,提出国策建言。通过上述团队和个人研究成果的不断积累,具有中国特色的国际经济法学科体系和理论体系初步成形,并正在逐步走向成熟。

一份有分量的长篇调查报告,客观地反映和记录了中国国际经济法学研究在陈安等中国学者群体多年努力开拓下欣欣向荣的现状和发展趋势,明确总结出:正是对外开放的国策推动了中国国际经济法学的迅速发展,充分肯定了中国国际经济法学作为独立法律学科地位的确立和学科体系的初步建立。同时指出:目前,中国各政法院校、大学的法学院和法律系一般都将国际经济法学作为一门主要的专业课程,一些大学的国际金融、世界经济专业也将国际经济法学列为必修课程。"国际经济法学所取得的丰硕成果及其对我国国际经济法律实践所产生的积极影响,初步证明了广义国际经济法学说的科学性,也展示了广义国际经济法学广阔的发展前景和强大的生命力。"[21]

(二) 创建"中国特色国际经济法学派"之首议(1993 年)

创建"中国特色国际经济法学派",此议最初可溯及至1993年在中国国际经济法珠海年会期间,由中国社科院法学所李泽锐教授和复旦大学法学院董世忠教授提出。此项创新建议得到陈安先生的高度认同。陈安先生认为:"这既符合于中国的国情,也符合于时代的需要。中国人当然不能妄自尊大,但也不必妄自菲薄。""创建中国的国际经济法学派,当然不能一蹴而就,也不可能期待在三五年、一二十年之中由几个人完全实现。要完全实现,并获得广泛的国际认同,需要几代中国学人群体的连续努力和不懈追求。中国人应当有这种志气和抱负,从现在就起步,朝这个方向迈步前进。"[22]正是在这样的远见卓识下,以陈安为代表的中国国际经济法学界,筚路蓝缕,一步一个脚印,配合国家的改革开放国策,经过三十余年的努力,秉持和代表第三世界共同立场和声音的中国国际经济法学者已然崛起。以陈安为代表的

---

[19] 对本书的学术评价,请参见中国商务部条法司来函:《立意新颖务实 分析缜密深入 理论实践交融——对陈安主编《国际投资法的新发展与中国双边投资条约的新实践》一书的评价》(商法投资函[2008]40号)。

[20] 其中发表于外国学术刊物的18篇英文长篇论文,均收辑于《陈安论国际经济法学》(第四卷),复旦大学出版社2008年版,第1723—2513页。

[21] 李双元:《中国国际经济法学研究的现状和发展趋势》,载《法学家》1996年第6期,第3—6页。以上各条注解所列主流媒体、同行学者对陈安教授论著的报道、评论等,均收辑于《陈安论国际经济法学》(第五卷),复旦大学出版社2008年版,第2515—2626页。

[22] 转引自张永彬:《陈安:知识报国,壮心不已》,载《中华读书报》2009年12月9日;陈安:《陈安论国际经济法学》(第一卷),复旦大学出版社2008年版,第104—108页。

中国国际经济法学派,以其创新、务实、丰硕的学术成果以及日益完备的理论体系,正在形成自己的独立风格和鲜明特色,为建立国际经济新秩序发出时代的强音。

(三) 1993 年始,长期执掌作为全国性一级学术社团的中国国际经济法学会及其会刊《国际经济法学刊》

除了个人的学术努力外,陈安先生还不负国内同行所托,在众多志士仁人的鼎力支持下,使中国国际经济法学会获得了中华人民共和国民政部批准,正式登记成为国家一级的民间学术社团,陈安先生也自 1993 年以来连选连任中国国际经济法学会会长,并通过这一学术平台,更有效地积极开展国际经济法领域的国内外学术交流,逐渐形成和确立了"以文会友,以友辅仁,知识报国,兼济天下"的学会宗旨和共识。陈安先生初创和主编的学会会刊《国际经济法学刊》,在全国同行、先进的积极参与下,已成为全国性、开放性的国际经济法领域优秀学术著述的集刊,由北京大学出版社出版,已连续出版 18 卷,每卷 4 期,先后发表了大量代表中国水平的高水准的国际经济法论文,其学术水平和社会影响受到国内外理论界和实务界的普遍肯定和赞誉,并已入选"中文社会科学引文索引"(CSSCI)学术数据来源集刊,成为国际学术交往和展示中国学者国际经济法学研究成果的交流平台。

(四) 锐意培养青年才俊,致力学术团队的建设与传承

1984 年 3—4 月,陈安教授应联合国教科文组织邀请,作为中国派出的"国际法教育考察组"成员之一,由北京大学国际法研究所所长王铁崖教授率领,一行三人,出访西欧和北美五国二十个城市,对西方发达国家的法学教育进行调研、考察,并与一百多位法学界有关人士进行交流。回国后,陈安教授依据此次考察见闻,结合中国国情,就国际法专业人才培养等方面的问题撰写"万言书",[23]提出许多具体的改进建议。诸如:(1) 派人员出国深造应考虑门类、品种和国别的多样化;(2) 应积极参加国际性的学术会议或学术团体;(3) 国际法课程的教学应注重培养学生解决实际问题的能力,强调大量的课前预习和活跃的课堂对话,开设模拟法庭课(Moot Court)、法律门诊课(Clinical Program in Legal Aid)或学生法律援助服务项目(Student Legal Aid Service);(4) 提倡由优秀研究生主办专业学刊,作为法学拔尖人才的摇篮;(5) 注重开发利用外籍华人和港台留学生中的法学人才资源;(6) 建立全

---

[23] 参见陈安:《改进我国国际法教育的"他山之石"——欧美之行考察见闻》,载《国际学术动态》1985 年第 4 期。

国性的国际法资料中心,资源共享,互通有无;(7)组织和推动全国国际法专业力量的合作,协同致力研究国家面临的外交、外贸问题,提供国策建言,实行"知识报国"。如今这些建议有的已被有关部门采纳,并行之有效;有的则尚待借鉴他山之石,付诸实践,俾使中国的国际法人才培养事业与时俱进,更上层楼。

陈安教授以厦大法学院为基地,在人才培养方面开创出了"寓教学于科研,溶科研于教学,使出人才与出成果并举"的研究生培养方法,强调"从难从严训练,成果人才并出"。[24] 他指出,培养研究生的目的是为国家输送高层次的专业人才,为了快出人才,出好人才,很有必要把出成果作为培养人才的手段。从研究生入学伊始,就从难从严出发,狠抓基本功训练,力争实现成果与人才同时并出。其基本训练方式包括:实行"大运动量"训练,敢于坚持严格要求,力排某些学生的怕苦"众议"和畏难"惰性",要求尽早过好法学专业英语关;提倡多学科交叉渗透,兼修相关相邻课程,建立合理的知识结构;强调理论联系实际,参加各类实践,提高实务工作能力;充分信赖,及时"压"担,严密组织,严格把关;赋予新设专业较大"成才自留权",加速形成"人才生产基地",提高人才生产力。

陈安教授主要负责博士生培养方案的设计,抓研究生师资队伍的学风和教风建设,带领有关教师和研究生申请承担国家有关科研课题,指导他们进行科研攻关,指导教师与研究生编辑《国际经济法学刊》,并积极指导年轻一代研究生导师的成长。多年来,陈安教授牵头采用这种方法,培养了数十名学有专长的硕士和博士,他们知识结构合理,综合能力较强,大多已成为各教学、科研单位的教学和科研骨干。以陈安教授为带头人的厦门大学国际经济法专业学术团队,经过二十多年的集体努力,在科研和教学方面均取得了突出的成果,在全国同一专业学科中居于领先地位,其所属的"厦门大学国际法学科"于2002年被评为国家重点学科。十年以来经数度中期审核、重评,均完全合格,一直保持学术青春和全国领先地位至今。

毕业后留校坚持与陈安教授在厦门大学合作共事、协力开拓的优秀研究生,如今均已成长为国内知名的中青年教授和新一代的博士生导师。其中成就突出的有曾华群教授(博士生导师)、廖益新教授(博士生导师)、徐崇利教授(博士生导师)、李国安教授(博士生导师)等。在其他高校执教的知名学者,如西安交通大学的单文华教授(院长)、西北政法大学的李万强教授(院长),当年都曾在厦大法学院师从陈安教授,积极参与团队科研,成绩优异,脱颖而出。当年在厦大攻读国际法学博士学位后投身实务界的执业人士,如赵德铭律师、林忠律师、傅明律师、谢岚律师等,如今也

---

[24] 参见刘智中:《从难从严训练,成果人才并出》,载《学位与研究生教育》1988年第5期。

都在中国涉外法律事务和国际法律事务中,善于运用专业知识,折冲樽俎,创业有成,成为同行中的佼佼者。

中国特色国际经济法学派的标志性成果

前述五卷本《陈安论国际经济法学》的问世,是中国特色国际经济法学派的标志性成果,标志着中国特色国际经济法学派的初步形成。

在五卷本《陈安论国际经济法学》问世之前,陈安教授所著两卷本《国际经济法学刍言》(北京大学出版社2005年版)首次整理汇集了陈安教授自改革开放以来二十余年间在国际经济法领域耕耘所开拓和收获的丰硕成果,并荣获第五届"吴玉章人文社会科学奖"一等奖。五卷本《陈安论国际经济法学》的推出,则更加系统地梳理了陈安教授在国际经济法学领域的学术追求和学术思想,更加突出显示了陈安教授在当代国际经济法前沿的新成果及其对该领域理论和实践中出现的新热点问题和难点问题的新探索。特别是,伴随着中国在"入世"后迅速崛起,面对各国对中国崛起所发出的不同声音,陈安教授站在建立国际经济新秩序的高度,旗帜鲜明地代表广大发展中国家依法仗义执言,力图为包括中国在内的当代第三世界争取国际经济公平权益和平等地位提供法学理论武器,提出了一系列具有鲜明中国特色的国际经济法学派的学术观点和主张,[25]从而初步形成了有独特风格、有独到见解的中国国际经济法学派。因此,五卷本《陈安论国际经济法学》堪称中国特色国际经济法学派的标志性成果。其最为突出之处在于:

(一)致力构建中国特色国际经济法学理论体系

《陈安论国际经济法学》全书约310万字,荟萃了陈安教授在中国实行对外开放基本国策30年来,研究国际经济法学这一新兴边缘学科所获的主要成果,系统、集中地展示了陈安教授30年来为创建中国特色国际经济法学所作的开创性学术建树。全书共分五卷八编,即国际经济法基本理论(一)、国际经济法基本理论(二)、国际投

---

[25] 全书从当代国际社会弱势群体即第三世界的视角,探讨和论证国际经济法学这一新兴的边缘性、综合性学科。诸如:阐明独立的、不同于发达国家学者的学术理念和学术追求;独到地探索建立国际经济新秩序的规律和路径;创新地论证当代国际经济法的基本原则;钻研中国古籍,深入探讨源远流长的中国对外经济交往史及其蕴含的法理原则;长期重点研究国际投资条约及其相关体制的实际运行,探讨发展中国家如何在这些体制中趋利避害,提供决策咨询建议和立法建言;率先剖析评议中国涉外仲裁监督机制立法的优点与不足,旁征博引,力排"众议",澄清学术讹传,提出建立严格监督体制、防阻执法腐败、保证公正仲裁的立法建议;秉持公正公平原则,具体研析涉外经贸争端仲裁典案,依法祛邪扶正,并撰文从理论上伸张正义;致力澄清和批驳外国媒体、政界和学界对中国的误解和非难。通过学术论证,努力维护中国的国家尊严、国际信誉和民族自尊,弘扬中华爱国主义。参见陈安:《陈安论国际经济法学》(第一卷),复旦大学出版社2008年版,自序。

资法、国际贸易法、涉台经济法、国际法教育、英文版论文选辑以及有关本书作者论著和学术观点的报道、评论和函件等。其中有关国际经济法基本理论的研究就占了全部五卷中整整两卷的篇幅,于此可以看出作者为构建中国国际经济法学科体系和基本理论体系倾注了大量心血,努力尝试开拓创新。全书虽为鸿篇巨制,但体系和脉络相当清晰。这些文字忠实地记录了自20世纪70年代末以来,陈安教授三十年如一日,不懈探索、辛勤耕耘,牵头引领同行学者们,共同将国际经济法这一当年很少人承认的法律部门,逐步开拓和发展成为对中国改革开放做出重大贡献的独立的法律部门。[26]

(二) 代表广大发展中国家力主建立国际经济新秩序(NIEO)

当代国际社会中时常流行形形色色力图阻挠或扭曲建立国际经济新秩序(NIEO)历史潮流的各种学说,诸如"新自由主义经济秩序"论、"WTO宪政秩序"论、"WTO体制有法必守、执法必严、违法危险、变法徒劳"论、"经济民族主义扰乱全球化秩序"论、"中国应当完成'角色转变':从现存国际经济秩序的革命者转变为维护者"论、"中国应当全盘接受美国领导的现存国际经济秩序,安分守己,才能从中获取更大利益"论等等。这类学说发源和流行于西方强权国家,而近年来"西风东渐",在中国国内不乏附和呼应之声,形成一种"时髦",甚至有教授对这类说教捧之为"精深而独到的见解",足以"开阔中国学者的眼界",不惜浓墨重彩,加以美化和拔高。这些似是而非的"时髦"理论确实造成了一系列新的思想混乱。陈安教授以敏锐的眼光、独立的思考和严谨的论证,对此类"时髦"理论逐一地、连续地加以批评剖析,力求澄清是非,排除误导,避免实践错误。[27]陈安教授强调:建立NIEO乃是20世纪50年代以来全球弱势群体数十亿人口争取国际经济平权地位的共同奋斗目标,也是邓小平1974年在联合国庄严讲台上向全球郑重宣布的中国战略目标。当代中国人应当秉持"科学的发展观",与时俱进、全面、完整、准确地加深理解邓小平的"韬光养

---

[26] 参见朱学山:《一剑淬砺三十年:中国特色国际经济法学的奠基之作——推荐〈陈安论国际经济法学〉》,载陈安:《陈安论国际经济法学》(第五卷),复旦大学出版社2008年版,第2537—2539页;李双元:《中国国际经济法学研究的现状和发展趋势》,载《法学家》1996年第6期。

[27] 详见陈安近三年来撰写的四篇系列论文:(1)《论中国在建立国际经济新秩序中的战略定位——兼评"新自由主义经济秩序"论、"WTO宪政秩序"论、"经济民族主义扰乱全球化秩序"论》(简称《一论》),收辑于陈安:《陈安论国际经济法学》(第一卷),复旦大学出版社2008年版,第109—134页;其修订文本发表于《现代法学》2009年第2期,第3—18页。(2)《旗帜鲜明地确立中国在构建NIEO中的战略定位——兼论与时俱进,完整、准确理解邓小平"对外二十八字方针"》(简称《二论》),发表于《国际经济法学刊》2009年第16卷第3期。(3)《三论中国在构建NIEO中的战略定位:"匹兹堡发轫之路"走向何方——G20南北合作新平台的待解之谜以及"守法"与"变法"等理念碰撞》(简称《三论》),发表于《国际经济法学刊》2009年第16卷第4期。(4)《中国加入WTO十年的法理断想:简论WTO的法治、立法、执法、守法与变法》(简称《四论》),发表于《现代法学》2010年第6期。

晦、有所作为"方针,将中国在构建 NIEO 历史进程中的战略坐标和基本角色,定位为旗帜鲜明、言行一致的积极推动者。中国理应进一步发扬传统的具有独特内涵的中华民族爱国主义,通过 BRICSM 类型的"南南联合"群体,坚定不移地成为建立 NIEO 的积极推手和中流砥柱之一。中国理应致力推动国际经济新秩序和国际经济法制逐步实现新旧更替、吐故纳新和弃旧图新,在"变法图强"、南北平等、和谐合作的前提下,谋求世界的共同繁荣。

(三) 抓住国际经济法的首要关键,深入剖析当代经济主权上的"攻防战"

早在 1981 年初,陈安先生便和在美国享有"中国通"美誉的哈佛大学法学院的柯恩教授在有关征收外资的问题上有过一场针锋相对的辩论。其时,柯恩教授来访厦门,在一场演讲中批评新中国政府不尊重私有财产,随意没收(confiscate)外国人资产;他认为,为了吸引外商来华投资,应当在立法中规定绝对不侵犯外国人一切财产。陈安先生当场指出,他的批评不符合中国的实际情况,并列举中国的有关法律规定逐一予以反驳,同时援引美国的相关法律和国际惯例,辨析"没收"(confiscation)与"征收"(expropriation)的区别。陈安先生认为,中国在涉外经济立法中,不宜、不必、不应、不容明文规定对外资绝对不实行征收或国有化。东道国在必要时有权依法征收境内外资并给予补偿,乃是当代国家经济主权权利之一,而且已是国际通行的立法惯例,中国不应通过立法自行"弃权"。相反,务必留权在手,但决不任意滥用。

柯恩教授当即表示:"你的知识补充了我的不足",并邀请陈安先生前往哈佛访问和讲学。后来,以此次辩论为基础,陈安撰写了相关的中英双语论文《我国涉外经济立法中可否规定对外资绝不实行国有化》,[28] 其中有关观点被后来的修订立法所吸收。[29]

2004 年,柯恩教授应邀来厦门参加国际学术会议,老友重逢,聚叙甚欢。"但我们之间又在美国单边主义与 WTO 多边主义之间矛盾冲突问题上,各持己见,激烈争

---

[28] 参见陈安:《我国涉外经济立法中可否规定对外资绝不实行国有化》,载《厦门大学学报(哲学社会科学版)》1986 年第 1 期。See also An Chen, "Should an Absolute Immunity from Nationalization for Foreign Investment Be Enacted in China's Economic Law?" *Legal Aspects of Foreign Investment in the People's Republic of China*, China Trade Translation Co. Ltd., 1988. 中英文本分别收辑于陈安:《陈安论国际经济法学》(第三、五卷),复旦大学出版社 2008 年版,第 1197—1209、2368—2387 页。

[29] 上述论文中文本发表四年之后,1990 年 4 月全国人大对《中华人民共和国中外合资经营企业法》加以修订,在第 2 条中增补了第 3 款:"国家对合营企业不实行国有化和征收;在特殊情况下,根据社会公共利益的需要,对合营企业可以依照法律程序实行征收,并给予相应的补偿。"此项新规定在国有化和征收问题上区分一般情况与特殊情况,分别对待。这完全符合当代发展中国家外资立法的通例,也与 1986 年陈安教授提出的看法和论证即"务必留权在手,但决不任意滥用"相一致。

辩"。陈安先生说,可以说,他们是"不打不相识"的"诤友",在互相尊重对方的基础上,通过国际性前沿问题的学术争鸣,实行知识互补,达到共同提高。

在经济全球化加速发展的条件下,各国经济主权的原则和观念是否应当弱化和淡化?这是当代国际论坛上颇有争议的一大理论问题和实践问题。如何看待各国经济主权,素来是国际经济法中首屈一指的关键所在,也是一大热点难点问题。长期以来,以曾经担任美国国际法学会会长的权威教授路易斯·汉金(Louis Henkin)为首的学者极力鼓吹弱国"主权过时"论、"主权有害"论;另一位被西方学界推崇为"WTO之父"的美国权威国际法教授约翰·杰克逊(John H. Jackson)则牵头极力倡导"美国主权(实为霸权)优先"论。针对美国权威教授们在国家经济主权这个关键问题上的似是而非、流行全球的理论观点,陈安先生作了针锋相对、有理有据的批评和剖析。他以WTO体制运作十年来美国单边主义与WTO多边主义交锋的三大回合作为中心,撰写中英双语的长篇学术论文,[30]综合评析美国"1994年主权大辩论"、1998—2000年"301条款"争端案以及2002—2003年"201条款"争端案的前因后果和来龙去脉,指出这三次交锋的实质都是美国经济"主权"(经济霸权)与各国群体经济主权之间限制与反限制的争斗,都是植根于美国在1994年"入世"之初就已确立的既定方针:力图在"入世"之后仍然推行其单边主义政策,以维护和扩大其既得的经济霸权,可以随时背弃其在WTO体制中承担的多边主义义务。

上述既定方针,是美国"1994年主权大辩论"得出的结论,它标志着在这第一回合大交锋中美国单边主义的胜利和WTO多边主义的败北。其后,在第二回合的大交锋中,审理"301条款"争端案的专家组执法不公,以模棱两可、"小骂大帮忙"的方式偏袒美国,实际上导致美国单边主义的再度获胜和WTO多边主义的再度败北。在第三回合的大交锋中,经过两审结案,美国终于在2003年11月败诉,这虽然标志

---

[30] 本长篇论文撰写并发表于2001—2004年,题为《晚近十年来美国单边主义与WTO多边主义交锋的三大回合:综合剖析美国"主权大辩论"(1994)、"301条款"争端(1998—2000)以及"201条款"争端(2002—2003)》,全文约6.5万字。其部分内容约1.5万字最初以《美国1994年的"主权大辩论"及其后续影响》为题,发表于《中国社会科学》2001年第5期。另一部分内容约2万字,题为《美国单边主义对抗WTO多边主义的第三回合——"201条款"争端之法理探源和展望》,发表于《中国法学》2004年第2期。此前,本文的英文本"The Three Big Rounds of U. S. Unilateralism Versus WTO Multilateralism During the Last Decade: A Combined Analysis of the Great 1994 Sovereignty Debate, Section 301 Disputes (1998-2000), and Section 201 Disputes (2002-2003)",发表于美国 *Temple International and Comparative Law Journal* 2003年第17卷第2期。英文稿发表后,引起国际人士关注。作者应总部设在日内瓦的62个发展中国家的政府间国际组织"南方中心"(South Centre)约稿,又结合"201条款"争端案终审结局,将上述英文全稿再次作了修订增补,由ICSID作为"T. R. A. D. E. 专题工作文件第22号",于2004年7月重新出版单行本,散发给"南方中心"各成员国理事以及WTO各成员常驻日内瓦代表团,供作决策参考;同时,登载于ICSID网站上(http://www.southcentre.org/publications/workingpapers/paper22/wp22.pdf),供读者自由下载。本文的英文本于2004年获得第十二届"安子介国际贸易研究奖"一等奖;中文本于2005年获得"福建省第六届社会科学优秀成果奖"一等奖。中英两种文本分别收辑于陈安:《陈安论国际经济法学》(第一、四卷),复旦大学出版社2008年版,第366—420、1725—1807页。

着美国单边主义的初步败北,固属可喜,但是充其量,只能把它视为十年来 WTO 多边主义此前两次事实上败北之后的"初度小胜",对其发展前景,实不宜过度乐观。因为,美国总统在"201 条款"争端案中败诉之后发表声明,对上述既定方针毫无改弦易辙之意,足见祸根未除,"病根"仍在,故其单边主义的霸权顽症可能随时复发,WTO 多边主义仍然前途多艰,可谓"庆父不去,鲁难未已"。鉴此,善良的人们不能不经常保持清醒,增强忧患意识,随时谨防美国单边主义大棒之卷土重来和再度肆虐。

另外,"201 条款"争端案中 WTO 多边主义之初度小胜,端赖与美国对垒的 22 个主权国家(包括中国在内),敢于和善于运用掌握在自己手中的经济主权,与经济霸权开展针锋相对的斗争。可见,所谓 WTO 正式运转之后,有关国家经济主权的原则和概念应当日益"淡化""弱化"云云,此类说辞,至少是不符合现实、不够清醒的,也是很不可取的;至于美国权威学者鼓吹经济主权"过时"论云云,则显然是居心叵测的理论陷阱,对此,不能不倍加警惕!

(四) 突出显示鲜明的中国特色

当今的国际经济法,其学科发展水平在某种程度上可以说是与一国在国际经济舞台上的实力相关联的。由于广大发展中国家在经济上的弱势,长期以来,以美国为首的西方国家的权威学者的某些学术观点流行全球,弥漫着或残留着浓烈的殖民主义、扩张主义、霸权主义的气息。作为发展中国家一员的中国的学者,陈安教授的论著立足于中国国情和国际弱势群体即广大发展中国家的共同立场,致力于探索和开拓具有中国特色的国际经济法学,提出诸多开创性见解,为国际社会弱势群体"依法仗义执言",提供维护其应有平等权益的法学理论武器,这是贯穿全书的学术理念和追求,也是该书的基本学术主张和论述主线。如书中提出的著名的"6C 轨迹"论,依据大量史实,探索建立国际经济新秩序的规律和路径;通过史论结合,有理有据地揭示近代史上的"殖民十恶",论证全球弱小民族坚持爱国主义,要求改变国际经济旧秩序和更新国际经济立法的正当性;强调当代国际经济秩序和国际经济法律规范的破旧立新,势必循着螺旋式上升的"6C 轨迹",曲折而又不断地向前发展;排除"速胜"论、"坦途"论和"瓦解"论的影响,令人信服地指出:要逐步更新国际经济立法,建立起国际经济新秩序,舍韧性的南南联合自强,别无他途可循。[31] 书中类似的开创

---

[31] 参见陈安教授的论文《南南联合自强五十年的国际经济立法反思:从万隆、多哈、坎昆到香港》(A Reflections on the South-South Coalition in the Last Half Century from the Perspective of International Economic Law-making: From Bandung, Doha and Cancun to Hong Kong)。本长篇专论有中、英两种文本。随着"多哈回合"谈判形势的发展,先后数度应邀增订或改写,被中国及有关国际组织机关公报等国内外六种权威学刊(含《中国法学》2006 年第 2 期、*The Journal of World Investment & Trade* 2006 年第 2 期等)相继采用、转载、转译,并被辑入英文学术专著。中英两种文本已分别收辑于陈安:《陈安论国际经济法学》(第一、四卷),复旦大学出版社 2008 年版,第 479—506、1808—1852 页。该论文于 2007 年获得"福建省第七届社会科学优秀成果奖"一等奖。

性见解还有很多。[32] 可以说，这些成果突出地显示了中国国际经济法学派的鲜明特色和理论水平。

（五）跻身国际前驱

作为国际知名的中国学者，五卷本专著中有近两卷的篇幅是陈安教授相继发表在国际权威期刊上的长篇英文版专题论文。[33] 中国国际法学界前辈权威学者郭寿康教授认为：这些用英语发表的作品，投身国际争鸣，弘扬中华学术，在国际上影响很大，既体现出发展中国家的主张与立场，也扩大了中国的国际影响，为中国国际经济法学赢得了国际声誉。[34]

国际知名人士 B. 戈索维奇（Branislav Gosovic）先生（曾长期担任发展中国家政府间组织"南方中心"秘书长），对陈安教授所撰《南南联合自强五十年的国际经济立法反思：从万隆、多哈、坎昆到香港》长篇专题论文给予很高评价，认为它标志着"对第三世界思想体系的重大创新来自中国"[35]，在世界上特别是第三世界产生了重大影响。

陈安教授在进行学术研究的同时，作为中国政府依据《华盛顿公约》于1993年、2004年、2010年三度遴选向"解决投资争端中心"（ICSID）指派的国际仲裁员，作为国际知名的商务仲裁员，还积极参与国际经济司法的实践。书中收录的其研析涉外或涉华经贸争端仲裁的典型案例，或深入探讨相关法理问题，提出创新见解；或依法据理，剖析批判，匡谬驱邪，伸张正义，留下了他在国际经济司法舞台上鲜明的刚正不阿的印迹。

另值得一提的是，全书文辞优美流畅，尤其是用英文撰写的文章如同用母语写出的文章一样生动，实为难得，充分显示出老一辈学者深厚的学养和扎实的功力。

概言之，五卷本《陈安论国际经济法学》积三十年之功而汇成鸿篇巨制，具有鲜明的中国特色，堪称"独树中华一帜，跻身国际前驱"。正如中国国际法学界前辈权威学者、100岁高龄的朱学山教授所言：这部新著既是创建中国特色国际经济法学理论的奠基之作和扛鼎之作，也是学术报国和经世致用之作。全书秉持陈安教授"三十年来一贯的学术追求，即体察当代南北矛盾的现实，依据和提炼第一手资料，运用

---

[32] 参见陈安：《陈安论国际经济法学》（第一卷），复旦大学出版社2008年版，自序。

[33] 这些发表于外国学术刊物的18篇英文长篇论文，均收辑于陈安：《陈安论国际经济法学》（第四卷），复旦大学出版社2008年版，第1723—2513页。

[34] 参见郭寿康：《弘扬中华学术 投身国际争鸣——推荐〈陈安论国际经济法学〉》，载陈安：《陈安论国际经济法学》（第五卷），复旦大学出版社2008年版，第2539—2540页。

[35] 转引自陈安：《陈安论国际经济法学》（第五卷），复旦大学出版社2008年版，第2540—2546页。

当代国际法理论,通过学术论证,致力为发展中国家弱势群体'依法仗义执言',为当代第三世界争取国际经济平权地位提供法学理论武器,三十年如一日,不懈不渝,可谓'一剑淬砺三十年'"[36]。

此外,五卷本《陈安论国际经济法学》的书名同样引人关注。这也是中国改革开放以来首次参照国际惯例以学者姓名命名的多卷本法学专著。在国际法学界,以学者个人姓名命名"××论××法",是国际上不少著名法学著作的命名惯例,如《奥本海国际法》(Oppenhein's International Law)、《戴西和莫里斯论冲突法》(Dicey & Morris on the Conflict of Laws)等等。五卷本《陈安论国际经济法学》的问世,未尝不是当代中国学者排除百年来形成的民族自卑残余,努力树立应有的"跻身国际前驱"的自信自强心志与正当追求。如此,具有鲜明特色的中国国际经济法学派的形成和存在,当在不远的将来为世所公认,并必将为世所重。

四、从陈安教授辛勤探索的结晶中感悟其治学之道

朱榄叶*

《陈安论国际经济法学》简介

《陈安论国际经济法学》一书(以下简称"五卷本")分列八编,含中、英双语专论78章,共约310万字,2008年由复旦大学出版社推出。其篇章结构和主要内容如下:

第一编,国际经济法基本理论(一)。含16章专论,分别从国际经济法学科的性质、基本原则、其产生和发展、国际经济法几种理论的批判、南北关系、南南合作等方面探讨了国际经济法基本理论问题。

第二编,国际经济法基本理论(二)。含13章专论,分别对中国国内国际经济法学界的不同观点展开了分析和评论,还包括对一些具体案件的评析。

第三编,国际投资法。含15章专论,探讨了多边投资担保制度、美国海外私人投资保护制度、中国吸引外资和对外投资制度,分析了涉及国际投资的几个具体案例。

第四编,国际贸易法。含7章专论,通过具体案例分析了国际贸易法中的一些具体问题,如合同无效、抵押及其争端管辖权、汇票承兑争端管辖权、商检结论等。

---

[36] 朱学山:《一剑淬砺三十年:中国特色国际经济法学的奠基之作——推荐〈陈安论国际经济法学〉》,载陈安:《陈安论国际经济法学》(第五卷),复旦大学出版社2008年版,第2537—2539页。

* 朱榄叶,华东政法大学教授、博士生导师,国际法学院前院长,WTO争端解决机构专家组指示性名单成员。本文原载于《西南政法大学学报》2012年第2期。

第五编,涉台经济法。含5章专论,对《台商大陆投资权益保障协议》《多边投资担保机构公约》对中国台湾地区的适用问题、中国"入世"后海峡两岸经贸问题"政治化"之防治等问题提出了作者的独到见解。

第六编,国际法教育。含4章专论,以作者从事法学教育半个多世纪的感悟,剖析了法学教育中一些发人深省的问题。

第七编,英文版论文选辑。这一部分包括了陈安教授原先发表于国外学术刊物上的18篇英文长篇专论。

第八编,附录。含有关本书作者论著和学术观点的报道、评论和函件等。

五卷本给读者的启示

面对厚厚的五卷本,虽当时一口答应复旦大学出版社参加笔谈,但真的坐下来,却觉得有些惶恐。要写一篇简扼的"书评",评介蕴含在这五卷本中的陈安教授的学术思想、学术理念和学术追求,谈何容易!笔者作为国际经济法学界的晚辈,早就听说了陈安教授的大名,也曾在许多会议上聆听过老师的高论,但有缘当面请教,还是12年前的事。自那以后,在每年的国际经济法学会年会或其他学术会议期间,都有幸听到老师的发言。看着手头这五卷书,笔者在思考着:我们从陈安教授辛勤探索的结晶中可以学到什么?

(一) 秉持鲜明立场,独树中华一帜

只要是读过陈安教授论文的人,都可以从中感受到他论述问题的鲜明立场。不管是他对国际经济新秩序"6C轨迹"的分析[37],还是"南南联合自强"的观点[38],都是鲜明地从发展中国家特别是中国的立场出发。陈安教授的观点并不一定每个人都能接受,但是他论述问题的坚定不移的出发点,却是我们很多学者所忽视,或至少不够重视的。这样的出发点,不是像时下有些人那样,在某篇论文的最后简单加上一个"我国的对策",而是贯穿于他研究和分析的全过程。陈安教授并不轻易否定国外的各种理论,但也绝不盲从。例如,陈安教授对美国国际法学权威学者杰塞普、洛文

---

[37] 关于该问题的详细论述,请参见陈安教授的文章《论国际济法的产生和发展》《论中国在建立国际经济新秩序中的战略定位》(简称《一论》)、《南南联合自强五十年的国际经济立法反思:从万隆、多哈、坎昆到香港》,载陈安:《陈安论国际经济法学》(第一卷),复旦大学出版社2008年版,第62—64、109—111、479—506页。

[38] 参见陈安:《旗帜鲜明地确立中国在构建NIEO中的战略定位——兼论与时俱进,完整、准确地理解邓小平"对外二十八字方针"》,载陈安:《国际经济法学刊》2009年第16卷第3期,第55—81页;陈安:《三论中国在构建NIEO中的战略定位:"匹兹堡发轫之路"走向何方——G20南北合作新平台的待解之谜以及"守法"与"变法"等理念碰撞》,载陈安:《国际经济法学刊》2009年第16卷第4期,第1—29页;陈安:《中国加入WTO十年的法理断想:简论WTO的法治、立法、执法、守法与变法》,载《现代法学》2010年第6期,第114—124页。

费尔德、汉金、杰克逊等人的某些关键性理论观点和学术主张,都秉持虚心学习、严肃对待的态度,通过独立思考、剖析批评,取其精华、去其糟粕。[39] 对任何一个问题,不是从表面现象看,而是作深层次的分析。比如《世纪之交在经济主权上的新争议与"攻防战":综合评析十年来美国单边主义与WTO多边主义交锋的三大回合》一文[40],将美国加入WTO之前的"主权大辩论"、美国"301条款"案(欧共体提出)、美国"201条款"案(欧共体、韩国、日本、中国、巴西、墨西哥、新西兰等提出的钢铁保障措施案),置放在美国一贯的经济霸权主义宏观背景下作了深刻分析。他指出,当代来自超级大国的国家经济主权"淡化""弱化"之类的时髦说法,既不符合现实,也是很不可取的;他提醒全球弱势群体国家,切忌轻信盲从,堕入理论陷阱。[41] 有了大量的事实和引证,这样的分析让人口服心服。何谓"独树中华一帜"?[42] 这就是一大典范。

(二) 力求查证原始资料,养成严谨治学习惯

浏览陈安教授的每篇论文,看到大量的注释,其中不但有马列著作,有中国的历史古籍,还有各个年代外国学者的著述,更有大量的第一手原始资料。[43] 但是,我们却较少看到他引用近期其他学者的论述。这并不是陈安教授不了解近期学术动向,更不是他不看别人的文章,而是他力求运用最直接的原始"证据"来支持自己的观点。笔者想起了最早和陈安教授探讨问题的一件事。2000年,笔者出版了第一本《世界贸易组织国际贸易纠纷案例评析》,其中就论及美国与欧共体之间关于"301条款"的案件。在评析该案时,笔者把它误认作了欧共体"荷尔蒙"案的续篇,在书中说:"1998年2月,DSB通过了荷尔蒙案专家组和上诉机构的报告,确认欧共体的某

---

[39] 关于该问题的详细论述,请参见陈安教授的文章《论国际经济法学科的边缘性、综合性和独立性》《世纪之交在经济主权上的新争议与"攻防战":综合评析十年来美国单边主义与WTO多边主义交锋的三大回合》,载陈安:《陈安论国际经济法学》(第一卷),复旦大学出版社2008年版,第12—16、34—37、370—378页。

[40] 关于该问题的详细论述,请参见陈安:《世纪之交在经济主权上的新争议与"攻防战":综合评析十年来美国单边主义与WTO多边主义交锋的三大回合》,载陈安:《陈安论国际经济法学》(第一卷),复旦大学出版社2008年版,第366—420页。

[41] 关于该问题的详细论述,请参见陈安:《陈安论国际经济法学》(第一卷),复旦大学出版社2008年版,第415—420页。

[42] 关于该问题的详细论述,请参见朱学山教授的文章《一剑淬砺三十年:中国特色国际经济法学的奠基之作》、吴焕宁教授的文章《独树中华一帜,跻身国际前驱》,载陈安:《陈安论国际经济法学》(第五卷),复旦大学出版社2008年版,第2537—2539、2556—2557页。

[43] 关于该问题的详细论述,请参见陈安教授所撰各篇专论,诸如《论国际经济关系的历史发展与南北矛盾》《论源远流长的中国对外经济交往及其法理原则》《论中国在建立国际经济新秩序中的战略定位》《论马克思列宁主义对弱小民族国家主权学说的重大贡献》《论"适用国际惯例"与"有法必依"的统一》《论中国的涉外仲裁监督机制及其与国际惯例的接轨》《再论中国涉外仲裁的监督机制及其与国际惯例的接轨》等等,辑于《陈安论国际经济法学》一书第一卷、第二卷。

些措施不符合《实施卫生与植物卫生措施协定》,要求欧共体修改这些措施。此后,美国就曾经扬言要根据301条款对欧共体实施报复。欧共体的申诉就是在这一背景下出台的"[44]。此后,陈安教授就不止一次打电话来,要笔者告诉他美国是在什么时候如何"扬言"的。在写此案的案件评析时,笔者原先仅仅凭着自己对一篇报道的记忆写出了上述的话。等到陈安教授细究,笔者找遍了所有材料,都无法找到美国何时、何地、如何扬言要报复欧共体"荷尔蒙"案的原始出处。后来笔者继续寻找,才搞清其实是美国对欧共体"香蕉案"的执行情况不满而要求报复,导致了欧共体的申诉。反观陈安教授的《世纪之交在经济主权上的新争议与"攻防战":综合评析十年来美国单边主义与WTO多边主义交锋的三大回合》一文,对这个同一案件的来龙去脉和前因后果却写得清清楚楚。[45] 从这件事可以看出,陈安教授在研究中,每一个细节都要努力搞清楚,这可能已经形成了习惯,但却是许多学人所不及的。

(三) 紧密关注当代国际事件,善于进行多维角度分析

紧密关注当代国际事件,并以法学理论加以分析,指出对待这些事件的正确态度,这是陈安教授的书给我们的又一启示。从1980年对苏联"有限主权论"的剖析[46]到多哈回合谈判[47],从不同仲裁案件的裁决[48]到中国台湾地区的WTO成员地位[49],再到对"黄祸"论——"中国威胁"论的批判[50],书中都不是就事论事的表面介绍,而都是理论结合实际的深入分析。陈安教授善于从历史渊源、国际政治、世界

---

〔44〕 朱榄叶编著:《世界贸易组织国际贸易纠纷案例评析》,法律出版社2000年版,第661页。

〔45〕 关于该问题的详细论述,请参见陈安:《世纪之交在经济主权上的新争议与"攻防战":综合评析十年来美国单边主义与WTO多边主义交锋的三大回合》,载陈安:《陈安论国际经济法学》(第一卷),复旦大学出版社2008年版,第382—385页。

〔46〕 关于该问题的详细论述,请参见陈安:《论社会帝国主义主权观的一大思想渊源:民族虚无主义的今昔》,载陈安:《陈安论国际经济法学》(第一卷),复旦大学出版社2008年版,第421—443页。

〔47〕 关于该问题的详细论述,请参见陈安:《南南联合自强五十年的国际经济立法反思:从万隆、多哈、坎昆到香港》,载陈安:《陈安论国际经济法学》(第一卷),复旦大学出版社2008年版,第479—506页。

〔48〕 关于该问题的详细论述,请参见陈安教授的文章《论中国涉外仲裁程序中当事人的申辩权和对质权》《就中国涉外仲裁体制答英商问》《论涉外仲裁个案中的偏袒伪证和纵容欺诈——CIETAC 1992—1993年个案评析》《论涉外仲裁个案中的越权管辖、越权解释、草率断结和有欠透明——CIETAC 2001—2002年个案评析》《论中国法律认定的"违法行为"及其法律后果——就广东省广信公司破产清算债务讼案问题答外商摩根公司问》等,载陈安:《陈安论国际经济法学》(第二卷),复旦大学出版社2008年版,第683—810页。

〔49〕 关于该问题的详细论述,请参见陈安:《中国"入世"后海峡两岸经贸问题"政治化"之防治》,载陈安:《陈安论国际经济法学》(第四卷),复旦大学出版社2008年版,第1650—1677页。

〔50〕 参见陈安:《"黄祸"论的本源、本质及其最新霸权"变种":"中国威胁"论——中国对外经济交往史的主流及其法理原则的视角》,载《现代法学》2011年第6期,第10—36页。See also An Chen, On the Source, Essence of "Yellow Peril" Doctrine and Its Latest Hegemony "Variant"—the "China Threat" Doctrine: From the Perspective of Historical Mainstream of Sino-Foreign Economic Interactions and Their Inherent Jurisprudential Principles, *The Journal of World Investment & Trade*, Vol. 13, No. 1, 2012, pp. 1-58.

经济和国际法的多维角度,广征博引,由此得出的综合结论不仅令人信服,而且所提出的相应对策也有理有据,成为政府有关部门决策的重要参考。[51]

结　论

近年以来,学术界真是奇闻不断,层出不穷,抄袭、造假"蔚然成风",阴暗角落的诸般"潜规则"似乎就要公然登堂"转正",一时间纯洁的、学术的校园氛围似乎已经凋零而不复存在。但是,细细揣摩陈安教授五卷本的论文,再看看周围的同事们辛勤刻苦的工作状态,笔者的心情顿时平静了许多:任凭乱云飞渡,人间学术正气,仍自岿然兀立,常在长青! 联想到近年来与陈安教授接触过程中的一些感悟,笔者深深感到,像陈安教授这样的人才是中国一代知识分子的楷模。

五、中国特色国际经济法学的理念与追求
——《陈安论国际经济法学》的学术创新与特色贡献

曾华群*

陈安老师积三十年之功蔚为大观的《陈安论国际经济法学》(五卷本)以马克思主义为指导,以南北问题为主线,站在中国和广大发展中国家的立场,坚持建立国际经济新秩序的目标,深刻论证国际经济法的基本原则,充分反映了作者创建中国特色国际经济法学的理念和追求。

以马克思主义为指导论述国际经济法学的基本问题

如所周知,中国特色法学理论是中国特色社会主义理论的重要组成部分之一,其指导思想和理论基础是马克思主义。作为中国特色法学理论的重要组成部分之一,中国特色国际经济法学尽管具有"国际性",其指导思想和理论基础同样是马克思主义。

早在20世纪40年代,作者在厦门大学求学时就开始接受马克思主义的启蒙和熏陶,50—70年代,曾专门从事马克思主义教学和研究。对马克思主义特别是民族

---

[51] 参见1987年至2008年期间中华人民共和国对外经贸部、商务部条法司以及中华人民共和国常驻世界贸易组织代表团团长孙振宇大使先后致陈安教授的函件,载陈安:《陈安论国际经济法学》(第五卷),复旦大学出版社2008年版,第2546—2547、2585—2591页。

* 曾华群,时任厦门大学法学院教授、博士生导师。本文原载于《西南政法大学学报》2012年第2期。

殖民地及主权理论学养深厚,是其致力创建中国特色国际经济法学的重要思想和理论优势。在 80 年代以来的国际经济法学研究中,作者援引马克思主义原著的精辟论述,分析国际经济关系的发展,以殖民掠夺史揭示南北问题的根源和实质及阐释马克思主义主权观。

(一) 分析国际经济关系的发展

国际经济关系既是国际经济法借以产生和发展的主要依据,又是国际经济法调整的主要对象。作者以辩证唯物主义和历史唯物主义详细分析国际经济关系发展的三大主要阶段(即早期的国际经济交往与国际经济关系的初步形成,资本主义世界市场的形成与国际经济关系的重大发展,社会主义国家的出现、众多弱小民族的独立与国际经济关系的本质变化),深刻指出,历史唯物主义的基本原理"是对人类社会长期发展进程客观事实的科学总结","是对各国社会进行解剖的利器,也是对国际社会实行科学分析的指南"[52]。

(二) 以殖民掠夺史揭示南北问题的根源和实质

基于历史事实,作者以激扬文字历数 15 世纪以来列强在亚非拉地区推行殖民主义的十大罪恶行径,称为"殖民十恶"(即"欺蒙诈骗,以贱易贵""明火执仗,杀人越货""践踏主权,霸占领土""横征暴敛,榨取脂膏""强制劳役,敲骨吸髓""猎取活人,贩卖奴隶""垄断贸易,单一经济""种毒贩毒,戕民攫利""毁灭文化,精神侵略"和"血腥屠杀,种族灭绝")[53],进而总结:"漫漫数百年,一部殖民史,就是一部弱肉强食史,也就是欧美列强和全世界众多弱小民族之间的国际经济关系史的主要内容。"[54]"15 世纪以来的数百年间,欧洲列强在亚、非、美广大地区实行殖民掠夺的历史,是一部火与剑的历史,也是一部血与泪的历史。"[55]

在中外国际经济法学论著中,居于道义制高点,以如此犀利笔触历数殖民之恶,似为仅见。或许有人会认为这是政治学或史学的内容,但笔者以为,殖民掠夺史在西方国际经济法学论著中讳莫如深,却是中国特色国际经济法学应有的立论根基。正本清源,温故知新。只有回顾和铭记历史,才能深刻理解南北问题的根源和实质,

---

[52] 陈安:《论国际经济关系的历史发展与南北矛盾》,载陈安:《陈安论国际经济法学》(第一卷),复旦大学出版社 2008 年版,第 40 页。
[53] 同上书,第 46—54 页。
[54] 同上书,第 53 页。
[55] 同上书,第 46 页。

认清西方列强罄竹难书的罪恶"发家史"及其对广大发展中国家所欠下的巨大"历史债务",也才能深刻理解建立国际经济新秩序的正当性、必要性和紧迫性,正确认识社会发展规律和国际经济关系的发展趋势和方向。在法理上,殖民掠夺史是经济主权、公平互利和全球合作等国际经济法基本原则的必要铺陈。

(三) 阐释马克思主义主权观

作者对马克思主义主权观的研究和论述,重点强调民族自决权和批判民族虚无主义。两者相辅相成,构成了作者研讨马克思主义主权观的核心主张,即十分强调尊重和维护广大发展中国家的主权,坚决反对社会帝国主义等形形色色的霸权主义。

在专著《列宁对民族殖民地革命学说的重大发展》(1981年)中,作者系统深入研究马克思、恩格斯关于民族殖民地问题的基本理论,列宁1895—1924年期间在弱小民族国家主权问题上的学说,重点探讨国际共产主义运动史上有关"民族自决"问题的长期论战,研究国际公法上有关弱小民族国家主权学说的争鸣辩论,侧重论述殖民地、半殖民地弱小民族国家主权——民族自决权问题在国际共产主义运动队伍中的论战过程及其发展历史。[56]

在专论《论社会帝国主义主权观的一大思想渊源:民族虚无主义的今昔》(1981年)中,作者回顾和缕述当年马克思、恩格斯和列宁与伪装成"国际主义者"的形形色色的民族虚无主义者多次论战的历史事实,追本溯源,探讨曾经猖獗一时的社会帝国主义主权观的理论基础和思想渊源,揭露它既是对国际法主权原则的粗暴践踏,又是对马克思主义主权观的彻底背离。[57]

应当指出,马克思主义主权观具有重要的现实意义。研究国际共产主义运动中的民族殖民地学说和国际法上的弱小民族国家主权学说,有助于理解当代发展中国家的历史来由、现实地位和发展趋向及南北问题的根源和实质。研究近代以来西方列强和社会帝国主义的霸权行径及相关学说,有助于认清当前全球化趋势下美国推行的霸权主义及西方学者否定或淡化主权的"理论先导"与前者的一脉相承或异曲同工。不难看出,作者在国际经济法基本理论研究中强调经济主权原则,深刻批判美国经济霸权及西方学者否定或淡化主权的谬论,源于对马克思主义主权观的深刻理解和研究积淀。

---

[56] 参见陈安:《列宁对民族殖民地革命学说的重大发展》,生活·读书·新知三联书店1981年版。该书已辑入《陈安论国际经济法学》(第一卷),题为"论马克思列宁主义对弱小民族国家主权学说的重大贡献",复旦大学出版社2008年版,第136—342页。

[57] 参见陈安:《论社会帝国主义主权观的一大思想渊源:民族虚无主义的今昔》,载陈安:《陈安论国际经济法学》(第一卷),复旦大学出版社2008年版,第421—443页。

站在中国和其他发展中国家的立场提出南北矛盾发展的"6C律"

不容否认,作为法学学科之一,国际经济法学具有普世价值,各国国际经济法学者当有共同的立场、价值取向和追求。基于此,各国国际经济法学者需要加强学术交流,增强共识,求同存异,共同促进世界性国际经济法学的发展和繁荣。

同样不容否认,作为法律规范之一,国际经济法既是发达国家巩固国际经济旧秩序的重要工具,也是发展中国家改革国际经济旧秩序、建立国际经济新秩序的重要工具。换言之,国际经济法规范体现了新旧法律规则并存、冲突的状况。在国际经济法的发展过程中,始终贯穿维护国际经济旧秩序与建立国际经济新秩序的斗争。相应地,各国国际经济法学者并非居于同一的、纯粹的、超脱的法的立场。在全球化背景下,由于国家利益、历史传统、意识形态、宗教信仰、文化等因素,各国特别是南北国家的国际经济法学者各有其不同的立场、价值取向和追求。西方国家国际经济法学者对其立场,或直言不讳,或犹抱琵琶。在国际经济法学研究中,作者一向旗帜鲜明地站在中国和其他发展中国家的立场,坚持和发展"三个世界"理论,坚持建立国际经济新秩序的目标,体现了"知识报国,兼济天下"的志向和胸怀。

(一) 坚持和发展"三个世界"理论

20世纪80年代末90年代初苏东剧变、冷战结束后,世界格局发生了重大变化。作者坚持和发展"三个世界"理论,明确指出:现在的世界实际上存在着互相联系又互相矛盾着的三个方面,从而使全球划分为三个世界:首先,美国、苏联是第一世界,苏联在1991年瓦解之后,美国遂成为第一世界中唯一的超级大国;亚、非、拉美发展中国家和其他地区的发展中国家,是第三世界;处在这两者之间的发达国家是第二世界。中国是一个社会主义国家,也是一个发展中国家,它和其他发展中国家,曾经有过共同的经历,当前又面临着共同的斗争。过去、现在和将来长时间共同的处境和共同的利害,决定了中国属于第三世界。[58] 作者进一步分析,世纪之交,国际经济秩序破旧立新的争斗进入新的回合。其主要特点有三:一是冷战已告结束,和平与发展成为当代世界主题;二是霸权主义和强权政治在各种新"包装"下有新的发展,"新干涉主义"和"新炮舰政策"不时肆虐;三是经济全球化趋势加速发展,南北矛盾日益突出,广大发展中国家的经济主权面临严峻挑战。[59]

---

[58] 参见陈安:《论国际经济关系的历史发展与南北矛盾》,载陈安:《陈安论国际经济法学》(第一卷),复旦大学出版社2008年版,第59页。

[59] 同上书,第60—61页。

对当前国际经济秩序,西方学界有不同的解读,诸如"新自由主义经济秩序"论、"WTO宪政秩序"论和"经济民族主义扰乱全球化秩序"论等,总体上是不提"三个世界"、南北问题和新旧国际经济秩序,另辟蹊径,以所谓"经济全球化""法律全球化"理论淡化或否定国家主权。作者针对上述各说,逐一辨析,言简意赅,切中肯綮。

针对"新自由主义经济秩序"论,作者指出,"宣扬全面自由化、市场化和私有化的新自由主义和'华盛顿共识'的本质是为国际垄断资本在全球扩张服务的";"'新自由主义经济秩序'的说教及其实践,实质上乃是殖民主义、资本主义、帝国主义三位一体的国际经济旧秩序在当代的更新和翻版,充其量只不过是'新瓶装旧酒'或'换汤不换药'罢了"。

针对"WTO宪政秩序"论,作者指出,"WTO宪政秩序"论的先天性缺陷和致命性弱点在于,它忽略了当代WTO体制及其规则缺乏坚实的、真正的民主基础;WTO体制虽然素来被称为摆脱了"权力导向",转而实行"规则导向",但其"立法"完全是"权力导向"之下的产物,带着先天的不公胎记,其"司法"和"执法"实践也出现过"财大者力大气粗"、霸权或强权国家不受约束或规避制裁的弊端,实际上体现了"规则导向"向"权力导向"的异化、转化;"WTO宪政秩序"论要求将贸易自由宪法化、最高化、绝对化的主张是不可取的。[60]

针对"经济民族主义扰乱全球化秩序"论,作者指出,其实质是以莫须有的"罪名",力图迫使国际弱势群体离开原定的建立国际经济新秩序的奋斗目标。他认为,把"经济民族主义"理解为全球各民族特别是各弱小民族坚持在经济上独立自主,坚持国际经济主权,是基本正确的。[61]

笔者以为,坚持和发展"三个世界"理论,是正确认识新时期中国在国际经济关系和国际体制的"立场"和"战略定位"问题的必要前提。基于"三个世界"理论,才能深入分析当前西方强势主导的形形色色的"国际经济秩序新论",也才能坚持和发展建立国际经济新秩序的理论。鉴于南北问题仍然是当前国际经济发展的重大问题,寻求建立公正的"国际秩序"和真正的"全球治理体系",[62]不能回避南北问题,更不

---

[60] 关于WTO体制的进一步剖析,请参见陈安:《中国加入WTO十年的法理断想:简论WTO的法治、立法、执法、守法与变法》,载《现代法学》2010年第6期,第114—124页。

[61] 关于该问题的详细论述,请参见陈安:《论中国在建立国际经济新秩序中的战略定位——兼评"新自由主义经济秩序"论、"WTO宪政秩序"论、"经济民族主义扰乱全球化秩序"论》,载陈安:《陈安论国际经济法学》(第一卷),复旦大学出版社2008年版,第120—134页。

[62] 近年来,西方学者除上述国际经济秩序论外,还提出了所谓全球治理论。如在国际投资法领域,提出了所谓"外国直接投资的全球治理体系"(the global governance system for FDI)的概念,并指出这一体系主要是由BITs构成的。See Axel Berger, China's New Bilateral Investment Treaty Programme: Substance, Rational and Implications for Investment Law Making, paper for the American Society of International Law International Economic Law Group(ASIL IELIG) 2008 Biennial Conference "The Politics of International Economic Law: The Next Four Years", Washington, D. C., November 14-15, 2008.

能回避改革国际经济旧秩序、建立国际经济新秩序这一根本性问题。

(二) 提出南北矛盾发展的"6C 律"

早在《国际经济法总论》(1991 年)中,作者即以马克思主义为指导,指出:"在国际经济和国际经济法的发展过程中,始终贯穿着强权国家保持和扩大既得经济利益、维护国际经济旧秩序与贫弱国家争取和确保经济平权地位、建立国际经济新秩序的斗争。这些斗争,往往以双方的妥协和合作而告终,妥协合作之后又因新的利害矛盾和利益冲突而产生新的争斗,如此循环往复不已,每一次循环往复,均是螺旋式上升,都把国际经济秩序以及和它相适应的国际经济法规范,推进到一个新的水平或一个新的发展阶段。"[63]

在专论《南南联合自强五十年的国际经济立法反思:从万隆、多哈、坎昆到香港》(2006 年)和专著《国际经济法学专论》(2007 年)中,作者总结万隆会议以来的南北斗争史,进一步提出了南北矛盾发展的"6C 律"及其特点,强调南南联合自强对建立国际经济新秩序的重大意义。其主要观点可概要如下:

国际经济秩序的新旧更替和国际经济法的破旧立新是在南北矛盾发展进程中产生的。南北国家之间既有互相矛盾、互相斗争的一面,又有互相依存、互相合作的一面。因此,南北矛盾斗争的每一个回合,往往以双方的妥协和国际经济秩序在某种程度上的除旧布新而告终。妥协之后经过一段时间,又在新的历史条件下产生新的矛盾斗争。南北矛盾上述规律性的发展进程,可概括称为螺旋式的"6C 轨迹"或"6C 律",即 Contradiction(矛盾)→Conflict(冲突或交锋)→Consultation(磋商)→Compromise(妥协)→Cooperation(合作)→Coordination(协调)→Contradiction New(新的矛盾)。当代国际经济秩序和国际经济法正是在此种"6C 律"的基础上和支配下,不断经历着新旧交替、吐故纳新、弃旧图新和破旧立新的进程。[64] 南北问题的根本解决取决于国际经济新秩序的建立,取决于南北国家基于经济主权、公平互利和全球合作等国际经济法基本原则的真诚合作。发展中国家要在南北经济关系中获得真正平等的地位,只有依靠独立自主和自力更生,提高本国的经济实力,才能提高和增强在南北合作中的谈

---

[63] 陈安:《论国际经济法的产生和发展》,载陈安:《陈安论国际经济法学》(第一卷),复旦大学出版社 2008 年版,第 64 页。

[64] 参见陈安:《南南联合自强五十年的国际经济立法反思:从万隆、多哈、坎昆到香港》,载陈安:《陈安论国际经济法学》(第一卷),复旦大学出版社 2008 年版,第 500—502 页;陈安主编:《国际经济法学专论(第二版)》,高等教育出版社 2007 年版,第 246、324—326 页。

判地位和能力。与此同时,要大力加强南南合作,以求联合自强和共同发展。[65]

"6C 律"的提出具有重要的理论和实践意义。首先,指明发展中国家"斗争中求生存,合作中求发展"的必由之路。南北国家之间矛盾、冲突之后是磋商、妥协、合作和协调,张弛有度,循环往复,反映了南北双方既相互矛盾、冲突又相互依存、合作的客观现实和南北矛盾运动的发展规律。第二,揭示发展中国家的持续斗争是促进国际经济秩序的新旧更替和国际经济法的破旧立新的原动力。发达国家为保持和发展其在国际经济交往中的优势地位,自然成为固守和维护国际经济旧秩序的守护神。而发展中国家为改变其在国际经济交往中的劣势地位,必然成为要求改革国际经济旧秩序、建立国际经济新秩序的主力军。第三,强调建立国际经济新秩序和国际经济法新规范的长期性和艰巨性。长远看来,在上述"6C 律"的发展过程中,国际经济秩序的新旧更替和国际经济法的破旧立新总体上处于上升态势。但在特定历史时期,由于南北国家在矛盾、斗争中此强彼弱,此消彼长,在发达国家占上风的情况下,则可能出现下行态势。对发展中国家而言,如同逆水行舟,每一个进步,都需要艰辛的斗争和努力,稍有懈怠,已取得的成果可能得而复失或名存实亡。对于建立国际经济新秩序和国际经济法新规范的长期性和艰巨性,发展中国家应有战略的眼光和充分的准备。

(三)新时期中国在国际经济关系和国际体制中的立场和战略定位

关于新时期中国在国际经济关系和国际体制中的立场和战略定位,特别是中国在建立国际经济新秩序中的地位与作用,中外学者见仁见智。近年来,随着中国经济的发展和国际影响力的提升,某些西方学者热衷于强调中国的"领导作用"和"大国责任",甚至提出"中国威胁"论,其用意发人深思。[66] 中国是现存国际经济秩序的最大受惠者、维护者、改良者、改革者,抑或革命者?众说纷纭。作者在国际经济法理论研究中的相关视角和论述富有启迪。

首先,是作者研究国际经济法问题的角度。在论述"我国涉外经济立法中可否规定对外资绝不实行国有化"问题时,作者指出:"从中国国情与国际舆情的结合上来考虑问题,从南北矛盾的历史与现实的结合上来考虑问题,从新、旧两种国际经济

---

[65] 关于南南合作问题的系统论述,参见 An Chen, Weak Versus Strong at the WTO, the South-South Coalition from Bandung to Hong Kong, *The Geneva Post Quarterly: The Journal of World Affairs*, 2006, pp. 55-107。

[66] 关于"中国威胁"论的历史考察,参见陈安:《"黄祸"论的本源、本质及其最新霸权"变种":"中国威胁"论——中国对外经济交往史的主流及其法理原则的视角》,载《现代法学》2011 年第 6 期。See also An Chen, On the Source, Essence of "Yellow Peril" Doctrine and Its Latest Hegemony "Variant"—the "China Threat" Doctrine: From the Perspective of Historical Mainstream of Sino-Foreign Economic Interactions and Their Inherent Jurisprudential Principles, *The Journal of World Investment & Trade*, Vol. 13, No. 1, 2012.

秩序的更迭兴替上来考虑问题,作为在世界上具有举足轻重地位的社会主义国家和发展中国家,作为第三世界的一个中坚成员,中国在本国关于经济特区和沿海开放城市的涉外经济立法中,显然不宜、不必、不应、不容明文规定对外资绝对不实行征用或国有化。"[67]由此可见,作者所主张的研究国际经济法问题的三个角度分别是中国国情与国际舆情的结合、南北矛盾的历史与现实的结合以及新、旧两种国际经济秩序的更迭兴替,对中国的明确定位是"第三世界中坚成员"。

其次,鉴于新时期中国在国际经济关系和国际体制中的立场和战略定位是新中国成立以来的延续,有必要考察新中国对外交往的一贯立场。作者指出:"独立自主和平等互利,乃是新中国对外经济交往中一贯坚持的最基本的法理原则和行为规范,也是中国对外经济交往健康发展的两大基石。"[68]

关于新时期中国在国际经济关系和国际体制中的立场和战略定位,作者在论述古代中国的自我定位和近现代中国历史形成的"中华民族爱国主义"独特内涵的基础上明确指出,中国应成为建立国际经济新秩序的积极推手,应致力于成为南南联合自强的中流砥柱之一,中国与全球弱势群体共同参与建立国际经济新秩序的战略目标,应当坚定不移,韧性斗争,百折不挠,即应当坚持战略原则的坚定性,又坚持策略战术的灵活性。[69]

概言之,历史已然成就了中国作为"第三世界中坚成员"的地位。作为"第三世界中坚成员",中国的基本立场理应是,奉行独立自主和平等互利原则,成为建立国际经济新秩序的积极推手,致力于成为南南联合自强的中流砥柱之一,坚持建立国际经济新秩序的战略目标。无论将来中国国际经济地位发生怎样的改变,应该有始终如一的、坚定的立场和目标。以国际投资关系为例,中国必须坚持和强调经济主

---

[67] 陈安:《我国涉外经济立法中可否规定对外资绝不实行国有化》,载陈安:《陈安论国际经济法学》(第三卷),复旦大学出版社2008年版,第1209页。

[68] 更详细的论述,请参见陈安:《论源远流长的中国对外经济交往及其法理原则》,载陈安:《陈安论国际经济法学》(第一卷),复旦大学出版社2008年版,第98页。

[69] 更详细的论述,请参见陈安教授的论文《论中国在建立国际经济新秩序中的战略定位——兼评"新自由主义经济秩序"论、"WTO宪政秩序"论、"经济民族主义扰乱全球化秩序"论》,载陈安:《陈安论国际经济法学》(第一卷),复旦大学出版社2008年版,第109—120页。在该文发表之后,作者相继发表有关中国在建立国际经济新秩序中战略定位的专论,包括:陈安:《再论旗帜鲜明地确立中国在构建NIEO中的战略定位——兼论与时俱进,完整、准确地理解邓小平"对外二十八字方针"》,载陈安:《国际经济法学刊》2009年第16卷第3期;陈安:《三论中国在构建NIEO中的战略定位:"匹兹堡发轫之路"走向何方——G20南北合作新平台的待解之谜以及"守法"与"变法"等理念碰撞》,载陈安:《国际经济法学刊》2009年第16卷第4期;陈安:《中国加入WTO十年的法理断想:简论WTO的法治、立法、执法、守法与变法》,载《现代法学》2010年第6期;An Chen, What Should Be China's Strategic Position in the Establishment of New International Economic Order? With Comments on Neoliberalistic Economic Order, Constitutional Order of the WTO and Economic Nationalism's Disturbance of Globalization, *The Journal of World Investment & Trade*, Vol. 10, No. 3, 2009; An Chen, Some Jurisprudential Thoughts upon WTO's Law-Governing, Law-Making, Law-Enforcing, Law-Abiding and Law-Reforming, *The Journal of World Investment & Trade*, Vol. 11, No. 2, 2010.

权、公平互利和全球合作原则,不能因为居于资本输出国地位就片面强调资本输出国的权益,要求资本输入国限制其主权。中国一向反对发达国家"以邻为壑""损人利己"的做法,同样也要引以为戒,严格自律。随着中国国际经济地位的改变,对外经济政策可以根据形势的变化而调整,但立场要坚定,不因经济地位的转变而变化,不因利益的诱导而变化。中国国际经济法学者进行学术研究应有"第三世界中坚成员"的"立场"意识,政府主管部门在国际经济实践中也应有"第三世界中坚成员"的坚定立场。

论证南北矛盾中形成的国际经济法基本原则

一般而言,国际经济法的基本原则指国际社会普遍接受的调整国际经济关系的最基本的法律原则。作者认为:"国际经济法的基本原则,指的是贯穿于调整国际经济关系的各类法律规范之中的主要精神和指导思想,指的是这些法律规范的基础和核心"[70];"在当代国际经济法基本规范或基本原则更新发展的全过程中,始终贯穿着强权国家保护既得利益、维护国际经济旧秩序与贫弱国家争取平权地位、建立国际经济新秩序的矛盾和斗争。这种矛盾斗争,乃是当代世界性'南北矛盾'斗争的主要内容。"[71]作者强调国际经济法基本原则是在南北矛盾中形成的,旨在强调其"发展性"和"动态性",强调发展中国家建立国际经济新秩序的目标,反映了中国国际经济法学的特色。以下概述作者有关经济主权原则、公平互利原则和全球合作原则的部分重要观点。

(一) 经济主权原则

如所周知,主权是国际法的基石。当前,为推进经济全球化,西方国家以理论为先导,提出了否定或淡化主权的种种理论。[72] 对于广大发展中国家而言,面临的首要任务是坚持和维护《联合国宪章》确立的国家主权原则。[73]

关于经济主权原则,作者重点研究了经济主权原则的形成原因及其基本内容、世纪之交经济主权"攻防战"及中国坚持经济主权原则的实践。

---

[70] 陈安:《论经济主权原则是当代国际经济法首要的基本规范》,载陈安:《陈安论国际经济法学》(第一卷),复旦大学出版社 2008 年版,第 344 页。

[71] 同上书,第 346 页。

[72] See John H. Jackson, *Sovereignty, the WTO, and Changing Fundamentals of International Law*, Cambridge University Press, 2006.

[73] See B. Boutros-Ghali, B. Gosovic, *Global Leadership and Global Systemic Issues: South, North and the United Nations in 21st Century World*, Transcend University Press, 2011.

1. 经济主权原则的形成原因及其基本内容

作者指出,发展中国家强调和坚持经济主权有其特定的历史原因和现实原因。从历史上看,大多数发展中国家在二战结束之前都处在殖民地、半殖民地地位;二战结束后,殖民地、半殖民地弱小民族相继挣脱殖民枷锁,取得政治独立,但经济上仍然遭受原宗主国的控制,不同程度地处于从属或附庸的地位。政治主权是经济主权的前提,经济主权是政治主权的保障。发展中国家强调经济主权实质上是全世界弱小民族反殖民主义斗争的必要继续和必然发展。[74]

根据 1974 年《各国经济权利和义务宪章》的规定,作者概括国家经济主权的主要内容,包括:各国对本国内部以及本国涉外的一切经济事务享有完全、充分的独立自主权利,不受任何外来干涉;各国对境内一切自然资源享有永久主权;各国对境内的外国投资以及跨国公司的活动享有管理监督权;各国对境内的外国资产有权收归国有或征用;各国对世界性经贸大政享有平等的参与权和决策权。[75]

2. 世纪之交经济主权"攻防战"

近年来,作者以马克思主义主权观为指导,针对当前全球化趋势下西方国家否定或淡化"主权"的理论和实践,进行了深入的专题研究。作者以 WTO 体制运作十年来美国单边主义与 WTO 多边主义交锋的三大回合作为中心,综合评析美国 1994 年"主权大辩论"、1998—2000 年"301 条款"争端案及 2002—2003 年"201 条款"争端案的前因后果和来龙去脉,指出这三次交锋的实质,都是美国经济"主权"(经济霸权)与各国群体经济主权之间限制与反限制的争斗,植根于美国早在 1994 年"入世"之初确立的其单边主义政策高于其 WTO 义务的既定方针;提出这场以经济主权问题为核心的激烈论战对发展中国家的重要启迪是:增强忧患意识,珍惜经济主权;力争对全球经贸大政决策权实行公平的国际再分配;善用经济主权保护民族权益,抵御霸权欺凌和其他风险;警惕理论陷阱,摒除经济主权"淡化"论。[76]

作者深刻指出:"主权'过时'论、主权'废弃'论的主旨在于彻底解除弱小民族的思想武装,好让当代霸权主义在全球通行无阻;'淡化'论和'弱化'论的'发展方向',正是归宿于'过时'论和'废弃'论。这种归宿,绝不是弱小民族之福,而是善良的人们不能预见其后果的理论陷阱"。[77]

---

[74] 参见陈安:《论经济主权原则是当代国际经济法首要的基本规范》,载陈安:《陈安论国际经济法学》(第一卷),复旦大学出版社 2008 年版,第 347—348 页。

[75] 同上书,第 351—359 页。

[76] 参见陈安:《世纪之交在经济主权上的新争议与"攻防战":综合评析十年来美国单边主义与 WTO 多边主义交锋的三大回合》,载陈安:《陈安论国际经济法学》(第一卷),复旦大学出版社 2008 年版,第 366—420 页。

[77] 同上书,第 420 页。

3. 中国坚持经济主权原则的实践

不言而喻,作为发展中大国,中国理应与广大发展中国家站在一起,坚持经济主权原则。作者主张,无论是在国内立法实践方面,或是国际条约实践方面,中国都要坚持经济主权原则。

针对中国涉外经济立法中可否规定对外资绝不实行国有化问题,作者主张,在中国经济特区和沿海开放城市的涉外经济立法中,不应明文规定在任何情况下都不对外资实行征用或国有化。其主要理由是,从外资国有化问题的论战史、中外签订的双边投资保护协定、西方国家对"国有化"的理解及中国的宪法精神和现有政策等方面看,不适宜、不必要、不应当、不容许作此规定。其结论是:"鉴于东道国在必要时有权依法征收境内外资,并且给予适当补偿,乃是当代国家经济主权权利之一,而且已经成为国际通行的立法惯例,中国不应通过立法自行'弃权'";"务必留权在手,但决不任意滥用!"[78]

在国际实践方面,作者主张,中国在"入世"谈判中应坚持经济主权原则,指出:"中国是主权牢牢在握的独立国家,中国人民十分珍惜自己经过长期奋斗得来不易的主权权利……尽管'复关'和加'入世'贸组织的谈判旷日持久,难关重重,中国坚持经济主权原则,有关加入多边贸易体制的基本立场和方针不变。"[79]

当前,国际投资法发展迅速,其趋向值得密切关注。传统国际投资法本来就是发达国家为保护其海外投资者的产物,带有与生俱来的片面维护资本输出国权益的烙印,其新近发展并未起到平衡发达国家与发展中国家之间、东道国与外国投资者之间的权利和利益关系,而是更加片面强调保护发达国家和外国投资者的权益,进一步限制东道国的主权。通过此类规范的不断强化,发达国家推动投资自由化,以实现其国家利益。近来,双边投资条约普遍规定接受"解决投资争端国际中心"(ICSID)的管辖,甚至规定投资者可以单方面启动 ICSID 程序。在经济全球化趋势下,中国的某些国际实践顺应了西方国家主导和推波助澜的所谓"时代潮流"。针对20世纪90年代以来中外双边投资协定的"争端解决"条款的新发展,作者明确提出,中外双边投资协定实践中的"逐案审批同意""当地救济优先""东道国法律适用"和"重大安全例外"四大"安全阀"不宜贸然拆除;[80]进而主张,区分南、北两类国家,实

---

[78] 陈安:《我国涉外经济立法中可否规定对外资绝不实行国有化》,载陈安:《陈安论国际经济法学》(第三卷),复旦大学出版社 2008 年版,第 1197—1209 页。

[79] 陈安:《论中国在"入世"谈判中应当坚持经济主权原则》,载陈安:《陈安论国际经济法学》(第一卷),复旦大学出版社 2008 年版,第 360 页。

[80] 参见陈安:《中外双边投资协定中的四大"安全阀"不宜贸然拆除——美、加型 BITs 谈判范本关键性"争端解决"条款剖析》,载陈安:《陈安论国际经济法学》(第三卷),复旦大学出版社 2008 年版,第 1079—1108 页。

行差别互惠,明文排除最惠国条款对争端程序的普遍适用,切实维护中国的应有权益。[81]

(二) 公平互利原则

公平互利原则是在"公平"这一传统法律概念基础上结合"互利"概念发展起来的国际经济法基本原则,强调实质上的平等,进一步明确了平等互利的含义,是平等互利原则的新发展。

关于公平互利原则,作者重点研究公平互利原则是平等互利原则的发展及公平互利原则的主旨。

1. 公平互利原则是平等互利原则的发展

作者在分析公平互利原则的形成过程中指出,在国际交往实践中,发展中国家认识到,仅仅从或主要从政治角度强调主权平等原则,往往只能做到形式上的平等,难以实现实质上的平等。在某些场合,发达国家往往以形式上的平等掩盖实质上的不平等。因此,应从经济角度、从实质上重新审视传统意义上的主权平等原则,赋予其新的时代内容,互利原则由此产生。国家之间的关系,只有建立在平等的基础上,才能做到互利;只有真正地实行互利,才算是贯彻了平等的原则,才能实现实质上的平等。[82]

把传统的国际法上分立的平等原则与互利原则结合成调整国际政治、经济关系的一项基本原则,标志着国际法上平等原则的新发展。[83] 作者特别指出了中国有关平等互利原则的实践对公平互利原则形成的贡献。在国内法实践方面,中国人民政治协商会议在 1949 年 9 月 29 日通过的《共同纲领》中,明确把平等互利规定为与外国建立外交关系的前提条件及对外经济交往、调整国际经济关系的基本准则。在国际法实践方面,1954 年 4—6 月,中国与印度、缅甸一起,率先把平等互利原则与互相尊重主权和领土完整、互不侵犯、互不干涉内政、和平共处等五项原则作为指导当代国际关系的基本准则,逐渐获得了国际社会的普遍认同。[84]

2. 公平互利原则的主旨

作者指出:"在国际经济交往中强调公平互利,究其主要宗旨,端在于树立和贯

---

[81] 参见陈安:《区分两类国家,实行差别互惠:再论 ICSID 体制赋予中国的四大"安全阀"不宜贸然全面拆除》,载陈安:《陈安论国际经济法学》(第三卷),复旦大学出版社 2008 年版,第 1109—1146 页。

[82] 参见陈安:《论国际经济法中的公平互利原则是平等互利原则的重大发展》,载陈安:《陈安论国际经济法学》(第一卷),复旦大学出版社 2008 年版,第 446—447 页。

[83] 参见周鲠生:《国际法》(上册),商务印书馆 1981 年版,第 213 页。

[84] 参见陈安:《论国际经济法中的公平互利原则是平等互利原则的重大发展》,载陈安:《陈安论国际经济法学》(第一卷),复旦大学出版社 2008 年版,第 444 页。

彻新的平等观。对于经济实力相当、实际地位基本平等的同类国家说来,公平互利落实于原有平等关系的维持;对于经济实力悬殊、实际地位不平等的不同类国家说来,公平互利落实于原有形式平等关系或虚假平等关系的纠正以及新的实质平等关系的创设。"[85]

在论证公平互利原则时,作者进一步指出:"这种新的平等观,是切合客观实际需要的,是科学的,也是符合马克思主义基本观点的。早在百余年前,马克思在剖析平等权利时,就曾经指出:用同一尺度去衡量和要求先天禀赋各异、后天负担不同的劳动者,势必造成各种不平等的弊病,并且断言:'要避免所有这些弊病,权利就不应当是平等的,而应当是不平等的。'马克思的这种精辟见解,对于我们深入理解当代发展中国家提出的关于贯彻公平互利原则、实行非互惠普惠制等正义要求,具有现实的指导意义。"[86]作者形象的结论是,对经济实力悬殊的国家,"平等"地用同一尺度去衡量,用同一标准去要求,实行绝对的、无差别的"平等待遇"的实际效果,"有如要求先天不足、大病初愈的弱女与体魄强健、训练有素的壮汉,在同一起跑点上'平等'地赛跑,从而以'平等'的假象掩盖不平等的实质"。[87]

(三) 全球合作原则

全球合作原则是 1974 年《建立国际经济新秩序宣言》和《各国经济权利和义务宪章》倡导的一项富有时代特点的国际经济法基本原则。基于南北问题的认识,要实现建立国际经济新秩序的目标,必须进一步强调、坚持和实践全球合作原则。

关于全球合作原则,作者重点论证南北合作是全球合作原则的中心环节和南南联合自强是建立国际经济新秩序的唯一路径。

1. 南北合作是全球合作原则的中心环节

作者指出,南北合作是全球合作原则的中心环节,是国际经济关系上众多弱者与少数强者之间在不同阶段的互相妥协和互相让步;就其内在实质而言,是国际经济关系中剥削者与被剥削者、强者与弱者之间的妥协,也是对弱肉强食规则缓慢的逐步否定。[88]

南北合作的依据是发达国家与发展中国家在现实经济生活中存在极其密切的

---

[85] 参见陈安:《论国际经济法中的公平互利原则是平等互利原则的重大发展》,载陈安:《陈安论国际经济法学》(第一卷),复旦大学出版社 2008 年版,第 449 页。
[86] 同上书,第 449—450 页。
[87] 同上书,第 448—449 页。
[88] 参见陈安:《全球合作的新兴模式和强大趋势:南南合作与"77 国集团"》,载陈安:《陈安论国际经济法学》(第一卷),复旦大学出版社 2008 年版,第 463—466 页。

互相依存和互相补益关系。这决定了南北国家"合则两利,离则两伤",促使南北国家在不同发展阶段的斗争中终究要相互妥协,作出"南北合作"的选择,从而解决各个相应阶段的南北矛盾。

南北合作的阻力来自发达国家,特别是来自第一世界的美国。相对而言,第二世界的政界、法界中,出现了一些能较冷静正视南北互相依存现实的明智人士。

关于南北合作的成效,基于对《洛美协定》和《科托努协定》的研究,作者在肯定南北合作生命力之后,深刻指出:"《洛美协定》式的南北合作,仍然远未能从根本上改变南北双方之间很不平等、很不公平的经济关系";"距离实现彻底公平互利的南北合作从而建立起国际经济新秩序的总目标,还有相当漫长、艰辛的路程"。[89]

2. 南南联合自强是建立国际经济新秩序的唯一路径

作者指出,南南合作是国际经济关系上众多弱者之间的互济互助,以共同应对或联合反抗来自强者或霸者的弱肉强食。作者在论述南南合作的战略意义中指出:现存的国际经济体制,是在经济实力基础上形成的。要改变它,首先也要靠实力;在经济上过分依赖发达国家,对发展中国家经济发展极为不利。加强南南合作,走弱者联合自强的道路,才是增强自身经济实力的可靠途径;南南合作,把各个分散的、在经济上相对弱小的发展中国家联合起来,凝聚成一股强大的国际力量,可望提高在南北对话中的地位和能力;南南合作是建立在弱者互助互济、公平互利的基础上,是全球合作的新兴模式和强大趋势,本身就是国际经济新秩序的体现。[90]

在专论《南南联合自强五十年的国际经济立法反思:从万隆、多哈、坎昆到香港》中,作者回顾近五十年来南北矛盾与南北合作的史实,总结贯穿全程并将长期存在的发展轨迹,深刻指出,南北矛盾和冲突,南北力量对比上的"南弱北强",势必在今后相当长的历史时期持续存在,鉴此,在南北角力的进程中,南南联合自强者务必树立起"持久战"的战略思想,逐步更新国际经济立法、建立起国际经济新秩序的唯一路径是南南联合自强。[91]

知识报国、兼济天下,发出中国和南方学者的时代强音

从作者的治学立场、理念和追求以及对中国特色国际经济法学的杰出贡献,我

---

[89] 参见陈安:《南北合作是解决南北矛盾的最佳选择》,载陈安:《陈安论国际经济法学》(第一卷),复旦大学出版社2008年版,第455—459页。

[90] 参见陈安:《全球合作的新兴模式和强大趋势:南南合作与"77国集团"》,载陈安:《陈安论国际经济法学》(第一卷),复旦大学出版社2008年版,第463页。

[91] 参见陈安:《南南联合自强五十年的国际经济立法反思:从万隆、多哈、坎昆到香港》,载陈安:《陈安论国际经济法学》(第一卷),复旦大学出版社2008年版,第479页。

们看到了老一辈知识分子的命运是如何与国家的命运紧密相连,更感受到老一辈知识分子"知识报国、兼济天下"的历史责任感、宽广襟怀、坚定的政治立场和鲜明的价值取向。作者强烈的学术使命感、历史与现实结合的研究方法及学术成果"国际化"的不懈努力尤其值得我们学习。

(一) 强烈的学术使命感

作者指出:"当今发达国家国际经济法诸多论著的共同基本特点,是重点研究发达国家对外经济交往中产生的法律问题,作出符合发达国家权益的分析和论证。反观中国,作为积弱积贫的发展中国家之一员,这样的研究工作还处在幼弱阶段,远未能适应我国对外交往的迫切需要和对外开放的崭新格局。"[92]作者正是怀着强烈的学术使命感,三十多年如一日,身体力行,殚精竭虑,致力于中国特色国际经济法学的创建。

中国国际经济法学主要是在引进和借鉴西方国际经济法学的基础上产生和发展起来的,国际经济法学的概念、术语、原则、规则等大多来自西方。汲取和借鉴西方国际经济法学理论,首先要有"扬弃"精神,"取其精华,去其糟粕"。作者之所以能取得独树一帜的国际经济法研究成果,成就中国和其他发展中国家的"一家之言",最重要的是坚持"扬弃"精神,独立思考,勇于创新,具有破旧立新的历史责任感、决心和勇气,不迷信权威,不附和所谓"主流理论",既能深入钻研西方国际经济法理论,又能摆脱西方学者立场、视野所决定的法律观念或思维定式,特别是摆脱阻碍建立国际经济新秩序的西方法律观念的羁绊,为建立国际经济新秩序而创建和发展新的法律概念、观念和理论。

(二) 历史与现实结合的研究方法

中国属于发展中的社会主义国家,中国特色国际经济法学的研究服务于建立国际经济新秩序和建立社会主义市场经济体制的目标,这决定了中国国际经济法学界在吸收西方国家有关研究成果的同时,应有符合本国国情和目标的研究方法。在种种研究方法中,对创建中国特色国际经济法学尤为重要的当是历史和现实结合的方法。

如前所述,作者对南北问题、中国的战略定位和国际经济法基本原则的论述,无

---

[92] 陈安:《〈陈安论国际经济法学〉自序》,载陈安:《陈安论国际经济法学》(第一卷),复旦大学出版社2008年版,第3页。

不采取历史和现实结合的研究方法。在这方面,中国国际经济法学界老一辈学者与中青年学者的关注点、敏感度和立场或有不同。老一辈学者曾经历过"三座大山"压迫下的旧社会,对西方列强的本质有深刻的认识和高度的警惕。而中青年学者在改革开放的新形势下,有更多的机会接受西方的法学教育或理论成果,更容易接受西方主导建构的所谓"主流理论"。对中国特色国际经济法学的一些基本问题,诸如南北矛盾、国家主权等的认识以及对西方理论的"扬弃"精神,中青年学者与老一辈学者尚有一定差距。这从一个侧面反映了历史和现实结合研究方法的重要性,我们需要更深入地了解西方国际经济法的缘起、发展及其实质,从中探求中国特色国际经济法学的历史使命和发展方向。

(三) 学术成果"国际化"的不懈努力

鉴于国际经济法学的学科特色,中国国际经济法学者应积极主动地开展国际学术交流和合作,在国际学术论坛上,对国际经济法学的重要理论和实践问题提出中国学者的见解,表明中国的立场,为世界性国际经济法学的发展和繁荣做出应有的贡献。

作者大学期间专攻法学,外语兼修英语一年,自学俄语、日语,1981年以"知天命"之年负笈于美国哈佛大学,即与国际学术同行开展平等交流和对话,受到该校东亚法学研究所所长 A. von Mehren 教授、副所长 F. K. Upham 教授的高度评价。[93] 作者一直力倡中国国际经济法学者的学术成果"走出国门"。自1981年在美国《国际法与比较法学报》首次发表英文论文以来,作者持续发表和出版英文论著,成果丰硕。[94] 特别是,2006—2010年在享誉国际经济法学界的《世界投资与贸易学报》(瑞士日内瓦出版)发表六篇重要论文,创该期刊同期发表论文数的最高纪录。[95] 其英文论著立场坚定,论证严谨,特别是具有鲜明的中国特色,因而产生了重要的国际学术影响。发展中国家智库"南方中心"秘书长 Branislav Gosovic 先生认为,作者有关南南联合自强的论述"能给人以清晰鲜明的方针政策性的启示,会使'南方中心'公报的读者们很感兴趣,特别因为这是您从一个正在崛起的举足轻重的大国发出的大

---

[93] 参见《(美国)哈佛大学法学院斯托利讲座教授、东亚法学研究所所长 A. von Mehren 教授致陈安教授函(1982年10月25日)》《(美国)波士顿大学法学院教授、哈佛大学东亚法学研究所前所长 F. K. Upham 教授致陈安教授函(1982年11月29日)》,载陈安:《陈安论国际经济法学》(第五卷),复旦大学出版社2008年版,第2613—2614页。

[94] 陈安教授的主要英文著述,载于《陈安论国际经济法学》(第四、五卷),复旦大学出版社2008年版,第1725—2513页。

[95] 参见康安峰、蒋围:《致力"走出去":厦门大学国际经济法研究团队科研"国际化"的初步实践》,载陈安:《国际经济法学刊》2011年第18卷第2期,第264—282页。

声呐喊"[96]。更为难得的是,来自发达国家的多边投资担保机构首席法律顾问 L. Weisenfeld 先生和 ICSID 法律顾问 A. Parra 先生等同样对作者的学术主张和水平表示由衷赞赏和信服。[97]

中国特色国际经济法学是世界性国际经济法学的一个重要组成部分。中国特色国际经济法学的发展和繁荣在一定程度上有赖于世界性国际经济法学的发展和繁荣,世界性国际经济法学的发展和繁荣也不能缺少中国特色国际经济法学的参与和奉献。中国特色国际经济法学的使命是,站在中国和广大发展中国家立场,紧密联系中国和国际实践,汲取具有普世价值的国际经济法学精华,维护和发展国际社会普遍认同的国际经济法原则,积极影响和促进国际经济法实践的健康发展。

这是一项长期的、宏大的理论工程,需要几代人矢志不移、坚持不懈的努力。陈安老师等老一辈国际经济法学者筚路蓝缕,为中国特色国际经济法学的创建和发展做出了开拓性的贡献,亦成为后学之师范。近年来,厦门大学国际经济法学术团队青年教师积极向国外学术刊物投稿,在国际学术界崭露头角,显示出较强的学术发展潜力。自 2002 年以来,厦门大学法学院辩论队连续参加 Willem C. Vis 国际商事模拟辩论赛、Jessup 国际法模拟法庭辩论赛(英文)和国际人道法模拟法庭辩论赛(英文)等国际性专业大赛,形成优良传统,屡获佳绩,如荣获 Jessup 国际法模拟法庭辩论赛"Hardy C. Dillard 最佳书状奖第一名"(2006 年)和"反方诉状第一名"(2011 年),为中国法学教育赢得了国际声誉,也给国人莫大的启示和鼓舞。需要明确的是,上述辩论赛均是在西方主导下进行的西式"游戏规则"的演练和竞争。鉴此,在研究和掌握这些规则以求"知彼"的同时,更需要独立思考,明确"己方"的信念、追求和使命,力求在"知己知彼"的基础上增强专业能力和创新精神,担负起建立国际经济新秩序的历史重任。相比老一辈国际经济法学者和我们这一代"老三届"学者,青年学者和学生后来居上,具有更好的基础、更高的起点、更好的发展环境和机会,专心致志,自强不息,在创建和发展中国特色国际经济法学方面当有更大的作为。

---

[96] 《南方中心秘书长 Branislav Gosovic 致陈安教授函(2006 年 2 月 1 日)》,载陈安:《陈安论国际经济法学》(第五卷),复旦大学出版社 2008 年版,第 2591—2592 页。

[97] 参见《"多边投资担保机构"(MIGA)首席法律顾问 L. Weisenfeld 致陈安教授函(2004 年 5 月 12 日)》《"解决投资争端国际中心"(ICSID)法律顾问 A. Parra 致陈安教授函(1990 年 3 月 22 日,1990 年 8 月 22 日)》,载陈安:《陈安论国际经济法学》(第五卷),复旦大学出版社 2008 年版,第 2599—2602 页。

六、中国参与经济全球化管理的战略思考
——评《陈安论国际经济法学》的主导学术理念

赵龙跃*

国际经济秩序是指在世界范围内建立起来的国际经济关系以及各种国际经济体系与制度的总和,是使世界经济作为有内在联系和相互依存的整体进行有规律的发展与变化的运行机制;其建立和变迁,取决于国际社会各类成员间的经济、政治和军事的实力对比。[98] 现行国际经济秩序是 20 世纪 40 年代以来,在以美国为代表的西方国家的主导和控制下建立起来的,首先体现的是美欧工业国家的利益和要求。随着经济全球化的深入发展,国际经济形势发生了重大的变化:发展中国家经济增长迅速,在世界经济中的比重不断提升;发达国家经济不仅增长乏力,而且面临巨额财政赤字和主权债务等种种危机。然而,国际经济秩序却没有随着世界经济格局的变化而进行相应的改革,发达国家继续掌控着主要的国际经济组织,竭力维持国际经济旧秩序,发展中国家被严重地边缘化。

长期以来,陈安教授致力于国际经济法学的教学与研究工作,高度关注国际经济秩序的改革与完善,取得了丰硕的成果。陈安教授于 2008 年 80 大寿之际,出版大型学术专著《陈安论国际经济法学》,共分五卷;其后在 2009 和 2010 年又连续发表了《论中国在建立国际经济新秩序中的战略定位》等系列论文四篇[99],从国际经济法学的角度,分析了现行国际经济秩序的特点,指出在国际经济秩序和国际经济法的发展过程中,始终贯穿着强权国家维护国际经济旧秩序与贫弱国家争取建立国际经济新秩序的矛盾,即南北矛盾。"南北矛盾冲突的焦点和实质,是全球财富的国

---

* 赵龙跃,时任南开大学周恩来政府管理学院教授、博士生导师,世界银行兼职研究员,美国乔治敦大学特聘教授。本文原载于《西南政法大学学报》2012 年第 2 期。

[98] 参见陈安:《论中国在建立国际经济新秩序中的战略定位——兼评"新自由主义经济秩序"论、"WTO 宪政秩序"论、"经济民族主义扰乱全球化秩序"论》,载陈安:《陈安论国际经济法学》(第一卷),复旦大学出版社 2008 年版,第 109—134 页。其修订文本发表于《现代法学》2009 年第 2 期,第 3—18 页。

[99] 陈安教授的四篇系列论文包括:《论中国在建立国际经济新秩序中的战略定位——兼评"新自由主义经济秩序"论、"WTO 宪政秩序"论、"经济民族主义扰乱全球化秩序"论》(简称《一论》),载《现代法学》2009 年第 2 期;《旗帜鲜明地确立中国在构建 NIEO 中的战略定位——兼论与时俱进,完整、准确地理解邓小平"对外二十八字方针"》(简称《二论》),载《国际经济法学刊》2009 年第 16 卷第 3 期;《三论中国在构建 NIEO 中的战略定位:"匹兹堡发轫之路"走向何方——G20 南北合作新平台的待解之谜以及"守法"与"变法"等理念碰撞》(简称《三论》),载《国际经济法学刊》2009 年第 16 卷第 4 期;《中国加入 WTO 十年的法理断想:简论 WTO 的法治、立法、执法、守法与变法》(简称《四论》),载《现代法学》2010 年第 6 期。

际再分配。而新、旧国际经济秩序的根本分野,则在于全球财富国际再分配之公平与否。"[100]呼吁中国应该旗帜鲜明地,积极与发展中国家一起"变法图强","通过BRICSM类型的'南南联合'群体",[101]改变不合理的国际经济旧秩序。陈安教授一系列独特的战略思想和政策建议,喊出了与时俱进、变法图强的最强音,非常值得我们重视和思考。

现行国际经济秩序存在严重的缺陷

现行国际经济秩序基本上是以布雷顿森林体系为核心,体现在联合国、世界银行、国际货币基金组织、关贸总协定以及世界贸易组织等国际机构的有关协定和组织管理中。二战以来,美国成为这些组织的"所有者"、操控者和经营者,享受着特殊的权利和利益。[102] 在过去的六十多年中,国际经济社会经历了巨大的变迁,国际经济管理体系也发生了一些变化,但是西方国家主导现行国际经济秩序的本质没有改变,体现为发达国家的"制度霸权"和"话语优势",严重地忽略了广大发展中国家的利益和要求。

发达国家"制度霸权"最明显也最直观的体现就是在国际经济组织中的人事权和决策权,美欧国家不仅始终控制着世界银行行长、国际货币基金组织(IMF)总裁和世界贸易组织总干事的职位,而且在决策程序上占有绝对的优势。以 IMF 为例,IMF 实行加权投票表决制,投票权由两部分组成,每个成员国都有 250 票的基本投票权和一定份额的加权投票权。因为基本投票权各国都一样,所以在实际决策中起决定作用的是加权投票权。最近几年,虽然 IMF 酝酿改革,希望增加新兴国家和发展中国家的投票权,但是美国仍然占有约 17% 的投票权。按照 IMF 宪章,重大议题表决需要 85% 以上的多数票才能通过,因此美国具有绝对否决权。陈安教授对此等制度设计评价为:"它使寥寥几个西方发达大国和强国加在一起,就可以操纵全球性重大经济事务的决策……众多发展中国家在这种极不合理、极不公平的决策体制下,往往陷入进退维谷的两难选择:一是被迫签字'画押',吞下苦果;另一是被迫退

---

[100] 陈安:《论中国在建立国际经济新秩序中的战略定位——兼评"新自由主义经济秩序"论、"WTO宪政秩序"论、"经济民族主义扰乱全球化秩序"论》,载陈安:《陈安论国际经济法学》(第一卷),复旦大学出版社 2008 年版,第 110 页。

[101] 参见陈安:《旗帜鲜明地确立中国在构建 NIEO 中的战略定位——兼论与时俱进,完整、准确地理解邓小平"对外二十八字方针"》,载陈安:《国际经济法学刊》2009 年第 16 卷第 3 期,第 80 页。

[102] See G. John Ikenberry, *Liberal Leviathan: The Origins, Crisis, and Transformation of the American World Order*, Princeton University Press, 2011.

出困境,自行孤立。"[103]

除了拥有制度霸权以外,发达国家还拥有强势的话语体系,通过鼓吹和宣扬利于自身的价值观念来维持现行国际经济秩序。2004年,在美国学界和政界都具有重要影响力的约瑟夫·奈发表了《软实力与美国外交政策》,他认为"软实力"的核心为一国文化的吸引力、价值观念和政策,并指出"当我们[美国]的政策在他人看来具有合法性时,我们的软实力就会得到加强"[104],其实质即为达到"不战而胜"的效果。由于其是一种隐形力量,作用是潜在的,但危害不可小视。陈安教授在其《一论》中,对这种西方主导的话语权进行了精彩的分析。

其实这种价值观念的输出在西方早就存在,在美国战略界,如经济学家罗伯特·吉尔平提出了"霸权稳定论",认为国际经济的稳定与发展取决于一个占绝对优势的霸权国存在[105];国际问题研究学者罗伯特·基欧汉提出了由美国操控的国际制度能降低合作成本促进合作[106],等等。由于美国占据学术研究的中心,这些思想在中国以及世界影响非常大。而这些思想的潜台词就是让发展中国家"自愿"维护现有的国际经济秩序,借用陈安教授的话就是让发展中国家自觉"守法"而不去"变法图强"。国际经济领域,此类思想更是层出不穷,比较有影响力的有"新自由主义经济秩序"论、"WTO宪政秩序"论、"经济民族主义扰乱全球化秩序"论等。"它们虽然在相当程度上激发了新的有益思考,却也造成了某些新的思想混乱。"[107]以"新自由主义经济秩序"论为例,它所突出宣扬的是所谓的"华盛顿共识"。诺姆·乔姆斯基曾明确指出华盛顿共识是由美国政府及其控制的国际经济组织所制定,并由它们通过各种方式进行实施。其奉行的教条是自由化、私有化和政府作用的最小化,"本质是为国际垄断资本在全球扩张服务的"[108],对发展中国家造成的伤害是非常严重的。"华盛顿共识"曾在拉美国家盛行,以阿根廷为例,在20世纪90年代实行全面的私有化、自由化与市场开放,结果在国际游资和国内问题的双重打击下,金融崩溃,政府垮台,社会动乱。颇具讽刺意味的是,"面对'华盛顿共识'在拉美国家制造的悲剧,新自由主义的经济学家缄默了"[109]。

---

[103] 陈安:《中国加入WTO十年的法理断想:简论WTO的法治、立法、执法、守法与变法》,载《现代法学》2010年第6期,第115页。

[104] Joseph S. Nye, Jr., Soft Power and American Foreign Policy, *Political Science Quarterly*, Vol. 119, No. 2, 2004, pp. 255-270.

[105] See Robert Gilpin, *War and Change in World Politics*, Cambridge University Press, 1981.

[106] See Robert O. Keohane, *After Hegemony: Cooperation and Discord in the World Political Economy*, Princeton University Press, 1984.

[107] 陈安:《陈安论国际经济法学》(第一卷),复旦大学出版社2008年版,第120页。

[108] 同上书,第121页。

[109] 房宁:《迷梦的远逝:"华盛顿共识"与拉美困境》,载《社会观察》2005年第3期,第11—12页。

在鼓吹和推行所谓的自由和民主"价值观"的同时,发达国家还不遗余力地攻击发展中国家的自我保护措施,将其贬斥为"经济民族主义乱序"。"'经济民族主义乱序'论的实质和效应则在于以莫须有的'罪名',力图迫使国际弱势群体离开原定的建立国际经济新秩序的奋斗目标。"[110]其实南方发展中国家在面对北方发达国家试图以各种"迷惑人心的口号"冲破主权限制和掠夺财富时,完全有理由保护自己,这一点是理直气壮和合情合理的,在西方发达大国的强势话语影响之下,切不可自先气短自乱阵脚。陈安教授明确指出:"全球弱势群体对此类含有精神鸦片或精神枷锁毒素的理论,亟宜全面深入剖析,不宜贸然全盘接受。"[111]

在国际贸易领域的情况完全类似。长期以来,世界贸易组织及其前身关贸总协定,虽然在规范和稳定国际贸易秩序、降低关税和非关税壁垒、促进国际贸易发展方面发挥了一定的作用,但是却严重忽略了广大发展中国家发展的不平衡问题。国际贸易规则主要是在发达国家的操纵下制定的,所以首先体现的必然是这些发达国家的利益。后来在发展中国家的共同努力下,关贸总协定增加了一些给予发展中国家差别待遇或优惠的条款。可是这些条款有些是有名无实,有些是形同虚设,基本没有得到预期的效果。世界贸易组织成立以来,主要受益者仍然是发达国家,那些看似平等的贸易条款所带来的利益仍然是不平等的。那么多哈回合是不是真的要解决这些问题,或者能不能解决这些问题?到目前为止,答案仍然是 NO。许多专家学者都怀疑多哈回合究竟是把促进发展中国家的"发展"作为谈判的实质内容,还是作为吸引发展中国家参与谈判的诱饵?美国前贸易代表巴尔舍夫斯基就曾经说过:"把多哈回合说成是'发展回合',只是一种乔装打扮而已。"[112]

面对拥有制度霸权和话语优势的发达国家,面对不平等的国际经济秩序,弱势国家应该怎么办?我们应该怎么办?是"韬光养晦",去满足于"搭乘全球化的便车"实现一定程度的发展,还是在力所能及的范围"有所作为",团结广大的发展中国家,争取推动国际经济秩序更加公平合理?陈安教授给出了一个肯定的答案:"中国人理应与时俱进,落实科学的发展观,全面、完整、准确地理解邓小平提出的'韬光养晦、有所作为'方针";"理应成为建立国际经济新秩序的积极推手"。[113]

---

[110] 房宁:《迷梦的远逝:"华盛顿共识"与拉美困境》,载《社会观察》2005 年第 3 期,第 130 页。
[111] 陈安:《旗帜鲜明地确立中国在构建 NIEO 中的战略定位——兼论与时俱进,完整、准确理解邓小平"对外二十八字方针"》,载陈安:《国际经济法学刊》2009 年第 16 卷第 3 期,第 79—80 页。
[112] Cf. Daniel Altman, Charlene Barshefsky on Doha (2007) Managing Globalization Weblog—The International Herald Tribune, http://blogs.iht.com/tribtalk/business/globalization/? p=342.
[113] 陈安:《旗帜鲜明地确立中国在构建 NIEO 中的战略定位——兼论与时俱进,完整、准确理解邓小平"对外二十八字方针"》,载陈安:《国际经济法学刊》2009 年第 16 卷第 3 期,第 80 页。

现行国际经济秩序不能适应新的国际经济形势

随着经济全球化的深入发展,国际经济形势发生了重大的变化,现行国际经济秩序已经不能适应新的国际经济形势,构建国际经济新秩序已经成为当前世界走出危机、重振经济的当务之急与必然选择。同时,在当今的国际形势下,出现了一些有利于推动国际经济秩序变革的条件,主要表现为新兴国家和发展中国家的实力在不断增强,而发达国家却面临新的经济和社会问题。

当今国际经济格局最突出的一个变化就是发展中国家经济增长迅速,在世界经济中的比重不断提升,一些新兴经济国家出现在世界经济舞台的中心,开始发出不同于西方国家的声音。从国际货币基金组织的统计数据来看,发达国家虽然在经济总量上仍然占有显著优势,但在经济增长速度上明显低于发展中国家和新兴经济国家。高盛公司曾经预测:"到2018年'金砖四国'和美国占全球GDP的比例将同为25%;而到2050年四国将一同跻身全球六大经济体之列,发展中国家和发达国家在全球经济总量中的份额将各占50%。"[114]有些学者认为:"进入21世纪以来,世界经济的最大特点是,新兴经济体群体性崛起……尤其是中国、印度等新兴大国名副其实成为世界经济的领头羊,在增强自身经济实力的同时,改变着世界经济发展的路径。"[115]

发达国家不仅经济增长乏力,而且面临巨额财政赤字和主权债务等种种危机。西方G7国家的主权债务持续走高,比世界平均水平高出近1倍,比新兴国家和发展中国家高出3到4倍。[116]美国2011年财政年度的财政赤字近1.3万亿美元,累计债务高达14.8万亿美元,几乎相当于全年的国内生产总值。欧盟国家的主权债务问题更加严重,希腊、西班牙、爱尔兰、葡萄牙和意大利,相继出现主权债务危机,不仅威胁着欧元区的经济稳定,而且影响着全球经济的健康发展。

除此之外,随着经济全球化的深入发展,很多全球性问题仅靠西方国家早已不能解决诸如国际能源安全、全球粮食安全、气候变化和环境问题等等。2008年金融危机以后,G7首脑峰会转为G20峰会,就是对这种情况变化的调整,为推动国际经济秩序的变革提供了新的机会。最近G20戛纳峰会所关注的主要议题,如解决经济失衡、加强金融监管、改革全球货币体系、改进全球监管治理等,都涉及对国际经济秩序的改进。中国国家主席胡锦涛在会上指出:"我们应该充分反映世界经济格局

---

[114] 佚名:《调整全球经济格局面临三大挑战》,载《上海金融报》2010年4月20日第A02版。
[115] 陈凤英:《新兴经济体与21世纪国际经济秩序变迁》,载《外交评论》2011年第3期,第1页。
[116] See IMF, World Economic Outlook, April, 2011.

变化,继续增加新兴市场国家和发展中国家在全球经济治理中的发言权,为发展中国家发展创造良好制度环境。"[117]

在推动国际经济秩序变迁的过程中,既得利益的大国与贫弱的国家之间,围绕国际经济制度设计和规则制定的斗争是非常复杂的,斗争的焦点是全球资源和财富的国际再分配。在发达国家主导的国际经济秩序中,全球资源和财富的国际再分配必然是不公平的,无论是分工还是交换,发展中国家都处于完全被动的局面,这正是现行国际经济秩序的最大问题。"从根本上看,世界经济发展的最大瓶颈在于广大发展中国家未能实现充分发展,使世界范围内有效需求增长未能跟上生产力发展步伐。长期以来,发达国家和发展中国家资源占有失衡,财富分配不公,发展机会不均,形成'越不发展越落后,越落后就越难发展'的恶性循环,最终制约了世界经济持久稳定增长。"[118]

面对不合理的旧秩序及其给世界经济带来的问题,思变求新是必然的选择。但是,在全球化深入发展、经济依存度越来越高的今天,发达国家占据技术优势、制度优势和话语优势,向它们争取平等合理的发展机会难度很大。面对当代国际社会"南弱北强"、实力悬殊的战略态势,面对国际强权国家集团在国际经济领域中已经形成的"霸业"格局和"反变法"阻力,国际弱势群体要求"变法"图强,当然不可能一蹴而就[119]。权益只有争取才会获得,而不是靠施舍。陈安教授通过分析南北关系,总结为螺旋式上升的"6C 轨迹"或"6C 律",说明过程虽然是曲折的,但是成果还是显著的。[120]"6C 轨迹"指在南北合作曲折行进的过程中,"国际经济秩序和国际经济法律规范的破旧立新、新旧更替,势必循着螺旋式上升,即 Contradiction(矛盾)→Conflict(冲突或交锋)→Consultation(磋商)→Compromise(妥协)→Cooperation(合作)→Coordination(协调)→Contradiction New(新的矛盾),逐步实现"[121]。弱势国家并不是完全无能为力的,而是可以有所作为的。

当然,机会总是与挑战并存,发展中国家包括新兴国家也面临很多国内外的问题和挑战。首先,美元主导的国际货币体系可以说是根深蒂固,很难撼动,"重建具

---

[117] 《胡锦涛在二十国集团领导人第六次峰会上的讲话》,http://finance.jrj.com.cn/2011/11/04054211487860.shtml。

[118] 同上。

[119] 参见陈安:《旗帜鲜明地确立中国在构建 NIEO 中的战略定位——兼论与时俱进,完整、准确地理解邓小平"对外二十八字方针"》,载陈安:《国际经济法学刊》2009 年第 16 卷第 3 期,第 66—67 页。

[120] 陈安教授对南北经济谈判过程与效果进行系统分析,可参见《南南联合自强五十年的国际经济立法反思》,载陈安:《陈安论国际经济法学》(第一卷),复旦大学出版社 2008 年版,第 479—506 页。

[121] 陈安:《论中国在建立国际经济新秩序中的战略定位——兼评"新自由主义经济秩序"论、"WTO 宪政秩序"论、"经济民族主义扰乱全球化秩序"论》,载《现代法学》2009 年第 2 期,第 4 页。

有稳定的定值基准并为各国所接受的新储备货币可能是个长时期内才能实现的目标"[122]。其次还是主权债务问题,发达国家政府赤字和债务问题在短期内很难解决,必将影响全球金融市场的稳定,这又不可避免地加大了新兴市场国家的债权安全与金融风险。美国的债务问题不仅仅是美国的问题,而是全球持有美债的债权人所担心的问题,必须警惕发达国家转嫁危机的风险。当然还存在贸易保护主义等其他问题,危机带来机遇,但带来的各种不确定因素与风险也须时刻注意。

G20为发展中国家争取推动国际经济秩序朝着公平合理方向变革提供了有利的条件,陈安教授通过对2009年G20匹兹堡峰会和匹兹堡峰会前后的重要国际会议的分析,认为"'匹兹堡发轫之路'之'新'值得重视,就在于它强调和指定历时整整10年的G20南北对话机制,应当从非正式机制开始转轨成为正式的、常规的、主要的机制,从而很可能进一步发展成为南南联合自强、建立国际经济新秩序的新转折和新起点"[123]。但是,"从历史上的经验教训看,全球公众却同时理应继续保持清醒头脑和敏锐目光,预测'匹兹堡发轫之路'今后发展的另一种可能前景:时过境迁,强权发达国家之'信誓旦旦'迅即转化为'口惠而实不至'的一纸空头支票"[124],而这个"空头支票"却有可能为发达国家换来大量的利益。

中国参与经济全球化管理的战略思考

当今世界正处在大发展大变革大调整时期,世界多极化、经济全球化深入发展。中国经济社会持续快速发展,融入全球化程度的不断提高,国际政治、经济环境对中国的影响越来越大,在国际事务中,中国面临的问题和挑战也越来越多。现行国际经济秩序不仅本身存在严重的缺陷,越来越不能适应当前世界经济发展的新形势,而且体系中有些条款本身就是用来牵制或限制中国发展的。中国拥有独特的政治、经济和社会体制,在世界上扮演着非常独特的角色。全面准确地把握国际经济秩序变革的动因和趋势,积极参与国际规则制定和经济全球化管理,不仅是维持并进一步开创有利于中国改革开放发展国际环境的需要,而且也是满足国际社会希望中国在国际事务中发挥更大作用,推动建设和谐世界,促进国际经济秩序朝着更加公正合理方向发展的需要。

"世界五分之四的人口在发展中国家,发达国家人口只占五分之一。人人都有

---

[122] 周小川:《关于改革国际货币体系的思考》,http://www.gov.cn/gzdt/2009-03/23/content_1266412.htm。
[123] 陈安:《三论中国在构建NIEO中的战略定位:"匹兹堡发轫之路"走向何方——G20南北合作新平台的待解之谜以及"守法"与"变法"等理念碰撞》,载陈安:《国际经济法学刊》2009年第16卷第4期,第1—29页。
[124] 同上。

平等的生存权利。如果广大发展中国家继续贫困,说明当今世界是不公平、不和谐的,也注定是不稳定的。"[125] 物不平则鸣,人亦然。[126] 面对不平等的国际经济秩序,"中国既是全球弱势群体的一员,又是最大的发展中国家之一。中国积极参与和努力推动建立国际经济新秩序,应属当仁不让,责无旁贷"[127]。

当然也有不同的看法,其中比较流行也最为荒谬的说法是中国的发展得益于现行的国际经济秩序,即中国享受了美国霸权提供的稳定的国际经济体系带来的发展机遇,享受了美国提供的"公共产品","搭了美国的便车"。[128] 因此,现在中国不是要推动国际经济体系的变革,而是要主动承担更多的义务,为现行国际体系提供更多的"公共产品",帮助美国维持现状。事实上中国不是"搭了现行国际经济秩序的便车",而是付出了很高的代价。陈安教授提出,面对建立国际经济新秩序的大势所趋,"中国的自我战略定位理应一如既往,继续是旗帜鲜明的积极推动者之一,是现存国际经济秩序的改革者之一,不宜只是现存国际经济秩序的'改良者'、南北矛盾的'协调者'"[129]。为此,必须处理好"韬光养晦"与"有所作为"的关系,处理好"守法适法"与"变法图强"的关系。

首先是"韬光养晦"与"有所作为"的关系。陈安教授明确提出应与时俱进,落实科学的发展观,全面、完整、准确地理解邓小平提出的"韬光养晦、有所作为"方针,批评了中国只应明哲保身、自顾自己发展,不顾外部是非的倾向。邓小平在提出"韬光养晦"的同时,一直坚持主张建立国际经济新秩序,坚持要"有所作为"。陈安教授也批评了建立国际经济新秩序的斗争已经式微,而中国应融入"蓬勃的新自由主义经济秩序"的错误观点,指出这种观点源于美国学界,目的是"瓦解南南合作的坚定信心和不懈实践,从而步步为营,维护少数经济强权国家在国际经济旧秩序和国际经济现有'游戏规则'下的既得利益"[130]。陈安教授的分析鞭辟入里,引人深思,事实也正是如此。"韬光养晦"不是目的,坚持"韬光养晦"是为了"有所作为",决不能为了"韬光养晦"而"韬光养晦",不能无原则地"软弱退让",更不能掉进西方的"话语陷阱",结果被洗脑跟着西方的战略走。在奉行"强者为王"竞争激烈的国际经济领域,

---

[125] 《温家宝在联合国千年发展目标高级别会议上的讲话》,http://www.fmprc.gov.cn/ce/cgstp/chn/zt_1/zgwj/t764048.htm。

[126] 韩愈在《送孟东野序》中说:"大凡物不得其平则鸣……人之于言也亦然。有不得已者而后言,其歌也有思,其哭也有怀。凡出乎口而为声者,其皆有弗平者乎!"

[127] 陈安:《旗帜鲜明地确立中国在构建 NIEO 中的战略定位——兼论与时俱进,完整、准确地理解邓小平"对外二十八字方针"》,载陈安:《国际经济法学刊》2009 年第 16 卷第 3 期,第 80 页。

[128] 参见〔美〕罗伯特·吉尔平:《国际关系政治经济学》,杨宇光等译,上海人民出版社 2006 年版。

[129] 陈安:《旗帜鲜明地确立中国在构建 NIEO 中的战略定位——兼论与时俱进,完整、准确地理解邓小平"对外二十八字方针"》,载陈安:《国际经济法学刊》2009 年第 16 卷第 3 期,第 80 页。

[130] 同上书,第 67 页。

良好的经济发展的环境只有争取才会得到保障,而不是简单地去追随强者,靠施舍绝不会自主更不会长久。"在建立国际经济新秩序的时代总潮流中,中国的自我战略定位理应一如既往,继续是旗帜鲜明的积极推动者之一,是现存国际经济秩序的改革者之一。"[131]

其次是"守法适法"与"变法图强"的关系。陈安教授认为,在国际经济关系中必须力行法治,但是从法理角度看,当代国际经济法的"立法"过程中决策权力的国际分配存在着严重不公。强者拥有"游戏规则"的制定权,必然造成全球财富的国际分配严重不公,不利于发展中国家。"国际经济法是巩固现存国际经济秩序的重要工具,也是促进变革旧国际经济秩序、建立新国际经济秩序的重要手段。"建立国际经济新秩序,就是要求改变、改革现存的有关"立法",就是要求"变法"。[132] 当然,"变法"是一个循序渐进的过程,不可能一蹴而就,要先"适应"和"守法",在"适应"和"守法"的实践检验中,不断加深认识。熟悉游戏规则,使其"为我所用",同时"又立足于国际弱势群体的共同权益,进行检验和判断,明辨其是臧否,思考其变革方向"[133]。当然,向强势国家争取"变法图强",免不了道路曲折反复,"但势必与时俱进,前景光明"[134]。

随着中国经济社会持续快速的增长,国际地位越来越高,国际影响越来越大,国际社会重视来自中国的声音,希望中国在参与国际规则制定和经济全球化管理方面发挥更大的作用,这是中国国际政治、经济、外交地位不断提高的必然结果,总体来说是一件好事。同时我们必须意识到,参与全球化管理意味着中国的国际责任和义务愈来愈大,面临的问题更加复杂,进一步提高中国经济外交能力和水平的要求更加迫切。参与经济全球化管理呼唤中国的调整,这里的调整不仅仅是经济结构的调整、发展模式的更新,还包括观念的转变和角色的转换。

第一,参与经济全球化管理,必须按照国际思维方式,研究制定科学的战略与策略,不断地提高国际谈判艺术和经济外交能力。特别是在国际谈判中,不能过多地受到中国文化的影响和束缚,不宜过早地暴露自己的底线,否则会造出被动局面,甚至付出更大的代价。

第二,参与经济全球化管理,需要研究制定一个长期的、整体的、系统的和一致

---

[131] 陈安:《旗帜鲜明地确立中国在构建 NIEO 中的战略定位——兼论与时俱进,完整、准确地理解邓小平"对外二十八字方针"》,载陈安:《国际经济法学刊》2009 年第 16 卷第 3 期,第 80 页。

[132] 参见陈安:《中国加入 WTO 十年的法理断想:简论 WTO 的法治、立法、执法、守法与变法》,载《现代法学》2010 年第 6 期,第 116 页。

[133] 同上书,第 119 页。

[134] 同上书,第 120 页。

的国际行动方案和指导原则,并贯穿于国家有关部门的日常国际事务中。经济全球化提高了参与国际事务的透明度和关联度,给中国参与国际合作交流提出了更高的要求。即使在研究制定双边的谈判和合作方案时,也需要考虑其对多边合作和区域合作的影响。目前中国的一举一动,与任何国家的谈判口径或合作行动,都将受到全世界的高度关注。

第三,参与经济全球化管理,需要大量的国际化的专业人才和对有关专题的深入研究。长期以来,中国政府部门所实行的那种近乎封闭式的用人机制将面临严峻的挑战,中国需要研究开放式的用人机制,既要加快培养体制内的相关人才,也要充分发挥现有专业人才的作用。根据国际合作的需要,从全国选拔最合适的专家学者,及时充实有关机构,把握机遇,争取主动。

同时我们还要重视为国际组织培养输送管理人才,研究疏通国际组织与国内机构人才互动的机制,把参与国际组织工作作为中国培养国内熟悉国际规则、具有国际领先水平管理人才的平台之一。在全球化的时代,国内事务与国际事务的界限变得越来越模糊,国内专家和国际专家交互使用,方能相得益彰。

第四,参与经济全球化管理,中国需要角色的转换,从过去强调熟悉和接受国际规则,开始转向修订、完善现有国际规则,并积极参与制定新的规则。现行规则往往具有发达国家的烙印,不完全是客观公正的国际规则。中国独有的经济体制,在世界上扮演着非常独特的角色,只能是由自己站出来,争取建立既适合于中国国情又有利于世界经济发展、公平公正的国际经济新秩序。

和而不同,与时俱进:我们学习的楷模

《陈安论国际经济法学》是一部巨著,全书分五卷共 310 多万字,全面汇集了陈安教授从中国改革开放三十多年来潜心国际经济法学教学和研究的经历、思想和成果。该书对于我们了解当代国际经济法学前沿的理论和动态,回顾中国国际经济法学理论的成长、实践和发展,展望建立国际经济新秩序所面临的机遇和挑战,都具有重要的学术理论价值和政策实践意义。拜读《陈安论国际经济法学》与《四论》以后,深切地体会到陈安教授数十年磨一剑,在独树中华一帜,跻身国际前驱方面的许多独到之处。特别是在以下三个方面,即对待国外国际经济法学理论和流派的态度、理论联系实际的学风以及知识报国、兼济天下的志向,非常值得我们晚辈学习。

第一,对待世界上各种国际经济法学的理论和流派非常重视,但不迷信。陈安教授非常重视研究世界上有关国际经济法学的理论和流派,但是从不迷信。陈安教授研究和引进国际经济法学的现有成果只是一种手段,而博采众长、消化吸收、开拓

创新、创立具有中国特色的国际经济法学体系才是目的。陈安教授一贯主张:"在国际学术论坛上,中国人既要谦虚谨慎,认真学习和吸收有益的新知,切忌闭目塞听,妄自尊大;又要敢于对外来的种种'权威'理论,根据国情和世情,深入探讨,独立思考,加以鉴别,乃至质疑,切忌妄自菲薄,盲目附和。"孔子《论语》中倡导的"和而不同"精神,在陈安教授的治学实践中随处可见。

第二,坚持理论联系实际,学以致用。陈安教授的教学研究工作密切联系中国和世界的实际,致力为中国的改革开放提供理论和法律支持。国际经济法学是规范国际经济关系中的法律和政策问题的综合性和边缘性的学科,过去在很长的一段时间里,中国参与的不是很多,或者可以说很少。随着中国改革开放发展程度的不断提高,中国面临的国际经济法律问题越来越复杂,亟须深入研究解决。陈安教授的研究成果,涵盖了有关国际贸易和投资、双边协定和多边公约以及相关国际组织和管理体制的多个方面,为中国政府有关部门处理国际经济法律问题,为保护中国有关企业的合法权益,提供了大量的战略思想和决策建议,具有重要的参考价值。

第三,坚持知识报国、兼济天下的志向。关于中国在建立新的国际经济秩序、参与国际规则的制定、促进南南合作方面如何发挥作用,陈安教授作出了重要的理论创新,致力为中国和全球弱势群体在国际经贸大政问题上争取平等的话语权和参与权。《陈安论国际经济法学》一书在探索建立国际经济新秩序的规律和路径方面旁征博引,史论结合,提出了螺旋式上升的"6C轨迹"理论,得到了国内外学者的广泛重视和认可。其中,《南南联合自强五十年的国际经济立法反思》一文为促进南南合作、丰富第三世界思想体系做出了重要贡献;《晚近十年来美国单边主义对抗WTO多边主义的三大回合》一文在美国杂志发表以后,被认为是"当前最受关注的、最引人入胜和最有创见的"文章,专门为发展中国家服务的国际组织"南方中心"将其收辑为中心的专题出版物——《贸易发展与公平》专题议程的系列工作文件之一,以单行本的形式重新出版发行。

随着中国经济社会持续快速的发展,在国际社会的地位和影响显著提高,如何才能继续维持并进一步开创有利于深化改革开放发展的国际环境,全面有效地参与国际规则制定与经济全球化管理,正成为中国迫切需要解决的问题。研究和借鉴陈安教授提出问题和解决问题的思路,对于中国更深入、更广泛和更有效地参与国际规则制定和经济全球化管理,具有更加重要的价值。

第 2 章 《中国的呐喊》书评荟萃

编者按：

陈安教授所撰《中国的呐喊》一书，自德国 Springer 出版社向全球推出以来，已引起国内外学界同行的广泛关注，学者们纷纷撰文评论与回应，迄今已经收到书评24篇，并已汇辑在一起，由北京大学出版社出版的《国际经济法学刊》第 19 卷第 2 期至 23 卷第 2 期特辟《中国的呐喊》书评专栏，以中英双语集中发表[135]，荟萃聚合，形成对外弘扬中华学术正气、追求国际公平正义的共鸣强音，借以进一步扩大其国内外的学术影响。

编者：陈　欣、杨　帆[136]
2017 年 6 月 10 日

Editorial Note：

After the publication of Prof. An Chen's monograph—*The Voice from China: An CHEN on International Economic Law* through world renowned Springer, it has attracted extensive attention and provoked intensive interest in the academic circles, both from domestic and abroad. Scholars have in succession responded with comments and reviews. As of today we have received 24 such book reviews, the bilingual (Chinese and English) versions of which are all ready to compile together and publish in a special book-review column for *The Voice from China* in the *Journal of International Economic Law* (China) through the Peking University Press. It is our wish that these leading comments will help to forge and converge a stream of strong resonances to advance and enrich the righteous viewpoints of Chinese scholars, and to pursue equity and justice at the international level.

June 10, 2017

---

[135] 其中，日本东京大学中川淳司教授所撰书评原为日文，现译为中英双语，同时保留日文，便于读者参考。

[136] 陈欣，厦门大学法学院国际经济法研究所副教授；杨帆，厦门大学法学院国际经济法研究所助理教授。

一、中国呐喊 发聋振聩

耄耋高龄的厦门大学法学院国际经济法学教授、中国国际经济法学会荣誉会长陈安教授所撰英文专著《中国的呐喊：陈安论国际经济法》(*The Voice from China: An CHEN on International Economic Law*)，新近由享有国际学术盛誉的德国权威出版社 Springer 向全球推出，在国际经济法学界引起广泛关注。

本书汇集作者自 1980 年以来三十多年不同时期撰写的 24 篇英文专论。全书 852 页，分为六部分，分别探讨和论证当代国际经济法基本理论和重要实践的学术前沿重大问题。这些英文专论原稿绝大部分发表于中外知名学刊，立足于中国国情，以马克思主义为指导，从当代国际社会弱势群体即第三世界的视角，有的放矢，针对当代国际经济法学科领域的基本理论以及热点难点实践问题，发出与西方强权国家主流观点截然不同的呼声和呐喊。在积极参与国际学术争鸣当中，大力宣扬众多发展中国家共同的正义主张和基本立场，有理有据地揭示某些西方主流理论误导之不当和危害，从而避免在实践上损害包括中国在内的国际弱势群体的公平权益。这也正是本书命名为《中国的呐喊：陈安论国际经济法》之由来。

这部英文专著文稿于 2013 年 11 月获得"国家社会科学基金中华学术外译项目"正式立项，据悉，这是中国国际经济法学界获得此立项的第一例。按照全国社科规划办公室文件解释，"中华学术外译项目"是 2010 年由全国社会科学规划领导小组批准设立的国家社科基金新的重大项目，旨在促进中外学术交流，推动中国社会科学优秀成果和优秀人才走向世界。它主要资助中国社会科学研究的优秀成果以外文形式在国外权威出版机构出版，进入国外主流发行传播渠道，增进国外对当代中国、中国社会科学以及中国传统文化的了解，提高中国社会科学的国际影响力。

诚如专家评审意见所指出的那样，这部英文专著"对海外读者全面了解中国国际经济法学者较有代表性的学术观点和主流思想具有重要意义。全书结构自成一体，观点新颖，具有中国风格和中国气派，阐释了不同于西方发达国家学者的创新学术理念和创新学术追求，致力于初步创立起以马克思主义为指导的具有中国特色的国际经济法理论体系，为国际社会弱势群体争取公平权益锻造了法学理论武器"。

陈安教授《中国的呐喊》一书，在展现作者中国特色学术思想和创新成果的同时，也为中国国际经济法学界向世界发声搭建了国际传播平台。本专著出版之后，反响强烈，国内外高端学者纷纷撰文评论与回应，迄今已经收到书评14篇，即将由北京大学出版社出版的《国际经济法学刊》第21卷第4期特辟专栏，以中英双语集中发表，荟萃聚合，形成弘扬中华学术正气、追求国际公平正义的共鸣强音。另外，鉴于此书出版后国际学术效应良好，德国Springer出版社又主动提出进一步开展学术合作的建议，要求陈安教授主持组织另外一套系列英文学术专著，总题定名为"**当代中国与国际经济法**"（Modern China and International Economic Law），遴选和邀请一批中外知名学者围绕这个主题，撰写创新著作，提交该出版社出版，每年至少推出两部。经认真磋商，双方现已达成协议，正式签署合同，并已启动执行。相信此举将会为进一步提升中华法学学术在世界学术界的知名度和影响力做出新的贡献。

中国国家主席习近平曾经指出，"文明因交流而多彩，文明因互鉴而丰富"；"文明是平等的，人类文明因平等才有交流互鉴的前提"[137]。近来他又强调中国在国际事务中应当积极"提出中国方案、贡献中国智慧"[138]。可以说，陈安教授上述力作向全球发行及其良好效应和后续举措，对于促进**中外不同特色**的文明在**平等前提下交流互鉴**，对于在国际事务中提出中国方案，提升中国的话语权，都将起到应有的积极作用。

（林伍/报道）

---

[137]《习近平在联合国教科文组织总部的演讲》，http://news.xinhuanet.com/politics/2014-03/28/c_119982831.htm。

[138]《习近平接受拉美四国媒体联合采访》，http://news.xinhuanet.com/world/2014-07/15/c_126752272.htm。

The Enlightening and Thought-provoking Voice from China

The English monograph of Prof. An Chen, an octogenarian prominent professor at School of Law, Xiamen University and the Honorary Chairman of Chinese Society of International Economic Law (CSIEL for short, a nation-wide academic society), was recently published by Springer, a Germany-located yet world-renowned Publisher, under a broad title "*The Voice from China: An CHEN on International Economic Law*". It has now entered the main disseminating channel of academic works, arousing extensive attention in the circles of international economic law.

This monograph, with a total six parts and a colossal volume of 852 pages, has compiled within it 24 of Prof. Chen's articles written in English since early 1980s. These English articles were mostly published by well-known academic journals in and out of China. Guided by Marxism, they are all based on a common stand of China's national conditions and a consistent perspective of world weak groups, endeavoring to speak up a completely different voice from those of mainstream Western powers as regards the fundamental theoretical problems and hot or controversial issues in practice in the field of contemporary international economic law. During his active participation in world academic debates, Prof. Chen persistently advocates for the just proposals of the many developing countries, and tries his best to reveal the improperness and potential hazard of those misguiding mainstream theories from the West, so as to protect the equitable rights and interests of world weak groups including China. This is why the monograph is entitled "*The Voice from China*".

This English monograph has successfully won the support of the Chinese Academic Foreign Translation Project (CAFTP), making itself the first of such kind within the academic circles of International Economic Law in China. According to the official specifications from the National Social Science Fund of China (NSSFC), CAFTP is one of the major categories of projects set by the NSSFC and approved by the National Philosophy and Social Science Planning Leading Group of China in

2010. This Project aims to promote Sino-foreign academic exchanges, and to facilitate the outstanding works as well as prominent scholars in the field of philosophy and social science towards the world's academic stage. For this purpose, a major part of such funding is allocated to sponsor the aforesaid achievements to be published in foreign language through authoritative publishers abroad. It is expected that, by such way of accessing and participating in foreign mainstream distribution channels, foreigners could have a better understanding of contemporary China, its philosophy and social sciences and its traditional culture. It is also expected that Sino-foreign academic exchange and dialogue would hence be more active, and the overseas influence of Chinese philosophy and social science would be enhanced.

In the Expert Review Report, some of the most professional peers opine that Prof. Chen's book "contributes vastly in the sense of introducing onto the world arena a series of typical academic views and mainstream ideas of Chinese International Economic Law scholars. The whole book is well and uniquely structured, and loaded with creative points of views. With its obvious Chinese character and style, this book has illustrated various innovational academic ideals and pursuits that are different from those voices & views preached by some authoritative scholars from Western developed powers. The author has endeavored to create a specific Chinese theoretical system of International Economic Law under the guidance of Marxism, to further serve as a theoretical weapon for the weak groups of international society to fight for their equitable rights and interests."

Apart from spreading the China-specific academic thoughts and creative achievements, Prof. Chen's monograph has also set up an international platform for Chinese scholars in international economic law to disseminate their viewpoints to the world. With the publishing of Prof. Chen's monograph, scholars as well as practitioners from domestic and abroad have one after another responded with book reviews and relating comments, which have now converged into a strong resonating voice of advancing and enriching China's academic justice and righteous proposals on international issues. As till now, 14 such reviews have been received and are to be published by Peking University Press as a special bilingual column in the forthcoming Chinese *Journal of International Economic Law* (Vol. 21, No. 4). In light of this favorable and positive outcome, Springer offered to build a further cooperative relation, by asking Prof. Chen to preside and organize a whole series of English monographs entitled "Modern China and International Economic Law". This brand new series will select and invite a batch of well-known scholars from China and abroad to contribute their innovative works around the theme of this series, at least two volumes of which will be published by Springer per year. After conscientious consultation, the two sides have reached and executed the final agreement. It is believed that such cooperation will make new contributions to promote the popularity and influence of China's legal academic research.

China's President Xi Jinping once pointed out in his speech in the UNESCO (United Nations Educational, Scientific, and Cultural Organization), that "[I]t is through communication that civilizations can show their multicolor, and it is through learning from each other that civilizations can be abundantly enriched ⋯ All civilizations are equal, which forms the very premise for the communication and mutual learning."[139] He further emphasized that we should actively "raise Chinese proposals and contribute Chinese wisdom" in international affairs.[140] It could be predicted that, the above-referred book of Prof. An Chen, together with its consequent influences and follow-up measures, will prove its positive utility in boosting the equal communication and mutual learning among civilizations of different characteristics, as well as in enhancing China's voice of contributing its own prescriptions as to world affairs.

（翻译：林　伍）

二、晨起临窗坐　书香伴芳菲
——喜览《中国的呐喊：陈安论国际经济法》

郭寿康*

昨天傍晚收到了一批书报杂志的邮件，今晨逐件拆封、翻阅时，忽然发现一本

---

[139] Xi Jinping's Speech at UNESCO Headquarts, http://news.xinhuanet.com/politics/2014-03/28/c_119982831.htm.

[140] Xi Jinping Was Interviewed by the Media from Four Countries in Latin America, http://news.xinhuanet.com/world/2014-07/15/c_126752272.htm.

* 郭寿康，时任中国人民大学资深教授、博士生导师，中国国际法学界的前辈权威学者，2012年获得"全国杰出资深法学家"荣誉称号。

装帧精美的全英文书。书名很别致,*The Voice from China*(《中国的呐喊》或《来自中国的声音》)。初想,平日与新闻、文艺各界接触很少,刚要放在一边,忽然发现,本书作者的署名,是大名鼎鼎的陈安教授,翻阅内容,主要是1980年以来陈老在国外著名刊物上发表的24篇关于中国国际经济法学的论文集合,这又是陈老的一大创举。

陈安老先生是中国国际经济法学界驰名中外的泰斗和大师,而且是中国特色国际经济法学科的创始人之一,发表了一系列有分量的扛鼎之作。陈老也在国外著名刊物上发表了许多影响很大的学术论文。但是,用时却很难找到。这一次集24篇在国内外发表的中国国际经济法学方面的论文成卷出版,给国内外业界专家提供了很大方便,使人们更便于听到来自中国国际经济法学界的声音,功德无量。

陈老这个头带得很好。据我所知,国内专家也有在国外报、刊发表学术作品,但往往难于寻找。在中国出版的五卷本《陈安论国际经济法》以及笔者的《郭寿康法学文选》中,都包括一部分在国外发表的论文作品,但全书用英文出版的,尚属罕见。希望有更多的学者,用外语在国外权威出版社出版学术专著,从而进入国外学术著作主流发行传播渠道,以满足世界上迫切需要听到"来自中国的声音"的日益强烈的要求。

(编辑:龚 宇)

By the Casement at Dawn, in the Fragrance of New Book
—A Joyful Browse of *The Voice from China*: *An CHEN on International Economic Law*

Guo Shoukang[*]

This morning when I was sealing off and leafing through a pile of newly received books, journals and magazines, a rather well designed English book suddenly caught my eyes. With its unconventional title: *The Voice from China*, it first occurred to me that I seldom had contacts with media and literature circles.

---

[*] Senior Professor of International Law, Renmin University of China; widely recognized predecessor within jurisprudential circle, awarded with the honorable title "National Eminent & Senior Jurist" in 2012.

When I was just about to put it aside, I suddenly saw that the author of this book is Prof. An Chen, a widely renowned scholar. After I skipped through the contents, I found it a compilation of 24 articles successively published by Prof. Chen since 1980 in foreign journals, all with a focus on the topic of Chinese school of International Economic Law(IEL). This should be deemed as another pioneering work of Chen.

Mr. An Chen, an elderly gentleman, is a master of the discipline of IEL, and has a worldly recognized reputation in this academic circle. He is also one of the founding members of the Chinese School of IEL, or IEL with Chinese characteristics, for he has published a series of heavy-weight masterpieces, as well as a number of research papers in well-known journals. These journal articles are, however, not that handy when people feel the need to refer to. Now that Prof. Chen's 24 articles on Chinese IEL are compiled into one volume, it will be bound to foster a more convenient way for peers, both from domestic and abroad, to hear a Voice from Chinese academic circle of IEL. The benefits that go along with this publication are definitely beyond measure.

Mr. Chen has set a very instructive leading example. As far as I know, there are other scholars of China who have also published their research results in foreign journals. But these articles share a common deficit of being inconvenient to find and collect. In the domestically published works such as *An CHEN on International Economic Law* (Five Volumes), and my *Guo Shoukang's Selected Works on Law*, there are some thesis written in English, too. But it is rather rare, at least for now, that a published book of Chinese scholar is all in English. It is my sincere hope, that more scholars of China can publish their works through authoritative foreign press, and enter the worldwide mainstream transmission channel of academic works, so as to fulfill the increasingly strengthened demands of world people to hear the "Voice from China".

（翻译：杨　帆）

三、弘中华正气 为群弱发声

曹建明[*]

中华人民共和国最高人民检察院

弘中华正气 为群弱发声

尊敬的陈安教授：

当我收到您的英文专著《中国的呐喊：陈安论国际经济法》，欣喜之外，更是一种感动和震撼。多年来，您一直希望我们以文会友、以书会友。这些年我先后收到了您的《陈安论国际经济法》5卷本、《国际经济法学刍言》上下卷等鸿篇巨著。我的书架上，整整齐齐排列着您主编的《国际经济法学刊》，至今已是第21卷！打开您《中国的呐喊》，更是让我感到份量很重、很重……

这是您的又一部力作。这部专著不仅深刻阐述了当代国际经济法的基本理论问题，而且紧密结合国际经济法理论与实践，深入探讨了构建国际经济新秩序的热点难点问题，自成体系，兼容并包，翔集事理。我知道，字里行间，凝聚的都是您几十年潜心学术研究之成果，是您又一部研精覃思的著作。这本专著作为国家社科基金中华学术外译项目以英文正式出版，对于促进世界更加了解和理解当代中国必将产生重要影响，无疑是中国国际经济法学界的一件大事。

让我感动的是，您在国际经济法学方面的造诣很深，学术成

---

[*] 曹建明，国际经济法教授，时任最高人民检察院检察长，原华东政法学院院长。

就斐然。但是，耄耋之年，您至今仍在孜孜不倦，辛勤耕耘，不断深入思考国际经济法学特别是中国国际经济法学的发展，并为之奉献了自己的全部心血和智慧。先生的精神实乃难能可贵，足以让那些心浮气躁、急功近利的后辈晚生汗颜。我们年轻一代，无论是法学研究工作者还是司法工作者，都应当学习和弘扬您这种严谨治学、学为人师的学术品格和行为风范。

世界多极化、经济全球化和社会信息化的趋势深入发展，科技进步日新月异，各种文化碰撞交融，使当今世界正经历着前所未有的历史性变革。中国已经历了30多年的改革开放历程，中国比以往任何时候更加重视国际法的研究，更加重视国际规则的制定和运用。全面推进依法治国，离不开法学理论的繁荣发展。构建开放型新经济新体制，离不开国际经济法的研究。可以说，摆在我们面前的一系列国际法问题包括国际经济法问题，既是理论研究，更是应用研究，我们必须理论联系实际。我们需要学习借鉴外国法学先进理论，更需要立足于复杂多变的国际形势和国际关系，立足于国际经济法理论与我国对外开放实践的紧密结合，积极推动建立公正合理的国际政治经济新秩序，有自己的思考和建议，并且敢于发出中国声音。

在这本英文专著第一编里，我看到其中一篇熟悉的文章，即《"黄祸"论的本源、本质及其最新霸权"变种"："中国威胁论"》。这篇专论我有幸在2012年就拜读过，它以史实为据，史论结合，深入剖析和批判"中国威胁论"的本质和危害，读了之后令人荡气回肠、拍案叫好。这些年来,您始终立足中国国情和广大发展中国家的共同立场,始终秉持国家经济主权原则,强调维护发展中国家利益,倡导公平互利、南北合作、南南合作,探索建立国际经济新秩序的规律和路径,实事求是,与时俱进,不断探索,追求真理,特别是敢于提出与西方国家传统观点乃至主流观点截然不同的观点,真正响亮地发出了中国的声音,不断推动着中国国际经济法学的理论创新与实践创新。从您的身上,我更是深深感受到了我们每一个国际法学者和法律工作者义不容辞的责任和使命。

真诚感谢您为国际经济法学界奉献了又一部力作!衷心祝愿您健康长寿!

2014 年 9 月 16 日

Spreading China's Justice, Voicing for the Global Weak

Cao Jianming[*]

Dear Esteemed Prof. An Chen

Upon receiving your recent published English writing monograph—*The Voice*

---

[*] Current Procurator-General of the Supreme People's Procuratorate, PRC; Professor.

from China: *An CHEN on International Economic Law*, I felt more touched and shocked than delighted. For decades, you have been encouraging us to meet friends through sharing our articles and books. I alone have successively received a number of big treatises of yours, such as *An CHEN on International Economic Law* (Five Volumes), and *CHEN's Papers on International Economic Law* (Two Volumes). On my bookshelf arrays neatly a complete serie of Chinese *Journal of International Economic Law* (from Vol. 1 to the present Vol. 21!). I can literally feel the heavy weight of your new book when I hold it in hand and turn over the cover...

  Undoubtedly this is your another masterpiece. It has not only elaborated in depth the many fundamental theoretical problems of contemporary international economic law (IEL), but also deeply discussed some hot and controversial issues regarding the establishment of a new international economic order (NIEO), with a close integration of relating IEL theory and practice. By adopting an all-inclusive approach to synthesize facts and reasonings, this new monograph has created a unique system similar to no other. As I see, this new monograph, which is pervaded among the words and lines with all your hard work, condenses your meticulous research and thorough thinking, and embodies your decades' devotion to and fruits of this subject. Supported by the Chinese Academic Foreign Translation Project of the China National Social Sciences Fund, the publishing of this English monograph must bring significant influence on promoting the global understanding of contemporary China, and is with no doubt a major event in the Chinese academic circle of international economic law.

  What moves me most is that, apart from your many academic accomplishments in the field of IEL, and despite of your **eighties-odd age, you have not yet ceased in thinking and writing on this subject, and still are tirelessly and entirely devoted your heart and wisdom to promoting the development of Chinese school of IEL. Such spirit of yours is quite rare and commendable,** and can shame all the youngsters who are impatient and eager for quick success. We younger generations of legal researchers and practitioners shall learn and carry forward such academic personality and behavioral demeanor of yours, to carry out meticulous research and to disseminate righteous knowledge or ideals.

  With the continuous deepening of world multipolarization, economic globalization and society informatization, as well as the fast innovation of science and technology, the collision and fusion of various cultures, contemporary world is now experiencing an unprecedented historical change. After over three decades of opening-up and reformation, China is now attaching importance more than ever before to the research of international law, and the making and application of international rules. The comprehensive promotion of managing state affairs according to law is indispensable to the prosperity of legal theoretical research. The establishment of a novel economic system that opens up to the world is indispensable to the research of IEL. A series of problems that we encounter, no matter regarding international law or IEL, are of theoretical research as well as of practical one. We must thus link theory to practice. Also, we need to learn and benefit from the foreign advanced theories; especially need to base on the complicated and changeable international situations and international relations, as well as a close combination of international economic legal theory with our past open-up practices. Furthermore, we also need to actively promote the establishment of a fair and reasonable new international economic and political order, to form our own thoughts and suggestions, and dare to express our own Voice from China.

I have found a familiar article in Part I of your English monograph, namely "On the Source, Essence of 'Yellow Peril' Doctrine and Its Latest Hegemony 'Variant'—The 'China Threat' Doctrine", which I had the fortune to read when it first came out in 2012. This article has carried out a very thorough dissection of and pointed critique against the "China Threat" Doctrine. Based on historical facts and with a well-organized integration of history and theory, this article is soul-stirring, making readers can't help striking the table and shouting bravo. For the past decades, you have been consistently standing on China's situations and the common ground of the vast developing countries, adhering to the principle of national economic sovereignty, emphasizing the preservation of national interests of the weak groups, advocating equity and mutual benefit, South-North Cooperation and South-South Cooperation, and exploring the rules and approaches to establishing a new international economic order. You have been persistently advancing with the times, keep exploring and pursuing the truth from facts, and especially daring to express thought-provoking viewpoints that are different from or even contrary to traditional or mainstream views from the West. Such resounding Voices from China of yours have been keeping pushing forward the innovation of international economic legal theory and practice with Chinese characteristics. You have set up a model, from whom I have deeply felt the responsibility and mission that every international law scholar and practitioner is bound to and shall undertake.

I sincerely thank you for contributing another new masterpiece to the academic circle of IEL, and cordially wish you good health and a long life!

CAO Jianming
September 16, 2014

（翻译：杨 帆）

四、老艄公的铿锵号子* 发出时代的最强音
——《中国的呐喊：陈安论国际经济法》读后的点滴感悟

曾令良**

金秋收获时节，欣悉《中国的呐喊：陈安论国际经济法》(*The Voice from China: An CHEN on International Economic Law*，以下简称《中国的呐喊》)面世。这部新著集中了中国国际经济法学奠基人之一陈安先生三十多年学术研究之精华，由举世闻名的国际权威出版社同时向全球推出纸质版精装本和电子版。晚辈获陈老前辈惠赠其巨著，受宠若惊，感激之余，不禁感叹如下数语，以飨读者。

创新远征 教材开路

陈先生不愧为学界泰斗，学术常青常新。他数十年如一日，研究不息，笔耕不止，出版和发表的著述字数以数百万计。根据晚辈初步观察，中国改革开放后的头20年，陈先生研究的重心主要是通过主编不同版本的《国际经济法》教材、创办和主编《国际经济法论丛》及其改版的《国际经济法学刊》，创立和不断完善中国的国际经

---

* 号子，指集体劳动协同用力时，为统一步调、减轻疲劳等阶唱的歌，通常由一人领唱，大家应和。参见《现代汉语词典》(第7版)，商务印书馆2016年版，第521页。

** 曾令良，时任武汉大学资深教授、"长江学者"特聘教授、国际法研究所所长。

济法学体系。此外,他还在国际商事仲裁和国际投资争端解决等领域著书立说。与此同时,陈先生在国(境)内外一系列重要学术刊物上就国际经济法基本理论和实践中的重大和热点问题分别用中文和英文发表了数十篇具有重要影响的论文。

"三步进行曲"与"陈氏国际经济法"

进入21世纪,陈先生的学术成就集中体现在其先后出版的三部巨著之中。这三部代表作可谓是陈先生近十几年来学术创新的"三步进行曲",节节攀升,直至巅峰。首先,由北京大学出版社于2005年推出《国际经济法学刍言》上、下两卷本,共计210余万字。三年后的2008年,在原有著述的基础上由复旦大学出版社推出了《陈安论国际经济法学》五卷本,共计300余万字。诚如先生自言:这部新著"并不是《刍言》的简单再版或扩容",而是作者"针对本学科领域新问题进行探索的心得体会的全面增订和创新汇辑"。更令人震撼的是,如今,虽然先生已85岁高龄,但是追求学术之壮心不已,再次由国际权威出版机构向全球推出其英文巨著《中国的呐喊》。至此,"陈氏国际经济法"不仅深深扎根和流行于华语世界,而且将在全球各种不同文化的国家和地区广泛传播和推广,必将产生深远的国际影响。

"三性"理论与"6C律"

《中国的呐喊》重申和再现了"陈氏国际经济法"。[141] 20世纪90年代初,陈先生率先提出了国际经济法学的"三性"基本特征,即"边缘性""综合性"和"独立性",并将这一新的理论贯穿于此后他主编的教材、出版的著作和发表的论文之中。"三性"理论科学地揭示了国际经济法学作为一门新兴学科的内涵和外延,阐明了国际经济法与其他相邻学科之间的区别与联系,论证了这一新兴学科体系上的综合性和相对独立性。如今,"三性"理论早已被国际经济法学界所普遍接受,广泛应用于中国的国际经济法教学与研究之中,结束了曾长期困扰学界的关于国际经济法学的定性之争。

《中国的呐喊》创造性地揭示了国际经济关系、国际经济秩序和国际经济法发展与更新"6C律"。"6C律"是陈先生通过洞察和总结数十年来围绕建立国际经济新秩序的南北斗争的历程而得出的规律性认识,并预言这一规律在全球化快速发展的当下和明天将持续下去。所谓"6C律"(依笔者看来,似乎是"7C律"),就是描述国际经

---

[141] See An Chen, On the Marginality, Comprehensiveness, and Independence of International Economic Law Discipline, in An Chen, *The Voice from China: An CHEN on International Economic Law*, Springer, 2013, pp. 3-29.

济秩序和法律规范破旧立新的螺旋式上升轨迹,即"矛盾"(Contradiction)→"冲突或交锋"(Conflict)→"磋商"(Consultation)→"妥协"(Compromise)→"合作"(Cooperation)→"协调"(Coordination)→"新的矛盾"(Contradiction New)。[142] 陈先生巧妙地运用7个英文单词的首字母予以概括和表述,既贴切,又便于记忆,其学术智慧可见一斑。

捍卫弱者主权 抨击国际霸权

《中国的呐喊》向国际社会阐释中国对外经济交往的法理内涵和原则,揭露当今美国等国宣扬的"中国威胁"论是近代西方列强"黄祸"论的翻版,二者的DNA一脉相承,其本质是"政治骗术",其目的是蛊惑人心,误导国际舆论,贬损中国。[143] 陈先生锋利的言辞依据的是历史和事实,秉持的是正义和公理,捍卫的是中国的正面形象和正当合法的利益。

《中国的呐喊》先后三论中国在建立国际经济新秩序中的战略定位。陈先生主张中国应成为"建立国际经济新秩序的积极推手""南南联合自强的中流砥柱之一";中国应"既坚持战略原则的坚定性","又审时度势,坚持策略战术的灵活性"。[144] 依陈先生之见,正在和平崛起的中国"不宜只是现存国际经济秩序的'改良者'、南北矛盾的'协调者',而应是'改革者'之一"[145]。我坚信,这一观点道出了中国和其他发展中国家及其国际经济法学界共同的心声,并且已经得到一些欧美学者的赞许。

旗帜鲜明、直抒己见,是陈先生为人、做事、治学的原则和特点,这同样贯穿于《中国的呐喊》之中。这里仅举一例。近年来,在改革现有国际经济法及国际经济秩序的问题上,西方国际法学界一度流行"新自由主义经济秩序"论、"WTO宪政秩序"论、"经济民族主义扰乱全球化秩序"论。对此,陈先生告诫中国和广大发展中国家及其学人,不可盲从或附和,应实行有鉴别的取舍,尤其要警惕西方"淡化""弱化"主权和鼓吹主权"过时"的"理论陷阱"。[146]

---

[142] See An Chen, A Reflection of the South-South Coalition in the Last Half Century from the Perspective of International Economic Lawmaking: From Bandung, Doha, and Cancún to Hong Kong, in An Chen, *The Voice from China: An CHEN on International Economic Law*, Springer, 2013, pp. 207-239.

[143] See An Chen, On the Source, Essence of "Yellow Peril" Doctrine and Its Latest Hegemony "Variant"—the "China Threat" Doctrine: From the Perspective of Historical Mainstream of Sino-foreign Economic Interactions and Their Inherent Jurisprudential Principles, in An Chen, *The Voice from China: An CHEN on International Economic Law*, Springer, 2013, pp. 45-99.

[144] An Chen, What Should Be China's Strategic Position in the Establishment of New International Economic Order? With Comments on Neoliberalistic Economic Order, Constitutional Order of the WTO, and Economic Nationalism's Disturbance of Globalization, in An Chen, *The Voice from China: An CHEN on International Economic Law*, Springer, 2013, pp. 167-206.

[145] Ibid.

[146] Ibid.

《中国的呐喊》将广大发展中国家描述为"全球弱势群体",强调这些弱势群体国家应"珍惜和善用经济主权",呼吁"南南联合自强",反对美国的单边主义和西方强势群体国家在国际经济和贸易关系中实行"双重标准",坚持多边主义,以争取和维护全球弱势群体在国际经济秩序中的平等地位和公平权益。[147]

旗帜鲜明 中国风格 中国气派 时代强音

总之,《中国的呐喊》具有鲜明的中国风格和中国气派,代表着中国国际经济法学先进的理论,发出的是全球弱势群体国家强烈呼吁建立公平、公正的国际经济新秩序的共同心声。《中国的呐喊》的出版,再次体现了一代宗师非凡的学术气度和追求学术卓越的精神。陈先生不愧为中国国际经济法学的舵手和国际经济秩序"破旧立新"的旗手。更重要的是,陈先生学术成就的重大意义和影响已经超越了国际经济法学本身,正如有关国际机构的高级人士所评价的,"《中国的呐喊》是对当代世界政治研究和认识的重要贡献";同时,"应成为了解和研究中西关系人士的必读物,尤其是应作为发展中国家的领导人、高级经贸谈判官员培训的指导用书",甚至作为这些国家高等院校的教材。[148] 总之,《中国的呐喊》无疑是中国国际经济法学界具有代表性的学术权威之音,是向世界发出的强音和高音。我坚信,这部巨著的出版将对国际经济法学的发展产生深远的影响!

(编辑:龚　宇)

The Sonorous Work Song of an Old Helmsman of International Economic Law
—Some Reflections and Thoughts After Reading *The Voice from China: An CHEN on International Economic Law*

Zeng Lingliang*

In this golden harvest season, it is delighted to know that *The Voice from*

---

[147] See An Chen, A Reflection of the South-South Coalition in the Last Half Century from the Perspective of International Economic Lawmaking: From Bandung, Doha, and Cancún to Hong Kong, in An Chen, *The Voice from China: An CHEN on International Economic Law*, Springer, 2013, pp. 207-239.

[148] See Branislav Gosovic, WTO Citadel Needs to Be Challenged by the South; An Important and Creative Contribution from China to the Ideology of Third World, both compiled in An Chen, *The Voice from China: An CHEN on International Economic Law*, Springer, 2013, Annex, pp. 754-765.

* Yangtse River Scholar Professor; Senior Professor of International Law, Wuhan University, China.

China: An CHEN on International Economic Law (hereafter referred as *The Voice from China*) was published by Springer, the world-wide well-known publisher, both in paper and electronic versions. This new monograph collects the very essence of academic research achievements of Professor An Chen for the past 30-odd years, who is one of the founders of Chinese international economic law. I, as a younger generation of the discipline and receiver of this great book, thank him for his kindness. In addition to gratefulness to him, I would like to make a few words of my superficial understanding of this book as follows:

Professor Chen has proved himself to be a leading scholar of the discipline of Chinese international economic law. His academic research is evergreen and often up-dated. He has never stopped studying and writing for several decades, producing numerous publications both at home and abroad. According to my preliminary observation, his studies in the first twenty years after China engaged itself in "reform-and-open policy", focused on creation and completion of the Chinese discipline of international economic law by means of compiling international economic law textbooks in various editions and founding Journal of International Economic Law in Chinese as editor-in-chief. In addition, some parts of his writings relate to theory creation in the areas of international commercial arbitration and international investment dispute resolution. At the same time, he published quite a number of articles on key and hot issues both concerning basic theories and practices of international economic law in some important academic journals in Chinese or English.

Since the 21th century, Professor Chen's academic achievements have been reflected intensively and respectively in his three masterpieces. These three magnificent masterpieces might be well-called as "trilogy" of his academic creation in the most recent twenty years, which steadily climbs up to the peak. He firstly published the monograph entitled *CHEN's Papers on International Economic Law* (two volumes) in Peking University Press in 2005. Three years later in 2008, he published the new expanded edition (five volumes altogether) entitled *An CHEN on International Economic Law* in Fudan University Press. This new edition, as its author described, "is not simply a re-edition or expansion in volume, but a collection of comprehensive revision and enlargement as well as creation made by the author after his continuous exploration of new issues arising in the discipline". Today, in spite of his age of 85, he continues pursuing his academic excellence by publishing his great work *The Voice from China* in English version in Springer who enjoys high international reputation. Hence, Chen's doctrines of international economic law not only has been deeply rooted and popular in the Chinese society, but also will spread and extend globally, thus resulting in far-reaching international influence.

The Voice from China reaffirms and reproduces the theory of "three basic features"[149] persistently advocated by Professor Chen for decades. This theory was first put forward by him in early 1990s, namely the marginality, comprehensiveness and independence of international economic law discipline. Since then on, he has penetrated and integrated the theory into his subsequent textbooks, monographs and published articles as well as various lectures on international economic law. This new theory scientifically brings to light the connotation and extension of international economic law as a newly-born discipline, and identifies the differences from and links to other neighboring disciplines. Nowadays, the theory of "three basic features" has been widely recognized by international economic law scholars and extensively applied in teaching and studying of international economic law courses in China's universities and colleges, thus ending the debates on definition of international economic law which had persecuted scholars ever before.

The Voice from China creates the "6C Track" or "6C Rule" format embedded in the law-making process of international economic relations since the end of the Second World War. The "6C" means Contradiction → Conflict → Consultation → Compromise → Cooperation → Coordination → Contradiction New. [150] It seems to be a "7C" process instead. This format description demonstrates via the author's critical eyes the track of struggles between the North and the South in establishing international economic order for the past several decades and expects that this track of development in spirals will be continuing in today's and future world of

---

[149] See An Chen, On the Marginality, Comprehensiveness, and Independence of International Economic Law Discipline, in An Chen, *The Voice from China: An CHEN on International Economic Law*, Springer, 2013, pp. 3-29.

[150] See An Chen, A Reflection of the South-South Coalition in the Last Half Century from the Perspective of International Economic Lawmaking: From Bandung, Doha, and Cancún to Hong Kong, in An Chen, *The Voice from China: An CHEN on International Economic Law*, Springer, 2013, pp. 207-239.

globalization. Professor Chen skillfully uses the seven key English words which all share the first letter "C" to summarize this circle development tendency, which is both precise and easy for memory. We could appreciate the wisdom of an academic master underlying it.

The Voice from China explains to the international society the Chinese jurisprudence and legal principles in international intercourses, exposes that "China Threat" Doctrine advocated by the U. S. and a few other countries today is in essence the refurbished version of "Yellow Peril" Doctrine advocated by the western powers in the past. He sharply observes that the DNA of the two theories is the same and their essence is a "political trickery".[151] His sharp words are based on history and facts, uphold the justice and generally acknowledged truth and maintain the positive image of China and its legitimate rights and interest.

The Voice from China contributes a special Part (part III) to analyze China's strategic position on contemporary international economic order issues. It proclaims that China, as the biggest developing country, should "play an active part in promoting the establishing of the NEIO", "become one of the driving forces and mainstays of the South-South Coalition".[152] In the course of establishment the NEIO, China should adhere to the firmness its strategic principles on the one hand and tactical flexibility on the other hand. In the view of Professor Chen, the peacefully rising China should not only be an "ameliorator" of the current international economic order and "intermediary" of the South-North contradiction, but also one of the "reformers" of the order,[153] which I believe expresses the common voice and wishes of the vast developing countries and their scholars and deserves the blessing of some European and American academics.

Up-holding clear-cut stand and speaking his mind is the principle and feature of

---

[151] See An Chen, On the Source, Essence of "Yellow Peril" Doctrine and Its Latest Hegemony "Variant"—the "China Threat" Doctrine: From the Perspective of Historical Mainstream of Sino-foreign Economic Interactions and Their Inherent Jurisprudential Principles, in An Chen, *The Voice from China: An CHEN on International Economic Law*, Springer, 2013, pp. 45-99.

[152] See An Chen, What Should Be China's Strategic Position in the Establishment of New International Economic Order? With Comments on Neoliberalistic Economic Order, Constitutional Order of the WTO, and Economic Nationalism's Disturbance of Globalization, in An Chen, *The Voice from China: An CHEN on International Economic Law*, Springer, 2013, pp. 167-206.

[153] Ibid.

Professor Chen in his behavior, research and dealing with matters, which is also reflected in *The Voice from China*. For instance, in recent years, theories of "neoliberalistic economic order", "constitutional order of WTO" and "economic nationalism's disturbance of globalization" have been popular in western academics of international law. However, Professor Chen warns China and vast developing countries and their international economic law scholars not to follow these theories blindly, but make choices identifiably, with special guard against "theories trap" which fades out and weakens sovereignty or claims sovereignty old-fashioned. [154]

The Voice from China describes the vast developing countries as the "global weak group" and stresses that these weak countries should "cherish and take a proper use of sovereignty". The author calls for the "South-South coalition and self-improvement" to oppose unilateralism of the U.S and "double standards" by the strong group of western countries and persist in multilateralism so as to strive for and maintain the equal rights and fair interests in the international economic order. [155]

In short, *The Voice from China* bears a distinctive Chinese-style ballet. The book represents the advanced theory of the discipline of Chinese international economic law and delivers the common voice of the weak group countries calling for the establishment of a new international economic order with fairness and justice. It reproduces a master's spirit of extraordinary academic tolerance and pursuing academic excellence. Professor Chen deserves the title of "helmsman" of Chinese international economic law and "the flag bearer" of the international economic order who promotes to "destroy the old and establish the new". What is more important is that the significance of his academic achievements surpasses the discipline of international economic law itself. Just as a retired official of the UNATAD observed, Professor Chen's work is "an important contribution to the study and understanding of contemporary world politics", and "should be made subject for

---

[154] See An Chen, What Should Be China's Strategic Position in the Establishment of New International Economic Order? With Comments on Neoliberalistic Economic Order, Constitutional Order of the WTO, and Economic Nationalism's Disturbance of Globalization, in An Chen, *The Voice from China: An CHEN on International Economic Law*, Springer, 2013, pp. 167-206.

[155] See An Chen, A Reflection of the South-South Coalition in the Last Half Century from the Perspective of International Economic Lawmaking: From Bandung, Doha, and Cancún to Hong Kong, in An Chen, *The Voice from China: An CHEN on International Economic Law*, Springer, 2013, pp. 207-239.

required reading and study by leaders and policy makers in all developing countries" and "should also be part of the curriculum in developing countries' ministries, universities, and institutes of higher learning that prepare new cadres and officials for participating and work in the multilateral sphere".[156] In conclusion, *The Voice from China*, just like the sonorous work song of an old helmsman, is undoubtedly a representative academic voice of the Chinese academics of international economic law as well as its high and strong voice to the whole world. I am confident that the publication of this master work will produce a far-reaching significance for the development of international economic law studies.

（翻译：曾令良）

五、天下视野 家国情怀 公平秉守
——读《中国的呐喊：陈安论国际经济法》

车丕照*

由国际著名出版社 Springer 出版发行的陈安先生的英文著作《中国的呐喊：陈安论国际经济法》(*The Voice from China: An CHEN on International Economic Law*)已经问世。该书汇集了陈安先生数十年来在国际经济法研究方面的重要学术成果，集中向世界展示了一位资深的中国国际经济法学者的立场、观点和方法。如果我们要对该书所反映出的陈安先生的学术思想与学术风格作一个简单概括，或许可以归结为这样三句话：天下视野、家国情怀和公平秉守。

天 下 视 野

国际经济法学者原本就应具有观察问题的天下视野。但事实上，许多学者的学术视野局限于西方发达国家的国际经济法理论与实践，甚至完全唯西方标准马首是瞻，以至于"法律全球化"成了"美国法的全球化"。[157]

陈安先生的研究虽然仍关注美国等西方发达国家的理论与实践，但却具有更为

---

[156] See Branislav Gosovic, WTO Citadel Needs to Be Challenged by the South: An Important and Creative Contribution from China to the Ideology of Third World. The above papers are both compiled in An Chen, *The Voice from China: An CHEN on International Economic Law*, Springer, 2013, pp. 754-765.

* 车丕照，清华大学法学院前院长，教授。

[157] 参见高鸿钧：《美国法全球化：典型例证与法理反思》，载《中国法学》2011年第1期，第5页。

广阔的视角,即国际经济秩序的视角。法律的首要价值是其秩序价值。"秩序构成了人类理想的要素和社会活动的基本目标。"[158]同样的道理,国际经济法的首要价值应该是其在确立国际经济秩序方面的功能。事实上,当今的国际经济秩序是在各种国际经济法律规范的共同作用下得以维系的。在这些法律规范中,既有国际法规范,又有国内法规范;既有私法规范,又有公法规范。陈安先生在二十多年前即已为我们清晰地描绘出这样一个支撑国际经济秩序的国际经济法体系。[159] 由于国际社会并不存在代表社会利益的"世界政府",因此,国际经济秩序的形成,即国际经济法律制度的形成是各国及其他各类实体长期行为积累的结果。由此形成的秩序,尽管优于无秩序,但却可能并非公平。正因为如此,从 20 世纪 60 年代起,世界上形成了以"公平"为价值追求的"建立国际经济新秩序"的思潮和运动。这场运动虽然尚未达到预期的效果,但仍旧取得了一些现实的成果。国际贸易领域中的"普惠制"和国际环境领域中的"共同却有区别的责任"就是其中的代表。中国国际经济法学者虽然也关注过国际经济新秩序的研究,但少有像陈安先生那样持续、深入地对国际经济新秩序加以探索和研究的。在中国老一辈国际经济法学者当中,陈安先生关于国际经济新秩序的研究应该是最具代表性的。尽管"建立国际经济新秩序"的运动在二十多年前即已开始陷入低潮,但陈安先生的相关研究依旧势头不减,并鼓励大家继续深化该领域的研究。在《中国的呐喊》中,陈安先生高瞻远瞩地指出:"建立国际经济新秩序乃是数十亿人争取国际经济平等地位的共同目标和行动纲领。自通过南南合作而建立国际经济新秩序的方针形成以来,弱势国家争取平等国际经济地位的努力,虽历经潮起潮落,但不断冲破明滩暗礁,持续向前。因此,应从长远的战略视角对这场运动予以分析和评估,而不宜从短期战术角度考虑其得失。"[160]中国优秀知识分子历来就有"先天下之忧而忧,后天下之乐而乐"的价值取向,而这样一种以天下为己任的胸怀,对于当代知识分子来说,首先就应表现为学术研究的"天下视野"。

家 国 情 怀

在以天下为视野的同时,陈安先生的学术研究也明显地表露出家国情怀。这种

---

[158] 张文显:《法哲学范畴研究》(修订版),中国政法大学出版社 2001 年版,第 195 页。

[159] See An Chen, On the Marginality, Comprehensiveness, and Independence of International Economic Law Discipline, in An Chen, *The Voice from China*: *An CHEN on International Economic Law*, Springer, 2013, p. 27.

[160] An Chen, What Should Be China's Strategic Position in the Establishment of New International Economic Order? With Comments on Neoliberalistic Economic Order, Constitutional Order of the WTO, and Economic Nationalism's Disturbance of Globalization, in An Chen, *The Voice from China*: *An CHEN on International Economic Law*, Springer, 2013, p. 203.

家国情怀主要体现为两个方面:一是对中国国家利益的深切关注,二是以国家为中心的研究进路。

陈安先生的学术研究始终表现出对中国国家立场和国家利益的关切。在《论中国在建立国际经济新秩序中的战略定位》(What Should Be China's Strategic Position in the Establishment of New International Economic Order?)一文中,陈安先生指出:"在建立国际经济新秩序的时代大潮流中,中国的自我战略定位理应一如既往,继续是旗帜鲜明的积极推动者之一,是现存国际经济秩序的改革者之一。不宜只是现存国际经济秩序的'改良者'、南北矛盾的'协调者'。"[161]在《中外双边投资协定中的四大"安全阀"是否应贸然拆除?》(Should the Four "Great Safeguards" in Sino-foreign BITs Be Hastily Dismantled?)一文中,陈安先生语重心长地建议:在中外双边投资协定谈判中,中国应坚持有关国际法授权的规定,善于掌握四大"安全阀"[162],以有效保护中国的国家利益,并在确立合理的外国投资法律规范及建立国际经济新秩序的过程中发挥示范作用。[163] 陈安先生的学术研究始终跟踪中国政府的相关实践。他所带领的学术团队与国家商务部等政府部门一直保持很好的互动关系。他的许多研究成果都得到中国相关政府部门的重视和采纳。陈安先生的学术研究中所包含的这份家国情怀令人感动、值得称赞。

陈安先生的学术研究中还表现出另外一种"家国情怀",即以国家为中心的研究进路。如前所述,陈安先生很早就界定了国际经济法的范围,指出:"由于国际经济法是用来调整各种公、私主体之间跨国经济关系的法律规范。所以,它并非专属于单一的国际公法,不单纯是国际公法的分支,不仅仅是适用于经济领域的国际公法。恰恰相反,它的内涵和外延早已大大突破了传统的国际公法的局限,与国际私法和国际商法交叉,并及于国内经济法、民法和商法,从而构成了一个多门类、跨学科的边缘性综合体。"[164]尽管如此,陈安先生的国际经济法研究基本上是以国家为中心展开的,而几乎不涉足私人之间交易的法律问题。于是,在《中国的呐喊》一书中,我们

---

[161] An Chen, What Should Be China's Strategic Position in the Establishment of New International Economic Order? With Comments on Neoliberalistic Economic Order, Constitutional Order of the WTO, and Economic Nationalism's Disturbance of Globalization, in An Chen, *The Voice from China: An CHEN on International Economic Law*, Springer, 2013, p. 204.

[162] 四大"安全阀"是指在处理东道国与外国投资者的关系时,有利于东道国的"逐案审批同意"权、"当地救济优先"权、"东道国法律适用"权和"重大安全例外"权。

[163] See An Chen, Should the Four "Great Safeguards" in Sino-foreign BITs Be Hastily Dismantled? Comments on Critical Provisions Concerning Dispute Settlement in Model US and Canadian BITs, in An Chen, *The Voice from China: An CHEN on International Economic Law*, Springer, 2013, p. 273.

[164] An Chen, On the Marginality, Comprehensiveness, and Independence of International Economic Law Discipline, in An Chen, *The Voice from China: An CHEN on International Economic Law*, Springer, 2013, p. 5.

看到陈安先生关于美国单边主义与WTO多边体制冲突的研究（The Three Big Rounds of US Unilateralism Versus WTO Multilateralism During the Last Decade）、对中国在建立国际经济新秩序中的战略立场的研究（What Should Be China's Strategic Position in the Establishment of New International Economic Order?）、对建立国际经济新秩序过程中南南合作的研究（A Reflection of the South-South Coalition in the Last Half Century from the Perspective of International Economic Lawmaking: From Bandung, Doha, and Cancún to Hong Kong）以及关于中国外资政策与法律的研究（To Open Wider or to Close Again: China's Foreign Investment Policies and Laws）等。即使是就具体案例所进行的研究，陈安先生也是围绕着国家与私人的关系而展开的。陈安先生的这种研究进路反映出他对国家这一国际社会的基本主体的重视。尽管私人之间的国际经济交往是国际经济法现实的和逻辑的起点：没有私人之间的国际经济交往，就没有国家对国际经济交往的管理；没有国家对国际经济交往的管理，也就没有国家之间的冲突、协调和合作。但与私人相比，国家是更为重要的国际经济法主体。在调整私人之间交易关系的民商法性质的规范逐渐趋同的情况下，国际经济法体系中更为活跃的部分是国际经济活动的国家管理制度及国家间的协调和合作制度。陈安先生归纳出的"6C律"：Contradiction（矛盾）→Conflict（冲突或交锋）→Consultation（磋商）→Compromise（妥协）→Cooperation（合作）→Coordination（协调）→Contradiction New（新的矛盾）[165]系统而准确地阐明了国家行为与国际经济法的关系及演变规律。

公 平 秉 守

陈安先生学术研究的另外一个特色就是对公平的执着秉守。

如果我们从国家层面观察国际经济法，如果我们将国际经济法的形式限定为制定法和习惯，那么，当今的国际经济法从整体上看只能达到"互惠"（reciprocity），而无法达到"公平"（equity）。"互惠"是相互对等的让与，而"公平"则要求考虑特定情形下的利益分配，这种分配并不要求是互惠和对等的。由于当今的国际经济法是历史上各类规则的积累，平等地适用这些规则，以致创设新的"互惠"规则，都无法在国际社会成员间实现真正的公平，因此，"建立新的国际经济秩序"也就是要"建立公平合理的国际经济秩序"。如前所述，陈安先生的研究所贯穿的一个基本思想，就是追

---

[165] See An Chen, A Reflection of the South-South Coalition in the Last Half Century from the Perspective of International Economic Lawmaking: From Bandung, Doha, and Cancún to Hong Kong, in An Chen, *The Voice from China: An CHEN on International Economic Law*, Springer, 2013, p. 234.

求国际经济秩序的公平合理。"公平"是比"秩序"更高一级别的价值。人类社会中的"秩序"仅仅表明稳定的社会关系的存在,而"公平"则深入到对"秩序"内容的评判或"秩序"模式的选择。在《关于 WTO 的法治、立法、执法、守法与变法的法理思考》(Some Jurisprudential Thoughts upon WTO's Law-Governing, Law-Making, Law-Enforcing, Law-Abiding, and Law-Reforming)一文中,陈安先生指出:"面对当今现存的各种国际经济立法,包括形形色色的国际经贸'游戏规则',国际弱势群体固然不能予以全盘否定,也无力加以彻底改造,但更不能全盘接受,服服帖帖,心甘情愿地忍受其中蕴含的各种不公与不平。"[166]关于建立公平合理的国际经济秩序的途径,陈安先生认为其根本途径在于弱小国家的团结合作。他认为:"在今后一系列全球性问题的国际论坛和多边谈判中,南方各发展中国家比以往任何时候都更加需要采取集体行动,才能赢得公平、公正和合理的结果。为了维护发展中国家共同的根本利益,必须适应形势的变化,通过精心研究和科学设计,调整和更新 77 国集团的纲领,协调不同的利益,以增强共识和内部的凝聚力。"[167]

陈安先生对国际经济秩序的公平与合理的不懈和热切的追求——无论建立国际经济新秩序的运动是处于高潮或低谷,除其他原因外,与其自身经历有关。他在《中国的呐喊》一书的前言中写道:"我年轻的时候,在学习中华灿烂文明的同时,也从教育中知晓并亲身感受到中华民族的悲惨危机。复杂的情绪逐渐培养起我强烈的民族自豪感和爱国主义的思想,我的反对国际霸权主义的决心,以及我的努力实现社会公正和支持世界上所有弱小国家的志向。"[168]

陈安先生与姚梅镇先生等一起在中国开创了国际经济法学这门学科,并继姚梅镇先生之后成为中国国际经济法学界的旗手。他在 90 年代初就系统地论述了国际经济法学的边缘性、综合性和独立性,[169]并对质疑国际经济法学的"不科学"或"不规范"论、"大胃"论或"长臂"论、"浮躁"论或"炒热"论以及"翻版"论或"舶来"论作出了系统的批驳,[170]为国际经济法学的发展奠定了坚实的基础。如今,陈安先生的英文著作又结集出版,在国际学界发出了中国国际经济法学者的声音。我们期待随着陈

---

[166] An Chen, Some Jurisprudential Thoughts upon WTO's Law-Governing, Law-Making, Law-Enforcing, Law-Abiding, and Law-Reforming, in An Chen, *The Voice from China: An CHEN on International Economic Law*, Springer, 2013, p. 246.

[167] An Chen, A Reflection of the South-South Coalition in the Last Half Century from the Perspective of International Economic Lawmaking: From Bandung, Doha, and Cancún to Hong Kong, in An Chen, *The Voice from China: An CHEN on International Economic Law*, Springer, 2013, p. 212.

[168] An Chen, *The Voice from China: An CHEN on International Economic Law*, Springer, 2013, p. v.

[169] See An Chen, On the Marginality, Comprehensiveness, and Independence of International Economic Law Discipline, in An Chen, *The Voice from China: An CHEN on International Economic Law*, Springer, 2013, p. 3.

[170] Ibid., pp. 32-43.

安先生的引领,中国学者将在国际社会发出更为响亮的和声。

(编辑:龚　宇)

Global Perspective, State Position and Equity Pursuance
—Introducing *The Voice from China : An CHEN on International Economic Law*

Che Pizhao[*]

Professor An Chen's book, *The Voice from China : An CHEN on International Economic Law*, newly published by internationally leading academic publisher Springer, contains representative articles written by the author over the past three decades, showing specific ideas of a senior and eminent Chinese scholar of international economic law. We may sum up the author's wisdom and style reflected in this book with several words, namely: the global perspective, the state position, and the equity pursuance.

1. Global Perspective

A scholar of international economic law is expected to observe issues with a global perspective. However, the views of many scholars are limited to the theories and practices of Western developed countries, and globalization of laws, for them, is the globalization of the laws of the United States.[171]

Although Professor Chen has been paying close attention to the theories and practice of the United States and other developed countries, he insists on studying from a broader perspective—the international economic order. The primary value of law is order. "Order constitutes the ideal element of mankind as well as the basic target of social activities."[172] Similarly, the most essential value of international economic law is its function on establishing international economic order. In fact,

---

　　[*] Professor of Law, former Dean of Law School, Tsinghua University, China.
　　[171] See Gao Hongjun, The Globalization of American Law, *China Legal Science*, Vol. 1, 2011, p. 5.
　　[172] Zhang Wenxian, *Studies on Basic Categories of Legal Philosophy* (revised edition), China University of Political Science and Law Press, 2001, p. 195.

the current international economic order is maintained by the co-function of various rules of international economic laws, which include both international law and domestic law, private law and public law. Such a system of international economic law maintaining the international economic order was first demonstrated to us by Professor Chen as early as more than 20 years ago. [173] Due to the absence of a world government to represent the interests of the international society, the formation of international economic order, as well as the international economic legal system is a result of historically accumulated practices of states and other actors. Such an order, though better than disorder, may be far from equity. This is why a trend of thought and movement of the new international economic order aiming at achieving equity was radically developed since 1960s. There have been some fruits from this movement, such as GSP arrangements in international trade law and the principle of common but differentiated responsibilities in international environment law, although there is still a long road to achieve its expected objectives. There are Chinese scholars paying attention to the study of the new international economic order (NIEO), but few like Professor Chen who keeps continuous and in-depth studies on the new international economic order. Among the senior generation of Chinese scholars in the area of international economic law, Professor Chen's study on the new international economic order may be the most representative one. Although the movement of establishing the new international economic order began to hit its bottom about 20 years ago, Professor Chen has never been disappointed; rather, he has consistently encouraged others to further study in this field. In *The Voice from China*, Professor Chen shows great foresight that "the establishment of NIEO is the common goal and program of action of billions of people who are striving for equal international economic status. Since the formation of the policy of establishing the NIEO by way of South-South Coalition, the movement of striving for equal international status of the weak states has undergone ebb and flow, and kept on progressing in a spiral course in spite of layers of barriers. Therefore, the analyses and evaluation of the movement should be carried out from a long-term

---

[173] See An Chen, On the Marginality, Comprehensiveness, and Independence of International Economic Law Discipline, in An Chen, *The Voice from China: An CHEN on International Economic Law*, Springer, 2013, p. 27.

strategic perspective, not from a perspective of gains or loss in the short run."[174] "Feeling anxious before all the others and enjoying happiness after all the others" is the creed of outstanding Chinese scholars in history. For today's scholars, to have the world in mind, should firstly keep a global perspective in academic studies.

2. State Position

While taking a global perspective, Professor Chen's book is an embodiment of the standpoint of the state. The state position is clearly expressed by his profound concern for China's interests and his state-centered research approach.

Professor Chen's academic study always shows his profound concern for China's interests. In "What Should Be China's Strategic Position in the Establishment of New International Economic Order", Professor Chen points out that "in the course of establishing the NIEO, China should adhere to her self-positioning, i. e., an active promoter who takes a clear-cut stand and a reformer of the existing international economic order, but not just an ameliorator of the existing order or an intermediary of the South-North Contradiction."[175] In "Should the Four 'Great Safeguards' in Sino-foreign BITs Be Hastily Dismantled?", Professor Chen advises earnestly that China, in the course of negotiating BITs, should insist on stipulating in related BITs such rights authorized by the relevant international law, to well control the four "Great Safeguards",[176] so as to effectively protect China's national interest as well as to play a model role in the course of establishing reasonable legal norms toward foreign investment and the new international economic order.[177] Professor Chen always combines his academic study with the practice of Chinese government, and his team has been working with the Ministry of Commerce of

---

[174] An Chen, What Should Be China's Strategic Position in the Establishment of New International Economic Order? With Comments on Neoliberalistic Economic Order, Constitutional Order of the WTO, and Economic Nationalism's Disturbance of Globalization, in An Chen, *The Voice from China: An CHEN on International Economic Law*, Springer, 2013, p. 203.

[175] Ibid., p. 204.

[176] The four Great Safeguards include the four rights of the host country in its relations with foreign investors, namely, the right to "consent case by case", the right to require "exhausting local remedies", the right to "apply host country's laws" and the right to invoke the "exception for state essential security."

[177] See An Chen, Should the Four "Great Safeguards" in Sino-foreign BITs Be Hastily Dismantled? Comments on Critical Provisions Concerning Dispute Settlement in Model US and Canadian BITs, in An Chen, *The Voice from China: An CHEN on International Economic Law*, Springer, 2013, p. 273.

China and other governmental departments smoothly. Many of his suggestions in his studies have been adopted by relevant governmental agencies. Professor Chen's patriotic ideas and feelings are really precious and deserve high praise.

Another embodiment of state position is Professor Chen's state-centered research approach. As mentioned earlier, professor Chen defined the scope of international economic law very early, saying that "as international economic law refers to legal norms that are used to adjust the cross-border economic relations of various public and private subjects, it can thus not be categorized solely to public international law and cannot be merely deemed as a branch of public international law that applies to economic issues. On the very contrary, its connotation and denotation have largely broken the constrains of public international law in its traditional sense and have crossed partially with private international law, international business law and relating domestic economic law, civil law, and commercial law. Thus, it formed an interdisciplinary marginal synthesis of multi-branches."[178] However, Professor Chen's study seems always focusing on state, and seldom concerned with transnational business transactions among individuals. Thus, in *The Voice from China*, we can find Professor Chen's analysis on the conflicts between US unilateralism and WTO multilateralism ("The Three Big Rounds of US Unilateralism Versus WTO Multilateralism During the Last Decade"), his insight on China's strategic position in the establishment of the new international economic order ("What Should Be China's Strategic Position in the Establishment of New International Economic Order?"), the study on South-South coalition in the process of establishing the new international economic order ("A Reflection of the South-South Coalition in the Last Half Century from the Perspective of International Economic Lawmaking: From Bandung, Doha, and Cancún to Hong Kong") and his study on China's policy and law on foreign investment ("To Open Wider or to Close Again: China's Foreign Investment Policies and Laws"). Even in the articles mainly adopting case-study, Professor Chen's analysis is also developed around the relations between the state and individuals. This approach reflects Professor Chen's attention on states, the basic actor of the

---

[178] An Chen, On the Marginality, Comprehensiveness, and Independence of International Economic Law Discipline, in An Chen, *The Voice from China: An CHEN on International Economic Law*, Springer, 2013, p. 5.

international society. Admittedly, transnational business transaction between individuals is in fact the logical starting point, as without individuals' business transactions there would be no governmental administration on them, and no conflicts and coordination among states concerning international economic transactions. However, compared with individuals, the state is a more important actor. While civil law and commercial law regulating business transaction tend to converge, the law regulating governmental administration becomes a more essential part of international economic law. The "6C rules" concluded by Professor Chen, namely Contradiction → Conflict → Consultation → Compromise → Cooperation → Coordination → Contradiction New[179], systematically and accurately expounds the relationship between state behavior and international law and their road of evolution.

3. Equity Pursuance

Another character of Professor Chen's study is his pursuance to equity.

If we observe international economic law from a perspective of international relations, and confine the law to international convention and custom, we may find today's international economic law in general is a system in the nature of reciprocity, but not equity. Reciprocity means mutual and equal concession between countries, while equity requires specific allocation of interests under particular situations, which does not necessarily require reciprocity. Since current international economic law is a legal system containing historically accumulated rules, it is difficult to achieve equity among members of the international society by applying those rules equally or establishing new reciprocal rule. Therefore, to establish a new international economic order is to establish an equitable and reasonable international economic order. As mentioned earlier, an idea permeated through Professor Chen's studies is pursuing the equity and reasonableness of international economic order. Equity is a value of law superior than order. Order only means stable social relations, while equity requires the judgment on the content of order or the choosing

---

[179] See An Chen, A Reflection of the South-South Coalition in the Last Half Century from the Perspective of International Economic Lawmaking: From Bandung, Doha, and Cancún to Hong Kong, in An Chen, *The Voice from China: An CHEN on International Economic Law*, Springer, 2013, p. 234.

of the pattern of order. In "Some Jurisprudential Thoughts upon WTO's Law-Governing, Law-Making, Law-Enforcing, Law-Abiding, and Law-Reforming", Professor Chen explains that "facing the existing IEL, including varieties of 'rules of game' for international economic and trade affairs, the international weak groups certainly cannot deny them all, nor are they capable of remaking the rules entirely. However, the weak groups cannot either accept all the therein embedded unfairness and injustice willingly, docilely, and obediently."[180] With respect to the road to establish an equitable and reasonable international economic order, Professor Chen believes the fundamental way lies in the cooperation among the small and weak countries. He holds that "in the later international fora and multilateral negotiations on a series of global issues, it is more necessary than ever for the developing countries of the South to take actions to win an equitable, justified and reasonable outcome. To defend the fundamental common interests of developing countries, it is imperative for the South to adapt itself to the change of circumstances, through delicate research and scientific design, and to reorient and renew the guidelines of the Group of 77, harmonizing various interests and reinforcing common understanding and internal cohesion."[181]

Professor Chen's unremitting pursuance to equity and reasonableness of the international economic order, no matter whether the movement for establishing the new international economic order is rising or falling, in addition to other factors, relates to his personal experiences. He recalls in the preface of *The Voice from China* that "when I was young, I was told of the glorious civilization of China, but I was also educated by and personally experienced the sad national crisis of China. Such complex emotions gradually nurtured my strong sense of national pride and patriotism, my determination to fight against international hegemonism, and my ambition to strive for social justice and to support all other weak countries in the world."[182]

---

[180] An Chen, Some Jurisprudential Thoughts upon WTO's Law-Governing, Law-Making, Law-Enforcing, Law-Abiding, and Law-Reforming, in An Chen, *The Voice from China: An CHEN on International Economic Law*, Springer, 2013, p. 246.

[181] An Chen, A Reflection of the South-South Coalition in the Last Half Century from the Perspective of International Economic Lawmaking: From Bandung, Doha, and Cancún to Hong Kong, in An Chen, *The Voice from China: An CHEN on International Economic Law*, Springer, 2013, p. 212.

[182] An Chen, *The Voice from China: An CHEN on International Economic Law*, Springer, 2013, p. v.

Together with other pioneers, such as professor Yao Meizhen, Professor Chen created the discipline of international economic law in China, and succeeded professor Yao as the standard-bearer of China's international economic law academia. He expounded and proved systematically that international economic law "formed an interdisciplinary marginal synthesis of multi-branches" as early as in the 90s of last century.[183] He also argued convincingly against queries towards the discipline of international economic law including the queries of "nonscientific or nonnormative", "polyphagian or avaricious", "fickle fashion or stirring heat" and "duplication version or importing goods",[184] and laid firm foundation for the discipline of international economic law in China. The publication of Professor Chen's works in English makes it more convenient for foreign readers to hear the voice from Chinese international economic law scholarships. We expect that following the voice from Professor Chen, there shall be a loud and clear cantata by much more Chinese scholars in international stage.

（翻译：车丕照）

六、"提出中国方案、贡献中国智慧"[185]的先行者
——评《中国的呐喊：陈安论国际经济法》

赵龙跃*

厦门大学陈安教授的英文专著《中国的呐喊：陈安论国际经济法》(*The Voice from China: An CHEN on International Economic Law*，以下简称《中国的呐喊》)，近期由在国际学术界享有盛誉的德国出版社 Springer 在全球出版发行，令人非常钦佩。作为中国国际经济法学界的学术泰斗，陈安教授耄耋之年，笔耕不辍，知识报国，堪称楷模。《中国的呐喊》顺应中国和平发展的要求，从积极参与国际规则制定

---

[183] An Chen, On the Marginality, Comprehensiveness, and Independence of International Economic Law Discipline, in An Chen, *The Voice from China: An CHEN on International Economic Law*, Springer, 2013, p. 3.

[184] Ibid., pp. 32-43.

[185] 习近平主席在接受拉美四国媒体的联合采访时表示，中国"将更多提出中国方案、贡献中国智慧，为国际社会提供更多公共产品"，详见《习近平接受拉美四国媒体联合采访》，http://news.xinhuanet.com/world/2014-07/15/c_126752272.htm。

* 赵龙跃，时任南开大学教授、美国乔治敦大学客座教授、世界银行咨询专家。

和全球治理的角度,就国际经济法的基本理论、当代国家经济主权的论争以及中国在构建国际经济新秩序中的战略定位等重大问题进行了独特的战略思考,提出了许多切实可行的政策建议。陈安教授立足中国国情和维护广大发展中国家合法权益的需要,学贯中西,独树一帜,从完善国际经济法的角度,为中国参与国际规则制定,建立国际经济新秩序发挥了重要作用,是中国为国际社会"提出中国方案、贡献中国智慧"的先行者。

随着经济全球化的深入发展,国际政治经济格局正在发生着深刻的变化,中国和广大发展中国家在国际舞台上的地位和作用日益重要。积极参与国际规则制定、参与全球经济治理,不仅是实现中华民族伟大复兴之中国梦的重要战略选择,而且也是满足国际社会希望中国在重塑国际经济新秩序过程中发挥更大作用的需要。

中国新一届党和国家领导人高度重视这项工作。习近平总书记在出任国家主席后的第一次对非访问中,就明确提出要推动建设全球发展伙伴关系、加强宏观经济政策协调、共同参与国际发展议程制定、推动国际秩序朝着更加公正合理的方向发展等倡议。[186]之后他在各种场合多次强调中国要全面参与国际规则制定、参与全球经济治理。

2014年7月,在出席金砖国家领导人第六次会晤,对巴西、阿根廷、委内瑞拉、古巴进行国事访问并出席中国—拉美和加勒比国家领导人会晤的前夕,习近平主席接受了巴西《经济价值报》、阿根廷《国民报》、委内瑞拉国家通讯社和古巴拉丁美洲通讯社的联合采访,就中国的国际作用回答记者的提问时,进一步承诺中国"将更加积极有为地参与国际事务,致力于推动完善国际治理体系,积极推动扩大发展中国家在国际事务中的代表性和发言权","将更多提出中国方案、贡献中国智慧,为国际社会提供更多公共产品"。[187]

2014年12月,习近平总书记在中共中央政治局第19次集体学习中指出,中国"是经济全球化的积极参与者和坚定支持者,也是重要建设者和主要受益者"。对于参与国际经贸规则制定、争取全球经济治理的制度性权力,中国"不能当旁观者、跟随者,而是要做参与者、引领者","在国际规则制定中发出更多中国声音、注入更多中国元素"。[188]

---

[186] 参见《习近平在金砖国家领导人第五次会晤时的主旨讲话(全文)》,http://politics.people.com.cn/n/2013/0328/c1001-20941062.html。

[187] 参见《习近平接受拉美四国媒体联合采访》,http://news.xinhuanet.com/world/2014-07/15/c_126752272.htm。

[188] 参见《加快实施自由贸易区战略 加快构建开放型经济新体制》,http://politics.people.com.cn/n/2014/1207/c1024-26161390.html。

从加入世界贸易组织以来,中国无论在学术研究方面,还是在政策实践方面,对参与国际经贸规则制定的认识和重视都还很不够,甚至还存在不同的看法,归纳起来可以分为"阶段参与论""能力不足论"和"避免麻烦论"等观点。[189]陈安教授对于现行的世界贸易组织体制和规则,以及中国参与国际经贸规则制定的问题一直有他自己的独立思考和鲜明观点,早在2010年便在他纪念中国加入世界贸易组织10周年的论文中作了全面的阐述,提出了立法、执法、守法和变法的辩证关系。[190]陈安教授在坚持国际经济关系必须力行法治的基础上,深入地剖析了国际经济立法中决策权力分配不公的事实,指出由此而形成全球财富分配严重不公的后果,即发达国家主导国际经贸规则的制定权,发展中国家权益严重受损。所以,中国和广大发展中国家弱势群体既要在现行的多边贸易机制中"守法"和"适法",熟悉运行规则,争取为我所用,最大限度地趋利避害;又要在实践中明辨是非,系统排查现行体制中对国际弱势群体明显不利和显失公正公平的条款、规则,研究探索变革方向,通过"南南联合",推行"变法图强",促使多边贸易体制和规则与时俱进,造福全球。

事实上,现行国际经贸体系主要是在20世纪40年代以后,在美欧等西方发达国家的主导下建立起来的,首先体现和维护的是西方国家的利益和价值。这些国际规则不仅没有考虑中国和其他发展中国家的实际情况,而且有些规则还是专门针对中国和一些发展中国家的,最为典型的例子就是所谓的"特殊保障条款",以及在贸易补救条款下的"非市场经济"地位。随着经济全球化的深入发展,现行国际经贸体系已经不能很好地适应新的国际经济格局。中国与世界的关系在发生变化,中国同国际社会的联动更加密切,中国和平发展追求的不仅是中国人民的福祉,也是世界人民共同的福祉,所以必须统筹考虑和综合运用国际国内两个市场、国际国内两种资源、国际国内两类规则。

陈安教授心怀报国之志,以强烈的学术使命感,长期奋战在国际经济法教学和研究的道路上,独立思考,积极探索,先后在国内外发表了一系列重要的学术论文和论著,包括"国际经济法学系列专著"、《国际经济法总论》和《陈安论国际经济法学》等鸿篇力作,为发展完善具有中国特色的国际经济法学做出了巨大的贡献。英文专著《中国的呐喊》的出版,不仅让国际社会听到了中国的声音,而且也正式揭开了中国学者全面系统地参与国际经济法学研究交流的序幕。

---

[189] 参见赵龙跃:《中国参与国际规则制定的问题与对策》,载《人民论坛·学术前沿》2012年第16期,第84—94页。

[190] See An Chen, Some Jurisprudential Thoughts upon WTO's Law-Governing, Law-Making, Law-Enforcing, Law-Abiding, and Law-Reforming, in An Chen, *The Voice from China: An CHEN on International Economic Law*, Springer, 2013, pp. 241-269.

在参与国际规则制定、构建新的国际经济秩序的过程中,发展中国家与发达国家必然会发生一些利益上的摩擦和碰撞。西方国家极力维护现存的体现其利益的经济秩序,发展中国家希望建立新的更加公平合理的国际经济秩序,改变全球资源和财富分配不合理的现状。围绕新制度的设计和相关规则的制定,南北方国家之间的斗争是非常激烈和复杂的,在国际经济法学界也出现了"新自由主义经济秩序"论、"WTO 宪政秩序"论和"经济民族主义扰乱全球化秩序"论等理论误区。陈安教授在《中国的呐喊》一书中,对这些西方理论界的误区逐一地进行了分析批判,并呼吁中国在构建国际经济新秩序中要发挥领导作用,坚持和平发展、合作共赢的原则,推动国际经济新秩序和国际经济法体制的新老交替,实现世界共同繁荣。[191]

随着经济全球化的不断深化,国家主权原则是否过时,成为当代国际法学界另一重大的理论和实践问题。20 世纪 90 年代前后,西方国家凭借自身经济实力的优势,出现了种种否定和淡化国家主权的思潮,美国国际公法专家、曾任美国国际法学会会长的路易斯·汉金教授就曾提出"主权过时论"和"主权有害论"。世界贸易组织成立以后,美国国会担心加入世界贸易组织可能影响美国的国家主权,从而引发了美国法学界关于国家主权的大辩论。美国另一位国际经济法学专家、被誉为"世界贸易组织之父"的约翰·杰克逊教授则提出所谓的"现代主权论"和"主权有效论",他认为传统主权的核心没有过时,仍然有效,现代主权的核心是权力的分配问题。[192]陈安教授对于美国的这场"主权大辩论"进行了深入的研究和分析,发现汉金教授的"主权过时论"和杰克逊教授的"主权有效论"貌似相反,实则相成:都是为了限制其他国家的主权,而维护美国的霸权地位。[193]

当我看到《中国的呐喊》第四章的时候,就不由地想起陈安教授与约翰·杰克逊教授就国家主权问题的一次面对面的精彩辩论,那是 2005 年在美国首都华盛顿,美国国际法学会举办的"国际贸易与和平、自由、安全"国际研讨会上。陈安教授是受邀出席该研讨会的第一位演讲嘉宾,他提交的论文就是《综合评析美国单边主义与

---

[191] See An Chen, What Should Be China's Strategic Position in the Establishment of New International Economic Order? With Comments on Neoliberalistic Economic Order, Constitutional Order of the WTO, and Economic Nationalism's Disturbance of Globalization, in An Chen, *The Voice from China: An CHEN on International Economic Law*, Springer, 2013, pp. 167-206.

[192] 参见〔美〕约翰·杰克逊:《国家主权与 WTO 变化中的国际法基础》,赵龙跃、左海聪、盛建明译,社会科学文献出版社 2009 年版,第 65—93 页。

[193] See An Chen, On the Implications for Developing Countries of "the Great 1994 Sovereignty Debate" and the EC-US Economic Sovereignty Disputes, in An Chen, *The Voice from China: An CHEN on International Economic Law*, Springer, 2013, pp. 159-163.

WTO多边主义交锋的三大回合》。[194]陈教授从美国随意使用"201条款"和"301条款"等国内贸易法规出发,揭示了美国实行单边贸易保护主义不仅是WTO多边贸易机制所面临的挑战,而且直接影响世界的和平、自由与安全。美国1994年主权大辩论的实质就是维护美国的霸权主义,限制其他国家的主权,从而将美国的主权和利益凌驾于其他国家和国际组织之上。陈教授的精彩演讲给当时在美国乔治敦大学任职的我以及与会的各国专家学者留下了深刻的印象,也使我有幸与陈安教授结下了忘年之交的深厚友谊。

实现中华民族伟大复兴的中国梦,积极参与国际规则制定和全球经济治理,推动完善国际机制,建立公正合理的国际经济新秩序,需要中国社会各界的努力合作。陈安教授耄耋之年,笔耕不辍,博览中外,厚积薄发,向世界国际经济法学界发出了代表中国的呐喊,不仅为国际社会了解中国国际经济法学的主流思想和价值取向提供了途径;为传播中华文化的先进思想和理念、建立完善中国国际经济法学派做出了杰出贡献;而且也为促进中外学术交流、丰富完善国际经济法理论做出了杰出贡献,堪为我们晚辈努力学习的楷模。

(编辑:龚 宇)

A Pioneer in "Providing China's Proposal and Contributing China's Wisdom"[*]
—Review on *The Voice from China*:*An CHEN on International Economic Law*

Zhao Longyue[**]

Professor An Chen of Xiamen University has recently published an English book *The Voice from China*:*An CHEN on International Economic Law*, which is distributed globally by Springer, a Germany press with high reputation in the

---

[194] See An Chen, The Three Big Rounds of US Unilateralism Versus WTO Multilateralism During the Last Decade: A Combined Analysis of the Great 1994 Sovereignty Debate Section 301 Disputes (1998-2000) and Section 201 Disputes (2002-2003), in An Chen, *The Voice from China*:*An CHEN on International Economic Law*, Springer, 2013, pp. 103-158.

[*] Xi Jinping Was Interviewed by the Media from Four Countries in Latin America, http://news.xinhuanet.com/world/2014-07/15/c_126752272.htm.

[**] Professor of Nankai University, Adjunct Professor of Georgetown University and the World Bank Consultant.

international academic circle. That should be greatly admired. As a leading magnate in China's international economic law and jurisprudential circle, the octogenarian, Professor An Chen has never stopped writing and been insisting on making contributions to our country with knowledge, who is an excellent model. The book complies with the requirements of peaceful development in China, particularly ponders such significant problems as the basic theory of international economic law, the debate on modern economic sovereignty and the strategic position of China in building a new international economic order, etc. and presents numerous feasible policy suggestions from the perspective of active participation in making international rules and global governance. Basing on the China's national conditions and the requirements of maintaining legal interests of developing countries, Professor An Chen is well versed in both Chinese and western learning, develops a school of his own and plays an important role in assisting China in participating in making international rules and building a new international economic order from the perspective of perfecting international economic law, who will be a Chinese pioneer in "Providing China's Proposal and Contributing China's Wisdom" for the international society.

In the wake of the in-depth development of economic globalization, international political and economic pattern is undergoing profound changes, China and other developing countries play an increasingly important position and role on international stage. The proactive participation in making international rules and global economic governance is not only an important strategic choice achieving Chinese dream of bringing about a great rejuvenation of the Chinese nation, but also a desire satisfying the international society that hopes China to play a greater role in rebuilding a new international economic order.

The new Chinese Party and State leaders have attached great importance to the work. The Party General Secretary Xi Jinping explicitly put forward suggestions in the aspects of promoting and constructing global development partnership, strengthening macroeconomic policy coordination, jointly participating in making international development agenda and driving international order toward a more just and rational direction during his first visit to Africa after he was elected as the president. [195]

---

[195] See Xi Jinping's Speech in the Fifth Summit of BRICS Leaders, http://politics.people.com.cn/n/2013/0328/c1001-20941062.html.

Afterwards, he has stressed that China should comprehensively participate in making international rules and global economic governance for several times in different occasions.

Chinese President Xi Jinping received the joint interview of Brazil *Valor Economico*, Argentina *National Newspaper*, Venezuela news agency and Cuba Latin America news agency on the previous day of attending the 6th summit of BRICS leaders for official visit to Brazil, Argentina, Venezuela and Cuba and attending the leaders' summit between China-Latin America and Caribbean countries in July, 2014. When answering the question of journalist about China's international role, he made a further commitment that China would further proactively participate in international affairs and perfecting international governance system, promote and enlarge the representative right and speaking right of developing countries in international affairs, present more Chinese schemes and contribute more Chinese wisdom and provide more public products for the international society.[196]

The Party General Secretary Xi Jinping indicated in the 19th collective learning of CPC Central Committee Political Bureau in December, 2014 that China is the active participant and firmed supporter and also the main constructer and beneficiary of economic globalization. China may act as a participator and leader rather than an onlooker and follower with regard to the institutional power participating in making international economic and trade rules and seeking for global economic governance. China may present more suggestions and implant more Chinese elements in making international rules.[197]

Since accessing to the WTO, China has not paid enough attention to the participation in making international trade and economic rules either in the aspect of academic research or policy practice. There were even various different views such as "theory of participation by stages", "theory of scarce capacity" and "theory of avoiding trouble", etc.[198] As for the existing WTO systems and rules and the

---

[196] See Xi Jinping Was Interviewed by the Media in Four Countries from Latin America, http://news.xinhuanet.com/world/2014-07/15/c_126752272.htm.

[197] See Accelerate Implementing Strategy of Free Trade Zone and Building New Open Economy System, http://politics.people.com.cn/n/2014/1207/c1024-26161390.html.

[198] See Zhao Longyue, Problems and Countermeasures of China's Participation in Making International Rules, *People's Tribune · Academic Frontiers*, No. 16, 2012, pp. 84-94.

problem regarding China's participating in making international economic and trade rules, Professor An Chen has his own independent thoughts and distinct viewpoints. He has comprehensively expounded the dialectical relationship between legislation, enforcement, law-abiding and law-reforming in the paper in memory of 10th anniversary of China's accessing to the WTO as early as in 2010.[199] On the basis of performing laws in international economic relationship, Professor Chen deeply dissected the fact of maldistribution in decision-making power in international economic legislation and pointed out the consequence of serious maldistribution in global wealth, namely the developed countries dominate the right of making international trade and economic rules and the rights and interests of developing countries are seriously damaged. China and the vulnerable groups in developing countries shall "abide by laws" and "make laws" in existing multilateral trading system and use the operation rules for ourselves and draw on advantages and avoid disadvantages to the maximum extent. They shall also distinguish right from wrong, systematically survey the articles and rules obviously disadvantageous to international weak groups and losing just and fair in existing system, explore and study the reform directions and promote the multilateral trade systems and rules to keep pace with the times and benefit the world through "South-South" Coalition and "law-reforming".

In fact, the existing international economic and trade system was built after 1940s under the leading of western developed countries inclusive of America and European countries, giving priority to safeguarding of benefits and value of western countries. These international rules do not take the actual conditions of China and developing countries into account, and also some rules especially direct at China and some developing countries. The most typical example is the so-called "special safeguards measures" and "non-market economy" position under trade remedy terms. Along with the in-depth development of economic globalization, the existing international economic and trade system can not well adapt to the new international economic pattern. The relationship between China and the world has been

---

[199] See An Chen, Some Jurisprudential Thoughts upon WTO's Law-Governing, Law-Making, Law-Enforcing, Law-Abiding, and Law-Reforming, in An Chen, *The Voice from China: An CHEN on International Economic Law*, Springer, 2013, pp. 241-269.

changing, and the linkage between China and international society is more frequent. What the peaceful development China pursues is not only the well-being of Chinese, but also the well-being of the world's people. Therefore, it shall overall consider and comprehensively utilize international and national markets, resources and rules.

With the will of serving the country and strong academic sense of mission, Professor An Chen has fought in the teaching and research road of international economic law for a long time. Upon independent thinking and proactive exploration, he has published a series of important academic papers and works successively at home and abroad, including Monographs of International Economic Law Series, *Pandect of International Economic Law* and *An CHEN on International Economic Law*, etc. He has made great contributions to developing and perfecting international economic law with Chinese characteristics. The English book of *The Voice from China* not only makes the international society hear Chinese voice, but also officially ushers the Chinese scholars comprehensively and schematically in participating the research and communication of international economic law.

Some interest frictions and collisions will certainly occur between the developing countries and developed countries during the process of participating in making international rules and constructing a new international economic order. The western countries make an utmost effort to maintain the existing economic order representing their benefits, while the developing countries are willing to build a fair and rational new international economic order to change the unreasonable distribution of global resources and wealth. The Southern and Northern countries fight intensively and complexly centering about the design of new systems and the making of relevant rules. The theoretical misunderstandings of "Neoliberalistic Economic Order", "Constitutional Order of the WTO" and "Economic Nationalism's Disturbance of Globalization" also exist in international economic jurisprudential circle. Professor An Chen seriatim analyzes and criticizes the misunderstandings in western theory field in this book, and appeals to China playing a leading role in building a new international economic order, insisting on the principle of peaceful development and win-win cooperation, driving the alternation of new international economic order and international economic law system and achieving co-prosperity in the world.[200]

Along with the deepening of economic globalization, whether the principle of state sovereignty is behind the times has become another important theory and practice problem in modern international jurisprudential circle. Before or after 1990s, the ideological trend of negating and fading state sovereignty appeared in western countries by virtue of their own economic strength. Professor Louis Henkin, an expert in American public international law and the former president of American Society of International Law has ever presented "a theory of outmoded sovereignty" and "a theory of harmful sovereignty". After setting up the WTO, United States Congress worried about influencing state sovereignty after accessing to the WTO, hereby giving rise to a mass debate about state sovereignty in American jurisprudential circle. Another American expert in international economic law, John Jackson with the reputation of "Father of the WTO" presented the so-called "modern theory of sovereignty" and "theory of effective sovereignty". In his opinion, the core of traditional state sovereignty is not outmoded and the core of modern state sovereignty is the power distribution.[201] Professor An Chen deeply researched and analyzed the "mass debate about sovereignty", discovering that Henkin's "theory of outmoded sovereignty" and Jackson's "theory of effective sovereignty" are opposite in appearance, while complementary in reality: both theories are presented to limit the sovereignty of other countries and safeguard the hegemony position of America.[202]

While reading Chapter IV of *The Voice from China*, I can't help thinking of the face-to-face and wonderful debate between Professor An Chen and Professor John Jackson about state sovereignty in the international conference on International Trade and Peace, Freedom and Security held by American Society of International

---

[200] See An Chen, What Should Be China's Strategic Position in the Establishment of New International Economic Order? With Comments on Neoliberalistic Economic Order, Constitutional Order of the WTO, and Economic Nationalism's Disturbance of Globalization, in An Chen, *The Voice from China: An CHEN on International Economic Law*, Springer, 2013, pp. 167-206.

[201] See John H. Jackson, *Sovereignty, the WTO, and Changing Fundamentals of International Law*, Cambridge University Press, 2006. Chinese version of this book is translated by Zhao Longyue, Zuo Haicong and Sheng Jianming, Social Sciences Academic Press, November, 2009, pp. 65-93.

[202] See An Chen, On the Implications for Developing Countries of "the Great 1994 Sovereignty Debate" and the EC-US Economic Sovereignty Disputes, in An Chen, *The Voice from China: An CHEN on International Economic Law*, Springer, 2013, pp. 159-163.

Law in Washington D. C. in 2005. Professor Chen is the first speaker to give a presentation in the conference. The paper he submitted is "The Three Big Rounds of US Unilateralism Versus the WTO Multilateralism During the Last Decade".[203] Professor Chen revealed that the unilateral trade protectionism of the United States not only threatened WTO multilateralism trade mechanism, but also directly influenced the peace, freedom and security of the world by taking the random use of "Article 201", "Article 301" and other domestic trade laws. The essence of sovereignty debate in 1994 is safeguarding the American hegemonism, limiting the sovereignty of other countries and outmatching American sovereignty and benefits above other countries and international organizations. The splendid speech of Professor Chen made a profound impression on me and the experts and scholars from different countries attending the conference. Since then, I have the honor to be a close friend of Professor Chen in spite of the big difference of age.

All sectors of society in China shall cooperate to achieve the Chinese dream of bringing about a great rejuvenation of the Chinese nation, proactively participate in making international rules and global economic governance, driving the perfection of international mechanism and building a fair and reasonable new international economic order. The octogenarian, Professor An Chen has never stopped writing whilst has been accumulating knowledge in China and foreign countries and uttering a voice to the circle of international economic law on behalf of China, not only providing channels for international society to understand the mainstream ideology and value orientation in China's international economic law and making great contributions to spreading advanced ideology and ideas in Chinese culture and to build China's own school of international economic law, but also making great contributions to promoting academic communication between China and foreign countries and enriching and perfecting the theories in international economic law. He is an excellent model from whom the young generations should learn.

（翻译：赵龙跃）

---

[203] See An Chen, The Three Big Rounds of US Unilateralism Versus WTO Multilateralism During the Last Decade: A Combined Analysis of the Great 1994 Sovereignty Debate Section 301 Disputes (1998-2000) and Section 201 Disputes (2002-2003), in An Chen, *The Voice from China: An CHEN on International Economic Law*, Springer, 2013, pp. 103-158.

七、追求全球正义　抵制国际霸权*

〔韩〕李庸中**

小　引

陈安教授经过长期刻苦钻研,完成了鸿篇巨著,邀请我撰写书评。对我而言,为这样一位令人敬仰的学者撰写书评,是喜出望外的殊荣。第一次见到陈安教授,可以回溯到 2011 年。当时,经蔡从燕教授推荐,我代表韩国《东亚与国际法学刊》(*Journal of East Asia and International Law*),专程前往厦门采访陈安教授。采访在厦门大学法学院的大楼进行。我还记得,厦门大学法学院靠近景色优美的海滨,整个厦门大学法学院的气氛非常专业化,稳重温文,具有合作精神。陈安教授和厦门大学法学院的其他教师如陈辉萍教授,以及陈安教授亲切和善的女儿陈仲洵的热情接待,给我留下深刻的印象,令我有宾至如归之感。我走进宽敞的会面房间,就看到陈安教授已经带着温暖的笑容在等我。我立刻意识到他是一位名副其实的学者,是一位具有深厚美德的"士",善于以其无比顽强的力量对抗任何压制真理(veritas)的行为。在我诚挚问候之后,他谦逊且友好地说:"李博士！我们之间有两个共同之处。首先,中国和韩国都曾经遭受日本军国主义的侵略。其次,我和你都推崇孔儒之道,因为你的名字'庸中'与一部儒家经典著作《中庸》密切相关。"确实如此,我们之间的会面访谈也正是在这些共识的基础上积极地展开的。

陈安教授在采访过程中提到的许多有趣故事,深深地吸引了我(整个采访的问答记录刊登在英文版《东亚与国际法学刊》第 4 卷第 2 期,并被辑入《中国的呐喊:陈安论国际经济法》(以下简称《中国的呐喊》)这本书的导言部分[204])。作为中国国际经济法的旗手学者,他具有卓越的才华和坚守的原则,思维清晰,博闻广识,严谨缜密,充满智慧。他对国际法的重要性具有深刻厚实的理解。

---

* 本篇书评对本书作者个人的学术理念、独到观点和学术创新加以全面概括,写得比较简明扼要和重点突出,故特同时移置于本书第一卷,作为"导言 I",冀能便于许多青年读者对照阅读中英双语文本,从中受益;也便于日后出版书评单行本时加以剪裁。请参看本书末"后记"第三点和第四点的说明。

** 李庸中(Eric Yong Joong Lee),韩国东国大学法学院教授,李僑(YIYUN)国际法研究院院长,《东亚与国际法学刊》(*Journal of East Asia and International Law*)主编。

[204] See A Dialogue with Judicial Wisdom, Prof. An CHEN: A Flag-Holder Chinese Scholar Advocating Reform of International Economic Law, *Journal of East Asia and International Law*, Vol. 4, No. 2, pp. 477-502; An Chen, *The Voice from China: An CHEN on International Economic Law*, Springer, 2014, pp. xxxi-lviii.

在我回到韩国之后，我们之间一直保持频繁的联系。2014年，陈安教授邀请我为《中国的呐喊》一书撰写书评。一开始我有所犹豫，因为我觉得自己不够资格为这样一位我从心底深深敬佩的杰出学者的著作撰写书评，这将会是我要承担的最艰难的任务之一。然而，最后我还是接受了陈安教授的提议，因为我觉得我有责任祝贺他把自己的学术主张传播到国际社会。我的评论本身也许并非对这一著作的确切评价，但我的粗浅评说却表达了一位年轻外国学者对作者的仰慕和敬意。

作者简介

陈安教授在1929年5月出生于福建省东北部的一个小山村，在其成长过程中，很大程度上受到父亲的影响和教育。他的父亲是位儒家学者和诗人，1945年辞世。1946年，17岁的陈安教授考进厦门大学开始学习法律。此后，由于历史的原因，自1953年起他的法学学习和研究令人遗憾地中断了27年，直到1980年厦门大学法学院重新建立。那时，陈安教授已经五十来岁。他敏锐地意识到中国不仅需要建立国内法律体系，而且，由于中国开始实施对外开放的战略，还需要有自己的国际经济法体系。陈安教授决定专注从事国际经济法的研究。然而，在那个时代，中国缺乏现代的法律教科书，更遑论有关国际经济法的各种文献。1981年，一个偶然的机会，陈安教授遇到美国的Jerome Cohen教授并与之就学术观点展开争论，最后，陈安教授被邀请到哈佛大学继续从事法学研究。从此之后，他利用所有到国外访问和参加学术会议的机会，带回大量相关的英文书籍和资料。辑入《中国的呐喊》一书的一系列专论就是其研究的主要成果。它们反映了陈安教授严谨的学术素养、爱国主义情怀和历史责任感。陈安教授是"新中国国际经济法学的奠基人之一"，他的学术生涯和中国改革开放的国策息息相关。在法学实践中，他又是一名国际商事领域的律师，多家跨国企业的法律顾问，同时还是ICSID、ICC、IAI和RIA的仲裁员。

除了国际经济法，陈安教授还爱好诗歌、文学和书法艺术。在东亚，一名完美的学者通常都有这些方面的修养。他性格温和、热心，有勇往直前的信念。他经历了中国被外国占领、内战和社会革命的历程。所有这些，都不能阻止他对人类社会真理、公平的追求。甚至可以说，这些磨难帮助他在中国学术乃至国际学术上达到难以超越的高峰。陈安教授经常论证对人类社会和平以及共同繁荣的崇高追求，不失为我们这个时代的一位杰出的良师益友。

著作内容

《中国的呐喊》这部专著，汇辑了陈安教授在过去30多年所撰写的24篇英文论文,是陈安教授从 1980 年开始多年从事国际经济法学术研究的代表作。这本书涵盖了中国所面临的有关国际经济法的许多疑难问题。在该书中,这 24 篇文章被分为 6 部分:当代国际经济法的法理;当代经济主权论;中国在当代国际经济秩序中的战略定位;当代双边投资条约;中国的涉外经济立法;当代中国在国际经济争端解决中的实践。各部分的内容相互联结并保持良好平衡。陈安教授的法理观念和学术见解在许多方面不苟同于美国和欧洲国际法研究的主流观点。《中国的呐喊》这本著作的出版具有相当重大的意义,因为它打造了中国在国际经济法领域话语权的坚实基础。通过陈安教授周全深入的研究,中国开始在世界上发出自己的声音,表达自己的理念。从这个意义上说,《中国的呐喊》这一标题有相当深刻的喻义。除了学术内容精彩独到之外,这本书由久负盛名的斯普林格出版社负责出版,编辑加工十分专业,装帧精美,封面设计也很典雅大方,值得称道。

"黄祸"论(Yellow Peril)

中国对于西方来说一直是个神秘的国度。其主要原因在于中国具有广阔的疆土,大量的人口,漫长的历史和古老的文明,现代的共产主义理念,而且在 1978 年之前一直坚持闭关锁国的政策。但是,更关键的是,在西方人思想的深处,曾经不知不觉地根植了所谓"黄祸"论的传言。最近,这种思想又从他们的潜意识中悄悄爬出来,进入真实的世界,变成为一个恶毒的说法,即"中国威胁"论。在《中国的呐喊》第三章,陈安教授分析了"黄祸"论以及其现代变种"中国威胁"论的起源、演变和在国际社会的法律意义。一些中国学者似乎也同样意识到这两个概念之间的历史联系。例如,中山大学陈东教授指出:"'中国威胁'论并非是在过去二十年才出现的新的概念。它可以回溯到 19 世纪,例如,在沙俄时代米哈伊尔·巴枯宁撰写的《国家制度与无政府状态》一书中,就谈到了'来自东方(中国)的巨大和可怕的威胁'。德皇威廉二世制作的形象漫画《欧洲人啊,保卫你们的信仰和家园》,就描述了 19 世纪末欧洲人对中国的普遍看法。"[205]陈东教授还指出:"'黄祸'论的根源在于一些欧洲人将黄色面孔的中国人视为'不文明的'和愚蠢的破坏者,他们对西方的'文明社会'可能造成巨大的威胁。"[206]

然而,单凭这种历史回溯的方法,往往还不是认识现今"中国威胁"论的关键所在。当代美国霸权版的"中国威胁"论最早出现在 20 世纪 90 年代中叶,其主要鼓吹

---

[205] Dong Chen, Who Threatens Whom? The "Chinese Treat" and the Bush Doctrine, *Journal of East Asia and International Law*, Vol. 7, 2014, p.32.

[206] Ibid.

者是布什政府下的美国政客和学者。到了 21 世纪的最初几年,这一谰言开始变得相当尖锐刺耳。看来当时布什政府是刻意地杜撰出"中国威胁"论这个口号,意在阻止经济和政治影响力迅速增长的中国进一步扩展,影响到亚洲—太平洋地区,以便于美国全盘统治东亚。对当时唯一的"超级大国"美国而言,中国可能是美国在这一地区军事和经济霸权主义的潜在威胁。"中国威胁"论正是在此种权力交替的国际环境中产生。"中国威胁"论可能不是"黄祸"论在当代的简单转型,因为"黄祸"论主要是欧洲人在特定环境下的看法,"黄祸"论的产生实际上起源于 13 世纪蒙古人入侵欧洲后,欧洲人面对黄色脸孔的中国人和中国文明产生的根深蒂固的自卑情绪。因此,"黄色"一词可能不是指亚洲人皮肤的颜色,它指的是蒙古骑兵在入侵过程中掀起的黄色沙暴。对当时的欧洲人而言,他们是魔鬼,只有全能的上帝能战胜他们。

这一假设在陈东教授的《谁在威胁谁?"中国威胁"论和布什政策》一文中得到很好的论证。陈东教授认为,布什政府抱有"单极世界的梦想"可以解释"中国威胁"论的来由。[207] 陈东教授引用伊肯贝利撰写的论文《美国的帝国野心》,指出,美国人将布什的政策视为"美国能保持单极世界从而没有任何竞争者的宏伟战略",但这有可能造成"世界更加危险和分裂,因此也会威胁到美国的安全"。[208] 陈东教授还特别援引福音教派的理论作为论证布什政策的基础。他认为,"中国威胁"论是布什构建以美国为中心的单极世界的实用工具。[209]

陈安教授在《中国的呐喊》一书中对前述布什政策下的种种"中国威胁"论作了概括总结。陈安教授认为:

> 它们是美国出现的层次最高、频率最繁、影响最大的美国官方版的"黄祸"论——"中国威胁"论。它们是美国国会、美国国防部、美国高层智囊"三结合"产物。美国国防部门的部门利益昭然若揭……(苏联解体)和冷战结束后,对于始终保持着"古怪癖好"的惯性思维的美国人而言……他们需要找到(苏联以外)另一个明确的、强大的新"威胁",而中国正好就是美国人一向极力虚构的危及美国安全的新的"严重威胁"。[210]

我十分赞同陈安教授对"中国威胁"论的看法,即"中国威胁"论就是"21 世纪美

---

[207] Dong Chen, Who Threatens Whom? The "Chinese Treat" and the Bush Doctrine, *Journal of East Asia and International Law*, Vol. 7, 2014, pp. 39-40.

[208] G. Ikenberry, America's Imperial Ambitions, *Foreign Affairs*, Vol. 81, 2002, p. 44.

[209] Dong Chen, Who Threatens Whom? The "Chinese Treat" and the Bush Doctrine, *Journal of East Asia and International Law*, Vol. 7, 2014, pp. 42-43.

[210] An Chen, *The Voice from China: An CHEN on International Economic Law*, Springer, 2014, pp. 64-65.另参见陈安:《评"黄祸"论的本源、本质及其最新霸权"变种":"中国威胁"论》,载《现代法学》2011 年第 6 期,第 20—21 页。

国霸权最新修订版的"黄祸"论,它体现为美国"鹰派"反华议员每年一度集中渲染"中国威胁"的《中国军力报告》,美中经济与安全审议委员会的《审议报告》,以及各种媒体的呼应鼓噪。[211]

经济主权

在《中国的呐喊》一书的第四章和第五章,陈安教授探讨了更为根本性的经济主权问题。随着经济全球化和各国间互相依存性的增强,单个国家的经济主权成为论战的焦点之一。陈安教授对WTO的多边主义和美国的单边主义作了对比分析。他非常精彩地比较分析了美国汉金教授和杰克逊教授关于美国单边主义和WTO多边主义的不同观点。他引用许多相关案例批判美国单边主义凌驾于其他国家主权之上。他的分析和评论有意识地涵盖《美国贸易法》中的201条款和301条款,WTO体系形成过程中的各种主权冲突,美国国内的1994年主权大辩论,美国的主权和其他国家的主权之间的关系,美国与欧盟之间经济主权的争夺,美国与日本之间的汽车争端,美国与欧盟之间的香蕉争端,WTO争端解决机构针对美国301条款的专家组报告等。

陈安教授探讨了多边体制时代各主权国家合作协调的问题。他的观点谅必建立在中国过往历史经验的基础上,包括被列强侵占的灾难和国内战争的痛楚,这些灾难和痛楚陈安教授都曾经亲身经历过。我完全赞同陈安教授的观点。绝大多数亚洲国家都曾经一度沦为殖民地,对亚洲人说来,"主权"不应该是个虚构的神话,它是民族自决的现实。

结 论

陈安教授《中国的呐喊》一书,无论对中国、整个亚洲,还是对国际社会,都是一项重大的成就和贡献。此书追求和论证的目标是,国家间应当在公平和均衡的基础上开展经济合作。这本著作的核心和焦点可以概括为:为世界群弱呐喊,追求全球正义,抵制国际霸权。

这也是"了解中国"系列专著的出发点,即从建立国际经济新秩序的角度来理解和看待中国。对于今后愿意追随陈安教授的学术界人士和实务工作者而言,《中国的呐喊》将会成为杰出的范本。就我而言,我正处在陈安教授开始从事国际法研究的年龄。他不渝不懈的努力和学术热情会一直激励着亚洲乃至全球的国际法工作

---

[211] See An Chen, *The Voice from China: An CHEN on International Economic Law*, Springer, 2014, pp. 67-68. 另参见陈安:《评"黄祸"论的本源、本质及其最新霸权"变种":"中国威胁"论》,载《现代法学》2011年第6期,第22页。

者。陈安教授的精神也一直鼓舞我保持永无止境的求知欲。无论何时,我都热切地期待未来新的一卷《中国的呐喊》问世。由于陈安教授老当益壮,依然矍铄健朗,我希望新书的出版不会等待太久。在这里,我再次对《中国的呐喊》一书出版,表达发自内心的深深的祝贺之忱。

(翻译、编辑:陈　欣)

Pursuing Global Justice Resisting International Hegemony

Eric Yong Joong Lee[*]

Introduction

It is an incredible honor for me to have this opportunity to review the product of a long and painstaking research conducted by an honorable scholar like Professor An Chen. My first encounter with Professor Chen traces back to 2011 when I visited Xiamen in order to interview him for the *Journal of East Asia and International Law* with the recommendation of Professor Congyan Cai. The interview was held in the building of School of Law, Xiamen University which is close to the coast of the beautiful ocean. The atmosphere of the School of Law was very professional, gentle and cooperative. I was fully impressed by the warmhearted hospitality of Professor Chen and other staff members of including Professor Huiping Chen and Professor Chen's lovely daughter Carol. It made me feel at home. When I entered the wide room for the interview, Professor Chen was waiting with his gentle smile. I could instantly recognize he is a true scholar and a man of immense virtue(士)with the invincible power against anything suppressing "veritas"(真理). After my deeply felt greetings, he modestly and friendly said: "Dr. Lee, We are sharing two common things. First, both of us(China and Korea)have suffered severely from Japanese militarism. Second, we(Professor Chen and Lee)in common respect Confucius, considering that your name Yong Joong(庸中)is related to one of the holy books of Confucius. The relating specific holy book is named with '中庸'

---

[*] Professor of Dongguk University College of Law, President of YIJUN Institute of International Law, Editor-in-Chief of the *Journal of East Asia and International Law*.

(Chinese pronounced as Zhong Yong)." Indeed, our interview started on a positive note based on these commonalities. Professor Chen spoke about many interesting stories during the interview sufficient to enthrall me (The transcript of the whole interview has been published in volume 4, number 2 of the *Journal of East Asia and International Law* as well as in the introduction section of *The Voice from China*[212]). As a flag-holder Chinese scholar of international economic law, he is a man of exceptional brilliance and principles with clear, broad, rigorous thinking and wisdom. He has a profound understanding of the importance of international law.

Since my return home, we have maintained frequent contact with each other. In 2014, Professor Chen requested me to review *The Voice from China*. I was hesitant at first because I thought I was not entitled to comment on something by an outstanding scholar whom I respect from the bottom of my heart. It would thus be one of the most difficult tasks I have endured. However, I finally decided to accept his proposal because it would be my duty to celebrate his voice toward the global community. My review may not contain an evaluation per se, but my humble comments as a young foreign scholar admiring the author.

The Author

Professor Chen was born in May, 1929 in a small mountainous town in northeast Fujian Province, China and grew up there profoundly influenced and educated by his father who was a Confucian scholar and poet, dying in 1945. He began studying law at Xiamen University in 1946 when he was 17 years old. Due to historical reasons, his legal studies were unfortunately interrupted for 27 years until 1980 when the Law School of Xiamen University was reestablished. By that time, he was already in his fifties. He had the keen insight to recognize that China would need to establish not only its domestic legal regime, but also international (economic) law, especially when China opened up to the world. Professor Chen decided to focus on international economic law (IEL). At that time, however, there were few modern legal reference texts in China, not to mention IEL literature. In

---

[212] See A Dialogue with Judicial Wisdom, Prof. An CHEN: A Flag-Holder Chinese Scholar Advocating Reform of International Economic Law, *Journal of East Asia and International Law*, Vol. 4, No. 2, pp. 477-502; An Chen, *The Voice from China: An CHEN on International Economic Law*, Springer, 2014, pp. xxxi-lviii.

1981, he occasionally met and argued with Professor Jerome Cohen and was finally invited to Harvard Law School to continue his legal studies. Afterwards, he took all opportunities of travelling abroad for conferences and visits to bring back relevant books and articles in English. The series works of *The Voice from China* are the main products of his research. They reflects his academic rigor, patriotism and historical responsibility. Professor Chen is "one of the founders of international economic law in new China" and his academic life is closely connected with reform and opening up. In his legal practice, he is also a concurrent lawyer of international business, legal adviser of several transnational corporations, as well as an arbitrator of the ICSID, ICC, IAI and RIA.

In addition to the IEL, Professor Chen likes poetry, literature and calligraphy, which are grounds to be an ideal scholar in East Asia. He is a true man of gentle, warmhearted and courageous personality. In his lifetime, China has experienced foreign occupation, civil war and the socialist revolution. All these, however, could not stop his longing for the truth and justice in human society. Rather, those trials have made him an insurmountable peak of Chinese as well as world academia. Professor Chen always tells his lofty messages and ideas for peace and co-prosperity of human society as a great mentor of our time.

Book

The monograph entitled *The Voice from China: An CHEN on International Economic Law*, is a collection of 24 English articles written by Professor An Chen over the past 30 years. *The Voice from China* is a representation of his academic life of IEL, starting from 1980. The book covers areas of IEL questions that China has been asking. These 24 articles are divided into six parts in his book, namely: Jurisprudence of Contemporary International Economic Law; Contemporary Economic Sovereignty; China's Strategic Position on Contemporary International Economic Order; Contemporary Bilateral Investment Treaties; China's Legislation on Sino-Foreign Economic Issues; and Contemporary Chinese Practices on International Economic Disputes; which are all very well balanced. His jurisprudential idea and academic opinions show different aspects of international law from those of the United States and Europe that were mainstream. This publication has great significance considering that it is the firm ground of Chinese discourse on IEL. With his thorough research, China began expressing her ideas in her own voice. In that sense, the title, *The Voice from China* has deep implications. In addition to academic contents, the book is professionally edited and beautifully bound by a highly renowned publisher, Springer. The cover design is also appreciable.

"Yellow Peril" Doctrine

China is a mysterious country to the western people. It is mainly due to her vast national territory, large population, long history and civilization, modern communism and her closed-door policy up until 1978. One more critical point is, however, the so-called "Yellow Peril" Doctrine, which is unconsciously rooted in the western mind. Recently, this "Yellow Peril" Doctrine began creeping out of their sub-consciousness into the real world as a poisonous concept of the so-called "China Threat" Doctrine. In Chapter 3 of *The Voice from China*, Professor Chen has analyzed the origin, evolution and international legal significance of the "Yellow Peril" Doctrine and the "China Threat" Doctrine, which is its modern style transformation. Some Chinese scholars seem to perceive these two concepts to be historically connected. For example, Professor Chen Dong at Sun Yat-sen University stated:

> The term "Chinese Threat" has not been a novel wording for the past twenty years. Its references date as far back to the nineteenth century, e. g., in Mikhail Bakunin's work entitled *On Statism and Anarchism*, which implies the "tremendous and dreadful threat from the East". Wilhelm II von Deutschland's vivid cartoon "The Yellow Peril" (Völker Europas, wahrt eure heiligsten Güter) depicted a common European perception of China at the turn of the nineteenth century.[213]

He also added:

---

[213] Dong Chen, Who Threatens Whom? The "Chinese Treat" and the Bush Doctrine, *Journal of East Asia and International Law*, Vol. 7, Iss. 1, 2014, p. 32.

The core of the "Yellow Peril" theory lay in the fact that some Europeans regarded yellow-faced Chinese as "uncivilized" and stupid locusts causing great, albeit potential, threats to the "civilized (western)" world. [214]

Such a historical approach is, however, not always the key to understanding the current recognition of the contemporary US hegemonic version of "China Threat" Doctrine, which was firstly referred to in the mid-1990s, mainly by US politicians and scholars under the Bush administration. It became shrill in the early 2000s. The then Bush administration seemed to intentionally fabricate the political slogan, "China Threat" Doctrine in order to dominate East Asia by preventing China whose economy and political influence were fast growing from expanding to the Asia-Pacific region. For the US, who was "the only superpower" at that time, China might be a potential threat to the American military and economic hegemony in the region. The concept, "China Threat" Doctrine seemed to be initiated under this global environment of power shift. The so-called "China Threat" Doctrine thus might not simply be a modern transformation of the "Yellow Peril" Doctrine, which was largely European oriented. The "Yellow Peril" Doctrine was actually coined because of the Mongol invasion of Europe in the thirteenth century which led to the deep-rooted inferiority complex of the Europeans toward Chinese (Yellow-faced Asian) people and civilization. Herewith, the word, "yellow" might not mean the skin color of Asian, but the color of sand storms that the Mongol cavalry made while aggressing. For the then Europeans, they were evils that could be surmounted only by the omnipotent God.

This hypothesis is well evidenced by Professor Dong Chen's article, "Who Threatens Whom? The 'Chinese Treat' and the Bush Doctrine". In his article, Dong Chen states "Bush's dream for the unipolar world" to explain the "China Threat". [215] Citing Ikenberry's article, America's Imperial Ambitions, he argues that Americans regard the Bush strategy as "a 'grand strategy' that begins with fundamental commitment to maintaining a unipolar world in which the US has no peer competitor," and that threatens to "leave the world more dangerous and

---

[214] Ibid.
[215] Dong Chen, Who Threatens Whom? The "Chinese Treat" and the Bush Doctrine, *Journal of East Asia and International Law*, Vol. 7, Iss. 1, 2014, pp. 39-40.

divided-and the US less secure."[216] Furthermore, Professor Dong Chen specially refers to evangelical Christianity as the basis of the Bush doctrine.[217] According to him, China Threat is an implementative tool of the Bush doctrine to build the unipolar world with the US in the center.

An abovementioned statement to that effect on "China Threat" under the Bush doctrine may be wrapped up in *The Voice from China*. Professor An Chen said:

> They could be fairly deemed as the official American versions of "Yellow Peril" and "China Threat" on the highest level, at the highest frequency… They are the outcome of the following triple sources: American Congress, the US Department of Defense, and various high-ranked think tanks… The departmental interests of American Department of Defense could be easily discerned in this regard… After the Cold War was over, it was always the inertial thinking of "curious" Americans… to find a definite and powerful new "threat". And China is the new "serious threat" on security that Americans have been endeavoring to establish.[218]

I would fully agree with the position of Professor An Chen that the China Threat is "the twenty-first century version of 'Yellow Peril' which has been repeatedly advocated by American hawkish anti-China congressmen, as evidenced in the annual Report of China's Military Power and in the annual Report of US-China Economic and Security, and the echoing of media along with them."[219]

Economic Sovereignty

In Chapters 4 and 5 of *The Voice from China*, Professor Chen discusses a more fundamental question of economic sovereignty. As the economic globalization and interdependency between nations are deepening, sovereignty of each nation State is

---

[216] G. Ikenberry, America's Imperial Ambitions, *Foreign Affairs*, Vol. 81, 2002, p. 44.

[217] See Dong Chen, Who Threatens Whom? The "Chinese Treat" and the Bush Doctrine, *Journal of East Asia and International Law*, Vol. 7, Iss. 1, 2014, pp. 42-43.

[218] An Chen, *The Voice from China: An CHEN on International Economic Law*, Springer, 2013, pp. 64-65. See also An Chen, On the Source, Essence of "Yellow Peril" Doctrine and Its Latest Hegemony "Variant"— the "China Threat", *Modern Law Science*, No. 6, 2011, pp. 20-21.

[219] An Chen, *The Voice from China: An CHEN on International Economic Law*, Springer, 2013, pp. 67-68. See also An Chen, On the Source, Essence of "Yellow Peril" Doctrine and Its Latest Hegemony "Variant"— the "China Threat", *Modern Law Science*, No. 6, 2011, p. 22.

getting to a point of controversy. Professor Chen refers to the comparison between the WTO multilateralism and the US unilateralism. He compares the ideas of Professor L. Henkin to those of Professor J. Jackson with regard to unilateralism (US) and multilateralism (WTO) very well. Professor Chen has cited pertinent cases in order to critically discuss the US unilateralism over the sovereignty of other states. His analytic statement purposefully covers Sections 201 and 301 of the US Trade Act, conflicts of sovereignties in the formation of the WTO system, the Great 1994 Sovereignty Debate, sovereignty of the US and other States, the US-EU economic sovereignty disputes, the US-Japan auto disputes, the US-EC banana disputes, the WTO/DSB Panel Report on the Section 301 case, etc.

Professor Chen discusses the coordination of national sovereignty in the time of multilateralism. His idea might be set up based on the China's historical experience including horrible foreign occupation and the civil war that Professor Chen himself got through in his lifetime. I fully second his opinions. For Asians, most of whom were once colonized, "sovereignty" is not myth; it is the reality to self-determination.

Conclusion

The *Voice from China* is a great achievement and contribution by Professor An Chen to China, to the whole of Asia, as well as to the global community, which is searching for a new discourse in the promotion of economic cooperation in a fair and balanced manner between states. The core and focus of this monograph could be summarized as Voicing for Worldwide Weaks, Pursuing Global Justice, Resisting International Hegemony.

It should be a triggering point for the series of "Understanding China" with a viewpoint of establishing a new international economic order. This publication will be an outstanding model of other academics and practitioners who are willing to follow him. Personally, I am now of the age in which Professor Chen began studying international law. His constant efforts and enthusiasm is a consistent stimulant for the passion of international lawyers in Asia as well as the whole world. My eternally curious mind is also deeply inspired by Professor Chen. I am eagerly awaiting a future volume of *The Voice from China*, whenever it is manifest. Since

Professor Chen is enjoying green old age, I hope it would not entail much waiting. Once again I extend the deepest and heartfelt celebration to the publication of *The Voice from China*.

八、国家主权等国际经济法宏观问题的深刻反思
——评《中国的呐喊:陈安论国际经济法》

〔加拿大〕帕特丽莎·沃特丝*

《中国的呐喊:陈安论国际经济法》一书的作者是中国国际经济法学界泰斗、厦门大学法学院陈安教授,该书汇集了作者自1980年以来三十多年不同时期撰写的24篇专论。该书的学术专论和案例分析论及国际法诸多议题,却又服务于一个共同的主题,即发出作者对国际经济法的独特的"中国声音"。

全书分为六个部分:当代国际经济法的基本理论;当代国家经济主权的"攻防战";中国在构建当代国际经济新秩序中的战略定位;当代国际投资法的论争;当代中国涉外经济立法的争议;若干涉华、涉外经贸争端典型案例剖析。该巨著共789页,含正文24章及参考文献和附录(包括对陈教授论著的各种书刊评论)。

读者开篇即可看出作者的主要意图——阐述自己对国际(经济)法的中国特色和独有路径的看法。"序言"开宗明义:

> ……中国学者不应盲目附和和全盘接受某些西方观点。正确的态度理应是独立思考,明辨是非,批判地吸收。秉持这一态度,我和我的中国同仁在晚近30年的研究和著述中,一直立足于中国国情和其他弱小国家的基本立场,努力剖析、辨别、探讨西方各种法学理论的真伪,从而决定取舍。除了对西方法律理论"取其精华,去其糟粕"外,我们还努力推陈出新,开拓创新,针对若干重大法律问题提出一系列自己的观点,积极参与国际学术争鸣,形成了自己的理论体系……我们的理论与现有的某些西方观点截然不同(第vi页)。

我的研究领域是国际水资源和国家主权理论,故急切想看看陈安教授在《中国的呐喊》一书中如何看待主权这一问题。本书索引列举了大量与主权有关的讨论,为探讨这一复杂问题提供了多种方便路径。例如,对**国家主权至上**这一问题,作者

---

* 帕特丽莎·沃特丝(Patricia Wouters),厦门大学法学院国际法教授、中国国际水法项目主任,英国苏格兰邓迪大学教授、UNESCO水法科学中心前主任。

主张:"在当代国际法的规范体系和理论体系中,国家主权原则乃是第一性的、居于最高位阶的基本原则。"(第 326 页)为此,作者认为:"从这个意义说,MFN 待遇原则乃是国家主权原则的衍生物,它应当附属于、服从于国家主权原则。"(第 326—327页)然而,"即使是居于最高位阶的国家主权原则,也可以依缔约主权国家的自由意志,通过平等磋商,作出适当的真正平等互惠的自我限制"(第 327 页)。虽然这一主张貌似夸大了国际法的基本原则,但作者以中国为例解释了为什么要对这些原则如此强调和全面阐释。在中国,"历史上丧权辱国的惨痛,人们记忆犹新"(第 327 页)。虽然作者在这里讨论的是国际经济法,其寓意却是深远的,特别有助于人们充分理解和领会中国对国家主权的立场。"如今,已经站起来了的中国人民,已经恢复和强化了完全独立自主的主权国家身份……"(第 317 页)

本书其他部分亦从不同角度探讨国家主权理论。由于本书主要论及国际经济法,大量论述的是"经济主权"(有 20 次之多),"单个国家的主权"讨论过一次,"永久主权"两次,"联合主权"两次,"国家主权"8 次。"主权"一词贯穿全书,通过剖析西方特别是美国的相关理论与实践,全面阐述中国对主权的立场。举例来说,陈教授质疑"跨国法"学说,认为这是一种否定弱国主权,鼓吹美国霸权的学说,是一种有毒的"舶来品"(第 38 页)。他认为:"杰塞普鼓吹的'跨国法',打着'世界政府''联合主权''国际法'优先的旗号,为觊觎、削弱、否定众多弱小民族的国家主权提供'法理依据',其宗旨在于促使弱国撤除民族与国家藩篱,摒弃主权屏障,从而使美国的国际扩张主义和世界霸权主义得以通行无阻。"(第 38—39 页)

本书附录收录了 Branislav Gosovic 的一篇论文,总结陈教授对国家主权的看法。他认为,国家主权理论是中国外交战略的基石(该战略在 1982 年《宪法》中确立,即"和平共处五项原则":相互尊重主权和领土完整、互不侵犯、互不干涉内政、平等互利、和平共处)。Gosovic 认为:"今后若干年,学者们可以用实践来检验陈教授的论点和论据,如果证明他是对的,则可对抗西方凡夫俗子思想模式下广泛流传的观点。"(第 773 页)"'西方'观点认定,中国的和平崛起会……演变为霸权主义、扩张主义和侵略主义,会仿效并追随过往的侵略者和殖民者,继而将全球瓜分为各自的势力范围。"(第 773 页)陈教授《中国的呐喊》一书则从中国的国际法观出发,作出了完全不同的论断。

换个角度说,陈教授的国家主权观是从中国实际出发,为我们理解中国的跨界水实践提供了新的洞见。跨界水问题是当今中国和亚洲地区迫在眉睫、亟待解决的问题。中国与 20 个主权国家和地区有 40 多条跨界河流,多数情况下中国处于上游,中国对这些河流的淡水使用和开发颇受质疑。争议的焦点是国家主权以及外交政策如何落实国家主权。具体而言,就是中国在管理跨界水资源时,如何根据国际法,既满足自身经济发展的需要,又考虑邻国的需求。虽然有不少外国研究者批评中国的跨界水实践有"霸权性质",说中国是(无情的?)地区"超级大国",只片面考虑自身利益,但是,如果仔细加以研究,会发现这些研究者大都有同样的重大疏忽,即没有探究中国的国际法观对跨界水问题的内在影响。用跨界水涉及的国际法规则来评估和分析中国的相关条约和国家实践,我们发现中国一贯采取相当一致的立场(虽然该立场尚未得到充分研究),这一立场符合中国的国家主权观,反映的是领土主权有限论(Wouters and Chen,2013;Xue,1992;Saul,2013)。陈教授在《中国的呐喊》中提出的强有力的法律论据,有助于人们更好地理解将来中国在跨界水实践方面的可能走向。的确,对于中国涉水行业的外国投资政策这一重要问题,现有研究极少(H. Chen,2015),今后需要更多细致研究。《中国的呐喊》一书充分展现出来的跨学科新思维,为更多的创新思路提供了基础。中国需要新的法律思维来管理跨界水资源,从而平衡经济发展与环境保护问题,环境问题现在已成为国内的重要议题。当今全球自然资源过度开发,缺乏保护。中国在该领域的国家实践,不仅对其自身的国家资源,而且对地区和全球经济和环境资源,都有重大意义。如何以支持经济发展的方式来解决全球水/能源/食品/环境等问题,是一个热点问题,也是世界经济论坛热议的话题。世界经济论坛是全球思想家和政策制定者的重要年度会议。在最近一次世界经济论坛会议上(2015年1月在达沃斯召开),中国总理李克强说:"文化多样性与生物多样性一样,是我们这个星球最值得珍视的天然宝藏。人类社会是各种文明都能盛开的百花园,不同文化之间、不同宗教之间,都应相互尊重、和睦共处。同可相亲,异宜相敬。国际社会应以海纳百川的胸怀,求同存异、包容互鉴、合作共赢。"(2015年1月23日,达沃斯)"中国提出'一带一路'建设,愿与相关国家需求相结合,合作推进。"中国如何在实践中,尤其是在面临诸多复杂挑战时,根据中国的国家主权观和国际法,实施这一雄心勃勃的外交政策,人们拭目以待。也许陈教授的洞见能够指点迷津?

　　对于解决这些相当复杂又颇有争议的问题,本书极富启迪意义。本书详加探讨的是国际经济法理论与实践,作者却常将之归依为国际公法的普遍问题。因此,《中国的呐喊》具有更宏大的魅力。本书还讨论了许多相互关联而又高度相关的国际法问题。诸如:南南合作发展战略("发展中国家对自己的自然资源应该享有和行使永久主权;对发展中国家的经济援助应该严格尊重受援国家的主权,不附带任何条件,施援国不得要求任何特权"(第176页)——论邓小平对国际经济新秩序理论的贡献);以理论联系实际的方法来研究国际经济法诸议题(包括外国投资),等等。作者反复呼吁并详细论证,国际(经济)法领域需要更加独立的研究和批判性思考。

对于那些对国际法感兴趣的人而言,《中国的呐喊》提供了广阔的天地,尤其是从中国的视角来看。以下前瞻性的论断,非常振奋人心,将激励学者们接受挑战:

> 学术上原无什么绝对的"专属区",更不该有什么"独家禁地",不许他人涉足。因此,中国法学界的志士仁人,不论其擅长或专攻何门类、何学科,似均宜摒除、捐弃任何门户之见,从各自不同的角度,各尽所能,齐心协力,尽力地开拓和尽多地产出具有中国特色的法学硕果和上佳精品,共同为振兴中国法学,跻身国际前列,并进而为世界法苑的百花争妍和绚丽多彩,做出应有的贡献!(第42—43页)

总之,我希望本书广传于世,激发更多人从更广阔的国际法维度研究国际经济法。此外,我们也需要更多人从事自然资源和涉水资源的研究,既考虑中国的见解,又参考国际最佳实践,综合评估各方意见。

来自中国的呐喊必须认真倾听。陈教授的专著及时问世,必将引发更多创新性的研究。

参 考 文 献

(详见本书评英文版)

(翻译:陈辉萍,校对、编辑:陈　欣)

Reflections on State Sovereignty and Other Grand Themes of International Law

Patricia Wouters[*]

The monograph, *The Voice from China: An CHEN on International Economic Law* is a collection of some 24 papers written over 3 decades (from the 1980s) by China's eminent professor in this field—Professor An Chen (School of Law, Xiamen University). It includes scholarly writings and case analyses, which together aim at consolidating the author's views on the distinctive "Voice of China" in the area of international economic law, touching also on a range of related themes in

---

[*] Professor of International Law, School of Law, Xiamen University; Director, China International Water Law Programme; former Director, University of Dundee UNESCO Centre for Water Law, Policy and Science, Scotland.

international law.

Presented in six parts—Jurisprudence of Contemporary International Economic Law; Great Debates on Contemporary Economic Sovereignty; China's Strategic Position on Contemporary International Economic Order Issues; Divergences on Contemporary Bilateral Investment Treaty; Contemporary China's Legislation on Sino-Foreign Economic Issues; Contemporary Chinese Practices on International Economic Disputes (Cases Analyses)—the work comprises 24 chapters, with references and an Annex that includes comments about Chen's writings. It is a large volume, covering 789 pages.

The reader quickly discerns the primary objective of the author—to present his personal views on the Chinese characteristics of, and approach to, international (economic) law. The preface provides:

> ... we Chinese law scholars, should not blindly follow and completely accept these Western opinions. Rather, a correct attitude is to contemplate independently and critically in order for us to be able to distinguish right from wrong. By holding such kind of attitude, in my later three decades of research and writing, I, together, with my Chinese colleague, have always bene trying to analyse, distinguish, ascertain, absorb, or reject Western legal theories while steadily taking into account the national situation of China and the common position of the weak countries. In addition to "keeping the essence while discarding the dross" of the Western legal theories, we have raised a series of our own innovative ideas and actively participated in international academic debates, which have helped us to shape our systematic theories on various legal subjects... Our theories are significantly and substantially different and independent from some of the existing Western ones. (p. vi)

As my own research looks at the notion of state sovereignty (in the context of international freshwater resources), I was keen to explore how Professor An Chen addresses this topic in *The Voice from China*. The index offers a list of sovereignty-related discourse, each providing diverse inroads on this complex notion. As just one example, on the particular issue of the supremacy of state sovereignty, the author asserts, "State sovereignty is still the primary rule and occupies the highest hierarchical position within the norm-system and theory-system of international law"

(p. 326). In accordance with this view, the author holds that MFN treatment is "merely a derivative of state sovereignty", "which should be subordinated to and serve the supreme principle of state sovereignty" (pp. 326-327). He continues by observing, "However, even if the principle of state sovereignty occupies the supreme place, it can still be appropriately constrained by the states themselves on the basis of real equality, reciprocity, willingness, and equal negotiation" (p. 327). While such an assertion might seem to over-state these bedrock principles of international law, the author explains why, in China's case, these need to be reiterated and fully understood. "The serious consequences of humiliation of nation [sic] and forfeiture of sovereignty are unfaded bitter lessons in history" (p. 327). Although this passage deals ostensibly with international economic law issues, its relevance is more broad-based, especially when one tries to fully discern and appreciate China's approach to state sovereignty. "Nowadays Chinese people have stood up and recovered and have also intensified the sovereignty status of complete independence..." (p. 317)

Other parts of the book also explore the notion of state sovereignty, albeit in different contexts. Understandably, considerable reference is made to "economic sovereignty" (with some 20 citations); "individual sovereignty" is discussed once; "permanent sovereignty", twice; "united sovereignty", also with two entries. "State sovereignty" garners some 8 mentions. A summary of these entries sprinkled throughout the book reveals a rather comprehensive elaboration of China's approach to sovereignty, discussed primarily vis-à-vis western thought and practice, especially US doctrine. As just one example, Professor Chen challenges the "Transnational Law Doctrine" (TLD) as "a doctrine that negates the sovereignty of weak nations, while preaches the hegemony of the United States and is thus a poisonous imported product" (p. 38). He continues, "Jessup's TLD, by flaunting the banners of 'world government', 'united sovereignty' and 'priority of IL' [international law], intends to provide the jurisprudential basis of coveting, weakening, and negating the state sovereignty of the vast nations. It purports to force the weak nations to discard the fence of nation and state sovereignty, so that the US expansionism and world hegemonism could go through without hindrance" (pp. 38-39).

Interestingly, Professor Chen's treatment of the theme of state sovereignty is summarised in a paper by Branislav Gosovic included in the Annex, where the notion is cast as the anchor for China's foreign policy strategy (defined in the 1982 Constitution—the so-called Five Principles of Peaceful Co-existence—"the mutual respect to each other's sovereignty and territorial integrity, mutual nonaggression, mutual non-interference in each other's domestic affairs, equality and reciprocity, and peaceful coexistence"). Gosovic argues that "In the years and decades to come, scholars will be able to test empirically Professor Chen's thesis and arguments and, if he is proven right, counter the widespread view in the realist mode of thinking, especially in the West" (p. 773). The "western" view is described as positing that China's declared peaceful rise will "... morph into a hegemonic, expansionist, aggressive mode of reasoning and planetary behaviour, imitating and following the former oppressors and colonizers with whom it will proceed to carve the planet into respective spheres of influence" (p. 773). *The Voice from China* suggests an entirely different outcome, based fundamentally on China's approach to international law.

In another vein, Professor Chen's treatment of the notion of state sovereignty (unabashedly from a Chinese perspective) provides new insights for China's transboundary water practice—a contemporary pressing issue for the country and the region. China, upstream on most of its 40 + major transboundary waters, shared with more than 20 other sovereign nations and autonomous regions, is often challenged with regard to its international freshwater use and development. At the heart of this debate is state sovereignty and how it is implemented in foreign policy, generally, and more specifically, as regards China's management of these transboundary resources in ways that, not only meet its own national economic imperatives, but also take into account the needs of its riparian neighbours, in accordance with international law. While there is a significant body of research that refers to China's transboundary state practice as "hegemonic", casting China as the regional (and ruthless?) "super-power" that acts unilaterally in its own self-interests, upon closer scrutiny, most of these studies suffer the same glaring oversight—they fail to interrogate the integral role that China's approach to international law plays in this domain. A critical analysis of China's treaty and state practice, evaluated in the light of rules of international law in this field, reveals a rather coherent, albeit not yet fully developed approach, aligned with China's approach to state sovereignty, and reflected in the theory of limited territorial sovereignty (Wouters and Chen, 2013; Xue, 1992; Saul, 2013). Professor Chen's "Voice of China" provides substantive legal arguments that contribute to a better understanding of how China might go forward with its transboundary water practice. Indeed, China's foreign direct investment policy on water-related matters needs more rigorous study, with few writings on this important topic (Chen, H. 2015). Such cross-over connected thinking, richly demonstrated in *The Voice from China*, provides a foundation for innovative approaches.

New legal approaches will be required in order to manage China's transboundary water resources in ways that balance economic growth with environmental issues is now high on the domestic agenda. As the world's natural resources continue to be over-exploited and under-protected, China's practice in this field will have a bearing, not only its national resources, but with respect to regional and global economic and environmental resources. Addressing global water/energy/food/environmental issues in ways that support economic growth is now a key topic debated at the World Economic Forum, the leading annual meeting of the globe's thinkers and policy-makers in this area. At the most recent meeting of the World Economic Forum (Davos, January 2015), Chinese Premier Li Keqiang stated that "Cultural diversity, like biodiversity, is a most precious treasure endowed to us on this planet... Like the vast ocean admitting all rivers that run into it, members of the international community need to work together to expand common ground while accepting differences, and seek win-win progress through inclusive cooperation and mutual learning." (Davos, 23 January 2015) "China has put forward the initiatives to build the Silk Road Economic Belt and the 21st Century Maritime Silk Road. China hopes to work with other countries to advance these initiatives and ensure that they are brought forward in ways that meet the actual needs of countries concerned." How China implements this ambitious foreign policy in practice, especially in the context of complex contemporary challenges, and in light of China's approach to state sovereignty and international law, will be watched closely. Will Professor Chen's insights offer guidance for the future?

The collected work sheds light on these highly complex and controversial topics through its elaborate discussion of international economic legal theory and practice, which the author often locates within more general themes of public international law. Thus, *The Voice from China* has broad appeal. A number of inter-connected (and highly relevant) international legal topics are touched upon—as just some examples: South-South development policies ("developing countries possess the right to exercise permanent sovereignty over their natural resources; economic aid to the developing countries should be strictly based on respect towards the aided countries' sovereignty, attaching with it no conditions or privileges for aiding countries' extra benefit", p. 176—reviewing Deng Xiaoping's contribution to the notion of a New International Economic Order); theoretical and practice-based approaches to international economic law topics (including foreign investment); and other areas, always with repeated calls and detailed justification for more independent and critical thinking in the field of international (economic) law.

The Voice from China provides a fascinating backdrop for all those interested in international law, especially from the Chinese perspective. It is compelling reading for scholars, who are wholeheartedly urged on by this forward-looking visionary to take up the research challenge:

> There is and shall be no "exclusive zone" or "prohibited area" for academic research, into which outsiders are forbidden to enter. As a result, all those Chinese scholars with far vision and lofty ideal [sic] shall discard any parochial prejudices, no matter which fields they are specialized in; shall do their best and make concerted efforts respectively from different fields; and coordinatingly endeavour to take exploration and produce as many china-specific research results as possible. In this way, we can make our significant contributions for the revival and prosperity of legal study in both China and the world. (p. 43)

In closing, it is the reviewer's hope that this collected work will be read by a wide audience and lead to more academic research in this area, considered within the broader canvas of international law. In particular, more scholarship in the field of natural and water-related resources is needed, infused with Chinese approaches, building on international best practice, rigorously evaluated.

China's voice must be heard—Professor Chen's book is a timely contribution that invites more innovative study in this field.

References:

H. Chen, The Human Right to Water and Foreign Investment: Friends or Foes? *Water International*, Vol. 40, Iss. 2, 2015; Manuscript on File with the Author.

Chinese Premier Li Keqiang's Speech at Davos 2015 (23 January, 2015), https://agenda.weforum.org/2015/01/chinese-premier-li-keqiangs-speech-at-davos-2015/.

B. Saul, China, Natural Resources, Sovereignty and International Law, *Asian Studies Review*, Vol. 37, Iss. 2, 2013, pp. 196-214.

Y. Su, Contemporary Legal Analysis of China's Transboundary Water Regimes: International Law in Practice, *Water International*, Vol. 39, Iss. 5, 2014, pp. 705-724.

S. Vinogradov & P. Wouters, Sino-Russian Transboundary Waters: A Legal Perspective on Cooperation, Stockholm Paper, Retrieved 12 02, 2014, http://www.chinainternationalwaterlaw.org/pdf/resources/20131216_001.pdf.

P. Wouters & H. Chen, China's "Soft-Path" to Transboundary Water Cooperation Examined in the Light of Two UN Global Water Conventions: Exploring the "Chinese Way", *Journal of Water Law*, Vol. 22, 2013, pp. 229-247.

P. Wouters & H. Chen, Editors' Introduction to the "China Water Papers", *Water International*, Vol. 40, Iss. 2, 2015, pp. 1-20.

P. Wouters, The Yin and Yang of International Water Law: China's Transboundary Water Practice and the Changing Contours of State Sovereignty, *RECIEL*, Vol. 23, Iss. 1, 2014.

Hanqin Xue, Relativity in International Water Law, *Colorado Journal of International Environmental Law and Policy*, Vol. 3, No. 1, 1992.

九、精当透彻的论证 尽显大师的风采

——简评《中国的呐喊：陈安论国际经济法》

黄雁明[*]

捧读陈安教授的皇皇巨著《中国的呐喊：陈安论国际经济法》，以下简称《中国的呐喊》（*The Voice from China: An CHEN on International Economic Law*），不禁为他的学术硕果与驾驭英文的能力所折服。

陈教授是中国国际经济法学界的大师、旗手，笔者曾是其麾下的普通成员。作为从事国际商事仲裁的工匠，笔者希图从此视角对《中国的呐喊》中的两宗案件的法

---

[*] 黄雁明，中国国际经济法学会理事，SCIA、CIETAC 以及上海国际仲裁中心仲裁员。

律意见书(第 20、21、22、23 章[220])略作评述。

案一,英国 X 公司 v. 英国 Y 保险公司。X 公司与中国 B 公司成为 1996 年 12 月成立的中国 C 电力公司的中外合作双方。Y 公司作为 X 公司的担保人,承保的风险中包括政府征用险。因中国国务院〔1998〕第 31 号通知与国务院办公厅〔2002〕第 43 号通知(以下简称"两通知"),依 Y 公司对 X 公司的保单,后者要求前者赔偿在保险期内因中国政府(可能)的征收而发生的损失,Y 公司拒绝,在仲裁案中列为被申请人。

陈教授应对的关键问题是"两通知"是否构成(中国政府)对 C 公司与对 X 公司在 C 公司的投资权益的征收;是否据此 X 公司可以向承保人 Y 请求赔偿,之后 Y 公司是否可以获得 X 公司的代位求偿权。或许还可以用另一种方式表述,即在 C 公司的合作合同符合当时的《中外合作企业法》规定而获得批准的前提下,被国际普遍接受的"当事人意思自治"与"法无溯及力"原则是否在作为法治国家的中国存在。

案二,厦门买方 Zhonghe v. 新加坡卖方 Bunge 于 2004 年 2 月 25 日签订销售合同,标的物是 5.5 万公吨巴西大豆,准据法是英国法。合同规定 Zhonghe 要在 Bunge 所接受的中国一流银行开立以后者为受益人的信用证。

陈教授的法律意见书涉及的核心问题是中国国家质量监督检验检疫总局(以下简称"检验总局")的禁令对中国进口公司、中国的银行及其海外分行是否具有强制性约束力;系争合同开立信用证义务的履行地是否在中国;系争合同的准据法是英国法,中国强制性规则对中国法人是否有约束力,上述禁令能否导致系争合同落空。

在法律意见中,陈教授对于以中国法为准据法的案件,关注从中国宪法的有关法条到与案件及争议问题密切相关的法律、法规、规章与行政命令等;对以英国法为准据法的合同,他根据《国际合同义务法律适用公约》(即《罗马公约》)、英国《1990 年合同法》、英国法院在长期的司法实践中所确立的判例、英国权威学者提炼与归纳的为国际社会所普遍接受的法律冲突规范,对它们的相互关系与不同效力层层分析,透彻论证自己的见解与观点。

他的结论是否定征收的构成与存在,确认法无溯及力等两项原则在中国同样有效;中国的强制性命令对中国法人有约束力,中国是合同开立信用证义务的履行地,

---

[220] See An Chen, The Truth Among the Fogbound "Expropriation" Claim: Comments on British X Investment Co. Versus British Y Insurance Co. Case; The Approach of "Winning from Both Sides" Used in the "Expropriation" Claim: Re-comments on British X Investment Co. Versus British Y Insurance Co. Case; On the Serious Violation of Chinese Jus Cogens: Comments on the Case of Importing Toxic Brazilian Soybeans into China (Expert's Legal Opinion on Zhonghe Versus Bunge Case); Isn't the Strict Prohibition on Importing Toxic Brazilian Soybeans into China "Illegal"? —A Rebuttal to Lawyer Song's Allegation, in An Chen, *The Voice from China: An CHEN on International Economic Law*, Springer, 2013, pp. 635-716.

前述强制性命令导致系争合同落空。

拜读之,笔者不禁想起1985—1986年中国改革开放与法制建设初期,曾经协助某前辈出具法律意见书的经历。其中一份意见书是给中国香港地区的银团出具的,涉及银团向国内某公司的贷款,贷款合同的准据法是美国纽约州的法律。银团律师聘请中国内地律师以查明与确认借款人与担保人的身份、营业范围、财政状况、关于借款与担保的偿还能力与各自董事会的决定、借款与担保获得国家外汇管理局批准的情况、各自委派的签约人等等。两家担保人中的一家是非金融企业,其主营业地在香港,并在香港拥有很高的商誉。但是,我们获悉其注册地是北京,因而要求其向国家外汇管理局申请批准对外债的担保,提供批准文件。当时中国的法规有限,要适用内部文件所涉及的有关政策。可见,在贷款合同的准据法为美国纽约州法律的情况下,中国法律涉及中国当事人的权利能力和行为能力的规定关系到涉外合同能否顺利履行。银团及其境外律师希望中国律师查明有关中国当事人的问题与中国法律的相关规定,包括当时的内部(红头)文件所载的政策,在意见书出具后,贷款协议才能正式签署。

案一,Y公司是明智的,及时请教中国法律专家为之提供有力的法律武器。若是X公司在怀疑所涉"两通知"的溯及力以及"两通知"对其在中国C公司的权益构成征收之时,在依据保险合同提请仲裁之前,同样请求陈教授为其出具法律意见书,那么效果是上佳的。毕竟若将争议提交仲裁,由于X公司的现金投资是1200万美元,保险额势必不少于该数额(可能另加10%);其仲裁请求断不少于此数额。而聘请律师要付费,向仲裁机构提请仲裁要交管理费(按请求金额的比例计算)、指定仲裁员的费用与仲裁庭的费用,与中国专家出具法律意见书的费用相比,后者是最合算的。

案二,根据笔者在前文提及曾经参与出具法律意见书的经历,在准据法是纽约州法律的情况下,对中国当事人的属人法,境外的律师从不敢掉以轻心,因为它关系到银团与借款人之间的贷款合同是否存在落空的危险;更不会如Bunge聘请的中国律师般漠视。

本案是国际货物销售合同的争议,双方均来自《联合国国际货物销售合同公约》(CISG)的签字国,CISG成为新加坡与中国法律的构成部分。若不明确排除或减损其效力,那么保留部分除外,CISG是否适用于本案?以英国法为准据法的合同争议是否排除CISG的适用?依据陈教授援引的《罗马公约》第3.3条:

当事人选择外国法这一事实,无论其是否同时选择外国法庭,如在选择时一切与当事情况有关因素仅同一个国家有关,不应影响该国法律规定的适用,即该国法律规定(以下称"强制性规定")之适用不得以合同废除之。

据此,上述法条表明,适用英国法不能构成对适用 CISG 的排除,那么 CISG 第 7(2)条规定:

> 本公约未明确解决的属于本公约范围的问题,应当按照本公约所依据的一般原则来解决,在没有一般原则的情况下,则应按照国际私法规定适用的法律来解决。

依照 CISG 的上述原则,系争合同 Zhonghe 的属人法,对其以及对中国的银行(包括它们的海外分行)的行为能力有约束力。在明知进口的食品(或食物的原料)被检验总局禁止的情况下,不得违反。对此,陈教授已经援引法条充分论证。

此外,是否还可以提及中国《合同法》第 127 条:

> 工商行政管理部门和其他有关行政主管部门在各自的职权范围内,依照法律、行政法规的规定,对利用合同危害国家利益、社会公共利益的违法行为,负责监督处理;构成犯罪的,依法追究刑事责任。

上述法条从另一角度再次表明中国法律体系中强制性规定的约束力与违反的严重后果。

或许还可以告诉案二的当事人,如果仲裁庭漠视中国法律体系中的强制性规范,裁决可以向中国出口含有高毒性致癌农药的巴西大豆,或者裁决 Bunge 胜诉,中国法院可以不承认与执行被申请人的胜诉裁决。因为危害消费者健康的食品是不可接受的。裁决书中严重的错误构成对公共政策的违反。[221]允许有重大缺陷的裁决书存在,不予更正,必将损害公众对仲裁整体的信赖。[222]这是国际上日渐流行的准则。这一准则现在已经鲜明地体现在联合国国际贸易法委员会《国际商事仲裁示范法》第 34 条与第 36 条之中。这里不妨援引一宗案例 Telkom SA Ltd. v. Anthony Boswood QC,涉及仲裁员的处理不当(misconduct)导致裁决书的撤销或搁置(setting aside):

> 南非高级法院查明仲裁员出现(适用)法律的错误(commit errors of law),构成仲裁的重大违法(或不当)行为(to amount to gross irregularities),而撤销

---

[221] See Michael Hwang and Amy Lai, Do Egregious Errors Amount to a Breach of Public Policy? *Arbitration*, Vol. 71, No. 1, 2005, pp. 1-24; Michael Huang, Do Egregious Errors Amount to a Breach of Public Policy? *Arbitration*, Vol. 71, No. 4, 2005, pp. 364-371.

[222] Michael Hwang and Amy Lai, Do Egregious Errors Amount to a Breach of Public Policy? *Arbitration*, Vol. 71, No. 1, 2005, p. 24.

(或搁置)裁决书。[223]

从陈教授的法律意见书中,仲裁员还可以学到些什么?在裁决书的仲裁庭意见部分,仲裁员论述争议焦点,交代与揭示其所查明或确认的事实,要全面、详尽、条理清楚;要论述当事人的请求与反请求成立与否的理由。如果仲裁员具备这样的能力,裁决才有说服力。

陈教授的法律意见书出具时间是 2006 年,当时中国与改革开放和市场经济建设相配套的法律法规已经基本齐全。意见书中提及的所有法规均在阳光下,"红头文件"的效力逐渐消退。问题在于一个法律专家是否真的是行家里手?若没有深厚的理论功底与对所涉问题的深刻理解,又对所涉法规不能了然于胸、融会贯通,便不能多角度多层面地分析与论述,鞭辟入里,结论清楚,释疑解惑。

时代给他提供了机会,他无愧于时代赋予的使命。作为杰出的法学家,他的声音在攀登的路上回响。

料想,陈教授必定熟知马克思所言:"外国语是人生斗争的武器。"他的英文著作代表中国国际经济法学界与中国国际商事仲裁界在国际上发声。非经多年的苦读与苦练,不能以地道的英文撰写专业文章并在国际仲裁的权威刊物上发表,进而得以结集出版。

《中国的呐喊》中披露,陈教授从 1953 年起作为年轻的法学教员转入马列主义的教学领域。1980 年,他年过半百后,才得以重回法学领域,研究国际经济法。盛年之时,在"应冲刺的年龄才起跑",也可以视为幸运。在中国改革开放与法制建设的春天,他"急起直追,以勤补拙"。据其弟子告知,陈教授往往工作到深夜或凌晨。三十多年中陈教授获得了广阔的舞台,在流逝的岁月中留下了深深的足印,为光辉的时代留下了华章。

2005 年他已 76 岁,犹以自勖诗句[224]表达其永不止步的决心:

蹉跎半生,韶华虚掷。青山满目,夕霞天际。
老牛破车,一拉到底。余热未尽,不息奋蹄!

诵读此诗,令人不禁想起美国诗人 Robert Frost 的诗《献身》(*Devotion*,汉蓉译):

---

[223] Michael Hwang and Amy Lai, Do Egregious Errors Amount to a Breach of Public Policy? *Arbitration*, Vol. 71, No. 1, 2005, p. 24. And note 21 on the same page: The errors considered material were that the arbitrator (1) failed to apply his mind properly to certain questions he had to decide; ...(4) failed to decide another material question, which effectively resulted in a ruling favoring one party (emphasis added). Ibid., paras. 10.8-10.84.

[224] 参见陈安:《国际经济法学刍言》,北京大学出版社 2005 年版,自序。

心灵视献身，不比海岸高。
守候岸曲线，永数潮涨消！

（编辑：龚　宇）

Precise and Thorough Analyses—Illustrating a Guru's Profound Knowledge
—A Brief Commentary on *The Voice from China*: *An CHEN on International Economic Law*

Huang Yanming[*]

Opening this great monograph titled *The Voice from China*: *An CHEN on International Economic Law* (*The Voice from China*), I am very delighted with and impressed by Prof. Chen's scholastic achievements on the subject and his skills in mastering English.

Prof. Chen is an eminent jurist and the forerunner of China's international economic law discipline. He was the Chairman of the Chinese Society of International Economic Law in which I was once a member of the Society and a mere subordinate under his supervision. I wish to touch and simultaneously share my views on some aspects of the cases and the Legal Opinions in *The Voice from China* (Chapters 20, 21, 22 and 23[225]) from the perspective of a craftsman—an arbitrator. In order to save space, abbreviated case names and subjects related would be applied.

Case 1, A UK Co. X v. a UK Insurance Co. Y. In December 1996, an entity from Cayman Islands and Chinese Co. B entered into a contractual joint venture

---

[*] Council member of the Chinese Society of International Economic Law; arbitrators with SCIA, CIETAC and Shanghai International Arbitration Centre.

The author is grateful to Brian C. W. Wong, Barrister of Hong Kong and Prof. Thomas Chiu of HKCT Institute of Social Science for their valuable pieces of advice, such as on idiomatical ways of saying things.

[225] See An Chen, The Truth Among the Fogbound "Expropriation" Claim: Comments on British X Investment Co. Versus British Y Insurance Co. Case; The Approach of "Winning from Both Sides" Used in the "Expropriation" Claim: Re-comments on British X Investment Co. Versus British Y Insurance Co. Case; On the Serious Violation of Chinese Jus Cogens: Comments on the Case of Importing Toxic Brazilian Soybeans into China (Expert's Legal Opinion on Zhonghe Versus Bunge Case); Isn't the Strict Prohibition on Importing Toxic Brazilian Soybeans into China "Illegal"? —A Rebuttal to Lawyer Song's Allegation, in An Chen, *The Voice from China*: *An CHEN on International Economic Law*, Springer, 2014, pp. 635-716.

agreement ("**the Agreement**") and a contractual joint venture ("**the CJV**") was established in China. Later Co. X replaced the Cayman entity. Under the insurance policy issued by Co. Y with Co. X as the assured, the risks undertaken cover losses arising out of acts of expropriation occurring during the policy period of February 20, 2001 to February 19, 2004. Due to the issuance of **Circular No. 31 〔1998〕** by the PRC's State Council and **Circular No. 43 〔2002〕** by the General Office of the State Council ("**the Two Circulars**"), Co. X claims that the Two Circulars constitute an **Act of Expropriation**, and therefore requesting compensation for losses from Co. Y by reference to the insurance policy that stipulated about (possible) compulsory take over by the Chinese government. Co. Y denies and Co. X refers the case to arbitration in British.

The key issues before Prof. Chen are whether the Two Circulars are of the nature or give such effects of an Act of Expropriation of the assets of the CJV; if the answer is affirmative, Co. X could base on the alleged Act of Expropriation to claim the coverage under the insurance policy, thereafter Co. Y would gain the subrogation (of insurer) from Co. X. In another word, the said issues could be expressed in a manner to cover situations where an agreement is in line with the provisions of the Act of PRC on Chinese-Foreign Contractual Joint Venture ("**CJV Act**") and has received approval by some competent governmental authorities of China. Under such circumstances, have those internationally accepted basic legal principles, such as "**autonomy of the parties' will**" and "**no-retroactivity of law**", been fully accepted by or already taken root in China as a country ruled by law?

Case 2, Xiamen Zhonghe Industry Co., Ltd. (Zhonghe) v. Bunge Singapore Pte. Ltd. (Bunge). Zhonghe as buyer and Bunge as seller on February 25, 2004 entered into the Contract S04-071("**the Contract**") with Brazilian soybeans of 55,000 metric tons as the subject matter. It is provided in the Contract that Zhonghe shall through a first-class Chinese bank acceptable by Bunge open a letter of credit in favor of the seller.

The kernel problems that Prof. Chen are faced with are whether **the prohibitions** (or **administrative ordinances, administrative prohibitive orders** or **mandatory regulations or rules**) by AQSIQ have comprehensive and powerful legal binding force over Chinese importers, Chinese banks and their respective branches overseas; whether China is the place of performance of the obligation to open the letter of credit under the Contract; **when English laws are applicable**, whether the mandatory rules or orders in Chinese legal system are of mandatory effects over Chinese legal entities and therefore the Contract was frustrated due to the said prohibitions and their binding force.

In his Legal Opinions, when dealing with issues pertaining to Case 1, Prof. Chen has not overlooked or missed out any provisions concerned from the Constitution to all the laws, acts, regulations, rules, and administrative orders and even the promises by China when entering into WTO. For instance, he lists some facts that as a member of WTO, China has not only promised to "ensure the full conformity of its laws, regulations, and rules with the provision of the WTO Agreement"[226], but also taken measures in this regard.[227] When treating the problems relating to Case 2, he respectively identifies the Contract and the clause that "English laws shall be applied", and that the Contract was signed by Bunge's subsidiary Bunge International Trading (Shanghai) Co., Ltd. ("**Bunge Shanghai**") residing in Shanghai with Zhonghe.[228]

Revealing his deep knowledge of the Convention on the Law Applicable to Contractual Obligations ("**Rome Convention**"), the effective Contacts (Applicable Law) Act 1990 (of British), the precedents established by English courts in their long established judicial practice and conflict of laws rules which have been refined and summarized by authoritative English scholars and widely accepted by the international community, analyzing their mutual relations and different forces, step by step, Prof. Chen discusses the issues and expounds his viewpoints by accurately referring to the relevant provisions of various acts or laws and legal theories.

Prof. Chen reaches his conclusion that in Case 1 the Two Circulars and their provisions are of no **Expropriation** effects, and confirms that the two major principles of law, ie., "**autonomy of the parties' will**" and "**non-retroactivity**" have

---

[226] An Chen, The Truth Among the Fogbound "Expropriation" Claim: Comments on British X Investment Co. Versus British Y Insurance Co. Case, in An Chen, *The Voice from China: An CHEN on International Economic Law*, Springer, 2013, p. 643.

[227] Ibid., pp. 643-646.

[228] See An Chen, On the Serious Violation of Chinese Jus Cogens: Comments on the Case of Importing Toxic Brazilian Soybeans into China (Expert's Legal Opinion on Zhonghe Versus Bunge Case), in An Chen, *The Voice from China: An CHEN on International Economic Law*, Springer, 2013, pp. 687-688.

actually taken root in China and are applicable to the case. And in Case 2, he firmly believes that the **administrative prohibitive orders** or **mandatory orders** contained in the Publication Announcements, such as the Announcements 71 by AQSIQ are of binding effects over Chinese legal entities concerned, that China is the place of performance of the obligation to have the letter of credit opened and the Contract was frustrated due to the mandatory orders.

Perusing the Chapters, the author cannot help recall the days when China was at the initial period of reform and began to rejoin the international community. It was also the initial period of the rule by law in China. In 1985-1986, I once assisted a senior superior in his rendering of legal opinions. One of the legal opinions was for a banking group of Hong Kong, relating to the banking group as lenders and a Chinese company as borrower and two Chinese corporations as guarantors to the loan agreement with the laws of New York State of the America as the governing laws. The lawyers engaged by the banking group had to engage some lawyer in the mainland China to carry out inquiries to identify and confirm the status, the business scope, the financial standing and other conditions of the borrowers and the guarantors; that the matters relating to the loan and guaranty were normal and in conformity with the laws, acts, regulations or policies of China; that the borrower and his guarantors had got consents from competent departments of China; and the decisions relating to the loan made by the boards of directors of the borrower and the guarantors and representatives who would sign the loan agreement and other documents concerned. The main business of one of the two guarantors had been in Hong Kong for over 100 years, nevertheless its registration place of the business was in Beijing. Though it was of good credit in Hong Kong, it was required according to the regulations by the State Administrative Bureau of Exchange Control to apply for approval for the guaranty and to obtain the approval certificate. At that time, there were few statutes enacted or promulgated by National People's Congress or its standing committee, instead there were quite a lot internal documents or official documents of red colored titles ("hong tou wen jian" in Chinese). But it was obviously, while the applicable laws of the loan agreement were the laws of the New York State, the banking group and their lawyers relied expressly upon the provisions of the laws, acts, regulations or even the then popular internal documents of China containing some policies in this regard. All the legal issues or matters identified and confirmed in the legal opinions issued by the lawyer from mainland China were the pre-conditions for the finally conclusion of the loan agreement. The signing of the loan agreement was done upon the receipt of the legal opinions by the banking group and its lawyers.

In Case 1, Co. Y acts in reasonable manner, timely asking a Chinese legal expert for advice which forms as his basis for defence. If Co. X, when in doubt of the retroactivity of the Two Circulars and whether it is of the nature of expropriation, should have acted as Co. Y in asking a Chinese legal expert for advice, Prof. Chen's legal opinions would have been issued for him and such legal opinions would have even better effect. After all, Co. X had referred the case to arbitration, as his sum of investment was USD 12,000,000.00, the coverage of the policy would not have been less than that sum or probably plus 10 per cent and the sum claimed would have not been less than the sum either. In this case, Co. X had paid fees for his lawyers, for the arbitration administrative charges closely relating to the time spent by the registrar and his deputies and the fees for the arbitrator(s). If Co. X had asked for advice before referring the case to arbitration, the sum paid for a Chinese legal expert and his legal opinions would be a very small proportion comparing with the fees and changes that he would have paid for arbitral process.

Concerning Case 2, I have mentioned above that I was once an assistant to a senior superior in rendering legal opinions to a banking group from other jurisdiction. When the governing laws were those of the New York State, the banking group's lawyers had never overlooked the lex personalis of the borrower and guarantors of other jurisdiction. In contrast, in Case 2, the Chinese lawyer engaged by Bunge has given me an impression that he did not take proper notice or even probably turned a blind eye to the laws or mandatory orders of China.

The lex personalis of Zhonghe should not have been neglected, such as those pertaining to the capacity for private rights or duties, any Chinese legal entities should abided by them or the Chinese legal entities must be subject to those laws, acts, regulations or administrative orders. If there are any prohibitions on the importing or exporting to China food or material for food processing with **pesticide**, knowledge about these prohibitions or the absence of such knowledge would have different serious consequences. Prof. Chen has proved that he is well professed of all aspects of the matters concerned.

I would like to stress that the Contract is of an important feature in international trade. For example, parties are from the contracting states to the CISG, then the provisions of the CISG will be regarded as being integrated into their respective national law of P. R. China and Singapore. If the parties do not expressly exclude the application of the CISG or derogate from or vary the effect of its provisions,[229] save the reservations, doesn't the CISG apply to the case? When the governing law is of English law, does it mean that the CISG could be absolutely excluded?

I am fully accept that Prof. Chen is correct in quoting Art 3(3) of the Rome Convention "[T]he fact that the parties have chosen a foreign law, whether or not accompanied by the choice of a foreign tribunal, shall **not**, where all the other elements relevant to the situation at the time of the choice are connected with one country only, **prejudice the application of rules of the law of that country which cannot be derogated from by contract, hereinafter called 'mandatory rules'.**"[230]

It seems to me that the application of the CISG to the case could not be excluded. If the parties don't exclude the application of the CISG in the Contract, it will be necessary to look at Art. 7(2) of the CISG:

> Questions concerning matters governed by this Convention which are not expressly settled in it are to be settled in conformity with the general principles on which it is based or, in the absence of such principles, **in conformity with the law applicable by virtue of the rules of private international law.**

If in the instant case the CISG could not be excluded, should we rely on the lex personalis of Zhonghe as Prof. Chen does and we may further refer to Art. 127 of the Contact Act of PRC:

> The Administration of Industry and Commerce and other relevant administrative authorities shall, within the scope of their respective the

---

[229] See Art. 6 of the CISG.
[230] An Chen, On the Serious Violation of Chinese Jus Cogens: Comments on the Case of Importing Toxic Brazilian Soybeans into China (Expert's Legal Opinion on Zhonghe Versus Bunge Case), in An Chen, *The Voice from China: An CHEN on International Economic Law*, Springer, 2013, pp. 687-689.

functions, supervise and deal with any unlawful conduct by way of contract prejudicial and detrimental to national or public interest. **If such conduct amounts to a crime, criminal responsibility shall be pursued according to laws.** [231]

The provision contained in Art. 127 above, once more from another angel reminds anyone of the binding effects of Chinese mandatory orders or rules and serious consequence of being against them.

In addition, I guess it might be better to tell Bunge and his Chinese lawyer, if they insists on the view that the mandatory rules or orders in the Chinese legal system could be ignored and the award should be made in favor of Bunge that under the Contract Brazilian soybeans containing highly toxic carcinogenic pesticide could be exported to China, the award should be set aside or its enforcement be refused. Some lines on a case revealing that misconduct of arbitrator "[W]hich justified setting aside an award Telkon SA Ltd. v. Anthony Boswood QC" are as follows:

> The South African High Court found that the arbitrator had committed **errors of law** (emphasis added) which amounted to gross irregularities in the conduct of the arbitration and set the award aside. [232]

We should be aware that nowadays any awards tainted with extremely serious or egregious errors amount to a breach of public policy. [233] To allow such fundamentally flawed awards to stand uncorrected would undermine confidence in the integrity of the arbitral process. [234] That concept or principle is expressly reflected in the Arts. 34 and 36 of the UNCITRAL Model Law on International Commercial Arbitration.

From the Legal Opinions by Prof. Chen, we arbitrators could get some

---

[231] Quoted from the English Edition of the Contract Act of PRC by Harmony Consultants Ltd.

[232] Michael Hwang and Amy Lai, Do Egregious Errors Amount to a Breach of Public Policy? *Arbitration*, Vol. 71, No. 1, 2005, p. 24. And note 21 on the same page: The errors considered material were that the arbitrator (1) failed to apply his mind properly to certain questions he had to decide; ... (4) failed to decide another material question, which effectively resulted in a ruling favoring one party (emphasis added). Ibid., paras. 10.8-10.84.

[233] Ibid., pp. 1-24.

[234] See Michael Hwang and Amy Lai, Do Egregious Errors Amount to a Breach of Public Policy? *Arbitration*, Vol. 71, No. 1, 2005, p. 24. And note 21 on the same page: The errors considered material were that the arbitrator (1) failed to apply his mind properly to certain questions he had to decide; ... (4) failed to decide another material question, which effectively resulted in a ruling favoring one party (emphasis added). Ibid., p. 24.

enlightenment. In our awards under the subtitle "the Opinions of the Tribunal", the tribunal should ensure that no issue and claim is missed out, all matters, key issues, facts and the merits of the case should be thoroughly explored. If arbitrators are short of that ability, failing to explain why a claim or counter-claim is sustained or refused, their awards rendered would be far from convincing in giving reasons.

It is in the 21 century that Prof. Chen issued his Legal Opinions. Sets of laws, acts, regulations or rules that are orientated towards the needs of a market economy have been basically enacted or promulgated. All the provisions he quotes are transparent in the sun. The effects of those "internal documents" are fading. Nevertheless, the problem lies in whether one is an old hand. Not familiar with all the aspects of the matters concerned, without profound knowledge and deep understanding of all the issues concerned, without skills in mastering in one's mother-tongue and English plus its legal terminology, one could hardly deal with those hard-nuts properly.

The era of reform and opening to the international community has provided Prof. Chen with a golden opportunity and in return for the era and on behalf of the discipline of the international economic law of China he advocates with admirable clarity and strength, his voice are echoing along the long road to the heights.

I guess Prof. Chen must be familiar with the saying of Karl Marx: "A foreign language is a weapon in the struggle of life." No pains no gains. Without decades of hard working, reading, writing and studying, no one is able to write in idiomatic English.

His professional papers are carried in authoritative journals and then collected in this monograph. Acting as a distinguish representative of discipline of the China's international economic law and the circle of China international arbitration, he has made his marks on the international stage and added academic literature thereon.

It is revealed in *The Voice form China*, that Prof. Chen as a junior teacher in 1953 shifted from law to Marxism and Leninism. When over 50 years old, in his prime years, he at last got the chance to return to the law field as he says that "Just stated to race at the age of spurt". On the other hand, it could be regarded as a matter of luck. In the spring of reform and opening to the outside, he has lost no chance to "rouse to catch up, overcome shortage by diligence". His doctorial candidates remember that he usually would not turn off his desk-lamp until midnight or early morning. In the past decades, he has never idled away. His brilliant works are reflecting the long road he has travelled.

In his poem of self-encouragement in 2005 even when he was aged 76, he revealed his determination that he would never stop in his academic researching and creating course:[235]

> Regretfully it is so late in a daytime,
> Half of a lifetime had been spent in vain,
> Thanks to the setting sun so brightly shines,
> The old ox insists in carrying a broken cart to the end,
> Never stop in speeding up its hoof-pace in time,
> As long as its surplus energy still remains.

That reminds me of the similar poem by an American poet Robert Frost:

> *Devotion*
> The heart can think of no devotion,
> Greater than being shore to the ocean,
> Holding the curve of one position,
> Counting an endless repetition.

（翻译：黄雁明）

十、独具中国风格气派 发出华夏学术强音
—— 评《中国的呐喊：陈安论国际经济法》

石静霞 孙英哲*

2013年，中国国际经济法学界的前辈陈安先生的英文版新书《中国的呐喊：陈安论国际经济法》隆重面世。该书汇辑了陈安教授自1980年以来不同时期撰写的24

---

[235] An Chen, *The Voice from China: An CHEN on International Economic Law*, Springer, 2014, pp. li-lii.

* 石静霞，对外经济贸易大学法学院教授、博士生导师，对外经济贸易大学法学院院长；孙英哲，对外经济贸易大学法学院2014级博士研究生。

篇精品专论,受"国家社会科学基金中华学术外译项目"支持,由国际著名出版社斯普林格(Springer)出版。

陈安先生学贯中西,素养精深,他就中国国际经济法学的基本问题提出了许多真知灼见,并多次代表中国国际经济法学界赴国外交流讲学,被誉为"中国国际经济法学的奠基人之一"。陈安先生并未拘泥于国际经济法学的理论探讨,而是积极投身实践,代表中国参与多项国际法律实务。特别是,陈先生曾经先后于1993年、2004年、2010年三度受中国政府指派,就任"解决投资争端国际中心"(ICSID)国际仲裁员,处理具体的国际投资争端。

陈安先生《中国的呐喊:陈安论国际经济法》一书共分六部分,系统梳理和分析了改革开放以来国际经济法学术前沿的重大热点和难点问题,在该书中,陈安先生将理论与实践紧密结合,始终坚持实事求是,并以公平正义作为自身观点的内在脉络。其中,以第十一章"对近期谢业深诉秘鲁政府案 ICSID 管辖权裁定的若干质疑:中国—秘鲁 BIT 是否应当适用于'一国两制'下的香港特别行政区"(Queries to the Recent ICSID Decision on Jurisdiction Upon the Case of Tza Yap Shum v. Republic of Peru: Should China-Peru BIT 1994 Be Applied to Hong Kong SAR Under the "One Country, Two Systems" Policy?)[236]尤为突出。

近年来,国际投资仲裁发展迅速,中国企业的参与度正在逐步增长。中国企业近年来提起了三起国际投资仲裁案,[237]其中包括两件 ICSID 仲裁案。因此,ICSID 仲裁实践对于中国投资,尤其是中国对外签订的双边投资保护协定(BIT)的具体落实具有重要意义。这篇文章以中国政府签署条约首次在 ICSID 涉案的谢业深诉秘鲁政府案(Tza Yap Shum v. Republic of Peru)的管辖权裁定为中心,探讨了 ICSID 仲裁庭裁决的不当之处。案件的核心问题之一是,香港人是否可以援引中国政府在香港回归之前与秘鲁政府签订的 BIT 来寻求投资保护。陈安先生对此持否定态度。陈安先生在着重分析《中英联合声明》《香港特区基本法》以及《维也纳条约法公约》(VCLT)等相关规定的基础上,主要从两方面论证了其观点:首先,考虑到中国政府

---

[236] See An Chen, *The Voice from China: An CHEN on International Economic Law*, Springer, 2013, pp. 337-372.

[237] See Ping An Life Insurance Company of China, Limited and Ping An Insurance (Group) Company of China, Limited v. Kingdom of Belgium, ICSID Case No. ARB/12/29; China Heilongjiang International Economic & Technical Cooperative Corp., Beijing Shougang Mining Investment Company Ltd., and Qinhuangdaoshi Qinlong International Industrial Co. Ltd. v. Mongolia, PCA; Beijing Urban Construction Group Co. Ltd. v. Republic of Yemen, ICSID Case No. ARB/14/30.

"一国两制"的大政方针和《香港特区基本法》中的具体规定[238],中国—秘鲁BIT不应自动适用于香港。其次,中国—秘鲁BIT于1994年签订时,香港尚未回归,因此不能适用于涉及中国的争议。

Lao Holdings N. V. v. Lao People's Democratic Republic案[239]也涉及类似问题,即澳门投资者是否可以援引中国—老挝BIT对老挝提起仲裁。Lao Holdings N. V.案仲裁庭在肯定了《关于国家在条约方面的继承的维也纳公约》(VCST)第15条"移动条约适用范围原则"(moving treaty frontiers rule)与VCLT第29条均为国际习惯法,并对二者区别以及在此案中的联系进行分析的基础上,认为中国—老挝BIT应当适用于澳门特别行政区。[240]该案裁决虽然与谢业深案的裁决思路存在差异,[241]但在基本立场上继承了仲裁庭在谢业深案中的立场,值得注意。首先,仲裁庭运用VCST第15条[242]对于国家继承问题所发展出的分析框架进行了论证。第15条分为一般条款和例外条款,仲裁庭认为,如果适用一般条款,中国—老挝BIT可以对澳门适用;但是,如果第15条的例外条款的规定得以满足,则中国—老挝BIT不得对澳门适用。仲裁庭采用反推的方法,证明第15条B项中的3项例外条款中的规定均未在该案当中得到满足。其中,在论证"中国—老挝BIT是否在另外被证明不能适用于中国领土全境"时,仲裁庭继承了谢业深案的观点。在谢业深案中,仲裁庭认为在中国与第三国已经签订BIT的情况下,香港自行与第三国缔结BIT的权力并不必然多余(necessarily redundant)。[243]该案中的仲裁庭认为,中国—老挝BIT与澳门—老挝BIT的立法目标都是保护外国投资者和东道国的经济发展。两个BITs如果同时对澳门适用,不仅不会造成阻碍,反而会对实现这两个BIT的立法目标产生促进作用。[244]除此以外,在对BITs重点概念的理解上,该案仲裁庭也基本认同谢业深案仲裁庭适用VCLT进行的论证分析。[245] 谢业深案仲裁庭认为,根据VCLT相关规

---

[238] 该法第153条规定:"中华人民共和国缔结的国际协议,中央人民政府可根据香港特别行政区的情况和需要,在征询香港特别行政区政府的意见后,决定是否适用于香港特别行政区。"
[239] See Lao Holdings N. V. v. Lao People's Democratic Republic, ICSID Case No. ARB(AF)/12/6.
[240] Ibid., pp. 232-269.
[241] 谢业深案的裁定仅援引了VCLT,并未引用VCST进行论证。
[242] VCST第15条"对领土一部分的继承"规定:"一国领土的一部分,或虽非一国领土的一部分但其国际关系由该国负责的任何领土,成为另一国领土的一部分时:(a)被继承国的条约,自国家继承日期起,停止对国家继承所涉领土生效,(b)继承国的条约,自国家继承日期起,对国家继承所涉领土生效,但从条约可知或另经确定该条约对该领土的适用不合条约的目的和宗旨或者根本改变实施条约的条件时,不在此限。"
[243] See Tza Yap Shum v. Republic of Peru, ICSID Case No. ARB/07/6, p. 76.
[244] See Lao Holdings N. V. v. Lao People's Democratic Republic, ICSID Case No. ARB(AF)/12/6, p. 295.
[245] Ibid., p. 329.

定,[246]在对中国—秘鲁 BIT 第 8 条第 3 款[247]中规定的"涉及"(involving)一词的"通常意义"(ordinary meaning)进行解释时,应当将"涉及"理解为"包含"(inclusive)而非"仅包含"(exclusive)。因此,不能仅仅从表面上将第 8 条第 3 款中规定的"涉及"简单理解为对于仲裁庭管辖权的限制。[248]

由此看来,陈安先生的主张虽然理由翔实,但并未受到国际仲裁实践的完全认可。陈安先生的论证重点在于《中英联合声明》与《香港特区基本法》,但仲裁庭显然对《中英联合声明》与《香港特区基本法》的分析着墨不多,而是着重于对 BITs 的分析。这启示我们,作为中国学者,应当对中外联合声明的国际法律地位以及特区基本法的内涵进行深入研究,从而能够引起国际关注。

陈安先生文章的最大特色在于论证充分,尤其是完整论证了 VCLT 第 31 条、第 32 条在具体适用中的问题。总体上看,陈安先生的论证不仅对后案有所影响,[249]同时还留下了一些值得深思的问题。首先,中国—秘鲁 BIT 不能对香港特别行政区生效,是否可以直接等同于香港公民(Chinese nationals who hold a HKSAR passport)不能援引中国—秘鲁 BIT?中国—秘鲁 BIT 中规定的"投资者"的范围是所有"依照中华人民共和国法律拥有其国籍的自然人"[250]。而根据中国《国籍法》相关规定,[251]香港公民具有中国国籍,则香港特别行政区的"高度自治权"是否可以阻碍香港公民凭借中国国籍,获取中国—秘鲁 BIT 项下的投资保护呢?其次,作为一种法律论证技术(lawyering skill),如果谢业深不能获得中国—秘鲁 BIT 项下的投资保护,他是否可以根据英国于 1993 年与秘鲁签订的英国—秘鲁 BIT(1994 年生效)来寻求投资保护呢?如果谢业深因为"旧法(1995 年生效的中国—秘鲁 BIT)不适用'新情况'[252]"而不能获得中国—秘鲁 BIT 的保护,则其是否可以依据"旧法(1994 年生效的英国—秘鲁 BIT)应当根据'过去的情况'[253]继续适用"的逻辑寻求英国—秘鲁

---

[246] 该法第 31 条第 1 款规定:"条约应依其用语按其上下文并参照条约之目的及宗旨所具有之通常意义,善意解释之。"

[247] 中国—秘鲁 BIT 第 8 条第 3 款规定:"如涉及征收补偿款额的争议,在诉诸本条第一款的程序后六个月内仍未能解决,可应任何一方的要求,将争议提交根据一九六五年三月十八日在华盛顿签署的《关于解决国家和他国国民之间投资争端公约》设立的'解决投资争端国际中心'进行仲裁。缔约一方的投资者和缔约另一方之间有关其他事项的争议,经双方同意,可提交该中心。如有关投资者诉诸了本条第二款所规定的程序,本款规定不应适用。"

[248] See Tza Yap Shum v. Republic of Peru, ICSID Case No. ARB/07/6, pp. 163-165.

[249] Ibid., p. 77.

[250] 中国—秘鲁 BIT 第 1 条第 2 款第 1 项。

[251] 该法第 3 条规定:"中华人民共和国不承认中国公民具有双重国籍。"第 4 条规定:"父母双方或一方为中国公民,本人出生在中国,具有中国国籍。"

[252] 回归后的香港在国际法意义上成为中国领土的一部分,香港公民获得中国国籍。

[253] 在英国与秘鲁签订 BIT 时,香港在国际法意义上仍然是英国的领土。

BIT 的保护呢？这些都是我们在陈安先生著作的启发下，可以进一步考察的重要问题。

此外，陈安先生在该文中还从中外投资争端的视角，详细论证了有关《中英联合声明》《中国宪法》《香港特区基本法》以及中外条约彼此之间的关系等问题[254]，明确指出，《中英联合声明》明文规定，中国政府决定于 1997 年 7 月 1 日对香港恢复行使主权，同日，英国政府将香港交还中国。从此时起，根据《中国宪法》第 31 条制定的"《香港基本法》构成管理香港特别行政区的宪政性文件"[255]，香港的一切事务均应按《香港基本法》行事。依据《中英联合声明》附件一第 XI 章以及《香港特区基本法》第 153 条规定，在"一国两制"的特定条件下，"中国与外国签订的各种国际协定在 1997 年后并不能自动适用于香港。相反，这些协定只在中国中央政府征询香港特别行政区政府的意见，并决定适用于香港特别行政区后，才能适用于香港特别行政区"[256]。这些论证，对于当前中国所面临的现实问题，包括任何人都无权借口《中英联合声明》干涉中国内政、应以法治方式解决香港"占中"危机等，均具有重大的现实参考意义。[257] 具体说来，情况如下：

据香港《文汇报》2014 年 11 月 18 日报道，英国下议院外交事务委员会 17 日举行有关《中英联合声明》的听证会。香港《南华早报》前总编辑范力行(Jonathan Fenby)在出席"作证"时称，中国中央政府希望紧紧控制香港政治和经济，香港特区政府比较重视与内地的关系，忽略港人的民主诉求。在港参与"占领"行动的香港大学学生 Hui SinTung 及香港中文大学学生 Tang Chi Tak 则称，中国**中央政府多次违反《中英联合声明》，包括"剥夺"内文订明港人能继续享有的新闻自由、集会自由及普及选举权利，英国应该迫使中国"履行"《中英联合声明》并作出谴责，甚至重启《南京条约》及《天津条约》**。此外，香港民主党主席刘慧卿 18 日也通过视像向英国国会"作证"，称英国有责任保障香港的自由和生活方式。另外，英美等外国势力一再插手香港内部事务，趁"占中"之机，他们插手频率更是有增无减。2014 年 9 月底，英国

---

[254] See An Chen, *The Voice from China*: *An CHEN on International Economic Law*, Springer, 2013, pp. 341-348. 同时参见《〈中国—秘鲁 1994 年双边投资协定〉可否适用于"一国两制"下的中国香港特别行政区》，载陈安：《陈安论国际经济法学》（第五卷），复旦大学出版社 2008 年版，第 1155—1162 页。

[255] An Chen, *The Voice from China*: *An CHEN on International Economic Law*, Springer, 2013, p. 344.

[256] Ibid., p. 343.

[257] 例如，由于《中英联合声明》并不对香港政府自动生效，因此香港政府的措施并不受《中英联合声明》的拘束，而只受到《香港特区基本法》及其项下法律法规的规制。因此，英国下议院于 2014 年 12 月 16 日对占中分子进行听证，并决定对香港政局作出调查的行为是于法无据的。See Evidence Session Announced with Protesters from Hong Kong, http://www.parliament.uk/business/committees/committees-a-z/commons-select/foreign-affairs-committee/news/hong-kong-evidence-wprotesters/.

时任首相卡梅伦称,"英国与中国达成的协议中提到了在'一国两制'框架下,香港拥有民主对未来的重要性",10月中旬他又宣称"英国应为香港人的自由权利站出来"。11月,当"占中"行动在香港已陷入穷途末路之际,继美中经济与安全审议委员会年度报告用了20页篇幅对香港政改胡诌一通外,美国国会中国问题委员会又召开听证会,邀请"末代港督"彭定康在伦敦透过视像卫星越洋"作证",称西方国家应公开对香港问题发声。英国外交事务委员会的议员则计划到港调查,结果被北京拒绝入境。对于英国的诸多谰言和花招,香港特区政制及内地事务局局长谭志源反驳说,英方对回归后的香港无主权、无治权、无监督权,不存在所谓"道义责任"。香港工联会议员王国兴说,香港部分反对派人员"应邀作证",是**公然配合外国势力干预香港内部事务,是丧失国格的行为,对中国人民、香港市民构成极大伤害**。香港金融界立法会议员吴亮星也说,香港事务是中国内政,其他国家无权指指点点,有香港反对派议员"配合"出席听证会,明显是招引外国势力干涉中国国家内部事务。[258]

中国政府对英国下议院外交事务委员会举行有关《中英联合声明》的听证会的荒唐行径,也连续予以严词谴责。早在2014年7月25日,中国外交部发言人洪磊就指出,香港事务属于中国内政,英方的做法是干涉中国内政,中国对此表示强烈不满和坚决反对。中国政府反对任何外部势力以任何借口进行干涉。[259] 2014年12月3日,外交部发言人华春莹更加明确指出,香港已于1997年回归中国,是中国的特别行政区。1984年的《中英联合声明》就中方恢复对香港行使主权和过渡期的有关安排,对中英双方的权利义务作了清晰划分。英方对回归后的香港无主权、无治权、无监督权,不存在所谓"道义责任"。英方有些人企图用所谓"道义责任"混淆视听,干涉中国内政,是不可接受的,也不可能得逞。[260]

显而易见,中国政府2014年的上述表态以及香港爱国人士2014年的上述主张,与陈安先生早先在2008年作出的前述详细论证,可以说是完全契合和互相呼应的。

陈安先生博学强识,书中很多对于国际经济法学重要问题的观点均来自于其毕生孜孜不倦的研习以及他与国际学术界的对话。陈安先生先后与Louis Henkin、Andreas F. Lowenfeld以及John H. Jackson等著名国际经济法学学家进行过深入

---

[258] 参见《香港大学生赴英"听证"声称英国应重启〈南京条约〉》,http://news.ifeng.com/a/20141219/42757765_0.shtml。

[259] 参见《英质询联合声明在港实施 中国强烈不满》,http://www.zaobao.com.sg/wencui/politic/story20140727-370611。

[260] 参见《2014年12月3日外交部发言人华春莹主持例行记者会》,http://www.fmprc.gov.cn/ce/cgct/chn/fyrth/t1216342.htm。

的研讨交流,不断更新自己的知识,并将中国国际经济法学界的新发展和新动向介绍给国外同仁。更可贵的是,在研究与实践的过程中,陈安先生深刻洞察到国外国际经济法学著作中所暗含的殖民主义气息和单边主义进路,尤其是美式双重标准(US-style double standards)等,因此他毕生以呼吁改造旧式国际经济秩序、建立新型国际经济秩序为己任,坚持实事求是的态度,不懈探索真理,三十年如一日,积累汇聚而成《中国的呐喊》一书。"全书结构自成一体,观点新颖,具有中国风格和中国气派,阐释了不同于西方发达国家学者的创新学术理念和创新学术追求,致力于初步创立起以马克思主义为指导的具有中国特色的国际经济法理论体系,为国际社会弱势群体争取公平权益锻造了法学理论武器。"[261]

党的十八届三中全会决议将"构建开放型经济新体制"上升到战略高度,加强中国国际经济法学研究、完善中国国际经济法治建设,已成为因应"一带一路""走出去"、创设金砖银行和亚洲基础设施投资银行的核心要求和必要保障。汪洋副总理撰文指出,应当加强涉外法律工作,积极参与国际规则的制定。[262]本书正是陈安先生植根于中华民族利益、中国特色社会主义制度以及中国作为发展中国家经贸大国的发展现状,对国际经济法基本理论和热点难点问题的重要回应。当前,多边贸易体系前行缓慢,双边、诸边贸易投资协定尤其是以跨太平洋伙伴关系协议(Trans-Pacific Partnership,TPP)、跨大西洋贸易与投资伙伴协议(Transatlantic Trade and Investment Partnership,TTIP)、区域全面经济伙伴关系(Regional Comprehensive Economic Partnership,RCEP)等为代表的巨型自贸协定(Mega-FTAs)以及数百个包含投资规则的 FTAs,正成为国际经贸法重构的重要体现。陈安先生在书中指出,"中外双边投资条约中的四大'安全阀'不宜贸然全面拆除"[263],这对于在中美、中欧BIT 谈判中如何保护国家、民族利益等具有借鉴意义。此外,陈安先生在其著作中引经据典,从中国古诗词到外国学界大师名著,可以很好地帮助读者更深入地了解中国国际经济法学者的独特学术视野。

我们相信,陈安先生的巨著《中国的呐喊》一书,将乘着全球化浪潮和中国经济高速发展的东风走向世界,代表中国国际经济法学人,在国际法舞台上发出华夏学术的强音。

(编辑:陈　欣)

---

[261] 全国哲学社会科学规划办公室下达"关于《中国的呐喊》书稿的专家评审意见",2013 年 11 月 22 日。
[262] 参见汪洋:《加强涉外法律工作》,载《人民日报》2014 年 11 月 6 日第 6 版。
[263] An Chen, *The Voice from China:An CHEN on International Economic Law*, Springer, 2013, p. 273.

Academic Voice with Chinese Characteristics
—A Commentary on *The Voice from China*:
An CHEN on International Economic Law

Shi Jingxia   Sun Yingzhe[*]

In 2013, the English version of the book *The Voice from China*: *An CHEN on International Economic Law*, sponsored by Chinese Academic Translation Program, was published by Springer, a distinguished publisher across the globe. The book is a collection of the 24 papers written by An Chen, an emeritus professor of Xiamen University, the former chairman of the Chinese Society of International Economic Law, and one of the co-founders of the Society, in different times since 1980s.

An Chen, with profound attainments and a thorough knowledge of both western and Chinese law in the field of international economic law, has been honored as one of the founders of the discipline of international economic law in China. He has put forward a lot of insights on the basic issues in China concerning international economic law and, for many a time, he went abroad for international academic exchange and overseas lecturing. Not just limited to the theoretic exploration, he also devoted himself to the practice in the field of international economic law. In particular, he was designated by the Chinese government in 1993, 2004 and 2010 respectively as an international arbitrator in the International Center for the Settlement of Investment Disputes (ICSID) and engaged in the specific settlement of investment disputes.

The book, composed of six parts, systematically presented and analyzed the major heat issues and perplexities concerning international economic law faced with China since its Reform and Opening-up Program. In this book, Mr. Chen has combined theory with practice, insisted the principle of seeking truth from facts

---

[*] Shi Jingxia, PhD Tutor, Professor of Law, Dean of Law School, University of International Business and Economics; Sun Yingzhe, 2014 Class Doctoral student of Law School, University of International Business and Economics.

unswervingly, and regarded fairness and justice as the backbone of his arguments. In Chapter 11, the paper entitled "Queries to the Recent ICSID Decision on Jurisdiction Upon the Case of Tza Yap Shum v. Republic of Peru: Should China-Peru BIT 1994 Be Applied to Hong Kong SAR Under the 'One Country, Two Systems' Policy?" is a particular case in point.

In recent years, with the rapid expansion of international investment arbitrations, China has seen an increasing engagement in the settlement of investment arbitration. Enterprises in the Chinese mainland have in recent years initiated 3 international investment disputes, two out of which involve ICSID arbitration. Therefore, the ICSID arbitration practice is of huge significance to China's overseas investment and, particularly, to the implementation of China's BITs negotiated with foreign countries or jurisdictions. This paper, revolving the decision on the jurisdiction issue in the case Tza Yap Shum v. Republic of Peru in which a BIT negotiated by China was involved in ICSID arbitration for the first time, has explored the inappropriateness of the ICSID arbitral tribunal's decision. One of the focuses in the case was whether Hong Kongese could seek investment protection under the BIT negotiated by the government of the Chinese mainland and that of Peru prior to Hong Kong's return to China. Mr. Chen adopted a negative attitude. After an analysis of the Joint Declaration of the Government of the United Kingdom of Great Britain and Northern Ireland and the Government of the People's Republic of China on the Question of Hong Kong (hereinafter referred to as "Sino-British Joint Declaration"), The Basic Law of the Hong Kong Special Administrative Region of the People's Republic of China (hereinafter referred to as "The Basic Law of the Hong Kong SAR") and the Vienna Convention on the Law of the Treaties (hereinafter referred to as "VCLT"), he based his argument on the two following aspects. The first was that Hong Kong had not returned back to China when the China-Peru BIT was signed in 1994, thus the China-Peru BIT could not be applied to Hong Kong; and the second was that in accordance with China's "One Country, Two Systems" policy and the relevant provisions in The Basic Law of the Hong Kong SAR, the China-Peru BIT could not be applied automatically to Hong Kong.

In the case Lao Holdings N. V. v. Lao People's Democratic Republic, a similar issue also arose whether investors in Macau may institute an arbitration against Lao under China-Lao BIT. The tribunal in the Lao Holdings N. V. case acknowledged both the Article 15 (moving treaty frontiers rule) of the Vienna Convention on Succession of States in Respect of Treaties (hereinafter referred to as "VCST") and the Article 29 of the VCLT as customary international law and held the view that the China-Lao BIT should apply to Macau SAR after distinguishing the above-mentioned two articles and analyzing the association therebetween in the present case. Although there existed differences in the jurisprudence between the two cases, it was noteworthy that the Lao Holdings N. V. case generally followed the positions adopted by the Tza Yap Shum tribunal. The Lao Holdings N. V. tribunal first used the Article 15 of the VCST to carry out the argumentation on the analytic framework developed by the state succession issues. Article 15 of the VCST includes general provisions and exceptional provisions. The tribunal observed that the China-Lao BIT may apply to Macau SAR if the general provisions were applied; but otherwise if the exceptional provisions were satisfied. The tribunal backwardly demonstrated that none of the three circumstances listed in Sub-paragraph B of Article 15 had been satisfied in the present case. To demonstrate that "the China-Lao BIT could not apply to all the jurisdictions of China", the tribunal had followed the Tza Yap Shum case. In the Lao Holdings N. V. case, the tribunal believed that under the circumstances where China has concluded BIT with a third country, Hong Kong's power to conclude of itself BIT with this third country was not necessarily redundant. In the tribunal's opinion, the legislative purpose of both the China-Lao BIT and the Macau-Lao BIT was to protect foreign investors and the economic development of the host state. If both of the above BITs could be applied to Macau, the legislative purpose, instead of being obstructed, may be otherwise facilitated. Besides, in terms of the understanding of some of the key conceptions in BITs, the Lao Holdings N. V. tribunal also basically followed the Tza Yap Shum case which used the VCLT argument. The tribunal of the Tza Yap Shum case believed that according to the relevant provisions of the VCLT, when interpreting the ordinary meaning of the word "involving" in Paragraph 3 of Article 8 in the China-Peru BIT, the word "involving" should be construed as "inclusive", but not "exclusive". Therefore, it would be inadvisable to simply take the word "involving" literally as a restriction to the tribunal's jurisdiction.

It thus appears that despite that Mr. Chen had provided a detailed and accurate argument, his argument had not been fully acknowledged by international arbitration practice. Mr. Chen concentrated on the Sino-British Joint Declaration and The Basic Law of the Hong Kong SAR, while the arbitral tribunal mainly drew on the BITs. It thus reveals that we as Chinese scholars need to delve into the international legal status of the Sino-British Joint Declaration and the intension of The Basic Law of the Hong Kong SAR, so as to attract the attention of the international community.

Mr. Chen's argument was sufficiently presented in his paper, and the issues around the specific application of Article 31 and 32 of VCLT were fully discussed in particular. Generally speaking, not only has his argument created important influence on subsequent cases, but his paper has also brought up quite some food for thought. To name a few. Is the fact that the China-Peru BIT cannot apply to Hong Kong SAR equivalent to that Chinese nationals who hold a HKSAR passport cannot invoke the same BIT either? The "investors" in the China-Peru BIT cover "all the natural persons who hold its nationality in accordance with the law of the People's Republic of China". Pursuant to the Nationality Law of the People's Republic of China, Hong Kongese possess Chinese nationality. Then, can Hong Kong's "high degree of autonomy" serve as an obstacle to Hong Kongese seeking investment protection under China-Peru BIT? In addition, as a lawyering skill, assuming that Tza Yap Shum cannot obtain the investment protection under the China-Peru BIT, whether there exists a possibility that it can get investment protection under the British-Peru BIT negotiated in 1993 (in force as of 1994)? If Tza Yap Shum cannot get protected under the China-Peru BIT because of the logic that "old law (the China-Peru BIT in force in 1995) cannot apply to 'new circumstances'", can it seek protection under the British-Peru BIT by the reasoning that "old law (the British-Peru BIT in force as of 1994) should continue to apply to 'past circumstances'"? These are all inspiring questions posed by Mr. Chen's paper that need to be further considered.

Moreover, Mr. Chen also, from the perspective of investment disputes between China and foreign countries, expounded the relationships between the Sino-British Joint Declaration, the Constitution of the People's Republic of China, The Basic

Law of the Hong Kong SAR as well as a series of treaties negotiated by China with foreign countries. He clearly pointed out that according to the Sino-British Joint Declaration, the Chinese government would resume the exercise of sovereignty over Hong Kong on July 1, 1997, and the British government would return Hong Kong back to China on the same day. Since then, "The Basic Law of the Hong Kong SAR formulated according to the Article 31 of the Constitution of the PRC would be the constitutive instrument governing the Hong Kong SAR", and all the affairs in Hong Kong shall be subject to The Basic Law of the Hong Kong SAR. According to Chapter XI of the Appendix to the Sino-British Joint Declaration and Article 153 of The Basic Law of the Hong Kong SAR, under the policy of "One Country, Two Systems", "international treaties entered into by China with third countries would not automatically apply to Hong Kong after July 1997. To the contrary, they would only apply to Hong Kong under the prerequisite that the Central Government of China decided to extend their application to Hong Kong after consultation with the Government of HKSAR." These crucial arguments are of huge practical relevance to tackling the current problems faced with China, including the attempt of interference with China's internal affairs by using the Sino-British Joint Declaration as a pretext and the crisis of "Occupy Central", etc. The specific circumstances are as follows:

As reported by Shanghai Mercury, Hong Kong on November 18, 2014, the Foreign Affairs Commission of the House of Commons on November 17 conducted a hearing on the Sino-British Joint Declaration. Jonathan Fenby, the former chief editor of South China Morning Post, expressed when "testifying" that the central government of China wished to keep a firm hand on Hong Kong's politics and economy and the government of Hong Kong SAR prioritized its relationship with the mainland over the appeal of the Hong Kongese for democracy. Hui Sin Tung from Hong Kong University and Tang Chi Tak from Chinese University of Hong Kong, students who participated in the "Occupy Central" movement stated that the central government of China had repeatedly violated the Sino-British Joint Declaration by depriving the Hong Kongese of the freedom of press and assembly as well as the universal voting rights as stipulated therein, and Britain should compel China to "honor" the Sino-British Joint Declaration, make condemnations, and even resume the Treaty of Nanking and the Treaty of Tientsin. In addition, Liu Huiqing, the chairman of the Democratic Party of Hong Kong also "testified" to the British Parliament by video on November 18 that Britain should be responsible for the maintenance of the freedom and lifestyle of Hong Kong.

External influences from Britain and America keep interfering with the internal affairs of Hong Kong and this has become more frequent since the "Occupy Central". In late September, the British Prime Minister Cameroon said, "the agreement between the UK and China mentioned the importance of Hong Kong's democracy under the framework of 'One Country, Two Systems'." In mid-October, he once again proclaimed that "Britain should stand up for the freedom of the Hong Kongese." In September, when the "Occupy Central" movement met the dead end, the United States used 20 pages in the annual report of the U.S.-China Economic and Security Council to fabricate wild tales on the political reform of Hong Kong. After that, the Congressional-Executive Commission on China conducted a "hearing", during which Peng Dingkang, the "Last Governor of Hong Kong" made an overseas "testification" in London through video satellite, claiming that western countries should speak out on Hong Kong issues. When the British MPs planned to conduct investigations in Hong Kong, Beijing denied their entry. Tan Zhiyuan, director of the Constitutional and Mainland Affairs Bureau refuted the British slanders and tricks, arguing that Britain has no sovereignty, nor administration and supervision powers over Hong Kong, and the so-called "moral responsibility" is nothing but nonsense. Wang Guoxing, a representative of Hong Kong Federation of Trade Unions, stated that the testification of the oppositionists in Hong Kong, overtly assisting foreign forces to interfere with the internal affairs of Hong Kong, was an act of losing national dignity and caused huge harms to Hong Kongese and the Chinese people at large. Wu Liangxing, a member of the legislative council on banking industry in Hong Kong, said affairs in Hong Kong belong to China's internal affairs with which other countries have no power to interfere, and the oppositionist senators who "cooperated" in the hearings conducted by foreign countries were obviously incurring foreign forces to do so.

The Chinese government also consecutively condemned the ridiculous hearings on the Sino-British Joint Declaration by the British House of Commons. As early as July 25, 2014, Hong Lei, the spokesman of China's Foreign Ministry, pointed out that affairs in Hong Kong belong to China's internal affairs with which the British hearings were interfering, and China would like to express strong dissatisfaction and resolute opposition to its actions. The Chinese government would oppose to any foreign forces interfering by any pretexts in China's internal affairs. On December 3, 2014, Hua Chunying, the spokeswoman of China's Foreign Ministry claimed in a more definite manner that Hong Kong had already returned back to China since 1997. Hong Kong is a special administrative region of China. It had been made clear on China's resumption of the exercise of sovereignty over Hong Kong and the relevant arrangements during the transition period in the Sino-British Joint Declaration of 1984. The respective rights and obligations of both China and Britain were also clearly defined. Britain had no sovereignty, nor administration and supervision powers over Hong Kong, and the so-called "moral responsibility" did not exist at all. It was unacceptable and untenable for Some British people attempted to use "moral responsibility" to confuse the public and interfere in China's internal affairs. This was unacceptable and untenable.

It is obvious that the statements made by the Chinese government and the patriots in Hong Kong in 2014 coincide perfectly with the detailed arguments brought up by Mr. Chen as early as 2008.

Mr. Chen is fast-learned and wealthy in knowledge, and many of his views in the book on international economic law come from his sedulous research and persistent dialogues with the international academia. He once had in-depth discussions about academic issues with distinguished scholars in international economic law, such as Louis Henkin, Andreas F. Lowenfeld and John H. Jackson. He keeps renewing his knowledge and trying to introduce the new developments of the international economic law in China to international peers. What's more commendable is that Mr. Chen has detected the colonialism and unilateralism, especially the U.S.-style double standards, in the books written by foreign scholars in international economic law. Therefore, he devoted all his life to the reform of the old international economic order and the establishment of a new international economic order. He insists the approach of seeking truth from facts and finished the book *The Voice from China: An CHEN on International Economic Law* after 30 years of hard work. "With an even structure and novel views, this book features

Chinese styles and characteristics by expounding innovative academic ideas distinct from those of the developed countries in the west. Dedicated to the initial establishment of the theoretic system of international economic law with Chinese characteristics under the guidance of Marxism, this book has forged a theoretical arm for the international underprivileged to struggle for equitable interests."

In the third plenary session of the 18th National Congress of the CPC, "to construct a new open-style economic system" has been promoted to a strategic level. To strengthen the research on, and to improve the rule of, international economic law has become the core requirements and necessary guarantees for the strategies of "One Belt, One Road" and "Going global", and the establishment of the BRICS Development Bank and the Asian Infrastructure Investment Bank. Wang Yang, the vice premier of the state council of China, pointed out in an article that we need to intensify the foreign-related legal work and proactively engage in the formulation of international rules. Deeply rooted in the national interests of the Chinese people, against the backdrop of the socialist system with Chinese characteristics, and based on the status quo of China as a developing economic and trade power, this book has served as an important response to the heated and difficult issues on the basic international economic law theories. At present, it has been dragging on over the multilateral trading system and, the mega-FTAs such as Trans-Pacific Partnership Agreement, Transatlantic Trade and Investment Partnership and Regional Comprehensive Economic Partnership and hundreds of FTAs with investment rules have reflected the reconstruction process of international economic and trade rules. Mr Chen pointed out in his book that "the four 'safety valves' in China's BITs with foreign countries should not be rashly dismantled", which is of critical relevance to protecting China's national interests in the negotiation of BITs with the United States and the Europe. Viewing the classics and ancient works cited in the book, no matter the ancient Chinese poetry or the masterpieces from the west, the readers can have a better appreciation of the peculiar perspective of a Chinese scholar in the field of international economic law.

Thus, we firmly believe that the book *The Voice from China: An CHEN on International Economic Law*, the monumental work of Mr. Chen, will surely be able to go global under the background of globalization and China's soaring economic growth, and the voice from China can certainly get heard in the international arena.

（翻译：张川方）

十一、把准南方国家共同脉搏的学术力作
——评《中国的呐喊：陈安论国际经济法》

孔庆江*

陈安先生的皇皇巨著 The Voice from China: An CHEN on International Economic Law（《中国的呐喊：陈安论国际经济法》，以下简称《中国的呐喊》）已由世界著名学术出版社 Springer 出版，此乃学界幸事。陈先生是中国国际经法学界的前辈，长期以来一直担任中国国际经济法学会会长（1993—2011）和荣誉会长（2012—），领导中国国际经济法学界同仁，引领中国国际经济法学研究的风气。陈先生大作刊行于世，我等晚辈同侪无不奔走相告，以先睹为快。

《中国的呐喊》由多篇专论构成，既独立成章，又相互支撑配合，形成一个相互关联的体系。纵览全书，主旨鲜明突出，即批评当今尚存重大合理性问题的现有国际经济秩序，并在此基础上，为构建著者心目中更公平合理的国际经济法律新秩序提供建言。

2007—2008 年全球金融危机后，旧的全球经济秩序的弊端凸显，如何重构全球经济秩序已经成为刻不容缓的问题。对此，大国之间也立即开展了新的国际经济规则主导权的竞争。中国作为最大的发展中国家和崛起中的大国，自当发出自己的声音，而《中国的呐喊》在此时代背景下应运而生，无论批评还是建言，都体现了著者对国际经济秩序推陈出新和破旧立新的人文关怀。在一众中外学者满足于貌似完美的以"自由主义"为基石的现存国际经济秩序的背景下，著者毫不隐晦其中国学者的身份，强调中国在国际经济秩序重构过程中应该有的大国责任和大国风范，即应积极参与到全球国际经济新规则的制定过程中。其视野其观点，都不脱著者心目中不可或缺的中国视角和中国利益。这一切，反映出著者作为国际经济法学家拳拳的爱国之心。著者的赤子之心，在字里行间呼之欲出。

值得一提的是，著者绝非狭隘的民族主义者，其观点无不浸润着对发展中国家弱势群体数十亿大众的利益关切和广阔视角。从全球范围内看，著者的这一巨著，

---

* 孔庆江，中国政法大学国际法学院院长、教授。

不啻是在国际经济秩序推陈出新和破旧立新方面,体现南方国家共同立场的学术力作。无论是对于现存国际经济秩序的理论剖析还是对于各方观点的细致评判,都见解独到而又发人深省。而在批判现存国际经济秩序的基础上提出的构建国际经济新秩序的视角,则体现了一个心怀天下的国际经济法大师的胸怀,为全球南方国家在这个破而后立的时代,点明了参与国际经济规则制定的方向。

《中国的呐喊》的学术价值,还在于勾勒了塑造中国国际经济法学发展面貌的诸多因素,丰满了中国国际经济法学发展维度的诸多细节,特别是指出了中国国际经济法学发展的方向。这不但对于国际学者正确全面理解中国特色的国际经济法学,而且对于中国国际经济法学者反思自己的研究路径,都具有指导性的意义。

我相信,一方面,《中国的呐喊》将与任何严肃著述一样,经得起历史风雨的考验;另一方面,该书的出版将使著者成为南方国家中有代表性的、有重大影响的国际经济法学家。

(编辑:龚 宇)

A Highly Recommendable Monograph that Senses the Pulse of the South

Kong Qingjiang[*]

The Voice from China: An CHEN on International Economic Law (herein referred to as *The Voice from China*), which was recently published by Springer, one of the world's leading academic publishers, is a dear gift for the academic society. Professor Chen, who served as the President (1993—2011) and is acting as the Honorary President (2012—) of the Chinese Society of International Economic Law (CSIEL), is a pioneering explorer of international economic law in China. He helps inspire the researchers in this new discipline and guide their academic pursuits. It is no exaggerating to say that the academia, particularly the young generation was jubilant to learn of the publication of this brilliant monograph.

The Voice from China is composed of several chapters. These chapters—either concerned with investment regime or trade issues—are independent yet mutually

---

[*] Professor of Law, Dean of International Law School, China University of Political Science and Law.

supportive and therefore form an integrated academic work. Throughout the book, outstanding is the theme, which mainly purports criticizing the existing international economic order for its lack of rationality, and, proposing the establishment of a fairer and more reasonable international economic order.

In the aftermath of the global financial crisis of 2007/08, the old global economic infrastructure turned out to be defective, making the reform of the infrastructure a pressing issue. Hereto, the world powers are found to engage in a new round of competition to grab the leadership of international economic rule-making. As the biggest developing country and a rising power, China has to make her voice be heard. Under this circumstance, *The Voice from China* came out timely to reflect the author's humanistic concerns over innovative international economic order regardless of critics and disagreements. Where an array of scholars, home and abroad, are comfortable with and boasting the existing international economic order that is based on the seemingly perfect "liberalism", the author is not shy to disclose his identity as a China-born-and-bred scholar, advocate China's responsibility to contribute to the emerging new international economic order, and call for a China active in participating the international rule-making process. The author's perspectives and opinions, which originate from China' indispensable national interest, reflect nothing but the author's true patriotism as an international economic law scholar.

It is worth noting that the author is not a narrow-minded nationalist at all. His publication is a best example of how international economic law can be full of humane concerns on the interests of developing countries and the breath of billions of vulnerable people therein. From the global perspectives, *The Voice from China* insightfully presents and addresses the common concerns of the South in fighting for a fairer international economic order, thus making itself a great contribution. The meticulous theoretical analysis of international economic order and blatant critics of various parties' arguments are both highly relevant and thought-provoking. From the criticism of existing international economic order, to the proposal to have in place a brand new international economic order, what is evident is the image of a compassionate master in the realm of international economic law, who has great care about the whole world. At a time of setting up new rules after breaking down the olds, *The Voice from China* helps guide the South as a whole how to get involved in the rule-making for international economy.

Another academic value of *The Voice from China* lies in that it either sketches or details the development of Chinese international economic law, especially in that it points to the direction of how to advance the Chinese international economic law. It is of instructive significance to help international law scholars fully and properly understand the international economic law with Chinese characteristics, as well as to sharpen their research skills for the studies of Chinese international economic law.

I firmly believe that *The Voice from China* will, like any solemn monograph, undergo harsh testing of history and moreover, make the author a representative authority with significant contribution to the studies of international economic law.

（翻译：于天琪）

十二、国际经济法研究的"中国立场"
——读《中国的呐喊》有感

李万强[*]

厦门大学法学院陈安教授以"余热未尽，不息奋蹄"的精神与斗志，在八十五岁高龄推出英文学术专著《中国的呐喊：陈安论国际经济法》（以下简称《中国的呐喊》），令人可叹可佩！该书是继 2008 年复旦大学出版社出版的中文五卷本《陈安论国际经济法学》之后，面向国际学术界对陈安教授学术成就以及学术生活的一次全景式、立体化展现。

陈安教授是中国最早从事国际经济法研究的学者之一。过去三十多年，陈安教授一直在这一领域辛勤耕耘，为中国国际经济法学学科地位的巩固与夯实做出了重大贡献。他以一家跨国公司的投资项目为例，从六大方面释明了国际经济活动所需依赖和遵守的国际法律规范与国内法律规范、公法性规范与私法性规范、程序性规范与实体性规范，以及贸易法规范、投资法规范与金融法规范等，指明国际经济法是应客观现实之急需，不拘泥于传统法学分科，在学科交叉渗透的基础上形成的独立

---

[*] 李万强，西安交通大学法学院"腾飞人才计划"特聘教授，原西北政法大学国际法学院院长。

的、有机的边缘性综合体。[264] 不仅如此,面对其他一些学者对初创的国际经济法学的四种误解与非议,即"不科学"或"不规范"论、"大胃"论或"贪食"论、"浮躁"论或"炒热"论以及"翻版"论或"舶来"论,他撰文一一澄清或驳斥,进一步论证了这一学科定位的"科学性、合规律性和旺盛活力"。[265]

国际经济法作为一种法律现象,可以有不同的研究视角和方法。陈安教授则"一贯坚持"南北矛盾的研究方法,"独树一帜",形成并引领了颇具中国风骨与特色的国际经济法学流派。这一立场,由于两个方面的原因而对中国具有独特的意义:一方面,崛起的中国已经触碰到了某些发达国家"脆弱的神经",它们对中国极力遏制;另一方面,中国由于实行不同的政治制度,被某些西方国家另眼相加,列入另册,它们对中国严加防范。因此,建立国际经济新秩序(NIEO),并在其中发挥积极的、建设性的作用,是陈安教授立足于中国实际所确立的国际经济法研究的指导思想。为贯彻这一指导思想,《中国的呐喊》在学术层面进行了充分的论证与法理构建:

(1) 身份:关于中国的国家"身份"问题,陈安教授的认识是一贯的。长期以来,他对国际经济法中的经济主权原则、南北矛盾与南南合作等问题倾注极大的心力进行研究,就是基于中国"作为全球最大的发展中国家以及全球弱势群体的一员"这一认识。[266]

(2) 定位:陈安教授提出,中国应当立足于自身的历史,把握现有国际经济秩序的大局,科学地、合理地从长远角度确立自己在建立国际经济新秩序过程中的战略定位。具体说来,中国理应成为建立国际经济新秩序的积极推手,在国际经济旧秩序尚未完全退出历史舞台的背景下,为了实现南北公平,中国作为发展中的大国之一,理应以公正、公平、合理的国际经济新秩序作为长远奋斗目标,积极倡导和参与建设和谐世界;中国理应致力于成为南南联合自强的中流砥柱之一,作为当代奉行和平发展方针的大国,应当具有大国的意识和风范,勇于承担,与其他发展中国家一

---

[264] See An Chen, On the Marginality, Comprehensiveness, and Independence of International Economic Law Discipline, in An Chen, *The Voice from China: An CHEN on International Economic Law*, Springer, 2013, pp. 8-12.

[265] See An Chen, On the Misunderstanding Relating to China's Current Developments of International Economic Law Discipline, in An Chen, *The Voice from China: An CHEN on International Economic Law*, Springer, 2013, p. 34.

[266] See An Chen, What Should Be China's Strategic Position in the Establishment of New International Economic Order? With Comments on Neoliberalistic Economic Order, Constitutional Order of the WTO, and Economic Nationalism's Disturbance of Globalization, in An Chen, *The Voice from China: An CHEN on International Economic Law*, Springer, 2013, p. 204.

起联合行动。[267]

（3）目标：陈安教授认为，中国与全球弱势群体共同参与建立国际经济新秩序的战略目标，理应坚定不移，始终不渝。面对当今现存的各种国际经济立法，包括WTO法制下的种种"游戏规则"，国际弱势群体固然不能予以全盘否定，但是显然也不能全盘接受，心甘情愿地忍受其中蕴含的各种不公与不平。对待当今现存的各种国际经济立法，正确态度理应是：以公正、公平为圭臬，从争取与维护国际弱势群体的平权利益的视角，予以全面的检查和审查，实行"守法"与"变法"的结合。凡是基本上达到公正公平标准，符合改造国际经济旧秩序、建立国际经济新秩序需要的，就加以沿用、重申，就强调"守法"；凡是违反这种需要的，就要强调"变法"，并通过各种方式和途径，据理力争，努力加以改订、废弃或破除。[268]

在国际弱势群体争取建立国际经济新秩序的过程中，国际学界也出现了一些颇为流行的理论，比如"新自由主义经济秩序"论、"WTO宪政秩序"论、"经济民族主义扰乱全球化秩序"论等。陈安教授研究指出，这些理论各有其合理内核，但其副作用亦不可小觑。"新自由主义经济秩序"论、"WTO宪政秩序"论可能是一种精神鸦片，会麻痹、瓦解国际弱势群体的斗志与信心；"经济民族主义扰乱全球化秩序"论可能是一种精神枷锁，会压制国际弱势群体的斗志与信心。要警惕这些"时髦"理论取代"建立国际经济新秩序"论！[269]

（4）途径：面对当代国际社会"南弱北强"、实力悬殊的战略态势，面对国际强权国家集团（七国集团之类）在国际经济领域中已经形成的"长达三十余年的霸业"格局，国际弱势群体要求"变法"图强，不应该单枪匹马，各自为政。实践反复证明：唯一可行和有效之途径就是南南联合，动员和凝聚集团实力，不渝不懈，坚持建立国际经济新秩序、"变法图强"的理念和目标，一步一个脚印地迈步前进。也正是由于中国等发展中大国的综合国力和国际影响的逐步提高，在WTO多哈会议、坎昆会议、香港会议、华盛顿会议、首尔会议的全过程中，中国与印度、巴西、南非和墨西哥等

---

[267] See An Chen, What Should Be China's Strategic Position in the Establishment of New International Economic Order? With Comments on Neoliberalistic Economic Order, Constitutional Order of the WTO, and Economic Nationalism's Disturbance of Globalization, in An Chen, *The Voice from China: An CHEN on International Economic Law*, Springer, 2013, pp. 174-175.

[268] See An Chen, Some Jurisprudential Thoughts upon WTO's Law-Governing, Law-Making, Law-Enforcing, Law-Abiding, and Law-Reforming, in An Chen, *The Voice from China: An CHEN on International Economic Law*, Springer, 2013, pp. 245-248.

[269] See An Chen, What Should Be China's Strategic Position in the Establishment of New International Economic Order? With Comments on Neoliberalistic Economic Order, Constitutional Order of the WTO, and Economic Nationalism's Disturbance of Globalization, in An Chen, *The Voice from China: An CHEN on International Economic Law*, Springer, 2013, pp. 190-204.

BRICSM 成员曾多次通力协作,折冲樽俎,使得国际霸权与强权不能随心所欲,操纵全局,从而为国际弱势群体争得较大的发言权、参与权和决策权。[270]

对于南南联合自强及其成功经验,陈安教授进行了历史的考察。从历史上看,通过南南联合自强,逐步建立国际经济新秩序的战略主张,最初开始形成于 1955 年的万隆会议,此后,建立国际经济新秩序的进程迂回曲折,步履维艰,尽管经历了多次潮起潮落,但其总趋向是始终沿着螺旋式上升的"6C 轨迹"或遵循"6C 律",即 Contradiction(矛盾)→Conflict(冲突或交锋)→Consultation(磋商)→Compromise(妥协)→Cooperation(合作)→Coordination(协调)→Contradiction New(新的矛盾)……每一次循环往复,都并非简单的重复,而都是螺旋式的上升,都把国际经济秩序以及和它相适应的国际经济法规范,推进到一个新的水平或一个新的发展阶段,国际社会弱势群体的经济地位和经济权益也获得相应的改善和保障。当然,盲目的乐观也是有害的。陈安教授提醒,建立国际经济新秩序的前途依然漫漫而崎岖,要使它进一步发展成为康庄坦途,坚持南南联合自强和南北合作仍是不二法门。必须假以时日,必须坚持韧性,二者不可缺一。[271]

《中国的呐喊》不单是不畏国际强权、力争国际公义的呐喊,更是陈安教授赤诚的现实关怀与报国情怀的完美结合。陈安教授"蹉跎半生而重返法学殿堂"(先生语),却思想活跃,能紧跟形势,与时俱进。面对中国的实际问题,陈安教授殚精竭虑,奉献了超凡的智慧。无论是在改革开放之初还是在"1989 年政治风波"之后,陈安教授都及时撰文,宣讲中国的开放政策,澄清事实,消除误解。[272] 在中国对外开放的复杂形势面前,一些学者和官员在国际投资法重大问题的立场方面出现了疑虑与彷徨。陈安教授多次撰文条分缕析,周密论证,阐述中国应当采取的立场与做法,提出四大"安全阀"不宜贸然拆除等真知灼见。[273] 在中国《仲裁法》颁布之初,陈安教授

---

[270] See An Chen, A Reflection of the South-South Coalition in the Last Half Century from the Perspective of International Economic Lawmaking: From Bandung, Doha, and Cancún to Hong Kong, in An Chen, *The Voice from China: An CHEN on International Economic Law*, Springer, 2013, p. 207.

[271] Ibid., pp. 233-238.

[272] See An Chen, To Open Wider or to Close Again: China's Foreign Investment Policies and Laws; To Close Again or to Open Wider: The Sino-US Economic Interdependence and the Legal Environment for Foreign Investment in China After Tiananmen, in An Chen, *The Voice from China: An CHEN on International Economic Law*, Springer, 2013, pp. 407, 453.

[273] See An Chen, Should the Four "Great Safeguards" in Sino-foreign BITs Be Hastily Dismantled? Comments on Critical Provisions Concerning Dispute Settlement in Model US and Canadian BITs; Distinguishing Two Types of Countries and Properly Granting Differential Reciprocity Treatment; Re-comments on the Four Safeguards in Sino-Foreign BITs Not to Be Hastily and Completely Dismantled; Should "The Perspective of South-North Contradictions" Be Abandoned? Focusing on 2012 Sino-Canada BIT, in An Chen, *The Voice from China: An CHEN on International Economic Law*, Springer, 2013, pp. 273, 309, 373.

即对中国的涉外仲裁监督机制进行了批判分析。[274] 在WTO运行一段时间后,陈安教授以其学术敏感,撰文综合评析十年来美国单边主义与WTO多边主义交锋的三大回合,揭示美国学者主权观的两面性以及当代条件下经济主权原则之不可动摇,为国内学界再次敲响警钟。[275] ……总之,作为中国国际经济法学界的泰斗级人物,在关涉中国国际经济法研究与实践的重大问题与重大事件时,几乎都有陈安教授振聋发聩的"呐喊"!

(编辑:龚　宇)

A Chinese School of Jurisprudence on International Economic Law

Li Wanqiang[*]

It is admirable that Professor An Chen finished his monograph in English at the age of 85. This monograph, titled as *The Voice from China: An CHEN on International Economic Law*, is a quintessence of his five-volume book series published by Fudan University Press five years ago and some of his articles thereafter. Nevertheless, it reflects a three-dimensional panorama of Professor Chen's academic achievement and activities to the international academia.

Professor Chen is one of the rare pioneers in the research field of international economic law (IEL). Since the inception of China's policy of reform and openness (CPRO), he has been concentrating his energies on the IEL and the CPRO. As a founding member and former Chairman of Chinese Society of International Economic Law, he has played a leading role in the establishment and enhancement of the discipline of the IEL in China. He takes an international investment project as an example to show how an international economic transaction may be governed by

---

[274] See An Chen, On the Supervision Mechanism of Chinese Foreign-Related Arbitration and Its Tally with International Practices, in An Chen, *The Voice from China: An CHEN on International Economic Law*, Springer, 2013, p. 581.

[275] See An Chen, The Three Big Rounds of US Unilateralism Versus WTO Multilateralism During the Last Decade: A Combined Analysis of the Great 1994 Sovereignty Debate Section 301 Disputes (1998-2000) and Section 201 Disputes (2002-2003); On the Implications for Developing Countries of "the Great 1994 Sovereignty Debate" and the EC-US Economic Sovereignty Disputes, in An Chen, *The Voice from China: An CHEN on International Economic Law*, Springer, 2013, pp. 103, 159.

[*] Professor of Law, Xi'an Jiaotong University, China; former Dean of International Law School, North-Western University of Political Science and Law, China.

international law and domestic law, public law and private law, substantive law and procedural law, as well as trade law, investment law, tax law and financial law etc. Based on this practical analysis, he points out that IEL is a novel branch of legal discipline in response to the objective reality. This legal discipline adopts an interdepartmental and interdisciplinary approach of investigation and is an organic marginal independent synthesis. [276] Facing some misunderstandings and suspicions to the IEL, such as so-called "nonscientific or nonnormative", "polyphagian or avaricious", "fickle fashion or stirring heat", and "duplicating version or importing goods", he wrote an article to rebut or correct these opinions one by one, which prove the scientific and normative nature and the strong vitality of the IEL from different perspectives. [277]

As a legal phenomenon, the IEL can be reviewed and treated from different approaches. What Prof. Chen has been taking consistently is the "South-North Contradiction" approach. Thanks to his achievements and influence, a Chinese School of Jurisprudence on the IEL featured by this approach has come into being in China. Based on two factors, this school of jurisprudence on the IEL is of special significance to China. One is that some developed countries adopt "containment strategy" in response to China's rise. The other is that some western countries treat China in an alien way because of China's political system. According to Prof. Chen, establishing New International Economic Order (NIEO) is a way for developing countries like China to be treated justifiably and China shall play an active and constructive role in this process. In checking and reshaping the IEL, the following points shall be adhered to:

Firstly, the identity of China as a developing country must be recognized. Prof. Chen holds it is a fact that China is one member within the disadvantaged groups as

---

[276] See An Chen, On the Marginality, Comprehensiveness, and Independence of International Economic Law Discipline, in An Chen, *The Voice from China: An CHEN on International Economic Law*, Springer, 2013, pp. 8-12.

[277] See An Chen, On the Misunderstanding Relating to China's Current Developments of International Economic Law Discipline, in An Chen, *The Voice from China: An CHEN on International Economic Law*, Springer, 2013, p. 34.

well as one of the biggest developing countries in the world.[278] Based on this standpoint, he has attached great importance to the study of the basic issues in IEL such as economic sovereignty, South-North conflicts and South-South cooperation.

Secondly, the goal China shall firmly pursue is the establishment of a just, fair and reasonable NIEO. Facing the existed IEL, including varieties of "rules of game" for international economic and trade affairs, neither "accepting all" nor "denying all" is a right attitude. Prof. Chen holds a full review and investigation shall be carried out from the perspective of campaigning for and maintaining the equal rights and interests of the international weak groups, and law-abiding and law-reforming shall be combined together. For each and every rule which is in violation of justice and fairness, the weak groups shall seek to reform, abolish, or eradicate it through all possible ways and approaches.[279]

Accompanying the advocacy for the NIEO, some other theories have prevailed to some extent, such as "Neoliberalistic Economic Order", "Constitutional Order of the WTO", and "Economic Nationalism's Disorder of Globalization". Although the core of these theories is reasonable in some sense and could be utilized critically, Prof. Chen reminds that the former two can be a kind of mental opium and disintegrate the unions of the weak states, while the latter one can be a kind of mental shackles and prevent the weak states from establishing the NIEO.[280]

Thirdly, the role China is playing in the course of establishing the NIEO shall be one of the driving forces. China shall act ideologically and in style as a large nation, be brave in assuming responsibilities, and join force with all other weak

---

[278] See An Chen, What Should Be China's Strategic Position in the Establishment of New International Economic Order? With Comments on Neoliberalistic Economic Order, Constitutional Order of the WTO, and Economic Nationalism's Disturbance of Globalization, in An Chen, *The Voice from China: An CHEN on International Economic Law*, Springer, 2013, p. 204.

[279] See An Chen, Some Jurisprudential Thoughts upon WTO's Law-Governing, Law-Making, Law-Enforcing, Law-Abiding, and Law-Reforming, in An Chen, *The Voice from China: An CHEN on International Economic Law*, Springer, 2013, pp. 245-248.

[280] See An Chen, What Should Be China's Strategic Position in the Establishment of New International Economic Order? With Comments on Neoliberalistic Economic Order, Constitutional Order of the WTO, and Economic Nationalism's Disturbance of Globalization, in An Chen, *The Voice from China: An CHEN on International Economic Law*, Springer, 2013, pp. 190-204.

states in advocating and participating in the establishment of a harmonious world.[281]

Lastly, the pathway to achieve the goal of establishing the NIEO is South-South Cooperation. Since the South is far weaker than the North in contemporary international society and the group of international powers (such as G7) has maintained the dominant position for as long as over 30 years in international economic fields, the international weak groups' demand for law-reforming to strengthen themselves up shall not be expected to be accomplished once and for all, nor shall they take actions dividedly and single-handedly. Prof. Chen points out the only feasible and effective way is through South-South Coalition to keep mobilizing and agglomerating the collective power unswervingly with the aim to establish the NIEO.[282]

The significance of the South-South Coalition has been embodied in the South-North Contradiction. For over 60 years, the struggles between the South and the North usually temporarily paused when the two sides reaching a compromise, after which new conflicts would arise from new contradictions. As for the historic course and practice of South-North struggle, Prof. Chen proposes a generalization of the "6C Track" or "6C Rule": Contradiction→Conflict→Consultation→Compromise→Cooperation→Coordination→Contradiction New... But each new circle is on a spiral upper level rather than on an exactly repetitive old one, thus pushing International Economic Order and the relating IEL towards a fairer level at a higher development stage. Consequently, the economic status and rights of the international weak groups are able to acquire corresponding improvements and safeguards.[283]

The Voice from China is not only an advocacy of struggling against international hegemony and striving for international justice, but also a convergence

---

[281] See An Chen, What Should Be China's Strategic Position in the Establishment of New International Economic Order? With Comments on Neoliberalistic Economic Order, Constitutional Order of the WTO, and Economic Nationalism's Disturbance of Globalization, in An Chen, *The Voice from China: An CHEN on International Economic Law*, Springer, 2013, pp. 174-175.

[282] See An Chen, A Reflection of the South-South Coalition in the Last Half Century from the Perspective of International Economic Lawmaking: From Bandung, Doha, and Cancún to Hong Kong, in An Chen, *The Voice from China: An CHEN on International Economic Law*, Springer, 2013, p. 207.

[283] Ibid., pp. 233-238.

of Prof. Chen's patriotism and realism. Although starting his legal research as late as the inception of China's Openness Policy, Prof. Chen has endeavored to keep pace with the times. He has dedicated vast energy and wisdom to the research of Chinese reality. He wrote papers to eradicate the misunderstandings and suspicions to China's Openness Policy both at the earlier stage of 1980s and 1990s.[284] Facing the complicated issues in international investment law, he presented constructive suggestions to the decision makers through his painstaking research work. For example, his viewpoint that the "Four Safeguards" in Sino-foreign BITs can not be hastily and completely dismantled is of great importance to the protection of China's economic sovereignty.[285] Soon after the enactment of China's Arbitration Law, he did a critical research on the law and proposed suggestions on how to reshape it.[286] He made an analysis on how America interacted with the WTO in the first decade of this organization and revealed America's "double standards" to the sovereignty. It is a reminder that the sovereignty shall be stuck to for developing countries at any time[287]... To sum up, as an authority in Chinese academia of IEL, Prof. Chen's voice can always be heard at each critical moment or about each critical incident concerning the IEL, which has always been an advocacy for the rights and interests of the international weak groups.

（翻译：李万强）

---

[284] See An Chen, To Open Wider or to Close Again: China's Foreign Investment Policies and Laws; To Close Again or to Open Wider: The Sino-US Economic Interdependence and the Legal Environment for Foreign Investment in China After Tiananmen, in An Chen, *The Voice from China: An CHEN on International Economic Law*, Springer, 2013, pp. 407, 453.

[285] See An Chen, Should the Four "Great Safeguards" in Sino-foreign BITs Be Hastily Dismantled? Comments on Critical Provisions Concerning Dispute Settlement in Model US and Canadian BITs; Distinguishing Two Types of Countries and Properly Granting Differential Reciprocity Treatment: Re-comments on the Four Safeguards in Sino-Foreign BITs Not to Be Hastily and Completely Dismantled; Should "The Perspective of South-North Contradictions" Be Abandoned? Focusing on 2012 Sino-Canada BIT, in An Chen, *The Voice from China: An CHEN on International Economic Law*, Springer, 2013, pp. 273, 309, 373.

[286] See An Chen, On the Supervision Mechanism of Chinese Foreign-Related Arbitration and Its Tally with International Practices, in An Chen, *The Voice from China: An CHEN on International Economic Law*, Springer, 2013, p. 581.

[287] See An Chen, The Three Big Rounds of US Unilateralism Versus WTO Multilateralism During the Last Decade: A Combined Analysis of the Great 1994 Sovereignty Debate Section 301 Disputes (1998-2000) and Section 201 Disputes (2002-2003); On the Implications for Developing Countries of "the Great 1994 Sovereignty Debate" and the EC-US Economic Sovereignty Disputes, in An Chen, *The Voice from China: An CHEN on International Economic Law*, Springer, 2013, pp. 103, 159.

十三、不为浮云遮眼 兼具深邃坚定
——评《中国的呐喊:陈安论国际经济法》

韩立余[*]

收到陈安教授惠寄的 Springer 出版的 *The Voice from China*:*An CHEN on International Economic Law*(《中国的呐喊:陈安论国际经济法》),不禁心潮澎湃。为其观点,为其成果,为其精神!

初次面见陈安教授是在 1998 年于深圳大学召开的中国国际经济法年会上。其时,陈安教授力倡"以文会友、以学报国",那铿锵有力的声音和抓铁留痕的信念深深地印记在我的脑海里。此后,几乎在每次年会上,或听取陈安教授的大会报告,或参与陈安教授主持的讨论,或是私下里的交流,我都沐浴在陈安教授的思想光辉中。作为后学,自己取得的些许研究成果,一定程度上与陈安教授的影响、关怀和鼓励是分不开的。虽由于生活经历、成长年代、求学背景、研究兴趣等的不同,也有与陈安教授不同的具体想法,但那份尊重和敬佩深植心中、依然如故。

如陈安教授自己所言,其英文巨著是在其五卷本中文版《陈安论国际经济法学》的基础上进一步修订、更新、补充而完成的。今将其思想、观点、成果以 *The Voice from China* 为题出版英文版,陈安教授在国际层面进一步践行了"以文会友、以学报国"的信念和追求。陈安教授的思想独树一帜,且一以贯之,不为浮云遮眼,兼具深邃坚定。这一特点在国内如此,在国际上亦如此。其思想观点并非一时心得,而是建立在扎实的历史事实和教训之上。正因为如此,其声已超出个人之音,而具有历史和现实之义,理应向国际传播。

由于多方面的原因,特别是由于历史和语言的原因,中国学者对中国社会的描述,对国际社会的看法,不能尽达于国际社会。即便有些著述,或因篇幅所限,或因渠道所困,或因话语语境,不能充分而全面地阐述中国学者的立场观点。国际上一些汉学学者,由于经历、环境不同及兴趣所限,亦不能很好地反映中国的情况和观点。陈安教授立足中国,放眼国际,不满足于国内取得的学术成就和影响,志在基于中国现实和视角向国际社会表达中国学人的立场和观点,努力地有计划地在国际刊物、国际场合发文出声。在年届耄耋之际,陈安教授深耕细作,集其观点大成,推出

---

[*] 韩立余,中国人民大学法学院教授,WTO 争端解决专家组指示性名单成员。

八百多页巨著 The Voice from China，向世人展示其中国观和世界观，学术生涯达到新的高度。令人敬佩的是，陈安教授在坚持自己观点的同时，积极倡导、推动学术争鸣，提携后进进行独立研究。虽德高望重，但平等待人、平等交流；坚持一家之言，鼓励百家之说。笔者个人认为，其英文著作名称取"The Voice from China"，而没有选取"The Voice of China"，亦体现了其虚怀若谷的风范。

作为中国国际经济法学的奠基人之一，陈安教授对国际经济法的诸多领域均有很深的造诣，并且以学者、律师和仲裁员三栖身份，言行一致地践行其观点。The Voice from China 收录的文章，既有对建立中国国际经济法学科的详细论证，也有对国家经济主权理论和国际经济新秩序的深刻剖析，还包括亲身参与国际仲裁和诉讼的睿智实录。透过各种重大议题，如国家主权、南北关系、国际秩序、国际投资、"一国两制"等，再现了中国改革开放以来的激荡历史和中国人民参与国际事务的伟大实践。有的文章成文虽早，但仍不失其现实意义，这进一步体现了陈安教授所见所期之远之大，亦为后学所敬仰追随。

The Voice from China，洋洋巨著，洒洒数百万言。任何介绍或评论性的文字都无法充分展示其丰富的内容和精髓。笔者在此也不作该等无谓努力，相信读者会从中见仁见智、相遇金屋玉颜。

最后，想对"国家社会科学基金中华学术外译项目"致以敬意，感谢其立项资助陈安教授将中文著作推广到英语世界，让英语世界的读者认识、分享其思想观点，并引发对中国问题更深入、全面的认识。没有这一资助，陈安教授的"以文会友、以学报国"的理念或许无法实现到今天这样的程度。

（编辑：龚　宇）

Never Covered by Cloud, Insisting Profound Insight
—Comments on *The Voice from China*

Han Liyu[*]

On receiving the monograph *The Voice from China*: *An CHEN on International Economic Law* of about 800 pages written by Prof. An Chen, published in 2013 by famous publisher Springer, I could not help being moved by the

---

[*] Professor of Law, Renmin University of China; Panelist of WTO/DSB.

book, the opinions, and the spirit of Prof. An Chen.

It was in 1999 when the annual meeting of Chinese Society of International Economic Law(CSIEL) was held in Shenzhen University that I first met Prof. Chen. This was also the first time I attended the activities of CSIEL, almost every attendants of the meeting being stranger to me, but I was deeply impressed by Prof. Chen, then the President of CSIEL, when he gave a speech in his characteristically robust style, calling for "meeting friends with writings and rewarding home country with knowledge". Since then, either during the annual meetings of CSIEL or in other occasions, it was normal to listen to speeches of Prof. Chen, seek advices from him, and discuss with him. To some extent, what I have achieved in my legal research should be attributed to the influence, care and encouragement of Prof. Chen, though he was not my academic adviser in strict sense. This does not mean that I fully agree with all opinions of Prof. Chen owing to diffident ages, education backgrounds, life experiences and research interests etc. between us, but my respect for Prof. An Chen lasts forever.

Just as Prof. Chen said himself in his book, *The Voice from China* was a updated English version of his five-volume *An CHEN on International Economic Law* in Chinese published by Fudan University Press in 2008. The English version not only reflects Prof. An Chen's deeper thoughts on International Economic law, but also his effort to voice Chinese message on international plane, which in broader extent puts into practice his belief "meeting friends with writings and rewarding home country with knowledge". Prof. Chen is determined and thoughtful, and his thoughts on International Economic Law are consistent, neither blocked by intricate developments nor for occasions. He has supported his conclusions with good reasons and facts. Readers, either domestic or international, will find perfect combination of historical lessons and modern thinking in *The Voice from China*.

For some time Chinese scholars' views on domestic issues and international affairs have been not easy to be heard and understood by international community because of various reasons, including factors of language, history, media, and cultural context. On the other hand, Sinologists, owing to lack of rich experience in China and having their own special research interests, cannot accurately and fully reflect the real views of Chinese scholars and the complex reality in China. Born in

Old China, experiencing the invasion of Japan, witnessing the change and development of China, and trained in Harvard Law School, Prof. Chen is in a good position to tell China's story to international community. Not satisfied with the reputation of one of most famous scholars in China, Prof. Chen has broken through and made his academic career to a new height at the age of more than 80, with *The Voice from China*, which is based on China's perspective and world outlook. As a matter of fact, this is not the first time for Prof. Chen to voice his views in international forums. For many years Prof. Chen has been doing his efforts to hold or attend international conference, to publish articles in international journals, so as to make voice from China to be heard by international community.

As one of noble character and high prestige and one with own special perspective on International Economic Law, Prof. Chen has been paying due respect for different opinions of different people in different ages. "Respect for different opinions" is his long-held belief. Prof. Chen always encourages younger scholars to express their own views, and the more difference with his views the more encouragement from him. As far as I know, many Chinese young scholars pay high respect for Prof. Chen, though they don't agree with Prof. Chen in some points. Prof. Chen is always modest, and in my judgment his book titled "The Voice from China", not "The Voice of China", also show his modesty.

Being one of the founders of CSIEL, Prof. Chen has an extremely good knowledge of International Economic Law. Besides a professor of Law, Prof. Chen is also an arbitrator and a lawyer active in the field of international transactions. The essays collected in *The Voice from China* include different focuses, not only arguments for separate status of International Economic Law discipline in China's law education system, theoretical analysis of state sovereign and the new international economic order, but also arguments with wisdom for international cases he handled. With discussion of important topics such as state sovereign, South-South or South-North relationship, international order, international investment, and "One Country Two System" etc., Prof. Chen has revealed the surging history of opening-up and reform in China and active practice of China's participation in international affairs since 1979, and made his own contribution in his own way as a Chinese scholar to the new international economic order. Some essays, though finished long time ago, still have inspirational implications for current international affairs, with deep insights into future. This also implies that the academic style of Prof. Chen sets an example for younger scholars.

It says that there are a thousand Hamlets in a thousand people's eyes. So I won't attempt to make detailed comments on the contents of *The Voice from China* of about 800 pages, and I know my any effort of this kind would be an effort in vain. I encourage readers themselves to read *The Voice form China*. I'm sure readers all over the world would find his own Hamlets from *The Voice from China*.

Last but not least, I want to express my own appreciation for the work of the National Social Science Fund of China. Without its project, i. e. the Chinese Academic Foreign Translation Project (CAFTP), *The Voice from China* would not, I guess, been published in English by international famous publisher; readers in English world would not have this privilege to have a better understanding of modern China through the lens of Prof. An Chen; and the dream cherished by Prof. Chen of "meeting friends with writings and rewarding home country with knowledge" would not come true so soon.

（翻译：韩立余）

十四、任你风向东南西北 我自岿然从容不迫
——国际经济新秩序的重思：以陈安教授的国际经济法研究为视角

何志鹏*

国际经济法研究的两大流派

作为法学的一部分，国际经济法的研究显然不可能完全脱离法学研究的主流路径而完全独树一帜。法学的主流研究模式分为实证法学派和自然法学派，[288]因而国际经济法的各种研究手段也可以大略总结为描述性研究和规范性研究两大流派。描述性研究主要是对既有的国际经济法律规范和组织、运行进行说明，通过语义分

---

* 何志鹏，2011 计划·司法文明协同创新中心成员，吉林大学法学院、公共外交学院教授。

[288] See Peter Malanczuk, *Akehurst's Modern Introduction to International Law*, 7th ed., Routledge, 1997, pp. 15-18.

析阐释规范的含义,通过数据统计分析揭示实际运行的状况,或者通过案例研究研讨规范在实践运行中取得的成就和存在的问题。[289] 这种研究是作为一般法学方法的实证主义研究在国际经济法中的体现。规范分析一般前设一套正当性原则,通过批判性、反思性地考察相关的规范或者实践,或者比较不同的规范、不同的实践或者进程,来判断相关的规则和实践是否正当,或者说明相关的国际经济法进步的领域和方向何在。[290] 这种研究方法是作为法学方法的自然法学派在国际经济法领域的具体体现,是一种显在的价值分析的研究方式。

这两种方法虽然表面上并不相同,实质上却有很多联系。一个令人信服的价值分析必须建立在扎实的实证研究基础之上,很多实证研究在背后也都隐藏着一些基本的价值判断。[291] 进而言之,偏好实证分析的学者和偏好价值分析的学者有必要保持相互尊重和欣赏,而不必偏执地认为,只有自己才是正确的,另一种方法则是错误的。所以,好的法学研究虽然会在研究手段上有所侧重,但二者不可偏废。

陈安教授作为中国顶级的国际经济法学者,不仅在国际投资法的实证研究上作出了很多重要的努力,而且在国际经济法的发展方向的批判研究上也进行了卓有成效的尝试,提出了很多发人深省的观点。其中,关于国际经济新秩序及中国的立场的研究就是非常具有代表性的部分。

国际经济新秩序的兴衰

陈安教授从历史实证的角度考察了建立国际经济新秩序的背景与进程,同时也探讨了现代社会中倡导国际经济新秩序的重要性。起源于 20 世纪 60 年代的国际经济新秩序运动,可以理解为殖民时期基本结束后自决权的延续和拓展。新独立的发展中国家不仅在历史上受到侵略和盘剥,在现实中也被国际经济体系所伤害。[292] 原来的宗主国,继而成为国际经济体系的主导者、国际经济法的主要制定者的发达工业国家确立起一套国际经济规则体系,继续将利益输送到发达国家,却使得多数发展中国家积贫积弱,这种法律体制很难说是公正的。[293] 正如陈安教授所揭示的,国际经济法立法过程最常见的三大弊端是:少数发达国家密室磋商,黑箱作业,缺乏国

---

[289] E. g., Andreas F. Lowenfeld, *International Economic Law*, 2nd ed., Oxford University Press, 2011.

[290] E. g., Andrew Land, *World Trade Law After Neoliberalism: Re-imagining the Global Economic Order*, Oxford University Press, 2011.

[291] See John Finnis, *Natural Law and Natural Rights*, 2nd ed., Oxford University Press, 2011, pp. 27-29, 281-285; Robert George, *In Defense of Natural Law*, Oxford University Press, 1999, pp. 108-109.

[292] 参见陈安主编:《国际经济法学专论》,高等教育出版社 2002 年版,第 31—32、38—39 页。

[293] See Philippe Sands, *Lawless World: Making and Breaking Global Rules*, Penguin Books, 2005, p. 95.

际民主;国际经济组织体制规章中存在不公平、不合理的表决制度;全球唯一的超级大国在世界性经贸大政的决策进程中,历来奉行的"国策"是"美国本国利益至上"和"对人对己双重标准"。[294]

国际经济新秩序的主张就是一种试图除旧布新、继往开来的努力。但是,这种努力显然会影响到发达国家的短期、局部利益,所以它们对于国际经济新秩序的主张反应并不积极。[295] 来自发达国家的学者也更倾向于论证载有国际经济新秩序主张的国际文件不属于国际法、没有约束力,不能确立国际义务。在很大程度上是由于 20 世纪 70 年代初能源危机的压力以及冷战政治平衡的需要,[296]发达工业国家才允诺了包括普惠制在内的一些推进国际经济新秩序的条件。

在冷战结束以后,发展中国家追求国际经济新秩序的声音马上被新自由主义和全球化这两个相互联系的浪潮所淹没。去除管制、私有化、自由市场成为压倒性的声音。以世界贸易组织、世界银行和国际货币基金组织为代表的国际经济体制也主要以这些自由主义的理念为尺度去确立新的国际经济法,国际经济法的发展似乎走向了自由主义一枝独秀的"历史的终结"。建立国际经济新秩序的努力进入了消沉的阶段。

实践是检验真理的唯一标准。历史显然没有终结,自由主义的普世宣讲不仅在很多时候没有造福于发展中国家,而且"金融创新"的泡沫使发达国家自己也陷入了麻烦之中。

国际经济法的未来,究竟何去何从?

国际经济法的中国立场

国际法的变化,既可以从实体规范的层面进行,也可以从程序规范的层面进行;既可以是全局层面的变化,也可以是局部领域的变化。但所有的变化,归根结底来自于行为体层面的推动。这种行为体,虽然包含国际组织、非政府组织、企业和个

---

[294] See An Chen, Some Jurisprudential Thoughts upon WTO's Law-Governing, Law-Making, Law-Enforcing, Law-Abiding, and Law-Reforming, in An Chen, *The Voice from China: An CHEN on International Economic Law*, Springer, 2013, pp. 243-244.

[295] "第二次世界大战结束以来,众多发展中国家强烈要求彻底改变数百年殖民统治所造成的本民族的积贫积弱,要求彻底改变世界财富国际分配的严重不公,要求更新国际经济立法,建立起公平合理的国际经济新秩序。但是,这些正当诉求,却不断地遭到了国际社会中为数不多的发达强国即原先殖民主义强国的阻挠和破坏。它们凭借其长期殖民统治和殖民掠夺积累起来的强大经济实力,千方百计地维持和扩大既得利益,维护既定的国际经济立法和国际经济旧秩序。由于南北实力对比的悬殊,发展中国家共同实现上述正当诉求的进程,可谓步履维艰,进展缓慢。"参见陈安:《中国加入 WTO 十年的法理断想:简论 WTO 的法治、立法、执法、守法与变法》,载《现代法学》2010年第 6 期。

[296] See John W. Yound and John Kent, *International Relations Since 1945*, 2nd ed., Oxford University Press, 2013, pp. 274, 303.

人,但最有力量、最有影响、行动方式最为方便的,显然是国家。如果一个国家不能够明确地形成自己的立场,并以学术、政治和法律的方式表述自身的观念,则国际体制的变革就会失去该国家的话语,不仅有可能有害于该国的利益,而且有可能影响整个国际法的发展进程。

正是站在不同的利益取向上,带有不同的国际机制设计观念的国家在一起通过协商、谈判而形成的国际法律机制才能在多样化的基础上做到相对均衡。当然,绝对的平衡是不存在的,只有相对的平衡。这是因为,即使在所有国家都表述自己观点的前提下,作为一种国际博弈,强国与弱国之间的力量差异会转化成谈判过程中的讨价还价能力的对比,并最终在国际法律体制中表现为绝对的不平衡。

在中国的发展与国际经济法的发展两者互动的进程中,中国面临着多重任务。在很多学者看来,融入现有体系、了解现有体系、参与现有体系就已经很不容易了,甚至是值得称道的成就,但是在陈安教授看来,中国还有一项更为艰巨、复杂,同时也非常伟大的任务,那就是变革现有体系。这项任务在有些学者看来似乎是不必要的,如果将WTO这样的国际经济法体制视为"模范国际法",或者国际法治的典范,那么变革现有体系的正当性就不明显。同样,如果认为中国的国家利益在当今的国际体制中并没有受到重大影响,那么中国自身要求变革的动力就不大。如果我们认为中国还不是一个具有话语能力和话语影响的国家,那么中国要求进行变革的影响也不大。

陈安教授显然不是这么认为的。他强调:"作为全球最大的发展中国家和正在和平发展中的大国,在建立国际经济新秩序的历史进程中,中国理应发挥重要作用。"[297]具体说来:"首先,中国应成为建立国际经济新秩序的积极推手。……其次,中国理应致力于成为南南联合自强的中流砥柱之一。……第三,中国与全球弱势群体共同参与建立国际经济新秩序的战略目标,理应坚定不移,始终不渝。……第四,中国在建立国际经济新秩序进程中自我定位,理应旗帜鲜明,和而不同。"[298]

WTO这样的国际经济法体制较之以往的体制,诚然取得了长足进步,但是至少

---

[297] 参见陈安:《论中国在建立国际经济新秩序中的战略定位——兼评"新自由主义经济秩序"论、"WTO宪政秩序"论、"经济民族主义扰乱全球化秩序"论》,载《现代法学》2009年第2期,第4页。

[298] 陈安:《论中国在建立国际经济新秩序中的战略定位——兼评"新自由主义经济秩序"论、"WTO宪政秩序"论、"经济民族主义扰乱全球化秩序"论》,载《现代法学》2009年第2期,第7—8页;《再论旗帜鲜明地确立中国在构建NIEO中的战略定位——兼论与时俱进,完整、准确地理解邓小平"对外二十八字方针"》,载《国际经济法学刊》2009年第16卷第3期;陈安:《三论中国在构建NIEO中的战略定位:"匹兹堡发轫之路"走向何方——G20南北合作新平台的待解之谜以及"守法"与"变法"等理念碰撞》,载《国际经济法学刊》2009年第16卷第4期。See also An Chen, What Should Be China's Strategic Position in the Establishment of New International Economic Order? With Comments on Neoliberalist Economic Order, Constitutional Order of the WTO, and Economic Nationalism's Disturbance of Globalization, in An Chen, *The Voice from China: An CHEN on International Economic Law*, Springer, 2013, pp. 169, 174-175.

就发展中国家的利益而言,其公平性仍然不足。[299] 乌拉圭回合之后对于发展中国家确立的一系列特别待遇,多为"软措施",或者予以"过渡期限",难以达到提升发展中国家发展能力的目标;[300]中国的"入世"议定书中存在着对于中国非常不利的条文,以往的一些案例已经展现了这些条文对中国的损害。而中国已经跃升为全球性的经济和政治大国,此时,如果仍然不能展现出一个大国的风范,担负起一个大国的责任,不能代表如中国一样科技、产业不够发达,人均 GDP 较低的众多国家,去争取更好的国际体制,则不仅中国自身的发展会受到负面影响,国际社会的公正、稳定、健康、持续发展也无以维系。

所以,中国必须有所作为。以陈安教授为杰出代表的学者们所提出的宏观立场和具体建议,恰恰是中国在国际经济法和国际经济秩序破旧立新进程中理应有所作为的学术表现和实践基础。

陈安教授的学术贡献

陈安教授勤于研究、认真思考,心怀理想、硕果累累。陈安教授在国际经济法基本理论、国际经济法的中国立场、国际投资法、仲裁法等领域都出版了大量的著作,其中既包括高水平的论文,也包括很多教材和专著。

从这些研究可以看出,陈安教授在对国际经济法进行价值分析方面提出了很多具有启发性的观点。对于那些认同和高度评价现有国际经济法体制的专家和学者而言,这些观点未必能获得他们的赞同,但应当是可以激起进一步思考和讨论的重要阐释。其中体现的对国家利益的关切、对国际经济法发展方向的关切、对国际社会未来的关切,既有着一个学者追求学术真理的理想成分,也有着对于国际社会格局坚实认知的现实基础。

陈安先生的研究成果是国际法律文化的重要组成部分,这些著作是他贡献给中国学界和国际学界的宝贵财产。作品中不仅相关的内容和论断值得我们一再学习,而且其显示的独立学术品格,深切民族关怀,以及批判的研究方法也值得我们认真对待和深入借鉴。换言之,陈安先生放眼全球,立足中国,任你风向东南西北,我自岿然从容不迫,坚毅探求国际经济秩序之公正合理发展,由此鼓呼中国之立场方向,此一大端,中外学人已受益或将受益者必多。

(编辑:龚 宇)

---

[299] See M. Matsushita, T. J. Schoenmaum, and P. C. Mavroidis, *The World Trade Organization: Law, Practice, and Policy*, 2nd ed., Oxford University Press, 2006, pp. 912-913.

[300] See E.-U. Petersmann, ed., *Reforming the World Trade Organization: Legitimacy, Efficiency, and Democratic Governance*, Oxford University Press, 2005, pp. 233-274.

Disregarding Whither the Wind Blows, Keeping Firm Confidence of His Owns
—A Revisit to Prof. Chen's Research on NIEO

He Zhipeng[*]

1. Two Mainstream Approaches of International Economic Law Research

As a part of the science of law, the studies on international economic law cannot really deviate from mainstream approaches of legal studies and create something totally new. Since the mainstream approaches of legal studies may be categorized into positivism and natural law theory,[301] the means of studying international economic law may also classified into two streams, namely, descriptive studies and normative studies. Descriptive studies mainly try to illustrate existing rules, organizations, and operation, to explain the meaning of rules through semantic analysis, to discover the status of operation by analyzing statistics, or demonstrate achievements and problems arising from the enforcement of rules in practice based on case studies.[302] Normative studies need a set of principles of justice as prerequisite, and then, their main task is to make judgments on whether relative rules and practices may be regarded as legitimate through a critical, reflexive examination of such rules and practices, or to specify the area and direction of international economic law for improvement.[303] This approach is the specific embodiment of natural law approach from the field of legal theories into the field of international economic law, and should be regarded as an express value analysis.

Although at the superficial level these two approaches are different, they are closely related in many ways. A convincing value analysis must be based on solid positive studies, and many positive studies may implicitly include some basic value

---

[*] Professor of Law, Collaborative Innovation Center of Judicial Civilization, Jilin University, China.
[301] See Peter Malanczuk, *Akehurst's Modern Introduction to International Law*, 7th ed., Routledge, 1997, pp. 15-18.
[302] E.g., Andreas F. Lowenfeld, *International Economic Law*, 2nd ed., Oxford University Press, 2011.
[303] E.g., Andrew Land, *World Trade Law After Neoliberalism: Re-imagining the Global Economic Order*, Oxford University Press, 2011.

judgments behind it. [304] Thus, those who prefers positive studies and those who prefers values analysis should respect and appreciate each other instead of regarding implacably their own studies as the right approach and the other approach as wrong. Therefore, a good legal study may emphasis in a certain approach, but not choose one and abandon the other.

Professor An Chen, as one of the top scholars in international economic law in China, has not only achieved a lot in positive studies in international investment law, but also tried much in critical studies in the orientations of international economic law, and put forward many inspiring points of view. The research on new international economic order (NIEO) along with the position of China in the process of it is a typical and representative part.

2. The Rise and Fall of NIEO

Professor An Chen examined the background and history of setting up NIEO, and probed into the importance of NIEO in international society even in the 21st century. The NIEO movement, originated in the 1960s, may be understood as the continuation and upgrading of self-determination after the end of colonial times. The new independent states were not treated fairly since they had been invaded and exploited in the history and were still harmed by the international economic system at the time being. [305] The former suzerains, now acting as the promoter of international economic system and the creator of international law, took welfare and interest to their own territory by the rules they established, and made the developing states poor and weak. Such system cannot be legitimized. [306] According to Professor An Chen, there are three most commonly observed defects of international economic law-making process: 1) It is up to the heads or representatives from several most developed countries to consult and manipulate secretly before a basic framework is determined. 2) Unfair and unreasonable voting mechanisms are enacted into the regime of global economic organizations in advance. 3) US, as the only superpower

---

[304] See John Finnis, *Natural Law and Natural Rights*, 2nd ed., Oxford University Press, 2011, pp. 27-29, 281-285; Robert George, *In Defense of Natural Law*, Oxford University Press, 1999, pp. 108-109.

[305] See An Chen (ed.), *Problems of International Economic Law* (in Chinese), Higher Education Press, 2002, pp. 31-32, 38-39.

[306] See Philippe Sands, *Lawless World: Making and Breaking Global Rules*, Penguin Books, 2005, p. 95.

of the world, has been constantly pursuing the policy of "the superiority of US national interests" and "double standards towards itself and others" in her participation in the decision-making process of global economic issues. [307]

The proposition of NIEO should be regarded as efforts to get away with the old and set up the new, as well as a critical examiner of past traditions and a trail blazer for future generation. However, these efforts would definitely influence short-term and local interest of the developed countries. Hence, the developed countries' reaction towards NIEO was far from enthusiastic. [308] Some scholars from developed countries are inclined to argue that the documents proscribing the advocates of NIEO are not legally binding and cannot establish international legal obligations. The developed industrialized states reluctantly accepted some conditions such as the Generalized System of Preferences (GSP) to carry forward NIEO, to a large extent due to the pressure of Energy Crisis during the 1960s-1970s, plus the need for political balance during the Cold War. [309]

As soon as the Cold War ended, the voice of developing countries seeking for NIEO was submerged by two interlinked waves, namely neo-liberalism and globalization. De-regulation, privatization, and free market became overwhelming voice in the world. Main international economic institutions in the world, such as the WTO, the World Bank, and IMF, engaged in the establishment of "new" international economic laws based on the liberalist notions. It seemed that the development of international economic law was in the track of unilateral hegemony of liberalism and went directly to the "end of history", meanwhile, the striving for NIEO was in a depressed stage.

Practice is the sole criterion for testing truth. The history has not meeting its end. The universal dissemination of liberalism, in many occasions, has not made benefit for developing countries, and even made developed countries themselves in trouble by the bubbles named "financial innovation".

---

[307] See An Chen, Some Jurisprudential Thoughts upon WTO's Law-Governing, Law-Making, Law-Enforcing, Law-Abiding, and Law-Reforming, in An Chen, *The Voice from China: An CHEN on International Economic Law*, Springer, 2013, pp. 243-244.

[308] See Peter Malanczuk, *Akehurst's Modern Introduction to International Law*, 7th ed., Routledge, 1997, pp. 27, 233-235.

[309] See John W. Yound and John Kent, *International Relations Since 1945*, 2nd ed., Oxford University Press, 2013, pp. 274, 303.

What should the future of international economic law be?

3. China's Position in International Economic Law

The change of international law may occur in substantive matters, or in procedural matters. The change may be in a general and overall dimension, or may be in a specific and regional level. However, all changes must be initiated by the will and activities of actors. Such actors, although including intergovernmental organizations (IGOs), non-governmental organizations (NGOs), multi-national companies (MNCs), and individuals, mainly appear as states. Because states are the most powerful, most influential, and most convenient to appear in international stage. If a State cannot form its own status clearly, and demonstrate it by academic, political, and legal means, the change of international regime may lose discourse of that state. This circumstance may not only affect the interest of a state, but the whole developing process of international law.

A comparatively balanced international legal system may only be possible based on the negotiation of states with various preference of interest and various idea of international mechanism, and such a negotiation may create deliberate democracy in international society. It is necessary to mention that an absolute balanced mechanism in international law never existed. Even in the case that all states have the opportunity to express their views, as a type of international game, the asymmetric powers of states may change into the contrast of bargaining power in international negotiation, and then result in a status that could be unfavorable for the weak parties.

During the course that China interacts with the current system of international economic law, China is faced with many tasks. For many scholars, it is a demanding mission, or even a considerable accomplishment for China to be involved in the current system, to understand the current system, and to participate in the current system. But for Professor An Chen, this is not adequate. China still faces a more arduous, complicated, and significant task, that is to change the current system. This task seems to be unnecessary to some scholars because they regard international economic law regimes like the WTO as "model of international law", or a perfect example of international rule of law. If it is really so, the change of the current system is not so desirable. Moreover, if the national interest of China is not substantially influenced by today's international regimes, China would not have the initiative to demand changing the present system. Further, if China is not a country with negotiation power and discourse influence, the impact of China's efforts on changing the present system would not be significant.

Surely, Professor An Chen doesn't think so. He stresses: "As the largest developing country peacefully rising in the world, China should play an important role in the historical course of establishing the NIEO."[310]

"Firstly, China should be the driving force of the establishment of the NIEO... Secondly, China should dedicate herself to becoming one of the mainstays of 'South-South Self-reliance through Cooperation'... Thirdly, China should adhere firmly to her strategic objectives and principles accompanied by cooperating with all the weak states in the course of the establishment of the NIEO... Fourthly, China should take a clear-cut stand and be in harmony with other countries while reserving differences in the course of establishing the NIEO."[311]

It is true that international economic regimes like WTO has made substantial progresses compared with what we had before. However, judging from the interest of developing countries, they still lack fairness.[312] The special treatment for developing countries in the WTO after the Uruguay Round cannot really achieve the goal of capacity building for developing countries since most of them are just "soft measures" or merely setting up period of transition.[313] There are provisions in the Protocol on the Accession of the People's Republic of China which are obviously unfavorable for China, and cases have already shown that such provisions may take disadvantages to China. Now, China has already gained the position of a political and economic great power in the global scale, if she cannot show the image as a great

---

[310] See An Chen, What Should Be China's Strategic Position in the Establishment of New International Economic Order? With Comments on Neoliberalist Economic Order, Constitutional Order of the WTO, and Economic Nationalism's Disturbance of Globalization, in An Chen, *The Voice from China: An CHEN on International Economic Law*, Springer, 2013, p. 169.

[311] Ibid., pp. 169, 174-175.

[312] See M. Matsushita, T. J. Schoenmaum, and P. C. Mavroidis, *The World Trade Organization: Law, Practice, and Policy*, 2nd ed., Oxford University Press, 2006, pp. 912-913.

[313] See E.-U. Petersmann, ed., *Reforming the World Trade Organization: Legitimacy, Efficiency, and Democratic Governance*, Oxford University Press, 2005, pp. 233-274.

power, assume the responsibility of a responsible states, cannot endeavor to establish a better international regime on behalf of a great number of states who, like China, are not advanced in science and technology, and not developed in industries, has a low GDP per capita, the development of herself would be negatively affected, and a just, stable, healthy, and sustainable development of international society would be difficult.

Therefore, China must take some positive actions. The position and specific suggestions that submitted by scholars of whom Professor An Chen is a distinguished representative, may lay a solid foundation in academic and practice level for China's discourse in the evolution and innovation of international economic law & international economic order worldwide.

4. Professor An Chen's Academic Contribution

Professor An Chen is very diligent in making research, he thinks about legal issues critically with a set of ideal based on third world interests, and has contributed a lot in fundamental theories of international economic law, the position of China in international economic law, international investment law, arbitration law and many other fields, by many works including high level articles as well as textbooks and monographs.

From these research works, it is not hard to find out that Professor An Chen has provided many inspiring views in critical analysis on international law. These works embodied the author's concerns on national interest, concerns on the orientation of international economic law, concerns on the future of international society. They expressed the ideals of a scholar's seeking for academic truth, as well as a solid realistic basis for the constellation of international society. For those who agree with international economic law mechanism status quo and highly endorse it, these views may not be acceptable; however, they definitely present important discourse arousing further thinking and discussion.

Professor An Chen's research achievements form an important part in international legal culture, and should be deemed as a treasure he contributed to the academia in China and the whole world. In his works, not only the substantive contents and conclusions are worth leaning repeatedly, but the independent academic spirit, deep concern on national interest, and critical research methodology are all worth taking seriously and drawing useful experiences. In other words, disregarding to whither the prevailing wind blows, Professor An Chen has kept a firm confidence of his owns. His contributions are saliently featured by holding a firm Chinese stand while taking a global broad view, and by insistently pursuing the fair and reasonable development of international economic order, and thus advocating for China's self-position and orientation during this process, regardless of all kinds of voices otherwise preaching. With no doubt, scholars of international economic law, domestic or abroad, have greatly benefited from Professor An Chen's works both in the sense of substantial viewpoints and methodological approach, and will keep benefiting therefrom in the future.

（翻译：何志鹏）

十五、老战士新呐喊 捍卫全球公义
——评《中国的呐喊：陈安论国际经济法》

王江雨*

《中国的呐喊：陈安论国际经济法》的出版，是国际经济法发展过程中一个里程碑性的标志。事实上，这本书是近年来论述国际经济新秩序问题最重要的著作。这本巨著800多页，从陈安教授过去30年取得的大量的学术成果中，遴选24篇代表性文章，汇辑而成。

该英文专著获得"国家社会科学基金中华学术外译项目"的立项。据悉，这是中国国际经济法学界获此立项的第一例。依据全国社科规划办公室文件解释，"中华学术外译项目"是2010年由全国哲学社会科学规划领导小组批准设立的国家社科基金新的主要类别之一，旨在促进中外学术交流，推动中国哲学社会科学优秀成果和优秀人才走向世界。它主要资助中国哲学社会科学研究的优秀成果以外文形式在国外权威出版机构出版，进入国外主流发行传播渠道，增进国外对当代中国、对中国哲学社会科学以及传统文化的了解，推动中外学术交流与对话，提高中国哲学社会科学的国际影响力。[314]

---

* 王江雨，新加坡国立大学法学院教授、亚洲法律研究中心副主任。

[314] 参见《国家社科基金中华学术外译项目申报问答》，http://www.npopss-cn.gov.cn/n/2013/0228/c234664-20635114.html。

"专家评审意见"认为,陈安教授的这部英文专著"对海外读者全面了解中国国际经济法学者较有代表性的学术观点和主流思想具有重要意义。全书结构自成一体,观点新颖,具有中国风格和中国气派,阐释了不同于西方发达国家学者的创新学术理念和创新学术追求,致力于初步创立起以马克思主义为指导的具有中国特色的国际经济法理论体系,为国际社会弱势群体争取公平权益锻造了法学理论武器"[315]。

《中国的呐喊:陈安论国际经济法》是陈安教授站在中国和国际弱势群体的共同立场,践行知识报国夙志,投身国际学术争鸣之力作,也是其命名为"中国的呐喊"之由来。

《中国的呐喊》全书分为六个部分,不仅分析国际经济法重大的理论问题,而且也从学理上讨论国际经济法的实际应用。它首先探讨国际经济法的一般理论原则,有力地论证了国际经济法的内涵。陈安教授认为,国际经济法乃是一门独立的学科,而不应仅仅被视为国际公法的一个分支。这部著作第一部分最有价值、犹如皇冠珠宝的地方,是针对当代经济主权的"大辩论"所作的精辟剖析。陈安教授批评了美国的单边主义,并将其与他所赞同的 WTO 多边主义加以比较,论证热烈而极具感染力。该著作还就中国对国际秩序诸多问题所持的各种主张加以仔细分析并进行辩护。它是迄今针对中国在国际秩序中所持态度最好的陈述。《中国的呐喊》第四、第五和第六部分,分别探讨了中外双边投资条约、中国的涉外经济立法以及中国参与国际经济争端解决等方面的法律问题。

《中国的呐喊》一书中的所有文章,都是陈安教授过去在各国发表的论文,它们具有三个共同特点。第一,从历史、政治和经济综合的角度对法律问题进行探讨。虽然该书较少对国际经济法中的具体规则和案例进行学理分析,因此不能成为实务律师的参考书,但这本书的独到智慧在于深入探讨剖析国际上聚讼纷纭的各种问题,如国家主权、管理体制、经济民族主义、美国单边主义、"中国威胁"论等等。第二,陈安教授从南方国家的视角来分析和论证各种问题,也就是说,在南北两类国家有关国际经济秩序的分歧中他支持发展中国家的观点。但是,和某些持有"第三世界思路"的国际法学者的僵硬观点不同,陈安教授赞同多边主义,并认为国际经济秩序可以由诸如 WTO 之类的各种国际组织来驱动和引导。他似乎并不认为新自由主义是一种具有"原罪"的理念,它代表发达国家富豪们的利益压迫发展中国家穷苦大众。陈安教授主要是反对一些西方国家,特别是美国鼓吹和实行单边主义。第三,

---

[315] 全国哲学社会科学规划办公室下达"关于《中国的呐喊》书稿的专家评审意见",2013 年 11 月 22 日。

陈安教授显然是一位爱国主义者,甚至是思想开明、毫无偏见的民族主义者。[316] 他为维护中国在国际舞台上的既定立场和行动举止进行辩护,其满腔热忱,令人印象深刻。

  本书作者陈安教授是中国最杰出的法律学者之一,他带头倡导从南方国家的视角(当然更多是从中国的视角)看待国际经济法问题。陈安教授出生于 1929 年,经历和见证了中国和全球在 20 世纪发生的许多最重要的事件。他在 1949 年之前的民国时代就接受了正规的法学教育,在 1979 年之后自学了中华人民共和国的法律体系和国际法。据报道,他在"文化大革命"之后,从 1981—1982 年开始致力于国际经济法的研究,并应邀到哈佛大学进行学术访问。[317] 他在 50 多岁才开始接触国际经济法却能够成为该领域全球最著名的学者之一,可谓奇迹。更难能可贵的是,除了从事学术研究,他在重建厦门大学法学院中发挥了重大作用。厦门大学法学院在 1953 年全国性"院系调整"中被撤销,中断 27 年之后,直到 1980 年才重新组建,但现在已发展成为中国最顶尖的法学院之一。总之,陈安教授堪称一位既博学多才又勤奋不息的天才人物。

An Old Warrior's New Defense of Global Justice
—Comments on *The Voice from China*

Wang Jiangyu*

  The publication of *The Voice from China*: *An CHEN on International Economic Law* represents a landmark development in the discourse of international economic law. As a matter of fact, it is the single most important book on the New International Economic Order (NIEL) published in recent years. This enormous book, featuring almost 800 pages, is a collection of 24 representative articles

---

  [316] The scientific and detailed analysis on nationalism by Prof. Chen, see An Chen, *The Voice from China*: *An CHEN on International Economic Law*, Springer, 2013, pp. 200-203. 对"民族主义"一词的科学解读和具体剖析,参见陈安:《陈安论国际经济法学》(第一卷),复旦大学出版社 2008 年版,第 130—134 页。

  [317] See Eric Yong Joong Lee, A Dialogue with Judicial Wisdom, Prof. An CHEN: A Flag-Holder Chinese Scholar Advocating Reform of International Economic Law, *The Journal of East Asia and International Law*, Vol. 4, No. 2, 2011, pp. 477-514. Korean Prof. Eric Lee is now the Editor-in-Chief of the said Journal. This long Dialogue with 28 pages is now compiled in the Introdction of the English monograph *The Voice from China* (Springer,2013,pp. xxxi-lviii).

  * Professor of Law, Deputy Director, Centre for Asian Legal Studies, Faculty of Law, National University of Singapore.

selected from the voluminous scholarship authored by Professor An Chen that spanned the past 30 years.

This English monograph has successfully won the support from the Chinese Academic Foreign Translation Project (CAFTP), making itself the first of such kind within the academic circle of International Economic Law in China. According to the official specifications[318] from the National Social Science Fund of China (NSSFC), CAFTP is one of the major categories of projects set by the NSSFC and approved by the National Philosophy and Social Science Planning Leading Group of China in 2010. This Project aims to promote Sino-foreign academic exchanges, and to facilitate the outstanding works as well as prominent scholars in the field of philosophy and social science towards the world's academic stage. For this purpose, a major part of such funding is allocated to sponsor the aforesaid achievements to be published in foreign language through authoritative publishers abroad. It is expected that, by such way of accessing and participating in foreign **mainstream** distribution channels, foreigners could have a better understanding of contemporary China, its philosophy and social sciences and its traditional culture. It is also expected that Sino-foreign academic exchange and dialogue would hence be more active, and the overseas influence of Chinese philosophy and social science would be enhanced.

In the Expert Review Report, some of the most professional peers opine that Prof. Chen's book "contributes vastly in the sense of introducing onto the world arena a series of typical academic views and mainstream ideas of Chinese International Economic Law scholars. The whole book is well and uniquely structured, and loaded with creative points of views. With its obvious Chinese character and style, this book has illustrated various innovational academic ideals and pursuits that are different from those voices & views preached by some authoritative scholars from Western developed powers. The author has endeavored to create a specific Chinese theoretical system of International Economic Law under the guidance of Marxism, to further serve as a theoretical weapon for the weak groups of international society to fight for their equitable rights and interests."[319]

---

[318] See Q&A upon the Application for the Chinese Academic Foreign Translation Project Under the National Social Science Fund of China, http://www.npopss-cn.gov.cn/n/2013/0228/c234664-20635114.html.

[319] See Expert Review Report on the monograph manuscript of *The Voice from China*, issued by CAFTP under NSSFC, Nov. 22, 2013.

The Voice from China: An CHEN on International Economic Law is a masterpiece of Prof. An Chen to practice his lifetime will of serving the home country with knowledge and participating in the international competition of academic views. The whole book is based on the common stand of China and other international weak groups, and is indeed a strong & just Voice from China.

Divided into six parts, this magnificent book discusses both grand theories as well as practical doctrinal issues in international economic law. It starts with discussions on the general theories of international economic law, including a vigorous effort to define the international economic law so that it can be an autonomous academic discipline and so that it should not be regarded as merely part of public international law according to Prof. Chen. However, the examination of the "Great Debates" on contemporary economic sovereignty forms the crown's jewels of this first part of the book. Prof. Chen's critique of U.S. unilateralism, contrasted with his praise of multilateralism represented by the WTO, is powerful and passionate. The book also carefully examines and defends China's position on various issues concerning the international order. It offers by far the best account of China's attitude in this regard. Parts IV, V and VI examine, respectively, legal issues concerning Sino-foreign bilateral investment treaties (BITs), Sino-foreign legislation and China's participation in the settlement of international economic disputes.

All the chapters, originally journal articles published by Prof. Chen in various places, have three common features. First, they all put legal issues in their historical, political and economic contexts. Although the book does not work much on doctrinal analysis of specific rules and cases in international economic law and hence it cannot be treated as such a reference book by practicing lawyers, its wisdom lies more in the examination of international controversial issues such as sovereignty, regulatory space, economic nationalism, U.S. unilateralism, the China threat theory, etc. Second, it reasons from Southern perspective, meaning it sides with the developing countries in the North-South division in the international economic order. However, unlike many of the diehards in the camp of the Third World Approaches to International Law, An Chen favors multilateralism as well as an international economic order driven and led by international institutions such as the WTO. He does not seem to view neoliberalism as an idea with the original sin of oppressing the poor people in the developing countries on behalf of the billionaires in the developed world. Rather, he is mainly opposed to the employment of unilateralism by some Western countries, especially the U.S. Third, Prof. Chen is obviously also a patriot and even an open-minded nationalist.[320] His passion to defend China's relevant positions and behaviors at the international level is remarkably impressive.

The author of the book, Prof. An Chen, is one of China's most prominent legal scholars and a leading advocate of the southern view of international economic law, of course more from a Chinese perspective. Born in 1929, Prof. Chen has experienced or witnessed many of the most important events in China and the world in the 20th century. His legal education walks from formal legal education during the Republic of China period before 1949 to self-education of the PRC legal system and international law after 1979. Reportedly, he started to devote his energy to international economic law during 1981-1982, when, after the disastrous and lawless Cultural Revolution, he was invited to be a visiting scholar at Harvard University.[321] It is however a miracle that he was able to turn himself into one of the world's most distinguished scholars in this field given that he only started to learn and work on international economic law after he was 50 years old. More mysteriously, besides his research, he also played a major role in reestablishing the school of Law, Xiamen University, which was once interrupted and dismantled for 27 years since the 1953 nationwide "School Adjustments" until 1980, and developed it into one of the very best law schools in China. By all means, Prof. Chen deserves to be called a genius who is both talented and hardworking.

（翻译、编辑：陈　欣）

---

[320] The scientific and detailed analysis on nationalism by Prof. Chen, see An Chen, *The Voice from China : An CHEN on International Economic Law*, Springer, 2013, pp. 200-203.

[321] See Eric Yong Joong Lee, A Dialogue with Judicial Wisdom, Prof. An CHEN: A Flag-Holder Chinese Scholar Advocating Reform of International Economic Law, *The Journal of East Asia and International Law*, Vol. 4, No. 2, 2011, pp. 477-514. Korean Prof. Eric Lee is now the Editor-in-Chief of the said Journal. This long Dialogue with 28 pages is now compiled in the Introdction of the English monograph *The Voice from China* (Springer, 2013, pp. xxxi-lviii).

十六、二十五年实践显示了1991年陈安预言的睿智 中美国际经贸关系需增进互补、合作和互相依存
——评《中国的呐喊》专著第十四章

〔美〕斯蒂芬·坎特*

我收到陈安院长新近出版的英文专著《中国的呐喊》[322]一书,并且有机会撰写书评,对此我感到特别高兴。这部重要著作包含二十四篇专论,汇集了陈安过去三十多年来研究中国与国际经济法的代表作,具有重大学术价值。中国自1980年开始对外开放,如今已经发展成为全球举足轻重的经贸强国之一。对于任何希望了解中国上述发展进程的人们来说,陈安这部著作乃是重要的信息来源。

陈安是一位杰出的学者,一个具有前瞻思维的教育家。他在中国重新融入世界经济和实行法治的三十多年进程中,始终发挥着至关重要的作用。他是许多中国年轻一代法学专业人才的导师,这些人才在过去三十多年中积极参与了令人振奋的全部发展进程。同时,他也一直是众多国际同行的好朋友,我自己也有幸身列其中。

我特别乐意重新阅读《中国的呐喊》一书的第十四章,即《是重新闭关自守?还是扩大对外开放?——论中美两国经济上的互相依存以及"1989年政治风波"后在华外资的法律环境》。[323] 这一章的基本内容是基于在"1989年政治风波"之后一年多(即1990年秋)陈安在一次国际学术会议上发表的演讲,见解深刻,而且富有洞察力。那次国际学术会议即由路易斯与克拉克西北法学院主办,而当时我正在担任该法学院的院长一职。

"1989年政治风波"曾经导致中美两国关系十分紧张,并且引起许多人怀疑中美两国之间开展的合作和经济互动能否持久。在这种环境下,陈安敢于大胆地、正确地提出自己的见解,雄辩滔滔,他断言:尽管问题多多,时时出现,今后中美两国间的经贸合作互动关系势必经久持续,而且日益增强。他明确指出中美交往已经给中美两国人民带来互惠互利的许多事实,并且列举当时中国正在进一步实行的六个方面的改革,它们势必为中美经济互相依存关系的进一步深化创造更加有利的基础。这

---

* 斯蒂芬·坎特(Stephen Kanter),美国俄勒冈州波特兰市路易斯与克拉克西北法学院法学教授(1986—1994年任该院院长)。

[322] See An Chen, *The Voice from China: An CHEN on International Economic Law*, Springer, 2013.

[323] Ibid., pp. 453-466.

些改革包括:修订了1979年的《中外合资经营企业法》,赋予外商更多权益;制定了适用于经济特区的《外商投资开发经营成片土地暂行管理办法》,放宽了土地使用权的转让,便于外商投资成片开发土地;开放和拓展上海浦东地区,扩大了外商投资极其重要的平台;统一了外商投资企业和外国企业所得税,使之对外商更为优惠;实施了《行政诉讼法》,使外商有权依法"民告官";接受了ICSID体制,使外商可以把投资争端提交ICSID进行国际仲裁。[324]

陈安在1991年提出的关于中美关系的上述预言,现在已被证实是正确的。可是,在20世纪80年代和90年代,我们美国大多数人士——即使是最乐观的人——也很难预见中国经济竟然会如此非同凡响地快速发展,而陈安这篇论文中所强调的上述这些改革措施,在中国经济如此快速发展的进程中确实起到了关键的作用。

回首前尘,自1979年中美全面恢复外交关系,迄今三十多年以来,中国和美国一直在民生的各个方面不断地发展更加密切的关系。除了在经济方面建立了互惠互利和互相依存关系之外,在文化、教育以及其他诸多人文领域,两国人民也一直分享着美好的互相交流成果。

在当今世界,我们正面临着许多严重的问题。这些问题,只能通过各国人民和各国政府之间的互相合作、互相尊重和共同努力,特别是各个大国人民和大国政府之间的互相合作、互相尊重和共同努力,才能成功地加以解决。中国和美国是全球最重要大国之中的两个。有幸的是,近几十年来我们两国的各届领导人都致力于建立这种关系,并不断取得进展。政府与政府之间不断接触、举行会谈以及解决各种层次的实质问题,这已经成为两国关系的常态特征。我们两国的首脑,美国总统奥巴马和中国国家主席习近平之间,已经建立起紧密的工作关系和个人关系,经常互相邀请和互相访问。2015年9月,习近平主席即将对美国进行重要的国事访问。这种友好和坦诚的氛围相当有利于逐步解决范围广泛的各种争议问题,包括国际冲突和世界和平问题、净化环境问题、能源安全问题、改善严重威胁人类的气候变化问题、加强互相理解和坦诚讨论各种分歧问题、改进健康和消减贫困问题。这种不断接触和加强沟通的模式,完全符合1991年陈安预言中提出的见解,是当前我们应当采取的正确途径,也是造福全球的必不可少的关键举措。

最后,在书评末尾我想谈谈个人的访华经历。1984—1985年,我曾经以美国富布莱特基金法学教授的身份,在中国的南京大学法律系讲学。我经常愉快地回忆起1985年春天,在陈安院长的盛情邀请下,我带着八岁的儿子到厦门访问,很高兴在厦

---

[324] See An Chen, *The Voice from China: An CHEN on International Economic Law*, Springer, 2013, pp. 459-465.

门大学做了几场学术演讲,会见了陈安指导的许多才俊学生,而其中一些人随后赴美留学成为我的学生,并在美国路易斯与克拉克西北法学院获得法学博士学位。在厦门期间,承蒙陈安及其家人和厦门大学法学院同行们的盛情款待。后来,陈安在1991年回访美国,我们共同在路易斯与克拉克西北法学院非常愉快地相处了一段美好时光。

陈安是我的老朋友。中美两国都有不少人士其职业生涯中始终致力于在中美之间确立建设性的和友好相处的关系,陈安是其中的重要人物之一。在他撰写的这部精彩著作出版之际,我向他表示祝贺,并且向读者们郑重推荐此书。

(翻译:杨　帆)

Twenty-Five Years of Experience Show the Wisdom of An Chen's 1991 Prediction of Increasing Complementarity, Cooperation and Interdependence of Sino-American International Business Relations
—Comments on Chapter 14 of Chen's Monograph

Stephen Kanter[*]

It is with special pleasure that I received and have had the chance to review Dean An Chen's recent volume, *The Voice from China*.[325] This important work contains twenty-four articles that represent a portion of An Chen's significant scholarship over thirty years on China and International Economic Law. It is an important source for anyone wishing to understand China, and the development of her initial opening to the wider world from 1980 to China's critical position as one of the most important economic and international trading powers today.

An Chen played a vital role throughout this period of China's reintegration into the world economic and rule of law systems as a prominent scholar, as a forward-thinking educational leader, and as a mentor to so many of China's young lawyers who have participated in all of the exciting developments of the last thirty years. He has also been a good friend to countless international colleagues. I consider myself fortunate to be among their number.

---

[*] Professor of Law (Dean 1986-1994), Lewis & Clark Law School, Portland, Oregon.
[325] See An Chen, *The Voice from China: An CHEN on International Economic Law*, Springer, 2013.

I am particularly pleased to revisit Chapter 14, To Close Again or to Open Wider: The Sino-US Economic Interdependence and the Legal Environment for Foreign Investment in China After Tian'anmen. [326] This chapter is based upon an insightful talk that An Chen gave as part of an International Law Conference held in Autumn 1990 and hosted at Lewis and Clark Law School, where I was serving as Dean, just over one year after the disturbing 1989 events in Tiananmen Square. These events created great tension in the Sino-American relationship and raised doubts about the durability of cooperation and economic interaction between our two countries.

An Chen boldly and correctly argued that the relationship would endure and grow stronger despite problems (even serious ones) that would arise from time to time. He pointed to the mutual benefits already accruing to both countries and noted six recent further reforms in China that he knew would provide the basis for deeper economic interdependence. These included revision of the 1979 Joint Venture Law, granting more rights and benefits to foreign investors; easing of land use transfer rights within Special Economic Zones, promoting foreign investors to land-tract development; simplification of the tax structure and improved tax incentives for foreign investors; the opening and development of Shanghai's Pudong district, extending a significant key platform for foreign investors; improved enforcement of the Administrative Procedure Law, allowing foreign investors easier to bring suits aganst Chinese governments; and accession to the ICSID international dispute resolution mechanism, allowing foreign investors to submit the investor-state disputes to ICSID for international arbitration. [327]

His predictions have been proven correct. Even the most optimistic among us in the 1980s and 1990s would have been hard pressed to envision the extraordinary pace of further development of the Chinese economy, and the reforms he highlighted in his article played crucial roles.

From the first days of the Shanghai Communiqué in 1972 and the restoration of full diplomatic relations in 1979 to the present, China and the United States have

---

[326] See An Chen, *The Voice from China: An CHEN on International Economic Law*, Springer, 2013, pp. 453-466.

[327] Ibid., pp. 459-465.

continued to develop closer relations in every aspect of life. In addition to mutually beneficial economic interdependence, our two peoples have shared cultural, educational and many other wonderful human experiences.

Our world faces many serious problems that can only be successfully addressed through mutual cooperation, respect and effort among peoples and governments, especially those of the world powers. China and the United States are two of the most important of these powers, and it is fortunate that the leaders of both of our countries are committed to building on the progress that has been achieved in recent decades. Government-to-government contacts, meetings and substantive problem solving at all levels have become a regular feature of our nations' relationship. Our two Presidents, Barack Obama and Xi Jinping, have a close working and personal relationship and they have exchanged invitations and visits. President Xi will be making an important state visit to the United States in September 2015. This friendly and candid atmosphere is conducive to progress on a wide range of issues from international conflicts and peace, to a cleaner environment and energy security while ameliorating the threat of severe climate change, to mutual understanding and open discussion of differences, and to improved health and the reduction of poverty. This model, consistent with Chen An's 1991 prediction, is the right one for our new century and is essential for the well-being of the whole world.

I want to close with a personal note. I served as Fulbright Professor of Law at Nanjing University Law Department in 1984-1985, and will always fondly remember the visit my eight-year-old son and I made to Xiamen at Dean Chen's kind invitation in the spring of 1985. I greatly enjoyed giving some visiting lectures, meeting a number of An Chen's talented students (some of whom subsequently were my students and obtained their J.D. degrees from our law school at Lewis and Clark), and experiencing the kindness and hospitality of An Chen and his family and law department colleagues. It is wonderful that he was able to return the visit and spend time with us at Lewis and Clark in 1991.

An Chen is a lao pengyou (old friend) of mine, and one of the important people who worked throughout his career for constructive and friendly Sino-American relations. I congratulate him on the publication of this fine volume and commend it to readers' attention.

十七、评陈安教授英文专著《中国的呐喊》：聚焦 ISDS 和 2015 中美 BIT 谈判

〔加拿大〕格斯·范·哈滕*

陈安教授是中国国际经济法学领域资历最深的学者之一，他撰写的英文专著《中国的呐喊》一书，针对中国与国际经济法学之间的互动关系，提出了议题广泛、学识精深的一系列看法。本书汇辑了陈安教授自 20 世纪 80 年代初期以来撰写的 24 篇专题论文，阐述了中国对有关问题的见解和看法，视角独到、引人入胜，涉及众多议题，既包括中国对国际经济法的总体看法和价值理念、概述中国遭受外国列强多次入侵和占领的惨痛历史，也包括对各种具体问题的探讨，诸如"安全阀"在投资条约中的作用问题、中国涉外商事合同争端解决问题、中国经济特区的法律法规问题、美国单边主义与 WTO 多边主义之间的紧张关系和矛盾冲突问题，等等。整体看来，陈教授的这些论文犹如一幅绚丽多彩的织锦挂毯，向我们展示了中国"重新崛起"（re-emergence）的总体理念和具体决策，以及中国与国际经济法律架构之间的互动关系。

全书的一个新颖独到之处在于：针对占据国际投资法论坛主导地位的有害观点，本书是一剂解毒良药，反对严重偏袒西方资本输出国的主导看法。这些主导观点竭力鼓吹：应当优先考虑跨国公司的利益；投资者与东道国争端仲裁中的律师们和仲裁员们所扮演的角色，应当是这些跨国公司利益的支持者；保护外国投资者享有的特权应当被视为一项全球化的指导性规范。与此同时，民主、民族自决和国家主权的价值观，却被轻描淡写，不受重视；或被横加诽谤诋毁，有时候甚至到了这种程度，即胡说什么民主、民族自决和国家主权的价值观会对人类福祉构成威胁，其负面作用甚至超过了跨国公司滥用权力、寡头政体、殖民主义。至少从这些主导看法中，人们几乎听不到批判殖民主义历史流毒的声音，也几乎听不到评论、剖析殖民主义历史流毒与当今"投资者—东道国争端解决机制"（Investor-State Dispute Settlement，以下简称"ISDS"）之间因果关联的声音。这种机制，归根到底就是由

---

* 格斯·范·哈滕（Gus Van Harten），加拿大约克大学奥斯古德堂（Osgoode Hall）法学院副教授，法学博士。此前，他曾任职于伦敦大学政经学院法律系，著有《投资条约仲裁与公法》（牛津大学出版社 2007 年版）、《主权选择与主权约束：投资协定仲裁中的司法限制》（牛津大学出版社 2013 年版）、《一边倒的交易：加拿大与中国投资协定评述》（国际投资仲裁与公共政策资助，作者自行出版，2015 年），并在投资法与仲裁领域发表诸多专论。作者的相关著述可通过社会科学研究网络（Social Science Research Network）获得。

ISDS 这一法律行业的从业者们以及北美和西欧各强国政府所积极推动的。

在此种占主导地位的大量国际法文献背景下，认真思考、鉴别来自饱受历代形形色色殖民主义祸害国家的考察家们的看法，显得尤为重要。陈教授的专著之所以被称作是"一剂解毒良药"，是因为他不仅深入洞察并强烈谴责肆虐于中国和其他国家的殖民主义，同时还颂扬中国人民在反对帝国主义和法西斯占领的斗争中取得的成就。基于此，他致力于将这一源于中国历史的价值理念引入国际经济法。例如，对中国饱受殖民主义荼毒的历史，陈教授不但没有讳言回避，反而大声疾呼："自臭名昭著的 1840 年鸦片战争以后，中国饱受西方列强欺凌和残暴日寇入侵，丧权辱国。"正是这种历史使命感激励他具有"强烈的民族自豪感和爱国主义情怀"，并"立志为本国和广大发展中国家弱势群体的正义要求，呐喊和鼓呼"。铭记殖民主义历史并致力于国际主义事业，尤其是为广大弱势群体大声疾呼，这种理念，迥异于那些专为豪富强势精英们的利益而粉饰殖民主义的大量学术文献。

同时触动我的是，陈教授这本专著也给中国学者们带来了挑战。我不想对另一个拥有独特历史和文化的国度作过多评论，但我想说的是，我看到了在中华民族自豪感和明显由西方规则主导的游戏战略之间存在的冲突，即希望西方强国被击败在他们自己设计的游戏里。陈教授强调"我们不能盲目地附和遵从西方学者的观点"，"应该以求真务实的态度，独立思考，明辨是非"，对此我十分赞同。但是，我认为中国目前面临的直接挑战是：必须机智地决定接受什么和拒绝什么，尤其是在西方强国的压力之下，该何去何从。

遗憾的是，我的母国——加拿大，当今的联邦政府是一个极度"右翼"且非常"不理智"的政府。正因为此，面对中国遭受的来自西方军国主义的诽谤诋毁，加拿大当局一直表现得更像是一个煽动者而非公正调停人。陈教授将西方军国主义对中国的中伤称为"中国威胁"谰言。晚近，这一谰言在北美被频频援引，目的是推动由美国主导的跨太平洋伙伴关系谈判（Trans-Pacific Partnership，以下简称"TPP"）项下处于保密状态的 ISDS 条款的达成，然而，美国国会和美国人民对该谈判却持怀疑态度。TPP 的支持者们并没有解释其中的 ISDS 机制是如何运行的，外国投资者享有的特权包含哪些内容，怎样做到在 ISDS 机制下优先保障公众利益而避免仲裁缺乏独立性、公正性、平衡性等问题；也没有对该机制所耗费的总成本以及给公众带来的风险作出说明。他们一心一意专注于将 TPP 塑造成"反华"的工具，以此满足自身的需要。

面对 TPP 项下以美国范本为蓝本的 ISDS 条款的扩张和其聚焦"反华"的宣传，特别是考虑到中国自己在过去 15 年时间里已经采纳的强有力 ISDS 机制基本上是参照美国范本建立的,此时,我们该如何应对?此外,中国赋予外国投资者的宽泛特权也有进一步扩张,诸如在"公平公正待遇"之类的灵活性术语的设置上,只给外国投资者设定有限的例外,便将本国的国家主权让渡给ISDS机制下那些往往依附成性、并非真正独立的仲裁员,这些仲裁员往往以国际法院的法官们显然不会采取的某种方式,依附于跨国公司和行政官员;相比其他国家的政府,跨国公司和行政官员与美国政府当局之间的联系要更为密切。这样看来,中国和美国开始同步并行,对权力让渡加以认可,使得权力从国家机构(包括立法、行政、司法机构)手中,转移至外国投资者以及那些以仲裁员身份坐堂审案的私家律师手中。尽管中美之间还存在差异,但在ISDS机制问题上中国却趋向于仿效美国的做法。然而,ISDS依旧被当作西方强国的工具,用以对抗那些不满ISDS给本国民主和主权构成威胁的弱小国家,也用以"反华",以满足自身的需要。就这一矛盾悖论(paradox)问题我还不能作出明确的阐释,但我相信它是一个值得关注的问题,不论对中国学者还是西方学者,都是如此。

我一向批判ISDS机制反对民主,在制度设计上存有偏袒,偏向于支持大型的公司和豪富的个体。接下来我想以学者的身份进行评论。从陈教授关于ISDS的论证中引发的一个最为迫切的问题是:中国在同美国谈判缔结双边投资条约(Bilateral Investment Treaty,以下简称"BIT")时该作何选择?中美BIT谈判将是继欧盟和美国"跨大西洋贸易与投资伙伴协议"(Transatlantic Trade and Investment Partnership,以下简称"TTIP")谈判以及上述TPP谈判之后最为紧要的谈判。正是因为ISDS的不断扩张,已经使其从之前一个微不足道的角色发展到如今在全球治理中占据绝对的优势地位。换言之,中美BIT与TTIP、TPP三者是相辅相成的,特别是TPP,不只是"反华",更主要是对国家主权的全盘否定。

中国在中美BIT谈判中面临的主要挑战是什么?中国会因为ISDS存在缺陷,而基于我前述的任何一项理由拒绝接受吗?我认为答案很可能是否定的。以中加投资条约为例,在我看来,加拿大在某种程度上扮演着牺牲品的角色,就像是"一只被献祭给华盛顿的羔羊"。中加投资条约中涉及的一些主要问题同样也是中美BIT谈判所面临的挑战。其中最为关键的就是市场准入问题。中国迄今既有的投资条约从未给予外国投资者以准入前的国民待遇(pre-establishment national treatment),中加投资条约也不例外。值得注意的是,中国却向美国表达了同意以准入前国民待遇为基础进行谈判的意愿。就美国而言,根据其所缔结的BIT来推测,它希望为本国投资者在中国争取到一个扩大版的市场准入权,但对中国投资者在美国享有的市场准入却施加诸多限制条件。一个最好的例证,就是美国和厄瓜多尔签订的 BIT 中就市场准入作出的例外规定,美国将涉及本国经济运行的主要行业部门均排除在准入前国民待遇的清单之列;相比之下,厄瓜多尔对准入前国民待遇所作的保留几乎等于零。[328] 从某种意义上讲,市场准入问题应被视为中美 BIT 谈判真正开始之前的首要问题,其中的关键在于中国愿意在市场准入方面对美国作出多大让步?而作为回报,中国愿意在市场准入方面接受美国作出的让步又是多么微乎其微?

陈教授在其专著中评论了 19 世纪美国和其他西方强权国家把不平等条约强加于中国的历史目的。他写道:"根据不平等条约,列强以苛刻的条件贷款给中国政府,并在中国开设银行,从而垄断了中国的金融和财政。"如今,美国这一目标改变了吗?尽管 BITs 和不平等条约在很多方面不能等同,但其基本主旨目标是永恒不变的,即通过层层加码的方式订立各种条款,使美国企业享有各种优惠,借以促进它们对中国经济的渗透。然而,这些优惠条件是怎样层层加码设置起来的呢?最为重要的一点是,双方同意将涉及条款的各种争端都提交 ISDS 机制去仲裁解决,但其中仲裁员的选择却最终是由世界银行(World Bank)的行政官员们决定的。试想想,如果仲裁员不是由世界银行选定,而是由某一家亚洲开发银行(an Asian Development Bank)来选定,而后者在投票权分配方面又相对有利于中国,那么,美国会举手赞成吗?我估计,美国会觉得这一提议根本不值得考虑。现在,中国愿意对美国作出让步的范围究竟有多大?可以探讨的是,中国在与其他国家(包括加拿大)缔结的 BITs 中,似乎已经朝着这一方向发展,在此类 BITs 中,中国通常处于资本输出国的地位。但到目前为止,中国尚未对美国作出重大让步。

中美 BIT 谈判还面临哪些其他挑战呢?因为加拿大当前是保守党执政,正如陈教授所讲的那样,"加拿大这些年跟美国一直如影随形,亦步亦趋",只有当石油行业的要求超过了美国政府优先关注的事项时才是例外。我们可以设想,2012 年中加 BIT 和一般北美范本在 ISDS 规定上的差别,体现的是中国而非加拿大的偏好。基于这样的设想,除市场准入议题之外,中国曾经尽其所能地支持国内产业,似乎并不赞同北美范本中相对开放的 ISDS 诉讼程序,也不允许原住民享有履行要求的例外,并坚持使用比美国范本还要宽泛的"拒绝授益"条款("denial-of-benefits" clause)[329]。

虽然陈教授对 2012 年中加投资条约的剖析有着深刻的见解,但其中却没有论及中加投资条约和美国 BIT 模式的差异。可以探讨的是,陈教授似乎过分强调了中国

---

[328] See Treaty Between the United States of America and the Republic of Ecuador Concerning the Encouragement and Reciprocal Protection of Investment,Protocol Articles 2,4. 美国对国民待遇事项作出的保留有 17 项之多,厄瓜多尔仅有 2 项。

[329] 参见 2012 年中加 BIT 第 16 条的规定。"拒绝授益"条款又译为"不予授益"条款或"不予施惠"条款。

与北美在路径上的差别。例如,陈教授认为中方在2012年中加投资条约路径方面的独特性时,强调的是征收"补偿"两种标准之间的差别,即"兴旺发达企业的价值"与"公平市场价值"之间的区分。我不想完全否定这种区分方法,但我猜测,很多ISDS的仲裁员在适用这两种标准时应该会采取在本质上相同的方式。再者,2012年中加投资条约项下的"税收例外"条款,实际上沿用了自《北美自由贸易协定》(North American Free Trade Agreement)以来北美模式中的规定;而"用尽当地救济"条款规定提出ISDS仲裁请求前的"等待期",也仅仅是四个月。这个等待期的长度实际上要短于其他采取北美模式的条约。

在最惠国待遇(Most-Favoured-Nation,以下简称"MFN")问题上,陈教授指出中国对该条款采用的是更为缩限的版本,因为2012年中加投资条约规定MFN条款不能适用于争端解决机制。但是,对MFN条款加以限制早在21世纪初期就已存在,之后被广泛运用于北美范本中。需要说明的是,2012年中加投资条约允许MFN条款适用于1994年以来中加两国所签订的许多其他投资条约,这不免是对该条款的一种扩大适用,这就意味着投资者可以选择适用自1994年以来中加两国所签订的许多其他投资条约中更为优惠的规定。然而,不论是中国还是加拿大,1994年之后缔结的BITs并未包含在中加投资条约中出现的各种例外和保留规定,直到发现MFN条款存在漏洞,才开始对其范围进行缩减,从而达到限制外国投资者权利的目的。就其本身而言,2012年中加投资条约对MFN条款所作的规定,看来实际上是降低和削减了针对平衡外国投资者权利和东道国主权利益问题所作出的适度改进。

陈教授强调中加投资条约是双方"利益互相妥协"的典例,这一点我非常赞同。不过,就ISDS条款的设置而言,中国似乎已经朝着ISDS西方范本的方向走得很远。基于这一立场,现在中国直接和美国进行BIT谈判时将会面临更大的挑战。尤其是在诸如市场准入、维护自己的国民经济战略规划、抵制同美国企业有紧密关系的世界银行对ISDS的管辖等问题上,中国都将被迫对美国作出各种让步。

我本着钦佩和尊敬的精神写了这篇书评。全球化给我们带来了许多积极正面的事物,其中之一就是让我这样一个居住在安大略湖畔静谧郊区的加拿大人,能够享有"特权"阅读一位来自被群山环绕的福建省的中国杰出学者所写的专著。为此,我心怀感激。我衷心地希望,陈安教授对国际经济法领域所做的贡献和他本人对人文价值所做的努力,能够有助于牵制中国轻率地走向西方强国设定的关于ISDS和给予外国投资者特权的游戏规则。

(翻译:谷婀娜)

Review on Prof. Chen's English Monograph
—Focusing on the ISDS & 2015 China-U.S. BIT Negotiation

Gus Van Harten[*]

The Voice from China, by An Chen, offers a wide-ranging record of intensive scholarship on China's relationship to international economic law. It provides access to a rare and intriguing perspective from China by one of the country's most senior academics in the field. The book collects 24 articles written by Professor Chen since the early 1980s. The articles cover broad topics such as Chen's proposed values to inform international economic law and an outline of China's bitter history in relation to foreign powers' invasions and occupations. The articles also examine specifics including the role of safeguards in investment treaties, dispute resolution in Chinese commercial contracts, legal aspects of special economic zones, and the tension between U.S. unilateralism and WTO multilateralism. As a whole, Chen's writings offer a rich tapestry of generalist ideals and specific decisions to represent China's re-emergence and interaction with the legal architecture of the international economy.

A refreshing feature of the book is its antidote to dominant themes of international investment law scholarship, which has a heavy bias toward a Western capital-exporting point of view. That dominant theme prioritizes interests of multinational companies—and the role of investor-state lawyers and arbitrators as supporters of those interests—by defending the privileging of foreign investors as a guiding norm of globalization. Meanwhile, values of democracy, self-determination, and sovereignty are downplayed or denigrated, sometimes to such an extent as to

---

[*] Gus Van Harten is an Associate Professor at York University's Osgoode Hall Law School in Toronto, Canada. He was previously a member of faculty at the London School of Economics. He has written three books on investment treaties: *Investment Treaty Arbitration and Public Law*(OUP, 2007), *Sovereign Choices and Sovereign Constraints: Judicial Restraint in Investment Treaty Arbitration* (OUP, 2013) and *Sold Down the Yangtze: Canada's Lopsided Investment Deal with China*(IIAPP, Self-published, 2015). Open access to his publications can be found at the Social Science Research Network and his research database on international investment arbitration and public policy can be found at IIAPP.

suggest these values are a greater threat to human welfare than corporate abuse of power, oligarchy, or colonialism. At least, one hears little about the legacy of colonialism, on the one hand, and on the other hand the links between that legacy and investor-state dispute settlement (ISDS) as promoted primarily by the ISDS legal industry and North American and Western European powerful governments.

In this context of such innumerable literature on international law, it is important to identify perspectives from observers in countries victimized by colonialism in its various iterations. Professor Chen's book offers a refreshing antidote because he acknowledges and condemns strongly colonialism in China and elsewhere and because he celebrates the achievements of the Chinese people in resisting imperialism and fascist occupation. In turn, he strives to introduce values emerging from China's history into international economic law. For example, he does not shy away from but rather calls out the "aggression and suppression by the Western powers and Japan for more than a century" as "a humiliation to all Chinese people". His historical awareness motivated him to have a "strong sense of national pride and patriotism" and a "determination... to strive for social justice" and "to contribute to [his] own country and to support all other weak countries". The connection between remembering colonialism and committing to internationalism, especially on behalf of the weak, is the flipside of air-brushing colonialism from academic literature in the interests of wealthy and powerful elites.

Yet it struck me that Professor Chen's approach also presents a challenge for scholars in China. I do not want to go far in commenting on another country with its own extraordinary history and culture but will say that I see a tension between Chinese national pride and the apparent strategy of playing by Western rules in the hope of beating the West at its own game. Chen stresses "we should not blindly follow and completely accept... Western opinions" but rather "contemplate independently and critically in order... to distinguish right from wrong". I could not agree more. However, I expect the immediate challenge in China is to decide what to accept knowingly and what to reject, especially under pressure from the West.

Regrettably, my own country of Canada—under an exceptionally right-wing and often tactless federal government—has been more an agitator than a moderator of Western militarism based in part on the vilification of China. Chen calls the latter the "China Threat Doctrine". This doctrine was often invoked most recently in North America to promote the secretive ISDS provisions in the U.S.-led Trans-Pacific Partnership (TPP) to a sceptical U.S. Congress and American people. Instead of explaining how ISDS—and the privileging of foreign investors it entails—offers a public benefit to outweigh the lack of independence, fairness, and balance in ISDS and its gross costs and risks for the public, the TPP's promoters instead focused on portraying the TPP as "anti-China" and desirable on that basis.

What are we to make of the expansion of a U.S. model of ISDS in the TPP and its advertisement as "anti-China", especially if viewed alongside China's own embrace over the last 15 years of a muscular version of ISDS based largely on the U.S. model? China has also extended extraordinary rights to foreign investors, has settled for limited exceptions to flexible concepts like "fair and equitable treatment" for foreign investors, and has conceded its national sovereignty to ISDS arbitrators who are dependent—in a manner that international judges clearly would not be—on multinational corporations and executive officials who are more closely connected to the U.S. Administration than any other country's government. It seems the joint approach of China and the U.S. is to endorse the transfer of power from national institutions—legislative, governmental, or judicial—to foreign investors and private lawyers sitting as arbitrators. There are differences in their approaches, but the Chinese way in ISDS tends to have followed the U.S. path. Even then, ISDS is still presented in the West—to counter those weaks upset by its threat to democracy and sovereignty—as anti-China and therefore desirable. I do not have a clear explanation for this paradox but I think it warrants attention from Chinese and Westerners alike.

I offer the next comment as an academic who has criticized ISDS as anti-democratic, institutionally biased, and lopsided in favour of large companies and wealthy individuals. I think the most pressing question to emerge from Chen's scholarship on ISDS involves China's choices in the proposed China-U.S. bilateral investment treaty (BIT). A China-U.S. BIT would be the most significant step, after the proposed Europe-U.S. Transatlantic Trade and Investment Partnership (TTIP) and TPP, in the expansion of ISDS from its minority role to a dominant position in global governance. In other words, a China-U.S. BIT complements the

TTIP and TPP; inter alia, the TTP is not merely anti-China but rather anti-sovereignty altogether.

What are the key challenges for China in such a BIT and will China reject ISDS on any of the grounds I have identified? I think the answer is likely not. Drawing from the example of the 2012 Canada-China investment treaty—where I see Canada partly as having played the role of a sacrificial lamb for Washington—there are a few major issues on which China and the U.S. will face challenges in negotiating a BIT. The most prominent is market access. China has not given market access on the basis of pre-establishment national treatment to foreign investors in its investment treaties, including the 2012 Canada-China treaty, but has signalled a willingness to do so with the U.S. For its part, the U.S., judging from its BIT record, will want an expansive version of market access for U.S. investors in China combined with more limited market access by Chinese investors to the U.S. economy. As an illustration, one can review the market access exceptions in the Ecuador-U.S. BIT where the U.S. exempted practically all of the major sectors of its economy from pre-establishment national treatment and Ecuador exempted virtually none in its own economy.[330] Having gone some way to allowing market access before the BIT negotiations really began, a key question is how much market access China will be willing to give up and how little China will be willing to accept in return.

Chen comments on the historical aim of the U.S. and other Western powers as reflected by the unequal treaties imposed on China in the nineteenth century. Chen says: "By establishing banks in China [they] monopolized the banking and finance of China". Has the aim changed? BITs differ from unequal treaties in many ways but a basic goal is constant: to facilitate the penetration of China's economy by U.S. companies on terms that are stacked in favour of the latter. How are the terms stacked? Most importantly, they refer disputes about the terms to ISDS where the choice of whom serves as an arbitrator is made ultimately by World Bank officials. Imagine if the arbitrators were chosen instead by officials at an Asian Development Bank based on an allocation of voting power relatively favourable to China, would the U.S agree with that? It would be a non-starter in the U.S., I expect. Will

---

[330] See Treaty Between the United States of America and the Republic of Ecuador Concerning the Encouragement and Reciprocal Protection of Investment, Protocol Articles 2, 4.

China accept a comparable concession to the U. S. ? Arguably, China has moved in this direction in other BITs, usually while occupying a capital-exporting position, with other countries including Canada. But the big concession to the U. S. is yet to come.

What about other challenges in a BIT with the U. S. ? Because Canada, as Chen puts it, tends to follow the U. S. path "like a shadow to a person"—certainly under the present Conservative government, except when U. S. government priorities are trumped by those of the oil industry—we can assume that the differences between the 2012 Canada-China BIT and the usual North American model of ISDS reflect Chinese, not Canadian, preferences. On this assumption, besides the issue of market access, it appears that China held onto its existing ability to favour domestic companies, did not agree to the North American model of relatively open ISDS proceedings, did not accept exceptions allowing for performance requirements that would support aboriginal peoples, and appears to have insisted on a broader version of the "denial-of-benefits" clause[331] than in the U. S. model.

While Chen's analysis of the 2012 Canada-China treaty is insightful, it does not address these divergences from the U. S. model. Instead, Chen arguably over-states the degree to which China varied from the North American approach. For example, in stressing the uniqueness of China's approach based on the 2012 Canada-China treaty, Chen emphasizes the distinction between standards of "going concern value" and "fair market value" in compensating for expropriation. I do not wish to dismiss the distinction outright, but I suspect many ISDS arbitrators will apply these standards in essentially the same way. Further, the taxation carve-out in the 2012 Canada-China treaty actually tracks the North American model since NAFTA, and the 2012 Canada-China treaty's provision for exhaustion of local remedies is little more than a four-month waiting period for ISDS claims. That length of waiting period is actually shorter than other treaties on the North American model.

On the topic of most-favoured-nation (MFN) treatment, Chen comments that China achieved a more limited version of this concept because MFN was not extended in the 2012 Canada-China treaty to dispute resolution procedures. But that limitation

---

[331] See 2012 Canada-China Treaty, Article 16.

on MFN has been present in the North American model since the early 2000s. More telling is the 2012 Canada-China treaty's extension of MFN to past BITs since 1994. For Canada and China, there are post-1994 BITs that do not include various exceptions and reservations in the 2012 Canada-China treaty that appear—until one considers the MFN loophole—to limit the scope of foreign investor rights. As such, the approach to MFN in the 2012 Canada-China treaty appears actually to roll back the modest improvements in balancing foreign investor rights with sovereign interests.

I sympathize with Chen's emphasize on 2012 Canada-China treaty as an example of "mutual compromise". Yet it seems that China has moved far already in the direction of the Western model of ISDS and will now face a greater challenge to its position in direct negotiations with the U.S. In particular, China will be pressured to make concessions to the U.S. on market access, its preserve a national economic strategy, and its past resistance to ISDS—under the authority of the World Bank—in its close relationship with U.S. corporations.

I offer this assessment in a spirit of admiration and respectful criticism. One of the positive things about globalization is that a Canadian from a quiet suburb beside Lake Ontario can have the privilege to review the writings of an eminent Chinese scholar from the mountains of Fujian Province. For that, I am grateful. I do hope the strength of Professor Chen's contribution to the field and his commitment to humanistic values may help to check China's imprudent move toward Western rules on ISDS and the privileging of foreign investors.

十八、矢志不渝倡导南南联合自强与国际经济新秩序
——评陈安教授专著《中国的呐喊：陈安论国际经济法》

陈辉萍[*]

《中国的呐喊：陈安论国际经济法》是陈安教授的新作，2013 年由 Springer 出版

---

[*] 陈辉萍，厦门大学法学院教授。1994—1999 年师从陈安教授，攻读国际经济法专业博士学位。

社出版。陈安教授是厦门大学法学院资深教授。三十多年来,陈安教授在国际知名期刊上发表了众多中文和英文论文,从其中精选出24篇进行翻译和改写,汇聚成这部852页的巨著。

2008年由复旦大学出版社出版的专著《陈安论国际经济法》(以下简称"2008年专著")含五卷,78篇论文,多数是用中文写成,也有少部分是英文论文。2013年新专著精选了24篇论文,其中5篇是在2008年至2013年期间完成的。

这两大专著可视为姊妹卷。新专著承继了陈教授的一贯学术追求和理念,但又显示出岁月沉淀下来的更为成熟和老练的立场和观点。作为陈教授曾经指导过的博士生,以及20来年的同事,我拜读了他几乎所有的论文和专著,对其学术水平和学术理念熟稔于心。2011年,我曾为他2008年的专著写过书评,[332]评论了陈教授的人品、独特的研究视角和写作风格以及他对国际经济法的重大贡献。2013年Springer推出的这部英文版新作,体现了中华法学学术代表作"走出国门"、进一步弘扬中华文明的努力追求,因此,我很乐意为它再写一篇书评。

新作全书分为六个部分,分别探讨和论证若干学术前沿重大问题:(1)当代国际经济法的基本理论;(2)当代国家经济主权的"攻防战";(3)中国在构建当代国际经济新秩序中的战略定位;(4)当代国际投资法的论争;(5)当代中国涉外经济立法的争议;(6)若干涉华、涉外经贸争端典型案例剖析。

该新作有两大特点:第一,它涵盖了国际经济法的诸多广泛议题;第二,在探讨这些议题时,作者是站在中国的立场,因而将中国的观点推介给了世界。故此,该书命名为《中国的呐喊》。本篇书评主要评论第二个特点。

陈安教授是中国第一个旗帜鲜明地提出"南南联合自强"理论的学者。陈教授看到中国和广大发展中国家在历史上遭遇的各种磨难,以及它们当前在世界上所处的不利处境和弱小的政治经济地位,就积极倡导南方国家在建立国际经济新秩序中要联合起来,依靠整体的力量,共同奋斗。"南南联合自强"理论最早由陈教授在《南南联合自强五十年的国际经济立法反思:从万隆、多哈、坎昆到香港》一文中率先提出并积极倡导。他认为,通过南南联合自强,各国通力合作,促进法律改革,不仅会使这些弱小国家群体改善处境,获得平权,也会促使当前的国际经济法律制度朝着有利于全世界的方向发展。金砖五国(BRICS,是巴西、俄罗斯、印度、中国和南非五个国家英文名称第一个字母的组合缩写)这个联合体的建立和承担的使命,以及新近成立的金砖国家开发银行和已经签署成立协定的亚洲基础设施投资银行,正是南

---

[332] 该书评发表在2011年秋季出版的《东亚与国际法学刊》第4卷第2期,第533—536页。《中国的呐喊》第lix—lxiii页再次刊登了该书评。

南联合自强的典范。

对于中国在南南联合自强中的作用,陈教授认为,中国作为主要的发展中大国之一,应该成为南南联合自强的强有力支持者,以及今后建立国际经济新秩序的积极推手和中流砥柱。这应该成为中国在当代国际经济法律议题上的战略定位。这一观点主要体现在他的《论中国在建立国际经济新秩序中的战略定位——兼评"新自由主义经济秩序"论、"WTO宪政秩序"论、"经济民族主义扰乱全球化秩序"论》一文中。

本着"中华民族的爱国主义"和国际主义的有机结合,陈教授宣称中国应该坚定地与广大发展中国家站在一起。陈教授提出这一定位的原因是,2009—2010年,一些外国学者和盲目附和的中国学者认为,根据"新自由主义经济秩序"论、"WTO宪政秩序"论、"经济民族主义扰乱全球化秩序"论等新理论,中国应该采取经济上更加"自由主义"的立场,俯首帖耳地完全接受西方"华盛顿共识"和全盘遵守WTO的各项规则。对这些"时髦"理论,陈教授并不苟同。相反,他认为,这些理论会误导中国在建立国际经济新秩序中的方向。本书的目的就是批判性地分析和抵制这些理论,从而澄清是非,保护中国的国家利益和国际声誉,并保障众多发展中国家的平等权利。

陈教授认为,中国在国际经济新秩序中的定位,也同样适用于WTO体制这一具体问题。他认为,中国与广大发展中国家对现有的WTO法制,不能仅限于"遵守"和"适应",而应当通过南南联合,凝聚力量,寻求对其中某些不公平不公正的"游戏规则"加以改变、改革和补救。陈教授认为,WTO争端解决机构充满了缺陷和不平衡。他认为,某些WTO体制本身在立法之初就存在不公平不合理,可概称为"先天不足",有一些是武断制定的,口惠而实不至,专门欺负弱小国家。他指出,WTO的某些专家组在执法实践中显示出"不公平和无能",采取"政治上很圆滑但法律上破绽百出"的方法,可概称为"后天失调"。他认为,中国应与这类不公平和不利于发展中国家的WTO规则做斗争,发展中国家应该联合起来,自助自立自强。这与他一贯倡导的南南联合自强理论是一脉相承的。陈教授提出的这一战略定位,独树一派,与西方学者和某些追随西方"时髦"理论的中国学者泾渭分明,大相径庭。

该书让人印象深刻的一点,是作者有力地反驳了西方对中国和平崛起和支持南南联合集体行动的偏见和攻击,其典例之一就是一些美国政客、军队和学界头面人物提出的"中国威胁"论。这一误导大众的说辞被许多发达国家甚至某些不明真相的发展中国家所接受,严重损害中国的国际声誉,甚至影响中国今后的政治经济发展。陈教授溯本追源,通过比较源远流长的中国对外关系的真实历史、19世纪欧洲和亚洲的历史以及当前美国的具体情况,他得出结论:当代"中国威胁"论是19世纪曾经甚嚣尘上的"黄祸"论的变种,"黄祸"论是俄国沙皇和德国皇帝威廉二世最先提出来的。陈教授指出,"中国威胁"论和"黄祸"论拥有相同的DNA,其目的都是为了曲解历史,曲解中外交往关系的传统主流,成为殖民主义和帝国主义的口号。在反击这类错误学说时,陈教授一方面充分运用其丰富的知识,以及对中国和美国、世界历史的全面而深刻的洞察;另一方面,运用其犀利的语言风格和"妙语连珠"的中国成语来强化自己的立场。这种风格在法律文献中比较少见,但这就是陈教授的风格。

南南联合自强学说受广大发展中国家欢迎。发展中国家在瞬息万变的国际政治和经济环境中,在传统上南方国家存在的正当性备受质疑的情况下,面临诸多共同的挑战,南方思想家提出针对"全球南方国家:50年回顾及今后走向"的议题,以国际论坛的方式加以讨论。[333] 南方委员会认为,努力争取更加公平的国际体制已经使南方国家更为团结,也强化了它们采取联合行动的决心。[334] 联合国前秘书长加利亲自来信邀请陈教授为该论坛撰文。加利是以联合国和平大学欧洲和平发展中心名誉委员会主席、全球法语区秘书长和南方中心委员会前主席的名义发出邀请的。陈教授欣然授受邀请,写了一篇题为《南南联合自强:年届"知命",路在何方?——国际经济秩序破旧立新的中国之声》的论文。[335]

陈教授的理论研究高屋建瓴,入木三分。他的著作新颖尖锐,雄辩滔滔,具有中国风范和中国气派,阐释了不同于西方发达国家学者关于经济主权和国际经济新秩序的创新学术理念和学术追求,为国际社会的弱势群体争取公平权益锻造了法学理论武器。正因为如此,该书获得中国"国家社会科学基金中华学术外译项目"的资助,他是国际经济法领域迄今唯一获此殊荣的学者。该项目的顺利完成,说明陈教授的学术水平已获得国际认同;而荟萃其三十多年来主要学术成果的代表作《中国的呐喊》进入国外主流发行传播渠道,势必大大促进各国对当代中国的了解和理解。故此,Springer出版社将该书列入"理解中国"系列丛书。

此书出版时,陈教授已年届85,这正是一般人安逸颐养天年的时候,陈教授却仍孜孜不倦,笔耕不辍。这对年轻学者们确是一种榜样和鞭策。

(编辑:杨　帆)

---

[333] 引自加利致陈教授函。

[334] See ECPD International Round Table "Global South: At 50 and Beyond", http://ecpd.org.rs/index2.php?option=com_content&do_pdf=1&id=185.

[335] 这篇英文论文发表在2015年春季出版的《东亚与国际法学刊》第8卷第1期第75—105页。该刊总主编Eric Lee评论道:"您对即将来临的国际经济秩序和全球性的南南联合自强的洞见和科学分析,给我留下了深刻印象。……您的论文从国际法的视角揭示了中国对21世纪全球社会的伟大愿景和中国对全球共享繁荣昌盛的胸怀。在国际法论坛上表达如此真诚的亚洲立场,极为鲜见和难能可贵。"参见Eric Lee 2015年3月4日致陈安教授函。

A Tireless Advocate for S-S Coalition and NIEO: Comments on Prof. Chen's Monograph

Chen Huiping*

The Voice from China: An CHEN on International Economic Law is a new monograph written by Prof. An Chen, published by Springer in 2013. Prof. An Chen is a senior eminent resident professor at Xiamen University Law School (China). This 852 page book is a collection and compilation of 24 carefully selected articles written by him in English and published in international leading journals over the past 30-odd years. This English book is partially based on and substantially updated from his previous monograph entitled *An CHEN on International Economic Law* published by Fudan University Press (China) in 2008 (hereafter referred to as "the 2008 monograph"). The 2008 monograph consists of five volumes with 78 articles published until 2008, most of which are in Chinese with some in English. The new monograph consists of 24 English articles, five of which were written and published during 2008 and 2013. These two monographs could be seen as sister books in the sense that this new monograph continues his consistent academic pursuit and ideas, but also goes further to show well-established, more sophisticated ideas and positions gained from his aged experience. As Prof. Chen's previous PhD student and colleague for 20 years, I read almost all his articles and books and thus quite familiar with his scholarship and academic pursuits. I wrote a book review for the 2008 monograph in 2011[336] covering broad comments including his personality, his unique research and writing approaches as well as his important contribution to international economic law. The new English monograph published by Springer in 2013 shows Prof. Chen's further efforts to promote the international exchange of Chinese legal scholarship and the dissemination of Chinese civilization. Therefore, I

---

* Dr. Huiping Chen is now Professor of International Law at the School of Law, Xiamen University. She was a Ph. D. candidate of international economic law under the supervision of Prof. An Chen during 1994-1999.

[336] This book review was published in *The Journal of East Asia and International Law* (*JEAIL*), Vol. 4, No. 2, Autumn 2011, pp. 533-536. It is reprinted in this new book *The Voice from China* at lix-lxiii.

am glad to write a sister review for this new book.

The 24 articles in this new monograph are organized under six subheadings: (1) Jurisprudence of Contemporary International Economic Law; (2) Great Debates on Contemporary Economic Sovereignty; (3) China's Strategic Position on Contemporary International Economic Order Issues; (4) Divergences on Contemporary Bilateral Investment Treaty; (5) Contemporary China's Legislation on Sino-foreign Economic Issues; (6) Contemporary Chinese Practices on International Economic Disputes (Cases Analysis).

This monograph has two features: first, the book covers a broad range of international economic law issues; second, the author is standing in the shoes of China when taking positions in these issues, and thus brings China's views to the world. Hence, this book is entitled *The Voice from China*. This book review focuses on the second feature.

Prof. An Chen is the first Chinese scholar who takes a clear-cut stand proposing the "South-South coalition doctrine". Realizing the historical suffers by China and the developing countries (the "South countries") and their current disadvantageous and weak political and economic positions in the world, Prof. Chen strongly advocates that the South countries should unite and rely on themselves as a whole in the establishment of a new international economic order (NIEO). This doctrine is first formulated and elaborated by him in his article "A Reflection on the South-South Coalition in the Last Half Century from the Perspective of International Economic Law-making: From Bandung, Doha and Cancún to Hong Kong". He suggests that through collaboration of individual power found in South-South coalition, and through the united promotion of legal reform, these disadvantaged groups will not only become stronger, but also impel the advancement of the current international economic legal system for the benefit of the whole world. The establishment and the mandate of the BRICS association (BRICS is the acronym for an association of five major emerging national economies: Brazil, Russia, India, China, and South Africa) and the newly founded Development Bank of BRICS and the Asian Infrastructure Investment Bank are examples of South-South coalition.

As to China's role in the South-South coalition, Prof. Chen suggests that China, as one of the major developing countries, should be a strong supporter of

South-South coalition and a driving force for the establishment of NIEO currently and in the future. This should be China's strategic position on contemporary international economic legal issues. This suggestion is mainly embodied in his article "What Should Be China's Strategic Position in the Establishment of New International Economic Order? With Comments on Neoliberalistic Economic Order, Constitutional Order of the WTO, and Economic Nationalism's Disturbance of Globalization".

Based on the organic combination of "patriotism of Chinese People" and internationalism, he argues that China should stand firmly together with the developing countries. The reason for Prof. Chen to raise this position is that, during 2009—2010, some foreign scholars and their Chinese followers suggested that China ought to adopt a more economically liberal position, fully accept "Washington Consensus" and comply fully with WTO rules based on doctrines such as the Neoliberal Economic Order, Constitutional Order of the WTO, and Economic Nationalism's Disturbance of Globalization. Prof. Chen does not agree with these "pop" doctrines, and instead believes that these doctrines would mislead China in the NIEO. The purpose of this book is to critically analyze and resist the application of these doctrines to China, so as to protect China's national interest and international reputation, as well as the equal rights of vast developing countries.

According to Prof. Chen, this position towards NIEO also applies in the specific context of the WTO regime. He argues that China and the international developing countries shall not be limited only to "abide by" and "adapt to" current WTO laws, but should also consolidate with each other under the "South-South Coalition" to strengthen the ability to seek changes, reforms and redress from some unfair and disadvantageous "rules of the game" among WTO laws. In his opinion, the WTO/DSB (dispute settlement body) is the embodiment of deficiency and imbalance. He claims that some of the WTO laws are deficient since they are unfair and unreasonable at the very beginning of their enactment, some of which are arbitrarily made, nominal promises and an accessory in bullying the weak. He also argues that these principles are imbalances since some specific DSB panels show "injustice and incapability", and take "politically astute but legally flawed" approaches in law-enforcement practices. He advocates that China should combat these unfair and disadvantageous WTO rules. He suggests, in this regard, that developing states unite and work together for collective self-help and self-reliance as a whole. This echoes his persistent ideas of the South-South Coalition doctrine. By keeping and suggesting the strategic position, he creates a separate school which is quite different from and probably unacceptable by some foreign scholars and their Chinese followers.

I am impressed with the book's strong and vigorous refutation and rebuttal to some biases and attacks on China's peaceful rise and support of collective action from the South. The current "China Threat" doctrine proposed by some American politicians, military leaders and academics is one example. This misleading idea is accepted by developed countries and even some developing countries which are ignorant of the facts. This misguided understanding will seriously damage China's international reputation and potentially further block its economic and political development. After tracing the history of China's foreign relations, the history of nineteenth century in Europe and Asia, and after conducting careful analysis of the current US situation, Prof. Chen determines that the current China Threat Doctrine is a variant of the once prevalent, yet problematic, "Yellow Peril" doctrine fabricated and advocated for by the Russian Tsar and German Emperor. Prof. Chen holds that these two doctrines share the same DNA in their goal to distort the historical understanding of Sino-foreign relations, and have been used as slogans of colonialism and imperialism. In the fight against these misguided doctrines, Prof. Chen employs his abundant knowledge and complex understanding of Chinese and world history including US history; on the other hand, he takes advantage of his excellent command and unique style of language, i. e., his sharp and incisive language, and series of Chinese idioms and allusions used to emphasize his position. This literature language style is quite rare in legal analysis articles. But this is his style.

This South-South coalition doctrine is inspiring and accepted especially among developing countries. A forum on the topic of "Global South: At 50 and Beyond?" is proposed to look at instances where "developing countries face many common challenges in a changed and rapidly evolving global political and economic environment, and when the traditional rationale of the South is being questioned and even doubted by some". [337] The South Commission concludes that "The struggle for a fairer international system has consolidated their cohesion and strengthened their resolve to pursue united action". [338] Prof. Chen was invited to contribute to the forum by H. E. Boutros Boutros-Ghali, in his capacity as the Chairman of the Honorary Council of the European Centre for Peace and Development (ECPD) of the UN University for Peace, and as the former UN Secretary-General, Secretary General of the Francophonie, and Chairman of the South Centre Board. Prof. Chen happily accepted this invitation and wrote the article "Global South: At 50 and Beyond? —The Voice from China for Establishing NIEO". [339]

Prof. Chen has conducted research from a strategically advantageous and high position and expressed fully his penetrating opinion. His book contains creative viewpoints, critical analysis and an eloquent plea, with a unique Chinese character, splendor and style. This book illustrates and elaborates his original and novel academic research, ideas which are substantially different from those of western academia. He had endeavored to fight for the rights and interests of the weak by providing theoretical weapons. These features illustrate the necessity and value of expanding upon and spreading the book across the world. For this reason the book was financially supported by the Chinese Academic Foreign Translation Project (CAFTP) sponsored by the Chinese Fund for the Humanities and Social Sciences. He is the only person so far who won this sponsorship among those in the international economic law circle. Through the CAFTP his scholarship and this book which is a collection of the essence of his scholarship with the 30 plus years have gained international recognition and have entered the primary channels of academic dissemination. The aim of this project is to promote Sino-foreign academic exchange, and to facilitate the global dissemination of high-level research for

---

[337] Quoted from a letter by H. E. Boutros Boutros-Ghali to Prof. An Chen.

[338] ECPD International Round Table "Global South: At 50 and Beyond", http://ecpd.org.rs/index2.php? option=com_content&do_pdf=1&id=185.

[339] This long Article has been published in *The Journal of East Asia and International Law* (*JEAIL*), Vol. 8, No. 1, Spring 2015, pp. 75-105. As *JEAIL*'s Editor-in-Chief Eric Lee commented: "It has totally impressed me with your insightful and scientific analysis on the newly coming international economic order, the global south-south coalition... Your paper is showing the great vision as well as Chinese mind for the common prosperity in the 21st century's global community through the angle of international law. We have rare seen such a genuine position of Asia in international law forum." See Letter from *JEAIL*'s Editor-in-Chief Eric Lee to Prof. An Chen, 2015/03/04.

scholars in the field of philosophy and social science, hence this book is included in the series books of "Understanding China" by Springer. This series commonly aims to spread the works regarding Chinese culture and civilization, so as to promote foreigner knowledge and understanding of modern China.

At the age of 85 when most people at the same age retire from work, Prof. Chen continues to work hard in research and teaching. This is a great encouragement to and acts as a driving force for young scholars.

（翻译：陈辉萍）

十九、中国呼声 理应倾听
——评陈安教授专著《中国的呐喊》

〔美〕洛林·威森费尔德*

两年前出版的一部鸿篇力作——《中国的呐喊》，时至今日，我才有机会拜读。该书的作者陈安教授曾经多年担任中国最好的学府之一——厦门大学的法学院院长，又是中国国际经济法学会的创始人之一，并长期担任该学会的会长。陈教授是中国国际经济法学领域最负盛名、最为杰出的学者之一，也是硕果累累、最为多产的学者之一。《中国的呐喊》这部内容深邃的专著，汇集融合了他三十多年撰写的24篇长篇学术专论，聚焦探讨国际贸易法与国际投资法领域聚讼纷纭的各种热点问题。

这部扛鼎之作应该收藏在亚太地区所有学界和政府部门的阅览室和图书馆，以供关注当前国际贸易与国际投资法律热点问题的学者们和政府官员们参考。

陈教授将其最新的著述取名为《中国的呐喊》，用意深远。在他的学术生涯当中，他一直积极学习研究西方学者们的原著，汲取其中有益的智慧，同时又质疑、批驳西方学界有关贸易与投资的某些主流观点。陈教授非常谦虚，他称自己的观点只不过是"具有中国特色的个人视角"，但应该指出的是，他的建议——特别是那些可能被视为"离经叛道"的异议——是深深植根于中国过去150年的苦难历史，其中很大一部分是他亲身经历过的切肤之痛。

在阅读专著中的专论时，西方的读者将会领略到贯穿其中的广泛主题。第一，

---

* 洛林·威森费尔德(Lorin S. Weisenfeld)，美国法学界资深人士，曾长期担任国际组织"多边投资担保机构"法律总顾问，现为Felsberg & Associates律师事务所华盛顿办公室主任。

阐述建设性的爱国主义精神,支持和拥护正在"和平崛起"的中国。中华文明可以追溯到五千多年前,有过灿烂辉煌的时期,也有过令人沮丧的衰落式微。1840—1949年是这个国家特别不幸的岁月,整个晚清阶段,正值西方帝国主义最嚣张之际,中国频频横遭屈辱,饱受欺凌,多次被迫投降,国家主权大部分沦丧。在20世纪初期革命已经成熟,但是又遭野蛮凶残的日本人入侵占领,二战之后,国内战争又接踵而至。

这些经历促使中国知识分子在接受西方学者提出的一系列经济学和法学理论过程中,心存戒惧,这就理所当然,不足为奇了。例如,中国比较迟才加入建立"解决投资争端国际中心"的《华盛顿公约》,就是其后果之一。基此,陈教授在上述专著中,反复多次回顾中国遭到发达国家列强不公平待遇的种种事实,以论证他对那些条约措辞或者法律学说提出的质疑和异议,在他看来,这些条约的措辞和学说只会加重"全球经贸大政决策权力在国际分配中的严重不公"。

贯穿于陈教授这部专著的另一个主要议题是,探讨如何纠正"南北之间"(即发达国家与那些被视为正在发展中的国家)之间的不平衡问题。陈教授所指控的不公平待遇,不仅中国身受其害,所有的发展中国家也都深受其害,它们在二战结束、殖民时代终结之后,不得不与资本输出国展开国际谈判。陈教授谈论"弱小民族",证论"南南合作",敦促贫穷国家联合起来"逐步争得经济平权地位"。只有努力纠正"全球经贸大政决策权力在国际分配中的严重不公",发展中国家才能有效抨击和改变"全球财富分配的不公"。陈教授认为,"权力分配与财富分配之间往往存在着不可分割的因果关系",因此,"必须改变权力分配的不公,以保证全球财富分配的公平"。

贯穿于陈教授这部专著的第三个主要议题便是探讨发展中国家在当前的贸易和投资谈判中应当持有的具体立场。概括起来说,《中国的呐喊》一书探讨如何在发达国家和发展中国家之间的各个领域实行更公平的经济权力分配,向发展中国家的学者们和政府官员们提供了各种具体建议。陈教授毕竟是一位博学的法学教授,他旁征博引,论据充分,资料翔实,论证严谨。因此,那些正在参加国际贸易谈判和正在就双边投资条约最新版本进行磋商的发展中国家的代表们,都可以从陈教授的见解中领悟到很好的忠告和教益。

陈教授认为,当经济强国和弱势国家两方聚集在一起进行贸易和投资条约谈判时,前者往往采取"双重标准"。诸如,发达国家一边强迫发展中国家取消对非农业产品的关税,把这些国家进一步融入世界经济中,另一边却反其道而行之,设立种种"环境"壁垒,阻碍来自发展中国家的农产品进口的贸易自由,这是很不公平的。

在投资激励方面也有类似的问题。西方资本输出国所推行的双边投资条约要求东道国给予海外投资进入东道国关键经济部门的"自由准入"权以及"国民待遇"。然而,恰恰又是这些国家针对来自发展中国家的某些投资设置所谓的"国家安全"壁垒。

晚近的不少实践中,西方国家屡屡以提高效率为名,主张将发展中国家的国有企业私有化。在很多情况下,这可能是个不错的建议。但陈教授担心的是,让外资进入国民经济的关键部门,会使得东道国容易受到"国际垄断资本主义的盘剥"。

西方读者可能只对陈教授的某些主张给予较大同情,对他的其余主张则未必尽然。在有关征收后的补偿问题的探讨中,陈教授主张应采用限制性的标准而不是许多西方国家准备采用的标准。当然,有关赔偿的计算方法,发达国家的学者们也见仁见智而尚无定论,但一般情况下,大多数会倾向于在条约中纳入"赫尔"原则(the Hull Standard)("充分"补偿)的措辞,而不是仅采用"适当"补偿的措辞。

类似的问题也出现在陈教授关于"用尽当地救济"原则适用于解决投资争端的讨论当中。在一个发展中国家的部分行为涉嫌征收外资的情形下,数亿美元投资可能面临危险时,几乎没有哪个资本输出国的律师会赞同首先到东道国偏远的中小省份的法院去寻求当地行政救济。他们不会认为,他们不愿意向一个从未审过征收案件的乡下法院寻求救济,实际上是在"变相地"剥夺东道国的"经济主权和司法主权"。相反,他们认为,直接诉诸国际仲裁,才能保护自己避免受害于经验不够丰富的法官作出"偏袒本地的裁决"。

需要强调的是,陈教授的著述绝非在鸡蛋里挑骨头,或者恶意攻击他人观点,甚至夸夸其谈,不切实际。无疑,他看问题有自己的立场。但他的目的只是在引导读者理解他所看到的国际经济谈判中的不平衡,这种不平衡一直存在于过去两代人的国际经济谈判之中。他的观点是乐观和积极的。正如他援引本国箴言所说,"千万别把娃娃与洗澡水一起泼掉"。他更愿意看到发达国家与发展中国家能够达成共识。例如,中国与加拿大新近缔结的 BIT,历经 18 年的漫长磋商才达成共识,便是如此。所有的努力都是值得的。

作为他这一代人中的中国国际经济法学的顶尖学者之一,陈教授是个相当难得、罕有其匹的人物。他来自福建省农村的一个知识分子家庭,但前半生在中国变乱动荡的时局下饱经沧桑。直到年逾半百,他才得以重返法学领域刻苦钻研,并开始认真学习英语,获得一个进入哈佛大学学习、研修的机会。

留美回国后,陈教授很快便成为厦门大学法学院的院长,这是中国国内顶尖的法学院。他作为中国国际经济法学会的创始人之一,历任会长多年。陈教授还荣获政府授予的"全国杰出资深法学家"称号。这一荣誉代表中国法学界的最高学术水平,自 1949 年以来,全国仅有 25 人获此殊荣。

在阅读陈教授的学术专论汇辑时,西方读者也许不能完全认同他的所有观点,但他们会从《中国的呐喊》当中认识一位治学严谨、富有思想的学者,其独树一帜、不同凡响的呐喊呼声,源自于他的祖国过去 150 年来在政治和经济方面的拼搏奋斗。对于发展中国家的人们来说,它是指明前路、鼓舞人心的呐喊。对于发达国家人们来说,它是一种要求公平待遇和互相尊重的呼声。总之,它是人们理应认真倾听的呐喊呼声。

(翻译:李庆灵,校对:陈辉萍)

China's Voice Deserves Hearing
—Comments on Prof. Chen's *The Voice from China*

Lorin S. Weisenfeld[*]

Although it was published two years ago, I have just had a chance to read Prof. An Chen's weighty volume, *The Voice from* China. Dean for many years of Xiamen University Law School, one of China's best, and a founder and long the head of the Chinese Society of International Economic Law, Prof. Chen is one of China's best known and most distinguished scholars in the field of international economic law. He is also one of its most prolific and productive. In *The Voice from China*, Prof. Chen has pulled together in one hefty volume 24 of his lengthy academic articles, written over the course of more than 30 years, on contentious issues in international trade and investment law.

The volume is a tour de force. It ought to be in the reference library of every scholar and government official in the Asia-Pacific Region concerned with current issues in the fields of international trade and investment law.

Prof. Chen calls his latest publication *The Voice from China* for good reason. Over the course of his career, he has taken issue with elements of the received wisdom on trade and investment law emanating from Western scholars. With modesty, he labels his ideas simply "personal views with Chinese characteristics",

---

[*] Mr. Weisenfeld, an American senior attorney, had been the General Counsel of the Multilateral Investment Guarantee Agency (MIGA) for a long period during last 1980s-2000s. He is the current head of the Washington office of Felsberg & Associates, a corporate law firm based in Sao, Paulo, Brazil.

but it should be noted that his proposals—particularly those that might be seen as iconoclastic—are deeply rooted in the troubled history of China over the past 150 years, a good part of which he has lived through and experienced personally.

A Western reader will note several broad themes running through the articles incorporated in this volume. The first is a notion of constructive patriotism in support of a China that is "peacefully rising". Chinese civilization extends back more than five thousand years, embracing extended periods of brilliance and dispiriting periods of decline. The years 1840-1949 were particularly unhappy ones for the country. Humiliated throughout the late Qing dynasty, repeatedly bullied by Western powers at their most imperialistic, and forced to surrender significant sovereign rights under insulting conditions, China was ripe for revolution at the beginning of the last century. To this mix should be added the brutal Japanese occupation during World War II and the civil war that followed.

It is not surprising that these experiences left Chinese intellectuals leery of accepting without question a range of doctrines in the fields of economics and law propounded by Western scholars. As a consequence, for example, China was relatively late to adhere to the treaty establishing the International Center for the Settlement of Investment Disputes (ICSID). Time and again, Prof. Chen returns to the shabby treatment received by China at the hands of industrialized powers to justify his questioning of treaty language or legal doctrines that, in his eyes, only reinforce "the severe unfairness in international power allocation in [the formulation of] global economic and trade policy making".

Redressing that balance between "North" and "South", the developed countries and those seen as developing, is another major theme that runs through this volume. The unequal treatment of which Prof. Chen complains has been experienced not only by China but by all developing countries that, following the demise 死亡，终结 of colonialism in the post-war period, have had to negotiate with capital-exporting states in international fora. Prof. Chen talks of "weak nations" and of "South-South cooperation", urging that poorer countries stand together to "gradually obtain equal economic rights". Only by seeking to redress the "severe unfairness in international power allocation in [the] global economic and trade policy-making processes" can developing countries attack "unfair global wealth distribution". Prof. Chen finds a "causality between the allocation of power and the allocation of wealth." Thus, "unfair allocation of power must be reformed to guarantee fair distribution of global wealth."

Taken together, the articles republished in *The Voice from China* offer scholars and government officials in developing countries concrete suggestions in multiple contexts for rendering more fair the distribution of economic power between industrialized and developing countries. Prof. Chen is, after all, a law professor, and he advances his views carefully and with voluminous support Specific positions that developing states might take in current trade and investment negotiations are, thus, a third major theme that emerges in this volume.

Those involved on behalf of developing countries in international trade negotiations and in negotiations over the latest versions of bilateral investment treaties would be well advised to have a good understanding of Prof. Chen's views.

Several examples will serve to illustrate the tensions that Prof. Chen sees—double standards, as he calls them—between economically powerful states and the weaker ones when the two sides gather to negotiate trade and investment treaties. It is not fair, he argues, that developing countries be pressed to eliminate tariffs on non-agricultural goods, to further the integration of these states into the world economy, when developed states turn around and erect "environmental" barriers that hamper free trade in agricultural commodities from developing countries.

A similar problem emerges with respect to investment encouragement. Western bilateral investment treaties demand "free access" to critical economic sectors in host countries and "national treatment" for their investments, but then these same states bar certain investments from developing countries for reasons of "national security".

There have been numerous examples in recent years of Western nations arguing for privatization of state-owned enterprises in developing countries in the name of efficiency. This may be a good idea in many cases, but Prof. Chen worries about the instances in which foreign investment in critical sectors has made the recipient state vulnerable to "the predations of international monopoly capitalism".

A Western reader will be more sympathetic to some of these arguments than to others. In discussing the issue of compensation following an expropriation, Prof. Chen argues for a narrower standard than many in the West are prepared to accept.

Of course, the measure of compensation is by no means a settled issue among scholars in developed countries, but in general terms, most would probably favor treaty language embracing the Hull standard ("adequate") as opposed language talking only of "appropriate" compensation.

The same point can be made regarding Prof. Chen's discussion of the role of the "exhaustion of local remedies" doctrine in the context of resolving investment disputes. In the face of allegedly expropriatory action on the part of a developing country, few lawyers in the capital-exporting states would support a requirement to first seek administrative remedies, often in a modest and distant provincial tribunal, when hundreds of millions of dollars may be at stake. They would not view their reluctance to go before a rural court that has never seen an expropriation case as a "disguised" effort to deprive the host country of its "economic and judicial sovereignty". Rather, they would see direct recourse to international arbitration as a way to protect themselves against "hometown decisions" by insufficiently experienced judges.

It should be underscored that there is nothing mean-spirited or vindictive or even doctrinaire in Prof. Chen's writings. He has a point of view, to be sure, but his objective is to guide his readers to an understanding of the imbalances as he sees them in international economic negotiations over the past two generations. His is an optimistic and positive view. As he notes in one of his homey references, he does not want to "throw out the baby with the bath water". Rather he wants to see a convergence between the industrialized states and the developing countries. If it took Canada and China 18 years to negotiate a new bilateral investment treaty, so be it. The result was worth the effort.

Prof. Chen is an unlikely figure to have emerged as one of the leading Chinese international economic law scholars of his generation. He comes from a family of intellectuals in rural Fujian Province, but he lived through all of the vicissitudes suffered by China for the first half of his life. It was not until the relatively ripe age of 50 that he was able to dedicate himself seriously to his field, when he began to learn English and secured an opportunity to study at Harvard.

Returning to China, Prof. Chen quickly became the dean of the Xiamen University Law School, a leading law school in the country. He was one of the founders of the Chinese International Economic Law Society, and for many years its head. Prof. Chen was awarded the designation by the government as a "Nationally Eminent and Senior Jurist", the highest academic honor in Chinese legal circles, one of only 25 such honorees since 1949.

Western readers will not agree with all of Prof. Chen's arguments as they read this compilation of his articles, but they will recognize in *The Voice from China* a serious and thoughtful scholar, whose distinctive voice has been shaped by the political and economic struggles of his country over the past 150 years. For those in the developing world, it is a voice of guidance and encouragement. For those in the industrialized countries, it is a voice calling for fair treatment and respect. It is a voice that deserves to be heard.

二十、魅力感召、法治理念与爱国情怀之和谐统一
——读陈安教授《中国的呐喊》有感

赵 云[*]

2013年，一本重要的国际经济法专著诞生。[340] 该书甫一出版立即引起来自世界各地的国际法学界人士的关注和兴趣，尤其是那些对中国国际经济法实践特别感兴趣的国际法学界人士。陈教授是国际经济法领域的世界知名学者。由于特殊的历史原因，他的专业研究工作只能在20世纪70年代末才得以展开。[341] 但从那时起陈教授撰写了许多国际经济法研究领域的优秀学术文章和书籍，这些学术成果对中国国际贸易和投资相关的法律制度的发展产生了重大的影响。

陈教授从过去30年间撰写的学术论文中精选24篇，汇辑成为一部专著，[342] 全面且充分地展示了其作为一名中国学者对国际经济法的理解。这是中国学者首次

---

[*] 赵云，香港大学法律学院教授，法律系系主任。感谢香港大学法律系博士研究生陈晖和陈志杰协助作者就本文写作进行的研究工作。

[340] See An Chen, *The Voice from China: An CHEN on International Economic Law*, Springer, 2013, pp. 593-594.

[341] See Eric Yong Joong Lee, A Dialogue with Judicial Wisdom, Prof. An CHEN: A Flag-Holder Chinese Scholar Advocating Reform of International Economic Law, *The Journal of East Asia and International Law*, Vol 4, No. 2, 2011, pp. 477-514.

[342] See An Chen, *The Voice from China: An CHEN on International Economic Law*, Springer, 2013, pp. xiv-xxvii.

向全世界全面表明中国在国际经济事务上的立场。陈教授是谈论这一事务最为合适的人选。实际上,这部专著的一个显著的特点是它从中国的视角系统性地审查和研究了国际经济事务。[343] 这正好与此专著的书名——《中国的呐喊》相呼应。因此,对于想知道中国学者对国际经济法持何种看法的读者而言,此专著是一份宝贵资料。

这部专著的论述几乎覆盖了国际经济法的所有领域,包括贸易、投资、区域经济一体化以及经济全球化之趋势。[344] 中国执行对外开放政策之后,首先面临的一个主要挑战是争端解决机制。外商投资者尤为关注中国的司法体制以及司法程序的公正与透明。在20世纪80年代,建立一套与国际实践互相接轨的争端解决机制,是极为迫切的任务。作为应对,中国迅速恢复商事仲裁制度,以在某种程度上减轻外商投资者的顾虑。[345] 1995年施行的《中华人民共和国仲裁法》(以下简称《仲裁法》)是中国仲裁制度发展的一块里程碑。[346]

但是,1995年《仲裁法》的内容引发了激烈的争论与批判,尤其是适用于中国国内与涉外仲裁裁决的双轨体制。[347] 在1995年《仲裁法》施行仅两年之后,陈教授及时地对该部法律作出评价。他在论文中审查了《仲裁法》施行之时双轨制度的合理性问题。文章扼要总结了针对涉外仲裁裁决实施不同制度的四种解释与理解,即与《中华人民共和国民事诉讼法》(以下简称《民事诉讼法》)互相接轨的必要性、[348] 与1958年《纽约公约》以及1965年《华盛顿公约》互相接轨的必要性、[349] 符合国际实践[350] 以及考虑中国特色[351]。陈教授有条不紊地剖析论争中的基本问题,即有关中国《仲裁法》的涉外仲裁监督规定与下述四个方面的接轨问题:

首先,在关于《仲裁法》中的涉外仲裁监督规定是否与相关的民事诉讼法互相接轨的争论上,陈教授认为,其核心问题就在于《仲裁法》中的双轨制度对国内与涉外的仲裁监督区别对待。[352] 具体而言,国内的仲裁裁决可以就程序运作和实质内容同时进行审查与监督,而涉外仲裁裁决则只限于程序运作。[353] 在与《民事诉讼法》比较

---

[343] See An Chen, *The Voice from China : An CHEN on International Economic Law*, Springer, 2013, p. vi.
[344] Ibid., pp. xiv-xxvii.
[345] Ibid., pp. 593-594.
[346] Ibid., pp. 594-595.
[347] Ibid., pp. 581, 590, 595-596, 617-618.
[348] Ibid., pp. 592-596.
[349] Ibid., pp. 596-600.
[350] Ibid., pp. 600-608.
[351] Ibid., pp. 608-618.
[352] Ibid., p. 590.
[353] Ibid., p. 581.

之后,陈教授指出 1995 年《仲裁法》的一个积极的方面是,它进一步扩大了管辖法院对国内仲裁裁决的监督权力范围,并授权法院在必要时可以裁定应予撤销仲裁裁决。[354] 但是,陈教授同时也强调,《仲裁法》将涉外裁决的监督范围限于程序范围之内,这可能导致在现行的仲裁监督制度下引发矛盾以及不公正的裁决。[355] 另外,《民事诉讼法》中明确规定的"公共利益"保护条款在《仲裁法》中毫未提及,因为在对涉外仲裁裁决的监督制度中并没有此类实质性规定。[356]

其次,陈教授在分析 1995 年《仲裁法》是否与国际条约有关规定接轨这一争论上审查了两个国际条约,即 1958 年《纽约公约》和 1965 年《华盛顿公约》。尽管有学者主张,"1958 年的《纽约公约》也只是允许作为裁决执行地的东道国的主管机关对程序上有错误或违法之处的外国仲裁裁决实行必要的审查和监督"[357],但陈教授指出,根据《纽约公约》第 5 条第 2 款的规定,[358]部分实体性问题比如"公共政策"[359]还是在公约中有所列举,这显然表明《纽约公约》对国际仲裁裁决中实体性内容的监督。另外,1965 年《华盛顿公约》促进了解决投资争端国际中心(ICSID)的设立,并在第 52 条[360]规定了其国际仲裁裁决的监督机制。通过这一监督机制,对实体性内容和程序性规定进行必要的审查和监督,以处理仲裁裁决的"终局性"与"公正性"这一对矛盾。[361] 同时,陈教授也指出,《华盛顿公约》第 52 条规定的,由 ICSID 对实体性内容进行监督,可以化解"南"与"北"之间的矛盾,因为弱势的一方(通常是发展中国家)可以借助这一条规定进行自我保护,以避免不公正的裁决。[362] 因此,鉴于中国 1995 年《仲裁法》在对涉外仲裁裁决的监督机制上并没有包含实体性内容,这很难与国际条约在这一事项上所规定的精神与实践相一致。

再次,在涉外裁决监督条款是否符合先进的国际惯例这一争论上,陈教授言简意赅地列举了国外在涉外仲裁裁决监督上的实践,如美国、英国、德国、日本和澳大

---

[354] See An Chen, *The Voice from China*: *An CHEN on International Economic Law*, Springer, 2013, p. 594.
[355] Ibid., pp. 595-596.
[356] Ibid., p. 596.
[357] Ibid., p. 597.
[358] 《纽约公约》第 5 条第 2 款规定,倘声请承认及执行地所在国之主管机关认定有下列情形之一,亦得拒不承认及执行仲裁裁决:(1) 依该国法律,争议事项系不能以仲裁解决者;(2) 承认或执行裁决有违该国公共政策者。
[359] See An Chen, *The Voice from China*: *An CHEN on International Economic Law*, Springer, 2013, pp. 597-598. 根据陈安教授的观点,1958 年《纽约公约》上述条文中使用了英美法系所惯用的"公共政策"一词,其含义相当于大陆法系中的"公共秩序"(public order),或中国法律用语中的"社会公共利益"(social public interests)。这些同义语的共同内涵,通常指的是一个国家的重大国家利益、重大社会利益、基本法律原则和基本道德原则。
[360] 《华盛顿公约》第 52 条规定,任何一方可以根据下列一个或几个理由,向秘书长提出书面申请,要求撤销裁决:(1) 仲裁庭的组成不适当;(2) 仲裁庭显然超越其权力;(3) 仲裁庭的成员有受贿行为;(4) 有严重的背离基本程序规则的情况;(5) 裁决未陈述其所依据的理由。
[361] See An Chen, *The Voice from China*: *An CHEN on International Economic Law*, Springer, 2013, p. 599.
[362] Ibid., p. 600.

利亚的仲裁立法。"他山之石,可以攻玉。"基于发达国家的仲裁立法,陈教授总结道,发达国家的仲裁监督机制以同一的、统一的标准及同等的必要性要求对待各自的国内仲裁裁决和涉外仲裁裁决。此外,陈教授亦指出发达国家的仲裁立法不仅赋权于管辖法院可以裁定"不予执行"裁决,而且在必要时可以裁定"应予撤销"。[363] 至于发展中国家的仲裁立法,陈教授表示其中许多是借鉴发达国家先进的仲裁实践经验,并同样建立了仲裁监督机制对它们国内和涉外仲裁裁决实行"一视同仁"的监督。[364] 另外,陈教授还援引了联合国国际贸易法委员会《国际商事仲裁示范法》[365]以证明对国内和涉外仲裁裁决实行监督的国际趋势应当是"单轨制"而非"双轨制"。显然,中国1995年《仲裁法》中关于涉外仲裁裁决监督的规定与发达国家和其他发展中国家的实践相左。

最后,在中国特色以及地方保护主义这一争论上,陈教授重申追求所谓的"一片净土"论会导致"缺乏应有的清醒和足够的警惕"。[366] 他还提到党和国家领导人的号召和指示以提醒人们一个事实,即一套有效的、健全的仲裁监督机制应当是打击和杜绝仲裁程序中的一切不法行为的。[367] 有些人可能认为当前涉外仲裁的仲裁员的素质相对较高,因此推测在审理仲裁案件期间很少会存在不法行为,[368]而管辖法院某些法官的素质却不够理想,不足以对这些案件形成有效的监督,且他们还可能受地方保护主义影响。对于涉外仲裁的"极少不法行为"的推断,陈教授不否认涉外仲裁的仲裁员的素质整体上具有较高水平且在仲裁的过程中会严以自律。[369] 然而,仲裁审理期间"极少失当行为"并不必然意味着据此就能否定对仲裁员在整个涉外仲裁过程中的不当行为实施监管的必要性。这种忽略审理涉外仲裁案件的仲裁员也可能会存在某些不法及舞弊行为的观点,显然不符合中国现代社会的法治思想以及深深地扎根在法律框架内的正义精神。陈教授不同意以"预防地方保护主义"作为维持目前的"单轨"仲裁监督机制的借口或护盾。这展示了他负责任的态度以及意图寻求一套有效的、健全的仲裁监督机制的决心,他也鼓励法学界、司法界、仲裁界

---

[363] See An Chen, *The Voice from China: An CHEN on International Economic Law*, Springer, 2013, p. 605.
[364] Ibid., pp. 606-607.
[365] See S. Zamora & R. A. Brand, eds., *Basic Documents of International Economic Law*, Vol. 2, CCH International, 1990, pp. 975-984. 作者在文中提到:"联合国大会于1985年12月11日通过专门决议,向整个国际社会郑重推介这部《国际商事仲裁示范法》,建议'全体会员国对这部示范法给予应有的考虑',以作为各国国内仲裁立法的重要参考和借鉴。这种郑重推介,客观上无异于承认了和进一步加强了示范法各有关条款作为国际通行做法(通例)的应有地位。"
[366] See An Chen, *The Voice from China: An CHEN on International Economic Law*, Springer, 2013, p. 610.
[367] Ibid., pp. 619-611.
[368] 这些不法仲裁行为包括:仲裁员在仲裁中凭伪证作出裁决或收受贿赂、舞弊,或者枉法裁决等。
[369] See An Chen, *The Voice from China: An CHEN on International Economic Law*, Springer, 2013, p. 612.

和商界更多的人投身到设计与完善当前的仲裁监督机制的洪流中。

在1995年《仲裁法》实施当时,存在对中国仲裁员素质的质疑以及涉外仲裁程序可能难以有效运行的诸多顾虑是可以理解的。因此,就仲裁制度在中国的正常运作以及排除外商投资者对中国争端解决机制的疑虑而言,一套适当的监督机制显得尤为重要。在这一背景下,陈教授继续就如何加强涉外仲裁程序的监督机制提出建言。诸如设立自律委员会、仲裁研究中心和专家委员会的此类设想,不仅旨在确保仲裁员和仲裁程序的公平公正,[370]而且有利于中国仲裁的有序发展,促进仲裁这一领域的学术研究。

仲裁的概念在商业世界中已被广泛认可,中国国际经济贸易仲裁委员会每年处理大量的商业争端案件。中国仲裁实务发展相当快速,其间也吸收了其他世界级仲裁机构的先进经验,增强了本土仲裁机构在世界仲裁市场中的竞争力。陈教授提出的观点和见解在指导中国仲裁的发展方面至今仍有借鉴意义。只有对仲裁理论与实务的不断研究,方能确保仲裁机构改善自身的仲裁管理与争端解决程序。研究机构等仲裁内部相关机构提供的支持,应当为相关的研究与合作提供一个有益的平台。

在如今的商业世界中,我们强调不同类型的纠纷解决机制共同存在的重要性。陈教授对这一问题也持开放的态度,而没有局限于传统的诉讼程序和仲裁机制。本专著里的论文也涉及解决投资争端国际中心(ICSID)和WTO争端解决机制分别针对国际投资和贸易争端而设立的纠纷解决机制。这些论文的讨论中,我们可以看到陈教授对待不同类型的纠纷解决机制采纳务实而开明的做法。通过研究这些机制的运作方式,陈教授就如何利用这些机制实现中国的最佳效益提出了自己的见解。例如,在分析WTO争端解决机构(DSB)这一法律执行机构时,陈教授提到,尽管WTO争端解决机制在所有现有的国际经济争端解决机制当中地位显著,但它仍然问题不少,"先天不足,后天失调"。[371] 具体而言,陈教授指出,争端解决机制的"先天不足"在于其所执之法中,如在农产品协议的"三大支柱"(即市场准入、国内支持和出口补贴)规则中均包含对国际弱势群体不利的"劣法"或"恶法"的内容,它们仍然不合理地在WTO争端解决机制中生效、运行。[372] 此外,正如其他发展中国家在"入世"时遭受不公正的待遇一样,中国作为世界最大的发展中国家,其已经基本建立了市场经济体制,但这一"双重经济身份"并没有得到WTO/DSB的考虑,还迫使中国接受一些"不利条款"。[373] 与之相反,有些发达国家则通过制定和执行WTO规则受

---

[370] See An Chen, *The Voice from China: An CHEN on International Economic Law*, Springer, pp. 608-618.
[371] Ibid., pp. 249-252.
[372] Ibid., p. 249.
[373] Ibid., pp. 249-250.

益。在301条款和201条款的相关案例中,陈教授指出美国在全球经济体系和WTO下的优势地位,如其在WTO守法方面的刚愎自用、霸权成瘾,进一步阻碍WTO/DSB朝着更为公平与公正的争端解决机制发展。上述两方面案例进一步反映了WTO/DSB是"后天失调"的。[374] 但是,陈教授强调,由于WTO主要由发达国家发起和构建,包括中国在内的发展中国家应该寻求更灵活的战略,以适应WTO的规则体系。发展中国家不应畏惧承担在现行WTO规则下所作出的不公正的承诺,而应共同努力以尽快熟悉WTO的各种"游戏规则",并在面临WTO不公正的立法、守法、执法、变法之时,共同为弱势群体鼓与呼。[375] 陈教授指出,WTO成员之间关系的核心特征在于贯穿于规则的确立、执行、遵守与改变始末的这一"成员驱动"(WTO所有的决议都是由其成员方共同作出)功能特征。因此,发展中国家作为"游戏规则"中的弱势一方,尽管力量有限但却是国际经济领域不可或缺的,它们应该凝聚集体力量,谋求更为公平的国际经济秩序和国际经济法大背景下经济上的平权。

从本书体现出的学术贡献来看,不难发觉陈安教授对于不同的司法体系都有深入的掌握及独到的见解。比如,在本书第二十四章《一项判决 三点质疑——评香港高等法院1993年第A8176号案件判决书》[376]中,陈安教授批判性地评论了香港高等法院的第A8176号案件,并且严格遵循"以事实为依据,以法律为准绳"原则对中国内地与香港地区不同的法律和司法体系作了比较。[377] 在本章中,陈安教授主要从三个方面,分析并质疑香港高等法院的这一判决,即该案管辖权、所谓的中国票据法自治原则以及诉讼程序中的被告答辩权等。[378] 该案原被告双方争议的焦点,[379]是案中的汇票能否绝对地"独立存在",具有"自主性",也就是所谓的"汇票自治原则"在国际法、中国国内法和1993年香港地区司法体系中是否具有法律依据。根据陈安教授的观点,该案的审理法官卡普兰(Kaplan)先生作出判决的依据却是原告方律师狄克斯(Dicks)先生提供的子虚乌有的规则。[380]

关于第一项质疑,即关于该案的管辖权,陈安教授提出了一个非常重要的有待回答的问题:该案的管辖权究竟应归属谁?它应由香港地区的高等法院通过诉讼方式处断,抑或是应由中国内地的CIETAC通过仲裁方式解决?[381] 陈安教授注意到,

---

[374] See An Chen, *The Voice from China: An CHEN on International Economic Law*, Springer, pp. 252-253.
[375] Ibid., pp. 254-258.
[376] Ibid., pp. 717-752.
[377] Ibid., p. 717.
[378] Ibid., p. 718.
[379] Ibid., pp. 718-723.
[380] Ibid., p. 717.
[381] Ibid., p. 723.

卡普兰法官把该案管辖权判归香港地区法院,无视合同当事人在该案中自愿选择了签约地、履行地、合同的仲裁管辖机构、适用的准据法(A158号合同[382])以及合同仲裁条款应当适用于10732C号汇票争端这些事实,从根本上违反了"有约必守"以及当事人"意思自治"这两大基本法理原则。[383] 香港地区《仲裁条例》(第2条、第34A条和第34C条[384])和英国参加缔结的、对香港地区有法律约束力的1958年《纽约公约》[385]均认可当事人"意思自治"的实践。[386] 诸如此类,该案裁决对已与国际惯例接轨的中国内地法律法规缺乏应有的尊重。[387] 对此,陈安教授总结为:"任何人,只要真心实意地尊重和遵循当事人'意思自治'和'最密切联系'这两大法理原则,就当然会认定中国内地的法律是解决A158号合同一切有关争端的唯一准据法;任何人,只要言行一致地承认中国内地的法律是解决本合同一切争端的准据法,并对此准据法给予起码的尊重,就绝不会对中国内地法律体制中有关涉外合同争议及其管辖权的一系列具体规定,弃置不顾。"[388] 因此,根据陈安教授对此问题的深入分析,该案审理中把汇票争端管辖权判归香港地区法院是缺乏法律依据的。

在第二项质疑,也就是关于中国内地法律"承认"该案汇票之"独立性"问题中,陈安教授指出,狄克斯先生(原告的代表律师,香港律师)在论证其论点时所援引的论据,即他所谓的"中国内地在汇票以及其他票据方面实施的各项法律原则",往往是"无中生有",或"化有为无",并不符合事实原貌或原文原意。[389] 为了进一步指出狄克斯先

---

[382] See An Chen, *The Voice from China: An CHEN on International Economic Law*, Springer, p. 726. 在A158号买卖合同第7条中,双方明确约定:"与合同有关的分歧通过友好协商解决。如不能达成协议,将提交中国国际[经济]贸易仲裁委员会仲裁。"

[383] Ibid., pp. 724-729.

[384] Ibid. 根据香港地区《仲裁条例》第2条、第34A条和第34C条的规定,涉及香港地区当事人的国际仲裁协议以及按国际协议进行的仲裁,应当适用联合国贸易法委员会于1985年6月21日颁行的《国际商事仲裁示范法》第一至七章。《国际商事仲裁示范法》第8条明文规定:(1)法院受理涉及仲裁协议事项的诉讼,为当事人一方在不迟于就争议实质提出第一次申述之际,即要求提交仲裁,法院应指令当事人各方提交仲裁。但法院认定仲裁协议无效、失效或不能履行者,不在此限。(2)已经提起本条第1款规定的诉讼,尽管有关争端在法院中悬而未决,仲裁程序仍可开始或继续进行,并可作出裁决。

[385] Ibid., p. 731. 1958年《纽约公约》第2条第3款明文规定:当事人就有关诉讼事项订有本条所称之(书面仲裁)协议者,各缔约国的法院在受理诉讼时,应依当事人一方的请求,指令各方当事人将该事项提交仲裁。但前述协议经法院认定无效、失效或不能实行者,不在此限。

[386] Ibid., pp. 729-730. 澳大利亚著名学者赛克斯(E. I. Sykes)和普赖尔斯(M. C. Pryles)在《澳大利亚国际私法》一书中也引证典型判例,对当事人选择仲裁地的法律意义作了更加明确的阐述:[在合同中]设立条款规定在某特定国家里提仲裁,这就仍然是一种强有力的推定:实行仲裁的所在地国家的法律就是合同的准据法。这种推定,只有另设明文规定的法律选择条款,或者另有其他具有绝对优势的综合因素表明应当适用其他法制,才能加以改变。因此,订有仲裁条款的合同的准据法,往往就是仲裁举行地当地的法律。

[387] Ibid., pp. 734-736. 陈安教授指出,该案判决缺乏对于"《中华人民共和国民法通则》第8章145条的规定""《中华人民共和国涉外经济合同法》第5条的规定""中国司法解释对'涉外合同争议'准据法的规定",以及"中国大学教科书对'涉外合同争议'准据法的基本主张"的应有尊重。

[388] Ibid., p. 739.

[389] Ibid., p. 740.

生在此方面的"无中生有"或"化有为无",陈安教授分别从五个角度进行了阐述:第一,中国内地法律中并不存在"汇票自治原则"这个生造出来的名词,也不存在狄克斯先生所推崇的汇票至高无上的"独立性";[390]第二,狄克斯先生援引中国内地的《银行结算办法》时,使用了断章取义的方法;[391]第三,狄克斯先生在转述郭锋先生论文时,阉割前提,歪曲原意;[392]第四,狄克斯先生的见解与中国内地票据法学术著作中公认的观点、有关的国际公约及中国内地票据法的具体规定,都是背道而驰的;[393]第五,狄克斯先生在援引《民事诉讼法》,以论证其所谓的"汇票自治原则"时,竟然篡改条文,无中生有。[394] 根据以上的五点,可以很自然地得出结论:狄克斯先生所呈递的虚假证词,诱使审理法官卡普兰先生落入对中国内地票据法律原则的误判和陷阱中。[395]

在第三项质疑中,陈安教授对于该案被告答辩权问题提出了疑问。关于法官卡普兰先生在判决中作出的阐释:"我拒绝了被告的申请,不接受他们提交的陈安教授所写的另外一份意见书,因为已经为时太晚,而且在特殊的环境下,对方的专家狄克斯御用大律师没有机会在足够的时间内作出答复",陈安教授指出此说法难以令人信服。[396] 首先,这种"为时过晚"论是站不住脚的,特别是考虑到法官允许狄克斯先生为原告提供的专家意见书一拖再拖,逾期整整三个月,[397]而被告针对狄克斯意见的答辩书距离狄克斯意见书的提交仅仅26天却被拒绝接受。从这个角度来说,法官卡普兰先生的"为时过晚"论缺乏令人信服的解释和足够的法律依据。其次,不给予被告充分的答辩权,是违反公平原则,违反国际诉讼程序惯例的。[398] 这一原则已经

---

[390] See An Chen, *The Voice from China: An CHEN on International Economic Law*, Springer, 2013, p. 740.

[391] Ibid., p. 741. 狄克斯先生任意阉割了适用第22条规定的法定前提:票据经过"背书转让",并且以移花接木和张冠李戴手法,把它强加于该案10732C号这份未经背书转让的汇票头上;同时忽略或"回避"了《结算办法》第14条第2款和第3款的规定,即对商业汇票使用范围及其票据权利加以重大限制。

[392] Ibid., pp. 743-744. 郭文探讨的主题乃是:票据经背书转让之后,票据债务人对于持票的善意第三人的票据债权,应当承担什么责任。换言之,全文的论述主题,特别在论述普通债权与票据债权的区别时,其大前提乃是:第一,票据已经背书转让;第二,已经出现持票的善意第三人……狄克斯先生在援引郭文这些论点用以论证他自己所极力强调的票据权利的autonomy时,却有意无意地忽略或删除了郭文立论的这两个大前提。该案涉讼的10732C号汇票,其票据双方当事人始终就是买卖合同原来的双方当事人,从未发生过"背书转让"情事,因此,这场票据纠纷的当事人也百分之百的就是原来买卖合同纠纷的当事人,丝毫不涉及任何持票的善意第三人问题。

[393] Ibid., p. 745. 在中国内地,1994年2月出版的《票据法全书》(全书1950页,约315万字)中就辟有一章专门论述"票据抗辩"。书中多处论证、肯定和支持票据债务人依法行使抗辩权,从而很不利于或否定了狄克斯先生论票据的绝对autonomy。中国内地学者的上述一贯观点和联合国上述公约所规定的票据法基本原则,不但已经体现在1988年《银行结算办法》的前引条文之中,而且尤其鲜明地体现在1995年5月10日通过的《中华人民共和国票据法》之中。它强调:票据的签发、取得和转让,都必须"具有真实的交易关系和债权债务关系"。

[394] Ibid., p. 748. 根据陈安教授的分析与对比解释,狄克斯先生转述了《民事诉讼法》第189—192条所规定的"督促程序",但狄克斯先生在转述这些条文的时候,将自己不正确的理解强加给中国内地的有关法律。

[395] Ibid., p. 740.

[396] Ibid., p. 750.

[397] Ibid.

[398] Ibid., p. 751.

在众多的国内和国际立法中有所体现,如英美诉讼法的理论和实践中的"自然公平准则"、中国民事诉讼法中的"以事实为根据,以法律为准绳",以及体现在1958年《纽约公约》和1985年联合国《国际商事仲裁示范法》中的"给予被诉人以充分答辩权"。[399] 总之,此案的判决依据是卡普兰先生和狄克斯先生擅自编造的规则,缺少法律依据,应当被认定为丧失其法律约束力。

在这一起案件判决的研究和分析中,陈安教授展现出了作为一名杰出的国际法学者应有的姿态,有力、有理、有节地抨击了该判决中的非正义。在对此案件分析和对判决质疑中,陈安教授不仅熟练和系统地运用相关的法律原则、实体和程序法律、学术著作,以及国际惯例,来发掘和批判该案判决中不合理和缺乏依据的事项。更重要的是,陈安教授此种遵照"以事实为依据,以法律为准绳"原则来对任何司法体系中存在的不公正行为进行据理力争的精神,体现了中国法律体制的核心价值理念,值得所有的法律学者去学习。

上述讨论也正对应陈教授此部专著的基调和核心议题——主权。二战之后,国际社会所重组的国际经济秩序牺牲了发展中国家的利益。中国作为最大的发展中国家,应当扮演改变这种不公正经济秩序的重要角色。以争端解决为例,陈教授深谙相关理论,并能够就如何重构一套国内的争端解决体制,以及发展国际经济并与其他国家保持贸易关系提出务实的见解。[400] 对于当下国际经济法立法、守法和变法的问题,陈教授坚持"正确的态度"[401]应当是公平公正地对待弱势群体。因此,我们不应将改革现有的国际经济秩序的呼声仅仅视为一种政治标语,而应将其视为一个"法律"概念以切实促进法律改革上的成果。此外,国际法环境下的弱势群体应当不断努力地主张及呼吁以消除现行国际经济法的不公平现象,因为正如现在的状况所印证的,发达国家不愿意兑现它们的承诺,即牺牲它们的经济优势去作法律的变革(如在WTO多哈回合谈判中,WTO中的发达国家成员国拒绝在农业谈判上妥协并迈出实质的步伐)。正是在这一严峻的国际经济法环境下,陈教授强调"南南合作"势在必行,因为"集体力量"是促进稳固和公正的法律变革的唯一可行和有效之途径。[402]

本专著中收集的每篇论文都鲜明地蕴含了主权这一主旋律。在鼓励国际交易与交流的同时,中国应该能够捍卫自身的主权以及经济自主。笔者个人在2015年底

---

[399] See An Chen, *The Voice from China*:*An CHEN on International Economic Law*,Springer,2013,pp. 751-752.

[400] Ibid., p. 167.

[401] Ibid., p. 111.

[402] Ibid., p. 207.

受邀前往厦门大学开展系列讲座,其间首次见到陈教授,他睿智的言辞就让我印象深刻。陈教授申明了青年一代国际学者积极地参与国际学术交流以及熟悉国际学术讨论的重要性。但是,他也指出中国的国际法学者不应该盲目地附和或顺从其他学者鼓吹的观点,而应当具有独立的见解并基于对中国大背景的考量提出建议。文如其人,这便是我对陈教授这样一位享有盛誉的学者的确切感受。因此,笔者在阅读他的专著期间甚为愉悦,而通过此书,读者们不仅可以获得国际经济法领域的中国学者视角,更为重要的是,拥有一个优良契机去欣赏陈教授这位国际知名学者的个人魅力感召与爱国情怀。

Harmonization of Charisma, Jurisprudence and Patriotism
—The Inspiration from *The Voice from China*: *An CHEN on International Economic Law*

Zhao Yun*

A major monograph on international economic law was produced in 2013,[403] immediately arousing the attention and interests from international lawyers around the world, in particular from those with special interest in the Chinese practice in the international economic field. Professor An Chen is a world-renowned scholar in the field of international economic law. Due to the special history, he could only start his research in late 1970s;[404] but since then, Prof. Chen has produced many excellent articles and books in the field, which exert a heavy influence on the development of the legal regime in China for international trade and investment.

Twenty-four carefully-selected articles written during the last three decades by Prof. Chen[405] effectively demonstrate the views of Prof. Chen, a Chinese scholar,

---

* Professor of Law, The University of Hong Kong. The author is grateful to two PhD candidates from the University of Hong Kong, Hui Chen and Zhijie Chen, for their research assistance.

[403] See An Chen, *The Voice from China*: *An CHEN on International Economic Law*, Springer, 2013, pp. 593-594.

[404] See Eric Yong Joong Lee, A Dialogue with Judicial Wisdom, Prof. An CHEN: A Flag-Holder Chinese Scholar Advocating Reform of International Economic Law, *The Journal of East Asia and International Law*, Vol 4, No. 2, 2011, pp. 477-514.

[405] An Chen, *The Voice from China*: *An CHEN on International Economic Law*, Springer, 2013, pp. xiv-xxvii.

on relevant issues on international economic law in a comprehensive manner. It is for the first time that a Chinese scholar comprehensively shows to the world China's position on international economic affairs. [406] Prof. Chen is exactly the right person to speak on the matter. Actually, one distinct feature of this monograph is its systemic review and study of international economic affairs from a Chinese perspective. This exactly corresponds to the title of this monograph—*The Voice from China*. Accordingly, this monograph is a valuable source for readers to know the Chinese views on international economic law.

This monograph touches on almost every aspects of international economic law, including trade, investment, regional economic integration and the trend of economic globalization. [407] One major challenge facing China after its implementation of the open-door policy was the dispute resolution mechanism at that time. Foreign investors were seriously concerned about the judicial system and the quality of judicial proceedings in China. The establishment of a dispute resolution framework to be in line with the international practice was an urgent task in the 1980s. [408] China was quick to respond by reinstating arbitration for commercial arbitration, which to a certain extent help to relieve the concerns of foreign investors. The milestone in the development of arbitration was the enactment of Arbitration Law in 1995. [409]

However, the contents in the 1995 Arbitration Law aroused heated discussions and criticism, especially the dual-track regime ("separate track") [410] for domestic and foreign-related arbitral awards. Prof. Chen was quick to make comments on the regime just two years after the enactment. He examined the reasonableness of the dual-track regime at the time when the Arbitration Law was enacted. Four types of interpretation and understanding for the separate regime for foreign-related arbitral awards were succinctly summarised in his paper, namely, the necessity of compliance with the Civil Procedure Law; [411] necessity of compliance with New York Convention of 1958 and Washington Convention of 1965; [412] following relevant

---

[406] An Chen, *The Voice from China: An CHEN on International Economic Law*, Springer, 2013, p. vi.
[407] Ibid., pp. xiv-xxvii.
[408] Ibid., pp. 593-594.
[409] Ibid., pp. 594-595.
[410] Ibid., pp. 581, 590, 595-596, 617-618.
[411] Ibid., pp. 592-596.
[412] Ibid., pp. 596-600.

international practices;[413] taking into consideration of the unique situation in China.[414] Prof. Chen methodically indicated the essential issues within the debates concerning the tallying provisions of Foreign-Related Arbitration Supervision of Arbitration Law with the four aspects below.

First, with regard to the debate over whether Arbitration Law provisions tallying with corresponding Civil Procedure Law in foreign-related arbitration supervision, the core issue mentioned by Prof. Chen concerning the separate track adopted by China's Arbitration Law is that it differentiates domestic arbitration supervision from foreign-related arbitration supervision.[415] That is to say, both procedural operation and substantive matters are allowed to be examined and supervised in the domestic awards, whereas in a foreign-related arbitral award, only its procedural operation is allowed to be examined and supervised.[416] In the comparison between the current Arbitration Law and the Civil Procedure Law of China, one positive aspect of the Arbitration Law, noted by Prof. Chen, is that it has further broadened the scope of the jurisdictional court's supervision power over domestic awards, thus empowering the court to set aside an arbitral award when necessary.[417] However, Prof. Chen also emphasized that this Arbitration Law limits the scope of the supervision over foreign-related arbitration awards to procedure operations only, and can lead to some contradictions and unjust awards under present arbitration supervision mechanism.[418] Moreover, the " public interest" protection, which is expressly enumerated in the Civil Procedure Law, is not appropriately reflected in the Arbitration Law as no such substantive content is listed in the supervision over foreign-related awards.[419]

Second, two international treaties, i. e. New York Convention of 1958 and Washington Convention of 1965, have been involved in the analysis of Prof. Chen regarding the debate over whether Arbitration Law provisions tallying with those of

---

[413] See An Chen, *The Voice from China: An CHEN on International Economic Law*, Springer, 2013, pp. 600-608.
[414] Ibid., pp. 608-618.
[415] Ibid., p. 590.
[416] Ibid., p. 581.
[417] Ibid., p. 594.
[418] Ibid., pp. 595-596.
[419] Ibid., p. 596.

international treaties correspondingly. Even though some people argued that "New York Convention of 1958 only allows the competent authority of a Contracting State where an enforcement is sought to carry out a necessary examination and supervision over foreign awards involving procedural errors or violations of law"[420], Prof. Chen indicated that based on the stipulation in Section 2, Article 5[421] of the New York Convention, some substantive issues such as "public policy",[422] are enumerated in this Convention and thus obviously manifesting that New York Convention stipulates the supervision over substantive contents in international arbitral awards. On the other hand, the Washington Convention of 1965, which facilitates the establishment of International Centre for Settlement of Investment Disputes (ICSID), also enumerates its supervision mechanism on international arbitration in Article 52.[423] This supervision mechanism is employed to strike a balance in the contradiction between the "finality" and "justice" of an award by conducting necessary examination and supervision over both the substantive contents and procedural operations.[424] Furthermore, Prof. Chen also indicated that including substantive matters to be supervised by ICSID in Article 52 can settle the contradiction between the "North" and the "South", based on the fact that the weaker party (frequently the developing countries) can resort to this article to protect themselves from unjust awards.[425] Therefore, considering the present

---

[420] See An Chen, *The Voice from China: An CHEN on International Economic Law*, Springer, 2013, p. 597.

[421] According to Section 2, Article 5 of New York Convention of 1958, if the competent authority in the country where enforcement is sought (the host country) finds that (a) the subject matter of the difference is not capable of settlement by arbitration under the law of that country or, (b) the recognition or enforcement of the award would be contrary to the public policy of that host country, recognition and enforcement of an arbitral award may be refused.

[422] See An Chen, *The Voice from China: An CHEN on International Economic Law*, Springer, 2013, pp. 597-598. According to Prof. Chen, the term "public policy" which is commonly used by common law systems is employed in the above stipulation of the New York Convention of 1958. Its meaning is equivalent to the term "public order" in a civil law system or to the term "social public interests" in Chinese law. The common implication of these synonyms usually refers to the fundamental interest of a state and society and the basic legal rules and basic moral rules of the country.

[423] According to Article 52 of the Washington Convention of 1965, either party can request annulment of the award by an application to the ICSID, on one or more of the following grounds: (a) that the tribunal was not properly consulted; (b) that the tribunal had manifestly exceeded it powers; (c) that there was corruption on the part of a member of the tribunal; (d) that there had been a serious departure from a fundamental rule of procedure; or (e) that the award had failed to state its reasons on which it was based.

[424] See An Chen, *The Voice from China: An CHEN on International Economic Law*, Springer, 2013, p. 599.

[425] Ibid., p. 600.

Arbitration Law of China has not included the substantive matters into the supervision mechanism over foreign-related arbitral awards, it is unlikely that this mechanism is in compliance with the spirit and practice of international treaties in this regard.

Third, in the respect of debating whether foreign-related awards supervision provisions in compliance with advanced international practices, Prof. Chen precisely and concisely enumerates the instances of foreign practice in terms of foreign-related awards supervision, i. e. the arbitration enactments of United States, United Kingdom, Germany, Japan, and Australia. As "stones from other hills may serve to polish the jade of this one", in view of the developed countries' arbitration enactments, Prof. Chen concluded that the arbitration supervision mechanism in developed countries treat the domestic arbitration and foreign-related arbitration with identical and unified standard and corresponding necessary requirements. Moreover, Prof. Chen also indicated that the developed countries' arbitration enactments not only empower the jurisdictional court to make an order to refuse the enforcement of an award, but set aside it when necessary as well.[426] As to the developing countries' arbitration enactments, Prof. Chen indicated that many of them draw on the advanced arbitration practice experience from the developed countries, and also set up arbitration supervision mechanism to conduct identical supervision towards domestic and foreign-related awards.[427] Besides, Prof. Chen also referred to the UNCITRAL Model Law on International Commercial Arbitration[428] to demonstrate the "same track" international trend instead of "separate track" concerning the foreign-related arbitration supervision and domestic awards supervision. It is obvious that the present provisions concerning foreign-related arbitral awards supervision in the Arbitration Law of China are not in compliance with neither the developed countries' arbitration enactment practices, nor the practices in the developing countries.

---

[426] See An Chen, *The Voice from China: An CHEN on International Economic Law*, Springer, 2013, p. 605.

[427] Ibid., pp. 606-607.

[428] According to Basic documents of international economic law, by S. Zamora & R. A. Brand, eds, *Basic Documents of International Economic Law*, Vol. 2, CCH International, 1990, pp. 975-984, the United Nations General Assembly adopted a special resolution on 11 December 1985, seriously recommending this Model Law on International Commercial Arbitration to the whole international society and suggesting that "all States give due consideration to the Model Law" as a main reference for national enactments on arbitration.

Fourth, over the debate upon the uniqueness and local protectionism of China, Prof. Chen reiterated that pursuing the so-called "a piece of pure land" can lead to "lacking a clear head and due vigilance". [429] He also referred to the calls and instructions of party and state leaders[430] to remind people of the fact that an effective and perfective arbitration supervision mechanism is expected to prohibit and fight any misconducts[431] in the arbitral proceedings. Some people may argue that the current arbitrators in the foreign-related arbitration are at relatively higher levels and thus are expected to commit few misconducts during these arbitrational cases, whereas some judges from jurisdictional courts are not high enough to effectively conduct supervision over these cases and may be influenced by "local protectionism". With regard to the "few misconducts" in the foreign-related arbitration, Prof. Chen admitted that arbitrators in the foreign-related arbitration are at relatively high level and may behave themselves well during the arbitration courses. [432] However, "fewer misconducts" being discovered during the arbitration proceedings does not necessarily mean that the whole process of foreign-related arbitration should not be supervised in terms of misconducts by arbitrators. Obviously, neglecting the possibility that certain misconducts and malpractices may be exercised by arbitrators in the foreign-related arbitration, is not in line with China's modern social rule-by-law thought and the spirit of justice rooted deeply inside the law. Prof. Chen disagreed with the opinion to manipulate the "local protectionism" as an excuse or a guarding shield for maintaining the present "separate track" arbitration supervision mechanism, which identifies his responsible attitudes and determined mind-set towards an effective and perfective arbitration supervision system, and encouraged more people from law circles, judicial circle, arbitral circles, and business circles to engage into the designation and perfection of the current arbitration supervision mechanism.

It is understandable at the time of the enactment of the Arbitration Law, a lot of concerns existed in China over the quality of arbitrators and possible

---

[429] See An Chen, *The Voice from China: An CHEN on International Economic Law*, Springer, 2013, p. 610.
[430] Ibid., pp. 619-611.
[431] Including awards made on the basis of perjury or an arbitrator's corruption, malpractice, distorting the text of law in the arbitration, etc.
[432] See An Chen, *The Voice from China: An CHEN on International Economic Law*, Springer, 2013, p. 612.

malfunctioning of the arbitration mechanism for foreign-related arbitration proceedings; consequently, a proper supervision mechanism appeared all the more important for the proper functioning of arbitration in China and dissipate the concerns of foreign investors over the dispute resolution system in China. Under this circumstance, Prof. Chen continued to make suggestions on how to strengthen the supervision mechanism for foreign-related arbitration proceedings. The ideas on the establishment of a Self-Disciplined Committee, Research Institute of Arbitration, and Expert Committee have their target to ensure the proper function of the arbitrators and the arbitration proceedings.[433] These ideas, moreover, support the smooth development of arbitration in China and promote academic research on the topic of arbitration.

The concept of arbitration has been widely accepted in the commercial world, with the CIETAC receiving large number of commercial cases annually. The arbitration practice has developed rather quickly, absorbing useful experience from other world arbitration institutions, adding in the competitiveness of the Chinese arbitral institutions in the world arbitration market. The ideas raised by Prof. Chen continue to be useful in guiding further development of arbitration in China. Only by continuous study of arbitration theory and practice, can the arbitration institutions improve on their arbitration administration and dispute resolution processes. The support of relevant internal organs, such as research institutes shall provide a useful platform for relevant research and cooperation.

In the commercial world nowadays, we emphasize the importance of the co-existence of different types of dispute resolution mechanisms. Prof. Chen was also open-minded on the matter, not limiting himself to the traditional litigation process and the arbitration mechanism. The papers in this monograph also touches on the ICSID and WTO dispute settlement mechanisms for international investment and trade disputes. From the discussions in these papers, we can see that Prof. Chen adopted a pragmatic and flexible approach in dealing with different types of disputes. By examining the functioning of these mechanisms, Prof. Chen was able to put forward his insights on how to make use of these mechanisms to realize the best

---

[433] See An Chen, *The Voice from China: An CHEN on International Economic Law*, Springer, 2013, pp. 608-618.

benefits of China. For instance, in the analysis of the WTO's law-enforcing body—the DSB, Prof. Chen mentioned that even though the WTO's dispute settlement system (DSS) has its distinctive status among all the available international economic dispute settlement mechanisms, it still owns "congenital deficiency and postnatal imbalance".[434] To be specific, Prof. Chen noted that the DSB system has "congenital deficiency" in the rules of agricultural products' "three pillars" (i.e. market access, domestic support, and export subsidy) all contains "bad or evil" contents that run against the interests of the weak groups, which still unreasonably take effect in the WTO's DSB system.[435] And just being similar to other unfair treatment occurring in the accession process of developing countries to the WTO, the WTO/DSB did not take into account the "dual economic identity" of China, which represented the largest developing country in the world with a basic system of a market economy, thus not confirming the market economy status in China and forcing China to accept some "disadvantageous articles".[436] On the contrary, some developed countries in the WTO have benefited from the partial law-making and law-enforcing in the WTO/DSB. It is in the cases of Section 301 and Section 201 that Prof. Chen indicated that the superior status of the United States both in the global economy and the WTO, i.e. the "self-willed and hegemony-addicted" behaviour in the WTO law-abiding, has further hindered the WTO/DSB from becoming a more balanced and justice dispute settlement mechanism. The two cases further reflected that the WTO/DSB system is "postnatal imbalance".[437] However, Prof. Chen emphasized that since the WTO has been found and designed mainly by developed countries, developing countries including China should seek for a more flexible strategy to adapt to the rule system in the WTO. It is not that the developing countries should be afraid of assuming the burden of unfair commitment responsibility under current WTO rule system. It is just that the developing countries should make collective endeavour to nurture proficiency in various "rules of the games" as soon as possible, and stand together to make advocating sounds for

---

[434] See An Chen, *The Voice from China: An CHEN on International Economic Law*, Springer, 2013, pp. 249-252.
[435] Ibid., p. 249.
[436] Ibid., pp. 249-250.
[437] Ibid., pp. 252-253.

the weak groups when confronting the unjustified law-making, law-abiding, law-enforcing and law-reforming circumstances in the WTO.[438] Prof. Chen mentioned this pivotal feature existing in the WTO membership, which is this "member-driven" characteristic functioning throughout the process of making, abiding, enforcing and reforming law. Therefore, the developing countries, acting as the weaker part in the "rules of the game" should combine their limited yet indispensable power in the international economic environment to pursue a level playing field in the context of a more balanced IEO and IEL background.

From the scholarly contributions reflected in this monograph, it is not difficult to find that Prof. Chen has unique insights and deep understanding of different judicial systems. For example, in chapter 24 of this monograph[439]—"Three aspects of inquiry into a judgment: Comments on the High Court Decision, 1993 No. A8176, in the Supreme Court of Hong Kong", Prof. Chen critically commented on the specific High Court Decision case 1993 No. A8176, and compared different laws and judicial systems in Mainland China and Hong Kong, strictly following the principle of "taking facts as the basis, and taking laws as the criterion."[440] In this chapter, Prof. Chen analysed and queried this High Court Decision in three major aspects, i.e. the jurisdiction of the case, the so-called principle of autonomy in the Chinese Bills Law, and the defendant's right of defence during civil procedure.[441] The subject matter in dispute[442] is whether the Bills of Exchange "can stand independently" and owned "autonomy", i.e. whether the so-called "principle of autonomy of Bills of Exchange" has legal basis from the perspectives of international law, domestic law in China, and the Hong Kong judicial system in 1993. According to Prof. Chen, the judge in this case, Justice Kaplan, made the judgment according to the presumptuously fabricated rules made by Mr. Dicks.[443]

With regard to the jurisdiction of the case, Prof. Chen indicated that the question that needs to be answered is whether this case should be decided by the

---

[438] See An Chen, *The Voice from China: An CHEN on International Economic Law*, Springer, 2013, pp. 254-258.
[439] Ibid., pp. 717-752.
[440] Ibid., p. 717.
[441] Ibid., p. 718.
[442] Ibid., pp. 718-723.
[443] Ibid., p. 717.

High Court of Hong Kong, or settled by the CIETAC through arbitration. [444] Prof. Chen noted that Judge Kaplan neglected the facts that both contracting parties in this case voluntarily chose the place of contracting, the place of performance, the entity for arbitration and the proper law (Contract A158[445]), and that the arbitration clause should be applied to the Bills of Exchange, thus violating the principles of Pacta Sunt Servanda and "Autonomy of Will". [446] Both the Hong Kong Arbitration Ordinance (Articles 2, 34A, and 34C[447]) and the New York Convention of 1958, [448] to which Hong Kong is legally bound, acknowledged the practice of party autonomy. [449] As such, the decision failed to pay due respect for Chinese Laws and Regulations that tally with international practice. [450] Prof. Chen summarized that "anyone who sincerely respects and complies with the major legal principles of 'autonomy of will' and 'the closest connection' will inevitably consider Chinese law as the only proper law to resolve all the relevant disputes arising from Sales Contract A, and anyone

---

[444] See An Chen, *The Voice from China: An CHEN on International Economic Law*, Springer, 2013, p. 723.

[445] Ibid., p. 726. According to Clause 7 in Contract A, they agreed that: "Any difference relating to the contract will be resolved by compromise. If compromise cannot be reached, it will be submitted to the China International (Economic and) Trade Arbitration Commission for arbitration."

[446] Ibid., pp. 724-729.

[447] Ibid., pp. 729-730. Under the provisions of Articles 2, 34A, and 34C of the Hong Kong Arbitration Ordinance (Cap. 341), an international arbitration agreement and an arbitration pursuant to an international arbitration agreement are governed by Chapters I to VII of the Model Law on International Commercial Arbitration adopted by the United Nations Commission on International Trade Law on 21 June 1985 (hereinafter "UNCITRAL Model Law"). Article 8 of the UNCITRAL Model Law explicitly provides: A court before which an action is brought in a manner which is the subject of an arbitration agreement shall, if a party so requests not later than when submitting his first statement on the substance of the dispute, refer the parties to arbitration unless it finds that the agreement is null and void, inoperative, or incapable of being performed; Where such an action has been brought, arbitral proceedings may nevertheless commenced or continued, and an award may be made, while the issue is pending before the court.

[448] Ibid., p. 731. Section 3 of Article II of the New York Convention of 1958 provides: The court of a Contracting State, when seized of an action in a matter in request of which the parties have made an (written arbitration) agreement within the meaning of this Article, at the request of one of the parties, refers the parties to arbitration unless it finds that the said agreement is null and void, inoperative or incapable of being performed.

[449] Ibid., pp. 729-730. Famous Australian scholars E. I. Sykes and M. C. Pryles also cited typical precedents in their work, Australian Private International Law, and made the precise statement that: Nevertheless, a clause specifying arbitration in a particular country remains a strong inference that the proper law is that of the country where arbitration is to be held. The inference can be displaced only by an express choice-of-law clause or by a fairly overwhelming combination of factors pointing to another legal system. Thus, often the proper law of a contract (including the arbitration clause) will be the law of the place where the arbitration is to be held.

[450] Ibid., pp. 734-736. Prof. Chen indicates that the Judgment is a lack of due respect for Article 145 of Chapter VII, General Principles of Civil Law of the People's Republic of China, Article 5 of the Law of the People's Republic of China on Economics Contracts Involving Foreign Interests, a judicial interpretation by the People's Supreme Court of the PRC, and also the Chinese collegiate textbook's basic position on the proper law of disputes arising from the economic contracts involving foreign interests.

who shows due respect to Chinese law and honestly recognizes and confirms it as the proper law... will definitely not disregard the series of specific provisions under the Chinese legal system."[451] Hence, Prof. Chen concluded that the judgment was lack of legal basis.

Regarding the issue of the recognition in Chinese law of the "Autonomy" of the Bills of Exchange, Prof. Chen indicated that the argument raised by Mr. Dicks (Hong Kong Barrister representing the plaintiff) in terms of legal principles applicable in China to bills of exchange and other payment instruments were fabricated or misrepresented and not in conformity with the reality and the original meanings.[452] In order to elaborate on Mr. Dicks' fabrication and misrepresentation, Prof. Chen elaborated from the following five points: first, Chinese law did not have strange expressions of "the autonomy of bills of exchange" and absolute "independence" of bills of exchange, as worded by Mr Dicks;[453] second, Mr. Dicks' citation from the procedures for bank settlements were out of context;[454] third, Mr. Dicks had emasculated its prerequisite and garbled its original meaning when citing Mr. Guo Feng's article;[455] fourth, Mr Dick's opinion ran counter to the generally accepted viewpoints of Chinese academic works on bill laws, the stipulations of relevant international conventions, and the bills law in China[456]; and fifth, Mr

---

[451] See An Chen, *The Voice from China: An CHEN on International Economic Law*, Springer, 2013, p. 739.

[452] Ibid., p. 740.

[453] Ibid., p. 740.

[454] Ibid., p. 741. He (Mr. Dicks) emasculates the prerequisite of Article 22 that the Bill of Exchange should have been "transferred by endorsement" and forcibly applies the garbled stipulation to the case of Bill of Exchange 10732C. Meanwhile, he neglects or, in another word, evades the provisions of paragraphs 2 and 3 of Article 14 which apply major limitations to the sphere of application of the rights to a bill of exchange.

[455] Ibid., pp. 743-744. The subject of Mr. Guo's article is the liability of the debtor on a payment instrument transferred by endorsement to the holder of the instrument who is a bona fide third party. In other words, the prerequisites of the argument of the whole article, inter alia those arguments on the differences between an ordinary debt and a debt upon a payment instrument, are that, firstly, the instrument has been transferred by endorsement; and secondly, it has been held by a bona fide third party... However, Mr. Dicks ignored or intentionally garbled the two prerequisites of Mr. Guo's article when citing it as evidence for his so-called autonomy of payment instruments. The Bill of Exchange has nothing to do with any third party because it has never been transferred by endorsement and the payee and the payer are consistently the original two parties of Sales Contract A.

[456] Ibid., p. 745. In China, the *1984 Complete Compilation of and Comments on Bill Laws* (with 1950 pages and about 3.15 million words) contains a chapter devoted to "The Defence Against Payment Instrument". In this book, there are many arguments for defence by the obligors of payment instruments; these are unfavourable to the absolute "autonomy" of payment instruments insisted on by Mr. Dicks... the above viewpoints and principles are embodies not only in the 1988 Settlement Procedures of Banks but also more explicitly in the Law of Bills of the People's Republic of China, promulgated on 10 May 1995, which stressed that the issue, obtainment, and transfer of a payment instrument (bill) shall all "be based on a real transaction and credit-debt relation".

Dicks had distorted the original text when quoting the Civil Procedure Law of PRC as evidence for the said "Autonomy of Bills of Exchange".[457] Based upon these five points, it was thus safe to conclude that Mr. Dicks had submitted ill-grounded affidavit which misled Justice Kaplan in respect of China's legal principles on payment instruments.[458]

Prof. Chen then moved further to question on the defendant's right of defence in this case. Regarding Justice Kaplan's explanation in the judgment that "I refused an application by the Defendant to produce an additional report by Professor Chen An on the grounds that it was too late and in the special circumstances there was no opportunity for Mr. Dicks Q. C., the expert on the other side, to reply to it in sufficient time", Prof. Chen opined that it was hardly convincing.[459] Firstly, the reason "It was too late" was not tenable. The Judge permitted the extension of "the time within which Mr. Dicks had to submit his expert evidence for the plaintiff many times",[460] while the defendant's defence to Mr. Dicks' evidence was rejected for only 26 days after the presentation of Mr. Dicks' evidence. Justice Kaplan obviously had no persuasive explanation and concrete legal basis on this issue. Secondly, denial of the right to defence was contrary to the principle of equity and international practice on litigation procedures.[461] This principle had been reflected in many domestic and international laws, including "the rule of nature" in the Anglo-American procedural laws, the principle of "basing on facts and taking laws as criteria" in the Chinese Civil Procedure Law, "the right to defence" in the New York Convention of 1958 and the 1985 UNCITRAL Model Law on International Commercial Arbitration.[462] To sum up, the judgment based on the presumptuously fabricated rules made by Mr. Kaplan and Mr. Dicks had no legal basis.

In this chapter, Prof. Chen demonstrated the firm gesture of a leading

---

[457] See An Chen, *The Voice from China: An CHEN on International Economic Law*, Springer, 2013, p. 748. According to Prof. Chen's analysis and comparison interpretation, Mr. Dicks restated his so-called supervisory procedure (procedure for hastening debt recovery) provided by Articles 189 to 192 of the Civil Procedure Law, but Mr. Dicks rewrite the original text of the aforementioned provisions in the Civil Procedure Law, in which he forced his incorrect understandings upon the law.
[458] Ibid., p. 740.
[459] Ibid., p. 750.
[460] Ibid.
[461] Ibid., p. 751.
[462] Ibid., pp. 751-752.

international law scholar to argue strongly, reasonably, and pertinently against any unjust grounds, which deserves to be learnt by all legal scholars. As reflected in this chapter, Prof. Chen not only has a comprehensive understanding of domestic and international laws in the field, but also can proficiently and systematically apply relevant legal principles, substantial and procedural rules, academic works, and international practice to critically comment on the inappropriate and ill-grounded issues in the judgment.

The line of the above discussions exactly corresponds to the basic tone of this monograph and the essential subject for Prof. Chen, which is sovereignty. After the Second World War, international society reconstructed international economic order at the sacrifice of developing countries. China, as the largest developing country, should play an important role to change the unfair economic order. Taking dispute resolution as an example, Prof. Chen, having a deep understanding of the international dispute theory, was able to come up with realistic ideas on how to reconstruct a national dispute resolution framework while developing international economic and trade relationships with outside world.[463] With regard to the relationship among law-making, law-abiding, and law-reforming of the existing International Economic Law (IEL), Prof. Chen insisted that "a correct attitude"[464] should not break the balance of treating the weak groups fairly and justly in terms of making, abiding and reforming IEL. Hence, we should not treat demanding reform of the established International Economic Order(IEO) merely as a political slogan, but as a "legal" concept so that real legal reforming achievements can be expected in the IEO. Moreover, the weak groups in the international law environment should fight for themselves to contribute more advocacy and appeal for eliminating the unfair status quo of rules system in the IEL, because as current situation reflects, the developed countries are not willing to enforce their commitment to sacrifice their superior economic status for a level playground in law-reforming (e.g. in the process of Doha Agenda in the WTO, the developed country Members of the WTO refuse to comprise in Agriculture negotiation, thus making real progress in this field unpromising). It is in such severe IEL environment that Prof. Chen emphasized that

---

[463] See An Chen, *The Voice from China*: *An CHEN on International Economic Law*, Springer, 2013, p. 167.
[464] Ibid., p. 111.

"South-South Coalitions" are imperative considering the "collective power" is essential to promote solidified and fairly law-reforming progress.[465]

This underlying tone of Sovereignty is obvious from each and every paper collected in this monograph. While encouraging international transactions and exchanges, China should be able to protect its sovereignty and economic autonomy. I have deepest impression from my first meetup with Prof. Chen by end of 2015 when I was invited to give a series of seminar at Xiamen University. Prof. Chen wisely made his statement that it is important for the younger generation of international lawyers to actively participate in international academic exchanges and be familiar with international academic discussions; however, Chinese international lawyers should not blindly follow whatever other scholars proposed. One should have an independent mind and make suggestions by taking into account of the Chinese circumstance. This exactly demonstrate the unity of Prof. Chen as a well-respected scholar with his papers. Accordingly, the reading process of this monograph has been an extremely pleasant one. Readers will not only obtain knowledge on Chinese views on international economic law, but more importantly, has the opportunity to appreciate the charisma and patriotism of Prof. Chen, as a world-renowned international lawyer.

（翻译：赵　云）

二十一、驳"中国威胁"论——史学、政治学与法学的视角
——读陈安教授《中国的呐喊》第四章

张祥熙*

《美国霸权版"中国威胁"谰言的前世与今生》是教育部立项遴选和定向约稿的哲学社会科学研究优秀成果普及读物之一，由江苏人民出版社 2015 年出版。全书从史学、法学和政治学的三维角度，综合地探讨和剖析"中国威胁"论的古与今、点与面、表与里。本书可视为陈安教授 2013 年在德国 Springer 出版社出版的英文专论 *The Voice of China: An CHEN on International Economic Law* 第四章的最新详细扩展。

---

[465] See An Chen, *The Voice from China: An CHEN on International Economic Law*, Springer, 2013, p. 207.

* 张祥熙，厦门大学南洋研究院博士生。本书评原发表于《中华读书报》2016 年 8 月 31 日第 10 版。

该书的基本内容原是作者 2011—2012 年相继发表于中外权威学刊的中英双语长篇专题论文,题为《"黄祸"论的本源、本质及其最新霸权"变种":"中国威胁"论》。发表以来,获得中外学术界广泛好评。该文的英文版本刊登于国际知名的日内瓦《世界投资与贸易学报》(The Journal of World Investmeat & Trade),该刊主编 Jacques Werner 认为论文融合史学、政治学和法学,文章见解精辟,"让我在审读中享受到乐趣,因此乐于尽快采用此文"。随即在该刊 2012 年第 1 期作为首篇重点论文刊出,篇幅达 58 页,占该期 1/3 以上。数十年来投身于"南南合作"事业的国际活动家、原"南方中心"秘书长 Branislav Gosovic 先生撰写专文对论文给予高度评价,认为它"乃是一篇力排'众议'、不可多得的佳作。这篇文章的确是一项研究与解读当代世界政治的重大贡献","分析透彻并且富有启迪意义。我衷心期待:中国乃至其他发展中国家的领导人、决策者和智囊舆论人士们,都能阅读并研究这篇文章,汲收其中的深刻见解和建议。对于那些想研究或理解当今中国与西方关系的人们来说,这也是一篇'必读'文章"。

此书引起韩国出版界密切关注,一家出版机构已与江苏人民出版社签订翻译出版合同,预定 2017 年推出韩文本。可以预期,其国际学术影响势必逐渐扩大。

所谓的"中国威胁"谰言,喧嚣迄今不止一百四十余年,其直观的表象即是以危言耸听和蛊惑人心的话语,故意渲染、夸大、曲解中国各个方面的历史和现状,胡说中国会给西方带来种种威胁。尽管这种罔顾事实的论调在实践中一再被证伪,但是基于西方中心主义的视角的强权政治依旧存在和维护西方话语霸权的需要,"中国威胁"论并不会随着时间的流逝而消失。学者们对于此种"真实的谎言"展开了各种研究与批判。厦门大学法学院陈安教授的《美国霸权版"中国威胁"谰言的前世与今生》一书无疑是这方面研究中的翘楚。

《美国霸权版"中国威胁"谰言的前世与今生》一书高屋建瓴,紧扣甚嚣尘上的"中国威胁"论这一重大问题,娴熟地运用跨学科的方法,探讨了"中国威胁"论的来龙去脉,深刻理解其本源和本质,实现了由现实追溯历史,又由历史回归现实的研究,提出了许多新观点,为国家外交决策和对外交往提供了有益的参考。

诚如作者在书中所言,"以史为师,以史为鉴,方能保持清醒头脑和锐利目光"[466]。

---

[466] 陈安:《美国霸权版"中国威胁"谰言的前世与今生》,江苏人民出版社 2015 年版,第 3 页。

正是基于其强烈历史使命感,作者追根溯源,对"中国威胁"论的本源进行了由古及今、由点到面和由表及里的全方位、多层次的系统考察和深入探讨,厘清了"黄祸"论—"中国威胁"论的历史演进进程,深刻指出当代"中国威胁"论就是19世纪中后期一度甚嚣尘上的俄国沙皇版的"黄祸"论和德国皇帝版"黄祸"论在新历史条件下的"借尸还魂"。

在廓清了"中国威胁"论的前世与今生后,作者又进一步在历史研究的基础上,运用政治学研究的视角,对"中国威胁"论的实质进行了鞭辟入里的分析论证。作者在查阅大量史料记载的基础上正本澄源,指出西方人所认为的"蒙古人两度西征对欧洲造成'黄祸'战祸和威胁"的说法是于史无据之谈。因为在中原大地建立元朝的蒙古统治者从未派兵入侵过欧洲,更遑论是讲礼让爱和平的中国汉人。紧接着,作者在分析了沙俄入侵中国、德国入侵中国和八国联军侵华,以及1949年中华人民共和国成立之后以美国为首的西方国家对中国推行的一系列敌视政策等历史事实的基础上,一针见血地指出,"黄祸"论—"中国威胁"论鼓吹者最惯用的伎俩是"贼喊捉贼",威胁者自称"被威胁",加害人伪装"受害人",其实质乃是鼓吹"侵华有理""排华有理""反华有理""遏华有理",而鼓吹排华、反华和遏华,往往先导于和归宿于军事行动上的侵华。正因为如此,无论是"黄祸"论还是其后的"中国威胁"论,都只不过是西方国家在强权政治和霸权体系下自说自话的谰言。

作者运用法学研究的视角,分析其中蕴含的基本法理与和平内涵,有力地驳斥了"中国威胁"论这一"真实的谎言"。作者在考察了自汉唐至明朝中国对外经济文化交流的大量史实后认为,中国人通过长期的独立自主和平等互惠的对外经济文化交往,既为自身经济、社会和文化的进步起到了促进作用,也为全球经济文化的不断进步、共同繁荣和丰富多彩,做出了重大的贡献。然而,鸦片战争之后,近代中国落后丧权、饱受欺凌。西方列强通过一系列条约的签订,迫使中国纳入到由西方主导的资本主义殖民体系之中。中国的对外经济交往,无论在国际贸易、国际投资、国际金融、国际税收的哪一个方面,无论在国际生产、国际交换、国际分配的哪一个领域都须受制于列强,低人一等。弱肉强食的丛林法则显露无遗。中华人民共和国成立之后,"中国开始在新的基础上积极开展对外经济交往,促使中国历史传统上自发的、朴素的独立自主和平等互利的法理原则,开始进入自觉的、成熟的发展阶段"。但"在这个历史阶段中,中国遭受两个超级大国为首的封锁、威胁和欺凌,中国依然是被威胁者、被侵害者,而包括美国在内的坚持殖民主义、帝国主义既得利益的列强,则仍然是无庸置疑的威胁者、加害者"。[467] 强权政治和丛林法则的影响也依然延续。正因为如此,冷战结束之后,中国积极融入世界政治经济体系,也迫切希望改变

---

[467] 参见陈安:《美国霸权版"中国威胁"谰言的前世与今生》,江苏人民出版社2015年版,第132页。

不公正、不合理的世界经济体系。

中国要实现中华民族伟大复兴的中国梦,需要努力营造一个长期和平稳定的国际环境,这就使得中国长期实行和平外交政策成了历史的必然。但作者也不忘提醒我们,历史发展之必然也犹如硬币之两面,既有顺应历史潮流的发展趋势,也有悖逆历史潮流的趋势。美国长期推行侵华反华的政策也非历史之偶然,这一点我们要有清醒的认识。例如,在美国支持下,菲律宾、越南等国在南海抛出的"中国南海威胁论"和日本抛出的"中国东海威胁论",以及美国"亚太再平衡"战略的推出就是最好的例证。这一历史必然的总根源在于美国的帝国主义经济体制。作者告诫善良的中国人切勿对"黄祸"论—"中国威胁"论的实践后果掉以轻心,切勿"居安而不思危"或"居危而不知危"。

余音尚未消散,我们的邻国韩国某些当权人士就不顾中国的强烈反对,一意孤行要在韩国部署"萨德"系统。"萨德"探测距离最远范围远远超出防御朝鲜导弹所需,不仅直接损害中国等国的战略安全利益,也会破坏地区和全球的战略稳定。不仅如此,韩国媒体也密集炒作"大国的报复",认为中国对韩国施压才刚开始。殊不知,韩国自身及其背后的美国才是这场风暴的肇事者,这不仅无助于东北亚局势的缓和,而且极大地伤害了中韩关系,渔利的是美国。欣闻本书的韩文版将在韩国面世,希望韩国的领导人、决策者、智囊、舆论界人士,乃至普通学者、普通百姓都能好好阅读此书,了解此书之富有洞见的观点和建议,重新审视"萨德"部署一事,切勿利令智昏,做出搬起石头砸自己的脚的事情。我想,这也正是此书重大现实意义的最好体现之一吧。

Rebutting "China's Threat" Slander from the Perspectives of History, Politics and Jurisprudence
—On Chapter 4 of Professor Chen's Monograph *The Voice from China*

"A Most Important Contribution to this Kind of Research at Present."
—Prof. B. Gosovic

Zhang Xiangxi[*]

The so-called "China Threat" slander has dinned in the Western world for more

---

[*] PhD Candidate, Research School for Southeast Asian Studies, Xiamen University.

than one hundred and forty years. Its most commonly adopted form is by using of the scaremongering and demagogic words to intentionally pile up, exaggerate and distort various aspects of China's history and status quo, with an aim to create an illusion that China will bring threats for the West. Although this kind of facts-ignoring argument has been falsified repeatedly in practice, it will not disappear with the passage of time, as there is still need from the western center of power politics to maintain the western intellectual hegemony at the global level. Scholars have made a variety of research and criticism on this "living falsehood", and with its Chapter 4, this book is undoubtedly the top of such kind.

The basic contents of this Chapter is based on a previous Article published in the internationally renowned journal, i. e. *The Journal of World Investment & Trade*, entitled On the Source, Essence of "Yellow Peril" Doctrine and its Latest Hegemony "Variant"—the "China Threat" Doctrine: From the Perspective of Historical Mainstream of Sino-Foreign Economic Interactions and their Inherent Jurisprudential Principles. For this 58-page article which accounted for more than a third of the whole issue's space, Jacques Werner, then Editor-in-Chief of that journal, noted its penetrating views, and "enjoyed reading it". Mr. Lorin S. Weisenfeld was happy to say that he found the work brilliant and fascinating, and it has pulled together a number of disparate areas for him and caused him to see things in a fresh light.

Mr. Branislav Gosovic, the former Secretary-General of the South Center, who has engaged in international activities for the cause of "South-South Cooperation" for decades, spoke highly of the article. He wrote in a review article that "it is stimulating to read such a rich and enlightening analysis coming from a developing country at a time when conformity, self-censorship or resignation vis-à-vis the reigning storyline is widespread in governments, the media, as well as the academia." And he "would like to see leaders, policy-and-opinion-makers, not only in China, but also in other developing countries, including those involved in Group of 77 and NAM activities, read and study Professor Chen's article and absorb the insights and conclusions presented by the author." Besides, "It is a 'must reading' for those who study or are trying to understand China-West relations of today. It helps one to appreciate China's sensitivities and reactions, as well as to grasp the

Western, US-led, global, all-azimuth offensive against this country, of which the 'China Threat' intellectual construct, as a contemporary iteration of the earlier 'Yellow Peril' Doctrine, represents the overarching framework."[468] So it can be expected that with the publication of this book, the academic influence of views the author put forward in the book will be bound to expand gradually at home and abroad.

This book holds tightly and makes a high level description of the rampant "China Threat", which is not only a historical issue, but also an important reality problem. The author sheds light on the roots, intellectual and policy antecedents, i.e. the "family tree", of the "China Threat" Doctrines by skillfully adopting the interdisciplinary approach from the perspectives of history, political theory and law. He also puts forward many new ideas and provides the beneficial reference for the national diplomatic decision-making and foreign communication. With great foresight and powerful writing, this book not only preserves the author's strong patriotic and sincere feelings, but also reflects his rigorous scholarly research attitude and profound knowledge.

As is stated in the book, it is only through taking the history as teachers and as mirrors can people keep sharp brain and incisive eyesight. Based on his strong historical sense of mission, the author is trying to carry out synthetic discussion and comprehensive dissection on the past and present, the points and facets, as well as the appearance and essence of "China Threat" Doctrine and clarifies the historical evolution process from "Yellow Peril" Doctrine to its new variant "China Threat" Doctrine. So in this book, the author profoundly points out that the contemporary "China Threat" Doctrine is nothing but a current "variant" under contemporary situations of the once clamorous "Yellow Peril" Doctrine fabricated and preached by Russian Tsar and German Emperor in 19th century.

After making clear all the ins and outs of the "China Threat" Doctrine, the author further makes a thorough analysis on the essence of the "China Threat" Doctrine from both the historical and political perspectives. By consulting a large

---

[468] Branislav Gosovic, China—"Threat" or "Opportunity"? Professor An Chen's Article on "Yellow Peril"/"China Threat" Doctrines—An Important Contribution to the Study and Understanding of Contemporary World Politics, *Journal of International Economic Law*, Vol. 20, No. 2, 2013.

number of the original historical records, the author clarifies matters and points out that it is nonsense in the history that the twice Mongolian Westward March was the biggest "Yellow Peril" war and threat, because Yuan Dynasty of China had never sent a single soldier to invade Europe during its 98 years of existence. So the popular yet vague statements such as that "Yuan Dynasty of China sent a large army to invade Europe and caused Yellow Peril" did not accord to historical facts, let alone the Han Chinese people who are modest and courtesy and love peace. Then, based on the analysis of the Russian invasion of China, the German invasion of China, the aggression against China by the Eight-Power Allied Force and a series of hostile policies towards China implemented by the US-led western countries after the founding of the People's Republic of China, the author puts it succinctly that various versions of "Yellow Peril" Doctrine have been playing their customary trick of a thief crying "Stop thief", and its essence and core lie at the preaching and justification of invading into China, excluding Chinese, opposing against China and containing China; and such exclusion, opposition and containment always come before and lead to a final invasion. From these evidence it could be fairly put that both the "Yellow Peril" Doctrine and its new variant "China Threat" Doctrine are nothing more than a self-talking slander under the Western-system of power politics and hegemony.

Then the author utilizes the perspective of economic jurisprudence to analyze the basic and inherent jurisprudential principles and the real meaning of peace which is contained in the long standing mainstream of Sino-Foreign economic interactions, and refutes effectively that the "Yellow Peril" Doctrine and its new variant "China Threat" Doctrine are downright "living falsehood". Based on his thorough investigation into the development history of the long standing mainstream of Sino-Foreign economic interactions from the Han through Tang Dynasty and till to the Ming Dynasty, the author points out that just through their long-term external economic interactions of an equal and reciprocal nature, Chinese had made significant contributions towards the continuous improvement, common prosperity and colorful enrichment of global economics and culture.

However, after the Opium War, modern China had to surrender its sovereign rights under humiliating terms and suffered from bullying. And thus China was forced into the capitalist colonial system dominated by the West. In this case, because its political and economic sovereignty were severely damaged, China's external economic intercourse from whichever aspects such as international trade, international investment, international finance or international taxation, and within whichever domains such as international production, international exchange or international distribution were always in an involuntary and coerced condition, under others' control, at others' service. So China always suffered from humiliation of inequality, and it had to undergo unequal exchange and exploitation. The law of the jungle is exposed completely here.

After the founding of the People's Republic of China, China has begun to actively carry out foreign economic exchanges on the new base, and it would inevitably prompt the spontaneous and plain traditional principle of equality and reciprocity in its external economic intercourse shift to a conscientious and mature stage. But during this historical stage, new China had been blocked, threatened and bullied by various countries led by then two superpowers. China was still the country which was threatened and invaded, while the big powers including the U.S., who insisted on their colonial and imperial vested interests, were still the undoubted menacers and injurers. The influence of power politics and the law of jungle also continues till that time. As a result, after the end of the Cold War, China has been actively integrated into the world political and economic system, and is also eager to change the unfair and unreasonable world economic system.

In order to fulfill the Chinese Dream of achieving the great renewal of the Chinese nation, China needs to strive to create a peaceful and stable international environment for a long time, which makes it inevitable for China to unwaveringly follow the path of peaceful development and the win-win strategy of opening-up.

The author does not forget to remind us that the trees may prefer calm but the wind will not subside. The development of world history is just like a coin of two sides, with one complying with the tide of historical development, and another rebelling against the historical trend. The author told us that we should have a clear understanding that it is not the accident of history for U.S. to implement the long-term anti-China policy. Supported by the United States, for example, the

Philippines, Vietnam and other countries have been vigorously preaching one after another the Doctrines of "China Threat in the South China Sea" and "China Threat in the East China Sea", and the United States having launched the strategy of "Asia Pacific Rebalancing" are all the best examples. The behaviors of the United States are rooted in its imperialist economic system. So the author has warned the kind and forgiving Chinese people must not treat the practice consequences of the "Yellow Peril" Doctrine and its new variant "China Threat" Doctrine lightly, and must prepare for danger in times of safety.

What the author warned has not been dissipated. Our neighbor, the Republic of Korea, disregarding the strong opposition from China, decided to deploy "THAAD" in South Korea. The furthest detecting distance range of "THAAD" is far beyond the needs of defense of North Korea's missile. Such decision not only directly harms the strategic security interests of the neighboring countries such as China, but also directly damages the regional and global strategic stability. Not only that, the medias in South Korea also densely hype the views of "revenge from the great power", and assume that the pressures putting on the South Kore from China has only just begun. However, South Korea and the United States behind him are just the troublemakers of the tense situation. The deployment of "THAAD" will not help to ease the tension as among northeast Asian region, while on the contrary, it would cause great damage to the Sino-South Korean relationship, with the United States being the only one profiting therefrom.

If the leaders, policy-makers, and also the common people in South Korea have a chance to read and study this book and absorb the insights and conclusions presented by the author, and reexamine closely the deployment of "THAAD", there is a reason to believe that South Korea will not be blinded by lust for "THAAD", and decides to lift a rock only to drop it on its own feet.

二十二、论国际经济法的普遍性

——评《中国的呐喊：陈安论国际经济法》

中川淳司*

国际经济法是从什么时候开始具有普遍性的？时至今日，世界贸易组织（WTO）的成员方业已超过 160 个[469]，双边投资协定（bilateral investment treaties，以下简称"BIT"或"BITs"）的总数已接近 3000 个[470]，因此，现在还提出这个问题，多少会显得有些奇怪。然而，如果把时钟回拨到 30 年前的 1987 年，这个问题的回答和今天的答案就迥然不同，而绝不仅仅是修辞上的差异。在 1987 年，WTO 还不存在，其前身"关税及贸易总协定"（GATT）所举行的旷日持久的第八回合多边贸易谈判（即"乌拉圭回合"）也是 1986 年才正式开始。在 1987 年，GATT 的缔约方仅有 91 个。时值冷战末期，包括苏联、中国在内的社会主义阵营国家大多数并没有加入 GATT[471]。BITs 在 1987 年时的总数也只有约 300 个[472]，而且大多是在西欧发达国家和发展中国家之间缔结的。第二次世界大战后，东西方国家之间的冷战很快表面化，在此国际背景下，构成当代国际经济法主体的各种国际组织和国际条约，其成员方/缔约国几乎全部都是西方的资本主义国家以及某些发展中国家，而绝大部分社会主义国家并没有参加这些国际组织和国际条约。这意味着，国际经济法获得当今这种普遍性可以说是直到冷战结束之后才开始形成的。

对于各个社会主义国家来说，冷战结束意味着其国内的经济体制需要引入与市场经济相适应的新制度。与此同时，在对外战略上，意味着需要正式加入之前由资本主义国家和某些发展中国家构成的国际组织和国际条约。对于社会主义各国来说，如何实行国内体制改革和承担新的国际义务，是需要仔细研究的课题。然而，对

---

* 中川淳司，东京大学社会科学研究所教授。

[469] 到 2017 年 2 月为止，WTO 的成员国为 164 个，另有 21 个国家正在进行加入 WTO 的谈判。See WTO, Members and Observers, https://www.wto.org/english/thewto_e/whatis_e/tif_e/org6_e.htm.

[470] 截至 2015 年末，BITs 的总数为 2946 个，除此之外，还有 358 个自由贸易协定（FTAs）。合计起来的国际投资协定（international investment agreements, IIAs）总数达到了 3304 件。See UNCTAD, World Investment Report 2016 Investor Nationality: Policy Challenges, Geneva: UNCTAD, 2016, p. 101.

[471] 有若干例外。除 GATT 原缔约国、1959 年革命后继续保留 GATT 缔约国身份的古巴以外，同样为原缔约国的捷克斯洛伐克、波兰（1967 年加盟）、罗马尼亚（1971 年加盟）、匈牙利（1973 年加盟）仍为 GATT 加盟国。

[472] See UNCTAD, Trends in International Investment Agreements: An Overview, Geneva: UNCTAD, 1999, p. 22, Figure 2.

于国际经济法学来说,更重要的研究课题是,在冷战结束后国际经济法普遍化的过程中,国际经济法发生了何种变化?

在思考这个问题时,以中国的经历为视角进行研究具有以下重大意义:第一,中国经历了国内体制改革以及承担了新的国际义务,是体验冷战结束后国际经济法普遍化的当事国之一。在邓小平理论的指导下,1978年12月,中国共产党第十一届三中全会提出"改革开放"的国策,决定由社会主义计划经济体制向市场经济体制转变。从此以后,与国内各项制度改革同时进行的,是对外开放政策的逐步推进。1986年,中国向GATT提出了"复关"申请,经过15年多的谈判,于2001年11月正式加入WTO。在这个过程中,中国以1982年3月与瑞典缔结BIT为开端,到2017年2月为止,共缔结了132件BITs。[473] 第二,以加入WTO和缔结BITs为象征,意味着中国开始接受国际经济法的制约,但并不是单单消极被动地接受原有的以资本主义各国和某些发展中国家为主体的国际组织和国际条约。正如Lim和Wang等人所指出的[474],在与中国加入WTO同时开始的WTO多哈回合会议上,中国已逐渐代表发展中国家与欧美等发达国家形成对峙。相比于过去GATT时代的多边贸易谈判以主要发达国家的合意为主而推进,如今WTO多边贸易谈判的力量对比关系已经发生了变化。发生这种变化的决定因素之一,实际上就是因为中国的加入。这意味着,比起中国成为当今国际社会关注的焦点,以冷战结束后国际经济法的普遍化过程及由此带来的变化为背景,中国更是思考和观察国际经济法未来发展前景的非常有益的基点。在这种历史背景下,本篇书评郑重推荐陈安教授于2013年在德国Springer出版社出版的《中国的呐喊:陈安论国际经济法》一书,这部专著收辑的多篇论文便是思考国际经济法未来发展前景的最好素材。

陈安教授是中国国际经济法学界的资深前辈、第一代国际经济法学研究的代表人物。陈安教授1929年生于福建省福安市,1950年从厦门大学法学院毕业后留校任教,1953年遵从当时中国的高等学校院系调整政策方针,研究方向改为马克思列宁主义。中国实行改革开放国策后,陈安教授1980年调回复办的厦门大学法学院再次担任法学教授,1981年至1983年应邀在哈佛大学法学院进行国际经济法研究。1999年从厦门大学退休后,作为名誉教授接受返聘,继续从事学术研究和博士生论文指导的工作。从1993年至2011年,他被连续推举担任中国国际经济法学会会长。2008年,陈安教授关于国际经济法学的研究成果整理汇辑为五卷本系列专著,由复

---

[473] See UNCTAD, International Investment Agreements Navigator, China, http://investmentpolicyhub.unctad.org/IIA/CountryBits/42#iiaInnerMenu.

[474] See C. L. Lim and J. Y. Wang, China and the Doha Development Agenda, *Journal of World Trade*, Vol. 44, Iss. 6, 2010.

旦大学出版社出版发行。本篇书评所评析的《中国的呐喊:陈安论国际经济法》这部英文专著,是陈安教授精选的关于国际经济法学的代表作论文集,收集汇辑了从1984年至2012年他撰写的二十四篇论文,分列以下六部分:

　　第一部分　当代国际经济法的基本理论(论文1—论文3)

　　第二部分　当代国家经济主权的"攻防战"(论文4—论文5)

　　第三部分　中国在构建当代国际经济新秩序中的战略定位(论文6—论文8)

　　第四部分　当代国际投资法的论争(论文9—论文12)

　　第五部分　当代中国涉外经济立法的争议(论文13—论文19)

　　第六部分　若干涉华、涉外经贸争端典型案例剖析(论文20—论文24)

　　限于篇幅,本篇书评无法对上述全部论文进行评析,而只能通过对各组成部分主要论文的介绍,以期让陈安教授关于国际经济法学的精华观点浮现于世人眼前。

　　《中国的呐喊》第一部分收录了三篇论文。(1)《论国际经济法学科的边缘性、综合性和独立性》(1991年第一次发表),论证国际经济法的定义和调整对象;(2)《对中国国际经济法学科发展现状的几种误解》(1991年第一次发表),论证国际经济法的独立性;(3)《"黄祸"论的本源、本质及其最新霸权"变种"》(2012年第一次发表),尖锐批判当今甚嚣尘上的"中国威胁"谰言。

　　论文1涉及的是国际经济法的定义和调整对象,介绍了国际经济法的"狭义说",即认为国际经济法只是用以调整国际经济关系的国际公法的一个新分支;[475]国际经济法的"广义说",即认为国际经济法乃是调整跨国经济关系的国际公法、国际私法、国内经济法以及国际惯例(软法)的总和。[476]接下来,陈安教授从跨国经济关系多数由各种私人主体(非国家主体)承担的现实出发,以求真务实致用(practicalities, starting from the reality, seeking truth from facts)哲学为基础,对"广义说"进行了论证和支持。虽然说"广义说"是美国国际经济法学界的主流学说,但陈安教授并没有无条件地接受这一学说。例如,2002—2008年,美国Lowenfeld教授发表了新版的国际经济法教科书,其中对《各国经济权利和义务宪章》(1974年)的法律效力给予了极低评价,陈安教授对Lowenfeld教授的这种看法进行了批判,根据二三十年来的事实,指出《各国经济权利和义务宪章》在2002—2008年当时在国际社会中已经获得广

---

[475] 陈安教授对其代表学说,列举了G. Schwarzenberger、金沢良雄、D. Carreau作为例子。See An Chen, *The Voice from China*: *An CHEN on International Economic Law*, Springer, 2013, p. 5.

[476] 陈安教授对其代表学说,列举了P. C. Jessup、H. J. Steiner & D. F. Vagts、J. H. Jackson、A. Lowenfeld、樱井雅夫作为例子。See An Chen, *The Voice from China*: *An CHEN on International Economic Law*, Springer, 2013, p. 6.

泛的承认,已经形成了共同的法律确信效力(opinio juris communis)。[477]

论文1的立场,系从求真务实致用的角度出发,深刻领悟国际经济法的真谛,从中国的实际出发,站在发展中国家的立场,批判由发达国家所倡导的各种错误观点。其实,论文1所持的这种立场,也是贯穿《中国的呐喊》一书始终的立场。

《中国的呐喊》第二部分中的论文4探讨当代国家经济主权的"攻防战"(2003年第一次出版),剖析WTO成立前美国国内进行的"1994年主权大辩论"(The Great 1994 Sovereignty Debate);剖析围绕着美国贸易法"301条款"引起的WTO争端案件;剖析围绕美国的钢铁产业保护措施引起的WTO争端案件。通过这些剖析,对美国为坚持自己的贸易主权而不惜损害WTO多边贸易体制进行了批判。

"1994年主权大辩论"是指1994年WTO成立前夕美国国会对《乌拉圭回合协定》文本的采纳与否而引发的"WTO争端解决程序是否会损害美国主权"的争论。[478] 依据乌拉圭回合所通过的《关于争端解决规则与程序的谅解书》,WTO的争端解决机构(DSB)有权设立争端解决专家小组,而且专家小组报告和上诉机构报告的通过均采取"反向协商一致"(negative consensus)决策原则,几乎就是赋予上述报告自动通过的法律效力。美国许多议员担心这会因此损害美国的主权。对于这些担心,美国John Jackson教授作了如下的解释和"澄清":依据美国法律,《WTO协定》在美国并不具有自动执行力,WTO专家小组报告和上诉机构报告同样如此,如果要执行这些报告,需要美国国会的立法授权;当美国国会不希望执行WTO专家小组报告和上诉机构报告时,根据美国宪法,美国政府仍然有权贯彻执行自己的意志。最坏的情况下,美国还可以退出WTO(参见《WTO协定》第15条第1款)从而不需要承担《WTO协定》中的义务。

通过剖析Jackson教授的以上观点,陈安教授敏锐地发现美国对于其主权(实为霸权)有着强烈的教义信条(creeds)。[479] 因此,在美国已经批准加入《WTO协定》后,美国国会仍然维持和推行其贸易法301条款,以此经常单方面启动贸易制裁措施(如1995年美日汽车摩擦案、1998年美欧香蕉案)。在美欧香蕉案中,欧共体针对美国的单边措施申请设立的WTO专家小组发布报告认为,美国贸易法301条款虽然乍一看是违反了《WTO协定》,但美国政府在通过《乌拉圭回合协定》时作出的《政府

---

[477] See An Chen, *The Voice from China: An CHEN on International Economic Law*, Springer, 2013, pp. 15-17.

[478] See John H. Jackson, The Great 1994 Sovereignty Debate: United States Acceptance and Implementation of the Uruguay Round Results, *Columbia Journal of Transnational Law*, Vol. 36, 1997, pp. 157-188.

[479] See An Chen, *The Voice from China: An CHEN on International Economic Law*, Springer, 2013, pp. 119-120.

行政声明》(Statement of Administrative Action，SAA)中，表明了其承诺限制 301 条款实施从而确保《WTO 协定》一致性的意愿。陈安教授虽然对此表示了一定程度上的理解，但是对于该专家小组报告抑制美国单边主义措施不力给予了尖锐的批评。[480] 在这之后，在美国钢铁保障措施案中 WTO 专家小组裁定美国败诉，被看作是多边主义初步小胜。[481]

《中国的呐喊》第三部分(论文 6—论文 8)论述了中国在构建当代国际经济新秩序(NIEO)中的战略定位，这些论文为考察中国的参与给国际经济法的组织与条约体制带来怎样的变化，提供了最为合适的素材。在此，我介绍一下概述中国在国际经济新秩序中立场的论文 6(2009 年第一次出版)。在论文的开头，陈安教授论证了从国际经济旧秩序(OIEO)发展到国际经济新秩序的"6C 轨迹"或"6C 律"，即矛盾(Contradiction)→冲突或交锋(Conflict)→磋商(Consultation)→妥协(Compromise)→合作(Cooperation)→协调(Coordination)→新的矛盾(Contradiction New)之"螺旋式上升"发展路径[482]；并且主张：中国作为和平崛起中的全球最大的发展中国家，应该致力于遵循以上路径，为促进实现国际经济新秩序而发挥重大的历史作用，实现和平崛起的目标。从 1955 年不结盟各国首脑会议("万隆会议")开始，经由 1974 年《建立国际经济新秩序宣言》，直至现在确立的 WTO 体制，陈安教授强调在国际经济法的上述发展进程中，中国应当强化发展中国家的地位，同时积极促进发展中国家之间的协作互助，成为"南南联合自强"的驱动力量和中流砥柱。[483]

论文 7(2006 年第一次发表)论述了在 WTO 多哈回合谈判过程中，以中国与印度、巴西为轴心的发展中国家所开展的团结合作，并阐明了陈安教授提倡的实现国际经济新秩序的中国积极战略。

《中国的呐喊》前面三个部分论文的探讨焦点，集中于国际经济法学一般理论和以 WTO 法为核心的国际贸易法。第四部分则主要探讨国际投资法。论文 9(2006 年第一次发表)论述了中国签订的 BITs 中的争端解决条款。该文发表时，中国已经缔结了 112 部 BITs，但是在投资争端交付国际仲裁解决程序上仍然秉承严肃认真和慎之又慎的立场。经过多年的调查研究、政策咨询和审慎考虑，中国直到 1990 年 2 月才签署了《华盛顿公约》，事后又经过三年的权衡利弊，才于 1993 年 1 月 7 日正式批准公约。在这之前，虽然中国签订的 BITs 中已有关于发生投资争端可以提交国

---

[480] See An Chen, *The Voice from China*: *An CHEN on International Economic Law*, Springer, 2013, pp. 148-156.

[481] Ibid., p. 157.

[482] Ibid., p. 168.

[483] 陈安教授曾提到为南南联合之目的协调金砖国家的立场。

际仲裁的条款,但是并没有规定具体的程序。即使在之后中国签订的 BITs 中,依旧采取了限制提交 ICSID 仲裁的案件范围,即仅限于东道国对投资者财产的征用补偿争端才可以提交 ICSID 仲裁。论文 9 还剖析了美国 2004 年 BIT 范本和加拿大 2004 年 BIT 范本中关键性的投资争端解决条款,并探讨了中国是否应该采用同样的规定。当时国际流行的大多数 BITs 都规定,对于外国投资者与东道国无法通过协商解决的所有投资争端,都允许外国投资者将争端提交国际仲裁。但是,陈安教授认为:这种条款反映的是作为资本输出国的发达国家权益,中国是资本输入国,采用此条款需要相当慎重。他建议,在谈判缔结 BITs 时,包括中国在内的发展中国家就投资争端解决问题应当坚持设置四大"安全阀",即应该承认东道国享有(1)就是否提交国际仲裁的逐案审批同意权,(2)当地救济优先权,(3)东道国法律优先适用权,(4)国家重大安全例外权。[484]

此论文公开发表于 2006 年,当时,中国已经不是单纯的资本或者投资输入国,因为第十一个五年规划(2001—2005 年)以来,中国开始采取积极的对外投资的战略(即"走出去"政策),如果总是从净资本输入国立场考量条约规定似乎已不合时宜。但是,陈安教授根据 2004 年底的官方统计数字,指出中国对外直接投资的总量(潜在债权)对比外国在华投资的总量(潜在债务),几乎"微不足道",其比率约为 4.5%:95.5%,因此,改变上述保留四大"安全阀"方针,为时尚早。[485] 同时,文章以阿根廷为前车之鉴,说明了其"不慎放权导致如潮官司",再次主张对投资争端交付国际仲裁应该继续采取慎重之方针。在本篇论文中,陈安教授基于求真务实致用的理念,考量当时中国仍然主要作为投资输入国的现实,其立论基调与前述第一至三部分多篇论文是一脉相承、一以贯之的。与此同时,鉴于将来中国的对外投资比重可能提高,本篇论文预期,日后中国对待投资争端交付国际仲裁的方针,也可能随之改变。从这个意义上说,陈教授的立场并不是教条主义,而是求真务实致用的。换言之,将求真务实致用在更长的时间维度上延伸,日后中国与接受中国投资的发展中国家签订的BITs,可以引入把投资争端交付国际仲裁的条款;但中国与作为资本输出国的发达国家签订的 BITs,则仍应继续维持慎之又慎、保留四大"安全阀"的方针。论文 10(2007 年第一次发表)再次提倡采取这种"区别对待"的办法。

《中国的呐喊》第五部分收录了与中国制定的涉外经济法相关的 7 篇论文。本篇书评介绍论文 16(1990 年第一次发表)。这篇论文以经济特区和沿海开放城市为例,

---

[484] See An Chen, *The Voice from China*: *An CHEN on International Economic Law*, Springer, 2013, pp. 282-287.

[485] Ibid., p. 289.

论述当时的中国经济发展和立法框架。需要注意的是,这篇论文发表于1990年。中国在1978年实行改革开放政策后,1980年开始依次设立了深圳、珠海、汕头、厦门、海南(1988年)5个经济特区(SEZs)。1984年进一步开放大连、天津、上海等14个沿海城市(COPOCIs),1985年以后设立珠江三角区、长江三角洲等沿海经济开放区(CEOAs),逐步推进经济改革政策。但是,因为"1989年政治风波",中国遭受很多国家的严厉指责,改革开放政策被迫一时中断。陈安教授于此时机执笔撰写此文,显然怀有向国内外宣告设立经济特区、沿海开放城市等开放政策之正当性的意图。当时中国国内有这样一种声音,即批判改革开放政策系战前"租界"死灰复燃。面对这种质疑,陈安教授认为无论从其目的(实现社会主义现代化),还是中国政府对于外国在华投资的管辖权来看,这些开放政策与曾经的"租界"都迥然不同。[486] 此文对改革开放政策实施十年以来中国国内外投资的飞跃性增长给予了高度评价。对于阶段性、渐进性开放进程中伴生的腐败现象,陈教授也赞扬了中国当局所坚决采取的惩治措施。论文接着从法律角度对经济特区这类开放政策进行详细解读,其目的是为了提升因政治风波而削弱的外国对华投资热情。这与《中国的呐喊》第五部分收录的从法律角度阐明中国对外经济政策的其他各篇英文论文具有共通之处。例如,论文18(1997年第一次发表)对中国《仲裁法》(1994年颁布,1995年实施)的剖析,论文19(2005年第一次发表)对中国承认、执行外国仲裁裁决的国内法令的剖析。

《中国的呐喊》第六部分收录了对在华投资纠纷仲裁若干案件的评论和剖析。这是陈教授作为专家接受咨询时撰写的5份意见书和解说。本篇书评介绍的论文20(2006年第一次发表),系应英国一家保险公司请求撰写的、对被保险人的代位请求权的鉴定意见书。此案具体案情为,一家英国投资公司与中国公司合资设立电力公司,在中外合作经营投资合同中,约定向该英国投资公司保证付给投资额18%的利润。但是,根据中国国务院1998年第31号通知,禁止向外国投资者分配固定利率的利润,导致该合同利润分配条款无效,于是该英国投资公司认为这相当于英资被中国政府"征收",并依据中国的《仲裁法》提请仲裁,请求该英国承保的保险公司支付风险事故赔偿金。陈安教授在鉴定意见书中认为,中国国务院通知的法律效力低于中国国内的制定法,《中外合作经营企业法》才是适用于本案的准据法。这就否定了变更《中外合作经营企业法》内容的国务院通知之法律效力。因此,在向英国保险公司请求代位求偿前,应该慎重调查是否确因"征收"产生相应损失。论文21(2006年第一次出版)是陈安教授对于英国保险公司再次咨询问题的回答,他重申本案中

---

[486] See An Chen, *The Voice from China: An CHEN on International Economic Law*, Springer, 2013, pp. 484-486.

采取的措施不是"征收行为",不应向该英国保险公司索赔。在这些鉴定意见书中,陈安教授对中国相关法律的解说清晰明快。此外,陈安教授在国际仲裁领域也发挥了相当大的作用。虽然在《中国的呐喊》这本书中没有提及,但实际上陈安教授被中国政府指派为 ICSID 的仲裁员。2011 年陈安教授被津巴布韦政府指定为两件 ICSID 仲裁案的仲裁员。[487]这表明,在投资争端仲裁实务中,中国政府非常信赖陈安教授。

以上介绍了《中国的呐喊》这部收录陈安教授 1984 年以来撰写的国际经济法领域论文的英文著作的概要。如同本篇书评开头提出的,冷战结束后国际经济法普遍化的过程中发生了什么变化?解答这个问题,可以从陈安教授的这部著作中获得启发,这也正是我撰写本篇书评的意图所在。我认为:

第一,作为《中国的呐喊》这本书"一以贯之"的立论主张,中国加入国际经济法的组织、条约体制,乃是中国推行改革开放政策的重要一环;同时,为进一步顺利推进改革开放,中国必须对国际经济法的内容有所权衡取舍,注意求真务实致用之基本取向。论文 9 最鲜明地表达了此种观念。这篇论文中论证了引入投资争端提交国际仲裁制度时,必须保持慎重态度。论文 10 则赞成在中国与吸收中国投资的发展中国家签订投资条约中,可以尝试采用把投资仲裁提交国际仲裁的制度。论文 7 探讨中国在 WTO 多哈回合谈判中的战略定位,论文 1 和论文 2 论证和肯定了国际经济法之"广义说",也都同样强调求真务实致用的取向。这是陈教授一以贯之的国际经济法学理念。对中国来说,参与多边贸易体制和缔结 BITs,一方面是向国内外表明中国坚持改革开放政策的承诺,同时也在促进外国投资和促进中国在国际贸易中的出口增长发挥了重要作用。但是,从计划经济体制向市场经济体制转变的过程,是一个伴随着巨大的阵痛和各种摩擦的过程,因此在接纳国际经济法的过程中,也应力求确保这种渐进式的体制转变得到应有的保障。本书中陈安教授贯彻始终的求真务实致用,是与中国的相关政策要求相吻合的。

第二,《中国的呐喊》清楚地表明,中国作为谋求和平崛起的最大发展中国家,坚决反对发达资本主义国家的专横霸道。这一观点在阐释中国在建立国际经济新秩序过程中的战略定位的论文 6 中已有明确的表述。此外,在批判当今最大的霸权主义国家美国屡屡滥用单边主义并将其凌驾于多边主义之上的一系列论文中,也旗帜鲜明地表达了这一观点。可见,陈安教授所提倡的国际经济法的理念与美国的单边

---

[487] 这两个案件是:Bernhard von Pezold and Others v. Republic of Zimbabwe(ICSID Case No. ARB/10/15);Border Timbers Limited,Border Timers International (Private) Limited,and Hangani Development Co. (Private) Limited v. Republic of Zimbabwe(ICSID Case No. ARB/10/25)。

主义是尖锐对立的。从这个意义上说,冷战结束后的国际经济法秩序的普遍化进程,实际上凸显了自诩为"多边主义代表"的美国,其实只是唯我独尊的"自我中心主义者"。然而,不可否认,中国在多哈回合谈判中的战略导致了谈判的长期化甚至停滞,造成多边贸易体制有效性减损的后果。中国在加入 WTO 历经 16 年之后,现已成为全球最大的贸易大国。作为多边贸易体制的最大受益者,中国难道不应该在谋求维持和发展该体制过程中发挥领导作用吗?

现在,美国新任总统露骨地宣扬"美国第一",就任第一天就宣告退出 TPP。与此相反,在 2017 年的达沃斯会议上,中国的习近平主席倡导推进全球化。普遍化的国际经济法今后将面临两个任务,一是抑制美国倡导的单边主义,二是中国在全球化进程中如何发挥领导作用。与此同时,陈安教授在《中国的呐喊》这本书中一贯提倡的求真务实致用,也势必会继续引起全球学术界的广泛关注和深入探讨。

(翻译:刘远志,校对:李国安)

On the Universality of International Economic Law
—Comments on *The Voice from China*: *An CHEN on International Economic Law*

Junji Nakagawa*

Since when has the international economic law (hereinafter "IEL") acquired universality? Nowadays, the World Trade Organization (hereinafter "the WTO") already has more than 160 members.[488] Meanwhile, the total number of bilateral investment treaties (hereinafter "BIT") has reached to around 3000.[489] So, it seems a little bit weird to raise such a question now. However, if we look back to 30 years ago in 1987, the answer to this question would be significantly different—and not only in the sense of rhetoric. In 1987, the WTO did not even exist, and its predecessor, the General Agreement on Tariffs and Trade (hereinafter "the

---

* Professor of International Economic Law, Institute of Social Science, University of Tokyo.

[488] As of February 2017, WTO has 164 members. In addition, 21 countries are in the process of negotiations to join the WTO. See WTO, Members and Observers, https://www.wto.org/english/thewto_e/whatis_e/tif_e/org6_e.htm.

[489] By the end of 2015, the total number of BIT is 2946. Besides, there are 358 Free Trade Agreement (FTA) with investment chapters. Accordingly, the total number of international investment agreements (IIAs) reaches 3304. See UNCTAD, World Investment Report 2016 Investor Nationality: Policy Challenges, Geneva: UNCTAD, 2016, p. 101.

GATT"), only began the time-consuming eighth round of multilateral trade negotiations (Uruguay Round) in 1986. Back then, the GATT had only 91 Contracting Parties. The Cold War was coming to its end, and most of the socialist countries, including the Soviet Union and China, did not join the GATT.[490] In 1987, the total number of BITs was about 300,[491] mostly concluded between developed countries in Western Europe and developing counties. The Cold War became worldwide immediately after World War II. In such an international context, the members/parties to international organizations and treaties, which constitute the majority of today's IEL, were almost always Western capitalist countries and some developing countries. Most of the socialist countries were not part of these international organizations and treaties. In other words, the universality of IEL as we see today was only established after the end of the Cold War.

For socialist countries, the end of the Cold War also implied the necessity to usher into their domestic economic systems a market economy model. In terms of international strategies, this means that the socialist countries needed to join the international organizations and treaties originally established by capitalist countries and several developing countries. How to conduct domestic institutional reforms and take new international obligations were two subjects that required careful research by these socialist countries. However, a more important subject for IEL is, what changes would be undergone by the IEL in its process of universality after the Cold War.

Taking this question into consideration, the study from the perspective of China's experience has the following significances: Firstly, China has undergone domestic institutional reforms and increasingly undertook new international obligations, and it is one of the many countries that experienced the universalization of IEL after the Cold War. Under the guidance of the "Deng Xiaoping Theory", in December 1978, the Third Plenary Session of the 11th Central Committee of the

---

[490] There are certain exceptions. In addition to Cuba, which remained as the GATT member after its revolution in 1959, Czechoslovakia, Poland (joined in 1967), Romania (joined in 1971) and Hungry (joined in 1977) are already contracting parties to the GATT.

[491] See UNCTAD, Trends in International Investment Agreements: An Overview, Geneva: UNCTAD, 1999, p. 22, Figure 2.

Communist Party of China put forward the national policy of "reform and opening up", and decided to change from the socialist planned economy system to the market economy system. Since then, the progressive opening up to the outside world was launched in parallel with its domestic institutional reform. In 1986, China applied to restore its identity as Contracting Party in the GATT. After more than 15 years' negotiations, China formally acceded to the WTO in November 2001. Since its conclusion of the BIT with Sweden in March 1982, China has entered into 132 BITs by February 2017.[492]

Secondly, the accession to the WTO and the conclusion of BITs means that China began to accept the binding force of the IEL, rather than to simply and passively accept the original international organizations and treaties dominated by capitalist countries and certain developing countries. In the WTO Doha Development Agenda, beginning in the same year as China's accession, China has gradually become the representative of developing countries and confronted the developed countries such as the United States and the EU.[493] Compared with the GATT era when the multilateral trade negotiations were promoted mainly by the intention of developed countries, the current WTO regime has seen a shift in negotiating powers. In fact, one of the decisive factors that has caused such shift was the accession of China. In other words, in the post-WWII context of the universality of the IEL and the accompanying changes, China serves as a very useful basis for observing and considering the future of the IEL. This should be more significant than simply regarding China as the focus of current international society. Under such circumstance, this Review strongly recommends the Chapters compiled within Prof. An Chen's book, *The Voice from China: An CHEN on International Economic Law*, published by Springer in Germany in 2013. These Chapters are the best materials and documents for considering the future of the IEL.

Prof. An Chen is the pioneer of Chinese scholars in the field of IEL in China and the representative figure of the first generation. Born in Fu'an City, Fujian Province in 1929, Prof. Chen graduated from the Law School of Xiamen University in 1950

---

[492] See UNCTAD, International Investment Agreements Navigator, China, http://investmentpolicyhub.unctad.org/IIA/CountryBits/42#iiaInnerMenu.

[493] See C. L. Lim and J. Y. Wang, China and the Doha Development Agenda, *Journal of World Trade*, Vol. 44, Iss. 6, 2010.

and started his teaching career in that same University. Due to historical reasons, he shifted his research field from law to Marxism and Leninism in 1953. When the Law Department of Xiamen University was reestablished in 1980 as a result of China's reform and opening-up, he was appointed as professor of law. During 1981 to 1983, he was invited to conduct research on IEL at Harvard Law School. Although he retired from Xiamen University in 1999, he continued to teach as honorary professor and engaged in academic research and PhD student supervision. He was elected as President of the Chinese Society of International Economic Law during 1993-2011. In 2008, Prof. Chen's achievements on IEL were compiled into a five-volume collection, published by Fudan University Press. The current English monograph that this book review focuses on is actually a collection of Prof. Chen's English Chapters on IEL. 24 selected and representative Chapters written during 1984 to 2012 are compiled in six parts:

Part I: Jurisprudence of contemporary international economic law (Chapters 1 to 3)

Part II: Great debates on contemporary economic sovereignty (Chapters 4 to 5)

Part III: China's strategic position on contemporary international economic order issues (Chapters 6 to 8)

Part IV: Divergences on contemporary bilateral investment treaty (Chapters 9 to 12)

Part V: Contemporary China's legislation on Sino-foreign economic issues (Chapters 13 to 19)

Part VI: Contemporary Chinese practices on international economic disputes (Case studies) (Chapters 20 to 24)

Due to length restriction, it is not possible to comment on all these Chapters. This review aims to show the essence of Prof. Chen's main viewpoints in IEL by introducing the major Chapters of each of the six Parts.

Part I contains three Chapters, including: Chapter 1 "On the Marginality, Comprehensiveness, and Independence of International Economic Law Discipline" (first published in 1991) that discusses the exact connotation and denotation of the science of IEL, Chapter 2 "On the Misunderstandings Relating to China's Current Developments of International Economic Law Discipline" (first published in 1991), in which Prof. Chen agrees with the independence of IEL, and Chapter 3 (first published in 2012) that discusses the source, essence of "Yellow Peril" Doctrine and its latest hegemony "variant", and criticizes the "China Threat" Doctrine from a modern perspective.

Chapter 1 deals with the conception and the subject matter coverage of IEL. According to this Chapter, the "narrow interpretation" doctrine would consider IEL as a novel branch of public international law that only regulates international economic relations;[494] while the "broad interpretation" doctrine advocates that IEL refers to all legal norms regulating cross-border economic activities.[495] Then, starting from the reality that a variety of the cross-border economic intercourse with individuals, Prof. Chen advocates for the "broad interpretation" on the basis of the philosophy of practicalities. Therefore, he concludes that IEL generally refers to all legal norms that regulate international economic relations, comprising public international law, private international law, domestic economic law and soft rules that originate from international business practices. Even though the "broad interpretation" is the mainstream theory of American IEL scholars, Prof. Chen did not unconditionally accept this doctrine. For instance, in 2002-2008, Professor Andreas F. Lowenfeld published and reprinted a treatise titled International Economic Law, in which he gave a rather low evaluation of the legal force of the Charter of Economic Rights and Duties of States (1974), Prof. Chen criticized this opinion based on the fact that the Charter has won widespread recognition by international society and has already formed opinio juris communis.[496]

The position of Chapter 1 is based on pragmatic approach. It profoundly comprehends the connotation and denotation of IEL, supports the position of China as a developing country, and challenges the legitimacy of the viewpoints advocated from the standpoint of developed countries. In fact, the position of this Chapter is consistently adhered to this monograph. Chapter 4 (first published in 2003) of Part

---

[494] For the "narrow interpretation", Professor Chen takes the opinions of G. Schwarzenberger, Kanazawa Yoshio and D. Carreau as example. See An Chen, *The Voice from China: An CHEN on International Economic Law*, Springer, 2013, p. 5.

[495] For the "broad interpretation", Professor Chen takes the opinions of P. C. Jessup, H. J. Steiner and D. F. Vagts, J. H. Jackson, A. Lowenfeld and Sakurai Masao as example. See An Chen, *The Voice from China: An CHEN on International Economic Law*, Springer, 2013, p. 6.

[496] Ibid., pp. 15-17.

II relates to the Great 1994 Sovereignty Debate in the United States prior to the establishment of the WTO. It also discusses the disputes over Section 301 of the US Trade Act and US safeguard measures on imports of certain steel products under the WTO, and criticizes that the adherence of the United States to its own economic sovereignty had incurred damages to the multilateral trade system.

The Great 1994 Sovereignty Debate mainly refers to the nationwide discussion in 1994 prior to the establishment of WTO, when the US Congress was focusing on whether or not the United States should accept and implement the Uruguay Round results, and more specifically, "whether the acceptance of the WTO dispute settlement mechanisms was an inappropriate infringement on the United States' sovereignty."[497] According to the Understanding on Rules and Procedures Governing the Settlement of Disputes (hereinafter DSU) adopted at the Uruguay Round, the Dispute Settlement Body (DSB) shall have the authority to establish panels, adopt panel and appellate body reports under "reverse consensus", whereby reports are entrusted with the legal force of being adopted automatically. Many members of the Congress worried that the sovereignty of the United States would be impaired because of DSU. In addressing these viewpoints, Professor Jackson provided the following explanations and clarifications: WTO agreements will not be self-executing in US law, nor do the results of panel reports or appellate body reports automatically become part of U. S. law. Instead, the United States must implement the international obligations or the result of a panel report, often through legislation adopted by the Congress. In the case that the US Congress is not willing to execute panel reports or appellate body reports, the US Government still has the power to resist to adopt them under the US Constitution. In the worst case, the United States has the right to withdraw from the WTO, and thus need not bear its obligations under the WTO agreements.

By dissecting the viewpoints of Prof. Jackson, Prof. Chen keenly discovered that the United States had strong creeds on its own sovereignty.[498] Prof. Chen

---

[497] See John H. Jackson, The Great 1994 Sovereignty Debate: United States Acceptance and Implementation of the Uruguay Round Results, *Columbia Journal of Transnational Law*, Vol. 36, 1997, pp. 157-188.

[498] See An Chen, *The Voice from China: An CHEN on International Economic Law*, Springer, 2013, pp. 119-120.

believes that is the reason for the US Congress to still retain and enforce Section 301 of US Trade Act after its ratification of the WTO agreement. And the U.S. often unilaterally initiated trade sanctions (for example, the 1995 US-Japan Auto case, the 1998 US-EC Banana case). In the US-EC banana case, the WTO panel report concluded that although Section 301 seems to violate WTO agreements at the first glance, the US Government had demonstrated in its Statement of Administrative Action (SAA), which was made in the process of adopting Uruguay Round agreements, that it committed to limiting the implementation of Section 301 to ensure the consistency of WTO agreements. Prof. Chen expressed a certain degree of understanding of the panel report. Meanwhile, he criticizes sharply on its incapability of restraining the unilateral measures of the United States.[499] After that, in the US-Safeguard Measures on Steel Products case, the WTO panel ruled against the United States, which is regarded as the first minor victory of multilateralism.[500]

Part III discusses China's strategic position in the establishment of new international economic order (hereinafter "NIEO"). The book provides the most appropriate materials for examining changes brought by China's participation to the organizations and treaties of IEL. Here, I would like to introduce Chapter 6 (first published in 2009) on China's position in the NIEO. At the beginning of this Chapter, Prof. Chen demonstrates the "6C Trace" or "6C Rule" that leads the old international economic order (hereinafter "OIEO") to the NIEO. This path shows a spiral-up development, namely Contradiction → Conflict → Consultation → Compromise → Cooperation → Coordination → Contradiction New.[501] Prof. Chen proposes that, as the largest developing country, China should be devoted to follow such development path, play an important role in the historical course of establishing the NIEO to realize the goal of peaceful rising. From the 1955 Summit of Non-Aligned Countries (Bandung Conference), through the 1974 Declaration on the Establishment of a New International Economic Order, to the final establishment of the WTO system, Professor Chen emphasizes that in the process of

---

[499] See An Chen, *The Voice from China: An CHEN on International Economic Law*, Springer, 2013, pp. 148-156.
[500] Ibid., p. 157.
[501] Ibid., p. 168.

developing IEL, China should strengthen the position of developing countries and become one of the driving forces and mainstays for the establishment of the NIEO in joint effort with the South-South self-reliance through cooperation, that is cooperation between developing countries and mutual assistance.[502]

Chapter 7 (first published in 2006) demonstrates the coalition of developing countries, led by China, India and Brazil, in the process of the WTO Doha Development Round, and explains China's positive strategy on establishing NIEO as advocated by Professor Chen.

The first three parts of the book focus on the general theories of IEL and international trade law centering on WTO law. Part IV mainly concerns with international investment law. Chapter 9 (first published in 2006) discusses the dispute settlement provisions in Sino-foreign BITs (hereinafter referred to as the Chinese BITs). By 2006, China had concluded 112 BITs, and it still adhered to serious and cautious attitude on investment dispute settlement provisions. After many years' investigation, policy consultation and prudent thought, China signed the Convention on the Settlement of Investment Disputes Between States and Nationals of Other States (hereinafter referred as "ICSID Convention") on February 1990. After three years' of weighing the pros and cons carefully, China finally ratified it on January 7, 1993. Before that, although there were arbitration clauses that investment disputes can be submitted to the international arbitration in Sino-foreign BITs, no concrete procedures were set. Even in the BITs signed after 1993, China still restricted the scope of cases which may be submitted to ICSID, only to disputes concerning the amount of compensation for expropriation. Chapter 9 also devotes in examining some critical provisions concerning dispute settlement in the US and Canadian 2004 Model BITs, and discusses whether China should adopt the same rules. Most of the prevailing BITs provide that foreign investors are allowed to submit investment disputes between them and the host country for international arbitration if the disputes could not be resolved through settlement. Prof. Chen regards the above provisions as reflecting the rights and interests of developed countries or capital exporting countries. However, he argues that China, being a

---

[502] Prof. Chen once mentioned that for the purpose of promoting South-South coalition, BRIC countries should coordinate their positions.

capital importer, needs to put special consideration on the adoption of such clause. Hence, he suggests that in the course of negotiating BITs, the host developing countries should stick to the following four "Great Safeguards", including (1) the right to consent to international arbitration on the case-by-case basis, (2) the right to require exhaustion of local remedies, (3) the right to apply the host country's laws as governing law, and (4) the right to invoke the exception for state's essential security.[503]

The above Chapter was published in 2006 when China could no longer be considered as merely a capital-importing country. Because since the eleventh five-year plan (2001-2005), China has begun to take active strategy promoting outward investment ("going-out" policy), it appeared to be no longer appropriate if China always concluded treaties from the position of a net capital importer. However, based on the official statistics by the end of 2004, Prof. Chen pointed that the ratio between China's outward investments (contingent credits) and its inward investments (contingent debts) is merely about 4.5% : 95.5%. Therefore, Prof. Chen thinks it is too early and too fast to change the policy.[504] Meanwhile, by taking lessons from the experience of Argentina, Prof. Chen explained that once a country loosens its jurisdiction imprudently, a tidal wave of litigations will follow. Therefore he asserted that China should take serious consideration again as to submitting investment disputes for international arbitration. In that Chapter, Prof. Chen still treated China as a major capital recipient, and continued to propose to make treaty based on practicalities. In this sense, the Chapter remains well connected with the foregoing Parts Ⅰ through Ⅲ. At the same time, in view that China's foreign investment proportion may increase in the future, he admits that the policy of investment disputes arbitration may also evolve. In this sense, Prof. Chen's position is not dogmatic, but practical. If we expand the philosophy of practicalities longer on the time dimension, investment arbitration clause may be prescribed in BITs between China and developing countries, but as to BITs between China and developed countries as capital exporter, we should remain prudent. Chapter 10 (first

---

[503] See An Chen, *The Voice from China: An CHEN on International Economic Law*, Springer, 2013, pp. 282-287.

[504] Ibid., p. 289.

published in 2007) also advocates for this kind of a differential treatment.

Part V includes 7 relevant Chapters, relating to China's legislation on Sino-foreign economic issues. Chapter 16 (first published in 1990) is about the development and legal framework of China's Special Economic Zones and Coastal Port Cities. It is important to note that the Chapter was published in 1990. China adopted a basic state policy of reform and opening up in 1978. Since 1980, China has consecutively established the Special Economic Zones (SEZs) in Shenzhen, Zhuhai and Shantou in Guangdong Province, Xiamen in Fujian Province, and the entire province of Hainan (1988). In 1984, China further opened 14 Coastal Port Cities (COPOCIs) including Dalian, Tianjin, Shanghai. Since 1985, mainland China created the Zhujiang River Delta, the Yangtze River Delta etc., which were generally called as Coastal Economically Open Areas (CEOAs). The economic reform in China was progressively promoted, until it was temporarily interrupted, by the Tiananmen Event of 1989, to which China suffered from serious criticism from many countries. To write such an article as this Chapter at that specific historical background, Prof. Chen intended to declare the legitimacy of opening-up policy to set up Special Economic Zones and Open Coastal Port cities both at home and abroad. There was a voice in then China that criticized the reform and opening-up policy as "leased territories" or "concession". Faced with such challenge, Prof. Chen pointed out that the opening-up policy is completely different from the "concession" either from the policy's purpose (Socialist Modernization), or China's jurisdiction over foreign investment.[505] In addition, Prof. Chen praised highly to China's internal and external investment leap growth in the past ten years since the opening-up policy. With regard to corruptions occurred in the process of gradual opening-up, Prof. Chen also praised the anti-corruption measures taken by the Chinese authorities. Then the Chapter makes a detailed explanation on opening-up policy such as the Special Economic Zones from legal perspective, with a wish to promote the enthusiasm of the internal and external investments that had been weakened due to Tiananmen Event. This is in common with other Chapters in Part V that interpret China's foreign economic policy from a legal perspective. For

---

[505] See An Chen, *The Voice from China: An CHEN on International Economic Law*, Springer, 2013, pp. 484-486.

example, Chapter 18 (first published in 1997) on China's Arbitration Law (issued in 1994, enforced in 1995), Chapter 19 (first published in 2005) on China's domestic law about acknowledgement and enforcement of foreign arbitral awards.

Part VI includes 5 comments and opinions, written by Prof. Chen as an expert when he offered consul service on investment arbitration cases in China. Chapter 20 (first published in 2006) is an "Expert's Legal Opinions" written upon the request by a British insurance company, regarding the subrogation right of the insured. The summary of the case is as follows: A British investment company and a Chinese enterprise established a power company, there were provisions of distribution of profit in the contractual joint venture (CJV) that constituted a guaranteed return in the ratio of 18% to the investment. But according to the State Council's Circular [1998] No. 31, a guaranteed fixed return to foreign investors in Sino-foreign joint ventures should be prohibited. Therefore, the provisions on distribution of profit in CJV were invalid and the British investment company claimed that the Circular constituted an act of expropriation. Then the British investment company initiated arbitration proceedings based on China's arbitration law, requested the British insurance company to pay insurance indemnity. Prof. Chen noted in the expert opinion that the legal effect of the State Council's Circular is lower than China's legislations. China's Contractual Joint Venture Law is the relevant governing legislation. Therefore, he denied the legal effects of the Circular that changed the contents of Contractual Joint Venture Law. Therefore, the British insurance company who insured the expropriation risk for British investment company should make careful investigation to check whether the covered risk has really happened and the assured has really suffered subsequent losses before relevant payment for subrogation claims.

Chapter 21 (first published in 2006) is the re-comments to the question raised by the British insurance company. Prof. Chen reiterated that the measures taken in this case are not "behaviors of expropriation", and the British investment company should not make subrogation claims toward the insurance company. In such expert's legal opinions, Prof. Chen explained Chinese law clearly as an expert on investment disputes in China. What's more, he has also played a considerable role in the international arena. Although it is not mentioned in this book, actually Prof. Chen is an arbitrator designated by the Chinese government in the panel list of ICSID, and was appointed as an arbitrator in two ICSID arbitration cases by the government of Zimbabwe in 2011.[506] It is indicated that in the investment arbitration practice, the Chinese government gives full trust to Prof. Chen.

Above offers a very concise introduction and summary of the Chapters written by Prof. Chen in the field of IEL since 1984. As the question raised at the beginning of this paper, what changes have taken place in the process of IEL's universality after the Cold War ended? It can be inspired by the Chapters of Prof. Chen. This is precisely also the intention of this review, which opines that:

Firstly, as the consistent stance of the book, China's accession to the organizations and treaty system of IEL is an important part for it to implement the policy of reform and opening-up. What's more, for the smooth progress of reform and opening-up, China has to weigh and balance different contents of IEL, and needs to pay attention to practicalities orientation. The most notable expression of this concept is included in Chapter 9, which recommends that China should maintain a cautious attitude when introducing the investment arbitration system. Chapter 10 is in favor of the proposal of trying to introduce investment arbitration system into investment treaty between China and developing countries in which China has foreign direct investment. The same practicalities also appear in Chapter 7, which discusses China's strategic position in the WTO Doha Round negotiations, and in Chapters 1 and 2, which support "broad interpretation" concept of IEL. These are Prof. Chen's consistent views on IEL. For China, it means to show the promise of the reform and opening-up policy both at home and abroad when participates in the multilateral trading system and enters into BITs, in order to promote China's products export in the future. However, in the process of transition from the planned socialist system to the market economy system, accompanying by huge pains and frictions, China should try its best to seek safeguards in the gradual

---

[506] Bernhard von Pezold and Others v. Republic of Zimbabwe (ICSID Case No. ARB/10/15); Border Timbers Limited, Border Timers International (Private) Limited, and Hangani Development Co. (Private) Limited v. Republic of Zimbabwe (ICSID Case No. ARB/10/25).

acceptance of IEL. Prof. Chen's practicalities throughout this book is in compliance with China's relevant policy requirements.

Secondly, as the largest developing country, China typically objects to the tyranny of developed capitalist countries on its road of "peaceful rise", a point clearly demonstrated in Chapter 6. Chapter 6 discusses China's strategic position in the establishment of NIEO, and criticizes today's biggest hegemonic power—the United States, who often takes unilateral measures over multilateralism. In other words, the ideas of IEL advocated by Prof. Chen are sharply opposite to the US unilateralism. After the Cold War, the process of universality of IEL highlights the fact that, the United States, although constantly praising itself as representative of multilateralism, is self-centered actually. On the other hand, it is undeniable that China's strategy has also drawn some criticisms, such as the cause of long-term or even stagnation of the WTO Doha Round, and the ineffectiveness of the multilateral trading system. After 16 years since its accession to the WTO, China has become the world's largest trading nation. As the biggest beneficiary of the multilateral trading system, shouldn't China play a leading role to maintain and develop the multilateral trading system?

The current President of the United States expressed a starkly view of "America First", and withdrew from the TPP on the first day he took office. On the contrary, in the Davos 2017 Conference, Chinese President Xi Jinping defended globalization once again. The universal IEL will face two tasks in the future: one is to curb the unilateralism advocated by the United States, and the other is how China should play a leading role in the process of globalization. Meanwhile, the practicalities advocated by Prof. Chen in the book *The Voice from China* will continue to attract wide concern and inspire deep discussion among the global academic circles.

（翻译：刘远志，校对：杨 帆）

国際経済法の普遍性について

― An Chen, *The Voice from China: An CHEN on International Economic Law*, Berlin/Heidelberg: Springer, 2013 を素材に

中 川 淳 司[1]

　国際経済法（international economic law）が普遍性を獲得したのはいつのことだろうか？ WTO（世界貿易機関）の加盟国が160を超え、[2] 二国間投資条約（bilateral investment treaties, BITs）の総数が3000近くに達した今日、[3] この問いかけはいささか奇異に響くかもしれない．しかしながら、時計の針をわずか30年前の1987年に戻してみると、この問いかけは今日とは異なり、単なる修辞以上の意味があった．1987年にはWTOはまだ存在しなかった．WTOの前身であるGATT（関税と貿易に関する一般協定）の下で8回目に当たる多角的貿易交渉（ウルグアイラウンド）がその前年にスタートしていた．1987年時点でのGATTの締約国は91であった．東西冷戦の末期であり、ソ連、中国を初めとする社会主義諸国の大半はGATTには加わっていなかった．[4] 二国間投資条約の総数は1987年時点で約300であり、[5] その多くは欧州の先進国と開発途上国との間で締結されたものであった．第二次世界大戦後まもなく本格化した東西冷戦の下で、今日の国際経済法を構成する主要な国際組織や条約はもっぱら西側の資本主義諸国と一部の開発途上国を構成員としており、社会主義諸国の大半はこれらの国際組織や条約には参加し

---

1) 東京大学社会科学研究所教授
2) 2017年2月現在のWTOの加盟国数は164である．この他に21の国が加盟交渉中である．参照、WTO, Members and Observers. Available at [https://www.wto.org/english/thewto_e/whatis_e/tif_e/org6_e.htm]
3) 2015年末時点で、BITの総数は2946である．この他に、自由貿易協定（FTA）で投資章を設けているものが358あり、これらを合計した国際投資協定（international investment agreements, IIAs）の総数は3304件に上る．参照、UNCTAD, *World Investment Report 2016 Investor Nationality: Policy Challenges*, Geneva: UNCTAD, 2016, p.101.
4) 若干の例外はあった．GATTの原締約国であり、1959年の革命後も引き続いてGATT締約国であったキューバの他、同じく原締約国であったチェコスロバキア、ポーランド（1967年加盟）、ルーマニア（1971年加盟）、ハンガリー（1973年加盟）は既にGATTに加盟していた．
5) 参照、UNCTAD, *Trends in International Investment Agreements: An Overview*, Geneva: UNCTAD, 1999, p.22, Figure 2.

ていなかった．その意味で，国際経済法が今日の普遍性を獲得するのは冷戦終結後のことであるといえる．

　社会主義諸国にとって冷戦の終結は，国内的にはそれまでの経済体制を改めて市場経済に親和的な諸制度を新たに導入することを意味した．それと同時に，対外的には，それまで資本主義諸国と開発途上国で構成されていた国際組織や条約に新たに加入することを意味した．国内の体制変革と新たな国際義務の受容を伴うこのプロセスを社会主義諸国がどのように通過したかは，それ自体として興味深い研究テーマである．しかし，国際経済法学にとってより重要な研究テーマは，冷戦終結後の国際経済法の普遍化の過程で国際経済法にいかなる変化がもたらされたかであろう．この問題を考える上で，中国の体験に焦点を当てることには以下の意義がある．第一に，中国は，国内の体制変革と新たな国際義務の受容を通じて，冷戦終結後の国際経済法の普遍化を当事者として体験した国である．中国は鄧小平の指導体制の下で，1978年12月の中国共産党第11期中央委員会第3回全体会議で改革開放政策を打ち出し，社会主義経済体制から市場経済体制への以降に踏み切った．それ以来，国内の諸制度の変革とともに対外開放政策を進め，1986年にはGATTへの加盟を申請，15年余りの交渉を経て2001年11月にWTOに加盟した．この間，1982年3月にスウェーデンとの間でBITを締結したのを皮切りとして，2017年2月までの間に132のBITを締結している．[6] 第二に，WTO加盟とBITの締結に象徴される中国による国際経済法の受容は，資本主義諸国と一部の開発途上国で構成されていた国際組織や条約を単に受け入れるという消極的受容ではなかった．中国のWTO加盟と同時に開始されたWTOのドーハ開発アジェンダでの中国の交渉スタンスを克明にフォローしたLimらが指摘するように，[7] 中国はドーハ開発アジェンダで次第に開発途上国を代表して米欧などの先進国に対峙するようになる．GATTの時代の多角的貿易交渉が主要先進国の合意を軸として進められたのに対して，WTOの多角的貿易交渉の力学は変化しており，変化の一翼を中国が担ったといえる．その意味で，中国に焦点を当てることにより，冷戦終結後の国際経済法の普遍化の過程で国際経済法に生じた変化とその背景，さらには国際経済法の将来を考える上で有益な多くの知見が得られるだろう．そのための格好の素材となるのが，本稿で取り上げるAn Chen, *The Voice from China: An CHEN on International Economic Law*, Berlin/Heidelberg: Springer, 2013（lxiii+789pp.）である．

---

6) 参照，UNCTAD, International Investment Agreements Navigator, China. Available at [http://investmentpolicyhub.unctad.org/IIA/CountryBits/42#iiaInnerMenu]

7) C. L. Lim and J. Y. Wang, "China and the Doha Development Agenda", 44 *Journal of World Trade* 1309 (2010).

著者の陳安教授は中国の国際経済法研究の第一世代を代表する人物である．1929年福建省福安生まれ，1950年に廈門大学法学部を卒業して教職に就くも，1953年には当時の共産党政権の高等教育政策方針に従い専攻をマルクスレーニン主義に変えた．改革開放開始後の1980年に復活した廈門大学法学部で再び法学を教授するようになり，1981年から1983年にハーバード大学ロースクールで国際経済法の研究に従事した．1999年に廈門大学を定年退職するが，その後も名誉教授として教育，研究と論文指導を行っている．この間，1993年から2011年まで中国国際経済法学会の理事長を務めた．陳安教授の国際経済法に関する著作は2008年に著作集5巻にまとめられ，復旦大学出版社から出版されている．本書は陳安教授の国際経済法に関する代表的な著作を収録する論文集である．初出時期で1984年から2012年にまたがる以下の6部・24篇の論文が収められている．

第1部　国際経済法の理論（第1論文〜第3論文）
第2部　国際経済法における主権論争（第4論文〜第5論文）
第3部　現代国際経済秩序における中国の戦略的な位置（第6論文〜第8論文）
第4部　二国間投資条約の多様性（第9論文〜第12論文）
第5部　中国の対外経済法（第13論文〜第19論文）
第6部　中国の国際経済紛争実践（事例分析）（第20論文〜第24論文）

紙幅の関係で，全ての論文を取り上げて論評することはせず，各部の構成と主要な論文の紹介を通じて，陳安教授の国際経済法学のエッセンスを浮き彫りにすることとする．

第1部には3本の論文が収められている．国際経済法の定義と対象範囲を論じた第1論文「国際経済法学の周辺性，包括性と独立性について」（1991年初出），「中国の国際経済法学の発展に対する誤解について」論じ，その学問としての独立性を擁護する第2論文（1991年初出），「黄禍論」の起源と本質を論じ，その現代的な表明として「中国脅威論」を批判的に論じる第3論文（2012年初出）である．第1論文は，国際経済法の定義と対象範囲について，国際公法に限定する狭義説[8]と国境を超える経済関係を規制する国際法と国内法の総体と把握する広義説[9]を紹介する．そして，国境を超える経済関係の多くが私人によって担われている現実を的確に把握する必要があるというプラグマティック

---

[8] 陳安教授は代表的な学説としてG. Schwarzenberger, 金沢良雄, D. Carreauを挙げる．参照, An Chen, *The Voice from China: An CHEN on International Economic Law*, Berlin/Heidelberg: Springer, 2013, p.5.

[9] 陳安教授は代表的な学説として，P. C. Jessup, H. J. Steiner & D. F. Vagts, J. H. Jackson, A. Lowenfeld, 櫻井雅夫を挙げる．参照, *ibid.*, p.6.

な理由から広義説を支持する．そして，国境を超える経済関係を規律する国際公法，国際私法，国内経済法，国際取引慣行から形成されたソフトなルールの総体で構成されるのが国際経済法であるとする．広義説は米国の国際経済法学における主流的見解といえようが，陳安教授はこれを無条件に受け入れるわけではない．例えば，Lowenfeld が 2002 年に刊行した国際経済法の教科書で諸国家の経済的権利義務憲章（1974 年）の法的効力について低い評価を下したことに対しては，同憲章は当時の諸国の共通の法的確信（*opinio juris communis*）を表明するものであったとして，これを批判する．[10]

　第 1 論文のスタンス，すなわちプラグマティックな観点から国際経済法をとらえるとともに，開発途上国としての中国の立場を擁護し，先進国の立場から唱えられる見解の歪みを批判するというスタンスは，本書に通底するスタンスである．第 2 部の第 4 論文（2003 年初出）は，WTO 発足前の米国で戦わされた主権論争，米国通商法 301 条の発動をめぐる WTO 紛争，米国の鉄鋼セーフガード措置の発動をめぐる WTO 紛争という 3 つのトピックを取り上げて，通商問題に関する米国の主権と多角的貿易体制の関係を批判的に論じる．主権論争とは，WTO 発足直前の 1994 年に米国議会でウルグアイラウンド協定法の採択に際して戦わされた「WTO の紛争解決手続に服することで米国の主権が損なわれることになるか」をめぐる論議を言う．[11] ウルグアイラウンドで採択された紛争解決了解により，WTO の下では紛争解決小委員会の設置，小委員会報告・上級委員会報告の採択がネガティブ・コンセンサス方式により半ば自動化された．これにより米国の主権が損なわれるのではないかとの意見に対して，Jackson 教授は以下の通り反論した．WTO 協定は米国法上で自動執行力を持たない．小委員会報告・上級委員会報告も同様であり，これらを実施するためには議会の立法措置が必要である．議会が小委員会報告・上級委員会報告の実施を望まない場合，米国憲法上議会はその意思を貫徹する権限を有する．最悪の場合，米国は WTO から脱退することで WTO 協定上の義務から離脱することもできる．陳安教授は，Jackson 教授のこの説明に主権に対する米国の強い信念（creed）を見出す．[12] そして，米国議会が WTO 発足後も通商法 301 条を維持し，一方的な発動を行ったこと（1995 年の日米自動車摩擦に際しての発動，1998 年の EU バナナ紛争に際しての発動）をもって，その現われとする．後者の発動に対して EU が行った WTO 申立てを扱った小委員会報告は，301 条の文言は一見すると WTO 協定に違反するが，米国行政府がウルグアウン

---

10) *Ibid.*, pp.15-17.
11) 参照，John H. Jackson, "The Great 1994 Sovereignty Debate: United States Acceptance and Implementation of the Uruguay Round Results", 36 *Columbia Journal of Transnational Law* 157 (1997).
12) 参照，An Chen, *supra* n.6, pp.119-120.

ド協定法の採択に際して行った行政府行動宣言（SAA）でWTO協定整合的な301条の実施を約束したことにより，WTO協定との整合性が担保されたと判断した．陳安教授はこの小委員会報告の判断に一定の理解を示しながら，米国の一方主義を抑止する上では十分でないとして，詳細な批判を加える．[13] 他方で，その後の米国の鉄鋼セーフガード措置をめぐるWTO紛争で小委員会が米国敗訴の結論を導いたことに多国間主義の勝利を見出す．[14]

現代の国際経済秩序における中国の戦略的な位置を論じた第3部は，中国の参加で国際経済法の組織と条約体制にどのような変化が生じたかを考察する上で好個の材料を提供する．ここでは，現代国際経済秩序における中国の立場を総括的に解説した第6論文（2009年初出）を紹介する．論文の冒頭で，陳安教授は旧国際経済秩序（OIEO）から新国際経済秩序（NIEO）への以降が「6つのC」の螺旋的な発展という経路を辿るとの見方を示す．即ち，矛盾（contradiction）→対立（conflict）→協議（consultation）→妥協（compromise）→協力（cooperation）→新たな矛盾（contradiction new）という経路である．[15] そして，平和的台頭を目指す最大の開発途上国である中国は，以上の経路に沿って新国際経済秩序の実現に向けて尽力すべきであると主張する．1955年の非同盟諸国首脳会議（バンドン会議）から1974年の新国際経済秩序樹立宣言を経て今日のWTO体制に至る国際経済法の発展を踏まえて，開発途上国の地位の強化のために他の開発途上国とも協力しながら積極的な役割を果たすことを強調する．[16]

WTOドーハ開発アジェンダにおける中国，インド，ブラジルを軸とする途上国連携（coalition）の展開を論じた第7論文（2006年初出）は，陳安教授が提唱する新国際経済秩序の実現に向けた中国の積極的な戦略を解説したものである．

第3部までの論考が国際経済法学一般とWTO法を軸とする国際貿易法に焦点を当てたものであったのに対して，第4部は国際投資法を取り扱う．本稿では中国が締結した二国間投資条約における紛争解決条項について論じた第9論文（2006年初出）を紹介する．同論文の刊行時点で中国は既に112の二国間投資条約を締結していたが，投資紛争解決手続についてはきわめて慎重な立場を維持してきた．中国が投資紛争解決条約（ICSID条約に署名したのは1990年2月のことであり，条約の批准にはさらに3年を要した．それ以前に中国が締結した二国間投資条約では，投資紛争を国際仲裁に付託する可能性に言

---

13) 参照, *ibid.*, pp.148-156.
14) 参照, *ibid.*, p.157.
15) 参照, *ibid.*, p.168.
16) 陳安教授は，そのための方策としてBRICSの協調に言及する．参照, *ibid.*, p.204.

及する一方で，具体的な手続の定めは置かれなかった．その後に中国が締結した二国間投資条約においても，受入国による投資家財産の収用に対する補償をめぐる紛争についてのみICSID仲裁への付託を認めるという限定的な方針が採られてきた．第9論文は，米国の2004年モデル二国間投資条約とカナダの2004年モデル二国間投資条約の投資紛争解決手続に関する規定を検討し，中国が同様の規定を採用すべきか否かを論じる．いずれも，二国間投資条約が規定するあらゆる事項に関して生じた投資紛争が外国投資家と投資受入国の協議により解決されない場合，外国投資家が紛争を仲裁に付託することを認めている．陳安教授はこの規定を資本輸出国である先進国の利害を反映したものであると評価し，外国投資をもっぱら受け入れる立場にある中国が同様の規定を採用することには慎重であるべきと主張する．そして，投資紛争解決に当たっては，受入国に，（ⅰ）紛争の仲裁付託に当たっての同意権，（ⅱ）国内救済原則，（ⅲ）受入国国内法の準拠法としての適用，（ⅳ）核心的な安全保障に関わる紛争の適用除外という4つのセーフガードが認められるべきであると主張する．[17]この論文が公刊された2006年の時点で，中国は一方的な資本輸入国・投資受入国であったわけではない．中国は第11次5カ年計画（2001年〜2005年）以来対外投資を積極的に展開する戦略（走出去）を採用するようになった．もっぱら資本輸入国としての立場から望ましい条約規定を提唱することには疑問なしとしない．これに対して，陳安教授は，2004年時点で中国の対内外国投資に比べて対外投資の比重はフロー，ストックともにきわめて小さいことから，上記の方針を転換することは尚早であると主張する．[18]それと同時に，国家債務の不履行をめぐり多数の投資紛争仲裁案件を提起されたアルゼンチンの事例を挙げて，投資紛争仲裁への慎重な方針を維持することを重ねて主張した．本論文における陳安教授の主張は，投資受入国としての中国の立場に配慮した現実的でプラグマティックなものであり，その姿勢は第1部〜第3部を貫くプラグマティズムに通じる．それと同時に，中国の対内外国投資と対外投資の比重に言及したことを踏まえると，将来中国の対外投資の比重が高まれば，投資紛争仲裁に対する方針も変わりうることが想定されている．その意味でも，教授の姿勢は教条的でドグマティックなものではなくプラグマティックであるといえる．このプラグマティズムを延長すると，中国が対外投資を行う途上国と締結する二国間投資条約と中国が投資を受け入れる比重が大きい先進国と締結する二国間投資条約を区別し，後者では投資紛争仲裁への慎重な方針を維持しながら前者には投資紛争仲裁条項を採用するという方針が導かれるだろう．第10論文（2007

---

17) 参照，*ibid.*, pp.282-287.
18) 参照，*ibid.*, p.289.

年初出）はまさにこの意味での二重基準を提唱する．

　第5部は，中国が策定した対外経済法に関する7本の論考を収める．本稿では，経済特区と沿海港湾都市に関する中国の制度の発展を解説した第16論文（1990年初出）を紹介する．この論文が刊行された1990年という時期には注意が必要である．中国は1978年の改革開放政策の開始後，1980年から順次，広東省の深圳，珠海，汕頭，福建省の廈門，海南島（1988年）に5箇所の経済特区（SEZs）を設置した．1984年にはさらに大連，天津，上海など14の沿海港湾都市（COPOCIs）を開放し，1985年以降は長江デルタなど沿海経済開放地帯（CEOAs）を設置し，開放政策を推進した．しかし，1989年の天安門事件で中国は諸外国から厳しい非難を浴び，改革開放政策は一時的に中断を余儀なくされた．このタイミングで執筆された本論文は，経済特区や沿海港湾都市などの開放政策の正当性を内外に示す意図があった．対内的には，開放政策が戦前の租界の復活につながるのではないかとの批判があった．本論文で陳安教授は，これらの開放政策が，その目的（近代化）から見ても，また外国投資に対する中国政府の管轄権の態様から見ても，かつての租界とは全く異なると主張する．[19]　そして，開放政策開始以来の約10年間で中国の対内外国投資が飛躍的に増大したことを高く評価する．教授が特に評価するのは，段階的・漸進的に開放を進めるアプローチをとったこと，その過程で生じた腐敗に対して当局が断固たる対応をとったことである．論文は次いで，経済特区などの開放政策の法的側面を詳細に解説する．天安門事件で勢いがそがれた対内外国投資の再活性化を広く訴えることが狙いであった．中国の対外経済政策の法的側面を英文で解説するという狙いは第5部に収められた他の論文にも共通する．例えば，第18論文（1997年初出）は中国の仲裁法（1994年公布，1995年施行）の解説であり，第19論文（2005年初出）は外国仲裁判断の中国における承認・執行をめぐる国内法令の解説である．

　第6部は対中投資に関わる仲裁等の紛争案件で専門家として意見を求められた著者が執筆した意見書や解説など5本を収める．本稿では，英国の保険会社の求めに応じて執筆された，被保険者の代位請求についての鑑定意見書として執筆された第20論文（2006年初出）を紹介する．事案は，中国会社との合弁で設立された電力会社に投資した英国企業が投資契約で投資額の18％の利益を保証されていたことに対して，外資合弁企業による固定利率での利益配分を禁じた国務院通知によりこの契約条項が取り消されたことが収用（expropriation）に当たるとして，同企業が中国仲裁法に基づく仲裁手続を提起し，英国の保険会社に保険金の支払を求めたものである．陳安教授は鑑定意見書で，国務院通知が

---

19) 参照, *ibid.*, pp.484-486.

中国国内法上制定法より低い効力しか認められていないとして，制定法である合弁法の内容を変更する趣旨の国務院通知の法的効力を否定した．そして，英国保険会社に対して，代位請求に先立って収用に当たる損失が生じているか否かを慎重に調査するよう勧告した．これを受けて英国の保険会社から追加の質問が陳安教授に出され，それに対して回答したのが第 21 論文（2006 年初出）である．教授は本件措置が収用とみなされないことを重ねて説き，保険会社に代位請求を行うべきでないと説示した．これらの鑑定意見書における陳安教授の関連中国法の解説は明快であり，教授が中国の対内投資に関連する紛争処理において鑑定人として果たした役割の一端を伝える．本書には収録されていないが，陳安教授は中国政府により投資紛争処理条約の仲裁人候補者として指名されており，2011 年にはジンバブエ政府により 2 件の ICSID 仲裁で仲裁人に任命されている．[20] 投資紛争仲裁の実務においても陳安教授に対する中国政府の信頼が厚いことを示している．

　以上，陳安教授が 1984 年以降に執筆した国際経済法分野の論考を収録した著作の概要を紹介した．本稿の冒頭に掲げた，冷戦終結後の国際経済法の普遍化の過程で国際経済法にいかなる変化がもたらされたかという問いかけに対して，陳安教授の著作から得られる示唆を指摘して，本稿の結びとしたい．第一に，本書を通じて一貫する姿勢として，中国が国際経済法の組織と条約体制に参加することが改革開放政策の遂行にとって重要であり，かつ，改革開放政策の円滑な遂行に資する限りで国際経済法の内容を取捨選択するという，プラグマティックな姿勢が読み取れる．それが最も明瞭に現れたのは，投資紛争仲裁制度の導入に慎重な意見を述べた第 9 論文であり，中国が対外投資を行う途上国との二国間投資条約においては投資紛争仲裁制度の採用を考えても良いという二重基準を示唆した第 10 論文である．しかし，同様のプラグマティックな姿勢は，例えば，WTO のドーハ交渉における中国のスタンスを論じた第 7 論文，さらに，国際経済法の概念について国内経済法なども含めた広義説を支持した第 1 論文にも現れており，教授の国際経済法学を貫く一貫した姿勢といえる．中国にとって，多角的貿易機構への参加と二国間投資条約の締結は，改革開放政策へのコミットメントを内外に表明し，対内投資を盛んにして世界貿易における中国の輸出を伸ばしてゆく上で重要な役割を果たした．ただし，社会主義体制から市場経済への体制移行は大きな痛みと摩擦を伴うプロセスであり，国際経済法の受容に当たっても漸進的な体制移行を可能とするセーフガードを極力確保することが求め

---

20) 以下の 2 件である．*Bernhard von Pezold and Others v. Republic of Zimbabwe* (ICSID Case No. ARB/10/15); *Border Timbers Limited, Border Timbers International (Private) Limited, and Hangani Development Co. (Private) Limited v. Republic of Zimbabwe* (ICSID Case No. ARB/10/25).

られた。本書を貫く陳安教授のプラグマティズムは中国のこのような政策要求と整合的であった。

第二に、平和的台頭を目指す最大の開発途上国として中国をとらえ、先進資本主義諸国の専横には断固反対するという姿勢も明瞭である。この姿勢は現代国際経済秩序における中国の立場を総括的に解説した第6論文で表明されているが、最大の覇権国である米国がしばしば一方主義を多国間主義に優先させることを批判した一連の論考にも鮮明に現れている。陳安教授が唱える国際経済法の理念は米国の一方主義と鋭く対立する。その意味で、冷戦終結後の国際経済法秩序の普遍化は、多国間主義の担い手としての米国が抱える自国中心主義の矛盾を際立たせる意味を持った。他方で、WTOのドーハ交渉における中国の戦略が交渉の長期化と停滞を招き、多角的貿易体制の有効性を減じる結果をもたらしたことは否定できない。WTO加盟から16年を経て中国は世界最大の貿易国となった。多角的貿易体制の最大の受益者である中国には、この体制を維持し発展させる上での指導力を発揮することが求められるようになっているのではないか。

「米国第一」を露骨に唱える大統領が就任し、TPPからの離脱を通告した。ダボス会議では中国の習近平主席がグローバル化の推進を訴えた。普遍化した国際経済法の将来は米国の唱える一方主義の封じ込めと中国の指導力の発揮にかかっているように見える。本書で陳安教授が唱えたプラグマティズムの真骨頂が問われている。

(なかがわじゅんじ)

二十三、一部深邃厚重的普及读物

——评陈安教授对"中国威胁"谰言的古今剖析[*]

徐 海[**]

大师写小书以飨大众

根据中央有关精神,2013年起,教育部正式启动规模宏大的"哲学社会科学研究普及读物"的编写与出版工程,动员全国高等院校一流的专家学者编写通俗易懂、

---

[*] 陈安教授撰写的《美国霸权版"中国威胁"谰言的前世与今生》是中国教育部特约立项的优秀科研成果普及读物。其原始蓝本是中英双语长篇学术论文《评"黄祸"论的本源、本质及其最新霸权"变种":"中国威胁"论》(On the Source, Essence of "Yellow Peril" Doctrine and Its Latest Hegemony "Variant"—the "China Threat" Doctrine),分别发表于中国《现代法学》2011年第6期和日内瓦 *The Journal of World Investment and Trade*, Vol. 13, No. 1, 2012。其英文本经改写收辑为英文专著《中国的呐喊:陈安论国际经济法》(*The Voice from China: An CHEN on International Economic Law*)第3章,由德国 Springer 出版社于2013年推出。

[**] 徐海,江苏人民出版社资深编审、总经理。

篇幅10—15万字左右的小书,内容涉及中国特色社会主义道路与中国梦、哲学、经济学、政治学、法学、文学、史学、美学等人文和社会科学全方位领域。与一般意义的学术研究和科普读物相比,教育部此项工程更侧重对中国特色最新理论的宣传阐释,更强调学术创新成果的转化普及,更凸显"大师写小书"的理念,努力产出一批弘扬中国道路、中国精神、中国力量的精品力作。所撰写的作品必须具备相当的理论深度,同时又能深入浅出,推陈出新。这套丛书在强调理论普及的同时,特别注重对中国现实的高度关注。

诚然,历代学富五车的鸿儒大师,不乏辉煌巨著,洋洋大观。司马迁的《史记》、司马光的《资治通鉴》、马克思的《资本论》……这些鸿篇巨制,即使多个世纪过去仍旧熠熠生辉。不过,纵观历史上的大量重要名篇,影响一个国家甚至世界多年的薄册,也比比皆是,数量绝不亚于鸿篇。哥白尼的《天体运行论》、马基雅维里的《君主论》、王国维的《人间词话》、毛泽东的《论持久战》……这些传之久远的著作,仅有不到10万字左右的规模,有的甚至仅有四五万字,《道德经》《金刚经》(鸠摩罗什译本)只有5000字,儒家经典四书《大学》2000字,《中庸》3000字,《论语》16000字,《孟子》只有38000字。

媒体报道,邓小平曾多次强调他反复阅读《共产党宣言》,每每温故而知新。1949年,百万雄师突破长江天险,直捣国民党南京"总统府"。在"总统府图书室",邓小平与陈毅曾纵论旅欧经历,都说是读了《共产党宣言》等启蒙书的缘故,才走上革命道路。1992年,邓小平在南方谈话中又语重心长地对大家说:"我的入门老师是《共产党宣言》。"有人计算过:这部迄今影响全球170年的伟大经典著作,也只有15000字左右。

借鉴中外历史经验,此项"大师写小书"的出版工程,由教育部精心遴选,定向组稿,并授权委托江苏人民出版社陆续推出。从目前已出版问世的40余本"小书"来看,基本体现了教育部的宗旨初心和严格要求。

题材独特、思想深刻、旁征博引、激情充盈

厦门大学陈安教授撰写的《美国霸权版"中国威胁"谰言的前世与今生》,是这批已出版的"大师写小书"中题材独特、思想深刻、旁征博引、激情充盈的作品,出版后深受广大读者欢迎,也引起了学术界的高度关注。该书不仅在一年内很快重印,而且引起了国际上的关注,海外出版公司即将翻译出版。2016年10月,在第十八届全

国社会科学普及读物经验交流会议上,这部小书被授予**"全国优秀社会科学普及作品"**荣誉称号。

陈安先生系中国国际经济法学界的泰斗,是享誉世界的学者。他钩沉140余年的历史,环顾世界发展进程的中外关系,穷本溯源,纵横网罗,探究"黄祸"论的来源、表现形式、发生原因及本质特点。作者指出,今天"中国威胁"论其实是一百多年来"黄祸"论一以贯之的延续,是近代以来荒诞观点的最新霸权变种。无论是历史上的"黄祸"论,还是今日甚嚣尘上的"中国威胁"论,本质上都反映了列强力图殖民、侵略、污辱中国直至消灭中国的罪恶企图,并通过编织和捏造这些谰言,欺骗世界,错导后人,离间世上爱好和平的各国人民。

"黄祸"论肇始于近代史上中国最贫弱、中华民族灾难最深重之时。当时的中国,内外交困、山河破碎、国门洞开。昏庸无能、专制腐败的封建清朝政府对内为非作歹、穷奢极欲、盘剥百姓,对外却卑躬屈节、软弱无力,与列强签订无数丧权辱国的不平等条约,频频割地赔款,致使国家领土支离破碎,民不聊生。大量贫民被迫背井离乡,近走南洋,远逃北美,从事极端危险和困难的劳动,充当低贱"苦力",筑路开矿,寄人篱下,糊口谋生。他们备尝艰辛,为所谓的"上帝选民""高贵白人"做牛做马,不但付出血汗,亦使家庭破碎,产生无数家破人亡悲剧。所谓的"高贵白人"不但不体恤远走他乡的华人的无奈与痛苦,更不深入探究他们这些"高贵白人"所在的列强侵略中国、掠夺中国财富也是导致中国贫民远走他乡糊口谋生的一个重要原因,反而时时恩将仇报,"卸磨杀驴",诬蔑**黄皮肤**的中国贫民为"黄祸",欺骗和唆使白人劳工投入残酷的排华、辱华、屠华活动。

陈安先生正是痛感昔日积贫积弱的旧中国同胞水深火热的生活,怒对列强当局及其御用智囊们肆意歪曲历史、颠倒是非之无耻,遂在耄耋之年,进行深入专题研究,以深厚的学术功底,高屋建瓴,深入浅出,从史学、法学和政治学的三维角度,综合地探讨和剖析"中国威胁"论的古与今、点与面、表与里,深刻揭露"黄祸论—中国威胁论"的来龙去脉。他指出:近十几年来,美国某些政客、军人和学者起劲地鼓吹的"中国威胁"谰言,日本右翼军国主义者不遗余力鼓噪应和的同类谬论,实则只不过是19世纪中后期一度甚嚣尘上、臭名远扬的俄国沙皇版"黄祸"论和德国皇帝版"黄祸"论在新历史条件下的最新霸权变种,它们之间的DNA,是一脉相承的。换言之,它们肆意歪曲和否定中国数千年来对外和平交往的历史事实,**贼喊捉贼**,危言耸听和蛊惑人心,只不过是为反华、侵华活动进行精神动员和舆论准备的"政治骗术"。

作者还依据大量历史事实,揭示了美国立国前后400年来向全球实行殖民扩张侵略的霸权行径,提醒中国人民,切勿"居安而不思危","居危而不知危";也提醒周边邻国,切勿忘恩负义,利令智昏,为美国霸权主义者火中取栗,以免自食其果。

本书的一大特色是,作者用心精选了极其生动鲜活的、与本书内容密切相关的137帧历史图片,穿插融入相关章节,并且不惮其烦,逐一作了大量脚注,说明所阐述的资料图片的来源和出处,谆谆善诱地引导广大青年读者扩大阅读面,增长知识,增强同仇敌忾之情。

作者运用大量事实,证明这样一个重要结论:与"黄祸"论相反,自古以来**黄皮肤**的中国人从来不是"祸",而是和平爱好者和对外交往的互惠者。新中国成立以来,特别是改革开放以来,中国结束了闭关自守的意识,努力做到与世界各国人民平等互利,一直是公正、合理的国际秩序的倡导者和执行者。

今天,经过改革开放三十余年的拼搏发展,中国正在不断崛起,已成为相对强大的国家。然而,我们极其遗憾地发现,伴随着中国的崛起,当年西方列强刻意渲染"长辫丑恶"的中国人的形象虽然已一去不复回,但由"黄祸"论变种的"中国威胁"论,在20世纪90年代却又聒噪频起,经过十来年的不断大声咆哮,近年来更是日益猖狂,并直接导致今日中国周围"事件"不断:美国霸权主义者与日本军国主义者互相勾结,狼狈为奸,进行所谓"中国威胁"的反华大合唱,其险恶居心与侵华图谋,犹如司马昭之心,路人皆知!究竟谁是真正的威胁施加者?谁是真正的威胁受害人?太平洋何以如此不太平?何以时时浊浪排空,周边鸡犬不宁?"中国威胁"谰言后面的实质是什么?细读陈安先生的这部图文并茂、雅俗共赏的优秀科普读物著作,读者自会找到最客观、最科学的答案。

总之,我确信:《美国霸权版"中国威胁"谰言的前世与今生》既是一部历史著作,又是一部现实作品;既是一部政治经济著作,又是一部法律外交作品;既严肃深沉,又通晓畅达;既可作为培养和增强中国人民特别是青少年爱国主义情怀的读本,又可向世界推广,让各国朋友认识一个历史上和现实中的真实中国。谨此郑重推荐,与广大读者共享。

A Profound but Popular Reading Material
—On the Anatomy of the "China Threat" Slander by Professor Chen[*]

Xu Hai[**]

A Concise Book for the Public by a Great Master

In accordance with the relevant initiative by the Central Committee of the CPC, China's Ministry of Education has since 2013 launched a large-scale project for the redaction and publication of Popular Reading Materials on the Philosophy and Social Sciences. Top-ranking experts and scholars from institutions of higher learning across the country have been mobilized to write some concise books that are easy to understand, with a word count from 100 to 150 thousand. The contents cover almost all fields in humanities and social sciences, including the road of socialism with Chinese characteristics, the Chinese Dream, philosophy, economics, political science, law, literature, history and aesthetics, to name a few. In contrast with ordinary reading materials on academic research and science popularization, this project aims to produce a crop of excellent works advocating the Chinese road, the Chinese spirit and the Chinese power, by placing more stress on the publicity and elucidation of the latest theories with Chinese characteristics, on the transformation and popularization of innovative academic achievements, and on the idea of great master creating concise books. Not only with theoretical depth, but the works must also feature being explained in simple words and bringing forth the new through the old. This book series has prioritized China's reality while focusing on the

---

[*] *The "China Threat" Slander's Ancestors & Its US Hegemony Variant* written by Professor Chen An is an outstanding popular reading material on scientific achievements sponsored by a special project of China's Ministry of Education. Its original version is the academic paper entitled "On the Source, Essence of 'Yellow Peril' Doctrine and Its Latest Hegemony 'Variant'—the 'China Threat' Doctrine" in both Chinese and English which was published in *Modern Law Science* (No. 6, 2011) in China and *The Journal of World Investment and Trade* (No. 1, Vol. 13, 2012) in Geneva, Switzerland respectively. The English version has been included after adaption as the third chapter of *The Voice from China: An CHEN on International Economic Law* published by Springer, a German publisher, in 2013.

[**] Xu Hai is a Senior Editor and General Manager of Jiangsu People's Publishing House.

popularization of theories.

Indeed, there were many great masters and learned scholars with spectacular works in the history of mankind, such as SIMA Qian's *Shih Chi* (Shi Ji), SIMA Guang's *History as a Mirror* (Zi Zhi Tong Jian), Marx's *Capital*, etc. These masterpieces have still been sparkling in the long process of human history after centuries of baptism. However, there were also a large number of famous articles or booklets that have over years been influencing a country and even the whole world at large. Like Copernicus's *On the Revolutions of the Celestial Orbiting* (De Revolutionibus Orbium Coelestium), Machiavelli's *The Prince*, WANG Guowei's *The Notes and Comments on Ci Poetry* (Ren Jian Ci Hua), and MAO Zedong's *On the Protracted War*, these long-lasting works are all below 100 thousand words, and some of them even with a word count of 40 or 50 thousand. Less still, *Tao Te Ching* (Dao De Jing) and *Diamond Sutra* (Kumarajiva version) has just around 5000 words for each. In addition, the Four Books on Confucianism, including *The Great Learning* (Da Xue), *The Doctrine of the Mean* (Zhong Yong), *The Analects of Confucius* (Lun Yu) and *Mencius* (Meng Zi), each has a word count of about 2000, 3000, 16000 and 38000 respectively.

It was reported that Mr. Deng Xiaoping on more than one occasion mentioned his experience of repeated reading of *The Communist Manifesto*, each time with a totally different new understanding. In 1949, millions of bold warriors of PLA strode over the Yangtze River and occupied the presidential palace of the Kuomintang (Chinese Nationalist Party) in Nanjing. In the library of the presidential palace, Deng Xiaoping and Chen Yi freely talked about their experiences in Europe and contributed their engagement in the revolution to such enlightenment book as *The Communist Manifesto*. In his south China tour in 1992, Deng Xiaoping addressed to the audience in sincere words and earnest wishes: "*The Communist Manifesto* is my first teacher in Marxism." This magnificent masterpiece which has been influencing the entire world for 170 years has, as calculated, only 15000 words.

Drawing lessons from historical experience both in China and abroad, this publication project of great master creating concise books has assigned the Ministry of Education to select qualified authors to write on designated topics and, has authorized the Jiangsu People's Publishing House to publish the works successively. Thus far, the already published more than 40 books have basically satisfied the original objectives and strict requirements of China's Ministry of Education.

Unique Theme, Profound Thoughts, Copious Arguments and Passionate Voice

The "China Threat" Slander's Ancestors & Its US Hegemony Variant, composed by Chen An, a professor of Xiamen University, was among the already published concise books. This book, with a unique theme, profound thoughts, copious arguments and passionate voice, has been highly popular and glued the attention of the academia. Reprinted within one year after its publication in China, this book has also aroused abroad interest and will soon be translated into English and published by an overseas publisher. In October 2016, this book was awarded as **"China's Excellent Popular Works on Social Sciences"** in China's 18th experience-exchanging meeting for popular reading materials on social sciences.

Mr. Chen An, a world-renowned scholar, is the leading authority in the Chinese academia of international economic law. In his book, Mr. Chen reviewed the Sino-foreign relations in the developmental process of the world history since 140 years ago and examined the origin, versions, causes and essential features of the "Yellow Peril" Doctrine by tracing its source and thorough search. He pointed out that the "China Threat" Doctrine today was actually the continuance of the "Yellow Peril" Doctrine some 100 years ago. It was nothing but a latest hegemony mutation inheriting the preposterous arguments in modern times. No matter the "Yellow Peril" Doctrine in history, or the rampant "China Threat" Doctrine today, they both in essence reflected the vicious intention of the imperialist powers to colonize, invade, ravage and even destroy China. They intended, by fabricating these slanders, to deceive the world, mislead the posterity and alienate the peace-loving people of all countries across the globe.

The "Yellow Peril" Doctrine started in a time when the disaster-ridden China was suffering the poorest and weakest downturn in the modern history. In that time, forced to open its doors, China became disintegrated and beset with troubles both internally and externally. Internally, the stupid, incompetent and highly corrupted Qing government implemented its autocratic ruling by doing evils to and exploiting the general public to satisfy the extreme luxury and extravagance of the aristocrats. Externally, the servile and spineless Qing government surrendered China's sovereignty and signed with the imperialist powers a series of unequal treaties by which China's territory was frequently ceded and substantial indemnities were paid, making China's territory fallen apart and the life of the Chinese people miserable. A large number of Chinese refugees were forced to leave their native land for as near as Southeast Asia and as far as North America to make a living under aliens' roof. They undertook the most dangerous and difficult jobs and served as cheap manual labor in road construction and mining. In the process of serving the so-called "God's chosen people" and "noble white people", they worked hard like horses, only to end up with tragedy where their family members were either dispersed or dead. Under this context, the so-called "noble white people" had never shown any solicitude for the helpless and painful Chinese refugees, as they hardly imagined that it was the imperialist powers in which they were domiciled that drove the Chinese refugees away from home by invading China and rapaciously plundering China's wealth. How dare the "noble white people" bite the hand that feeds them, defame the Chinese refugees with yellow skin as "Yellow Peril" and even instigate the white workers to oust, humiliate and exterminate the Chinese refugees working there! How dare they!

It was out of the sympathy for the miserable life suffered by the Chinese compatriots in the then poor and weak China and the anger at the distortion of history and turning the facts upside down by the imperialist powers as well as their think tanks that Mr. Chen as an octogenarian delved into the monographic study on this theme. In a strategically advantageous position, with profound academic foundation and from the perspectives of history, law and political science, he in simple terms explored the past and today, the individual and general, the exterior and interior of the "China Threat" Doctrine, and deeply disclosed the origin and development as well as the cause and effect of the "Yellow Peril-China Threat" Doctrine. Mr. Chen pointed out in his book that the "China Threat" slander preached by some of the U. S. politicians, militants and scholars and the similar absurd defame clamored by the right-wing militarists in Japan are nothing but the latest hegemony mutations of the notorious "Yellow Peril" Doctrine fabricated by the Russian Tsar and the German emperor—each with a different version—in the middle and late 19th century. The "Yellow Peril" Doctrine and the "China Threat" slander shared the same DNA and came down in one continuous line. In other words, by recklessly distorting and denying the historical facts of China's peaceful external exchanges, they were just weaving sensational "political frauds" confusing people's minds in preparation for their invasion into China. They were the thieves crying "stop thief"!

In the book, the author also revealed, based on quantities of historical facts, the U.S. hegemonic actions that invade and colonize across the world in a span of 400 years before and after the founding of the United States. He reminded the Chinese people to be prepared in times of safety and sober in times of danger; he also alerted China's neighboring countries not to cut down the tree that gave them shade or pull chestnuts out of the fire for the U.S. hegemonists for the fear that they may reap what they had sown.

One of the features of the book is the careful selection of 137 vivid pictures that are relevant to the contents of the book. The pictures are properly inserted into the related chapters and sections, with many footnotes illustrating the sources of the pictures in an attempt to guide the young readers to enlarge their knowledge through extensive reading and to share a bitter hatred against the enemy.

Through volume facts, the author has drawn an important conclusion: contrary to the "Yellow Peril" Doctrine, since ancient times, the yellow-skin Chinese people has never been a peril, but a peace-loving benefactor in its external exchanges. Since the founding of the People's Republic of China, and since the Reform and Opening-up Policy in particular, China has ended its self-seclusion policy and has been an advocate and performer of a fair and justified international order by observing the principle of equality and mutual benefit in its international exchanges with people of all countries in the world.

Today, China has become a relatively big power after over 30 years of development since the Reform and Opening-up Policy, and it is still on the peaceful rise. The image of the Chinese people with a "long ugly braid" intentionally depicted by the western imperialist powers has already been a thing of the past. However, we feel regrettable to find that the "China Threat" slander as a mutation of the "Yellow Peril" Doctrine has again emerged since the 1990s. After 10 years of clamor, it has become increasingly rampant and caused many "incidents" surrounding China. The U.S. hegemonists and the Japanese militarists orchestrated in collusion an anti-China chorus of "China Threat". Their vicious intention of invading China was as obvious as a louse on the head of a monk. Who is the true inflicter of threat? Who is the true sufferer of threat? Why are there so many undercurrents and turbid waves in the Pacific Ocean? What is the essence behind the "China Threat" slander? To find the most objective and scientific answer to these questions, the captioned book authored by Mr. Chen An, which is excellent in both its texts and accompanying pictures and which suits both the refined and the popular tastes, provides an access.

In conclusion, I firmly believe that the book entitled *The "China Threat" Slander's Ancestors & Its US Hegemony Variant* is a historical work, but more of a reality book; it is not only a book on political economy, but also a book on law and diplomacy; it has a serious and grave theme, but also a familiar and smooth style of literature; it can not only serve as a reading book that cultivates patriotism of the Chinese people and the young generation in particular, but also as a medium via which peace-loving friends from all over the world can better understand a true Chine both in history and in reality. I hereby sincerely recommend this book to the reading public and would like to share it with you.

(翻译：张川方)

二十四、揭露"中国威胁"论的本质：三把利匕剖示美霸谰言真相

蒋围[*]

陈安教授的《美国霸权版"中国威胁"谰言的前世与今生》一书，是教育部遴选立项、定向约稿、统一由江苏人民出版社出版的优秀科研成果普及读物之一。在"大师写小书"系列已经问世的几十种书中，这本书题材独特、有的放矢、切中时弊、思想深

---

[*] 蒋围，时任西北政法大学国际法研究中心讲师。

刻、激情充盈、图文并茂、雅俗共赏，出版后深受广大读者欢迎，也引起了学术界的高度关注。

此书以史为鉴，以史为师，探讨了"中国威胁"论的本源、本质及其最新霸权"变种"——美国霸权版"中国威胁"论。针对国际上东海版、南海版"中国威胁"论，陈安教授摆事实、讲道理，廓清形形色色"中国威胁"论的迷雾，批判国际强权政治和霸权主义，弘扬中华正气，弘扬中华民族爱国主义。

5年前，笔者有幸参与此书的资料收集工作，事后又经反复精读本书，领悟到其中史论结合、夹叙夹议、有理有据、言简意赅、辛辣犀利的层层论证，旗帜鲜明，犹如三把锋利匕首，戳中错误言论的要害：

第一把锋利匕首：戳中和剖开"中国威胁"论的"层层画皮"，揪出其臭名昭著的列祖列宗，摆明其族谱世系，把140多年来形形色色"中国威胁"论的原始杜撰者以及花样翻新的后继者们分门别类，条分缕析，把他们的错误言论及危害本质公之于众。

第二把锋利匕首：戳中和剖开错误言论持有者的"躯体动脉"，从严复检，揭示美国立国前后400多年来的殖民扩张历史，劣迹斑斑，罪行累累，指出美国霸权主义者当今强化在全球的侵略扩张行径，绝非历史的偶然，而是其祖祖辈辈基因的必然传承和恶性发展。

第三把锋利匕首：戳中和剖开错误言论持有者的"大脑和心脏"，即在唯物史观的指引下，剖析美国400多年来借以立国的经济基础及其上层建筑，揭示当今美国极力推行的侵略扩张国策，乃是深深植根于美国的垄断资本主义——帝国主义的经济体制，也深深植根于美国主流社会意识和价值体系。

综上，可以说，陈安教授正是通过回顾历史，摆出事实，讲明道理，创造性地运用上述三把锋利的理论匕首，戳穿层层伪善画皮，全面深入解剖"美利坚帝国"的躯干、动脉、大脑、心脏，令人信服地揭示了美国长期推行侵华反华政策绝非历史的偶然，而是"美利坚帝国"建国前后400多年来的恶性殖民扩张的历史延伸和必然结果，乃是国际反华势力逆时代潮流而动的最新表现。

基于此，陈安教授特别强调，世人应当以史为师，以史为鉴，方能保持清醒头脑和锐利目光，避免遭受"黄祸"论21世纪最新变种——美国霸权版"中国威胁"论的欺蒙和利用。同时，也郑重提醒中国周边国家善良的人们，切勿见利忘义，利令智昏，为霸权主义者及其盟友火中取栗。

当前，面对某些国家边"笑容可掬，握手言欢"，边"调兵遣将，巨舰军机，频频入侵"的两面派手法，人们不能不认真学习和师承前辈革命家对付帝国主义和一切反动派的丰富斗争经验，牢记和践行其一系列的谆谆教导，诸如：必须"丢掉幻想，准备斗争","以斗争求和平则和平存,以退让求和平则和平亡";必须针锋相对,必须"人不犯我,我不犯人;人若犯我,我必犯人",必须发挥高度的政治智慧,善于做到策略的灵活与原则的坚定结合。

近两年来,面对复杂多变的国际形势和中国周边东海南海的风云变幻,我们作出了一系列重要的判断,诸如:"要善于运用底线思维的方法,凡事从坏处准备,努力争取最好的结果,做到有备无患、遇事不慌,牢牢把握主动权";中国人"决不拿国家主权和核心利益做交易",中国人"不惹事,但也不怕事";中国人民解放军必须加强战备,随时"能打仗,能打胜仗"等,显然都是既学习、师承和发扬前辈革命家的斗争经验和谆谆教导,又在新的历史条件下"与时俱进",加以发展、丰富和创新。

中国人今后也势必更加自觉地继承和发扬中华民族数千年来的"铁骨铮铮,岿然屹立,不畏强权,抗暴自强"的优良传统,为保卫国家领土主权的独立和完整,开展更有力更顽强的斗争。

"China Threat" Slander's Ancestors & Its US Hegemony Variant: Dissecting with Sharp Daggers

Jiang Wei[*]

The book, *The "China Threat" Slander's Ancestors & Its US Hegemony Variant*, written by Senior Professor of Law Mr. Chen An and published by the Jiangsu People's Publishing House, is one of the popular books selected from excellent social science research achievements. This publishing program is approved and sponsored by the Ministry of Education of the People's Republic of China. Among these published popular books, this one is objectives-oriented, with unique subjects, full of passion and sharp insights. The author has utilized both text and graphics to address the international community problems of the times, well suiting both refined and popular tastes. It has caused the high attention of the academic community, and is popular among the readers.

This book explores the origin, essence of "China Threat" theories and its

---

[*] Dr. Jiang Wei is a lecturer at International Law Research Center, Northwest University of Political Science and Law.

newest US hegemony variant through taking history as teachers and as mirrors. In terms of "China Threat" theories on the South China Sea and East China Sea situations, the author, by means of presenting facts and reasoning, tries to clarify the origin and essence of the problem, to rebut international power politics and hegemony behind them, as well as to carry forward China's national righteousness and promote Chinese patriotism.

Five years ago, I had the opportunity to take part in collecting materials for this book. I have also repeatedly read its finalized and published version. From the way I understand, there are three well-grounded and sharp systematical arguments expressed in the book. Through concise and comprehensive language, and by integrating narrative and comments, these three arguments stick at the heart of "China Threat" theories as three sharp daggers.

The first argument serves as a sharp dagger that stabs and rips off the masks of "China Threat" theories layer upon layer. It discloses their absurd opinions and harm essence by pointing out their notorious ancestors, their developing venation, the lineage of consanguinity, as well as originators and successors of various versions for over 140 years.

The second argument serves as a sharp dagger that stabs and splits the advocates' body and artery. It points out that the global aggression and expansion behaviors taken and strengthened by American hegemonists are not a historic accident, but an inevitable lineage and malignant development from its ancestral gene, by recalling and revealing the sleaze and criminality of American notorious colonial expansion history for over 400 years before and after it has been founded.

The third argument serves as a sharp dagger that stabs and splits the advocates' heart and brain. It discloses that American aggressive national policy is deep rooted in its monopoly capitalism, an imperialistic economic system, and in American leading social consciousness and value system, by analyzing its economic foundation and super structure which are the foundation of the United States for over 400 years from the perspective of the historical materialism.

In a word, it may be said that through looking back into the history, laying out the facts on the originators and successors of "China Threat" theories, clarifying their harm essence, Professor Chen creatively utilizes above-mentioned three systematic arguments. Just like three sharp daggers pierce through the American hypocritical masks layer upon layer and dissect its truncus, artery, brain, as well as heart, they have disclosed that American aggression against China and its anti-China policy in a long time are no accident, but a continuation and an inevitable result of the malignant colonial expansion for over 400 years before and after the American Empire has been founded. The American hegemonic version of "China Threat" is the newest manifestation of the international anti-China forces against the trends of the time.

Thus, Professor Chen particularly calls upon that common people should keep a clear mind and sharp-sight through taking the history as mirrors and teachers, to avoid being blinded and utilized by the American hegemonic version of "China Threat", the newest variant of "Yellow Peril" doctrine in the twenty-first century. Through careful reflection on the past, he reminds kind-hearted people in our neighboring countries not to forget moral principles on the sight of profits, and nor be blinded by lust for money, acting as cat's paw for American hegemonists and its allies.

At present, some countries play a double game. While they are smiling and shaking hands with our country, they also deploy forces, warships and military aircrafts to intrude our territory in the South China Sea. People in China must learn and inherit abundant fighting experiences against imperialists and all reactionaries from their revolutionary predecessors, bearing in mind the good instructions from revolutionary predecessors. We should "discard illusion and prepare to fight"; and know "fighting for peace, peace existing; concession for peace, peace perishing", as well as "tit for tat is fair play". We should give play to high politic wisdom to be good at combining tactical flexibility with a firmness in principle.

In recent two years, facing with a complex and changeable international situation and a rapidly ever-changing situation in the East China Sea and South China Sea, our country has made a series of important judgments. Among them are, for example, that "making good use of the bottom-line thinking, preparing for the worst, striving for the best, so as to make well preparation and keep unflappable facing difficult affairs, as well as firm grasp the initiative"; that Chinese people "never take the national sovereignty and core interests to make a deal"; that Chinese

People's Liberation Army must strengthen war preparedness, so as to have the ability to fight and win a fight at any time etc. These judgments obviously not only are learned, inherited and promoted from, but also are a development, enrichment and innovation in the new historical circumstances of the revolutionary predecessors' fighting experiences and earnest instructions.

Chinese people certainly will inherit and develop good Chinese traditions for thousands of years of "firm and unyielding character corpse, no afraid of power, opposing violence", strongly struggling for protecting their country's territorial integrity and independence.

(翻译:蒋 围)

第3章　陈安早期论著书评荟萃（1981—2008）

一、立意新颖务实　分析缜密深入　理论实践交融
——对陈安主编《国际投资法的新发展与中国双边投资条约的新实践》一书的评价*

中华人民共和国商务部条法司

厦门大学法学院：

收到你院寄来《国际投资法的新发展与中国双边投资条约的新实践》一书后，我司组织相关业务处室进行了认真的研读。同志们普遍感到该书立意新颖务实、资料翔实充分、分析缜密深入，是一本国内目前少有的研究双边投资条约理论与实践问题的专业书籍，对于我司的商签投资保护协定工作能够起到良好的参考作用。特别是在第三编"中国双边投资条约新实践"中，对我国双边投资保护协定谈判遇到的新问题的性质认定、应对技巧以及发展方向进行的深入分析，更具有现实意义。

特以此函表示谢意，并望你院教师一如既往地以更多的学术创作支持我国国际经济法理论与实践的发展。

商务部条约法律司
2008年4月28日

---

* 这原是中华人民共和国商务部条法司致厦门大学法学院的一份公函"感谢信"，文号为"商法投资函〔2008〕40号"。标题为本书作者所加。

二、内容丰富 系统完整 洵是佳作
——《美国对海外投资的法律保护及典型案例分析》评介*

游 斌

1985年1月,在武汉召开的"中、美、加三国学者关于国际投资与贸易法律讨论会"上,一篇题为《美国对海外投资的法律保护及典型案例分析》的长篇论文,得到与会者的交口称誉。法学界权威韩德培教授指出,这篇论文"以中国人的眼光来谈美国对海外投资的法律保护问题,确可谓独具新意,不落窠臼"。已故《中国国际法年刊》主编、北京大学陈体强教授曾称之为"内容丰富,系统完整,洵是佳作"。

这部专著的作者、厦门大学陈安教授治学严谨,在完成书稿后并不急于付梓,而是先将文稿的主要部分分两次在《中国国际法年刊》上登载,广泛听取意见,经过认真修改,再三润色,然后才交鹭江出版社出版。

作为世界上最大的发达国家和最大的海外投资国家,美国对其遍及全球的海外投资,历来是不遗余力地实行法律保护的,并精心设计了一整套法律保护体制。这一体制的核心内容就是设置了一个特殊的政府机构——官办的"海外私人投资公司",充分发挥了它的特殊职能,对于保护海外美资来说,是切实有效的。美国的上述体制已被联邦德国、日本、英国、加拿大等十多个发达国家所师法和仿效,因此,它具有相当广泛的典型意义。

该书的一大特点,是以大量的篇幅,对于有关海外美资风险事故的典型索赔案例,从法令与事实、理论与实践的结合上加以剖析。另一特点,是以更大的篇幅,编译和附录了相当丰富和珍贵的英文原始文档。

这部书有理有据地揭示了美国怎样通过法律手段在对外投资方面为资产阶级利益服务。对我们来说,这部书的最大价值就在于对今后我国的吸引外资的谈判、签约以及研究涉外投资纠纷案件的处断,能起到殷鉴作用。

1986年5月

---

* 本篇书评原发表于《福建日报》1986年5月10日。作者是当时鹭江出版社社长兼总编辑。

三、评陈安主编的国际经济法系列专著(1987年版)*

余劲松

我国实行对外开放政策以来,对外经济交往事业蓬勃发展。为研究和解决在对外经济交往中出现的一系列新的法律问题,国际经济法学作为一门新兴的、综合性的边缘学科,在我国应运而生,并逐步发展。数年来,我国法学界已陆续发表了一些研究国际经济法的文章、单科教材和专著,做出了开拓性贡献。1987年11月,由厦门大学陈安教授主编,并由他和安徽大学朱学山教授,南开大学高尔森教授、潘同珑副教授,以及复旦大学董世忠教授分别审订的我国第一套国际经济法系列专著成套出版,在我国国际经济法学术研究领域中做出了新的贡献。

这套国际经济法系列专著分为5卷,即《国际投资法》《国际贸易法》《国际税法》《国际货币金融法》以及《国际海事法》,共约150万字。《国际投资法》对保护、管制和鼓励国际投资的法律制度,中外合营企业的法律问题,中国境内外资企业的法律制度,中外合作开采海洋石油资源的法律制度,以及国际投资争端的解决等7个专题分别加以论述。该书联系我国实际,概括了国际投资法的主要内容。《国际贸易法》论及国际货物买卖法以及与之有关的国际货物运输、保险、国际结算和产品责任方面的法律,国际技术贸易方面的法律以及各国政府管制对外贸易的法律。《国际税法》共有9章,前6章介绍国际税法的基本理论和一般制度,其中论述了国际税法的概念、对象及渊源、国际税收管辖权、国际双重征税及其解决、国际双层征税及其解决、防止国际逃税避税、国际双重税收协定等内容;后3章介绍中国的涉外所得税法律制度,包括中国对外国投资人的征税、中国对外国个人的征税以及中国对外国投资人征税的税收优惠和征收管理制度。《国际货币金融法》包括外汇交易的法律问题、国际证券交易的法律问题、国际贷款协定、国际信贷实务的其他法律问题、国际货币的法律制度等5章。《国际海事法》分为16章,分别介绍和阐述了中国的海事立法与海事制度、船舶、船员及水域、提单运输、租船运输、海上旅客运输、船舶碰撞、海上救助、共同海损、海上人员伤亡及赔偿、海上留置权与船舶抵押权、责任限制、海洋环境保护与油污事故处理、海上保险合同、海事争议的解决、国际海事法的发展趋势、国

---

* 本篇书评原发表于《中国国际法年刊》,法律出版社1988年版,第407—502页。作者余劲松当时在武汉大学法学院执教,现为中国人民大学法学院教授、博士生导师。

际海事组织等内容。

这套系列专著,内容丰富、涉及面广。通观全书,具有如下特点和优点:

一是密切联系中国实际,注意从中国的立场来研究和评析国际经济交往中的有关法律问题。美国纽约大学法学院教授洛文费尔德编写的一套以"国际经济法"命名的六卷本丛书,是近年来在世界国际经济法学术界具有一定影响的著作。其基本特点之一,是立足于美国的实际,以美国的利益为核心,来分析美国涉外经济法以及国际经济法的各种问题,阐述和论证了西方发达国家对这些问题的基本观点。陈安教授主编的这套国际经济法系列专著,则从中国的实际出发,把对中国涉外经济交往法律问题的研究放在重要地位;同时,注意阐述和论证第三世界发展中国家对有关法律问题的立场。

作者在这套专著中除系统介绍国际投资、贸易、货币金融、税收、海事等方面的法律制度外,还用相当篇幅结合论述我国这些领域中的涉外法律规范。例如,在《国际投资法》中,以3章的篇幅专门论述了中外合营企业的法律问题、中国境内外资企业的法律制度以及中外合作开采海洋石油资源的法律制度;在《国际税法》中,将中国对外国投资人的征税、对外国个人的征税以及对外国投资人征税的税收优惠和征收管理制度,分别列为专章加以阐述;《国际海事法》则在开头第一章就介绍中国的海事立法与海事制度。

与此同时,作者还注意从中国的角度和第三世界的立场来研究和评析国际经济交往中的法律问题。例如,在《国际投资法》中,对国有化及补偿争议问题的评介,对中外合营企业管理权分享的具体安排、技术转让、产品销售安排等问题的剖析,都注意从中国立场出发,论证和维护中国权益。又如,在《国际税法》关于国家税收管辖权问题的论述中,强调利润所得来源国税收管辖权优先原则;在论及国际双重税收协定内容时,否定了西方某些学者要求给予外国人以所谓"国际最低标准"的税收优惠待遇的观点,认为为了促进国际经济交往,可采取"无差别待遇"原则,但是,对"无差别待遇"原则不能作绝对的理解,等等。这些观点是符合中国立场和利益的。

二是本套系列专著中的《国际货币金融法》一书,在我国第一次系统地论述了国际货币与金融法律制度,填补了我国在这方面的空白。我国以前在这方面的著作,有的是专门论述国际货币制度的,如盛愉的《国际货币法》;有的是论述国际融资的法律问题的,如沈达明、冯大同编的《国际资金融通的法律与实务》。而《国际货币金融法》一书则从国际货币买卖法、国际信贷法以及国际货币合作法三个方面来安排体系,从而把国际货币法与国际金融诸法律问题结合起来,既符合历史与逻辑相一致的原则,又能使读者对国际货币金融法律制度有系统的了解。

三是本套系列专著在我国现有其他教材、专著的基础上,增添了许多新的内容。例如,以前的有关国际税法方面的著作,对于国际双重征税问题,主要论及两个以上主权国家就同一征税对象对同一纳税人行使税收管辖权而造成的双重征税,即所谓"法律上的双重征税",而对国际上有些学者提出的所谓"经济上的国际双重征税",即两个国家对在经济上具有同一性或联系性的不同纳税人,就相同的征税对象征税,则论述不多。而本套系列专著中的《国际税法》一书,除介绍了前一种国际双重征税外,还在第4章专门对后者进行了介绍,并阐述了解决的措施和方法。同时,还专辟第5章论述了防止国际逃税和避税问题,这是国际经济交易中一个引人注目的问题,因为跨国纳税人总是寻找各种机会通过滥用转移定价以及利用避税港逃避税收。我国实行对外开放和吸收外资中也会遇到这些问题,而我国以前的著作对此也论述不够。此外,在本套系列专著的《国际贸易法》一书中增加了产品责任法的内容,《国际海事法》中还专门叙述了关于海洋环境保护与油污事故处理、国际海事组织等新内容。

四是材料丰富、新颖。这套系列专著在论述取材上,力求其新,广泛吸收国内外的最新学术成果。许多资料直接来源于近来的国外最新出版物,并综合了国内的最新研究成果,从而反映了目前国际投资、贸易、货币金融、税收及海事等法律领域中的最新动态和学术观点。此外,这套专著各书在正文外,还分别翻译和辑集了一些重要的原始文档,作为附录,这给读者学习、研究和查证原文提供了方便。

五是理论与实务相融通,介绍与分析相结合。这套系列专著既涉及国际投资、贸易、货币金融、税收、海事等领域中的法律理论问题,也涉及大量的法律实务问题。作者在介绍基本理论的基础上,又辅之以许多事例加以说明,并尽可能援引和评析国际经济法律讼争的具体案例,深入浅出,有助于读者掌握基本理论知识和提高解决实际问题的能力。

当然,这套国际经济法系列专著在某些方面还可以进一步加以考虑和完善,表现为以下几方面:

一是作为国际经济法系列专著,有关各书对国际经济法的概念、范围、体系等都没有予以论述和说明。在国内外学者中,对国际经济法的概念、性质、范围、解释不一,尚无定论。主要有两种观点:一种观点认为国际经济法属于国际公法的范畴,是经济领域的国际公法,属于国际公法的一个分支,各国国内的涉外经济法规范应排除在国际经济法之外;另一种观点认为,国际经济法不限于、不等于经济领域的国际公法,而应综合调整国际经济关系的国内法规范和调整国际经济关系的国际法规范,成为一门新的独立的法学部门。从这套系列专著的内容和体系安排来看,作者显然是赞成后一种观点,并据此来安排整套专著的体系。因此,似应在本系列专著开头对此阐明自己的观点和看法。

二是作为国际经济法系列专著,有关各书在内容安排上尚需作某些协调,以避免重复。作者在这方面注意到了这个问题,例如,关于国际支付、国际结算等法律问题,本应属于国际货币金融法的范围,但考虑到《国际贸易法》一书中对这些问题已有详尽的论述,因而在《国际货币金融法》一书中就从略了。但对于其他某些问题似乎还有疏忽,例如,关于国际海上货物运输和海上货物运输保险问题,在本系列专著中的《国际贸易法》和《国际海事法》两书中几乎都以相当的篇幅谈到了这一问题(尽管内容详略有所不同),造成某些重复。这部分内容似可考虑在《国际贸易法》一书中从略,而由《国际海事法》一书来详细叙述。

三是有些问题还可以进一步考虑和探讨。例如,《国际投资法》一书依国际投资法律制度的不同作用(保护、管制、鼓励)来分章论述,体系安排新颖。但是,一项法律制度有时同时具有几种作用,既是保护性的、鼓励性的,也是管制性的。例如,关于货币自由汇兑问题,许多国家在管制的前提下,又规定在某种条件下允许自由汇出,这既是一种管制措施,又是对外资实行的鼓励和保护。我国与某些外国政府签订的关于鼓励和相互保护投资协定中,也规定了这一内容。因此,似以综合论述为好。此外,对于我国涉外经济交往实践中尚待解决的问题,例如,关于中外合作经营企业的税收问题、债务责任问题以及某些其他有关的法律问题,还可从理论上进一步深入探讨。

总的来说,这套国际经济法系列专著是具有中国特色的、开拓性的好书,结构合理,条理分明,内容充实,材料新颖,理论与实际相结合,法律与实务相融通,既可作为高等学校学生的教材,也是从事国际经济法教学和研究的人员以及涉外法律实务工作者有价值的参考书。

四、新视角:从南北矛盾看国际经济法
——评陈安主编的《国际经济法总论》*

徐崇利

近年来,我国学术界对国际经济法这门新兴边缘学科的研究逐步深入,有关国

---

* 本篇书评原发表于《厦门大学学报(哲学社会科学版)》1992年第3期,第132—134页。作者徐崇利现为厦门大学法学院教授、博士生导师。

际经济法各分支学科以及专门问题的著述陆续出版。然而,在此期间,还没有一本对国际经济法最基本的理论和实践原则加以概括和综合论述的专著。1991年5月法律出版社出版、厦门大学法律系陈安教授主编的《国际经济法总论》(朱学山教授、曾华群教授、刘智中讲师参加撰稿,以下简称《总论》)一书,填补了我国在这方面研究的空白。

《总论》作为高等学校法学试用教材出版,具有体系完整、结构合理、内容全面、材料翔实、文笔流畅等特点。通观全书,人们不难发现,本书同时不失为一部颇有研究深度的学术专著。

当前,在西方学术界,用以维护发达国家利益的国际经济法学说层出不穷,而由于历史的原因,广大发展中国家长期以来缺乏自己的国际经济法理论体系,难以适应建立国际经济新秩序斗争的现实需要。《总论》一书作者在对国内外国际经济法两大基本学派的观点作了深入细致的分析之后,在方法论上肯定了"广义说",但又不囿于纯理念上的探讨,而是进一步论证了这一学派某些代表学者的根本立场,以美国的杰塞普和洛文费尔德为例,说明他们在许多理论问题上貌似持平公正,不偏不倚,实则主要是以本国资产者利益为最终依归的本质;其中许多观点和论据,渗透着、散发出浓烈的霸权主义和强权政治的气息。析微而知著,作者提出,对待现有的国际经济法知识和体系,应当兼采"拿来主义"和"消化主义"两种方法,即在"拿来"之后,认真咀嚼消化,吸收其营养,剔除其糟粕,逐步创立起以马克思主义为指导的、体现发展中国家共同立场的、具有中国特色的国际经济法学科新体系。《总论》作者正是以此作为主线和导向,力求建立自己的理论体系。

这种努力首先体现在本书对当代国际经济法发展历史的论述上。作者就我国一些学者对20世纪40年代以来建立的布雷顿森林体制多加溢美的倾向悉心论证,当时广大发展中国家在政治上尚未完全独立,在经济上仍处于不合理的国际分工体系之中,它们的利益和愿望在该体制中不可能得到应有的反映和尊重。以《关税及贸易总协定》为例,由于发展中国家和发达国家经济发展水平悬殊,无条件实行"互惠",完全"对等"地大幅度削减关税,只能导致发展中国家国内市场的丢失、民族工业的受害和对外贸易的萎缩。因此,作者认为,对这一时期建立起来的国际经济秩序不宜估价过高,更不能认为它"具有划时代的意义"。随后,作者又详加论述,从1955年万隆会议发端,到20世纪70年代联合国大会通过《建立国际经济新秩序宣言》和《各国经济权利和义务宪章》(以下简称《宣言》和《宪章》),广大发展中国家在创立国际经济法新规范的几个回合斗争中,逐步取得胜利,昭示了当代国际经济立法发展的历史新趋势。

作者的上述努力又在本书对国际经济法基本原则的阐述中得到进一步体现。国际经济法基本原则是国际经济法各种法律规范的核心。作者牢牢抓住这个核心，泼墨论述了国际经济法中的四大基本原则，即经济主权原则、公平互利原则、全球合作原则以及有约必守原则。其中对于《宣言》和《宪章》，作者在关于国际经济法发展史的阐述中，已经论证和确认它们是国际经济法新旧更替、破旧立新过程中的一项重大飞跃和明显转折。在这一章中，进一步从历史到现实，详尽论述了这两个纲领性文件中所包含的国际经济法基本原则，从而大大深化了人们对《宣言》和《宪章》历史意义的认识。由于整章论述紧扣维护发展中国家利益这一主题，给人以浑然一体的感觉：为了维护得来不易的政治主权，发展中国家势必要争取经济上的主权；在有了经济主权之后，由于各国在经济上的相互依存关系，发展中国家势必也要谋求全球间的"南北合作"和"南南合作"；在合作过程中，由于经济实力对比悬殊，发展中国家势必要求在公平互利的基础上与发达国家进行经济交往；为了保证这种经济交往得以正常进行，又势必要求双方做到有约必守。

此外，《总论》的主旨在全书的其他各大章节均有体现。篇幅所限，兹不赘述。

由于国际经济法是一门新兴的边缘性学科，有许多理论问题需要加以深入的研究和探讨，而国内外学者对其中的一些问题又存有不同程度的争议。由此，《总论》一书作者在建立自己理论体系的过程中，就诸多理论问题，特别是重大的基本理论问题，提出并论证了自己的观点。

有关国际经济法的含义问题。国内外学术界历来有"狭义说"与"广义说"之分，前者主张国际经济法是调整国际经济关系的国际法规范的总和，是国际公法的一个新分支；后者主张国际经济法是调整国际经济关系的各种法律规范的总和，是综合有关国内法和国际法规范的边缘性的独立法律部门。作者认为，由于对国际经济法调整对象——"国际经济关系"一词理解不同，也由于观察角度和研究方法上的差异，以致形成上述两大学派。这种提法综合了国内外学者的观点。值得注意的是，作者的研究并不仅仅停留于此，在详细评述两种学说之后，作者提出在方法论上"广义说"可取的观点，最后把支持该说的根据提高到划分法律部门和法学部门分类标准的高度去认识，阐明从"狭义说"到"广义说"的发展，正是国际经济法分类办法和分科标准从"以传统的法律类别为中心"到"以现实法律问题为中心"的转变。同时，这种转变颇有助于解决国际经济法与国际法、国际私法等相邻学科之间长期以来因划分标准混乱而造成的界限不清、分野不明的问题。

有关国际经济法的范围问题。不同于其他著述，作者不但把国际商务惯例作为国际经济法的渊源之一，而且把它列为与国际经济法相邻的法律部门，认为这种由各种国际性民间团体制定的用以调整国际私人经贸关系的商务规则,是国际经济法这一边缘性综合体的有机组成部分。但是,就其特点来看,又大大有别于国际经济法整体中的其他组成部分(诸如国际法、国际私法以及各国涉外经济法等范畴),而自成一类;作者还专题探讨了国际经济法与国内经济法的关系问题。从"广义说"的方法论出发,作者认为各国涉外经济法也是国际经济法的有机组成部分,批判了来自某些强权发达国家的一种有害倾向,即藐视弱小民族东道国涉外经济立法的权威性,削弱这些法律规范对境内涉外经济关系实行管辖的"域内效力";与此同时,作者又提醒人们,要注意防止和抵制发达国家强化和扩大本国涉外经济立法"域外管辖"或"域外效力"的另一种有害倾向。作者密切注视当代全球性"南北矛盾"的普遍存在以及强权政治倾向仍在顽固地表现自己的客观现实,从涉外经济法和国际经济关系的角度,即从"涉外"到"国际"应有的科学内涵及其合理的外延界限来论述这一问题,其研究的角度可谓"慧眼独具"。

有关国际经济法的发展阶段问题。国内外有关著述一般都以二战以后布雷顿森林体制建立作为划界标准。作者始终认为对该体制不宜评价过高,相应地也没有采用这一通例,而是沿着"南北矛盾"的历史渊源及其现实发展这一客观轨迹,详细回顾国际经济关系发展史,提出在此基础上划分国际经济法历史发展阶段的主张。作者认为,从宏观上分析,迄今为止国际经济法经历了萌芽、发展、转折更新三大阶段。从公元前一直到15世纪,国际经济交往的发展节奏比较缓慢,形式比较简单,规模也比较有限,国际经济法由于规范种类不全,数量不多,只是处在"萌芽"的阶段;16世纪以后,资本主义世界市场逐步形成,国际经济交往空前频繁,用以调整国际经济关系的国际条约、国际习惯大量出现,日益完备,延续到20世纪40年代,国际经济法一直处于不断"发展"的阶段;二战结束以后,发展中国家纷纷独立,构成第三世界,作为一支独立的力量登上国际政治经济舞台,它和第一、第二世界既相互依存,又相互争斗,国际经济法发展进入"转折更新"的阶段。需要指出的是,作者在这里虽然也把二战结束作为划界的时间,但在划界标准上却与其他人不同:一是以"布雷顿森林体制建立"为准,一是以"发展中国家兴起"为准,二者的基本着眼点及其历史意义截然不同。

有关国际经济法的基本原则问题。国内有关著述一般都限于简单援用国际公法一般概念的提法,把"平等互利原则"作为国际经济法的基本原则之一,而缺少深入具体的科学论证。作者则以联合国大会通过的《宣言》和《宪章》这两大纲领性国际文献作为根据,以马克思在《哥达纲领批判》一书中关于"平等"观的著名论断作为指导,提出创见,阐发了"公平互利原则",认为国际经济法中的"公平互利原则"与国际法中传统意义上的"平等互利原则",既有密切联系,又有重要区别。"公平"和"平等"有时是近义的,但在某些场合,表面上的"平等"实际上是不公平的,而表面上的"不平等"却是公平的。例如,《国际货币基金协定》依据各国缴金份额多少决定投票权大小的做法,貌似"平等",实际上往往导致"以富欺贫"现象的发生;反之,貌似对发达国家"不平等"的普惠制,实际上却是十分公平合理的。可见,"公平互利原则"是对"平等互利原则"的重大发展。另外,作者把"有约必守原则"纳入国际经济法基本原则之列,这也是其他著述所没有的。该原则之所以成为国际经济法基本原则之一,是由国际经济关系本身的基本要求所决定的。国家间、不同国籍的当事人之间签订的各种经济条约、经济合同,只有在缔约国各方或合同各方诚信遵守和切实履行的条件下,才能产生预期的效果,才能维持和发展正常的国际经贸交往和国际经济关系,从这个意义上说,"有约必守原则",乃是国际经济法必不可少的主要基石之一。另外,作者又强调:"有约必守原则"须受"所约合法"以及"情势变迁"两项条件的制约,这就加深了对"有约必守原则"的全面理解。

《总论》一书理论体系的建立以及许多观点的提出,都是建立在对国际经济关系历史回顾基础之上的。本书开篇设置了"国际经济关系的历史发展与南北矛盾"一节,就当代国际经济关系中的主要矛盾——南北矛盾,从历史到现实,阐明其症结渊源和发展进程,进而剖析当前国际经济秩序除旧布新、破旧立新的时代趋向。这样的安排颇具匠心,它是经济与法律关系的唯物史观在国际经济法研究中的具体运用,也是由国际经济法总论的特点所决定的。评断现行国际经济法的基本规范和实践原则,一则需要回溯历史,从中寻找其存在的根据,例如,如果不懂得近代殖民主义者对弱小民族兴兵索"债"的历史,就无法理解拉美国家长期以来坚持"卡尔沃主义",要求西方国家在特定条件下放弃"外交保护权"的坚定立场。二则需要回溯历史,从中寻找其现实意义,例如,如果不懂得近代殖民主义者对弱小民族疯狂掠夺的历史,就无法理解广大发展中国家要求对境内一切自然资源享有"永久主权"的重大意义。三则需要回溯历史,从中寻找判别是非的标准,例如,如果不懂得殖民主义者对弱小民族盘剥的历史,就无法理解发展中国家为恢复和维护经济主权,在必要时,对外资实行国有化并给予适当补偿的合理性。从研究方法来看,由于现行的国际经济法律新规范是发展中国家和发达国家长期斗争和妥协的结果,不采用历史的研究方法不足以反映其来龙去脉和发展轨迹。这一点尤其突出地表现在对历届联合国大会关于建立国际经济新秩序的一系列决议精神的前后对比上。

在所难免,本书也有某些不足之处。例如,有关国际经济法的构成体系问题,国内外学者的观点不尽相同,作者根据"以现实法律问题为中心"的分类标准,把国际经济法划分为国际贸易法、国际投资法、国际货币金融法、国际税法以及国际经济组织法等若干大类,并且认为,每一大类还可以进一步划分为若干较小的专门分支和再分支。由于缺少进一步的理论探讨,给人以意犹未尽的感觉。又如,本书在个别用词上前后不一,如"国际商务惯例"和"国际经济惯例"交叉使用,容易引起误解。对于此类不足之处,如在本书再版时能予补正,则可使其臻于完善。

五、独树中华一帜 跻身国际前驱
——评陈安主编的《MIGA 与中国》*

吴焕宁

厦门大学陈安教授牵头撰写的《MIGA 与中国:多边投资担保机构述评》一书由福建人民出版社出版后,引起了国内外有关各界瞩目。

本书是"国家社会科学基金项目"和国家教委"国际问题专项科研基金项目"的主要研究成果。

众所周知,政治风险,如战争、内乱、国有化和征收、禁兑等,一向是跨国投资者最为担忧的问题之一。而 20 世纪六七十年代发展中国家国有化风潮的兴起,更使得政治风险成为跨国投资,尤其是对发展中国家投资的严重阻碍。至 80 年代初期,发展中国家的直接投资流入量直线下降。建立一个世界性的专门承保跨国投资政治风险的保险机构,以消除跨国投资中的非商业性障碍,已成为时代之亟需。在这种背景下,经世界银行筹划,多边投资担保机构(MIGA)于 1988 年成立了。该机构包含了一套精心设计的国际投资政治风险保险机制,对于消除跨国投资的非商业性障碍、促进国际资本向发展中国家流动,能够起到重大的促进作用,因而受到了全球南、北两大类国家的普遍欢迎。可以说,该机构的成功设立,是近年来国际投资法领域最为重要的成就。

在 MIGA 酝酿组建期间,中国就对它采取积极支持的态度,并于 1988 年成为该机构的首批成员国之一。在短短几年内,MIGA 在我国的业务量不断攀升,这对于改善我国的整体投资环境,促进外资源源流入,产生了不可忽视的积极影响。

但是,国内对这样一个重要的国际经济组织的研究,除了已经发表的数篇论文

---

* 本篇书评原发表于《文汇读书周报》1996 年 3 月 23 日。作者吴焕宁现为中国政法大学国际法学院教授、博士生导师。

之外，几乎是一片空白。厦门大学陈安教授所牵头的科研群体，经过数年钻研，撰写了《MIGA与中国：多边投资担保机构述评》一书，立足于中国国情，紧紧扣住"南北矛盾"这一主线，从发展中国家的共同利益出发，对MIGA的渊源、机制、运作状况及其与我国的诸般关系，多角度、多层面地进行了周全的介绍和精辟的剖析，从而使我国对MIGA的研究由几近空白一跃而跻身于世界先进水平。可以说，在国际上研究MIGA的众多论著中，本书能"发他人之所未能发"，独树一帜，颇具中国特色。

从该书的内容可以看出，这部专著的资料丰富翔实，并且十分新颖。其中许多系采用有关国际组织专门提供的第一手材料，反映了相关领域中的最新信息和学术动态。同时，MIGA法律部首席顾问Lorin Weisenfeld先生直接参与该书的创作，世界银行资深副行长、MIGA缔造者之一Shihata先生拨冗作序，更为该书添色不少。

同时，由于该书对MIGA经营机制的阐述相当全面和透彻，并对中国加入MIGA的利弊得失作了深入而独到的探讨和论证，因而具有很高的科学性和可靠性，使得该书对于我国有关部门的外资决策和外资立法，具有重大的、不可替代的参考价值。

总而言之，这部专著堪称我国国际经济法学界的一部力作，是厦门大学国际经济法专业诸多学人对我国法学事业做出的新的重要贡献。

六、深入研究 科学判断
——《"解决投资争端国际中心"述评》简介*

单文华

《"解决投资争端国际中心"述评》一书是中国国际经济法学会会长、厦门大学政法学院院长、博士生导师陈安教授等接受我国对外经贸部的国策咨询，参与有关论证和研究的一项科研成果，也是国家教委博士点专项基金选定的重点科研项目的成果。1994年该书荣获福建省第二次哲学社会科学优秀科研成果一等奖。

"解决投资争端国际中心"（ICSID）是根据1965年《关于解决国家与他国国民之间投资争端公约》（以下简称《华盛顿公约》）设立的一个国际机构，总部设在美国华盛顿。截至1994年6月底，全球已有130个国家签署（其中113国已批准）《华盛顿

---

* 本篇书评原发表于《福建日报》1995年3月31日。作者单文华当时在厦门大学法学院攻读博士学位，现为英国牛津布鲁克斯大学法学院和西安交通大学法学院教授、博士生导师。

公约》。中国应否参加《华盛顿公约》、接受 ICSID 体制,事关既要贯彻对外开放国策,与国际惯例接轨,又要维护中国国家主权的问题,这是一对"矛盾"。因此,国内法学专家约于 1985 年开始展开国策咨询讨论,见仁见智,歧议甚多,但可大体归纳为两种主张:(1)促进开放,从速参加。(2)珍惜主权,不宜参加。陈安教授在对外经贸部条法局主持的专家讨论会上,提出了第三种主张,即(3)积极研究,慎重参加。他认为,在参加《华盛顿公约》、接受 ICSID 体制问题上,既不能过于保守,举棋不定,又不可掉以轻心,盲目从事。要作出正确和科学的判断,就必须在对外开放基本国策和独立自主的一贯立场的综合指导下,抓紧对《华盛顿公约》和 ICSID 体制的历史、现状以及它们在实践中的具体运作情况开展全面、深入的研究,并且在充分了解有关实况和全貌的基础上,慎重地决定应否参加、如何参加。这第三种主张,获得许多学者的赞同。

该书就是针对上述问题进行"积极研究"的初步成果。全书的主要特点是:立足于理论与实际的紧密结合,在研究大量原始资料和典型案例的基础上,对 ICSID 体制的实际运作情况进行评介,并密切联系中国的具体国情,就中国加入《华盛顿公约》、接受 ICSID 体制所可能遇到的若干主要问题进行预测,初步探讨了基本对策和防范措施,向中国的有关决策部门提出了一些有价值的、可供参考的建议。具体说来,本书论证了对《华盛顿公约》和 ICSID 加以深入、全面研究的现实必要性,提出了待决的诸多问题;评论了 ICSID 的管辖权问题;剖析了 ICSID 仲裁的法律适用问题;阐述了中国加入《华盛顿公约》、接受 ICSID 体制的可行性以及应当采取的主要对策;提出了对《华盛顿公约》及其体制应作的保留、限制以及应当采取的其他相应措施等。

《"解决投资争端国际中心"述评》一书是我国第一部也是目前唯一一部比较系统、深入地研究 ICSID 体制的著作,不仅其实践价值得到充分肯定,其学术价值在国内和国际学术界也备受推崇。1990 年 2 月,国家经过对该国策咨询成果的审议,采纳了其建议,正式加入了《华盛顿公约》;国家有关部门还多次来函称赞该成果"对我们立法工作有莫大帮助"。1993 年 8 月,我国政府正式委派陈安教授出任中国向 ICSID 选派的四名国际仲裁员中的首席仲裁员,再一次肯定了这一学术成果在理论与实践上的重要价值。

七、国际投资争端仲裁研究的力作
——评《国际投资争端仲裁——"解决投资争端国际中心"机制研究》*

张乃根

自1979年7月1日第五届全国人民代表大会第二次会议通过《中外合资企业法》以来,中国以吸收外国(外商)直接投资(FDI)为突破口,实施对外开放、对内改革的基本国策,已取得了举世瞩目的伟大成就。中国早已成为全球吸收外资的一片"热土"。为了切实保障外商在华投资的合法权益,中国政府于1993年2月6日正式成为世界银行集团管辖的《关于解决国家与他国国民间投资争端公约》(又称《华盛顿公约》)缔约国,并庄严声明中国将把由征收和国有化而引起的有关补偿的争端提交解决投资争端国际中心(ICSID)仲裁解决。

尽管迄今尚未发生一起在ICSID仲裁解决的中国政府与外商投资者的争端,但是,作为《华盛顿公约》的重要缔约国,中国如何在该公约机制内发挥一个负责任的大国应有的作用,非常值得全面、深入的研究。由我国著名国际经济法学者、中国国际经济法学会会长、厦门大学法学教授、博士生导师陈安先生主编,复旦大学出版社于2001年9月出版的《国际投资争端仲裁——"解决投资争端国际中心"机制研究》(以下简称《仲裁》)一书,堪称国际投资争端仲裁领域的一部力作。该书与同时出版的《国际投资争端案例精选》相辅相成,填补了该领域研究的一项空白。

该书包括绪论和三编。由陈安教授撰写的绪论以独特的笔触,提出了一个鲜明的问题:在中国境内的涉外投资争端中,外国的"民"可否控告中国的"官",这使读者顿感似乎是深奥莫测的国际投资争端解决,其实就是我们身边经常发生的寻常事。根据《中华人民共和国行政诉讼法》和《中华人民共和国行政复议法》,外商投资者在华对于各级政府及其主管部门违反有关法律、法规或不当的具体行政行为,均可通过行政诉讼或行政复议程序提起争端解决。既然如此,允许外商投资者到国际上去诉告中国政府,岂不多此一举?对于读者可能产生的这一疑问,陈安教授以其亲身经历的当年围绕中国是否加入《华盛顿公约》的争论,澄清了问题的实质,即首先要了解ICSID的体制,"对于中国应否加入上述《华盛顿公约》以及在何种保留条件下

---

* 本篇书评原发表于《中国图书评论》2002年第5期,第43—45页。作者张乃根现为复旦大学法学院教授、博士生导师。

方可参加这个《华盛顿公约》的问题,中国人应当尽早做到情况明了,胸有成竹,慎重决策,果断行事"(《仲裁》第41页)。这是非常务实的立场。正是基于这样的立场,陈安教授及其研究团队,通过三年紧张的研究,发表了《"解决投资争端国际中心"述评》一书,为中国政府决策加入《华盛顿公约》提供了不可多得的国际法学理依据。事实证明,中国政府仅将征收与国有化而产生的有关补偿的争端提交 ICSID 管辖,是完全正确的。这既通过中国加入《华盛顿公约》表明其对外开放、保障外商在华投资利益的坚定立场,又最大限度地避免了外商投资者在 ICSID 诉告中国政府的可能性,因为中国实行开放政策、吸收外资以来,从未发生过任何征收在华外资与国有化事件。陈安教授在绪论中审时度势,提出中国在面临新的国内外形势下是否应对 1993 年所作的保留再作适当的调整。根据《华盛顿公约》第 25 条第 4 款,任何缔约国可以在正式加入该公约之后的任何时候,决定本国增加或减少接受 ICSID 管辖的争端。在跨入 21 世纪的今天,这一提示,如同在 20 世纪 80 年代中期提出是否加入该公约的问题一样,促使中国人,尤其是中国的国际法学人开展脚踏实地的研究。

该书第一编分"管辖权""法律适用""临时措施""裁决撤销"(英文"annulment"可译为"取消""使无效")、"裁决的承认与执行""比较研究"六部分详细分析了 ICSID 的法律制度,构成了全书的核心内容。管辖权是 ICSID 受理国际投资争端的前提,法律适用是解决争端的关键,临时措施是保障争端当事方合法权益的必要手段,裁决撤销是作为国际仲裁机构的该中心内部特有的审查机制,裁决的承认与执行是维系仲裁成效的最终环节。

任何国家加入《华盛顿公约》,意味着将或多或少地接受该中心的仲裁管辖权。从国际法的角度看,主权国家接受国际司法或仲裁机构的管辖,属于让渡主权的行为。任何一个国家都不能迫使另一个国家接受国际司法或仲裁机构的管辖。是否让渡其部分主权,本身是国家行使其主权的表现。《华盛顿公约》第 25 条第 4 款规定,任何缔约国可以在加入时声明,或加入后的任何时候增减同意接受 ICSID 的管辖权范围。这与国家主权原则是一致的。关键在于 ICSID 解决的主权国家与他国国民之间的投资争端。在传统国际法上,个人不是国际法的主体。但是,在国际投资领域,由于《华盛顿公约》的存在,个人根据国际公约的规定,有权诉告主权国家,因而成为国际法上的主体。这是国际法的重大变化。如何从国际法的一般原理上,对这一法律现象作深入分析,是推进《华盛顿公约》研究的理论意义之一。

基于国际仲裁的特点,ICSID 在决定法律的适用问题上,首先尊重争端当事方的协议选择准据法,然后在没有这种协议选择的情况下,由仲裁庭决定可适用的法律(包括争端当事方的实体法与冲突法,或国际法规则)。无论在哪种情况下,作为主权国家的一方和争端当事方,都会面临适用他国法律或国际法的可能性。《仲裁》一书花费一定笔墨分析了与之相关的国内法与国际法问题,认为"从理论上讲,国内法与国际法应是协调一致的。不应存在冲突的情况,自然也不存在效力高低之分。一些国家规定国内法与其所订立的条约抵触时,优先适用条约规定,是国家协调整个法律体系的主动意愿的表现,并非国际法自然优先于国内法"(第159页)。这是中国国际法学界的一般观点。不过,正如该书所指出的,在 ICSID 的实践中,当适用国内法不能给投资者充分补偿时,国际法往往处于优先地位。这与《华盛顿公约》第1条规定的"根据本公约"解决各缔约国与其他缔约国国民之间投资争端这一宗旨是相吻合的,因为任何缔约国加入《华盛顿公约》就意味着在其接受管辖的投资争端领域,将让渡其部分主权,这本身就是国际法优先。可见,研究《华盛顿公约》的法律文本及其实践,对于我们进一步理解国内法与国际法的关系,不无裨益。

临时措施是《华盛顿公约》第47条所规定的一项授予仲裁庭在必要时采取的程序性措施。《仲裁》一书根据 ICSID 的实践,并结合 ICSID《仲裁程序规则》新增第39条第5款认为,除非双方当事人另有特别约定,ICSID 仲裁庭对临时措施申请享有排他的管辖权。这说明,该项程序性措施如同争端当事方接受 ICSID 的管辖,都取决于双方的约定。尤其是新增的第39条第5款表明先前仲裁庭在行使自由裁量权时存在偏差,因而需要法律本身的调整,以完善 ICSID 体制。这也证明该体制处在动态的完善过程中,需要我们跟踪研究,而不能只停留在原先的了解水平。

ICSID 的撤销程序是指对仲裁庭不当构成、裁决明显越权、仲裁员受贿等严重违法情况,任何一争端当事方可以申请撤销仲裁,由 ICSID 行政理事会主席从该中心仲裁员名单中指定成立的三人"专门委员会"(an ad hoc committee)审理,决定是否撤销。显然,这是 ICSID 内部独特的监督机制。《仲裁》一书对该机制作了很深入的剖析,并提出国际上已有通过研究来自 ICSID 的仲裁实践,反过来对其实践又起着重要影响的案例。这种影响会越来越重要,我们必须对这一问题予以足够的关注,以便应对今后中国在 ICSID 的可能争端裁决。

与一般的国际仲裁裁决承认与执行(如《承认及执行外国仲裁裁决公约》)不同,ICSID 的裁决等同于缔约国国内法院的最终判决,每一缔约国都应予以承认和执行,不得以任何理由(包括公共秩序保留)拒绝承认和执行裁决。这使得整个 ICSID 的机制具有了畅通的实施渠道,即只要是缔约国接受管辖,争端当事方愿意提交 ICSID 解决的国际投资争端,最后由仲裁庭裁决,且没有被撤销的,都可在当事国内得到执行。由此可见,《华盛顿公约》是一个具有强约束力的国际法体系。

相比上述各部分的研究,"比较研究"显得有些内容上的重复,如果在体系上将其比较有机地纳入各部分,可能更好一点。

《仲裁》的第二编对 ICSID 解决的阿德里昂诺·加德拉公司诉科特迪瓦共和国政府案、班弗努蒂和邦芬特公司诉刚果人民共和国政府案、阿姆科(亚洲)公司等诉印度尼西亚共和国、克劳科纳公司诉喀麦隆政府案、大西洋特里顿公司诉几内亚人民革命共和国案、南太平洋房地产(中东)有限公司等诉阿拉伯埃及共和国案、国际海运代理公司诉几内亚人民革命共和国案七个成案的评述,可使读者具体了解 ICSID 的运作机制。该书第三篇汇编了 ICSID 的基本法律文献,可供读者查阅。

八、俯视规则的迷宫
——读陈安教授主编的《国际经济法学专论》*

车丕照

国际经济法学在法学各分支当中属新兴学科,其边缘性和综合性决定了所覆盖内容的广博和复杂,也成为接触和研究本学科的难点和障碍。初识者往往畏其艰巨,感到难以入手;而研究者中则少有能够纵横各领域,融会精通诸多问题的全才。学习国际经济法学只有先大体掌握有关的基础知识,再进一步扩大学术视野和专业知识面,由浅入深,循序渐进。这就有赖于高水准的教材的引导。

《国际经济法学专论》是厦门大学陈安教授等编写的一部专门针对研究生的教材,单看其参编人员名单和目录就能感觉到阵容之强大,内容之专深。本书所意图面向的读者,"主要是为法学、经济学以及管理学这三个一级学科的硕士研究生","他们既有进一步学习国际经济法学的共同需要,而其原有的知识结构和理论基础又各有不同"。这样的设计定位,在目前的教材中即使不是绝无仅有,也当属少见,因为读者对这一专业的知识既有可能是初次接触,也有可能已经具备了相当的基础,要兼顾两者,则是对编撰提出了颇有难度的考验,正如作者们自己所说,"是一种新的任务和新的尝试"。

从我们做学生、做教师的体验来看,一部好的法学教材至少应具有体系化的结构设计、启迪性的理论阐述和与时俱进的实践追踪。也就是说,作为教材,它必须肩负着引领入门的功能,保证将学科内容完整地呈现于前,使读者对该学科基本知识形成系统化认识。《国际经济法学专论》一书承继了诸多优良教材的传统,同时基于

---

* 作者车丕照现为清华大学法学院教授、博士生导师。

其特殊的定位,该书又强调基础理论的分析,并有意在各章节的篇幅安排上,"侧重于对当代国际经济法学科领域中重大的理论争议问题、前沿性的热点难点问题以及具有重大意义的实务问题,做出比较深入的剖析和评介"。从这些方面来看,本书又不囿于教材的框架束缚,而力图以新颖的视角"激发读者进一步学习的兴趣和热情,自行加深钻研当代新鲜有益的知识和追踪国际前沿的学术发展",因此,这套书也可看作对深入研究本学科具有启迪作用的专门著作。

笔者对这部教材只是通读了一遍,但也为其鲜明的个性特色所吸引。通观下来,其内容和结构上的独特之处至少有以下几个方面:

一是这部教材对国际经济法学的知识覆盖达到了相当的广度和深度,在借鉴和吸收国内外现有的理论研究成果的基础上,系统地阐明了本学科的基本原理。作为教育部研究生工作办公室推荐的第一批研究生教学用书之一,这套书首先应具有教材的功用,须具有教材严密清晰的逻辑体系结构。法学是一门特别讲求逻辑严谨的学科,体系思维作为法学的方法由来已久。借助体系,不但有助于保证一门学科内容的完整性,形成对该学科基本知识的全面认识,而且可以通过体系本身的逻辑推理获取新知。这套教材体例结构上共分十章,上下两编各含五章。上编为"国际经济法学总论",系统阐述了国际经济法的基本理论,包括国际经济法的含义、主体、渊源和基本原则等;下编为"国际经济法学分论",包括国际贸易法、国际投资法、国际货币金融法、国际税法和国际海事法,概述了国际经济法各分支学科的基本知识,分别探讨了各分支的重要理论问题,并有重点地介绍一些主要的难点和热点问题。全书的安排,对有关知识板块是全面完整的,使读者能够从宏观上对国际经济法整个学科有概括的了解,即使是初学者也不会有片面和偏颇的理解,可对专业全貌了然于胸,不至于有以管窥豹之虞。

二是书中所引用的背景资料翔实新颖,跟踪和反映了国际经济法学科的最新发展。强调这一点是因为,国际经济法学相对其他法学科目而言是一门新兴的学科,紧跟和关注国际学术前沿显得尤为重要。本书的各位作者长期关注国内外的学术研究状况,从而可以在这套教材当中自如地援引和评判国外的研究成果。例如,本书在国际经济法的基本原则"经济主权"一节中所简介的由世界贸易组织体制而引发的美国"1994 年主权大辩论",大量引用了汉金教授和杰克逊教授著作中的内容,尽可能地贴近事实原貌和第一手材料,将辩论过程的来龙去脉娓娓道来,使读者能够比较客观详尽地了解事情的始末。而后,作者又对这次主权大辩论和美国的"301 条款"加以评论并且对其后续影响进行概括性的分析,所有这些都是基于 2000 年前后事态的最新局势作出的论述。在该小节末了,作者又深刻剖析了这场激烈论战的实质和核心,笔锋回转到经济主权对于发展中国家的重要性主题上来,这样在充分鲜活的证据上得出的结论确凿可信,一反这种纯理论问题空洞口号式的面目,读之使人顿感耳目一新、视野大开。如此行文布置,正是本书面对特定读者的匠心所在,冀以提供新的视角,引发深层思考。

三是这套教材十分重视国际经济法的总论部分,独立成编,有五章之多,在篇幅上占全书的 40% 强。当下的国际经济法教材大多不很重视总论部分的论述,究其原因,大概是由于国际经济法学本身还是一门新兴的边缘性学科,其内容范围、法律规范的源起和发展、与相邻法律部门的关系等基本问题都仍然存在诸多歧义,学术界众说不一。仅以"国际经济法"的含义和范围为例,就有认定其为国际公法新分支的狭义说和认为是调整国际经济关系的国际国内法综合体的广义说两种学术观点,前者以英国的施瓦曾伯格、日本的金泽良雄以及法国的卡罗为代表,后者则为美国的杰塞普、斯泰纳、瓦格茨、杰克逊、洛文费尔德以及日本的樱井雅夫所主张。虽然以往的国际经济法学教材也都会在总论部分力求给读者一个学理上的说明,但是像这套书这样对总论施以浓墨重彩的尚不多见。比如上面的例子,书中不仅介绍了两种学说的分歧,归纳了每位代表学者各自的观点,还对两大学派观点进行了整体分析。整个上编都以这种细致的态度将国际经济法学的概念、渊源、主体、基本原则以及国际经济争端的解决梳理透彻。这对于读者深入了解国际经济法学科无疑是大有裨益的。

四是本书在分论中将国际海事法以专章纳入,扩大了学科的研究范围,体现了本学科体系的广博复杂。如前所述,国际经济法的综合性代表着它必然与诸多相邻门类有多方面的相互交叉、相互渗透和相互融合的关系,这些复杂的关系也是学界历来关注的重点之一。本书没有拘泥于国际经济法传统意义上的分支归类,转而采取"以现实法律问题为中心",以某种国际经济法律关系或某类经济法律问题为中心的研讨途径或剖析方法,将国际海事法归为国际经济法的一个组成部分。海事法通常被认为属于商法范畴,但是,本书认为"航海贸易活动和海事行为由于其国际性或者涉外性极强而成为一种国际经济现象,应该属于国际经济法学的研究范畴"。因此,本书从研究实际问题的角度出发,探讨了有关国际航运的法律法规的现状及其理论研究状况,涉及国际海事关系包括航海贸易的国际公约和国际惯例。对于这样的划归各家当然可以见仁见智,但实际上,很多国际经济法领域是离不开海事法的相关内容的,尤其是海上运输、海上保险、共同海损以及海事赔偿责任限制等,几乎是与国际贸易如影随形的问题。既然如此,将国际海事法写进国际经济法的教科书中,也是顺理成章的事情。

五是这套书在内容上密切联系中国实际,结合中国国情,剖析了南北矛盾的发展和国际经济新秩序的进程,反映出中国国际经济法学的特色。任何法学学科研究最终的目的还是要服务于社会实践,国际经济法这样一个实践性很强的学科尤应如此。各国的国际经济法学者通常也都是从本国实际出发,研究本国政府和私人在对外经济交往活动中所涉及的国际法和国内法问题。本书在总论中对中国对外经济交往及其与学习国际经济法学的关系,乃至中国目前国际经济法学的研究概况都有介绍,在分论中所有重要的法律问题后面都对中国目前的相关情况加以概括和评析,并对中国未来应采取的立场和对策提出了建议,这些已经在书中奠定为基本的研究方法和思维方式,贯彻全书始终。

当然,一部教材要做到"雅俗共赏",令不同读者各有收益、各取所需实非易事。尽管编著时可能已经竭尽所能在内容编排和知识材料上精益求精,但是仍然有值得商榷和探讨的地方存在。从书本身的定位来说,其创意堪称上佳,然而书名既为"专论",无妨专业性再加强一些,在教材的普及性和专著的深入性之间向后者再稍作倾斜,突显研究生教育术业专攻的特色。加强专业理论的同时,一些史料性的常识作适当的指导即可,引导读者以本书为纲,展开延伸性的阅读,充分发挥研究生的自主学习研究特性,有选择和有重点地传道授业。另外,书中某些具体的说法似乎还可推敲。例如,在分析中国《关于外商投资举办投资性公司的暂行规定》第10条时,本书认为,由于投资性公司尽管为外国投资者设立,但仍然是中国法人,不符合《中外合资经营企业法》第1条有关"外国合营者"的定义,因此,允许投资性公司或投资性公司与其他外国投资者在中国投资的外汇投资比例占注册资本25%以上的企业享受外商投资企业待遇,是与《中外合资经营企业法》的有关规定相抵触的。其实,此处"享受外商投资企业待遇"并不意味着就将其划归为中外合资企业,只是在待遇上给予相同的优惠。准用类似规定,并无定性的意图,应该不存在相互抵触的问题。

总体说来,这是一套高水准的教材。作学科启蒙之用,她可以给读者以准确而全面的引导;作专业研讨之用,她又可以不时地激发学术争鸣。综观目前国内的本学科教材,就质量而言能达此高度进而出其之右者可谓鲜矣。

九、"问题与主义"中的"问题"
——读《国际经济法学专论》*

车丕照

自20世纪五四运动以降,中国理论界呈现为"问题与主义"之间的巨大分野,个中分殊使得所持论者成家、成言、成派。这种先决研究导向的对峙始终伴随着理论界的发展,或可与我们文化传统中在乎的名分、大统攸攸相关。然而,在"百家争鸣""百花齐放"中恢复活力的中国法学界,"问题"与"主义"间的"杯葛"的确为复兴的法学研究贡献了氛围、繁荣乃至前进的动力。究竟什么是我们的研究范围?我们的研究范围是先于问题而设定呢,还是通过问题来圈定我们的研究边界?我们研究的意义在何处?这些"问题与主义"的设问现在看来已经颇具历史气息,却曾经缠绕着许多学科,国际经济法学作为法域中的后起之秀在此间的摇摆尤为激烈。在这个论域中,如果将坚守国际法传统学科划分的学人们比作"主义"的倡言人,那么号召国际经济法以问题导向而应自成体系的则是"问题"一派。无疑,陈安教授是"问题"一派的领军人物和杰出代表,先生多年来孜孜以求,著述等身,为"问题"下了一个个有力的注脚。而《国际经济法学专论》,正是先生为"问题"所下注脚的鲜活教案。

(一)

对"主义"论者而言,范围设定的优先性先于问题,在他们看来,是范围制约了问题的寻找和解决。与之相对应,"问题"论者眼中的范围却因问题而设,是问题廓清了研究范围的边界。于是,学科的划定及其任务的纷争就在"问题与主义"的屋檐下展开。透过"问题与主义"的对话与对峙,我们见到的是方法论之间的交锋。如果只是纯粹从价值角度出发,殊难判别两种方法间的优劣高下。然而,结合国际经济法生成历史来看,却别有一番韵味。如书中开篇所示,国际经济法所调整法律关系的外延因不同的历史时期而呈现扩大的趋势。从罗得的商人习惯法、罗马法、中世纪《康索拉多海商法典》,经历了近现代的双边、多边的商务规约和习惯,乃至现今的转折、更新阶段的专题公约和惯例,有两条重要线索的延伸方向值得我们关注,一是量

---

* 本篇书评原发表于《政法论坛》2005年第1期,第189—191页。作者车丕照现为清华大学法学院教授、博士生导师。

的累积,即法律关系所涉范围的不断扩大;二是质的递进,即从习惯到条约所带来的约束力和确定性增加。两条线索铺陈了国际经济法所调整法律关系由简到繁的成长路径,这个历程也是国际经济法律关系所涉问题不断产生的过程。显然,如书中对这个学科发展的描述,这是一条"转折尚在更新"中的道路,要先决式地确立自己的研究范围,进而又能通过设定成熟的方法普适地解决其中问题仍显过早。

由此看来,我们甚至可以说,国际经济法学是一个在问题产生和问题解决链条上不断延伸中形成的学科。或许在这根链条能够延伸到足够远时,我们才能确定它的边界。

(二)

究竟什么是国际经济法学所关注的"问题"呢？作者从历史的视角,比较、总结前人的研究之后认为,国际经济法"是一个涉及国际法与国内法、公法与私法、国际私法以及各国涉外经济法、民商法等多种法律规范的边缘性综合体"。这一定义对国际经济法学中"问题"的特点进行了抽象和概括,是在实证层面进行了充分论证之后得出的结论。为此,书中以一家跨国公司为例证,从六个方面对国际经济活动中可能衍生问题的方向进行了具体阐释,其中的法律关系从效力层面来看有条约法律关系、合同法律关系;从经济活动范围层面来看,有投资法律关系、买卖法律关系、税收法律关系以及争端解决等等。所涉法律关系阡陌纵横,既包含平权的国家与国家、私人与私人、国家与私人之间的法律关系,也包含非平权的国家与私人间的法律关系。这些"问题"构成要素的交错和边缘化,使得人们无法从传统国际法的单一视角出发找到问题的解决方法。此时,一个开放、全方位的审视就显得突出而必要。因此,如作者所言,"国际经济法是根据迫切的现实需要'应运而生'的综合性法律部门,从而,国际经济法学乃是一门独立的边缘性法学学科。这门新兴学科的边缘性和综合性,并非出于人为的任意凑合,而是国际经济法律关系本身极其错综复杂这一客观存在的真实反映,也就是科学地调整这种复杂关系,对其中复杂的法律症结加以综合诊断和辨证施治的现实需要"。这是全书"问题"意识最为直接的表达。

全书的上下两编分别为总论与分论,互有分工,互为映衬。两编有着相同的"问题"观,从体例安排上彻底将"问题"体系化。从内容上看,上编对"问题"进行了全面的统摄,囊括的所有内容由一条主线统领,这条主线牵扯了针对"问题"全部共有属性的总结。从国际经济法内涵的界定、规范的渊源澄清、主体范围的归纳,到所有"问题"共戴原则的分析以及与"问题"相关的争端解决机制,作者在对理论上的存疑、争论梳理的过程中破立相承,逐渐阐明了对待"问题"的开放态度,从而固守了

"国际经济法学这一新兴学科具有边缘性、综合性和独立性"的立场。而下编的内容则是对"问题"的具体化,将问题落实在几个实在的分支中,包括国际贸易法、国际投资法、国际货币金融法、国际税法和国际海事法,这种横向的布局使得所涉领域几乎涵盖了全部的国际经济活动。可以看出,在"问题"的引导中形成的国际经济法学,并非一个自足自闭的体系,然而上述"开放式"的体例安排却为新"问题"的产生和旧"问题"的延展提供了足够的空间。

(三)

在解决"问题"的过程中,我们应该持有怎样的态度和立场呢?这关涉到学科研究的效用和命运。对此,笔者认为有两个方面值得关注,其一是"问题"的定位,这实际上是对"问题"进行"识别";其二是解决"问题"的立场,到底我们应该为谁服务?毫无疑问,立场关系到我们看待"问题"的价值评判并制约着解决方案的产生。

该书在对国际经济法进行了"边缘性、综合性"的学科定位之后,通篇以实际的议论对"问题"解决方法赋予了多学科、多部门的大视野。这意味着,当一个具体的问题摆在我们面前时,我们面临的首要任务就是"识别"。只有将其归入某类法律部门范畴,才有可能从权利义务的角度对这个问题进行剖析。同时,还要关注这一问题是否还兼具其他部门或学科的特点。这是因为国际法与国内法、私法与公法对待权利义务的看法并不一致,对待权利冲突的方式也各不相同。例如,涉及国家在国际经济法中的地位问题时,如果将国家放在国与国之间的关系的背景下加以研究的话,那么我们所面临的其实是国际公法的问题,应用于问题解决的方法自然要从国际公法的立场出发。如果把国家放在与国际交往的当事人法律关系的背景下加以考察,此时所面临的问题则主要是内国法的非平权主体间的法律问题。由此可以看出多视角对于一个边缘学科发展的重要意义,而书中所论的最大特点就是很好地贯彻了这一基点。

在国际经济法学中,如果说明晰"问题"中的多元化因素是从客观上澄清"问题"的症结,无疑,对待"问题"的立场表达则是从主观上寻找"问题"解决的努力。显然,立场将决定我们到底维护着怎样的利益。二战后,所有的发展中国家面临着一个秩序难题,即如何推倒一个旧有经济秩序和重塑一个新经济秩序,这是战后国际政治经济格局巨变给民族国家造成的影响。对这一历史潮流,书中通过对"经济主权原则""公平互利原则""全球合作原则"的描述,着重强调发展中国家的身份对国际经济新秩序的贡献和塑造,一再重申了发展中国家的立场。对此,笔者认为,尽管发展中国家身份是开展国际经济法研究时不可忽略的一种身份,然而作为民族国家的身份才是我们参与经济活动最原始、最根本、最核心的身份,而民族国家的立场则是我们开展研究的基础和出发点。这是因为,虽然发展中国家有改造经济秩序的初衷和动力,但是秩序的改变终究依靠的是实力的对比。随着时间的推移,秩序中所谓南北力量的博弈并没有出现发展中国家所期待的那般消长。此外,随着全球化进程的加快,国家之间的利益连接较之过往更加密切,也使得发展中国家共同的利益越来越模糊。当发展中国家的身份无助于我们对现行秩序的改变时,就只有以民族国家的身份加强对现行秩序的参与。况且,这种强调民族国家立场的地方性共识越来越成为全球化过程中的主流话语了。

(四)

为"问题"构筑一个体系是本书作者们的治学观。对国际经济法学而言,这是一个开放的"问题"体系,"问题"的发展和更新对体系的完善不可或缺,而本书在这方面的作为令人称道。"问题"的归纳、演绎、衔接被作者把握得非常流畅,例如,议论经济主权时谈及由 WTO 体制引发的美国"1994 年主权大辩论",就大量引用了汉金(Henkin)教授和杰克逊(Jackson)教授著作中的内容,尽可能地利用第一手材料,将辩论过程准确地描述出来,使读者能客观详尽地了解事情的始末。而后,作者针对主权大辩论和美国的"301 条款"进行评论以及对其后续影响进行概括性的分析时,都是基于 2000 年前后的最新态势作出的论述。

面对问题丛生的国际经济法律实践,多谈些"问题",少谈些"主义",让我们在寻找"问题"答案的过程中,且行且珍惜。相信水到渠成,这个过程本身就寄寓了寻找"问题"边界的意义。这份务实态度和成熟的"问题"观不仅是我对作者欣赏的理由,而且为我们的贡献指明了方向。

十、高屋建瓴 视角独到
——推荐《晚近十年来美国单边主义与 WTO 多边主义交锋的三大回合》*

戚燕方

陈安教授撰写的《晚近十年来美国单边主义与 WTO 多边主义交锋的三大回合》(The Three Big Rounds of U. S. Unilateralism Versus WTO Multilateralism During

---

* 本篇评论是《中国法学》杂志社戚燕方副编审撰写的参评推荐意见。现征得作者同意,辑入本书。

the Last Decade)原以英文发表于美国天普大学《国际法与比较法学报》2003 年第 17 卷第 2 期(Temple International & Comparative Law Journal, Vol. 17, No. 2, 2003),全文约 65000 字。其后,应本刊约稿,陈安教授摘取其中部分内容约 20000 字,并增补最新信息,题为《美国单边主义对抗 WTO 多边主义的第三回合——"201 条款"争端之法理探源和展望》,发表于《中国法学》2004 年第 2 期。

文章从此次"201 条款"争端说起,首先简要回顾了晚近十年来美国单边主义与 WTO 多边主义交锋的三大回合,然后从宏观上综合探讨了其中蕴含的原则碰撞和法理冲突,并对今后可能的发展进行了预测。作为本文中文版的责任编辑,我认为,该文高屋建瓴、视角独到,具有极强的现实针对性和学术理论性,其资料翔实全面,逻辑严谨,说理透彻,是这一学术领域中研究相关问题不可多得的佳作。

据我们获得的信息,陈安教授撰写的上述论文相继发表后,引起了较大反响,获得了国内外的广泛好评。在国内,中国国际法学会 2004 年 4 月的研讨会和中国法学会世界贸易组织研究会 2004 年 5 月的研讨会,均将上述中文版论文收入专辑文集,引起广泛重视。

在国际上,美国上述学报的责编 Laura Kolb 指出,该刊选择发表的论文,是他们认为"当前最受关注的、最引人入胜和最有创见的"文章。陈教授的这篇文章"论证有理有据,主题紧扣时局,资料丰富翔实","雄辩犀利,发人深思","会使国际法理论界和实务界都大感兴趣"。总部设在美国华盛顿的"多边投资担保机构(MIGA)"首席法律顾问 Lorin Weisenfeld 认为这篇文章"确实是具有头等水平的佳作","论据充分,雄辩有力",促使他全面反思近年来布什政府在国际舞台上的所作所为和霸道行径。特别值得注意的是:总部设在日内瓦的政府间国际组织"南方中心"是由 61 个发展中国家(含中国)签署国际协定共同组建的"思想库"和"智囊机构"。最近,其秘书长 **Branislav Gosovic** 来函告知:拟将这篇文章作为"南方中心"的专题出版物,即"贸易发展与公平"专题议程(T. R. A. D. E.)的系列工作文件之一,重印和扩大发行,使广大读者均能看到,特别是提供给众多发展中国家政府,作为议事决策参考。同时拟将本文列入"南方中心"的专门电子网站,供读者自由免费下载。据我们所知,中国法学家的长篇学术论文能有如此国际影响并引起国际政府间组织如此重视者,并不多见。

综上情况,我们郑重推荐陈安教授的上述中、英文版论文,参加申报学术评奖。

2004 年 6 月 6 日

十一、以史为师 力排"众议" 说理透辟
——推荐《南南联合自强五十年的国际经济立法反思》*

戚燕方

WTO第六届部长级会议2005年12月在中国香港地区召开,重启"多哈发展回合"多边谈判。对此次香港会议的结局及其发展前景,国际舆论见仁见智,褒贬不一:或"乐观",认为WTO多边体制从此步入坦途;或"悲观",认为WTO多边体制濒临瓦解;或畏难,或失望,或茫然。

陈安教授多年来跟踪研究南北矛盾和南北合作问题,积累丰厚,他全面地收集、整理香港会议后国际上出现的各种看法和见解,有的放矢地加以综合剖析,撰写了英、中两种文本的长篇论文。英文本题为"Reflections on the South-South Coalition in the Last Half Century from the Perspective of International Economic Lawmaking",中文本题为《南南联合自强五十年的国际经济立法反思》,先后投寄国外学术期刊和《中国法学》本刊。

作者主张:应当认真回顾五十年来发展中国家在南北矛盾中实行"南南联合自强"、力争更新国际经济立法的主要史实和曲折进程,以史为师,从宏观上总结经验,学会运用历史的慧眼,正视当代"南弱北强"和"南多北寡"的客观现实,自觉地认识和运用五十年来南北矛盾和南北合作中反复出现的螺旋式"6C律",排除"速胜"论、"坦途"论和"瓦解"论的影响,多一份冷静、耐心和韧性,少一些脱离实际的盲目"乐观"或无端"悲观"。即使香港会议之后,多哈回合各项重大难题的谈判再次出现"拉锯"或僵局,甚至再次不欢而散,也早在意料之中,国际社会弱势群体即众多发展中国家应早作思想准备,继续以南南联合自强的韧性奋斗精神和灵活多样的策略,从容应对,力求"多哈发展回合"的新一轮多边谈判在其后续的2006年底,或更迟一些,得以在公平互利、南北合作的基础上全面完成。总之,要逐步更新国际经济立法、建立起国际经济新秩序,舍韧性的南南联合自强,别无他途可循!

我作为本文中文本的责任编辑,在审阅过程中,深感此文旗帜鲜明,站在国际弱势群体的共同立场,以史为据,以史为师,史论结合,视角独到,"力排众议",颇多创新,具有极强的现实针对性和学术理论性。其资料翔实全面,逻辑严谨,说理透彻,

---

* 本篇评论是《中国法学》杂志社戚燕方副编审撰写的参评推荐意见。现征得作者同意,辑入本书。

论证雄辩,是这一学术领域中不可多得的力作和佳作。

有关信息资料显示此文在本刊发表后,获得读者广泛好评。其英文本在日内瓦引起广泛重视,先由国际组织"南方中心"机关报发表了其中的核心部分,并公布于ICSID网站,扩大宣传;另有两家国际性学刊相继全文刊载。据我们所知,中国法学家撰写的长篇学术论文,能引起国际组织和国际性学刊如此重视、具有如此国际影响者,尚不多见。

综上,我们郑重推荐陈安教授的上述中、英文版论文,参加申报学术评奖。

2006 年 5 月 31 日

十二、紧扣学科前沿 力求与时俱进
——推荐《国际经济法学》(第三版)*

杨立范

厦门大学陈安先生主编的《国际经济法学》一书,综合反映了国际经济法学这一新兴边缘学科的基本理论和基本知识,是对国际经济法主要内容的精心浓缩和精辟论述。全书内容科学、立论独到、取材新颖、涵盖全面、重点突出,在国内同类出版物中达到领先水平,深受读者喜爱。本书第一版自 1994 年 12 月由北京大学出版社出版以来,迄 2001 年 3 月,先后重印 7 次,累计 51520 册。由于本书具有以上特点和优点,又被全国高等教育自学考试指导委员会指定为全国高等教育自学考试统编教材,并于 1994 年 12 月至 2001 年 3 月,先后重印 12 次,印数达 231100 册。以上两项合计,迄 2001 年 3 月为止,印数共达 282620 册。

2001 年 4 月,本社推出《国际经济法学》(第二版),由作者们依据本书第一版推出后七年来的形势发展,对原书加以认真修订、增补,添加了大量新鲜知识和前沿信息,进一步提高了学术水平,并继续作为高等学校法学教材以及全国高等教育自学考试指定教材被广泛采用。第二版问世以来短短三年半,经过 31 次印刷,两种印数共 230200 册。与第一版总印数合计,两版总印数 512820 册,足见本书很受广大读者欢迎。

2004 年 1—8 月,本书作者们又根据经济全球化加速发展和中国加入世界贸易

---

* 本篇评论是《国际经济法学》一书的责编、北京大学出版社杨立范副总编撰写的参评推荐意见。现征得作者同意,辑入本书。

组织后出现的国际经济政治秩序的最新格局,并结合近十年来本书在全国高等教育教学实践中被广泛采用的效果和经验,对本书内容再次作了全面的修订、增补和更新。

本书第三版于 2004 年 11 月底以崭新面貌问世,全书共 73.3 万字,首印 8000 册,在两个多月内迅即售罄,随即在 2005 年 2 月第 2 次印刷 12000 册,市场需求继续看旺;经作者们再稍加修订,近期内即将进行第 3 次印刷。十年来本书前后三种版本的累计印数,已达 532820 册。这种情况表明:十年来本书内容的不断更新和提高,确实做到了"紧扣学科前沿,力求与时俱进",因而切合当代中国高校读者学习新知的需要,具有旺盛的学术生命力。

基于以上情况,兹特郑重推荐上述著作参加省部级、国家级优秀科研成果及优秀教材评奖活动。

2005 年 3 月 15 日

第4章　群贤毕至，少长咸集，
　　　　坐而论道，畅叙旧情

2009年5月，陈安教授八十诞辰之际，厦门大学法学院国际经济法专业历届博士生学友，从全国各地风尘仆仆赶来母校，济济一堂，举行"中国国际经济法的研究方法暨陈安教授学术思想"研讨会，犹如王羲之《兰亭序》所说"群贤毕至，少长咸集"，坐而论道，畅叙友情。会后厦大《校友通讯》整理了九篇发言稿，集中刊发。作为历史资料，辑录于本书第六编，以飨同道，并祈惠正。

一、在"中国国际经济法的研究方法暨陈安教授
　　　　学术思想"研讨会上的致辞

辜芳昭[*]

尊敬的陈安教授、尊敬的各位来宾、老师们、同学们：

上午好！

今天，我们欢聚一堂，共同庆贺陈安教授80华诞暨从教58周年，隆重召开"中国国际经济法的研究方法暨陈安教授学术思想"研讨会。这是厦门大学的一件喜事，也是一件盛事。在这里，请允许我代表厦门大学向陈安教授表示热烈的祝贺和崇高的敬意！向前来参加大会的社会各界朋友、校友表示热烈的欢迎！同时祝贺"中国国际经济法的研究方法暨陈安教授学术思想"研讨会隆重召开！作为陈安教授多年的同事和晚辈，还想借此机会向陈安教授表示我良好的祝愿！

陈安教授是我国法学界知名的学者，也是德才双馨的名师。陈安教授1950年7月毕业于厦门大学法律系，随后从事过短暂的司法审判工作，于1951年1月调回母

---

[*] 辜芳昭，时任厦门大学党委副书记、副校长。

校厦门大学法律系任教,从此与厦门大学的教学事业结下了不解之缘。

陈安教授是厦门大学国际经济法学科的创建人和学术带头人。早在我校法律系复办伊始,陈安教授与法律系的其他同仁为适应改革开放之急需,确立了创建国际经济法专业的学科发展战略,并先后于1982年、1985年和1986年获准招收国际经济法专业的硕士生、本科生和博士生。1987年,陈安教授主编出版的国内第一套国际经济法系列著作,为我校国际经济法学科的发展奠定了基础。陈安教授是中国特色国际经济法的奠基人之一,也是这个学科永不知疲倦的开拓者。1993年起,陈安教授连选连任中国国际经济法学会的会长。陈安教授还是中国国际经济法实践的先行者之一。他承担、承办了许多重要的国策咨询和典型的国际经贸仲裁司法案件,是我国政府根据《华盛顿公约》遴选向"解决投资争端国际中心"(ICSID)指派的国际仲裁员。我们都知道,陈安教授是改革开放之初,我国较早走出国门在国际舞台同外国同行同台竞技、同台抗辩的一位出色学者,他的作为为厦门大学赢得了荣誉,为国家争得了尊严。

今天,我们在这里庆贺陈安教授80华诞暨从教58周年,就是要学习他为人师表的典范和追求科学的精神。陈安教授孜孜不倦地追求着学术,而科学的高峰是无止境的,攀登这座高峰,不仅需要坚韧的毅力,也需要一种不畏劳苦的勇气。古人常说"学海无涯苦作舟",陈安教授就是一位在学海中不畏艰险、乘风破浪的掌舵手。陈安教授著作等身,他的鸿篇巨著《国际经济法学刍言》和《陈安论国际经济法学》,以及发表于海内外权威学术期刊上的中英文学术论文,忠实地记录了他对学术的执着和对中国特色国际经济法学的杰出贡献。陈安教授现虽已80高寿,但仍然以老骥伏枥、志在千里的精神从不懈怠,从事着他钟爱的学术活动。这种坚持、这份追求永远是我们学习的榜样。

陈安教授学为人师、行为示范。他对大学讲坛的敬重,对教学的认真,同样令我们敬佩。陈安教授热爱教师职业,喜爱他的学生。记得我在法学院工作的多年时间里,陈安教授已经是一名很有名望的教授,也已经不是一位很年轻的教授。但他不仅带好他的研究生,还经常腾出时间给本科生开设讲座。这也正是我们厦门大学现在一直提倡和要求的,即教授要给本科生开课。凡是有缘于陈安教授授课的学生,对他讲课的严谨和讲课的精彩,以及从课堂上所获取的知识与能力,都会留下终生难忘的印象。我知道在这个精彩的背后,付出的是十倍的艰辛。愿意这样付出的老师源于他对教育事业的忠诚,对学生的责任,这种精神是我们应该提倡和学习的。陈安教授既教书又育人,对他的学生既言传又身教,诲人不倦,以提携后人为己任。他真诚地关心每一位学生的成长,指导了众多的青年教师。我相信在座的很多人,都曾经得益过、受惠过陈安教授的教诲与关心。从教58年来,陈安教授和他的团队已经为国家和社会培养了一大批优秀的、出类拔萃的人才。这批人,大多在教学、科研、政府机关、企事业单位成为中坚力量,为国家做出了突出的贡献。

借此机会,我要再次恭祝陈安教授健康长寿、学术之树常青;预祝"中国国际经济法的研究方法暨陈安教授学术思想"研讨会取得圆满成功!谢谢!

二、我与陈安教授

赵龙跃[*]

我认识陈安教授的时间并不长,那是在四年前的一次国际学术会议上。

2005年2月,在美国国际法学会举办的国际年会上,我非常荣幸地认识了陈安教授。陈教授在大会上的精彩演讲,观点鲜明、论据翔实,直接抨击了美国实行单边贸易保护主义的危害。再加上他那纯正的美国英语发音、层次分明的演示框架,给包括我在内的所有与会的各国专家学者留下了深刻的印象;陈教授的机智反应,以及与世界著名国际经济法学专家、被誉为"WTO之父"的约翰·杰克逊教授的一番精彩辩论,更是让我们深深地折服。那次陈教授在华盛顿访问不到一个星期,日程安排得很紧张,每天晚上我都要开车到陈教授下榻的饭店,开怀畅谈,一谈就谈到深夜,大有如遇知音、相见恨晚之感。但是,无论从陈教授的身体状况,还是从他充满追求的精神状态,我都没有想到他已经是一位快到80岁的人了。

这次我非常荣幸能应邀参加"中国国际经济法的研究方法暨陈安教授学术思想"研讨会,我觉得活动举办得十分成功,具有重要意义。我相信每一位校友和在校的师生都和我一样,受到了极大的鼓舞和鞭策。我十分羡慕陈教授为我国国际经济法学的创立和发展,为厦门大学法学院学科建设和人才培养所做出的巨大贡献;羡慕陈教授学富五车、著作等身、桃李满天下的丰硕成果。从事教育工作,成就是可以叠加和倍增的,这种成就带来的欣慰和满足,是从事其他工作所难以得到的。

出席今天会议的嘉宾,从各个方位给陈教授作了一个全面的总结,如知识渊博、学贯中西、治学严谨、疾恶如仇、知识报国、兼济天下等,对这些我深有同感。另外,我觉得陈教授还有几个很独特的方面,非常值得我们学习。一是老骥伏枥、志在千里;二是思想活跃、开拓创新;三是立足中国、放眼全球。陈教授虽然已经是80高龄,

---

[*] 赵龙跃,国际贸易政策专家、世界银行国际贸易问题咨询专家、美国乔治敦大学特聘教授。

但是他的思想依然非常活跃,很容易接受新鲜事物;面对困难不畏缩,解决问题不机械。陈教授年过半百后才到哈佛大学学习,回国后就着手国际经济法学的教学与研究工作。当时在没有师资、没有教材、没有学生的情况下,他先从培养师资入手,招收了4名研究生,然后才招本科生;先翻译引进美国的原著,然后又编写了我国自己的国际经济法学教科书;学生从无到有,现在厦门大学法学院培养的学生已经都成为我国法学界的骨干,有的是兄弟院校的校长或法学院的院长,有的是活跃于我国各地律师事务所的法律工作者,以及世界各地法学界的教授和学者。这是陈教授策划和推进的一项多么伟大的工程。我们今天庆祝陈教授80寿辰,就是要学习他的这种精神,要有理想要有追求,争取多为社会做一些有意义的工作。同时,陈教授的成功对我们今天的年轻人来说也是一个巨大的鼓舞,我们生活在这么好的年代,有这么好的条件,所以应该也相信你们会做得更好。

三、诲人不倦 师道悠悠

钟兴国[*]

陈安教授从事教学科研60年,60年在人类历史的长河中是非常短暂的一刹那,但是陈安教授教学科研的60年却向人们展示了一幅"学而不厌,诲人不倦,格物致知,修身成德"的精彩画卷,真可谓:道德文章,堪称楷模;释疑解惑,独具一流。

陈安教授的教学科研,首先致力于传道。他以自己从善如流、疾恶如仇的做人品格,格物致知、锲而不舍的做学问的风格直接影响着他的同事、学生。我是一名公务员,每当谈到党内、社会上的一些腐败现象和个别干部庸俗的行为时,陈安教授总是声色俱厉、鞭辟入里地提醒我一定要勤政、廉政,恪守从政之道;我是一名从外文专业转攻法学的博士,每当谈到个别学生不求甚解、巧言令色、只图文凭、不求学问的习气,陈安教授总是谆谆教导我要囊萤映雪,寒窗苦读,恪守求学之道。真可谓:师道尊严。

陈安教授的教学科研,特别精攻于授业。他学识渊博、学富五车、逻辑缜密、辩才无碍,读他的著作常常感到如饮甘泉,唇齿留芳;听他的讲课常常觉得醍醐灌顶,茅塞顿开;与他的交谈常常使人豁然开朗,疑团顿消。真可谓:师道睿智。

陈安教授的教学科研,尤其擅长于解惑。他有教无类、因材施教;他妙语连珠、

---

[*] 钟兴国,厦门大学1999届国际经济法专业博士毕业生,时任中共厦门市委常委、海沧区委书记。

妙音解惑;他教会学生知识,更交给学生打开知识宝库的钥匙;他教会学生知识之其然,更教会学生知识之所以然。课堂上,他是个良师;课堂外,他是个益友。他待人处事既严肃认真,又不失诙谐幽默。真可谓:师道可亲。

尊敬的陈老、亲爱的老陈、敬爱的陈安教授,我们衷心地祝福您:幸福、快乐、健康、长寿!

四、陈安老师与中国国际经济法事业

徐崇利[*]

在中国,国际经济法可以说是法学中最年轻的学科,应改革开放之运而生。陈安老师是中国国际经济法事业的先行者和奠基者之一,他与北京大学的芮沐、中国人民大学的刘丁、武汉大学的姚梅镇、复旦大学的董世忠、南开大学的高尔森和上海社科院的周子亚等老先生一道,开创了中国国际经济法的科学研究和人才培养事业。

20世纪80年代初,在中国国际经济法学科始创之时,人才匮乏。包括陈安老师在内的一批老先生于1984年在江西庐山开办了中国国际经济法讲习班,培养了中国最早的一批国际经济法人才。现在,他们中的许多人已成为名享中国法学界的学者,包括厦门大学国际经济法学科的学术带头人曾华群教授和廖益新教授。这次讲习班被后人誉为是推动中国国际经济法事业起步和发展的"黄埔军校"。

早在1981—1983年,陈安老师就赴美国哈佛大学研究、讲学,为系统地将国际经济法学科引入中国做了充分的准备。回国后,陈安老师组织学术团队,结合中国实际,精研国外最新成果,经过数年的努力,于1987年在国内首次推出了国际经济法系列专著——《国际投资法》《国际贸易法》《国际货币金融法》《国际税法》和《国际海事法》。这套专著以及后来出版的《国际经济法总论》为学界提供了系统化的国际经济法知识,对构建中国国际经济法学科体系做出了历史性的贡献。通过这套专著的撰写,厦门大学国际经济法学科也初步搭建了一个比较完整的学术团队。至今,学术梯队的完整性仍然是厦门大学国际经济法学科的优势所在。

1992年起,中国国际经济法学界公推陈安老师担任中国国际经济法学会常务副会长、会长,这是学界同仁对陈安老师学术地位的高度承认。自此,在陈安老师的精

---

[*] 徐崇利,厦门大学1996届国际经济法专业博士毕业生,时任厦门大学法学院院长、教授、博士生导师。

心组织下,中国国际经济法学会的工作更上层楼,成为推动中国国际经济法事业发展的一个重要的全国性学术平台,并经中国民政部注册登记成为国家一级学术团体,其法人住所和秘书处设在厦门大学。17年来,一年一度的中国国际经济法学会年会成了汇聚海内外学科精英进行学术研讨的盛会。

1998年以来,陈安老师又亲自担任主编,主持出版了《国际经济法学刊》(原《国际经济法论丛》),连续11年未有中断。现在,学刊已成为汇辑国际经济法领域优秀学术著述的另一重要的全国性学术平台,也是目前国内唯一一个国际经济法综合性学术集刊。2006年,学刊首批入选CSSCI学术数据来源集刊。在国际上,学刊也已逐步成为一个反映中国国际经济法研究动向和水平的学术品牌。

30年来,陈安老师为中国国际经济法事业的发展笔耕不辍,始终立基于中国国情和发展中国家的共同立场,开科立派,致力于开拓具有中国特色的国际经济法学科。此次80华诞汇集出版的《陈安论国际经济法学》共5卷300余万字,记载了陈安老师对中国国际经济法事业的巨大学术贡献,也展示了一个老知识分子毕生以知识报国为己任的辉煌学术历程。

对于我们来说,最宝贵的学术基业是陈安老师开创的厦门大学国际经济法学科。在京城之外的诸多综合性大学的法学院中,能够白手起家,将一个学科发展成全国领先的法学学科,迄今恐怕也只有厦门大学的国际经济法学科。

学科要发展,人才是关键。20世纪八九十年代,全国高校难以吸引优秀人才,国际经济法又是一个应用性很强的法学学科,出国、从商、为官者众多,甘于在高校"坐冷板凳"者寥寥。因此,在全国的绝大多数高校中,都没能建立一个比较稳定的国际经济法学术团队。同期,厦门大学的国际经济法学科虽然也经历了大量的人才流动,但在陈安老师的苦心经营下,始终保持着一个比较完整的学术团队,这是厦门大学国际经济法学科起步和发展的根基。本人就是在陈安老师的感召下,1990年从上海社科院硕士研究生毕业后回母校任教,加入这个学术团队的。

从某个角度上讲,创业维艰,守业更加困难。当下,全国法学学科竞争激烈,学科建设不进则退。如何守护和提升厦门大学国际经济法学科的学术地位,已成为交到年轻一代团队成员手中一份沉甸甸的责任。只有凝练队伍,居安思危,潜心学问,团结协作,奋力进取,才能使厦门大学国际经济法学科成为一个富有生机和活力、长久不衰的中国国际经济法学术重镇。

五、知识报国 后学师范

曾华群*

在祝贺陈安老师 80 华诞和从教 58 周年的时刻,抚今忆昔,令人感慨。从陈老师的奋斗历程和奉献,我们深切感受到老一辈知识分子的爱国情怀、责任意识和价值取向。

80 年岁月峥嵘。在民不聊生、战乱频仍的旧中国,陈老师少年立振兴中华之志,勤奋用功。第二次世界大战后考入厦门大学,修习法学之余,开始接触和接受马克思列宁主义的启蒙和陶冶。1951 年以来,陈老师任教于厦门大学,法律系停办期间,由法学转为马克思列宁主义领域。改革开放 30 年,是陈老师学术生涯的黄金时期。1981 年,陈老师以"知天命"之年,远赴重洋,进修和讲学于哈佛大学,开始了专攻国际经济法的漫漫征程。

陈老师是厦门大学国际经济法学科的创建人和学术带头人,1979 年我校法律系复办伊始,与陈朝璧教授、盛新民教授、胡大展教授等同仁,为适应改革开放形势之急需,及时确立了以国际经济法专业为重点的学科发展战略。先后于 1982 年、1985 年和 1986 年获教育部批准招收国际经济法专业硕士生、本科生和博士生,并于 1987

---

* 曾华群,厦门大学 1990 届国际经济法专业博士毕业生,现任中国国际经济法学会会长、厦门大学国际经济法研究所所长,教授、博士生导师。

年主编出版了国内第一套国际经济法系列著作,为我校国际经济法学科的发展奠定基石。

陈老师是中国国际经济法学会的创建人之一。在1984年庐山国际经济法讲习班讲学期间,与上海市社会科学院周子亚教授、武汉大学姚梅镇教授、复旦大学董世忠教授、南开大学高尔森教授和中国社会科学院盛愉教授等发起创立了国际经济法研究会(即中国国际经济法学会的前身)。1993年起,陈老师连选连任中国国际经济法学会会长。26年来,作为国际经济法领域的全国性民间学术团体,学会发展之路关山重重。陈老师身先士卒,筚路蓝缕,团结全国学界和实务界同仁,积极开展国际经济法领域的国内外学术交流,逐渐形成和确立了"以文会友,以友辅仁,知识报国,兼济天下"的学会宗旨和共识。

陈老师是中国特色国际经济法学的奠基人之一。在潜心治学中,一向坚持马克思列宁主义,追求公平正义的法治精神,积极倡导"知识报国,兼济天下"的治学理念。一介书生,位卑未敢忘忧国,为振兴中华竭尽心力。一介书生,时刻关注天下大势,始终不渝地坚持改革国际经济旧秩序、建立国际经济新秩序的目标和立场,奋力为饱受欺凌压迫的广大发展中国家弱势群体的正义要求呐喊和鼓呼。天道酬勤。陈老师创办和主编的《国际经济法学刊》、撰写的鸿篇巨制《国际经济法学刍言》和《陈安论国际经济法学》以及发表于海内外权威学术刊物的中英文学术论文,忠实记录了其"板凳甘坐卅年冷"的执着和对中国特色国际经济法学的杰出奉献。

陈老师还是中国国际经济法律实践的先行者之一。在教学研究百忙之中,承担和承办了一系列重要的国策咨询和典型国际经贸仲裁、司法案件,是中国政府根据《华盛顿公约》遴选向"解决投资争端国际中心"(ICSID)指派的国际仲裁员。

艰难困苦,玉汝于成。陈老师在长达58年的执教生涯中,以其坚韧不拔的精神和持之以恒的努力,成就了利国利民的不平凡业绩,实现了其报效国家人民之志,亦成为后学之师范。

得益于陈老师的言传身教,经过近三十年的发展,厦门大学国际经济法学科及学术团队逐渐形成其传统和特色。主要表现在:

第一,立足中国国情,理论紧密联系实际。与商务部等政府部门和涉外经贸实务界长期保持密切的合作关系,结合改革开放实际,力图较全面、深入研究我国在国际投资、国际贸易、国际货币金融和国际税务等方面的法律问题,为我国法治建设和改革开放事业做出应有贡献。

第二,关注南北问题,坚持第三世界立场。在全球化背景下,铭记作为中国学者的历史责任和使命,坚持改革国际经济旧秩序、建立国际经济新秩序的目标和立场,重视研究国际经济法基本理论,特别是经济主权、公平互利和合作发展等国际经济法基本原则的理论和实践问题,努力维护发展中国家的权益。

第三,追求严谨学风,重视学术道德修养。深知为人师表,道德文章须经得起历史的检验。潜心钻研学问,崇尚淡泊明志,宁静致远。提倡学术民主,博采众长,百家争鸣。注重学术规范,严格自律,以身作则。

第四,勇于开拓创新,促进国际学术交流。创建厦门国际法高等研究院并连年举办"国际法前沿问题研修班",连续参加"Willem C. Vis 国际商事模拟仲裁庭辩论赛"(维也纳)和"Jessup 国际法模拟法庭辩论赛"(华盛顿特区)并屡获佳绩,持续在国际性专业刊物和出版社发表学术论著等,均反映了本学科师生走向国际的初步努力。

第五,强化团队意识,凝聚学科建设合力。在本学科建设的各项工作中,如《国际经济法学刊》的编辑、中国国际经济法学会秘书处事务、国际专业大赛辩论队的指导,以及厦门国际法高等研究院行政事务等,本学科师生基于共同的世界观和价值观,甘当"义工",勇挑重担,体现了强烈的事业心、责任感和团队意识。

光阴荏苒,时不我待。祈望本学科广大师生志存高远,继往开来,为学科和厦门大学的进一步发展,为中国的民主法治事业而不懈努力。

六、春分化雨育新人

林　忠[*]

光阴似箭,博士毕业已经将近十三年了。回想在陈安教授指导下攻读学位的日子,印象最深或说受益最大莫过于陈老师的正直为人以及他的认真严谨的学术态度。

在跟随陈老师的 6 年中,我见过不少"达官富豪"慕名前来要求做他的博士生,但他从来不因为对方是何权贵而作任何妥协或"通融"。在对待学术问题上,他对于他的学生,不论是何种背景,一律严格要求,不作任何妥协。对于应考者,也是同样要求按统一的录取标准。但是,陈老师的"苛刻"并不是刻板。对于付出努力的学生,他总是予以充分认可,并给予各种支持和培养。陈老师的确是疾恶如仇。他不能容

---

[*] 林忠,厦门大学 1996 届国际经济法专业博士毕业生,毕业后曾留校任教,现为上海瑛明律师事务所合伙人、律师。

忍的是请托求情和为非作歹。对于任何违规违法的事情,他总是坚决抵制并毫不留情地予以严厉批评。在市场经济时代,这样做似乎不太迎合潮流,甚至得罪了某些人。但是,陈老师首先自己行得正,坐得直,他的强烈的正义感染了很多人,也让我们做学生的学到了为人做事的真谛。如果中国像这样的知识分子多一些,我们的社会风气应当会有很大的不同。

陈老师让人印象深刻之处,还在于他的平易近人。身为学术界的权威,陈老师对于同道乃至晚辈学生都是十分客气,从来没有摆出一副权威的架子。他总是以理服人,谆谆教诲。对于不同的观点,他总是认真倾听,兼收并蓄。

陈老师的治学态度非常严谨。他撰写或主编的书稿不计其数。但他数十年如一日,每一部学术著作、每一篇文章都是认认真真校对,每一处引用、注解都按规范严格要求。对学生如此要求,自己也是这样做的。出版社的编辑感叹,陈老师经手的文章著作,他们这些编辑都不用复校了。

陈老师让人感动之处还在于他对国家、对学校和对学术的热爱。对于国际经济活动中涉及维护国家主权的事宜,他总是挺身而出,大声疾呼。对于经济霸权主义等各种损害我国国家或企业利益的事情,他总是如秋风扫落叶一般进行严厉抨击。对于厦门大学,他可以说是倾注毕生精力,去为她添砖加瓦。对于学科建设,他是鞠躬尽瘁,呕心沥血。可以说,陈老师堪称"中国的脊梁骨"的知识分子的典范。

七、八十感怀*

陈　安

回首近八十年蹉跎岁月,不无点滴感悟。概而言之,就是以勤补拙、羡鱼结网、薄技立身、赤子情怀、知识报国。

若论天赋,我自幼虽非愚鲁不堪,也绝非颖聪过人,平平庸庸而已。五岁随同兄姐入学,一次考试遇若干填空选择题,一头雾水,但硬着头皮"填上"空格,居然侥幸全数正确,得了"满分"。慈母闻讯揽入怀中,爱抚、期许有加。严父得悉侥幸实情,则表扬期许之余,又有批评教诲:"为人、做事、治学,来不得半点侥幸取巧。天赋平庸,可以以勤补拙。事事如此,日日如此,方能真正成长。"

---

* 本文原是复旦大学出版社 2008 年 12 月出版的《陈安论国际经济法学》(五卷本)的作者自序。限于篇幅,编入时有较多删节和适当改动。

日常见同侪中突出优秀者,读史中慕博学广识者,常有艳羡之言。又获严父耳提面命:"临渊羡鱼,不如退而结网。"家境清贫拮据,但父亲仍勉力送诸子女入学,谆谆相告:"我家无恒产,日后不可能留下什么遗产。现在送你们入学,便是我日后赠给你们的唯一遗产。积财千万,不如薄技在身,学得薄技,方能立身不败。学必恃勤,技必求精。"

时值日寇侵华,国难当头。师长、家长反复喻以至理:爱我中华,不畏强暴;多难兴邦,众志成城。身为稚童,弱腕无力握大刀杀敌,唯有勤奋掌握知识,日后方能参与振兴中华,报效祖国。服膺儒学的父亲,对历史上毁家纾难、忠贞殉国、视死如归的文文山,更是推崇备至,且对其《正气歌》作独到解读:"'天地有正气,杂然赋流形。下则为河岳,上则为日星;于人曰浩然,沛乎塞苍冥。'——这是千古不朽的座右铭。文天祥那般光照日月的浩然正气,虽非人人可及,却是人人可学、应学、应养。个人的刚正,赤子的情怀,民族的气节,都要从大处着眼,从小处着手,长期自律自养,才能逐步走向孟轲所倡导的'富贵不能淫,贫贱不能移,威武不能屈'之境界。"家长和师长的此类教诲,点点滴滴,沁入稚嫩心田,此后数十年来未尝或忘,成为做人和治学南针。

抗日战争胜利前夕,父亲病逝。翌年,我考入厦门大学。此后三年,大学图书馆丰富的图书以及地下党领导的多次反美反蒋爱国学生运动,使我开始接触和接受马克思列宁主义的启蒙和陶冶。1949年10月新中国成立,鸦片战争以来百余年中国罹受的民族灾难和丧权辱国惨痛,终于结束。那时那种"四海欢腾,普天同庆"的情景,至今记忆犹新。

正是在这样的历史环境下,我逐步形成了个人基本的理念定位、价值坐标和观察视角,并在大学毕业后迄今五十八年的粉笔生涯和偷闲爬格过程中,历经寒暑风雨,始终未变,又有所发展。平生著述不敢侈言丰硕,唯幸能以"知识报国,兼济天下"自勉不懈,尤其在蹉跎半生而重返法学殿堂之后,三十年来更是废寝忘餐,焚膏继晷,不息笔耕,博采、消化和吸收中外新知,力求开拓创新,其主要特色可略举数例如下:

• 阐明特定的学术理念和学术追求。当代发达国家国际经济法诸多论著的共同基本特点,是重点研究发达国家对外经济交往中产生的法律问题,作出符合发达国家权益的分析和论证。反观中国,作为积贫积弱的发展中国家之一员,这样的研究工作还处在幼弱阶段,远未能适应中国对外交往的迫切需要和对外开放的崭新格局。因此,我们必须实行"拿来主义"和"消化主义",在积极引进和学习西方有关国际经济法学新鲜知识的基础上,密切联系中国国情,站在中国和当代国际弱势群体即第三世界的共同立场,从第三世界的视角,认真加以咀嚼消化,取其精华,弃其糟粕,逐步创立起以马克思主义为指导的,具有中国特色的国际经济法学这一新兴边缘性、综合性学科的体系和理论体系,努力为国际社会弱势群体提供维护应有平等权益的法学理论武器。当然,完成此等大业,需要几代中国学人的共同刻苦钻研和齐心奋力开拓。

• 探索建立国际经济新秩序的规律和路径。当今国际经济秩序和国际经济法律规范的破旧立新,势必循着螺旋式上升的"6C 轨迹",即 Contradiction(矛盾)→Conflict(冲突或交锋)→Consultation(磋商)→Compromise(妥协)→Cooperation(合作)→Coordination(协调)→Contradiction New(新的矛盾),依靠群体力量,联合奋斗,步履维艰,迂回曲折地逐步实现。既不能盲目"乐观",期待"毕其功于一役";也不能盲目"悲观",遇到挫折就灰心丧志;更不能奢望只凭孤军奋斗,即可克敌制胜。总结历史,以史为师,国际弱势群体争取和维护平权地位和公平权益,舍韧性的"南南联合自强",别无他途可循。

• 论证当代国际经济法的首要基本原则。当代国际经济法贯穿着四大基本原则,其中经济主权原则是首要的基本规范,全球弱势群体务必增强忧患意识,珍惜和善用经济主权以确保和维护民族正当权益,警惕当代霸权主义的"双重标准"和伪善本质,切忌懵懵然地附和、接受当今颇为"时髦"的、来自西方霸权主义国家的经济主权"淡化"论、"弱化"论和"过时"论,切忌坠入理论陷阱。作为中国人,同时还应当加深认识当代中国实行对外开放基本国策的历史渊源和深厚积淀,从而更加自觉推动其优良历史传统及其独立自主、平等互惠的法理原则"与时俱进"。

• 研究国际投资条约及其相关体制。笔者长期重点研究有关国际投资的双边协定、多边公约以及相关的 OPIC、MIGA、ICSID 等基本体制及其实际运行,探讨中国和其他发展中国家如何在这些体制中趋利避害;并依据研究成果,努力践行知识报国素志,多次应邀积极向国家主管部门提供决策咨询建议和立法建言。

• 澄清和批驳外国媒体等对中国的误解和非难。多年来,笔者有的放矢,针对外国媒体、政坛和法学界对中国的各种误解和非难,撰写多篇双语专论,予以澄清和批驳;通过学术论证,努力维护中国的国家尊严、国际信誉和民族自尊,弘扬中华爱国主义。

较之海内外同行先进,笔者学术途程起步甚晚,实为"后学",积淀殊薄。承学界同行专家厚爱,评议认为笔者近三十年来所论,堪称"跻身国际前驱,独树中华一帜",乃是创建具有鲜明中国特色的国际经济法学理论的奠基之作,为创立具有中国特色的国际经济法学理论体系开了先河;其特点是运用当代国际法理论,致力为包括中国在内的发展中国家弱势群体"依法仗义执言",力争成为当代第三世界争取国际经济平权地位的法学理论武器,可谓"一剑淬砺三十年"。笔者理解:学界同仁的上述溢美之词,是对本人"薄技立身、赤子情怀、知识报国"感悟的认同、鼓励和最新鞭策。如今已届耄耋之年,满目青山,夕霞天际,益感"老牛最解韶光贵,不待扬鞭自奋蹄"。

八、高山仰止
——写于陈安老师八十寿诞之际

单文华[*]

海上仙山

光阴似箭。初次接触陈安老师的场景如同昨日,却已经是十六年以前的事情了。这十六年里,虽然大多数时间有重洋阻隔,我与先生的联系却从未中断过。可以说,大洋之外,我知道先生之冷暖,先生也知道我的忧乐。

再过几天,就是先生的八十寿诞。厦大师友来信嘱我就当年师从先生求学之经历心得略写一二,以为纪念。我惊喜之余,颇觉惶恐。去国十余年,外文或有些许长进,国文功夫却日见荒疏。开口提笔,时感词不达意,深恐写坏了,写偏了。然时间所迫,义不容辞,且记三事(求学、在读、毕业)以为纪念。不确不妥之处,还请先生及诸师友惠正。

海上仙山

我求学先生之路,并不平坦。1991年初,我在暨南大学经济学院读研究生,导师是经济法系的系主任张增强教授。张老师特别强调国际经济法学的学习,并很推崇陈安老师的著作。当时同学院有一位会计学的硕士生学业优异,提前一年毕业考取了厦大会计学的博士,令在读硕士生同学们十分艳羡。我当时便想,能不能也效法一下,争取两年毕业,提前攻博。于是便尝试着与厦大研招办联系。研招办的老师(我记得是关筱燕主任)很热情,告诉我虽然正式的报考期限已过,但我如能得到陈安老师的同意,他们还可以接受我的报名。关老师并建议我最好能前往厦门拜访一下陈先生。于是,1993年5月1日,我登上了广州去厦门的海轮。这是我生平第一

---

[*] 单文华,厦门大学1996届国际经济法专业博士毕业生,毕业后曾留校任教。1998年赴英国剑桥大学留学,获法学博士学位。现任英国牛津布鲁克斯大学法学院国际法教授、西安交通大学法学院院长、"腾飞人才计划"特聘教授、博士生导师。

次坐轮船。在海鸥翔集、波涛汹涌之际,凭栏望远,想着很快就要登上厦门这座海上仙山,见到令人景仰的陈安老师,心情十分激动。

然而,我那次并没有见到陈老师。5月2日抵达厦门之后,我直接入住厦大的凌云招待所。或许是因为过于兴奋,一夜未眠,又或许是因为不习海风,我竟然感冒了。尽管如此,我一住下便给陈老师家打电话,告知我到了厦门,想去拜见他。谁知陈老师却并不让我去见他,只让我在下午3点钟时给他去电话详谈。3点整,我在凌云招待所楼下公用电话室里拨通了陈老师家的电话。电话那头传来了陈老师亲切中透着威严的声音。通话持续了一个多小时。陈老师不仅询问了我的经历、学习的课程,还问了许多专业上的问题,我都一一认真作答。当时厦门天气很热,我感冒在身,衣着甚厚,加之那次与先生通话十分紧张,打电话时浑身热汗直流。临了,先生说了一句:"你可以报考了。"我心中一块石头落了地,感冒好像也立时好了。事后得知,原来先生极不喜欢那些可能送"见面礼"的考生,故特设此严格的"预防措施",以杜绝此类陋习。接下来是紧张的复习、考试,所幸最后考上了——我终于成了厦门大学陈安教授的一名学生!

后来我才知道,陈老师的严格是出了名的。这种严格,在招生环节就表现得十分明显,比方说他主张"逢进必考",不喜欢招收保送生之类的免试生,更不喜欢与政府官员或大款、大腕们拉"关系""走后门",在博士入学方面开绿灯。我记得他后来还专门写了篇短文《"博士"新解》,讽刺这种种不正常的现象。

"板凳愿坐十年冷"

现在回想起来,厦大三年博士生期间,是我这辈子最快乐的时光之一。我们住在高高的凌云楼上(凌云三608),每天看着海阔天空、云卷云舒,时感壮怀激烈。几乎每天下午,楼上会有人吼一声"打球啰",我们便离巢出动,奔赴篮球场。打完球回来,有时球友们还会在芙蓉湖边小坐,谈天说地。大多数时间则直接奔回宿舍,很快冲凉房便响起此起彼伏的歌声。

生活而外,更大的收获是学业上的。陈老师平时给我们说得最多的一句话是"板凳愿坐十年冷",要求我们守得住清贫,耐得住寂寞,因为学术之路、博士之路注定是清贫而寂寞的。在具体的教学方法上,令我印象深刻的是,陈老师从不拘泥于那种刻板的上课模式,而是强调人才培养与科研项目的结合、言传与身教结合,做到出"人才"的同时出"成果"。这种方法很能发挥研究生的主动性与积极性,取得了很好的效果。记得我的第一门专业课叫作"国际经济法文献精读选择",课程主要是练习翻译一部关于多边投资担保机构(MIGA)的英文专著的若干章节。第一次翻译外文专业文献，感觉难度很大，初时几乎是寸步难行。译稿先经同学校勘，修改后再由陈老师批阅，多次反复修改后方能交卷。一开始我并不理解这种训练的意义，认为它有点费而不惠，因为翻译是天大难事，译出来的东西却又不算是原创性的成果，费时费力，却又成效不彰。直到我过后再次尝试去阅读和翻译其他英文著作，才发现其中妙处。这种训练贵在让你认真揣摩原文中每一句话的句法结构，对加强英文专业文献的阅读能力，提高阅读速度大有裨益。难怪先生对此十分看重，并告诉我们这也是北大王铁崖等国际法先生们最常用的学术训练方法之一。后来我在译稿的基础上作了进一步的研究、更新和修正，写成一篇文章，收入陈老师主编的一部专著。专著的出版令我深受鼓舞，我研读原始国际经济法文献的兴趣也由此大有增强。

这三年里令我同样记忆深刻的是我有幸给先生做了一些他自己文稿的校对工作。先生学贯中西，识见宏深，每有心得，往往写成一篇传世佳作；加之课题不断，著作等身，时有新著出版，或旧著更新。我作为他为数不多的弟子之一，时时往返于先生白城的家里与经济学院打印室之间，传送文稿，并对打印稿作初步校对。记得先生每次对文稿的质量都精益求精，几近苛刻。当时经济学院经常为我们打印文稿的是一位叫作"小翁"的姑娘，在打字员中当属极为细心和有耐心的一位。有一次她偷偷地跟我说，她其实"最怕"打先生的文稿，不仅因为过于专业、难以理解，所以打字较慢，更因为先生在每次校对稿上都会有许多处新的添加或修改，这些又都需要经过一而再再而三的校订。我后来意识到，这种校对工作其实是一种很好的学术训练，它使我不仅有机会接触一流的学问与作品，更重要的是知道这样的学问与作品是怎样做出来的。我体会到全面广泛的资料，深入的研析，创新的思维和精益求精、一丝不苟的治学态度，是所有好作品的不二法门。

另外，十分难得的是，先生虽然学高于世，对我们这些学生等所秉持的是一种完全平等的态度。例如，有时我会斗胆对他文中的个别字句作点修改，他不但不怪我冒犯威严，反而时时褒奖有加，称我为"一字之师"。这种大家风范至今令我感动。

后来，我有一次去威尔士旅游，在一家纪念品商店看到一张父亲节节日贺卡，上面写着："谢谢您，父亲。因为您不仅指明了星星的所在，还告诉我怎样去找到它们。"一日为师，终身为父。我常常想，陈老师就像我学业上的"严父"，不仅让我知道什么是大学问和大学问家，还让我体会到怎样才能成就大学问和大学问家。这些年来，我虽然谈不上取得了什么成就，但陈老师的这种种言传身教，却一直是鼓励我进取向上的一种强大的精神力量。

凤凰花开

凤凰花是厦大的校花,年开二度,一度迎新,一度送旧。迎新的花季洋溢着喜悦,但送旧的凤凰花却总让离校的厦大学子无限惆怅。

1996年7月,又是凤凰花开的时节,众生惜别依依之际,我也面临着生命中一次不大不小的抉择。当时我曾联系过去北大法学院做博士后,或去清华法学院做讲师。两个地方都已表示接受。同时,蒙先生抬爱,母校表示希望我能留校任教。一方是京畿法学重地,另一方是恩师与母校,这个选择不可谓不艰难。然而,我没多少犹豫便选择了后者,且始终不后悔自己的这一选择。根本原因,是出于对恩师与母校的一种深深感恩与无限眷恋。

许多人不理解先生早年执行的"博士生留校"政策,认为有"近亲繁殖"之嫌。对此,先生作了有力的反驳。我记得先生常常跟我说,厦大法学学科属于后发后进学科,研究人才严重缺乏,而每年招研究生的名额又极其有限,他如果不这么做,就形不成"生产力",产不出"产品"。厦大法学不仅不能发展繁衍,甚至会有"断子绝孙"的危险。事实证明,先生的做法是明智和卓有成效的。厦大国际法学科20世纪80年代建立博士点,90年代以来获得飞速发展,先后取得了博士后流动站和国家重点学科等重大突破,其中一个最重要的因素,便是先生当年下大力气打造的一支强有力的国际法学术梯队。现在,当我在思考如何在欠发达的西北地区建设一个后发的法学院时,我更能深刻体会到先生当年的苦衷。是一份对厦大国际法学事业的坚强信念与执着追求支撑了先生这些不寻常的举措,而正是这些不寻常的举措为厦大国际法学科近年来在全国脱颖而出,并在国际上崭露头角奠定了基础。

"高山仰止,景行行止。"每年5月的这个日子,都是我特别感怀的一个日子。而今年这个日子更有特别重要的意义。令我遗憾的是,由于与伦敦一个国际会议的时间相冲突,我将不能赶赴盛会,当面表达我的感念和祝福。但愿这篇小文能于此有所弥补。

谨此敬祝先生生日快乐,龙马精神!

谨祝母校事业蒸蒸日上,迭创辉煌!

九、五"严"源自一"爱"

李万强*

今天我们齐聚一堂共祝陈安老师八十华诞,并对中国国际经济法研究方法暨陈安老师的学术思想进行深入研讨。在此场合,由于时间所限,我无法描述陈老师在学生心目中的全貌,由于能力所限,我也不敢尝试综述陈老师的成就与影响。思之再三,还是摘取片段的印象和感受与大家分享。

陈老师为人很严,"严格""严厉""严谨""严肃",都可以用来形容陈老师,甚至不乏一点点"严酷"。与陈老师相处的日子里,他即使是卧病在床也不肯收受学生聊表心意的一点薄礼。对学生论文当中的一点文字差错他都会"上纲上线"加以批评。还有在我们博士生当中传闻颇广的陈老师的"魔鬼训练法",那时候我们常常觉得陈老师"不近人情"。

2001年由于一些个人的原因,我不顾学科建设的需要离开了厦大,在最初的一段时间里,即使是在逢年过节的时候,我也不敢和陈老师联系。然而,这些年来,陈老师通过各种方式为我提供非常难得的机会,在学术上给予我很大的支持,包括发表论文、参加学术会议等等。我渐渐体会到了陈老师"五严"的另一层意蕴。的确,这种对青年学生和同行在学术上与事业上的关心与提携,难道不是一种超越凡俗、至纯至真的大大人情?!

陈老师爱好独立思考和学术争鸣。一直以来,都会或耳闻或眼见他与国内外同行大家学术论辩的事例。他甚至放下"身段",平等地、认真地与年轻学者"交手过招"。几年前,他与一位年轻学者平等、认真的学术争鸣催生了他洋洋几万言的学术成果——系列论文,并且获得了国家人文社科最高奖。前几日,又看到陈老师发表在《现代法学》上的一篇论文,尽管在这篇文章当中没有指名道姓,但其笔锋所指一目了然。该文对学界当前对于WTO的盲目推崇进行了严肃的学术批评,足够令人或幡然醒悟,或由衷叹服。仔细想来,陈老师在学术上的"不依不饶"不正是对学术高度负责的体现,不正是对青年学者另一种真挚的关爱吗?

著作等身的陈老师、行事低调的陈老师、辩才出众的陈老师、文才横溢的陈老

---

* 李万强,厦门大学1999届国际经济法专业博士毕业生,毕业后曾留校任教。时任西北政法大学国际法学院院长、教授。

师、爱憎分明的陈老师、信念坚定的陈老师、倡导学术道德的陈老师、极具现实关怀的陈老师,在学生心中有一位说不尽的陈老师,陈老师不仅是引领中国国际经济法学界的学术旗帜,更是散发着无穷魅力的人生灯塔。

1996年,我刚来厦大读书的时候听到一个故事:厦大法学院有一位学生对陈老师无比崇拜,常常以朗读陈老师的文章为乐事;同时,每当别人提起陈老师的时候,如果他当时正躺着或坐着,一定会立即起身肃立以示敬仰。这个故事是真是假我没有考证。但是,我想,即使这个故事是杜撰的,那么杜撰在陈老师身上,又有谁会怀疑它的合理性呢?

祝陈老师健康长寿,学术青春永驻!

第七编
有关陈安学术活动的报道、函件等

第 1 章 媒 体 报 道

一、在哈佛的讲坛上
——访厦门大学政法学院副院长陈安[*]

陈福郎

哈佛，美国这所国际性的名牌大学，云集着来自全球各地的访问学者。哈佛一个豪华而又雅致的会议厅里，正在举行午餐会。一位中国法学学者正用流利的英语演讲。四十多位听众中，主要是美国、日本的教授和学者，还有西欧、澳洲、东南亚诸国以及我国台湾地区的留美研究生。他们来自地球的不同角落，对中国的对外开放和吸收外资政策，内心都隐伏着程度不同的疑虑以及形形色色的惶惑。

……由于中国政府近来对经济犯罪采取必要的打击措施，一些外国人就猜疑中国的风向正在变：似乎是天刚放晴不久又要下雨了。美国一家报纸的社论甚至推断说："中国现在正在返回到教条主义"。有些外国朋友担心中国现行的对外开放和吸收外资政策不久就会变，他们告诫其他人，向中国投资要谨慎小心，看看再说，免得遇上麻烦，甚至发生风险……

演讲者陈安，是厦门大学法律系的副教授。他于1981年底以访问学者身份，前来哈佛大学法学研究院，研究国际经济法。

今天演讲的题目是：《是进一步开放？还是重新关门？——评有关中国吸收外资政策法令的几种议论》。

当时是1982年秋，国内正开展打击经济领域重大犯罪的斗争。一些外国人对于这场斗争议论颇多，啧有烦言，间夹非难。我国的对外开放政策正受到一些人的误解和曲解。有的赞成重新关门，有的担心重新关门，有的希望继续开放。作为来自社会主

---

[*] 本篇报道原发表于《生活·创造》1985年第12期，第6—8页。作者陈福郎时任厦门大学出版社总编辑。

义中国的法学副教授,陈安的办公室经常有人来叩门,种种发问,把他搅得心神不宁。

祖国的对外开放政策正在坚定贯彻,方兴未艾,绝不能为外人所误解,甚至歪曲。陈安强烈的责任感油然而生,他想,是时候挺身而出,作一番公开的澄清、解答甚至驳斥了。他明白,以一个中国法学学者的身份,在这个国际学术讲坛上发言,论述涉及中国的法律问题,是外国法学家们所无法替代的。我们在国际论坛上必须占得自己应有的席位。

中国法学学者那潇洒的风度、雄辩的说理、精辟的阐析,紧紧地攫住了听众的心。

……对所有正派、诚实和守法的外商来说,打击行贿、受贿、索贿,打击走私活动,仅仅意味着:中国对他们打开了一扇更宽敞的大门,开辟了一条更平坦的道路。因为,横在正路和正门上的路障和垃圾被清除了,非法的"竞争"手段和勒索行径被禁止了……

这场将近两小时的专题学术演说,系统阐述了我国有关政策法令的历史根据、立法精神和条款内容。讲演以事实为根据,从法学理论上说明我国今后既要继续坚持对外开放政策,进一步积极吸收外资,保护合法外资、外商;又要继续严肃认真地打击同吸收与外资有关的一切经济犯罪行为,从而为建设中国特色社会主义服务。

午餐会上的气氛渐渐活跃起来。有的快速记录,有的会心微笑,有的频频颔首。

在听众中,有一位日本访美研究员、金融经济专家杉原启示,他所服务的日本国家石油公司系日本政府国营机构,已向中国投资参加中日合作开发渤海湾及鄂尔多斯地区石油。他原来疑团满腹,可现在脸上却露出愉悦的神情。演讲一结束,他就索要了一份英文讲演细纲。事后,他送来一封短简,并附一份日文摘译,说已将"先生日前发表的高见……迅速摘译要旨,并已速送日本国家石油公司参考"。

演讲结束了,大厅里响起热烈的掌声。这掌声,是属于中国的。这天恰是1982年10月1日,祖国人民正在欢度国庆,而陈安则在地球的另一面,通过自己的声音,让世界了解中国,一种欣慰之情涨满了他的心怀。有位台湾地区留美研究生挤到他身旁说:"佩服!佩服!外国人给你鼓掌,掌声这么响,作为中国人,我们也有份,觉得很体面!"在哈佛修习"中美商务法律问题"课程的许多研究生,因为有课未能参加,纷纷要求为他们补讲。他想,要调动国外各种积极因素,支持我国"四化"建设,就必须增进外国人对我国的了解和信任。重讲诚然辛苦,却是当仁不让。

在此之前,他还在哈佛课堂上,对近百名哈佛法学研究院研究生及旁听的外国访问学者,做过另一场演讲。那次演讲的题目是《是棒打鸳鸯吗?——就"李爽案件"评〈纽约时报〉报道兼答美国法学界同行问》。这篇英文演讲稿经整理,在纽约法学院《国际法与比较法学刊》杂志上发表。杂志主编艾姆林·希加(Emlyn H. Higa)

对此文的评价是:"您的文章提出了人们所殷切期待的答案","您对于美国和中国的刑事法制所作的比较分析,是特别有教益和富有启发性的"。

20世纪50年代之初,陈安毕业于厦大法律系,当过一段审判员,随后回校任教。1953年院系调整时,厦大法律系撤销了,他奉命转行,一晃就是27年。1980年厦大复办法律系,他才重新回到自己的本行。随着我国对外开放政策的实行,国际经济法这一新兴边缘学科中的许多崭新课题深深地吸引了他。他的英语学习已中断30年。为了探索新知,以应祖国"四化"急需,他日夜兼程,训练口语,并以"半百"之年参加出国考试。好心的朋友说:你已是副教授了,何必如此自苦!他说:职称只是探索新知的新鞭,不是故步自封的包袱。在哈佛,为了准备这两场演讲,陈安副教授付出了多少劳动!他面对的是美国听众,对美国的历史背景和社会制度、法令规章和类似的案例处断,不能不预先作一番认真的研究和查索,他没日没夜地查找和研究资料,眼窝更加深陷,身形愈益瘦削,但是他换来的是祖国的荣誉,他感到生活的充实。陈安副教授在哈佛的20个月中,还写成了学术论文《论美国对海外美资的法律保护》,全文5万余字,寄回国内。这篇论文对于今后我国吸收外资的谈判、签约以及研究涉外投资纠纷案件的处断有重要的现实意义。有关出版社已建议扩大篇幅,作为专著出版。他还为瑞士日内瓦国际研究所教授哈里什·卡普尔(Harish Kapur)选编的一本书《中国闭关自守的终结》(*The End of Isolation*)撰写专章,论述中国吸收外资的基本政策和法律体制。此书即将在海牙问世,发行欧美。

去年,他参加了由教育部和司法部联合选派的"中国国际法教育考察团"。在近两个月的时间里,这个三人代表团历访了西欧、北美五个国家三十多个学术单位。回国后,同事们问他有什么新的收获和体会,他说:"国际法学新知,可谓琳琅满目。但愿常如干海绵,涓涓滴滴,能吸即吸,俾为我国所用。我赞成这样的'螺旋式'循环:学而后知不足,知不足而后学。"

二、他把法的目光投向世界与未来
——访厦门大学法律系陈安教授*

甘景山

开拓法律科学新领域

"铛,铛,铛……"清晨,厦门大学校园的钟声响了。我走进海滨新村六楼402号

---
* 本篇报道原发表于《福建司法》1988年第5期。作者甘景山当时是《福建日报》资深记者。

房间,这是法律系陈安教授的家。房间里到处都是书,他在书的海洋里生活。

窗外的大海在强烈的阳光照耀下,闪射着刺眼的光芒。我提出看看有关资料,他抱来两三包他撰写的著作、论文。

我打开纸包,一本又一本翻过。当我翻到一本封面为天蓝底色衬着白色世界地图图案的《国际经济立法的历史和现状》时,立即被吸引住了。这是由陈教授编译、法律出版社出版的国际经济法新书。

国际经济法是法学中新兴的学科,是边缘性学科,是国际法学科中一个新的重要分支,国内外学者还在探索中。我问陈教授:

"您怎么会想起去开辟这个新领域呢?灵感从何而来?"

"说来话长。'国际经济法'这个名词,是美国的一个法学专家洛文费尔德1976年才提出的。1979年,武汉大学七十多岁的法学老教授姚梅镇也开始了研究。"

"那您是哪年开始的?"

"也是79年。"

"您的步子真快。"

"研究国际经济法是形势的需要。现在,旧的世界经济秩序开始打破,新的经济秩序开始建立,国际经济交往日益频繁,打国际官司也在增加,为了在签订协议、合同,违约索赔,以及处理投资、贸易、关税、金融等法律纠纷时,不受外商愚弄或欺骗,为保护国家权益不受损失,一定要加强国际经济法的研究。今后,需要大量通晓国际经济法的专业人才。"

我听了以后明白了,他想的是世界,是祖国的未来。厦大法律系1981年就开始招收国际经济法研究生,到现在这个学科的研究生已有几十名,其中已毕业的几名在答辩中名列前茅,写出了高质量的学术论文。

在全国国际经济法学科中,厦大法律系已遥遥领先。经国家教委批准,厦大法律系率先正式设置国际经济法专业,从1985年开始每年招收一个本科生班。

为了创立国际经济法新的法学科学领域,陈教授呕心沥血;现在,为了发展和服务于这个领域,更是废寝忘食,四处奔忙。他除了自己搞科研、讲授"国际经济法概论"等数门课程外,还有许许多多的社会活动和行政工作,请看他的累累头衔:厦门大学政法学院院长、厦大法律系国际经济法教研室主任、中国国际经济法研究会副会长、中国经济法研究会理事、全国高等教育自学考试委员会委员、厦门经济特区法律顾问、福建省华侨律师事务所法律顾问、福建省保险公司法律顾问、美国国际法学会会员、福建省人大常委,等等。这些头衔,是社会对他的评价。在短短的数年里,他脱颖而出,走向全国,走向世界。

1982年10月1日，他在美国做了题为《是进一步开放？还是重新关门？——评有关中国吸收外资政策法令的几种议论》的讲演，阐述了我国有关政策法令的历史根据、立法精神，解释我国参加签订的保护外国投资的国际协定；从法理上说明我国今后既要继续坚持对外开放，进一步积极吸收外资，保护合法外资和守法外商，又要继续严厉地打击一切经济犯罪行为，从而消除了外国友人的顾虑和驳斥了个别人的攻击。不久，此篇论文被收进了海牙马尔丁出版社出版的《中国闭关自守的终结》一书。

此外，他还在《中国国际法年刊》上撰文，让世界人民了解中国的法律。

当铺路的石子

我翻阅着陈教授案头上的《访美小结》，其中有一段语重心长的话："建议今后在国内加紧培养年轻的专业人员（他在'年轻的'下面打了三个着重号），从中择优送往国外深造。"

在另一份考察欧美的报告里疾呼："关于国际法专业人才的培养，感到数量少、质量低，与西方国家相比，与十亿人口泱泱大国举足轻重的国际地位相比，差距极大，培养这方面的人才是当务之急，急中之急！"

这时，陆续来了几位国际经济法专业的研究生，有的拿论文给陈教授修改，有的打报告要陈教授批准出外调查等等。陈教授指了指其中一位戴眼镜的瘦个子说："我们要给年轻人压担子，他刚刚毕业，因为他学得好，系里已经研究确定，国际经济法教研室准备让他负责。我们这些老头子已经不行了，因此要把希望寄托在年轻人身上。我还不够格当人梯，可是我可以当铺路的石子，尽快填补人才断层。"

他无私的心深深地感动了我。

为了提高教学质量，加速培养高质量的法学人才，陈教授提倡加强国际交流，力避"近亲繁衍"，见闻受囿，他提倡"拿来主义"，吸收外国的好经验，教学、科研要不断创新。他根据美国哈佛大学的教学经验，逐步纠正"纯理论"的偏向，引导学生研究分析典型案例，活跃课堂对话。厦大法律系还组织学生办刊物，刊名是《法学与现代化》。他把这种学生办的刊物称作"拔尖人才的摇篮"。

陈教授还告诉我，厦大法律系招收国际经济法本科生，采取高分定向招生法，即向开放城市和特区定向招生，吸引那里的优秀生报考厦大法律系。在学期间，到香港、特区实习，同外商、港商打交道，"真刀真枪"打官司。对于优秀生，将分期分批送往国外深造。

我在陈教授的一本书里看到一张收据，原来是陈教授在出国期间将节省下来的两千多美元都买了法律书籍,分别赠送给学校图书馆和法律系资料室,为师生提供研究资料。我还看到一份报告,是陈教授联系了外国的几个图书馆赠送给厦大大批法律书籍,要求上级解决运输问题的。总之,他一切想着法律系,想着学生,想着人才,想着"四化"建设。最后,我问陈教授有什么打算,他谦虚地说:"我也是刚刚起步,盛名之下,其实难副,主要靠大家……"

当采访将要结束的时候,我望着窗外的大海,不免心潮起伏。我想,还是引用陈安教授写的"小结"末段来结束本文:"今后,我定将更加谦虚谨慎,继续努力,为社会主义法学繁荣和祖国四化事业尽绵薄之力。"

三、适应对外开放和发展外向型经济需要,国际经济法系列专著问世

林鸿禧　陈有仁

本报讯　由厦门大学政法学院院长陈安教授主编的我国第一套国际经济法系列专著《国际投资法》《国际贸易法》《国际货币金融法》《国际税法》《国际海事法》已由鹭江出版社出版。这是我国涉外经济法律的重要学术论著。它为我国高等院校提供了涉外经济法律的新教材。

陈安教授早年毕业于厦门大学法律系和复旦大学政治学研究生班,1981—1983

---

* 本篇报道原载于《光明日报》1988年4月26日。作者林鸿禧当时是厦门大学校长办公室主任、《光明日报》通讯记者,陈友仁当时是《光明日报》资深记者。在此之前,中国新闻出版总署主办的《新闻出版报》1988年1月9日在《人以少胜多,书以优取胜》一文中率先报道了鹭江出版社推出陈安教授一系列专著的信息,并作了评论,指出:该社"出版了《美国对海外投资的法律保护及典型案例分析》及其姊妹篇《舌剑唇枪——国际投资纠纷五大著名案例》,在学术界和社会上引起很大反响。法学界权威韩德培教授赞曰:'以中国人眼光来谈美国对海外投资的法律问题,确可谓独具新意。'已故北大教授陈体强生前称赞该书:'内容丰富,系统完整,洵是佳作。'最后,鹭江出版社又出版了一套国际经济法的系列专著,即《国际金融法》《国际贸易法》《国际海事法》《国际投资法》,为创立具有中国特色的国际经济法学科体系开了先河。这套专著被国家教委拟作推荐教材,并获得了厦门大学颁发的'南强奖'。"接着,《中国青年报》1988年5月11日在"法制与社会"专栏的一则短讯中向全国读者推荐说:"这套系列专著在论述取材上,力求其新,许多资料直接来源于近年的国外最新出版物。在吸收国外有关研究成果和介绍有关基本理论的基础上,力求从中国的实践出发,从中国人的角度和第三世界的立场来研究和评析当代的国际经济法,同时,每一分册都用相当篇幅结合论述我国在相应领域中的涉外法律规范,注意及时反映我国涉外经济立法的最新进展和总结有关的实践经验。"随后,上述报道引起了《人民日报》(海外版)记者张安南和陈树荣的注意,并继推在该报1988年10月26日和1991年12月31日的两篇专访中一再地向读者推荐陈安教授撰写和主编的上述一系列专著。前一篇专访仍题为《人以少胜多,书以优取胜》,指出:"《美国对海外投资的法律保护及典型案例分析》和《舌剑唇枪——国际投资纠纷五大著名案例》姐妹篇,还有包括《国际投资法》《国际贸易法》《国际货币金融法》《国际税法》《国际海事法》五册一套的国际经济法系列专著,是国家教育委员会博士点专项基金选定科学研究项目的初步成果。鹭江出版这套系列专著,为创立具有中国特色的国际经济法学科体系开了先河。而且,在短时间内集中出版同一研究领域的多部学术专著,这在地方出版社中也是罕见的。"后一篇专访为《厦门大学发挥师资的优势,为特区建设积极培养人才》,其中指出:"上述系列专著是我国第一套涉外经济法律的最新专著,对我国发展外向型经济具有理论研究和实用价值。"

年应邀在美国哈佛大学从事国际经济法研究。

这套155万字的涉外经济法律学术专著收集了当今世界主要国家有关经济立法的最新资料,并在引进新鲜知识的基础上,结合我国涉外经济交往的实际,对改造国际经济旧秩序、建立国际经济新秩序所面临的各种法律问题进行分析论证,观点新颖,条理分明。目前已有多所大学的法律系准备将这套书作为教材。

四、为对外开放铺路
——记厦门大学法学教授陈安*

杨亚南

"陈安教授:感谢你赠送的五本巨作。当前全省上下议外向、想外向、干外向的形势下,外向知识何等重要又何等贫乏。这五本书可算及时雨,大大有助于人们提高外向型知识,推动沿海开放事业发展……"

福建省副省长游德馨在这封亲笔谢函中提到的五本书是:《国际投资法》《国际贸易法》《国际货币金融法》《国际税法》《国际海事法》。这五本由厦门大学法学教授陈安主编的书,是我国第一套国际经济法系列专著。

陈安1950年毕业于厦大法律系。3年后,中断法学生涯,开始了长达27年的马克思主义政治理论、历史等方面的研究与教学。1980年,半百之年的他重返法学领域。

在应冲刺的年龄才起跑,他带着闽北山区人的执拗与狠劲,硬是在法学界占了一席之地。重返法学界6年之后,他成为国务院学位委员会评定的国际经济法专业全国最年轻的博士生导师。他现在是厦大法学院院长、国际法比较学会国际委员会委员、中国国际经济法研究会副会长、中国国际法学会理事、中国经济法研究会理事、全国高等教育自学考试指导委员会法律专业委员、中国国际经济贸易仲裁委员会仲裁员。

陈安于改革开放之始重返法学界,他的学术生命从此与改革开放紧密相连。

"……由于中国政府近来对经济犯罪采取必要的打击措施,一些外国人就猜疑中国的风向正在变:似乎是天刚放晴不久又要下雨了。"1982年秋,陈安以高级访问

---

* 本篇报道原载于《人民日报》(海外版)1992年7月7日。作者是当时国家教委干部、《人民日报》(海外版)专栏撰稿人。

学者的身份站在哈佛大学的讲坛上,面对美、日等国的学者及西欧、澳洲的研究生慷慨陈词:"对所有正派、诚实和守法的外商来说,打击行贿、受贿,打击走私活动,仅仅意味着中国对他们打开了一扇更宽敞的大门,开辟了一条更平坦的道路。因为,横在正路和正门上的路障和垃圾被清除了……"演讲后的热烈掌声证明,陈安为中国的开放事业又赢得了一些国际上的信任和理解。

1991年,美国俄勒冈州路易斯与克拉克西北法学院《律师》杂志上刊载了一篇论文《是重新闭关自守?还是扩大对外开放?》。论文原是陈安教授的演讲稿。演讲后他收到了中国驻美领事馆官员的来信:"很欣赏你的智慧、才干和勇气。此举很有意义。由此,使我联想到,如果我们的学者和学生中能有一批像你这样的民间大使,对反驳美政坛对我国的非难,以及消除一些美国友人的疑虑和误解,无疑将起到非同一般的影响和作用……"

这些年,陈安教授时刻注视着中国开放实践中的法律问题,写出了一篇篇论文,为开放事业提供了有效的法律武器。

"法律领域是40年来最枯萎的一朵花,而对外经贸中的法律则更是萎缩……"陈安教授对我国法学研究的现状充满焦虑。"应当建立具有中国特色、体现第三世界共同立场的国际经济法学科体系和理论体系",这不仅成为他的主要学术主张之一,也成为他的奋斗目标。

他指出,在许多发达国家中,已经出版了有关国际经济法的大量著作,相继建立了相应的学科体系和理论体系。其基本特色之一,是立足于本国的实际,以本国利益为核心,重点研究本国对外经济交往中产生的法律问题,作出符合其本国立场和本国权益的全面分析和系统论证。反观发展中国家,由于历史的和现实的原因,尚未形成比较成熟的、能够充分反映第三世界共同立场的国际经济法学科体系和理论体系。因此,应当在积极研究当代国际经济法新知识、新成果的基础上,从第三世界的共同立场出发,逐步创立起具有中国特色的、维护第三世界众多弱小民族利益的国际经济法学科体系和理论体系,借以加速国际经济法律秩序新旧更替的进程。

"对于中国法学界来说,这是责无旁贷的历史职责!"陈安教授10年来出版了十余部系列专著。为了博采他山之石,10年来,他11次出国,足迹遍布五大洲十多个国家。新思想、新成果,每次他都满载而归。去年他回国时,自费运回三十余箱共788本书,全部捐给了学校,价值近十万元。

国际经济法是厦门大学的重点专业,作为学科带头人,陈安教授和他的同事及学生们日夜兼程。他的胃切除了2/3,他却乐观地说:我要干到80岁。目前,他有一个强烈的愿望,就是他们的国际经济法专业争取早日进入全国重点学科的行列,以求得对外交流、科研经费等方面更大的支持。"一个学科体系的建立需要几代人的不懈努力",他说,"我愿意做铺路石。"

五、就闽台两省结拜"姊妹"一事,厦门大学法学教授发表看法[*]

记者 张 莉

中新社福州电 据台湾《经济日报》报道:我国台湾地区"立委"沈世雄于4月16日提出一项书面质询,呼吁台湾地区"行政院"在"海峡两岸人民关系法"(即"台湾地区与大陆地区人民关系暂行条例",下同)尚未制定实施以前,先行与福建省结为"姊妹省",签订"自由贸易协定"。此事引起福建各界关注。

为此,记者走访了厦门大学法学教授、福建省人大常委会委员陈安。

记者:台湾地区的沈先生建议闽台两省结为"姊妹省",您有何看法?

陈:据考证,台湾省居民70%以上祖籍为福建,台湾地区政要李登辉等人的先辈都是福建人,闽南话至今仍是通行台湾的主要方言。因此,闽台两省间的兄弟姊妹关系无须"结拜",早就是"天生"形成的了。

记者:您对关于闽台两省签订"自由贸易协定"的动议持何评价?

陈:"自由贸易协定"主要内容为货物、人力、资金的自由流通以及税捐平等互惠等四方面。其基本着眼点是从切实保障台商合法权益出发,要求率先在闽台间建立平等互利的经济关系。这个建议具有前瞻性和开拓性,有利于促进两岸经济共同繁荣,符合孙中山先生提倡的"人尽其才、地尽其利、物尽其用、货畅其流"精神,体现了"孙文学说"中的一项基本原则,即行事应当"适于世界之潮流","合乎人群之需要"。

记者:闽台两省间的"自由贸易协定"在法律上属什么性质?

陈:中国只有一个。福建和台湾两个省级地方立法机构都有依照法定程序制定本省地方法规的立法权。闽台签订"自由贸易协定",实质是两省地方立法机构共同立法,即适用于两省全部地区的单行性地方经济法规。这种省际地方立法一旦正式生效,就成为用以调整两省经济交往和贸易投资活动的行为规范和行动守则,对于两省的有关经贸活动都具有法律上的约束力。

记者:从报端消息看,沈先生建议的两省"自由贸易协定"的签订和实施,是在"海峡两岸人民关系法"正式制定和实施之前。若上述协定签订之后,"关系法"亦出

---

[*] 本篇报道原载于《人民日报》(海外版)1989年5月8日。

台,两者之间如何协调一致？

陈：这就看台湾当局的决心和"立委"们的立法技巧了。若台湾地方当局不同意扩大推行,则不妨仍保留上述两省协定,作为与"关系法"这一普通法并存的特别法。

六、理性务实的学术交流盛会
——1993年两岸法学学术研讨会综述*

记者 姚小敏

海峡两岸法学专家、学者日前聚首北京,交流学术,探讨两岸交往、交流中衍生的有关法律问题。此次研讨会荟萃了海峡两岸一百六十余位颇具名望的法学教授、律师,规模之大,前所未有,可说是两岸关系发展中的一件盛事。

两岸法学学术交流始于1988年,当时仅是单向的,只有我国台湾地区学者来大陆。到去年11月,大陆11位法学家应台湾东吴大学之邀,首次赴台参加两岸法学学术研讨会,迈出了两岸法学双向交流的第一步。

此次研讨会是上次会议的继续和发展。在这次会议上,两岸学者针对近年来两岸交往中出现的一些法律问题展开务实而理性的探讨,提出了一些富有建设性的建议。

保障台商权益大陆有法规

台商投资大陆,近年来可谓高潮迭起。到今年4月底,台商在大陆投资达1万多项,累计协议金额逾90亿美元。由此,台商权益的保障问题,成为两岸经贸关系中的一个"焦点",亦成为此次研讨会的议题之一。

台湾当局1987年11月开放民众赴大陆探亲。在此之后半年多,我国及时制定并颁布了《国务院关于鼓励台湾同胞投资的规定》,即"二十二条",迄今施行5年有余,绩效显著。但台湾地区某些人士认为,此项法规不过是行政规定,"很容易说变就变","不足以保障台商的权益",因而希望将"以行政命令方式"保障台商权益的"二十二条""提升至双方签署协议的位阶"。

对此,厦门大学法学教授陈安、讲师彭莉指出,中国的成文法按其地位的高低依次分为宪法、法律、行政法规和地方法规。根据现行《宪法》,"行政法规"是指最高国

---

* 本篇报道原载于《人民日报》(海外版)1993年8月27日。

家行政机关国务院制定的一种规范性文件,它是成文法的重要渊源之一,是具有普遍约束力和相当稳定性的行为规范和行动准则,并非某些台湾人士所想象的,是什么"说变就变"的行政命令。

至于两岸签署有关保障台商权益的协议需要何种条件或说障碍何在?陈安、彭莉认为,一个重要的障碍在于,台湾当局至今依然坚持"间接、单向"的交流原则,不准台商直接以自身的名义赴大陆直接投资。因此,现有在大陆投资的一般台商从法律"身份"上来说都是"外商"或"港商"。这种"名实不尽一致"的微妙身份,使得一般台商在实践中不但可以享受"二十二条"的优待,而且可以获得大陆有关外商投资的一系列法律、法规的全面保护;此外,还可以获得大陆和该台商投资经由的第三地区所属国家签署的投资保护协定的保护。可见,在台湾地区现行的大陆经贸政策下,两岸签署共同保障台商权益的法律文件并没有名正言顺的适用对象,也不具有实质性的意义。他们认为,解开这一症结的途径显然在于:台湾当局尽早抛弃"国统纲领"中所设的人为局限,实现两岸经贸的"直接、双向"交流。

保护知识产权需两岸努力

近年来,海峡两岸人民知识产权时有受到对方单位和个人侵犯的现象发生。因此,保护知识产权的问题日渐引起人们的关注。

研讨会上,两岸学者均肯定两岸在知识产权制度的建立和改进方面所作的努力。

台湾学者刘绍梁认为,大陆这几年来有关知识产权体制的发展可说是突飞猛进,相当值得台湾学界深思、学习。但他也指出,两岸知识产权的发展似乎都在急速地建立制度,以因应经济发展的需求,然而在执行方面,或许都还不算完备。

大陆学者种明钊、李昌麒比较了两岸专利法律制度的异同后认为,两岸专利法律制度各有特色,就台湾地区专利制度而言,规定得比较详尽具体,更早地接近了国际保护标准。大陆地区的专利法律虽然起步较晚,但起点较高,立法技术比较先进,特别是修改后的《专利法》,正如国外所评论的,是"一部在各方面堪称典范的专利法"。种、李二位先生指出,无论从立法技术和立法内容上讲,还是从进一步完善两岸专利法律制度来讲,两岸彼此都有互相借鉴之处。

这两位学者认为,现在摆在两岸法学家面前的一个重要任务,就是要进一步研究扩大两岸经济技术交流和合作的法律问题,其中包括建立两岸技术专利信息系统以及互相提供专利保护等问题,以使两岸的经济技术合作得到进一步发展。

两岸律师携手合作此其时

随着两岸人民交往的增进,引发和衍生了许多法律问题,其中不少问题两岸互涉性强,因之,两岸律师的协作日益突出和重要。

台湾学者李念祖分析比较了两岸不同法律制度下的律师从事业务合作的诸种方式,认为目前两岸律师以个案合作方式较具可能性,即相互介绍办案、委托办案或共同办案。

大陆学者张斌生在研究两岸律师具体合作方式时,所得结论与台湾学者大体相同。张斌生设想的协作方式有:互相提供咨询意见、相互介绍业务、相互委托、转委托业务、共同协办案件或法律事务、签订业务合作协议、成立联名的两岸法律服务机构等等。

张斌生认为,在目前两岸关系现状下,以律师的渠道办理两岸互涉的有关法律事务,不仅可以增进双方当事人的信赖程度,而且可解决目前官方渠道所暂时无法通融的问题。

综观此次研讨会,自始至终充盈着一种理性、务实的学术气氛。研讨会的时间虽短,但成果颇丰。两岸学者在讨论中所提出的一些富有建设性的意见将可供有关方面参考。这对于进一步加强两岸法学交流,促进两岸关系发展大有裨益。

七、春风吹拂紫梅 白鹭振翅腾飞
—— 陈安教授谈厦门获得立法权[*]

记者 翁黛晖 黄文启

八届全国人大二次会议通过了授予厦门立法权的决定。当前,我市首先要做的是什么呢?中国国际经济法学会会长、厦门市人民政府法律顾问陈安教授在接受记者采访时强调:厦门目前最急需做的,应是"为贯彻自由港某些政策立法",使人们谈论已久的"自由港某些政策"具体化、明朗化、规章化和法规化,从而依法治市,依法治港。

陈安教授说,中央授予立法权,这当然是厦门市的一大殊荣,但这也意味着厦门要担当起更大的责任。中央允许厦门实施自由港某些政策,这在全国是"仅此一

---

[*] 本篇报道原发表于《厦门日报》1994年3月27日。

家"。厦门应当沿着中央指示的这个大方向,"敢为天下先",充分发挥最新开辟的"立法试验区"的作用,"胆大心细"地为贯彻自由港某些政策进行立法,加大改革开放力度,为建设现代化港口城市提供法律依据、法律保证和法律规范,要担当起既为改革开放服务,又为全国探索新路子的双重任务。

中央说的"自由港某些政策",其中的"某些"两字,据陈安教授理解,就是要求我们根据中国的国情和本市的市情,对世界各地的自由港政策,有所抉择,有所取舍,既要博采众长,又忌盲目照搬。给了立法权,我们就要去研究,去探索,摸着石头过河,立足于国情、市情,参照世界各地自由港的有关法规和章程,取其精华,弃其糟粕,制定出具有中国特色的自由港法规和规章。在立法中,既要遵循我国宪法和其他基本法律原则,又要体现出"中国式自由港"的某些特色,具有较大的前瞻性和开拓性,在厦门地区率先试行。按照法律上的说辞,"特别法优先于普通法",在厦门特区内实行某些特别法,将更有助于特区经济建设的长足发展。实行自由港的某些政策,就应当认真考虑在国际经贸往来、商品流通、金融流通、资金流转、人才流通、人员进出境和旅游方便等方面,通过法规和规章的保证,具有更大的"自由"度和规范性。

党的十四大明确提出建立社会主义市场经济体制的改革目标,全方位对外开放。陈教授认为,建设社会主义市场经济,需要有一系列相应的体制改革、政策更新、法律调整与完善,才能在更大的广度与深度上参与和拓展国际经贸往来,充分利用国际市场经济所提供的各种资源和机遇,更卓有成效地促进我国社会主义经济建设。这就要求我们在对外经贸交往实践及其行为规范方面更多、更好、更快地与国际经贸惯例接轨。因此,应当"适时修改和废止与建立社会主义市场经济体制不相适应的法律和法规,加强党对立法工作的领导,完善立法体制,改进立法程序,加快立法步伐,为社会主义市场经济提供法律规范"。陈安教授熟练地引用了党的十四届三中全会决定中的这段话。

陈安教授是厦门大学政法学院院长,著名的国际经济法教授。由于他有很深的学术造诣,他已被列入英、美等五种版本的国际名人录。据说,他的讲座总是座无虚席,甚至其他专业的师生也常被吸引。在接受记者采访时,他就显示了其深厚的知识功底和灼见。在谈到"与国际惯例接轨"这一问题时,陈安教授特别强调了"适用国际惯例与有法必依"的辩证关系,他说,厦门特区对外开放以来,"按国际惯例办事"和"与国际惯例接轨"的观念,日益为人们所接受。它开阔了人们的视野,更新了人们的观念,使人们勇于和善于吸收外国的先进经验和有效的举措。但是,在参照和吸收适合我国需要的国际惯例,进一步改善、完善我国涉外经济法律体系过程中,对于法定的立法程序,务必严格遵守,做到依法"变法",依法"改法"或依法立法。有法必依,决不能以言代法或乱闯法律禁区。

随后,陈安教授对"适用国际惯例"与"有法必依"作了如下阐述:中国具有独特的综合性国情,它既是发展中国家,又是社会主义国家,既是全球人口最多的国家,又是当前全世界经济发展最快的国家之一。面对形形色色的国际惯例,在深入研究和认真鉴别的基础上,只要它确实有利于促进中国社会主义市场体制的建立,就应当大胆地"拿来"。拿来之前要鉴别,拿来之后要消化。原则是:立足国情,以我为主;博采众长,为我所用,趋利避害,取精华而弃糟粕。某些在西方国家盛行的国际惯例,如出版发行淫秽书刊和视听作品、卖淫嫖娼、开设赌场等,在当地是合法的,在我国则是违法或犯罪的行为。因为它们毒化社会风气,败坏公序良俗,危害民族健康,刺激作奸犯科。对于此类国际惯例,自应依据我们的现行法律,予以抵制和排斥。对于那些以"适用国际惯例"为借口,为谋私利或逞私欲"以身试法"的当事人,则应予以制裁和惩罚,这就是"有法必依"的体现。

陈安教授还强调:厦门在争取特区立法权方面虽然曾经失去了一点时机,但是,"后来者居上",事在人为。在春风吹拂之下,三角梅(厦门市市花)定将绽放得更加姹紫嫣红,白鹭(厦门市市鸟)也势必凭借这股风力,扶摇直上,飞向新的、更新的高度。

八、第十二届"安子介国际贸易研究奖"颁奖大会圆满结束[*](摘要)

记者 蓉 一

【对外经济贸易大学】宣传部讯 注重学术含量与社会价值的"安子介国际贸易研究奖"(以下简称"安奖")第十二届颁奖大会,12月16日在诚信楼三层国际会议厅隆重举行。本届有7部著作、12篇论文分获优秀著作、优秀论文奖,17人获学术鼓励奖。

商务部副部长廖晓淇、外贸司司长鲁建华,教育部社政司副司长袁振国、北京大学校长助理海闻,我校校长、"安奖"评委会主任陈准民教授出席大会。校办主任刘园主持大会。

第十二届"安奖"共收到参评著作28部、参评论文67篇,共有33名学生参评学

---

[*] 本篇报道原发表于对外经济贸易大学网站(http://www.uibe.edu.cn/),2004年12月18日。

术鼓励奖。经过严格评选,7部著作获优秀著作奖,其中一等奖空缺,二等奖2部,三等奖5部;12篇论文获优秀论文奖,其中一等奖1篇,二等奖3篇,三等奖8篇;17人获学术鼓励奖。

陈准民校长在致辞中特别强调,"安奖"作为我国经贸研究领域的最高学术奖,在国内外享有很高声誉。为继续提高"安奖"评选的科学性、公平性和严肃性,本届评委会对"安奖"评奖的指标体系作了系统调整和完善,注重从选题、内容、创新和成果等方面综合评价研究成果,从而进一步优化评奖机制。本届"安奖"评选继续遵循公正、公开、回避、择优的原则,确保了"安奖"评选结果的学术性和权威性。

据悉,本届获奖作品的特点是,选题范围广泛,涉及大经贸领域的许多重大前沿问题、热点和难点问题;内容新颖,创新程度较高,作品的学术性和社会价值十分突出。厦门大学陈安教授撰写的论文"The Three Big Rounds of U.S Unilateralism Versus WTO Multilateralism During the Last Decade",以其高度的理论与实践意义获得优秀论文一等奖。

颁奖在十分热烈的气氛中进行。"安奖"评委王林生教授宣读本届"安奖"获奖名单,廖副部长、鲁司长、袁副司长、陈校长先后为获奖者颁奖。

九、第十二届"安子介国际贸易研究奖"颁奖*

记者 刘 菲

本报讯 近日,第十二届"安子介国际贸易研究奖"颁奖大会暨学术报告会在对外经济贸易大学举行。"安子介国际贸易研究奖"是由已故全国政协副主席,香港著名实业家、社会活动家、学者,对外经济贸易大学名誉教授安子介先生于1991年出资设立的,该奖自1992年第一届评选以来,已成功举办了十二届。

经多年努力,"安子介国际贸易研究奖"已有了较高的学术含量,在国际经贸研究领域声誉卓著,被视为中国经贸领域中的最高学术奖。

本届"安子介国际贸易研究奖"共收到参评著作28部、参评论文67篇,另有33名学生参评学术鼓励奖。其中评出优秀著作奖7部,优秀论文奖12篇,学术鼓励奖17人。本届参评作品和获奖成果的质量较以往明显提高。获奖作品的共同特点是选题与时俱进,涉及经贸领域的许多前沿问题、重大问题、热点问题和难点问题,内

---

* 本篇报道原发表于《人民日报》(海外版)2004年12月21日。

容新颖,创新程度较高,成果的学术价值含量和社会价值突出。获得本届优秀论文一等奖的厦门大学陈安教授的论文《晚近十年来美国单边主义与WTO多边主义交锋的三大回合》,被总部设在日内瓦的发展中国家政府间组织"南方中心"列为出版物之一,并在该机构网站上全文公布。

十、中国特色国际经济法学的探索者和开拓者
——陈安教授*

记者 陈 浪

厦门大学最高荣誉奖项"南强奖"每两年评选一次。2008年"南强奖"特等奖获得者陈安是法学院教授、国际经济法专业博士生导师。1929年5月出生,1950年从厦门大学法律系毕业,1951年初应聘返回厦大工作,57年来,陈安坚持"以知识报国,为厦大增光"的理念,为厦大的法学教育辛勤耕耘,特别是近30年来,始终立足中国国情,致力于对国际经济法这一新兴边缘学科进行探索和开拓,为我国的国际经济法学科做出了影响深远的贡献。

在教学方面,陈安牵头组织撰写并及时修订国际经济法各版教科书,被全国高校广泛采用,据此开设的我校"国际经济法学"课程入选为"本科国家级精品课程";创办《国际经济法学刊》并长期担任主编,成绩显著,使该刊成为全国性专业同行交流和争鸣的重要学术平台,并于2006年入选为"中国社会科学引文索引"(CSSCI)学术数据来源集刊。陈安还参与创建"中国国际经济法学会"并长期担任会长,成绩显著。2006年7月,该学会获得民政部登记发给社团法人证书,成为全国性一级学术社团,法人住所设在厦门大学。迄今,陈安连续主持召开了该学会1993—2007每年年会。

在科研方面,陈安著作等身,撰写和主编的主要著作有:《中国大百科全书——法学卷(修订版)》中"国际经济法"分支学科词条、《国际经济法学(第1—4版)》《国际经济法总论》《国际经济法学新论》《国际经济法学专论(第1—2版)》(教育部主管司推荐的研究生教材)、"国际经济法系列专著"(含《国际贸易法》《国际投资法》《国际货币金融法》《国际税法》《国际海事法》全套五卷)、《美国对海外投资的法律保护及典型案例分析》《"解决投资争端国际中心"述评》《国际投资争端仲裁:ICSID机制研

---

* 本篇报道发表于《厦门大学报》2008年5月3日第1版。记者陈浪根据相关材料整理。

究》《MIGA 与中国：多边投资担保机构述评》《国际投资法的新发展与中国双边投资条约的新实践》等等。陈安教授经常自谦：这些论著都是他所牵头带动和积极参与的学术团队多年来通力协作，集体攻关，与时俱进所取得的成果。

2007 年 10 月，陈安根据自己 30 年来研究国际经济法这一新兴边缘学科取得的主要成果独立撰写的《国际经济法学刍言》（北京大学出版社出版，分上、下卷，212 万字）获第五届"吴玉章人文社会科学奖"一等奖。该奖面向全国，每五年评奖一次，是全国性高档次文科奖项之一，自该奖项设立 20 年来，厦大教授首次获得该奖项一等奖。专家评议认为，本书是创建中国特色国际经济法学这一新兴边缘学科理论体系的奠基之作，是第三世界国家争取国际经济平权地位的理论武器。

除了专著，近两年来，陈安的论文《南南联合自强五十年的国际经济立法反思：从万隆、多哈、坎昆到香港》（载于《中国法学》2006 年第 2 期）获得"福建省第七届社会科学优秀成果奖"一等奖。另外，近两年来他撰写的 5 篇英文论文，均发表于《世界投资与贸易学报》《日内瓦天下大事论坛》《南方公报》等权威性国际学术刊物，在海外具有一定的学术影响。

近两年，陈安承担了两项科研课题。其中，以陈安、曾华群为课题组组长承担了商务部条法司关于《中华人民共和国双边投资保护协定范本》的委托项目，该课题为国策咨询项目，将于今年底完成；以陈安为课题组组长承担并完成了全国"法学精品教材建设规划"委托研究开发项目《国际经济法学新论》系列。

陈安旗帜鲜明地站在全球发展中国家和弱小民族的共同立场，把握当代南北矛盾的实质，遵循建立国际经济新秩序的发展方向，来探讨当代国际经济法学所面临的各种理论和实践问题，从而为构筑具有中国特色的国际经济法学理论框架和学科体系做出了重要的开拓性贡献。改革开放以来，他先后作为中国各类法学代表团成员或法学界知名教授，多次出国访问，前往美国、加拿大、德国、英国、瑞士、比利时、澳大利亚、韩国、法国等国家和地区参加国际法学术会议或讲学，积极开展国际交流。

近 30 年来，陈安的各项工作成果，均取得了较大的全国性影响和一定的海外影响，基本达到了国内先进水平，取得了较显著的社会效益，为我校赢得了荣誉，陈安先后获得国家级、省部级科研成果一等奖 11 项，国家级、省部级科研成果二等奖 7 项，合计 18 项。2007 年，陈安教授被我国媒体"大学评价课题组"评选为"2007 中国杰出社会科学家"。

十一、十位厦大学者入选中国杰出社会科学家*

记者 王瑛慧

12月24日,由中国校友会网"大学评价课题组"编制的《2007中国杰出社会科学家研究报告》正式发布。报告公布了505名入选"2007(首届)中国杰出社会科学家"名单的学者。我校10人入选,入选数名列第十二。从杰出社会科学家的毕业院校分布来看(仅统计1952年以后),我校和中山大学各8人并列第十。

我校入选的十位学者是:陈安(法学)、陈诗启(历史学)、陈振明(公共管理)、葛家澍(应用经济学)、胡培兆(理论经济学)、钱伯海(应用经济学)、曲晓辉(工商管理)、邬大光(教育学)、吴世农(工商管理)、庄国土(政治学)。

据介绍,此次遴选依照的指标有6项:一是国家社会科学基金项目优秀成果奖二等奖以上第一完成人;二是中国高校人文社会科学研究优秀成果奖一等奖以上第一完成人;三是国务院学位委员会委员;四是教育部社会科学委员会委员;五是中国社会科学院学部委员;六是"长江学者奖励计划"特聘教授。

课题组负责人指出,此次遴选采用成果评价仅有国家社科基金奖和高校社科优秀奖的重大奖励成果,一些在某学科领域内较有影响力的基金奖因为评奖数量过多、奖励没分等级等原因暂未被采纳,从而使一些学者未被纳入最终名单。这也从侧面反映出,我国人文社会科学成果评价机制存在缺陷,亟待改进。

《2007中国杰出社会科学家研究报告》由中国校友会网、《大学》杂志和《21世纪人才报》等联合完成,是我国首个针对人文社会科学领域的杰出学者展开的调查研究报告。报告呼吁国家及社会各界应尽早遏制普遍存在的"重理轻文"现象,尽快设立"文科院士"和"国家级社会科学奖励"制度,以真正体现国家和社会对于人文社会科学价值的肯定和重视。

---

* 本篇报道由厦门大学党委宣传部于2007年12月27日编发,宣传部王瑛慧综合报道。

第2章 学界来函

一、来函概述

中国实行改革开放基本国策以来,陈安教授开始立足中国国情和国际弱势群体的共同立场,致力于中国特色国际经济法学的学习、探索和研究。陈安教授于1981—1983年应邀在美国哈佛大学从事国际经济法研究,兼部分讲学工作。1990—1991年以"亚洲杰出学者"名义应聘在美国俄勒冈州路易斯与克拉克西北法学院担任客座教授,兼任该学院国际法研究项目顾问。

自1981年至2007年,除在美国上述两所大学从事三年多的研究、讲学外,陈安教授先后十几次应邀和奉派出国,参加国际性法学学术活动,前往比利时(欧共体总部)、瑞士(联合国欧洲总部)、联邦德国、加拿大、美国、澳大利亚、荷兰、英国、法国、韩国等国家和地区,参加国际学术会议,为东道国和当地多所大学法学院和律师事务所讲学,宣讲中国改革和开放的政策、法律和法规,积极开展国际学术交流。在此期间,先后在外国学术刊物上或法学合著中发表了多篇论文或论著专章。与此同时,又接受中国政府有关部门的委托,有的放矢地从事专项科学研究,并以研究成果提供决策参考。以下选辑近三十封信件[1],从一个小侧面,具体而微地反映了陈安教授的上述学术活动以及国内外人士对这些学术活动所作的评价。大体上可归纳为以下八项事例:

(一) 对《国际经济法学刍言》[2]一书的评价

中国法学界老前辈韩德培先生、朱学山先生以及郭寿康先生于2005—2007年先后来函对本书惠予良好评价,并对本书作者鼓励、鞭策有加。韩老先生认为:"短短

---

[1] 这些函件的原件均收藏于厦门大学国际经济法研究所资料室,存档备考。
[2] 《国际经济法学刍言》一书于2005年由北京大学出版社出版,上、下两卷共约212万字,2007年获第五届"吴玉章人文社会科学奖"一等奖。其大部分内容经进一步全面增订更新,辑入《陈安论国际经济法学》一书,该书篇幅约311万字,由复旦大学出版社2008年出版,2009年获"福建省第八届社会科学优秀成果奖"一等奖;又于2013获"第六届高等学校科学研究优秀成果奖(人文社会科学)"二等奖。

二十余年,竟有如此丰硕研究成果,实属少见";朱老先生函称:"我已将其常置案头,以供不时研读,我一向以为您的文章是耐得百回读的,何况这些文章全是中国国际经济法学理论的奠基之作,应该反复研读。"郭老先生认为本书作者"是中国国际经济法的奠基人之一,也是中国国际经济法这门前沿学科的领军人物"。改革开放以来,作者"积极倡导建立中国国际经济法这门课程与学科,逐步形成了中国国际经济法的体系",《国际经济法学刍言》一书,是作者"二十余年来其著作的精华与代表,也是本学科发展中又一里程碑"。该书"为当代国际社会弱势群体争取经济平权地位提供有力的理论武器。尤其是用英语发表的作品,在国际上影响很大,既体现出发展中国家的主张与立场,也扩大了我国的国际影响,为我国的国际经济法学赢得了国际声誉"。(见本章后附"来函选辑"A部分之(一)(二)(三))

(二) 对《南南联合自强五十年的国际经济立法反思》[3]一文的评价

本文全文约6.4万字。发展中国家的政府间组织"南方中心"秘书长 Branislav Gosovic 教授收阅本文的英文版后,于2006年2月来函称:"我认为它能给人以清晰鲜明的方针政策性的启示,会使《南方中心公报》的读者们很感兴趣,特别因为这是您从一个正在崛起的举足轻重的大国发出的大声呐喊!"[4]因此决定把本长篇论文的核心内容(即第四部分,约7000字),以纸面版和电子版同时发表于该机关理论刊物,以扩大全球读者受众范围,增强其学术影响。(见本章后附"来函选辑"C部分之(三))

日内瓦《世界投资与贸易学报》《日内瓦天下大事论坛》的编辑 Jacques Werner 先生阅读本篇论文后,于2006年1月和2月两度来函,前函称:"我们发现您的《南南联合自强五十年的国际经济立法反思》论文,对于当前 WTO 正在进行的谈判磋商,作了很有创见和雄辩有力的评析,充分反映了您的见解,因此,我很乐于采用,并即将发表于本刊2006年4月这一期。"后函续称:"我发现,您的这篇文章令人很感兴趣,因此想要把它另行发表于我所编辑的另一种学刊,即《日内瓦天下大事论坛》季刊。这另一种学刊面向更加广泛的读者对象,包括联合国各种机构中的公务人员、外交人员、国际公司中的高层执事等等。……我们认为,这是一个良好的机会,让您的见解传播给更加广泛的公众,因而期待您能同意我的上述建议。刊载您这篇文章的《日内瓦天下大事论坛》季刊预定于2006年4月26日出版。"(见本章后附"来函选

---

[3] 本文于2007年获得"福建省第七届社会科学优秀成果奖"一等奖。本文的中、英两种文本已分别收辑于《陈安论国际经济法学》(五卷本)第一编之XV、第七编之II,由复旦大学出版社2008年出版。两种文本可资互相对照。

[4] 《南方中心秘书长 Branislav Gosovic 致陈安教授函(2006年2月1日)》,载陈安:《陈安论国际经济法学》(第五卷),复旦大学出版社2008年版,第2591—2592页。

辑"C部分之(一))

本文的中文版原稿曾刊登于《中国法学》2006年第2期,其责任编辑戚燕方副编审认为:"此文旗帜鲜明,站在国际弱势群体的共同立场,以史为据,以史为师,史论结合,视角独到,力排'众议',颇多创新,具有极强的现实针对性和学术理论性。其资料翔实全面,逻辑严谨,说理透彻,论证雄辩,是这一学术领域中不可多得的力作和佳作。""据我们所知,中国法学家撰写的长篇学术论文,能引起国际组织和国际性学刊如此重视、具有如此国际影响者,尚不多见。"(见本书第六编"陈安早期论著书评荟萃"第3章之十一)

随着时间的推移,本长篇论文得到了国际学术界更多的关注。其修订版已被翻译成韩语,并于2006年6月发表在韩国重要的学术刊物 The Journal of Inha Law 第9卷第2期。翌年,本文修订后的英文版又被收录在 Yong-Shik Lee 教授主编的 Economic Law Through World Trade: A Developing World Perspective 一书,列为该学术专著的第二章,由国际知名的法学学术出版社 Kluwer Law International 出版。

2008年1月,前"南方中心"原秘书长 Gosovic 教授得知本篇长文的全文连续数度增订并由多家国际性学刊发表或转载,又满怀同道热情,特意附函寄来他撰写的书评,对本文进一步加以推介。他认为:这篇长文所作的理论分析和雄辩论证,是"对第三世界思想体系的重大创新性贡献",其"重大意义就在于,它为当代全球弱小民族国家提供了用以抗衡强权和抵制霸权的理论利器和实践工具"。他强调:"尽管关于 WTO 的故事随着香港部长级会议的落幕而暂时告一段落,但是这并不会让陈安教授的这篇论文显得过时。恰恰相反,香港会议以后出现的种种事态发展,已经充分说明这篇论文依据历史所阐明的有关主题主旨仍然合理有效,并且具有深远的影响。因此,陈安教授的这篇论文不仅仍然可以作为学生和学者的标准读物,而且对于许多决策者和参与 WTO 等谈判磋商和日常活动的人士说来,也是可供参考的标准。同时,还可以指望它能对促进南南合作,加强南南合作的机制和组织机构,产生积极的影响。"(见本书第一卷卷首"前辈大师评论"之 IV)

(三) 对《晚近十年来美国单边主义与 WTO 多边主义交锋的三大回合》[5]一文的评价

这篇英文论文长达6.5万字,原先发表于美国天普大学《国际法与比较法学报》

---

〔5〕 本文及其"姊妹篇"中、英两种文本,先后部分或全文分别发表于中外数种权威性学术刊物,因其引起国内外广泛关注,具有较大学术影响,于2004—2006年相继获得第十二届"安子介国际贸易研究奖"一等奖、"福建省第七届社会科学优秀成果奖"一等奖、第二届"全国法学教材与科研成果奖"一等奖,以及第四届"中国高校人文社会科学研究优秀成果奖"二等奖(见本书第七编第4章"陈安教授论著、业绩获奖一览(以倒计年为序/2016—1960)")。本文的中、英两种文本经再次综合整理和增订,已分别收辑于《陈安论国际经济法学》(五卷本)第一编之 X、第七编之 I,由复旦大学出版社2008年出版。两种文本可资互相对照。

2003年第17卷第2期。它援引十年来的大量事实,针对美国在加入WTO多边主义国际协定后仍然顽固推行其传统的经济霸权政策和单边主义立法,进行系统的理论分析和深入批判。本文发表后引起国际上有关人士广泛关注。2004年6月,作者应国际组织"南方中心"要求,作了修订、增补,于2004年7月由该中心将本文作为T. R. A. D. E.专题"第22号工作文件"重印发行,分发给世界各国或地区常驻日内瓦WTO总部的代表团,并刊登在该中心网站上,供读者自由下载。(见本章后附"来函选辑"C部分之(二)(三))

"南方中心"是亚、非、拉美众多发展中国家缔约共同组建的政府间国际组织,总部设在日内瓦,发挥"国际思想库"和"国际智囊团"作用,中国政府是其核心成员之一。中心的主要工作是向国际社会宣传发展中国家的政治和经济主张、思想观点和理论文章,设计和论证发展中国家在各种南北谈判中的共同立场,并提供给各国政府作为决策参考。

(四) 对《"解决投资争端国际中心"述评》[6]一书的评价

"解决投资争端国际中心"(ICSID)是一个国际机构,根据1965年的《华盛顿公约》设立,是"世界银行"的五大成员机构之一,总部设在美国华盛顿。该机构的业务与中国的对外开放和吸收外资国策关系密切。中国已于1990年2月正式签署参加《华盛顿公约》,并于1993年1月提交了缔约批准书,同意接受ICSID体制。

陈安教授于1987年开始承担和主持国家教委博士点基金专题科研项目,就中国是否应当参加《华盛顿公约》接受ICSID体制问题,为对外经贸部提供国策咨询。其集体科研成果《"解决投资争端国际中心"述评》一书于1989年12月出版。

1990年陈安教授受聘在美担任客座教授期间,曾将上述著作一本连同全书目录英文译文一份寄赠设立在美国华盛顿的ICSID总部,该总部反应如下:

1. 世界银行副总裁、"中心"秘书长希哈塔(Shihata)委托"中心"法律顾问帕拉(Parra)来函表示"非常感谢",并称:"我们将在最近一期的《'中心'讯息》刊物上宣布您这部著作的出版消息,并将在下一版的《'中心'论著书目》中将这本书正式列入。"

---

[6] 陈安教授参撰并主编的这本书,约25万字,是中国人针对《华盛顿公约》及其"解决投资争端国际中心"(ICSID)机制开展系列研究的第一部创新成果,1989年12月由鹭江出版社出版,1994年获得"福建省第二届社会科学优秀成果奖"一等奖。其后,在组织新的博士生学术团队进一步深入研究的基础上,陈安教授又参撰并主编了另外两本"姊妹书",即《国际投资争端仲裁——"解决投资争端国际中心"机制研究》与《国际投资争端案例精选》,共约117万字,2001年由复旦大学出版社出版,2002年先后获得中国司法部颁发的"第一届全国法学教材与科研成果奖"一等奖以及中宣部、国家新闻出版总署、中国出版工作者协会联合颁发的"中国图书奖"。以上三部专著中由陈安教授撰写的部分,已经综合整理和增订,收辑于《陈安论国际经济法学》(五卷本)第三编之IV,题为《ICSID与中国:我们研究"解决投资争端国际中心"的现实动因和待决问题》,由复旦大学出版社2008年出版。

(Parra 1990 年 3 月 22 日致陈安教授函)

2. 1990 年《"中心"讯息》第 7 卷第 1 期宣告:"中国正式签署参加《'中心'公约》(即《华盛顿公约》)",同时,在《有关"中心"的近期最新论著》专栏中,列出世界各国近期出版的有关"中心"的新著 6 种,把陈安教授主持撰写的上述专著列在首位。

3. 1990 年 8 月,"中心"法律顾问帕拉写信给陈安教授,附函寄赠上述刊物一份,并称:"您论述'中心'的新书,已在本期的《'中心'讯息》上宣布了有关的出版消息。**根据本书内容目录的英文译文来判断,这肯定是一部极其有益的著作。**"(见本章后附"来函选辑"C 部分之(五))

中国政府有关主管部门对本书的出版也给予很大的鼓励和良好的评价,认为:"该书的出版无疑会推动我国学术界对于《华盛顿公约》和'解决投资争端国际中心'的理论研究,同时亦对我们研究加入该公约的工作具有积极的参考价值和借鉴作用。""您的大作,对我们的立法工作帮助很大。"(见本章后附"来函选辑"B 部分之(十)(十一))

(五)对《是重新闭关自守?还是扩大对外开放?——论中美两国经济上的互相依存以及"1989 年政治风波"后在华外资的法律环境》[7]一文的评价

"1989 年政治风波"发生后,美国某些政客掀起阵阵反华叫嚣,诬蔑中国对外开放政策即将"寿终正寝",外资在华处境"恶化",并一再威胁要中断对华"最惠国待遇",以示"惩罚"和"制裁"。美国社会上许多对华友好人士也因不明真相而产生各种疑虑和误解。1990 年 9 月 25 日,时值陈安教授应聘在俄勒冈州担任客座教授抵美不久,即应邀在路易斯与克拉克西北法学院校友会和俄勒冈州律师集会上进行专题演讲,并与美国"福特基金会"原驻北京官员马克·赛德尔(Mark Sidel)教授展开辩论。陈安教授列举大量事实,力排众议,论证中国对外开放与吸收外资的基本国策不但未有改变,而且因"1989 年政治风波"以后又相继制定了许多新的法律、法规,而使外资在华的法律环境进一步改善,导致大量新的外资投入中国;并论证一旦取消对华"最惠国待遇",美国经济本身势必首先受害。其后,陈安教授将上述演讲稿整理成文,发表于俄勒冈州《律师》杂志 1991 年第 10 卷第 2 期(中文版收辑于本书第三编"国际投资法"第十二章)。

美国俄勒冈州唐肯(Tonkon et al.)律师事务所首席律师欧文·布朗克(Owen D. Blank)曾与会聆听上述演讲,后来又阅读了上述论文。他致函陈安教授称:"您针

---

[7] 本文的中、英两种文本,已分别收辑于《陈安论国际经济法学》(五卷本)第三编之 IX、第七编之 XIII,由复旦大学出版社 2008 年出版。两种文本可资互相对照。

对中国与美国经济互利关系所作的分析,切合实际,令人耳目一新。您对于中国继续实行开放政策所作的论证,很有必要加以广泛、普及的宣传,以促使美国的许多公司恢复信心——它们在'1989年政治风波'以前本来已经很好地确立了这种信心。"(见本章后附"来函选辑"C部分之(六))

中国驻美国西海岸旧金山总领馆负责人朱又德先生收读上述论文后,致函陈安教授称:"很欣赏你的智慧、才干和勇气。此举很有意义。由此,使我联想到,如果我们的学者和学生中能有一批像你这样的民间大使,对反驳美政坛对我国的非难,以及消除一些美国友人的疑虑和误解,无疑将起到非同一般的影响和作用。谢谢你利用讲学、研究之余,抽时间、寻机会为宣传中国所做的工作。"(见本章后附"来函选辑"B部分之(九))

(六)对参加俄勒冈州"第三届国际商法研讨会"宣讲中国投资法的评价

1988年10月底,陈安教授应邀参加美国俄勒冈州"第三届国际商法研讨会",在会上做了专题学术报告《中国涉外投资法十年来的发展》,并印发了长篇演讲文稿。

会议主持人美国路易斯与克拉克西北法学院院长斯蒂芬·坎特教授(Stephen Kanter)会前(1988年9月12日)来函称这个报告选题"极好"(perfect),"我们希望您在本届研讨会上做开幕演讲"。会议通告将陈安教授列于八位在会发言人的首位。

研讨会结束,陈安教授回国后,路易斯与克拉克西北法学院"律师进修班"主任劳丽·梅普斯(Laurie B. Mapes)于1988年11月29日来函称:"我代表本法学院对您光临参加'第三届国际商法研讨会'表示感谢。此次学术活动取得巨大成功。我们收到许多反映,夸奖赞扬此次研讨会以及您的演讲——《中国涉外投资法十年来的发展》。我们深切感谢您对本次出色活动所做的贡献,它给我们法学院带来了很高的荣誉和声望。"(见本章后附"来函选辑"C部分之(七))

(七)对《是进一步开放?还是重新关门?——中国吸收外资政策法令述评》[8]一文的评价

1982年秋,中国政府在继续对外开放的同时,大张旗鼓地打击同吸收外资有关的一切经济犯罪活动。国际上当时曾因此盛传:中国对外开放的"风向"已经改变,

---

[8] 本文的英文文本已收辑于《陈安论国际经济法学》(五卷本)第七编之XVII,由复旦大学出版社2008年出版。

即将恢复"教条主义",重新实行"闭关自守"政策。陈安教授当时正在美国哈佛大学从事研究和讲学,遂于1982年中国国庆节应邀在该校发表专题学术演讲《是进一步开放?还是重新关门?》,旨在澄清美国、日本学者对中国吸收外资有关政策法令的疑虑、担心或非难,答复他们的询问,并以事实为根据,从法学理论上说明中国今后既要继续坚持对外开放政策,进一步积极吸收外资,保护合法外资和正当外商,又要继续严肃认真地打击同吸收外资有关的一切经济犯罪行为,从而为建设具有中国特色的社会主义服务。事后,陈安教授将演讲稿整理成文,发表在纽约法学院《国际法与比较法学报》1984年第6卷第1期上。

此次演讲由哈佛大学法学院助理院长兼该校东亚法学研究所副所长斯奈德(Frederick E. Snyder)主持。事后他索赠文稿,并来函称:"这次演说非常打动人心,很能发人深思,令人兴趣盎然。您的文稿中对于保护外国投资的两种不同做法的有关论述,也相当深刻周详。我认为,您针对美国(保护海外投资)的立场得到(某些国家)追随而又遭到(许多国家)挑战这个问题所作的论述,是特别有意义的。我殷切地期待您能把这篇文章公开发表,从而使国际法学界有更多人可以从您的深刻见解中获得教益。"(见本章后附"来函选辑"C部分之(八))

哈佛大学法学院权威老教授、该校东亚法学研究所所长亚瑟·冯·墨伦(Arthur von Mehren)在阅读上述演讲文稿以及陈安教授的另一篇文章[9]之后,来函称:"我认为这两篇文章对于有关主题所作的论述,都是很有教益和很有创见的。两篇文章都写得条理分明,行文妥善。每一篇都大大有助于促进美国的读者加深理解您所论述的问题。我们东亚法学研究所的同事,大家都知道您在这里的工作中,一向是干劲充沛和专心致志。您的两篇论文就是令人钦佩的例证,说明您的研究工作的质量和成就。我们高兴的是:如今您在美国帮助我们理解中国的法律和社会,日后回到中国,您有能力在那里以同样的方式向您的同事以及学生们阐明有关美国法律和美国社会的各个方面。"(见本章后附"来函选辑"C部分之(九))

日本访美研究员、日本国家石油公司金融经济专家杉原启示先生于听讲后索要演讲稿,并来函称:"我认为,日前先生发表之高见对于日本国民理解中国之政策精神,颇具参考价值,故已将先生惠赠之讲演原文(英文)稿件,迅即摘译要旨,径送日本国家石油公司参考。"(见本章后附"来函选辑"C部分之(十))

---

[9] 即《是棒打鸳鸯吗?——就"李爽案件"评〈纽约时报〉报道兼答美国法学界同行问》,其中文、英文两种文本已收辑于本书第五编第4章。

(八) 对《是棒打鸳鸯吗？——就"李爽案件"评〈纽约时报〉报道兼答美国法学界同行问》[10]一文的评价

1981年秋冬间，中国政府对中国公民李爽（女）与法国外交官贝耶华（Bellfroid，有妇之夫）在法国使馆公开姘居一案作了严肃处理，将李爽收容劳教两年。法国媒体借此攻击中国当局，美国《纽约时报》也对此案作了错误报道。哈佛大学法学院曾将该报的两篇报道列为参考教材，散发给研究生"学习"，引起在哈佛进修的各国学者议论纷纷，对中国的涉外政策法令、个人婚恋自由、知识分子政策、劳教条例以及案件审理程序等，颇有非议。陈安教授应邀在哈佛课堂上对近百名研究生及旁听的日、澳、德等国的访问学者做了专题演讲，从法学理论、国际条约、国际惯例以及中国法令具体条文规定上，论证中国有关当局在处理此案时，不但维护了民族尊严和国格，而且严格依法办事，做到合情、合理、合法，从而澄清问题，以正视听。事后，陈安教授将演讲稿整理成文，发表在纽约法学院《国际法与比较法学报》1981年第3卷第1期上（见本书第五编"国际经济法热点学术问题长、短评"第4章）。

该学报主编艾姆林·希加来函评论说："您这篇论文的主题是评论刊载于《纽约时报》的克利斯托弗·雷恩所写的两篇报道。这些报道曾经引起人们对中华人民共和国政府当局处理李爽案件的做法，啧有烦言，纷纷非难。您的文章提出了人们所殷切期待的答案。这种答案，来自中华人民共和国的一位公民，来自一位像您这样卓越出色的中国法学学者，是再恰当不过的了。您的这篇论文从中国的风俗习惯、志向抱负、政治和社会的奋斗目标的角度，从反映着这些因素的法律体制的角度，条理分明、令人信服地剖析了李爽案件。我不能设想有比这更加雄辩透彻的解释说明。您对于美国和中国的刑事法制所作的比较分析是特别有教益和富有启发性的。不过，我认为最能发人深思的还是您所使用的方法，即把李爽案件放置在中国的社会主义理论、社会主义实践以及社会主义目标的背景之中，加以剖析。"（见本章后附"来函选辑"C部分之（十一））

美国波士顿大学法学院教授弗兰克·K.阿帕姆（Frank K. Upham）索赠上述论文后，来函表示感谢，并称："我认为，您的论文以一个中国法学学者的敏锐眼光，对这桩案件作了引人入胜的、相当精辟的阐述。您那精心细致、沉着冷静的分析，提出了一些重要的课题，它们将郑重提醒美国的法学研究生们必须注意另外一种法学观点，这种法学观点往往同他们原有的观点迥然相异，并且难得有人能够妥善确切地加以论述阐明。我的研究专业虽是日本的法学，但我仍然打算今后要求我的研究生

---

[10] 本文的中、英两种文本，见本书第五编第4章。

们阅读您的这篇论文。因为这篇论文是如此妥帖完善地阐明了中国法制与美国法制之间的基本区别和某些相似之处,而这两种法制对于日本法制的形成,向来是有促进作用的。"(见本章后附"来函选辑"C部分之(十二))

二、来 函 选 辑

A　前辈大师来函

(一) 武汉大学教授韩德培老先生致陈安教授函

陈安同志好友:

　　日前承惠赠大著两卷,非常感谢!翻阅后不胜敬佩!我曾认为足下是闽南一位才子,短短二十余年,竟有如此丰硕研究成果,实属少见。

　　您在自序中说"古稀逾六,垂垂老矣"。其实,您还不能说"老",在我的心目中,您还是在"奋发有为"时期,毫无老的迹象。我现在已95岁,真可说是一个"老人"或"老朽"。虽然学校不让我退休,我还在带些博士研究生,但也只能量力而为。我在90岁时,曾在一首诗中说"鞠躬尽余热,接力有来人",真的,只有寄希望于"来人"了。

　　厦大的许多老朋友,请代问候。

　　敬祝

　　冬安

韩德培　敬启
2005年11月30日

(二) 安徽大学教授朱学山老先生致陈安教授函

陈安同志:

　　新春好!敬祝您身体健康,阖家幸福!

　　返抵合肥后见到大著《刍言》,不胜欣喜!我已将其常置案头,以供不时研读,我一向以为您的文章是耐得百回读的,何况这些文章全是中国国际经济法学理论的奠基之作,应该反复研读。

　　关于"庆父不去,鲁难未已",我对您谈过。现将谈话底稿奉上,以供参考。在年会上我提交的短文《小问题》,您没见到,现亦寄上,以便您了解一些情况,并祈教正!

专肃,即颂

著安!

朱学山再拜
2006 年 1 月 15 日

(三) 中国人民大学教授郭寿康老先生致陈安教授函及附件

【评奖推荐书】 陈安教授是中国国际经济法的奠基人之一,也是中国国际经济法这门前沿学科的领军人物。我国传统法学(包括中华人民共和国成立前和成立后)只讲授国际公法与国际私法,没有开设过国际经济法课程。国外法学院系也大体如此。改革开放以来,陈安教授积极倡导建立中国国际经济法这门课程与学科,逐步形成了中国国际经济法的体系。万事开头难,陈安教授为创建中国国际经济法,费尽心血,成绩卓越,发表了大量的优秀论文、教材与专著,做出了重大的具有历史意义的贡献。2005 年由北京大学出版社出版的《国际经济法学刍言》(上、下两卷,211 万字),是二十余年来其著作的精华与代表,也是本学科发展中又一里程碑。

《国际经济法学刍言》这部专著是国际经济法学这门学科的扛鼎之作。不但显示出作者知识渊博、深思熟虑,而且多有创新之见。二战后,逐渐兴起的国际经济法学,阵地多为发达国家的作者、专家所占领,发展中国家声音微弱,居于劣势。陈安教授这部专著旗帜鲜明地站在国际弱势群体即广大发展中国家的立场,理直气壮地阐明对国际经济法学中的热点问题观点,持之有故、言之成理,为当代国际社会弱势群体争取经济平权地位提供有力的理论武器。尤其是用英语发表的作品,在国际上影响很大,既体现出发展中国家的主张与立场,也扩大了我国的国际影响,为我国的国际经济法学赢得了国际声誉。

书中论证的螺旋式上升的"6C 轨迹"论,无疑是作者多年研究的创新之论。

这部著作理论密切联系实际,对我国政府有关部门处理国际经济法律问题,有重大参考价值。这从商务部条法司和我国常驻 WTO 使团团长孙振宇大使的有关函件里,可以清楚地看到。

2007 年 6 月 7 日

(四) 对外经济贸易大学教授沈达明老先生致陈安教授函

陈安同志:

谢谢你寄来的新著《美国对海外投资的法律保护及典型案例分析》。内容非常丰富,在近期内将细细拜读。我国近年来出版的涉外法律书籍都是些简论、浅说、基础知识等科普性的书。科普很重要,但没有专著,科普就缺乏基础。你的大作在走向专著的道路上定能起带头作用。

世界银行在成立"解决投资争端国际中心"之后,又有成立"多边投资担保机构"的计划。我手头有草案的英文本。不知你有没有这些材料。如需要,可告知,以便寄上。

再次谢谢来信,致

敬礼

沈达明

1985 年 9 月 16 日

(五) 中山大学端木正教授致陈安教授函

陈安同志:

您好!

别来三个月,不知苏州会议参加了没有?

收到大著《美国对海外投资的法律保护及典型案例分析》一册,喜出望外。近年国人自著如此专书,尚属罕见,实为阁下对我国学术界一大贡献,可喜可贺!

长春和北京之会又可面叙,谨先函谢,顺颂

旅安

端木正上

1985 年 11 月 30 日

※　※　※

B 中国政府官员来函

(一) 中华人民共和国外交部条法司司长徐宏致陈安教授函

尊敬的陈安教授:

您好!

来信收悉。感谢惠赠专著!陈老耄耋之年仍笔耕不辍,著此大作,面向国际社会弘扬中华学术、发出中国声音,您深厚的学术功底、严谨的治学态度、真挚的爱国热情令人钦佩。专著内容丰富,不仅具有很高的学术和理论价值,对实务部门参加国际谈判、解决实际问题也具有重要参考意义。

祝身体安康!

徐 宏
2014 年 9 月 12 日

(二) 中华人民共和国外交部美洲大洋洲司司长谢锋致陈安教授函

尊敬的陈安教授:

你惠赠的《评"黄祸"论的本源、本质及其最新霸权"变种":"中国威胁"论》一文我已拜读。感谢你心系国家发展,关心支持国家外交工作。

从"黄祸"论这一独特历史视角探究"中国威胁"论的根源,令人耳目一新。与几百年前相比,今天的"中国威胁"论涉及因素更复杂,包括地缘政治、意识形态、历史偏见等。这是实现中华民族伟大复兴和中国和平发展必须破解的外部障碍。我坚信,正如"黄祸"论最终被历史所唾弃,当代"中国威胁"论终将随着中国的持续繁荣发展被丢入历史的垃圾堆。

祝工作愉快,阖家幸福!

谢 锋
2012 年 8 月 6 日

(三) 中华人民共和国外交部条法司司长黄惠康致陈安教授函

尊敬的陈安教授:

七月五日您致杨洁篪部长和我本人的来函及附文敬悉。

我认真拜读了《评"黄祸"论的本源、本质及其最新霸权"变种":"中国威胁"论》一文,深感文中所列史料丰富、分析精辟、论述深刻,读后启发良多。我已请我司主管处认真研究此文,以冀从中撷取有益建议,为外交工作提供指导参考;并加强外交一线工作者特别是年青后辈对"中国威胁"论的历史及现实联系的认识,践行您在文中所提"以史为师、以史为鉴"的建议。

同时,您值耄耋高龄依然关心国家外交事业发展并为此笔耕不辍,我深感敬佩。我谨代表广大外交工作者对您的关心和指导表示由衷感谢,也希望您能继续为外交事业发展建言献策、启微发瀚。

顺祝

安好!

黄惠康
2012 年 7 月 30 日

(四) 中华人民共和国常驻世界贸易组织代表团团长易小准大使致陈安教授批复函

纪文华学友并转呈中国驻WTO使团团长易小准大使：

邮上拙作中、英文本各一份，讨论热点问题，直抒管见。谨请惠予批评指正。

英文本是在中文本基础上增补改写而成。

收到后，请简复。谢谢！

感谢你多年来惠予的关注和支持。

顺祝

健好

陈 安

2011年3月30日

陈会长：

我非常同意您的观点，WTO作为一个重要的国际贸易法律体系，也需要与时俱进。这就是我和我的同事们在多哈谈判中肩负的责任。

谢谢您对WTO问题的关注！

易小准

2011年4月27日

(五) 中华人民共和国商务部办公厅主任姚坚致陈安教授函

尊敬的陈老，您好！

您寄来的论国际经济法学丛书收悉，非常感谢！

作为中国国际经济法学科的重要奠基人、领头人，您始终立足于中国国情和广大发展中国家的共同立场，致力于探索和开拓具有中国特色的国际经济法学科。您潜心所著的《陈安论国际经济法学》奠定了学科基础，提出的学术理念和学术追求深受国内外学界的推崇。

拜观"人过半百再出发"专辑，深为您抱持的"余热未尽，不息奋蹄"之精神所感动，您至今仍在教学和科研战线上不懈耕耘，培养法学人才，推动学术研究。更为难能可贵的是，在教学科研任务繁重、领衔众多学术团体的同时，仍紧密跟踪国际学术界和实务界的最新动态，及时向国内实务部门反映并提出了大量深具价值的对应之策。前次您专程到商务部洽商工作，让我们受益匪浅。作为商务战线上的一员，我谨向您致以崇高的敬意。

敬祝

安康!

姚 坚 谨复
2009 年 5 月 19 日

(六) 中华人民共和国商务部条法司杨秉勋致陈安教授文[11]

由于工作关系,前两日到了一处仙乡好所在——厦门大学,她周遭山清水秀,背靠南普陀,旁边就是仙风道骨的南普陀寺,飞檐走角,蓝色的寺庙屋顶和青山相得益彰;她面迎无际的大海,天光碧海,海风飒爽,有渔舟片片,当真治学乐土,人间仙境……

得益于一位有着绵绵学术追求的领导,组织了一场有众多知名学者参加的研讨会,诸如复旦的陈治东、董世忠两位先生,人大的余劲松先生,教过我的车丕照先生等等,诸位先生纵谈国际投资法、世界大势、国家利益、国际法律原则,收益颇丰,先生们的治学态度和卓越风采令人起敬,然而给我印象最为深刻的是厦门大学的老先生陈安教授。

老先生,福建人,今年虚岁八十,著作等身,精神矍铄。先生于 20 世纪 50 年代毕业于厦门大学,修政治学于复旦大学,80 年代在哈佛大学从事国际经济法研究,兼部分讲学,90 年代以"亚洲杰出学者"名义应邀在美国俄勒冈州路易斯与克拉克西北法学院担任客座教授,曾任中国政府根据《华盛顿公约》遴选向"解决投资争端国际中心"(ICSID)指派的首席国际仲裁员、中国国际法学会顾问等。

千金难买老来瘦,老先生很瘦,虽然衬衫塞在腰带里,举手投足还是带出了道道褶皱,似乎有学识之气在隐隐流动。马可·奥勒留说:"我们必须抓紧时间,这不仅是因为我们在一天天地接近死亡,而且因为对事物的理解力和消化力将先行消失。"我看到这句话时有点 cry 的冲动,然而老先生给了这句话相反的注解,他讲话似乎不多,但是每句话都透露出览胜高一层的睿智。老先生眼睛不大,但是讲话时目光锐利,将真诚、平实的感觉凝聚到你的心里。以前曾有人说某位学术巨擘是时代的号角、岁月的良心,老先生也表现出这样的特征,他擅用成语、平实的话语点缀出高洁之士的俊彩,他并不忌讳自己被人称作"保守派",他认为国际投资协定不宜走得太

---

[11] 本文最初于 2008 年 9 月 12 日发表在新浪博客(http://blog.sina.com.cn/s/blog_4389bff20100w80s.html),原题为《说说厦大的那位老先生——陈安先生》,作者署名"Benthamyang",即杨秉勋。

快,毕竟我国相当长一段时间内没有改变投资东道国的身份,"走出去"战略才刚刚开始;他用了"贻害无穷""居安思危""亡羊补牢""陈述管见"……他又是一个尊重科学的人,他说:"知识分子说话虽然不一定中听,但是知识分子说话都是有根据的,是科学的,也许你会认为它片面,但是一个个的片面加起来就是全面,……任何事情都是兼听则明,偏听则暗……"

也许我是一个怀旧的人,我喜欢吴经熊,喜欢梁任公,所以我也喜欢陈安先生的话语风格,其实比较一下就知道他们都是学贯东西的人,然而保留了中华民族的传统话语风格,骨子中一以贯之的是对于国家的热爱,对普通大众的关怀,对真理的孜孜不倦。

这里有一段陈安先生的趣事:

1981年春,哈佛大学法学院柯恩教授来厦大访问。在一场座谈会上,柯恩教授批评道:"外国人来中国投资有顾虑,因为中国政府不尊重外国人的财产,会随便没收。"尽管对方来自世界最著名的大学,又是全球知名的学术权威,还是哈佛大学法学院副院长,而陈安老师当时只是个副教授,但他根本没想到"身份"的差别,立刻展开了辩论:"我认为你说错话了。"陈安当时只会讲点"蹩脚"英语,还好柯恩教授会一点中文。陈安就以夹杂着中文的英语,向柯恩教授详解中国法律:"在中国,任何外商,只要遵纪守法,不触犯刑法和海关法规,他的财产绝不会被没收。"柯恩教授脸红了,他辩道:"但是,中国政府还是有可能会将外国人的财产拿走呀!"陈安知道他讲的是"征收制度"。他反问道:"难道美国没有征收制度吗?"他引用美国的许多例子,反问柯恩教授:"美国人在美国本国都不能保证财产在任何情况下绝对不被征收,何以到中国来就要求享受绝对不被征收的特权?"美国人素来坚持"在真理面前没有权威"。柯恩教授对陈安老师产生了兴趣。座谈会一结束,他立刻走到陈安面前:"我打算邀请你到哈佛讲学,讲中国的法律,讲你的思想。"

陈安教授初到哈佛,一度讲的是中华人民共和国成立前的"山沟沟英语",甚至连"中国式英语"都谈不上,外国人经常听不懂。在哈佛大学讲坛上,一个旁听的美国教授当众嘲笑他。陈教授用英语反问他:"我能讲英语,讲一点美国式英语,尽管讲不好,但是你能讲中文,会讲中国的北京话吗?"那位教授脸红了,他承认:"我不会。"后来,那位美国教授对陈安教授尊敬三分,路上见到老远就打招呼:"嗨!陈教授,你好!"经过发奋图强,到美国讲学的第二年,陈安教授再站上哈佛的讲台时,英语已经非常流利。1982年秋,他做了一场演讲:《是进一步开放?还是重新关门?——评有关中国吸收外资政策法令的几种议论》。他的雄辩说理、精辟阐析,紧紧地抓住了听众的心。演讲结束后,全场响起了雷鸣般的声音,一位我国台湾地区留美研究生挤到陈教授身旁,说道:"佩服!佩服!外国人给你鼓掌,掌声这么响,作为中国人,我们也有份,觉得很体面。"

(七)中华人民共和国商务部条法司致陈安教授函(2005年9月27日)

中华人民共和国商务部

尊敬的陈安教授:

籍第九届中国国际投资贸易洽谈会期间,我司与您领导下的厦门大学国际经济法研究所再一次就国际投资协定问题进行了深入地研讨和成功地交流,收到了很好的效果。多年来我司与厦大国际经济法研究所紧密合作取得丰硕成果,离不开您的鼎力支持,我司特此,并代表商务部和双边投资保护协定的谈判团队,向您致以诚挚的感谢。

您是新中国国际经济法学的奠基人之一,并在国内最早进行有关国际投资协定和国际投资争议解决的开创性研究,著作等身,立言煌煌,为我国国际法学作出了重大贡献。您在学术研究中始终将维护国家利益放在首位,把正义和法治作为不懈诉求,代表中国和广大发展中国家法学界在国际上发出了建立国际经济新秩序的强有力呼声。近年来,您在教学科研任务繁重、领衔众多学术团体的同时,仍紧密跟踪国际学术界和实务界的最新动态,及时向国内实务部门反映并提出了有价值的应对之策。

另一方面,您一直呕心沥血,辛勤耕耘,以培育英才为己任,以教诲学生为乐事。春风化雨,暑去寒来,一批又一批的国际法人才在鹭城涌现、成长,成为中国国际法学界的新一代中坚。在您的启发和指引下,厦门大学一批年轻学者

中华人民共和国商务部

投身国际投资法的研究，组成了充满活力而富有钻研精神的学术团队，使国际投资法的研究欣欣向荣。市场经济的大潮对法律人充满诱惑，而您和您的团队始终坚守着对学术的执着追求，在国际投资法这一片园地里辛勤劳动、精耕细作。厦大国际经济法研究所在这一领域内已拥有雄厚的研究力量和突出的研究成果。

我司与您和厦大国际经济法研究所开展合作可以上溯至上世纪八十年代。改革开放之初，您和厦大国际经济法研究所的学术梯队成员就曾多次接受原外经贸部条法司的专题委托或专题咨询，提供有关"解决投资争端国际中心"（ICSID）体制和双边投资保护协定的专题委托或专题咨询。为我国对外商签双边投资保护协定和加入《华盛顿公约》、接受 ICSID 机制提供了重要的理论支持和决策依据。您与我司历任司领导多次深入研讨，厦大学术梯队与我司谈判团队间也始终保持交流切磋，双方间的合作堪称学术研究机构与政府决策部门互相配合互相支持的典范。在我们的最新合作中，我们又一次感受到了您和这一学术梯队的宽广视野和深厚功底，以及您所立意营造的宽松和谐、鼓励争鸣的学术氛围。目前，我国已与 112 个国家签署了双边投资保护协定，对吸引外商来华投资、贯彻我"走出去"战略发挥了越来越

中华人民共和国商务部

重要的作用,在这背后您和厦大学术梯队的学术铺垫和政策建言发挥了重要的作用。

最后,再次衷心感谢您在此次活动中的盛情款待,以及您对我国商务法律工作的长期支持和重大贡献,并期盼在今后与您和厦门大学国际经济法研究所继续紧密合作。祝您身体健康,工作顺利!

商务部条法司

2005年9月27日

(八) 中华人民共和国常驻世界贸易组织代表团团长孙振宇大使致陈安教授函

陈安同志:

您好!感谢您的来信及大量重要资料。

我反复拜读了您的学术报告《中国入世后海峡两岸经贸问题"政治化"之防治》,受益匪浅,足见您对 WTO 规则研究功力之深,所提建议极具参考价值。

信中所提另一篇英文大作[12]我没有收到,十分想了解您对美国以单边主义对抗WTO多边主义的见解与分析,如能寄来,将十分感激。

作为WTO中的新成员,我们对WTO规则的学习以及对WTO的认识还是十分肤浅的,急需国内有关的学术科研机构的协助与支持,如果贵学会能就中国作为一个新成员如何有效地应对由于广泛的加入承诺与一些不利条款给我国带来的挑战,以及中国作为一个发展中的大国如何在新一轮谈判中发挥应有的作用开展一些研究工作,将是对我团工作的重大支持。

我也会积极考虑选一些有一定分量的调研报告在贵会的学刊上发表,达到互相交流的目的。

顺致谢意。

孙振宇

2004年4月16日

(九)中国驻美国西海岸旧金山总领馆负责人朱又德致陈安教授函

(中华人民共和国总领事馆)

Consulate General of

the People's Republic of China

1450 Laguna Street

San Francisco, California 94115

(415) 563-1718

陈安老师:

你好!

来信并演讲摘要已悉。很欣赏你的智慧、才干和勇气。此举很有意义。由此,使我联想到,如果我们的学者和学生中能有一批像你这样的民间大使,对反驳美政

---

[12] 指英文稿"The Three Big Rounds of U. S. Unilateralism Versus WTO Multilateralism During the Last Decade: A Combined Analysis of the Great 1994 Sovereignty Debate, Section 301 Disputes (1998-2000), and Section 201 Disputes (2002-2003)"(《晚近十年来美国单边主义与WTO多边主义交锋的三大回合:综合剖析美国"主权大辩论"(1994)、"301条款"争端(1998-2000)以及"201条款"争端(2002-2003)》,全文约6.5万字),发表于美国天普大学《国际法与比较法学报》2003年第17卷第2期(Temple International & Comparative Law Journal, Vol. 17, No. 2, 2003)。应孙振宇大使要求,陈安教授补寄了该长篇论文的单行本。事后获悉:孙大使要求中国驻WTO代表团专业人员认真阅读本文并开展讨论。

坛对我国的非难,以及消除一些美国友人的疑虑和误解,无疑将起到非同一般的影响和作用。谢谢你利用讲学、研究之余,抽时间、寻机会为宣传中国所做的工作。

我已将你的演讲摘要转有关领导阅,并拟抄报国内有关部门及你的国内工作单位——厦门大学。

顺致

安好。

朱又德
1991 年 5 月 23 日

(十) 中华人民共和国对外经贸部条法司致陈安教授函

陈教授:

您好!

来函收悉,十分感谢您对我们工作的关心与支持,您的大作,对我们的立法工作帮助很大,急盼早日得之,如果可能的话,我局有关同志共需约 10 本,冒昧相求,望谅解。

关于"ICSID"目前国务院已原则同意加入,正在做最后阶段的准备工作,待我国一旦加入后,"实施条例"不久可望出笼,当然还要广泛征求意见,争取一个比较好的立法,既利用了公约的好处,又不损我国权益,这点我与您也有同感。在这方面,还盼您及贵校大力支持。

此致

敬礼

经贸部条约法律司
1989 年 12 月 15 日

(十一) 中华人民共和国对外经贸部条法司致陈安教授函

厦大法学院并陈安院长:

欣闻贵院拟出版《"解决投资争端国际中心"述评》,在此表示祝贺。

目前,我国政府正在研究加入"国际中心"的可能性,并进入了最后阶段。该书的出版无疑会推动我国学术界对于《华盛顿公约》及"解决投资争端国际中心"的理论研究,同时亦对我们研究加入该公约的工作具有积极的参考价值和借鉴作用。

我们感谢贵院对我司工作的支持并期待大作早日出版。

此致

敬礼

经贸部条约法律司

1989年8月29日

(十二) 中华人民共和国对外经贸部条法局致陈安教授函

陈教授：

您好！

很高兴收到您寄来的大作"国际经济法系列专著"。对您的辛勤耕耘而结出的累累硕果，我们表示钦佩和祝贺。也对您为国际经济法研究做出的贡献表示感谢。

在实践中，我们碰到过许多理论上的课题，而理论工作者也需了解实际工作的需求，并为实践服务，在理论与实践相结合的道路上，您和您领导的厦大法学院做了很出色的工作。"国际经济法系列专著"对我们无疑是一套可以信赖的有价值的业务参考书和工具书。

过去，在我局的有关事务中，您给予了很大帮助，今后还希望厦大的法律工作者对我们的工作继续给予支持。

国际经济法与我局业务密切相连。我局办公室愿与贵院资料室建立联系，互换资料，以便更好地为国际经济事业服务。

最后，再次向您表示谢意，并预祝您取得更大的成绩。

此致

敬礼

经贸部条约法律局

1988年1月30日

(十三) 中华人民共和国对外经贸部条法局致陈安教授函

陈安教授：

您好！

关于我国是否加入《华盛顿公约》(ICSID)之事，征求意见已初步结束，在这项工作中，得到了您及贵校法律系的大力支持，再次表示谢意。

加入公约是一项理论性和实践性都很强的工作，既要有实际工作部门同志的研究，也要有理论方面的同志配合，这一点已从我们过去的工作中得到了充分的印证。

您对我国是否加入公约的意见,经过研究和讨论,使我们受益很大,我们认为从下述几方面对我们有启示作用:

1. 从国际法的角度,全面分析公约条文及产生的背景、机构和作用,由此分析我国加入的利弊;

2. 重点提到了公约本身应引起重视的地方,如"法律适用""同意的形式""费用"等;

3. 客观地分析一旦加入公约后,我国可能提交中心仲裁的范围;

4. 提出研究公约案例的研究方法。

您的意见对我们做好这项工作帮助很大,还望今后继续得到您及贵系的支持。

此致

敬礼

经贸部条约法律局
1987 年 3 月 1 日

※　※　※

C　外国学界来函

(一)《世界投资与贸易学报》《日内瓦天下大事论坛》季刊主编致陈安教授函(摘译,原文附后)

陈教授:

感谢您于 2006 年 1 月 27 日发来的电子邮件。我们发现您的《南南联合自强五十年的国际经济立法反思》论文,对于当前 WTO 正在进行的谈判磋商,作了很有创见和雄辩有力的评析,充分反映了您的见解,因此,我很乐于采用,并即将发表于本刊 2006 年 4 月这一期。

…………

Jacques Werner[13] 编辑
2006 年 1 月 31 日

---

[13]　Jacques Werner 先生是日内瓦著名的编辑兼出版人,主持编辑和出版四种国际性学术刊物。

From: Werner & Associes
To: chenan
Sent: Tuesday, January 31, 2006 11:02 PM
Subject: contributing an article

Dear Prof. Chen,

Thank you for your email of last January 27. It was good to hear from you again. We found your article "A Reflection on the South-South Coalition in the Last Half Century from the Perspective of International Economic Law-making" a thoughtful and vigorous assessment of the current WTO negotiation, reflecting your views. I am pleased consequently to accept it for publication in our coming April 2006 issue.

Please confirm that, in accordance with our policy, we will have exclusive publishing rights.

Your article will need a lot of linguistic editing and you will hear in due time from my editorial assistant, Mr. Jim Boyce.

We provide authors with 50 off-prints of their article. You may order additional off-prints on your own account, in which case, please advise my editorial assistant within the coming three weeks. Please note that off-prints are usually dispatched four weeks after the issue has come out. Mr. Boyce will get in touch with you concerning your article.

Best regards,

Jacques Werner
Editor

陈安先生:

您的论文《南南联合自强五十年的国际经济立法反思》一文即将发表于《世界投资与贸易学报》4月这一期。我发现,您的这篇文章令人很感兴趣,因此想要把它另行发表于我所编辑的另一种学刊,即《日内瓦天下大事论坛》季刊。这另一种学刊面向更加广泛的读者对象,包括联合国各种机构中的公务人员、外交人员、国际公司中的高层执事等等。

……

我们认为,这是一个良好的机会,让您的见解传播给更加广泛的公众,因而期待您能同意我的上述建议。刊载您这篇文章的《日内瓦天下大事论坛》季刊预定于2006年4月26日出版。

....

Jacques Werner 编辑

2006年2月20日

From: wernerp@iprolink.ch
To: chenan@xmu.edu.cn
Cc: james.e.boyce@wanadoo.fr; wernerp@iprolink.ch
Sent: Monday, February 20, 2006 10:38 PM
Subject: Your Recent Article on the South-South Coalition

Dear Mr. Chen,

I found your article "A Reflection on the South-South Coalition in the Last Half Century from the Perspective of International Economic Law-making", which we are going to publish in the coming April issue of the *Journal of World Investment and Trade*, so interesting that I would like to re-publish it in another Journal which I edit, called *The Geneva Post Quarterly—The Journal of World Affairs*. This Journal is aimed to a wider readership of civil servants in the United Nations Organization, diplomats, executives in international corporations, and the like.

The style of this Journal is along the line of the well known US-based publication *Foreign Affairs*, and has no footnotes. We have consequently made a new version of your article, incorporating footnotes in the text itself, as well as taking into consideration the final changes you made to your original article. This new version is enclosed.

We think it would be a good opportunity to have your views disseminated to a wider public and hope that you will consequently agree with my proposal. The date of publication of the issue of *The Geneva Post Quarterly* where your article is planed is April 26, 2006.

Please let me have your consent to the above.

Best regards,

Jacques Werner

Editor

(二) 天普大学《国际法与比较法学报》学术论文编辑 L. K. Kolb 致陈安教授函(摘译,原文附后)

陈安教授:

　　…………

　　我作为学术论文责任编辑,曾与本学报主编共同审阅全部来稿,并从中选择我们认为当前最受关注、最引人入胜和最有创见的文章,尽快发表。

　　我们确实十分高兴能在本学报 2003 年秋季这一卷发表你的这篇学术论文,题为《晚近十年来美国单边主义与 WTO 多边主义交锋的三大回合》。这篇论文论证有理有据,主题紧扣时局,资料丰富翔实。同时,它针对当前特别重大和特别令人关注的争端问题展开论述。简言之,选用本文是由于我们认为它的论点论据雄辩犀利,发人深思,并且紧扣当前热点话题,相信它会使国际法理论界和实务界都大感兴趣。

　　…………

Laura K. Kolb

美国天普大学《国际法与比较法学报》学术论文编辑

2004 年 6 月 3 日

From: Lkathkolb@aol.com
To: chenan@xmu.edu.cn
Sent: Thursday, June 03, 2004 8:43 AM
Subject: Re: your article

Hello,

　　...

　　As Articles Editor, I reviewed all submissions to the Journal and together with the Editor-in-Chief, facilitated the publication of those papers we found to be the most topical, interesting and original.

　　We were truly pleased to publish your article entitled "The Three Big Rounds of U.S. Unilateralism Versus WTO Multilateralism During the Latest Decade" in our Fall, 2003 issue. The thesis was well-developed and the topic both timely and informative. In addition, the article addressed issues that are of particular import and interest at the present time. In short, we chose the article because we found the argument provocative and topical and believed that it would be of interest to those involved in the study and practice of international law.

......

Best regards,

Laura K. Kolb

Articles Editor, *TICLJ*

（三）日内瓦"南方中心"(South Center)秘书长 B. Gosovic 致陈安教授函（摘译，原文附后）

陈安教授：

我从"南方中心"向您问候致意！

我极其欣赏您的这篇论文，阅读时确实觉得是一种享受。我已建议我的同事们把这篇论文列为我们"南方中心"的出版物之一，纳入我们的"贸易发展与公平"专题议程（Trade-Related Agenda, Development and Equity, T. R. A. D. E），作为系列工作文件之一印刷发行，以便使它能更广泛传播，为公众所周知，特别是让它在我们发展中国家的广大读者和各国政府中，能够广为传播，普遍周知。

不知您是否同意这样做，是否可以结合最近〔WTO〕针对美国"201 条款"案件的裁断情况，对本文加以修订更新？特此征求您的意见。

············

等候您的回音。

谨致问候！

Branislav Gosovic

"南方中心"秘书长

2004 年 6 月 2 日

附言：我们还打算把您的这篇论文发表在"南方中心"的电子网站上。

From: gosovic@southcentre.org

To: chenan@xmu.edu.cn

Sent: Wednesday, June 02, 2004 12:26 AM

Subject: from south centre

Dear Professor An Chen,

Greetings from the Centre.

I was extremely pleased with your article and really enjoyed reading it. I have suggested to my colleagues that we print it as a South Centre publication in our T. R. A. D. E. working paper series and thus make it more widely known and accessible, in particular to our readers in the South, including especially the governments.

So, my question to you is whether you would agree with this and whether it would be possible for you to update the paper to take into account the recent ruling regarding the US.

...

Looking forward to your reply.

With best regards,

Branislav Gosovic
Head of the Secretariat
South Centre

PS: We would also like to place your article on our website.

陈安教授:

我刚读到您的来信,谢谢! 本星期以来我一直忙于参加"南方中心"的董事会会议和理事会会议。您的论文已于上星期四出版,并已在"中心"的理事会上分发;同时也已送交各国常驻世界贸易组织的代表团。我们将给您寄去一批(单行本)。

谨致问候!

Branislav Gosovic
2004 年 7 月 24 日

From: gosovic@southcentre.org
To: chenan@xmu.edu.cn
Sent: Saturday, July 24, 2004 7:31 PM
Subject: Re: the new version

Dear Professor An Chen,

Thank you for your message, which I just read. I was busy all week with the meetings of the Board and the Council. It was ready last Tuesday and it was distributed at the Council and sent to Permanent Missions. I will send you a supply.

Best regards,

B. Gosovic

（四）"多边投资担保机构"（MIGA）首席法律顾问 L. Weisenfeld 致陈安教授函（摘译，原文附后）

陈安教授：

上星期我在飞往南美多米尼加共和国的长途航程中，阅读了你评论美国单边主义的学术论文。这篇文章确实是具有头等水平的佳作。它论证充分，雄辩有力，析理透彻，紧扣当前话题，引人关注。你发表了这样一篇经过精心研究写成的论文，请接受我的祝贺。

你的论文使我耳目一新，促使我更好地反思许多有关国际贸易的问题，更新观念，过去我虽然知道这些问题，但从未认真深入探究。平日我阅读的大多是英国和美国的信息资料，一旦被迫从另一种迥然不同的角度观察同类问题，就会感到面临挑战。……有时，我发现自己不得不重新思考长期以来我认为"理所当然"而未加探究的某些传统观念。

总的说来，我不得不同意你的雄辩论证。在我的职业生涯中，这么迟才得出这样的结论，未免使我感到惭愧，特别是因为我在东南亚各国工作过程中，长期以来听到人们对美国的"301 条款"抱怨连连，可是一直到我阅读你的这篇论文以前，我始终没有认真思考过全面的情况。因此，我认为，对于集中半年或一年时间研修国际贸易法的学生说来，认真阅读你的这篇论文，谅必会受益不浅。

在当今布什当政时期，美国在各种国际场合的言行促使我反复思考我自己这个国家在国际舞台上的所作所为。理所当然，现在布什政府在有关环境条约、贸易制裁、国际刑事立法等方面所采取的立场，我一直是不能苟同的。而你在论文中所援引的各种事例，对于非专业人士而言虽较为生疏和不很熟悉，但却是美国对待国际经济法的"布什程式"的重要组成部分。

…………

总之，你的这篇论文是深思熟虑，催人猛醒的。我认为，它对于（国际法）这个学术领域做出了有益的贡献。厦门大学法学院可以为写出了如此高质量的论文感到自豪，你确实已经为这个学术机构增添了光彩。

…………

Lorin Weisenfeld
MIGA 首席法律顾问
2004 年 5 月 12 日

From: Lweisenfeld@worldbank.org
To: chenan@xmu.edu.cn
Sent: Wednesday, May 12, 2004 4:26 AM
Subject: Warmest Congratulations

Dear Prof. Chen,

I went last week to the Dominican Republic, and your article on U. S. unilateralism kept me company on the long flight down. It was an absolutely first rate piece. The article was well-argued, well-written, timely and even interesting. Please accept my congratulations for having turned out such a well-researched piece.

Your article refreshed my memory, helped me to put into better focus issues that I have read about but not been forced to dwell on, and sharpened my thinking about these trade questions. Because so much of my reading is of Anglo-Saxon sources, it is challenging to be forced to look at certain familiar issues from quite a different perspective... Every once in a while, I found myself forced to rethink notions that I had long taken for granted without further examination.

By and large, I have to agree with your argument. I suppose that I should be embarrassed to be reaching this conclusion so late in my career, particularly since I have been hearing complaints in Southeast Asia over Sec. 301 for a long time, but I never really stopped to think long about the whole picture until I read your article. I can imagine, therefore, the benefits of reading your article that will acree to a student of international trade law, who is spending a concentrated semester or year trying to get a handle on the subject. Your article will be very helpful.

The behavior of the United States in international fora under this Bush administration has made me think about my own country's behavior on the international scene. Certainly, this Bush administration has taken positions — the environmental treaty, the trade sanctions, the international criminal code, etc. — with which I disagree. The instances that you cite, more arcane and less familiar to laymen, are part and parcel of the Bush approach to international economic law.

...

Of course, if one looks back over the history of the United States, one sees that our views of ourselves in the larger world have ebbed and flowed over time. In the middle of the last century, we were said to be "jingoistic", with our notions of Westward expansion, "manifest destiny", "54′40″ or fight", "Remember the Maine!", etc. Lord knows that Mexico has still not gotten over our attitudes of the last century. Then, in this century, we shifted to a proudly isolationist approach to international relations, safe behind "Fortress America". No matter how hard he tried, President Wilson could not bring the U.S. into the League of Nations. As a kid, I remember the bombastic Sen. Knowland of California with his isolationist dogmas. And now the pendulum has swung once again. Messrs. Bush, Cheney, et al. have found a doctrine of "preemptive war" somewhere and are quite happy operating from the position of what the French scornfully call a "hyperpower". History will judge the results.

...

Your paper, in sum, was thoughtful and provocative. I think that it has made a useful contribution to the field. Xiamen Law School can be proud that writing of this quality is produced within its halls. You have made the institution look good, indeed.

It turns out that, for a change, I have an enormous amount of news regarding MIGA. We had a significant change in management on May 3, resulting in the replacement of the executive vice president and two of the four senior managers. A new team has taken the reins, and the institution is in the process of a thorough reorganization. I believe, personally, that we had a number of managerial problems in recent years, and I sincerely hope that the changes being implemented will reinvigorate the organization. I support and welcome them. Yet, all change of this sort brings tensions and transitional issues, as well as temporary uncertainty. Our transition has been a bit rocky, but I assume that matters will settle down in due course. I will bring you up to date on these changes in MIGA when I see you in June.

One of the difficulties that we need to traverse at the moment is an increase in the work-load in the face of a diminished budget. This has affected all of us. I have had to postpone my trip to China from May to June because of more pressing difficulties affecting our clients, and now I am hoping, as we near the end of our fiscal year, that we have enough money left in the till to be able to afford the trip that I propose to take in June. In theory, I will arrive in Beijing on June 16. I hope to arrive in Xiamen on June 18. Regrettably, I will only be able to stay for a day. I will be able to confirm these arrangements when I return to the office in early June from Eastern Europe.

Prof. Chen Huiping has been a good friend and colleague and I will send her a copy of this e-mail, together with a separate note responding to her last two e-mails. I am without a secretary now, since Lucy has left for greener pastures and we are not in a position to replace her. That makes production more difficult than formerly.

I look forward to seeing you all in June.

Cordially,

Lorin Weisenfeld

Principal Counsel, MIGA

(五)"解决投资争端国际中心"(ICSID)法律顾问 A. Parra 致陈安教授函(中文摘译见前"来函概述"之(四),原文附后)

March 22, 1990

Professor An Chen

Dean and Professor of Law

School of Politics and Law

Box 978

Xiamen University

Xiamen

Fujian, China

Dear Professor An Chen,

Further to Mr. Shihata's January 30 letter to you, I would like to renew our gratitude to you for so kindly sending us your article on whether an absolute immunity from nationalization for foreign investment should be enacted in China's law concerning the Special Economic Zones and Coastal Port Cities.

As Mr. Shihata is currently away on business, I would like to take this opportunity to thank you very much on his behalf for sending him the copy of your new book on ICSID. We will be announcing the book's publication in the upcoming new issue of News from ICSID, and plan also to list it in the next edition of the ICSID Bibliography.

The new issue of News from ICSID will also be reporting China's signature of the ICSID Convention on February 9, 1990. In case you would like to have a copy, I am pleased to enclose the news release that we issued on this important occasion.

With best regards,

Sincerely yours,
Antonio R. Parra
Managing Editor
ICSID Review

※　※　※

August 22, 1990

Professor An Chen

Visiting Professor

Northwestern School of Law

Lewis & Clark College

10015 S. W. Terwilliger Boulevard

Portland, Oregon 97219

Dear Professor An Chen,

On behalf of Mr. Shihata, I would like to thank you very much for your letter of July 12. I also am grateful for your separate letter to me. We are looking forward to reading your book that you kindly sent us on the legal aspects of foreign investment in China. I hope that we can have it reviewed for the ICSID Review.

...

The article that you also kindly sent to us on foreign investment laws of China is circulating amongst my colleagues in the Editorial Committee of the ICSID Review, and I will be writing to you again in due course on the possibility of our including it in a future issue.

Pursuant to your request, I am meanwhile pleased to enclose a copy of the issue of News from ICSID announcing the publication of your new book on the Centre. Judging from the translation of the table of contents of this book, it must be a most useful work.

I am looking forward to keeping in touch with you.

With best regards,

Sincerely yours,
Antonio R. Parra
Legal Adviser

(六) 美国唐肯(Tonkon et al.)律师事务所首席律师 O. D. Blank 致陈安教授函(摘译,原文附后)

陈安教授:

非常感谢您寄来最近发表在《律师》杂志上的论文。您针对中国与美国经济互利关系所作的分析,切合实际,令人耳目一新。您对于中国继续实行开放政策所作的论证,很有必要加以广泛、普及的宣传,以促使美国的许多公司恢复信心——它们在"1989 年政治风波"以前本来已经很好地确立了这种信心。

…………

O. D. Blank
1991 年 7 月 5 日

July 5, 1991

Professor An Chen
Northwestern School of Law
Lewis & Clark College
1015 S. W. Terwilliger Blvd.
Portland, Oregon 97219

Dear Professor Chen,

I greatly appreciate receiving the copy of your recent article in *The Advocate*. Your analysis of the mutual interests of China and the United States is refreshingly practical. The evidence regarding China's continued "open-door" policy needs to be widely disseminated in order for U. S. companies to regain the confidence that was building so well prior to the Tiananmen Event.

China and the United Stated both face complex political dilemmas. As China reaps the benefits of the open-door policy and of becoming a more significant "player" in the world, it must deal with the "burden" of having its external as well as internal policies subject to scrutiny by others. The world is getting smaller. As it does so, sovereignty is constantly being smaller. As it does so, sovereignty is constantly being redefined by the increased amount of political, cultural, economic and social interchange.

It is my hope and belief that by maintaining good relations between the United States and China, the peoples of both nations will benefit from the positive aspects of each nation and will learn that constructive criticism from friends is not intrusion. Rather, it is a way friends help each other.

I hope you are enjoying your visiting professorship at Lewis & Clark Law School. I look forward to seeing you in the near future.

Very truly yours,
Owen D. Blank

(七) 美国路易斯与克拉克西北法学院律师进修班主任 L. B. Mapes 致陈安教授函(中文摘译见前"来函概述"之(六),原文附后)

November 29, 1988

Professor An Chen

P. O. Box 978

Xiamen University

Xiamen, Fujian

People's Republic of China

Dear Professor An Chen,

On behalf of the Law School, I thank you for your participation in our Third Annual International Business Law Seminar: Contract Negotiations with China in the 1990's, on October 28, 1988. The program was a tremendous success, as you know. We have received many compliments on the seminar and on your speech, "One Decade of Chinese Foreign Investment Laws." We are grateful to you for your contribution to a fine program that has brought great honor and prestige to the Law School.

Thank you also for participating in many activities with our faculty, students, and friends of the Law School. We are very grateful that you were able to spend some time here in Portland; we only wish you could have stayed longer. It was our pleasure to have you here with us.

I know that I speak for the entire Law School when I say that we are delighted that we have developed a close relationship with you and with the Xiamen University School of Law and Politics. We hope that our exchange will grow in the future.

I appreciated the opportunity to become acquainted with you. Thank you again for your beautiful gifts, which I will treasure and which will remind me of your visit here.

Copies of the videotapes of the seminar will arrive in a separate package. I hope that you will find them useful—perhaps your colleagues at Xiamen University School of Law would like to see them.

Again, thank you for traveling so far to participate in the Third Annual International Business Law Seminar. Your presence at the seminar and at the Law School afterward enriched the lives of many people.

Sincerely,

Laurie B. Mapes, Director

Continuing Legal Education

(八) 美国哈佛大学法学院助理院长、东亚法学研究所副所长 F. E. Snyder 致陈安教授函（中译，原文附后）

陈安教授：

承赠送您在东亚法学研究所午餐会上学术演讲文稿一份，非常感谢。正如我曾经对您说过[14]，这次演说非常打动人心，很能发人深思，令人兴趣盎然。您的文稿中对于保护外国投资的两种不同做法的有关论述，也相当深刻周详。我认为，您针对美国（保护海外投资）的立场得到（某些国家）追随而又遭到（许多国家）挑战这个问题所作的论述，是特别有意义的。我殷切地期待您能把这篇文章公开发表，从而使国际法学界有更多人可以从您的深刻见解中获得教益。

祝一切顺利！

F. E. Snyder

哈佛大学法学院助理院长

哈佛大学东亚法学研究所副所长

1982 年 10 月 19 日

---

[14] 斯奈德助理院长当时是这场演讲会的主席（主持人），他曾在演讲结束时当场作过一些评论。

October 19, 1982
Professor An Chen
Pound 419

Dear An:

Many thanks for sending me a copy of your East Asian Legal Studies luncheon lecture. The talk was, as I mentioned to you, very stimulating, very provocative, very interesting. The discussion in your written text of the two different approaches to the protection of foreign investment is, similarly, very thoughtful. I found your discussion of the extent to which the American position has been followed and challenged to be especially helpful. It is my firm hope that you will be able to publish this piece so that more members of the international legal community will be able to benefit from your insights.

With all good wishes,

Sincerely,

Frederick E. Snyder

Assistant Dean and Associate Administrator

East Asian Legal Studies

(九）美国哈佛大学法学院斯托里讲座教授[15]、东亚法学研究所所长 A. von Mehren 致陈安教授函（中译，原文附后）

陈安教授：

您以访问学者身份逗留哈佛大学法学院以来，即将届满一年。我的同事们以及我自己都非常高兴有机会逐渐地亲自了解和熟悉您，并且从您这里学到了许多有关中华人民共和国法律规章和生活实际的知识。

我获悉您曾在几种场合对本院的学生和教员们做过演讲。此外，我还阅读了您写的题为《是进一步开放？还是重新关门？》的文章，论述同中国吸收外国投资有关的各种认识问题和法律问题；也阅读了您那篇将于11月发表在纽约法学院《国际法与比较法学报》上评论李爽案件的文章。

---

[15] 在美国，"讲座教授"是一种学术上的荣誉称号。美国大学往往把这种称号授予学术成就卓著的权威教授。斯托利（Joseph Story），19世纪中叶美国的法学权威，曾任美国最高法院大法官三十余年，哈佛大学名教授。用他的姓氏命名讲座，以示纪念。

我认为这两篇文章对于有关主题所作的论述,都是很有教益和很有创见的。两篇文章都写得条理分明,行文妥善。每一篇都大大有助于促进美国的读者加深理解您所论述的问题。

我们东亚法学研究所的同事,大家都知道您在这里的工作中,一向是干劲充沛和专心致志的。您的两篇论文就是令人钦佩的例证,说明您的研究工作的质量和成就。我们高兴的是:如今您在美国帮助我们理解中国的法律和社会,日后回到中国,您有能力在那里以同样的方式向您的同事以及学生们阐明有关美国法律和美国社会的各个方面。

您能同我们一起度过本学年剩下的时间,我们都感到高兴。我们盼望:我们同您之间已经建立起来的个人接触和学术联系,在您返回中国之后仍能继续下去,并且欣欣向荣,开花结果。

谨致高度敬意。

Arthur von Mehren
斯托里法学讲座教授
哈佛大学东亚法学研究所所长
1982 年 10 月 25 日

October 25, 1982

Professor An Chen

Harvard Law School

Pound 523

Cambridge, Massachusetts 02138

Dear Professor An Chen,

It will soon be a year since you began your stay at Harvard Law School as a Visiting Scholar. My colleagues and myself have enjoyed greatly the opportunity to come to know you personally and have learned from you much about law and life in the people's Republic of China.

I have heard you speak on several occasions to student and faculty groups here. In addition, I have read your paper entitled "To Open Wider or to Close Again?" in which you discuss various of ideological and legal problems that arise in connection with China's approach to foreign investment, and your discussion of the Li Shuang case which will be published in November in the New York Law School's Journal of International and Comparative Law.

I found both of these papers instructive and thoughtful treatments of their respective subjects. Both papers are clearly and well written. Each advances significantly the understanding of an American audience with respect to the issues that you discuss.

All of us associated with the East Asian Legal Studies Program know the energy and devotion with which you have carried on your work here. Your two articles are admirable examples of the quality and success of your studies. We are delighted that when you return to China you will be in a position to explain to your colleagues and students there various aspects of American law and society in the same way as you have helped us to understand Chinese law and society.

We are delighted that you will be with us for the remainder of this academic year and we hope that the personal and intellectual contacts that we have established with you will continue and flourish after your return to China.

With high regard,

Yours sincerely,

Arthur von Mehren

Story Professor of Law and Director,

East Asian Legal Studies Program

(十) 日本访美研究员、金融经济专家杉原启示致陈安教授函（中译，原文附后）

陈安教授阁下敬启者：

1982年10月1日，适值中国革命纪念日之际，能聆听教授阁下有关中国吸收外资政策之讲演，深受教益。通过先生之讲演，我得以加深理解当前中国一方面继续坚持一贯奉行之自力更生路线，另一方面又利用外国技术与资本，旨在以中国独特之方式方法，实现社会主义现代化。

我服务于日本国家石油公司。该公司系日本政府国营机构，目前已经以投资参加中日合作之方式，正在中国渤海湾以及鄂尔多斯地区积极推进石油开发事业。我认为，日前先生发表之高见对于日本国民理解中国之政策精神，颇具参考价值，故已将先生惠赠之讲演原文（英文）稿件，迅即摘译要旨，径送日本国家石油公司参考。

我相信，就日中两国关系而言，今后必将在经济与文化两个方面继续通力合作，共谋发展。我得以在美国哈佛大学此地与先生邂逅相识，今后如能继续交换意见,则不胜荣幸!先生善识日文,故今日谨以日文书写此感谢信,特此表示谢忱。请恕草草。

杉原启示 拜上
哈佛大学(日、美)交换研究员、
日本国家石油公司金融经济专家
昭和五十七年(1982年)10月30日

厦門大学法学部国際経済法研究科主任、
厦門大学学術委員会委員
陳安教授殿

　拝啓　中国の革命記念日に当たる1982年10月1日に陳安教授より中国の外資導入政策についての講演を聞き、大変有益でした。先生の講演を通じて、現在の中国が従来の自力更生路線を続行しつつも、海外の技術と資本を利用し、中国独自の方法で社会主義の近代化を目ざしていることがわかりました。
　私の会社が石油会社という日本政府機関で、現在既に渤海湾とオルドス地方で中日協力により石油開発事業を推進しておりますが、先生のご意見は日本側が中国の考え方を知るのに対して大変参考になると思っております。先生から頂いた原稿を早速要旨を書いて日本会社宛に送付しておりました。
　今後も日中関係の経済？文化両面での協力をしつつ、発展していくと思います。米国ハーバード大学でお知り合いになった上、今後も前向きに意見交換できる関係を継続していただければ幸甚で存じます。先生が日本語がお上手なので、本日は日本語でお礼の手紙を書かせていただきました。
　草々をご了承いただけますようお願いします。

杉原啓示
ハーバード大学交換研究員、日本石油会社・金融エコノミスト
昭和五十七年10月30日

(十一) 美国纽约法学院《国际法与比较法学报》主编 E. H. Higa 致陈安教授函(摘译,原文附后)

陈安教授:

　　　………

　您感到诧异,何以一家美国法学杂志愿意发表由一位中华人民共和国公民撰写的文章,批评一家美国报纸的新闻报道。但是,事实上我们很高兴采用这篇论文,并且引以为荣。

....

您这篇论文的主题是评论刊载于《纽约时报》的克利斯托弗·雷恩所写的两篇报道。这些报道曾经引起人们对中华人民共和国政府当局处理李爽案件的做法,啧有烦言,纷纷非难。您的文章提出了人们所殷切期待的答案。这种答案,来自中华人民共和国的一位公民,来自一位像您这样卓越出色的中国法学学者,是再恰当不过的了。

您的这篇论文从中国的风俗习惯、志向抱负、政治和社会的奋斗目标的角度,从反映着这些因素的法律体制的角度,条理分明、令人信服地剖析了李爽案件。我不能设想有比这更加雄辩透彻的解释说明。

您对于美国和中国的刑事法制所作的比较分析是特别有教益和富有启发性的。不过,我认为最能发人深思的还是您所使用的方法,即把李爽案件放置在中国的社会主义理论、社会主义实践以及社会主义目标的背景之中,加以剖析。

我简要地说明了我对您这篇论文的看法,希望这能敦促您继续向本刊投寄您的精辟论著,并且向您的同事们恳切说明我们美国人(特别是本刊同仁们)怀有重大的兴趣,期待收到中华人民共和国这些饱学的法学教授们投寄具有创见的法学学术论文。

谨致最友好的敬意。

Emlyn H. Higa

纽约法学院《国际法与比较法学报》1981—1982 年主编

1982 年 11 月 19 日

November 19, 1982

Prof. An Chen

423 Pound Hall

Harvard Law School

Cambridge, Massachusetts 02138

Dear Prof. Chen,

...

This is in response to your inquiry, made on behalf of your colleagues in the People's Republic of China, regarding my reasons for accepting your article on the Li

Shuang case for publication in the *New York Law School Journal of International and Comparative Law*. I am honored to have received the request and delighted to respond.

Although you expressed surprise that an American law journal would publish an article written by a citizen of the People's Republic of China that was critical of an American newspaper story, the fact is that we were pleased and honored to receive it.

...

The United States, as you well know, is a country born of rebellion and suckled on controversy. We are like a large, ill-mannered family whose members wranle loudly and sometimes violently with each other, seeming not to care that our neighbors may be disturbed by our domestic squabbling. But what binds us together is our common belief in the principle that for knowledge and wisdom and understanding to increase, debate must be open and free. Genuine doubts must always be voiced and responsible criticism is never improper.

We are a young nation. And with the restless enthusiasm and arrogant scepticism of youth, we are always greedy for new knowledge, straining to hear a new voice, or to see a new viewpoint. Therefore, when a charge is made, everyone waits and listens for the answer.

Christopher Wren's articles in the *New York Times*, which are the subject of your article, evoked much criticism of the way that the authorities in the People's Republic of China handled the Li Shuang Case. Your article provides the much awaited answer. An answer that can come from no one other than a citizen of the People's Republic of China and can come from no more appropriate citizen than such an eminent legal scholar as you.

Your article very clearly and responsibly explains the Li Shuang Case from the perspective of the customs, expectations, the political and social ambitions of the People's Republic of China, and the legal structure that expresses them. And I cannot imagine a more eloquent explanation.

Your comparative analysis of the criminal systems of the United States and of the People's Republic of China is particularly helpful and illuminating. But what I consider most thought-provoking is the way that you place the Li Shuang Case within the context of Chinese socialist doctrine, practice and purposes.

I hope that this abbreviated explanation of my attitude toward your article will encourage you to submit more of your excellent work to the Journal; and that you will urge upon your colleagues the great interest we in the United States, and particularly we at the Journal, have in receiving thoughtful, scholarly legal writing from such learned law professors in the People's Republic of China.

With much friendship and respect,

Emlyn H. Higa

Editor-in-Chief (1981-1982)

(十二) 美国波士顿大学法学院教授、哈佛大学东亚法学研究所前副所长 F. K. Upham 教授致陈安教授函

陈安教授：

非常感谢您在 1982 年 11 月 4 日寄来信件，并附赠有关李爽案件的论文清样。

我认为，您的论文以一个中国法学学者的敏锐眼光，对这桩案件作了引人入胜的、相当精辟的阐述。您那精心细致、沉着冷静的分析，提出了一些重要的课题，它们将郑重提醒美国的法学研究生们必须注意另外一种法学观点，这种法学观点往往同他们原有的观点迥然相异，并且难得有人能够妥善确切地加以论述阐明。我的研究专业虽是日本的法学，但我仍然打算今后要求我的研究生们阅读您的这篇论文。因为这篇论文是如此妥帖完善地阐明了中国法制与美国法制之间的基本区别和某些相似之处，而这两种法制对日本法制的形成，向来是有促进作用的。

趁此写信机会，让我另外向您致谢，感谢您上学年（1981—1982）在我担任哈佛东亚法学研究所副所长期间（Upham 教授于 1982 年 9 月离开哈佛，应聘在波士顿大学执教）所给予我的支持帮助。您是一位优秀出色的同事，我盼望今后能继续保持我们之间的友好关系。

谨致最良好的祝愿。

Frank K. Upham

哈佛大学东亚法学研究所 1981—1982 年副所长

1982 年 11 月 29 日

November 29, 1982

Professor An Chen

East Asian Legal Studies

Harvard Law School

Cambridge, MA 02138

Dear An Chen:

Thank you very much for your letter of November 4, 1982, and for sending me the proofs of your article relating to the Li Shuang Case.

I found your article fascinating and an excellent presentation of the case from the perspective of a Chinese legal scholar. Your careful, calm analysis raises the important issues in a way that will alert American law students to a view of law often very different from theirs and seldom well articulated. Even though my specialty is Japanese law, I plan to have my students read your article in the future because it so well presents the underlying differences and similarities in the Chinese and American legal systems that have both helped form Japan's.

On a different topic, let me take this opportunity to thank you for your support last year (1981-1982) while I was Associate Director of East Asian Legal Studies. You were an excellent colleague, and I hope we can continue our relationship in the future.

With all best wishes,

Frank K. Upham

Visiting Professor

Associate Director, East Asian

Legal Studies, 1981-1982

第3章　陈安学术小传及历年主要论著目录(以倒计年为序)

一、陈安学术小传

陈安,福建人,厦门大学法学院前院长和国际经济法研究所所长(1987—1998年),法学教授、博士生导师,国际知名的中国学者。主要学术兼职:中国国际经济法学会荣誉会长(2011年至今),中国政府依据《华盛顿公约》于1993年、2004年、2010年三度遴选向"解决投资争端国际中心"(ICSID)指派的国际仲裁员等。1950年厦门大学法律系毕业,1957年复旦大学政治学理论研究生班毕业。

1981—1983年应邀在美国哈佛大学从事国际经济法研究,并兼部分讲学。1990—1991年以"亚洲杰出学者"名义应聘担任美国俄勒冈州路易斯与克拉克西北法学院客座教授兼国际法研究学术顾问。先后多次应邀赴美、加、比(欧共体总部)、瑞士(联合国欧洲总部)、德、英、澳、法、韩等国家和地区参加国际学术会议或讲学。

在法律实务方面,陈安教授是兼职资深国际商务律师,跨国公司法律顾问;中国国际经贸仲裁委员会(CIETAC)仲裁员,国际商会(ICC)国际仲裁案件仲裁员,法国国际仲裁协会(IAI)仲裁员,美国国际仲裁员名册(RIA)仲裁员等。

近四十年来,陈安教授立足于中国国情和国际弱势群体即广大发展中国家的共同立场,致力于探索和开拓具有中国特色的国际经济法学这一新兴边缘学科。撰写和主编的主要著作有《中国的呐喊:陈安论国际经济法》《陈安论国际经济法学》《国际经济法学刍言》《美国对海外投资的法律保护及典型案例分析》《国际经济立法的历史和现状》《国际经济法总论》《国际经济法学》《国际经济法学专论》《国际投资法》《国际贸易法》《国际货币金融法》《国际税法》《国际海事法》《国际投资争端仲裁——"解决投资争端国际中心"机制研究》《MIGA与中国:多边投资担保机构述评》等44种,合计约25000余万字。另在《中国社会科学》《中国法学》、国际政府间组织"南方中心"机关学刊《南方公报》(South Bulletin)、美国纽约法学院《国际法与比较法学报》、天普大学《国际法与比较法学报》《威拉梅特大学法律评论》、日内瓦《国际仲裁学刊》《世界投资与贸易学报》等国内外学术刊物上发表多篇论文。多项学术论著获国家级、省部级科研优秀成果一等奖[16],或被指定为全国性高校本科生、研究生法学教材或教学参考书。

此外,陈安教授还兼任全国性的国际经济法专业优秀学术论文的汇辑《国际经济法学刊》的主编、《中国大百科全书·法学》(修订版)国际经济法分支的主编。

陈安教授1960年被评为福建省劳模,1992年获国务院政府特殊津贴。1987、1994、2003、2006年先后四次获得厦门大学最高荣誉奖"南强奖"一等奖;2008年又获"南强奖"特等奖。

《人民日报》(海外版)、《光明日报》《法制日报》等报刊以及国务院学位委员会刊物《学位与研究生教育》先后多次报道他的学术观点和有关事迹。[17] 美国、英国多种《国际名人录》均列有陈安教授的个人小传。

二、陈安历年主要论著

(一) 书籍

1. 《美国霸权版"中国威胁"谰言的前世与今生》(专著),江苏人民出版社2015年版。

2. The Voice from China: An CHEN on International Economic Law(英文版专著,中文名《中国的呐喊:陈安论国际经济法》),德国Springer出版社2013年版。

3. 《陈安论国际经济法学》(五卷本)(专著),复旦大学出版社2008年版。

4. 《国际经济法学专论》(上、下两卷)(主编),高等教育出版社2004年第一版、2007年第二版。

5. 《国际经济法学学刊》(原名《国际经济法学论丛》,2004年改用现名,第1—23

---

[16] 详见本书第七编第4章"陈安教授论著、业绩获奖一览(以倒计年为序/2016—1960)"。
[17] 例如,(1)《适应对外开放和发展外向型经济需要,国际经济法系列专著问世》,载《光明日报》1988年4月26日;(2)《就闽台两省结拜"姊妹"一事厦门大学法学教授发表看法》,载《人民日报》(海外版)1989年5月8日;(3)《为对外开放铺路——记厦门大学法学教授陈安》,载《人民日报》(海外版)1992年7月7日;(4)《理性务实的学术交流盛会——1993年两岸法学学术研讨会综述》,载《人民日报》(海外版)1993年8月27日;(5)《当代经济主权问题纵横谈》,载《法制日报》1997年3月22日;(6)《第十二届"安子介国际贸易研究奖"颁奖》,载《人民日报》(海外版)2004年12月21日。以上这些报道,均已收辑于《陈安论国际经济法学》第八编之 I "媒体报道"。

卷)(主编),法律出版社、北京大学出版社 1998—2017 年版。

6.《国际经济法学》(第一版至第七版)(主编),北京大学出版社 1994—2017 年版。

7.《国际经济法学资料选萃》(主编),高等教育出版社 2007 年版。

8.《国际投资法的新发展与中国双边投资条约的新实践》(主编),复旦大学出版社 2007 年版。

9.《国际经济法》(主编),法律出版社 1999 年第一版、2007 年第二版。

10.《国际经济法学新论》(主编),高等教育出版社 2007 年版。

11.《国际经济法学资料新编》(上、下两卷)(主编),北京大学出版社 2008 年版。

12.《中国大百科全书·法学》(修订版)之国际经济法分支学科(主编),中国大百科全书出版社 2006 年版。

13.《国际经济法学刍言》(上、下两卷)(专著),北京大学出版社 2005 年版。

14.《国际经济法概论》(第一版至第四版)(主编),北京大学出版社 1995—2010 年版。

15.《国际投资争端案例精选》(主编),复旦大学出版社 2001 年版。

16.《国际投资争端仲裁——"解决投资争端国际中心"机制研究》(主编),复旦大学出版社 2001 年版。

17."国际经济法学系列专著"(总主编,五卷),北京大学出版社 1999—2001 年版(含《国际投资法学》《国际贸易法学》《国际货币金融法学》《国际税法学》《国际海事法学》)。

18.《海峡两岸交往中的法律问题研究》(主编),北京大学出版社 1997 年版。

19.《台湾法律大全》(主编),中国大百科全书出版社 1998 年版。

20.《MIGA 与中国:多边投资担保机构述评》(主编),福建人民出版社 1995 年版。

21.《涉外经济合同的理论与实务》(主编),中国政法大学出版社 1994 年版。

22.《国际经济法资料选编》(主编),法律出版社 1991 年版。

23.《国际经济法总论》(主编),法律出版社 1991 年版。

24.《台湾涉外经济法概要》(主编),鹭江出版社 1990 年版。

25.《"解决投资争端国际中心"述评》(专著),鹭江出版社 1989 年版。

26."国际经济法系列专著"(主编,五卷),鹭江出版社 1987—1989 年版(含《国际投资法》《国际贸易法》《国际货币金融法》《国际税法》《国际海事法》)。

27.《舌剑唇枪:国际投资纠纷五大著名案例》(主编),鹭江出版社 1986 年版。

28.《美国对海外投资的法律保护及典型案例分析》(专著),鹭江出版社 1985 年版。

29.《国际经济立法的历史和现状》(日文、英文编译),法律出版社 1982 年版。

30.《列宁对民族殖民地革命学说的重大发展》(专著),生活·读书·新知三联书店 1981 年版。

31.《印度特仑甘纳人民的斗争及其经验教训》(英文译著),生活·读书·新知三联书店 1977 年版。

32.《修正主义反对无产阶级专政学说》(俄文译著),生活·读书·新知三联书店 1962 年版。

33.《反对修正主义》(俄文译著),生活·读书·新知三联书店 1961 年版。

34.《现代资产阶级社会学关于阶级和阶级斗争的各种反科学理论》(俄文译著),上海人民出版社 1958 年版。

(二) 论文

1.《"左公柳"、中国魂与新丝路》。

2.《建构中国特色国际法学理论》,载《人民日报》2017 年 5 月 8 日第 15 版学术版。

3.《向世界展现中国理念》,载《人民日报》2016 年 6 月 5 日第 5 版学术版。

4.《朝着合作共赢方向发展 推动国际经济法理念变革》,载《人民日报》2016 年 11 月 7 日第 16 版学术版。

5.《小议对外学术交流的三种"大忌"》,载《光明日报》2015 年 7 月 31 日第 2 版评论·观点版。

6. A Reflection on the South-South Coalition in the Last Half Century from the Perspective of International Economic Law-making: From Bandung, Doha and Cancún to Hong Kong,原发表于 *The Journal of World Investment & Trade* (Geneva)2006 年第 7 卷第 2 期。经增订更新,被收辑于在海牙、纽约、伦敦同时推出的学术专著《从第三世界视角看通过贸易谋求经济发展》(*Economic Development Through Trade:A Third World Perspective*),由 Kluwer Law International 于 2007 年 12 月出版。

7.《区分两类国家,实行差别互惠:再论 ICSID 体制赋予中国的四大"安全阀"不宜贸然全面拆除》,载《国际经济法学刊》2007 年第 14 卷第 3 期。

8. Distinguishing Two Kinds of Countries and Granting Differential

Reciprocity: Re-comments on the Four Safeguards in Sino-Foreign BITs Not to Be Hastily and Completely Dismantled, *The Journal of World Investment & Trade* (Geneva), Vol. 7, No. 2, 2007.

9. Should the Four Great Safeguards in Sino-Foreign BITs Be Hastily Dismantled? *The Journal of World Investment & Trade*, Vol. 7, Iss. 6, 2006.

10. Weak Versus Strong at the WTO, *The Geneva Post Quarterly: The Journal of World Affairs*, Vol. 1, No. 1, 2006.

11.《中外双边投资协定中的四大"安全阀"不宜贸然拆除》,载《国际经济法学刊》2006年第13卷第1期。

12.《南南联合自强五十年的国际经济立法反思:从万隆、多哈、坎昆到香港》,载《中国法学》2006年第2期。

13. Be Optimistic, or Be Pessimistic? The Fork Confronting DDR and WTO After Its Hong Kong Ministerial Conference, *South Bulletin*, No. 120, 2006.

14.《外商在华投资中的"空手道"融资:"一女两婿"与"两裁六审"》,载《国际经济法学刊》2005年第12卷第3期。

15.《外贸代理合同纠纷中的当事人、管辖权、准据法、仲裁庭、债务人等问题剖析——韩国C公司诉中国X市A、B两公司案件述评》,载《国际经济法学刊》2004年第9卷第2期。

16.《美国单边主义对抗WTO多边主义的第三回合——"201条款"争端之法理探源和展望》,载《中国法学》2004年第2期。

17. The Three Big Rounds of U. S. Unilateralism Versus WTO Multilateralism During the Last Decade: A Combined Analysis of the Great 1994 Sovereignty Debate, Section 301 Disputes (1998-2000), and Section 201 Disputes (2002-2003), *Temple International and Comparative Law Journal*, Vol. 17, No. 2, 2003. 后该文经修订增补,由国际组织"南方中心"(South Centre)作为其"工作文件"第22号,于2004年7月以"单行本"形式发行,并全文公布于该中心的网站。

18.《论涉外仲裁个案中的越权管辖、越权解释、草率断结和有欠透明——CIETAC 2001—2002年个案评析》,载《国际经济法论丛》2003年第7卷。

19.《中国"入世"后海峡两岸经贸问题"政治化"之防治》(增订本),载《国际经济法论丛》2002年第6卷。

20.《中国"入世"后海峡两岸经贸问题"政治化"之防治》,载《中国法学》2002年第2期。

21.《世纪之交围绕经济主权的新"攻防战"——从美国的"主权大辩论"及其后续影响看当代"主权淡化"论之不可取》,载《国际经济法论丛》2001 年第 4 卷。

22.《美国"1994 年主权大辩论"及其后续影响》,载《中国社会科学》2001 年第 5 期。

23.《评对中国国际经济法学科发展现状的几种误解》,载《东南学术》1999 年第 3 期。

24.《再论中国涉外仲裁的监督机制及其与国际惯例的接轨》(增订本),载《国际经济法论丛》1999 年第 2 卷。

25.《指鹿为马,枉法裁断——评港英高等法院 1994 年的一项涉华判决》,载《升华与超越:大学生文化素质教育讲座集锦 3》,高等教育出版社 1998 年版。

26.《论国际经济法的边缘性、综合性和独立性》,载《国际经济法论丛》1998 年第 1 卷。

27.《中国涉外仲裁监督机制申论》,载《中国社会科学》1998 年第 2 期。

28.《英、美、法、德等国涉外仲裁监督机制辨析》,载《法学评论》1998 年第 5 期。

29.《再论中国涉外仲裁的监督机制及其与国际惯例的接轨》,载《民商法论丛》1998 年第 10 卷。

30.《论中国涉外仲裁的监督机制及其与国际惯例的接轨》(英文),载《国际仲裁学刊》(日内瓦)1997 年第 14 卷第 3 期。

31.《一项判决 三点质疑》(中文增订本),载《民商法论丛》1997 年第 8 卷。

32.《一项判决 三点质疑:香港高等法院 1993 年第 A8176 号判决评析》(英文),载《国际仲裁学刊》(日内瓦)1996 年第 13 卷第 4 期。

33.《台商大陆投资保险可行途径初探》,载《中国法学》1995 年第 5 期。

34.《论中国涉外仲裁的监督机制及其与国际惯例的接轨》,载《比较法研究》1995 年第 4 期。

35.《中国涉外仲裁监督机制评析》,载《中国社会科学》1995 年第 4 期。

36.《论国际经济法的涵义及其边缘性》,载《中国国际法年刊》,中国对外翻译出版公司 1996 年版。

37.《论适用国际惯例与有法必依的统一》,载《中国社会科学》1994 年第 4 期。

38.《论有约必守原则在国际经济法中的正确运用》,载《东亚法律·经济·文化国际学术讨论会论文集》,中国大百科全书出版社 1993 年版。

39.《"台商大陆投资权益保障协议"初剖》,载《台湾研究》1993 年第 4 期。

40.《论国际经济法中的公平互利原则》,载《中德经济法研究所年刊》1992 年卷。

41.《是重新闭关自守？还是扩大对外开放？——论中美两国经济上的互相依存以及"1989 年政治风波"后在华外资的法律环境》(英文)，载《律师》(*Advocate*)杂志(美国俄勒冈州)1991 年第 2 期。

42. Special Economic Zones and Coastal Port-Cities：Their Development and Legal Framework, *Chinese Foreign Economic Law：Analysis and Commentary*, International Law Institute，1990.

43.《两种"两岸人民关系法"之对立与统一——兼谈"闽台自由贸易协定"之可行》，载《台湾研究集刊》1990 年第 2、3 期。

44.《某些涉外经济合同何以无效以及如何防止无效》(英文)，载《威拉梅特大学法评论》(美国)1987 年第 23 卷。

45.《我国涉外经济立法中可否规定对外资不实行国有化》，载《厦门大学学报》(哲学社会科学版)1986 年第 1 期，其英译本收辑于《在华投资的法律问题》，由香港中贸翻译公司 1988 年出版。

46.《从海外私人投资公司的体制和案例看美国对海外投资的法律保护》，载《中国国际法年刊》，中国对外翻译出版公司 1986 年版。

47. China and Foreign Capital：The Legal and Organizational Framework, in Harish Karpur(ed.), *The End of an Isolation：China After Mao*, Martinus Nijhoff Publishers，1985.

48.《是进一步开放？还是重新关门？——中国吸收外资政策法令述评》(英文)，载《国际法与比较法学报》(美国)1985 年第 1 期。

49.《从海外私人投资公司的由来看美国对海外投资的法律保护》，载《中国国际法年刊》，中国对外翻译出版公司 1985 年版。

50.《是"棒打鸳鸯"吗？——就"李爽案件"评〈纽约时报〉报道兼答美国法学界同行问》(英文)，载《国际法与比较法学报》(美国)1981 年第 3 卷第 1 期。

51.《论社会帝国主义主权观的一大思想渊源》，载《吉林大学社会科学学报》1981 年第 3 期。

52.《试论和平共处与反帝斗争》，载《厦门大学学报》(哲学社会科学版)1960 年第 2 期。

第4章 陈安论著、业绩获奖一览
（以倒计年为序／2016—1960）

一、国家级、省部级一等奖

序号	获奖论著/业绩名称	奖励名称及等级	获奖时间
1	美国霸权版"中国威胁"谰言的前世与今生	全国社会科学普及工作组委会授予"优秀社会科学普及作品"荣誉称号	2016年
2	批判"黄祸"论的美国霸权版变种："中国威胁"论	福建省第十届社会科学优秀成果奖一等奖	2013年
3	为中国法学理论体系建设和法治建设做出杰出贡献	全国杰出资深法学家	2012年
4	论中国在建立国际经济新秩序中的战略定位	福建省第九届社会科学优秀成果奖一等奖	2011年
5	中国加入WTO十年的法理断想：简论WTO的法治、立法、执法、守法与变法	重庆市第十一届社会科学优秀成果奖一等奖	2011年
6	陈安论国际经济法学（复旦大学出版社出版，五卷本）	福建省第八届社会科学优秀成果奖荣誉一等奖	2009年
7	国际经济法学刍言（北京大学出版社出版，两卷本）	第五届"吴玉章人文社会科学奖"一等奖	2007年
8	南南联合自强五十年的国际经济立法反思：从万隆、多哈、坎昆到香港	福建省第七届社会科学优秀成果奖一等奖	2007年
9	美国单边主义对抗WTO多边主义的第三回合——"201条款"争端之法理探源和展望	司法部第二届全国法学教材与科研成果奖一等奖	2006年
10	美国单边主义对抗WTO多边主义的第三回合——"201条款"争端之法理探源和展望	福建省第六届社会科学优秀成果奖一等奖	2005年
11	The Three Big Rounds of U.S. Unilateralism Versus WTO Multilateralism During the Last Decade	第十二届"安子介国际贸易研究奖"一等奖	2004年

(续表)

序号	获奖论著/业绩名称	奖励名称及等级	获奖时间
12	有关涉外仲裁监督机制的系列论文(共约22万字)	第三届中国高校人文社会科学研究优秀成果奖一等奖	2003年
13	国际投资争端仲裁——"解决投资争端国际中心"机制研究	司法部第一届全国法学教材与科研成果奖一等奖	2003年
14	国际投资争端仲裁——"解决投资争端国际中心"机制研究	中国图书奖	2002年
15	MIGA与中国:多边投资担保机构述评	福建省第三届社会科学优秀成果奖一等奖	1998年
16	"解决投资争端国际中心"述评	福建省第二届社会科学优秀成果奖一等奖	1994年
17	国际经济法学系列专著(五卷本)	福建省第一届社会科学优秀成果奖一等奖	1988年
18	福建省文教战线红旗手	福建省省级劳动模范	1960年

二、国家级、省部级二等奖

序号	获奖论著名称	奖励名称及等级	获奖时间
1	陈安论国际经济法学(复旦大学出版社出版,五卷本)	第六届高等学校科学研究优秀成果奖(人文社会科学)二等奖	2013年
2	南南联合自强五十年的国际经济立法反思:从万隆、多哈、坎昆到香港	司法部第三届全国法学教材与科研成果二等奖	2009年
3	世纪之交围绕经济主权的新"攻防战"——从美国的"主权大辩论"及其后续影响看当代"主权淡化"论之不可取	第四届中国高校人文社会科学研究优秀成果奖二等奖	2006年
4	国际经济法学专论(两卷本)	福建省第五届社会科学优秀成果奖二等奖	2003年
5	美国1994年"主权大辩论"及其后续影响	福建省第五届社会科学优秀成果奖二等奖	2003年
6	台湾法律大全	福建省第四届社会科学优秀成果奖二等奖	2000年
7	论中国涉外仲裁监督机制及其与国际惯例的接轨	福建省第四届社会科学优秀成果奖二等奖	2000年
8	国际经济法学	福建省第三届社会科学优秀成果奖二等奖	1998年
9	中国涉外仲裁监督机制评析	福建省第三届社会科学优秀成果奖二等奖	1998年

三、国家级三等奖

序号	获奖论著名称	奖励名称及等级	获奖时间
1	*The Voice from China：An CHEN on International Economic Law*（《中国的呐喊：陈安论国际经济法》，英文版专著，德国 Springer 出版社出版，852 页，"国家社会科学基金中华学术外译项目"重要成果）	第七届高等学校科学研究优秀成果奖（人文社会科学）三等奖	2015 年
2	*Weak Versus Strong at the WTO：The South-South Coalition from Bandung to Hong Kong*（《世贸组织中群弱抗衡强权》，英文专论）	第五届中国高校人文社会科学研究优秀成果奖三等奖	2009 年

四、厦门大学最高荣誉奖

1	厦门大学南强杰出贡献奖	厦门大学最高荣誉奖	2015 年
2	南强奖特等奖（个人）	厦门大学最高荣誉奖	2008 年
3	南强奖一等奖（个人）	厦门大学最高荣誉奖	2006 年
4	南强奖一等奖（个人）	厦门大学最高荣誉奖	2003 年
5	南强奖一等奖（个人）	厦门大学最高荣誉奖	1994 年
6	南强奖一等奖（团队集体）	厦门大学最高荣誉奖	1987 年

以上合计：获得国家级、省部级一等奖 18 项；国家级、省部级二等奖 9 项；国家级三等奖 2 项；厦门大学最高荣誉奖 6 项。总共 35 项。其中 33 项均为 1988—2015 年获得。在这 33 项中，有 26 项是陈安教授 1999 年退休后获得的。

(2016 年 12 月 12 日整理)

索　引

索引词条体例说明：(1) 按音序排列；(2) 词条设置三级；(3) 为查索方便，主要词条设置上互有交叉，互相呼应；(4) 主要案例列于 A 部分"案例剖析"词条项下；(5) 外国学者姓名中英文对照列于 W 部分。

A

案例剖析

　　1966 年韦布斯特出版公司索赔案 1280
　　1967 年瓦伦泰因石油化工公司索赔案
　　　　1262—1265
　　1967 年中央大豆公司索赔案 1289—1290
　　1968 年印第安头人公司索赔案 1253—1257
　　1971 年贝尔彻木材公司索赔案 1257—1258
　　1972 年华尔施建设公司索赔案 1291—1292
　　1973 年佐治亚太平洋国际公司索赔案
　　　　1284—1286
　　1974 年雷诺尔德斯金属公司索赔案
　　　　1258—1261
　　1974 年南美国际电话电报公司索赔案
　　　　1293—1300
　　1977 年阿纳康达公司及智利铜业公司索赔案
　　　　1265—1273
　　1978 年列维尔铜矿及铜器公司索赔案
　　　　1273—1279
　　1979 年阿格里科拉金属公司索赔案
　　　　1286—1289
　　1980 年卡博特国际投资公司索赔案

　　　　1261—1262
　　"201 条款"争端案 0626—0678
　　"301 条款"争端案 0626—0678
　　CIETAC 1992—1993 年个案 1088—1131
　　CIETAC 2001—2002 年个案 1132—1182
　　巴塞罗纳公司案 1235—1236
　　菲律宾"南海仲裁案" 详见 N 部分 **南海问题**
　　广东省广信公司破产清算债务讼案
　　　　1183—1191
　　韩国 C 公司 v. 中国 X 市 A、B 两家公司案 详见 W 部分 **外贸代理合同纠纷**
　　就外资企业"设董"自主权问题答英商问
　　　　1199—1204
　　就中国涉外仲裁体制答英商问 1078—1087
　　美国约克公司 v. 香港北海公司案 详见 W 部分
　　　　外贸汇票承兑
　　美—日汽车市场争端案 0642
　　欧—美经济主权争讼案 0642—0667
　　香港百利多投资有限公司诉香港克洛克纳东亚有限公司案 1068—1077
　　香港东方公司 v. 香港泰益公司案 详见 W 部分
　　　　外商在华投资
　　香港居民谢业深 v. 秘鲁政府征收投资案 详见

索 引

G 部分 国际投资争端解决

香港某债务讼案 1192—1198

香港上海汇丰银行有限公司 v. 厦门建设发展公司案 详见 W 部分 外商在华投资

意大利古西公司 v. 香港图荣公司案 1868—1881

英国 FOSFA 裁决 2014—2054

英商 X 投资公司 v. 英商 Y 保险公司案 详见 W 部分 外商在华投资

中国 A 市 MX 公司 v. 韩国 HD 株式会社案 1949—1966

中国深圳市中方四公司 v. 泰国贤成两合公司案 详见 W 部分 外商在华投资

中国中禾公司 v. Bunge 公司案 2014—2054

B

霸权主义 0006，0008，0013，0028，0035，0059，0061，0080—0084，0104—0106，0112，0124，0150，0159，0162，0189—0190，0197—0199，0202—0203，0217—0218，0230—0232，0241，0264，0336，0346，0350，0368—0371，0374，0406，0410—0411，0503—0504，0506，0574，0577，0581，0595，0631，0633，0637，0641，0678，0681，0692，0703—0704，0706，0708—0709，0719，0741—0742，0755—0756，0779，0793，0807，0812，0815，0888—0899，0907，0909，1226，1327，1546，2113，2129，2133—2134，2143，2147，2151，2152，2158，2202，2213，2223，2233，2371，2396，2403，2414，2445，2447

C

曹建明 0004-1—0004-2，2185

车丕照 2198，2209，2424，2428，2488

陈辉萍 2220，2235，2317，2326，2329

陈氏国际经济法 2191

　"6C 律"（"6C 轨迹"）2191—2192

　第一代：《国际经济法学刍言》(2005 年北京大学出版社两卷本) 2191

　第二代：《陈安论国际经济法学》(2008 年复旦大学出版社五卷本) 2191

　第三代：*The Voice from China：An CHEN on International Economic Law*（2013 年德国 Springer 出版社英文专著）2191—2193

　第四代：《中国特色话语：陈安国际经济法学》（2018 年北京大学出版社四卷本）0008—0009

　"三步进行曲" 2191

　"三性"理论 2191—2192

陈仲洵 0025，1391，2220

D

单边主义 0314—0334，0626—0676，0678，0745—0775，2141—2143，2158—2159

邓小平理论 0260—0281，0810，0888—0897，2363

帝国主义 0159—0197，0198—0233，0379—0577，0683—0705，2121—2122，2151—2153，2357—2358，2403

第三世界 0241—0259，0336，0353，0759—0592，0813—0819，0821—0834，0861—0898

对外开放 0130—0134，1672—1689

　"引进来" 1466—1467，1501，1535

　"走出去" 0894，1466—1467，1484，1501，1513，1525，1527，1535

多边主义 0243，0271，0626—0676，0859，2129，2142—2044，2158—2159

F

发达国家 0085—0106，0240，0247—0248，

0776—0786，0787—0819，0820—0834，
0835—0860，0861—0898

发展中国家 0085—0106，0240，0247—0248，
0776—0786，0787—0819，0820—0834，
0835—0860，0861—0898

法律不溯及既往 1695，1748—1749，1758，1774

法治 0307—0334，0355，0974—0975，1078—
1087，2174

　依法治国 0974，1041，1045，1083，2074

　有法可依，有法必依，执法必严，违法必究
0945—0946

非政府组织 0114，0852，1358，1532，2287

G

公平互利原则 0581，0776—0786，0905—0906，
0909，1340，1529，1697，2415—2417，2430

　公平 0776—0786，0306—0334，0379—0577，
0787—0812，0814—0819，0821—0834，
0836—0860，0862—0898

　互利 0085—0106，0144—0145，0148—0152，
0155，0157—0158，0184—0194，0776—
0786，0813—0819，0821—0834，0839—
0841，0858—0898

　普遍优惠待遇 0782

辜芳昭 2436

谷婀娜 1536，2311

郭寿康 0003，0021，2144，2475，2483

国际惯例 0913—0927，0937—0941，0942—0977，
0989—1057，1073，1690—1707

国际合作 详见 Q 部分 全球合作

国际经济法学 0049—0073，0075—0084，
2436—2454

　广义说 0051—0052，0058，0072，0900，2366，
2371，2414—2416，2426

　国际公法 0050—0057，0062—0066，0075—
0081，0109，2059，2069，2133—2134，
2200，2297，2366，2412，2415，2426

　国际经济法 0049—0073，0075—0084，0108—
0129，0131—0134，0578—0592，0776—
0786，0900—0910，2425—2426，2436—2454

　国际商务惯例 0052，0055—0056，0070—0071，
0114—0115，0124—0125，2415，2418

　国际私法 0051—0052，0054，0056，0062，
0064—0066，0071，0075—0081，0579，
0904，2059，2069，2200，2366，2415—
2416，2429

　内国经济法 0067—0070，0072

　狭义说 0050—0052，2366，2415，2426

中国特色国际法学理论 2117

中国特色国际经济法学 0008，0019，0030，
0040，2127，2132—2144，2149—2150，
2162—2165，2183，2437，2443，2472—2175

国际经济关系 0050—0073，0086—0106，0108—
0129，0235，0247，0307—0308，0322，
0777—0786，0820—0834，2150，2153，
2155—2157，2415—2417

国际经济秩序 0006，0008，0012，0020，0027，
0033，0037—0039，0061，0074，0081，
0086，0099，0101—0102，0105—0106，
0108—0109，0117，0120—0123，0128，
0133，0234—0236，0239，0242，0245—
0251，0259—0260，0264—0270，0273，
0278，0281，0283—0284，0287—0288，
0291，0294—0299，0301，0303—0305，
0308—0311，0332，0350，0354，0357，
0362—0367，0581，0585，0591—0592，
0597—0598，0614，0764，0795—0796，
0798，0799，0816，0821，0825，0830—
0831，0839，0841—0842，0855，0860—
0866，0868—0870，0886，0890，0893，
0896，0909，0919，0925，1220，1226，
1231，1232，1236，1274，1301，1304，

1328，1340，1395，1659，1666，1671，
2116，2126，2140，2143，2153—2155，
2166—2174，2176，2191—2193，2199—
2202，2212，2222，2260，2269—2270，
2273，2275，2289，2297，2320，2338，
2341，2417，2447，2546

"6C律" 0012，0021，0023，0033，0037，0128，
0235，0291，0306，0308，0320，0331，
0764，0836，0854—0857，0869—0870，
0925，2128，2143，2146，2152，2154—
2155，2171，2176，2191，2195，2201，
2207，2275，2279，2368，2378，2433，
2447，2484

"WTO宪政秩序"论 0038，0234—0235，0246，
0250—0252，0254—0255，0258，0260—
0261，0269，0280—0282，0349—0350，
0353，0364，2140，2153，2156，2166—
2168，2171，2192，2212，2274，2288，2319

霸权主义 详见B部分 **霸权主义**

国际金融新秩序 0244，0271—0273，0286—
0287，0892

 布雷顿森林体系 0244—0245，0272，0276，
0279，0286，0341，0880—0882，0892，
0896，2167

 国际货币基金组织 0056，0117，0245，0274，
0279，0288，0298，0309，0341，0344，
0591，0596，0679，0826，0880，0895，
1320，1538，1576，2167，2170，2287

 世界银行集团 0884，1305，1334，1347，
1352，1353—1356，1366—1367，1374，
1381，1392，1394，1395，1398，1414，2421

国际经济旧秩序（OIEO） 0006，0008，0012，
0033，0060，0081，0085，0090，0099，
0103—0104，0105，0106，0108，0117，
0119，0120—0122，0129，0148，0187，
0235，0239，0244，0247，0250—0251，
0262，0268，0272，0286，0295—0297，
0299，0304，0309—0310，0323—0324，
0333，0349，0356，0362，0364—0365，
0580—0581，0592，0777，0784，0790，
0792—0793，0813，0815，0816，0823，
0827，0836，0838—0839，0855，0860，
0863—0865，0872，0874，0892，0896，
0899，0906，0909，0919，1270，1300—
1301，1327，1329，1340，1446，1666，
2143，2152，2153—2155，2157，2166—
2167，2173，2273—2274，2287，2368，
2443，2463，2378

国际经济新秩序（NIEO） 0006，0012，0020，
0030，0333，0037—0039，0060，0075，
0090，0105—0106，0108，0117，0119—
0123，0128—0129，0155，0192，0234—
0236，0238—0242，0244—0246，0248，
0250，0255—0256，0258—0264，0268，
0271，0274，0278—0283，0286，0288，
0291—0292，0294—0297，0299—0301，
0303—0306，0310，0312，0324，0327，
0333，0335，0349—0351，0353—0356，
0362—0364，0369，0378，0579—0581，
0583，0585，0588，0596，0744，0751，
0764—0765，0776—0778，0780—0781，
0783—0784，0786，0792—0795，0799，
0808—0809，0813—0816，0819—0821，
0823—0825，0829，0834，0840—0841，
0858—0859，0863—0867，0870，0872，
0874，0877，0889—0890，0892—0893，
0905—0906，0919，1270，1300，1304，
1335，1340，1446，1470，1498，1501，
1529，1535，1541，1580，1590，1666，
2116，2128，2131，2133，2137，2139—
2141，2143，2146—2147，2149，2151—
2152，2153—2157，2161—2163，2165—

2167，2169—2176，2188，2191—2193，
2199—2202，2204—2205，2210，2212—
2213，2224，2232，2234，2270，2273—
2275，2277—2279，2282，2285—2288，
2290—2292，2294，2296，2318—2319，
2320—2321，2323，2325，2366，2368，
2371，2378—2379，2384，2414，2417，
2427，2430，2433，2443，2447，2463，
2473，2525

变法 0282—0283，0294，0297，0299—0300，
0302，0306—0308，0310—0312，0316，
0319—0323，0327，0329，0331—0332，
0349—0350，0354—0356，0358，0362—
0363，0365—0366，0744，0764—0765，
0808，0862，0864，0870，0873，0876—
0877，0879，0886—0887，0893，0896，
0913，0925—0926，2116，2140—2141，
2146，2153，2156，2166—2168，2171—
2174，2202，2211，2274，2287—2288，
2338，2341，2470，2525

立法 0012—0014，0020，0022，0027，
0033—0034，0055，0059—0064，0066—
0071，0075，0080—0082，0098，0107—
0108，0110，0114—0116，0123—0124，
0126—0127，0130，0132，0129，0140，
0175—0176，0180—0181，0221，0229，
0235—0236，0240，0242，0245，0247，
0251，0253，0262，0265，0267，0270，
0278，0283—0284，0297，0299—0300，
0306—0308，0310—0311，0313，0317—
0318，0320—0322，0329，0331—0333，
0350—0352，0355，0362—0363，0374，
0392，0438，0530，0579—0580，0585，
0601，0603，0627，0634—0636，0638—
0643，0646—0648，0651—0652，0654—
0655，0657—0658，0661，0664—0668，
0674—0675，0678，0711，0736，0764—
0765，0784，0823，0828—0831，0835—
0844，0849，0854—0855，0858，0862，
0864—0870，0872，0879，0893，0901，
0903，0907，0913—0914，0918—0926，
0928—0931，0934—0944，0946—0953，
0957—0963，0965—0975，0977—0984，
0988，0991—0995，0998—0999，1003，
1005，1007，1010，1012—1014，1016，
1018，1021—1025，1030—1031，1034，
1036，1039—1040，1042—1046，1049，
1055—1064，1067，1069，1079，1086—
1087，1110，1113，1132，1151，1156，
1178，1186—1187，1201—1203，1208，
1210，1213，1218，1221，1223—1224，
1227，1229，1231，1235，1239—1240，
1269，1271，1274，1276，1293，1300—
1303，1305，1310，1313，1327，1335，
1338，1358，1366，1376，1394，1397，
1399，1400—1402，1404，1406，1409，
1411—1414，1419，1421，1429，1431，
1433，1440—1442，1444，1452—1453，
1462—1463，1465，1470—1471，1473，
1479，1491—1492，1494，1499—1501，
1504—1505，1518，1520，1522，1552，
1555—1556，1559，1568，1571，1573，
1578，1579，1581，1618，1620，1622，
1623，1637，1641，1648—1649，1659—
1664，1669—1671，1681，1684，1686，
1688，1690—1694，1697，1698，1704，
1706—1707，1743，1747—1748，1751，
1753，1766，1771—1773，1776，1778，
1835，1842—1843，1857，1863—1864，
1873—1874，1876，1896，1906，1913，
1929，1943，1947，1994，2011，2025—
2027，2035—2036，2039—2040，2047，

2050—2052，2070—2071，2091，2128—2129，2131，2135—2136，2139，2141，2143，2144，2148，2153—2156，2159，2162，2168，2171，2174，2176，2202，2211，2222，2232，2256，2259，2274，2286，2287，2297，2309，2318—2319，2236，2338，2341，2366—2367，2370，2410—2411，2414—2416，2419—2420，2433，2447，2458，2460，2462—2463，2465—2470，2473，2476，2478—2479，2494，2497，2502，2518，2521，2522，2524—2526

守法 0147，0187，0282—0283，0294，0297，0299—0300，0306—0308，0310—0312，0319—0322，0331，0349—0350，0354—0356，0358，0362—0363，0624—0625，0744，0764—0765，0808，0864，0893，0922，0971，0984，0988，1036—1037，1055，1084，1130，1152，1359，1670，1768，1770，1843，1854，1866—1867，1956，2023，2044，2048，2050，2052，2140，2146，2153，2156，2166，2168，2172—2174，2202，2211，2274，2287—2288，2338，2341，2458，2461，2464，2489，2525

执法 0013，0044，0132，0176，0253，0306—0308，0312，0316—0320，0322，0350，0355，0362，0374，0601，0627—0628，0644，0646，0649，0654—0655，0658，0664，0708，0725，0727—0728，0764—0765，0864，0870，0918—0920，0926—0927，0946，0949，0950，0952，0970，0984，1001，1034，1036，1045，1122，1229，1248—1249，1283，1285，1422，1426，1436，1445，1461，1552，1555，1556，1585，1671，1743，1752，1765，1771—1772，1875，1912，1917，1945，2006—2009，2027—2028，2031，2033，2035—2036，2044—2045，2050—2052，2083，2089，2112，2139—2140，2142，2146，2153，2156，2166，2168，2174，2202，2211，2287，2319，2338，2525

华盛顿共识 详见 G 部分"新自由主义经济秩序"论

经济民族主义 0038，0234—0235，0246，0248，0255—0258，0260—0261，0280—0282，0350，0353，1247，1300，2140，2153，2156，2166—2169，2171—2192，2212，2274，2288，2297，2319

"经济民族主义扰乱全球化秩序"论 0038，0234—0236，0255，0258，0260—0261，0280—0282，0350，0353，2140，2153，2156，2166—2168，2171，2192，2212，2274，2288，2319

"新自由主义经济秩序"论 0038，0234—0251，0255—0256，0258，0260—0261，0265，0269，0280—0282，0349—0350，0353，0364，2140，2153，2156，2166—2168，2171，2173，2192，2212，2272，2288，2319

国际贸易法 0003，0016，0051，0073，0124，0864，0896，2001，2016，2059，2069，2071，2131，2133，2140，2145，2326，2368，2410，2412，2413，2418，2425，2430，2440，2462，2463，2472，2487，2502，2518，2520

国际商会（ICC） 0056，0070，0114，0125—126，1398，1431—1432，1967，1970，1984，2001，2016，2518

国际投资条约 0013，1402，1422—1423，1433，1453，1473，1475，1504—1505，1510，1532，1549，1551，1560，1573，1577—1578，1583，1586，1602，1644，1651—

1652，2139，2447

北美自由贸易协定（NAFTA）1453，1477—1479，1493，1521—1522，1555，1565，1571，1580，2311，2316

多边投资协定（MAI）0878，1478，1570—1571，1593

友好通商航海条约（FCNT）0114，0117，1216—1221，1237，1471

国际投资争端解决 0036，1596，1600，1602，1608，2191，2421

国际投资法庭（ICS）1591—1592，1595—1597，1600—1604，1606，1608

国际投资争端仲裁 0057，0956—0957，1061—1063，1417，1419，1468—1469，1473—1475，1496，1504—1505，1522—1523，1561—1562，1565，1575—1577，1591—1598，1601—1603，1629，2135，2421，2472，2478，2519—2520，2526

解决投资争端国际中心（ICSID）0013，0015，0026，0057，0597，0879，0932—0933，0954，0956—0957，1058，1061，1305，1310—1311，1377—1378，1384，1391—1392，1394，1396—1398，1417—1419，1421，1423—1424，1426—1433，1435，1448，1452—1455，1458—1466，1468—1470，1472—1475，1477，1479，1482—1483，1485—1486，1488—1493，1496，1497，1499—1500，1503—1506，1508，1509，1512，1515—1517，1519—1525，1527，1532—1534，1541—1542，1549，1555，1571—1572，1577—1578，1582，1587—1588，1594，1596，1598—1599，1601，1603，1606，1609—1613，1629，1632—1636，1638—1639，1641，1643，1646—1650，1653—1658，1673，1687—1688，1703，1706—1707，2001，2016，2070，2131，2135，2142，2144，2159，2165，2221，2227，2255—2257，2261—2262，2303，2305，2330，2327，2335，2337，2345，2348，2369，2371，2345，2348，2379，2383，2419—2424，2434，2437，2443，2447，2469，2471—2472，2478—2479，2485，2488，2494，2505—2506，2518，2520—2521，2526

解决国家与他国国民间投资争端公约（华盛顿公约）0057，0597，0932—0934，0954—0957，1003，1059—1061，1063，1396，1417—1418，1422—1423，1426—1433，1435，1437，1439—1447，1453—1454，1461—1469，1471—1475，1477—1481，1489—1491，1496—1497，1500，1503—1507，1512，1519—1520，1523—1524，1548，1555，1589，1592，1594，1598—1600，1604—1606，1610，1627—1634，1638—1639，1643—1644，1646—1648，1658，1687—1688，1703—1704，1706—1707，2001，2016，2070，2131，2135，2144，2327，2334—2335，2368，2419—2423，2437，2443，2478—2479，2488，2518

香港居民谢业深 v. 秘鲁政府征收投资案 1609—1658

香港特别行政区 0013，1192，1463—1464，1609—1610，1612—1613，1615—1616，1618，1619—1623，1625—1627，1635，1658，2255—2258

香港特别行政区基本法 1463—1464，1610，1615—1616，1619—1620，1622，1421，1567，1573，1576—1577，1579

一国两制 0013，0604，0767，1463，1512—1513，1610，1612，2255—2256，2258—2259，2282

中英联合声明 1610，1616—1620，1625，

1864，2255，2257，2258—2259

国有化 0013(fn.6)，0034，0054(fn.9)，0122，0584—0585，0587，0589—0590，0794—0795，0840(fn.9)，0871，0925(fn.21)，1032，1194，1218，1228，1232—1233，1252，1259，1267—1268，1272，1282，1293，1342，1367，1400，1424，1425(fn.17)，1432，1436，1444，1462，1465—1466，1485(fn.32)，1487，1515(fn.41)，1517，1545(fn.26)，1629—1630，1635，1639，1642，1646，1659—1669，1671，1681，1693—1694，1701—1702，1704，1707，1756，2129，2141，2155—2156，2159，2411，2417—2418，2421—2422，2524

国有企业 0114，0246，0248，0801，1136，1138，1141，1151，1155，1337，1341，1351—1352，1360—1361，1381，1586，1637，1695，1771，2328

H

韩德培 0003，0015，0018，0076，0917，0955，1022，1208，1209，1861，1862，1863，1887，1926，1933，1978，2049，2135，2409，2462，2475，2483

韩立余 0667，2281，2285

和平崛起 0005，0038，0135，0147，0152，0156，0158，0159，0160，0162，0187，0191，0192，0193，0194，0249，0265，0300，0338，0339，0346，0361，0363，0373，0709，0861，0864，1498，1535，1537，1584，1590，2122，2192，2233，2319，2327，2368，2371

何志鹏 2285，2296

胡锦涛 0120，0133，0152，0160，0191，0243，0244，0245，0246，0270，0271，0272，0273，0274，0275，0279，0285，0286，0287，0288，0289，0290，0301，0324，0349，0359，0859，0880，0891，0892，0893，1535，2170，2171

黄雁明 1174，2241，2254

J

江泽民 0083，0084，0106，0123，0127，0152，0191，0604，0682，0891，0943，0963，0964，0974，0987，1041，1045，1048，1054，1535

蒋围 0706，0804，2164，2402

K

孔庆江 1628，1631，1632，2269

跨国商品代销 1868

 越权抵押 1868

 争端管辖权 1430，1431，1473，1491，1494，1502，1504，1520，1521，1522，1527，1531，1532，1533，1549，1551，1555，1582，1651，1653，1868，1872，1882，1918，1928，1929，1930，1932，1933，2145，2339

跨国投资保险体制 1303，1304，1306，1310

 多边投资担保机构(MIGA) 1303—1306，1311，1312，1314，1315，1318，1319，1321，1322，1327，1328，1330，1335，1336，1340，1343，1344，1391—1393，1396，1398，1404，1409，1410，1412，1422，1433—1435，1454，1463，1467，1704—1706，2135，2165，2326，2418，2419，2432，2449，2473，2485，2502，2518，2520，2526

 多边投资担保机构公约(汉城公约) 1305，1344，1391，1393，1398，1409，1410，1422，1433—1435，1454，1463，1467，1704

 海外私人投资公司(OPIC) 1207—1216，1219，1223，1225，1226，1230，1236—1254，

1255, 1257—1262, 1265, 1267—1269, 1271—1273, 1275—1279, 1284—1289, 1291—1299, 1300—1302, 1307—1309, 1311, 1343, 1344, 1354, 1370, 1387, 1392, 1579, 1666, 1668, 1705, 2409, 2524

中美投资保险和投资保证协定 1208, 1212

L

李庆灵 0039, 0306, 0801, 1536, 1559, 1577, 1583, 2329

李万强 1463, 1522, 2138, 2272, 2280, 2452

联合国（UN） 0003, 0022, 0023, 0055, 0056, 0058, 0060, 0061, 0063, 0085, 0103, 0106, 0109, 0116, 0117, 0120—0124, 0127, 0128, 0133, 0172, 0196, 0214, 0215, 0220, 0241, 0250, 0253, 0256, 0257, 0264, 0268, 0296, 0313, 0324, 0327, 0328, 0333—0336, 0341, 0344, 0351, 0352, 0355, 0359, 0363, 0367, 0368, 0369, 0370, 0379, 0578, 0583, 0584, 0585, 0587, 0590, 0594, 0596, 0615, 0616, 0620, 0622, 0628, 0629, 0663, 0676, 0678, 0684, 0685, 0711, 0713, 0715, 0716, 0717, 0731, 0735, 0736, 0738, 0740, 0749, 0750, 0751, 0767, 0769, 0777, 0778, 0780, 0781, 0783, 0793, 0794, 0795, 0796, 0806, 0809, 0810, 0813, 0814, 0815, 0820, 0823, 0825, 0826, 0827, 0828, 0830, 0839, 0840, 0841, 0861, 0865, 0866, 0868, 0870, 0871, 0872, 0873, 0876, 0877, 0879, 0882, 0886, 0888, 0889, 0891, 0895, 0896, 0898, 0901, 0905, 0925, 0936, 0937, 0961, 0962, 0979, 0980, 0982, 0990, 0991, 0992, 0993, 0998, 1007, 1023, 1029, 1030, 1031, 1032, 1033, 1058, 1228, 1229, 1231, 1232, 1233, 1234, 1235, 1236, 1247, 1274, 1297, 1309, 1334, 1383, 1398, 1425, 1426, 1431, 1432, 1443, 1453, 1477, 1487, 1490, 1499, 1500, 1505, 1509, 1530, 1538, 1539, 1541, 1545, 1561, 1568, 1569, 1576, 1598, 1610, 1624, 1633, 1643, 1644, 1647, 1650, 1651, 1665, 1666, 1667, 1670, 1694, 1909, 1910, 1915, 1928, 1942, 1943, 2001, 2046, 2050, 2057, 2058, 2064, 2113, 2117, 2137, 2140, 2157, 2167, 2173, 2179, 2243, 2244, 2320, 2336, 2339, 2340, 2341, 2414, 2416, 2417, 2475, 2476, 2497, 2518

安理会 0214, 0220, 0825, 0839, 0865, 1231, 1439, 1666

各国经济权利和义务宪章 0060, 0063, 0121, 0122, 0296, 0297, 0327, 0333, 0578, 0583, 0590, 0596, 0778, 0795, 0813, 0814, 0821, 0840, 0866, 0870, 0872, 0901, 0905, 0925, 1231—1234, 1335, 1444, 1529, 1541, 1545, 1666, 1667, 1694, 2158, 2161, 2366, 2414

建立国际经济新秩序宣言 0121, 0122, 0242, 0258, 0264, 0296, 0297, 0327, 0363, 0578, 0585, 0596, 0778, 0795, 0813, 0814, 0820, 0821, 0840, 0866, 0870, 0890, 0905, 1335, 1529, 1541, 2161, 2368, 2414

联合国国际贸易法委员会（UNCITRAL） 0124, 0936, 0961, 0980, 0992, 1398, 1477, 1490, 1598, 1624, 1633, 1643, 1644, 1928, 2244, 2336

联合国海洋法会议（UNCLOS） 0735, 0736

联合国贸易与发展会议（UNCTAD） 0022,

1058，1472，1487，1500，1509，1510，1511，1531，1532，1561，1562，1565，1566—1568，1601，1641，1646，1651，1652

两岸经贸问题 0599，0600—0604，0606，0608，0613，0617—0619，0621，0622，0624，0625，2146，2148，2492，2522

两手准备 0378，0745

  两手并重 0706，0707，0744

  两手措施 0807

  两手应对 0787，0807

  两手战略 0812

  两手政策 0233，0348，0371

列宁 0007，0011，0013，0082，0083，0092，0100，0102，0104，0208，0228，0238，0256，0257，0258，0379，0380，0383，0384，0402，0411—0415，0417—0424，0428—0432，0434—0437，0440—0467，0469—0471，0474—0481，0484—0498，0500—0518，0521—524，0528—0556，0560—0577，0683，0685，0688，0689，0693—0704，0790，0807，0888，0895，0903，0923，0945，1056，1528，1581，2147，2151，2365，2442，2443，2446，2521

林忠 0017，2000，2019，2020，2138，2444

领事裁判权 0059，0068，0146，0186，0212，0541，1059，1423，1473，1504，1627，1628，1636，1647

罗马公约 1980，1982，2011，2012，2036，2037，2242，2243

M

马克思列宁主义 0011，0013，0083，0238，0256，0257，0258，0379，0453，0466，0517，0521，0523，0542，0555，0556，0574，0685，0697，0790，0807，0888，2147，2151，2365，2442，2443，2446

马克思主义 0008，0010，0012，0040，0041，0061，0082，0134，0155，0192，0224，0225，0227，0257，0319，0327，0347，0352，0366，0377，0378，0379，0398，0403，0406，0411，0412，0418，0419，0420，0421，0424，0426，0427，0428，0431，0435，0437，0438，0439，0440，0441，0443，0445，0446，0447，0449，0450，0454，0455，0456，0457，0458，0460，0461，0462，0463，0464，0465，0466，0468，0474—0479，0481，0485，0486，0490，0491，0493，0494，0495，0497，0499，0500，0501—0508，0511—0513，0523，0528，0529，0531，0537，0541，0542，0543，0547，0548，0554，0558，0559，0561，0562，0565，0568，0569，0573，0574，0683，0689，0690，0693，0695，0696，0697，0699，0701，0702，0703，0782，0874，1153，1212，1528，1529，1581，1628，1663，2118，2149，2150，2151，2154，2158，2161，2178，2179，2260，2297，2414，2447，2463

毛泽东 0077，0082，0082，0083，0105，0136，0145，0177，0185，0233，0265，0335，0336，0348，0355，0359，0366，0371，0377，0516，0518，0525，0689，0792，0793，0885，0887，0888，0890，0891，1528，1581，1627，1628，1636，2113，2394

毛泽东思想 0083，0265，0377，0890，0891

贸易保护主义 0330，0370，0751，0754，0761，0762，0764，0796，0800，0801，0868，2172，2213，2438

N

南北合作 0074，0235，0242，0251，0265，0269，0272，0282—0283，0291，0294，0300—0304，0331，0350，0354，0365，0578，0598，

0801，0808—0809，0813—0817，0819—0823，0826，0855—0858，0860，0863（fn. 3），0866，0891，0896，1304，1334—1335，1340，1531，1650，1705，2140（fn. 27），2154，2161—2162，2171，2175，2415，2433

南北矛盾 0012—0013，0020，0038，0074，0085，0090—0091，0105—0106，0121，0127—0128，0133，0234—0235，0240，0242，0245，0249—0250，0256—0257，0259，0261—0262，0264—0265，0267，0269，0272，0279，0281，0301—0303，0324，0330，0378，0578—0579，0581，0681，0777，0784，0787—0788，0790—0794，0796—0798，0800—0803，0805—0808，0811—0812，0813，0815—0816，0819，0826，0828，0835—0837，0839—0840，0842，0844，0854—0857，0864—0866，0870，0890—0891，0933，0957，1237，1300，1340，1531，1536—1538，1540—1542，1549，1556—1558，1569，1578，1650，1659，1666，1671，1705，2131，2135，2144，2147，2150，2152，2154—2157，2162，2164，2166，2173，2192，2200，2273，2413，2416—2417，2419，2427，2433，2473

南方中心（South Centre） 0015（fn. 11），0022（fn. **），0034，0626（fn. *），0803（fn. 49），0828—0829，0834，0835，0840—0841，0852，0862，0866—0867，0898，1540，2128，2142（fn. 30），2144，2164，2176，2320，2356，2432，2434，2472，2476—2478，2500—2501

南海问题 0005，0710—0717，0740，0741，0753，0759，0761，0765，0804

 巴拿马诉意大利案 0743

 东帝汶与澳大利亚调解案 0743

 黄岩岛 0376，0709，0721，0724，0726—0734，0740，0753，0761，0766，0804，0811

 历史性权利 0707，0719—0721，0726，0729—0730，0738—0739

 南海仲裁案 0706—0708，0712—0719，0728—0730，0739—0744，0804

  阿基诺三世 0708，0711—0712，0714，0719，0741，0804

  柳井俊二 0706，0712—0714，0716—0717

 南沙群岛 0707—0708，0717—0719，0721—0724，0729—0730，0733—0735，0741，0744

 低潮高地 0719，0721—0722，0727—0730，0734—0735，0737

 美济礁 0719，0721，0725—0731，0737—0738，0741，0744

 仁爱礁 0719，0721，0725—0730

 太平岛 0724，0729

南南合作 0007，0022—0024，0125，0243，0251，0270—0271，0274，0285—0286，0329，0335，0340，0345，0355，0360，0362，0365，0369，0753（fn. 28），0809—0810，0820—0827，0829（fn. 13），0830—0831，0834，0841—0842，0859—0860，0862—0864，0867—0868，0870—0871，0877—0878，0880，0886—0887，0892，0894—0896，1304，1334，1340，2131，2145，2155，2162，2173，2176，2199，2234，2273，2327，2341，2356，2415，2477

南南联合 0013，0022—0023，0033—0034，0038—0039，0234—0236，0238—0240，0242—0246，0250—0251，0258—0260，0262—0263，0269—0274，0278—0281，0283—0288，0291—0294，0300，0303—0307，0312，0319，0321—0322，0324，0336，0347，0353—0355，0359，0361，0365，0378，0823，0829—0830，0833，

0835—0843，0845，0854—0867，0869—0873，0878，0881，0885—0887，0889，0891—0893，0895，2128，2141，2143—2144，2146，2154，2156，2161，2162，2164，2167，2172，2176，2192—2193，2211，2273—2275，2288，2317—2320，2368，2433，2447，2473，2476，2496—2497

P

普世价值 1536，1538，1542—1543，1548，1556，2152，2165

Q

戚燕方 2431，2433，2477

全球合作 0081，0359（fn. 14），0581，0793—0812，0813—0819，0820—0834，0863（fn. 3），1304，1335（fn. 60），1340，2131，2151，2154，2157，2161—2162

北北串联 0283，0292，0303—0305

南北合作 详见 N 部分 **南北合作**

南方中心（South Centre）详见 N 部分 **南方中心（South Centre）**

南南合作 详见 N 部分 **南南合作**

南南联合 详见 N 部分 **南南联合**

匹兹堡发轫之路 0282—0283，0288—0294，0303—0305，0312（fn. 7），0350，0354，0808(fn.69)，0893，2172

八国集团（G8）0243，0245(fn. 19)，0270—271，0273，0275—0276，0279（fn. 43），0285，0287，0289，0291，0294（fn. 25），0341(fn. 15)，0359(fn.14)，0858—0859

二十国集团（G20）0273，0275—0277，0279（fn. 43），0282，0284，0286—0292，0303，0305，0330，0341—0345，0354，0359—0360，0750，0801，0808，0881，1600

全球化 0029，0037—0038，0106—0108，0127—0129，0131，0132—0133，0152，0191，0230，0234—0235，0247—0248，0255，0258，0260—0261，0280，0309，0320，0330—0331，0342，0353，0365，0368—0369，0580—0581，0605，0626，0628—0629，0644，0678—0682，0745—0748，0750—0751，0765—0766，0771，0794，0798—0799，0808，0829，0840—0841，0854，0856，0867，0898，0926，1343，1383，1459，1537，1556，1595，2115，2117，2140，2142，2151—2152，2157，2159，2166，2168—2172，2174—2176，2191—2192，2198，2210—2212，2224，2260，2274，2287，2307，2311，2319，2334，2372，2431，2434，2443

全球治理 0006—0008，0130，0132，0134，0156，0335—0336，0338—0341，0343—0345，0348—0350，0355—0356，0359—0362，0367，0373，0768，0770，0801，0808，1591—1593，1600，1602，1608，2113—2118，2126，2153，2210，2309，2546

霸权垄断 0768，0797

中国特色全球治理理念 0007，0335—0336，0339—0340，0345，0350，0355，0360，0367，2114

S

单文华 0017，0941，1057，1491，1520，1555，1635，2135，2138，2419，2448

商务部条约法律司 1543，2408

涉外经济合同 0014，0067，0902—0904，0914，0921，0955，1085—1087，1093，1102，1114，1122，1187—1190，1420，1695—1696，1724，1726—1727，1733，1736，1746，1749，1753，1781，1786—1787，1820，1826，1841—1843，1847—1854，

1858，1862，1864—1867，1885—1888，1893，1897—1898，1915，1919，1932—1935，1979—1980，2069—2070，2339，2520，2524

合同必须信守原则 1841—1843，1867

合同无效 0904，1114，1145，1155—1156，1162，1187—1189，1724，1727，1736，1841，1843，1848，1850，1852—1853，1858，2145

"违法合同自始无效"原则 0904，1841—1843

身份混同 0801，1559—1590

　法律身份混同 1559，1562

　经济身份混同 1559，1562

　身份混同非均衡化 1559，1565

石静霞 2254

市场经济地位 0763

世界贸易组织（WTO） 0128，0234，0239，0242，0245，0250—0254，0265，0280，0283，0300，0306—0334，0349，0355，0595，0601—0626，0627—0677，0681，0755，0762—0766，0801，0829，0831—0835，0836—0861，0869—0870，0879，0892，1176，1191，1487，1517，1531，1546，1569—1571，1605—1606，1620，1649，1748，1776，1975，2111—2112，2129，2140—2143，2146—2148，2157—2158，2166—2168，2176，2192，2200—2201，2212—2213，2224，2274—2276，2288，2297，2307，2319，2337—2341，2364—2372

多哈发展回合（DDR） 0242，0253，0262，0265，0316，0801，0831—0833，0836—0845，0855，0858—0861，0869—0870，0892，1569，1649，2341，2365

坎昆会议 0239，0242，0262，0265，0331，0833—0835，0837—0839，0844—0845，0855，0871，0892

香港会议 0239，0242，0262，0265，0330，0839，0845—0855，0859，0861，0871，0892

关税及贸易总协定（GATT） 0118，0251，0315，0322—0332，0606—0615，0620—0622，0625，0632—0633，0639—0640，0645—0653，0660—0661，0669—0773，0828，0830，0853，0857，0873—0877，0887，0896，1531，1649

关于争端解决规则与程序的谅解（DSU） 0603，0618—0625，0633，0641—0673

与贸易有关的知识产权协定（TRIPs） 1704

争端解决机构（DSB） 0307，0312—0319，0603，0605，0618—0619，0622—0625，0633，0640—0680

　上诉机构 0318，0623—0624，0633，0671

　专家组 0317—0318，0611—0612，0623—0624，0633—0634，0647—0671，0877，2362

中国入世议定书 0314，0316，0763—0765

双边投资协定（BIT） 0801，0878—0879，1470—1657，1755—1756，2197，2252—2254，2304—2308，2325，2361—2368

加拿大 BIT 范本 1477—1481，1652

美国 BIT 范本 1477—1481，1500

争端解决条款 1471—1479，1495—1496，1500—1505，1523—1524，1533，1576，1578，1582，1611—1612，1628—1630，1638，1642—1643，1653—1655，1972

差别互惠 1470，1499—1501，1524—1534，1578，1589，1651

"当地救济优先"权 1470—1471，1479—1480，1496，1499—1500，1504—1506，1523，1548

"东道国法律适用"权 1470，1479—1480，1496，1499—1500，1504—1506，1523，1548

"重大安全例外"权 1470，1479，1481，1496，1499—1500，1507，1523

"逐案审批同意"权 1470，1479，1499—1500，1504—1506，1548

征收补偿条款 1543—1548

    补偿标准 1536，1544—1548，1580，1693，1699

    补偿额估算 1537，1545—1548

中外双边投资协定 1470，1499，1502，1542，1586

    中国—巴巴多斯 BIT 1496，1501，1523，1631，1633

    中国—秘鲁 BIT 1609—1657，2252—2254

    中国—德国 BIT 1482，1497，1499，1642—1643，1665

    中国—加拿大 BIT 0801，1536—1558，2325

    中国—瑞典 BIT 1422，1472，1490，1505，1618，1624，1632，1666—1667，1699—1701，2361

    中国—英国 BIT 1485，1508，1515，1756—1757

最惠国待遇条款 1497，1549，1644，1700

溯及既往 1653，1695—1696，1747—1757，1771—1775，1787

T

特殊与差别待遇 0253，0851，1531，1650，1651(fn.100，101)

投资者—东道国争端解决 详见 G 部分 国际投资争端解决

W

外国学者姓名中英文对照

    安德里斯·洛文费尔德（Andreas H. Lowenfeld，美国）0035，0052，0059—0060，0297(fn. 28)，0310(fn. 4)，0332—0333，0872，1235(fn. 75)，2129，2134，2146—2147，2411，2414，2426，2460

    布拉尼斯拉夫·戈索维奇（Branislav Gosovic，南斯拉夫/塞尔维亚）0022—0024，0034，0039(fn. 8)，2128，2144，2164—2165，2193(fn. 8)，2233，2356，2476，2500—2501

    菲利普·杰塞普（Philip C. Jessup，美国）0052—0053，0058—0059，0080—0082，0163(fn. 8)，0704，0705(fn. 67)，2062，2146，2233，2414，2426

    格斯·范·哈滕（Gus Van Harten，加拿大）1548(fn. 36)，1595，2307

    杰尔姆·柯恩（Jerome A. Cohen，美国）0034，2082(fn. 6)，2129，2141，2489

    李庸中（Eric Yong Joong Lee，韩国）0025，2220

    路易斯·汉金（Louis Hankin，美国）0029，0035，0630—0632，0636—0637，2142，2147，2212，2224，2425，2431

    洛林·威森费尔德（Lorin S. Weisenfeld，美国）1336(fn. 62)，1340，1395，1401(fn. 50)，1403，1463(fn. 66)，2326

    帕特丽莎·沃特丝（Patricia Wouters，加拿大）2232

    斯蒂芬·坎特（Stephen Kanter，美国）2302，2480

    约翰·杰克逊（John H. Jackson，美国）0029，0035，0052，0632，0634—0637，0679，2142，2147，2212，2224，2431，2425—2426，2438

    中川淳司（Junji Nakagawa，日本）2177(fn. 135)，2364

外贸代理合同纠纷 0014(fn. 8)，1967

    韩国 C 公司 v. 中国 X 市 A、B 两家公司案 0014(fn. 8)，1967—1999

外贸汇票承兑 0014(fn. 8)，1882

    美国约克公司 v. 香港北海公司案 0014(fn. 8)，1882—1948

争端管辖权冲突 0014(fn. 8),1882

外贸转售合同作伪 0014(fn. 8),1949

中国A市MX公司 v. 韩国HD株式会社案 0014(fn. 8),1949

外商在华投资 0013(fn. 6),0014(fn. 8),1151,1213—1214,1311(fn. 13),1314(fn. 17),1327(fn. 36),1337,1342,1347,1361,1365,1387,1388,1391—1392,1394,1402,1406—1407,1410—1414,1417,1436,1438,1441,1670,1691—1692,1694—1695,1699—1701,1703—1704,1707,1718,1743,1757—1758,1772,1788,1790,2369—2370,2421—2422,2522,2524

担保与反担保 0014(fn. 8),1718

香港上海汇丰银行有限公司 v. 厦门建设发展公司案 0014(fn. 8),1718—1742

海外私人投资公司法案 1225(fn. 39, 42),1240(fn. 93, 95),1242(fn. 101),1243(fn. 106, 110, 111),1244(fn. 112),1250(fn. 139, 140)

金融票据诈骗 0014(fn. 8),1708

香港东方公司 v. 香港泰益公司案 0014(fn. 8),1708—1717

"空手道"融资 1790

外资企业法 0068,1151(fn. 17),1194,1199—1202,1420(fn.6),1639—1640,1693—1694

外资企业"设董"自主权 1199

英商X投资公司 v. 英商Y保险公司案 1743—1789

"征收"索赔 1743,1772

中国深圳市中方四公司 v. 泰国贤成两合公司案 1790—1838

中外合资经营企业法 0068,1084,1108,1151(fn. 17),1199,1201,1212,1402(fn. 51),1419(fn. 1),1420(fn. 3),1640,1659,1673,1681,1688,1693,1695,1747,1750,1756,1764,1850,2141(fn. 29),2303,2427

中外合作经营企业法 0068,1151(fn. 17),1199,1202,1419(fn. 4),1640,1693,1746,1748—1750,1753,1756,1764,1773,1798,1821,1823—1824,1830,2370

王海浪 0015,0017,1483(fn. 24),1508(fn. 20),1532(fn. 68),1536(fn. *),1591,1626,1654(fn. 110)

王江雨 2296

违法必究 0927,0931,0940,0946,0948,0953,0970,0975,0983,1035—1036,1057,1774

维也纳条约法公约 0063,0615,0617,0652,0658,0661,0738—0739,0899,0901,0905,0907—0909,0924(fn. 20),1247,1309,1479,1482,1506,1508,1532,1610,1645—1646,1649,1651,1656,1697(fn. 2),2255

乌拉圭回合 0023,0128,0252—0253,0302,0315(fn. 15),0323(fn. 31),0327(fn. 37),0328,0606,0607(fn. 22),0627,0629,0631—0633,0635,0640,0648—0649,0652—0653,0661,0666(fn. 90),0670(fn. 97),0679,0828,0830,0832(fn. 20)0840,0842,0857,0876(fn. 29),1556,1704,2289,2364,2367

吴焕宁 2418

X

习近平 0007,0041,0134,0147(fn. 27),0153,0231—0232,0233(fn. 96, 97),0339—0340,0342—0345,0347—0348,0350—0351,0356,0358—0360,0361(fn. 18, 21),0363,0365,0367—0370,0371(fn. 37),0372,0376—0378,0744(fn. 185),0745—

0747，0749，0750（fn. 10—15），0751（fn. 17，19，20），0756—0757，0765（fn. 67，68），0767（fn. 73—75），0769，0771，0808，0809（fn. 71，72），0810—0811，0812（fn. 86），0882—0883，0893—0895，1585，1586（fn. 85），1592，2113，2122，2179，2209（fn. 185），2210，2303，2372

徐崇利 0017，0055（fn. 11），0069（fn. 31），0081（fn. 9），0799（fn. 35，36），0878（fn. 39），1303（fn. *），1304（fn. 1），1312（fn. 14），1321（fn. 31），1340，1545（fn. 29），1547（fn. 32），1580（fn. 65），1602（fn. 36），1620（fn. 19），1625，1629（fn. 52），1630（fn. 61），1635，1644，2135（fn. 13），2138，2413，2440

徐海 2393

Y

鸦片战争 0011，0097，0111（fn. 3），0143，0145，0147，0153—0154，0157—0159，0163—0164，0169，0183，0185，0187，0193，0230，0234，0237—0238，0261，0346，0390，0393，0397，0401，1059，1473，1504，1581，1617，1627，1636，2111，2121，2308，2357，2446

杨帆 0039—0045

杨立范 2434

意思自治 0904，0944，0951，0972，0984，1006，1037，1161—1162，1190，1438，1532—1533，1654，1743，1747，1749，1754，1758，1772，1774，1862—1863，1874，1876，1885，1897，1901，1918，1924—1925，1928—1930，1932，1936，1979—1980，1997—1998，2242，2339

用尽当地救济 0801，1003，1474，1537，1549，1554，2311，2328

忧患意识 0013，0035，0128，0230，0348，0372，0627，0675，0677—0678，0681，0707，0744，0763，1467，1470，1483，1489，1498—1499，1501，1509，1518—1519，1535，1551，1555，1558，1586，1589，2143，2158，2447

游斌 2409

有约必守原则 0581，0900—0906，0908—0909，2415，2417，2523

余劲松 1551（fn. 44），1602（fn. 36），2131，2134（fn. 10），2410，2488

Z

曾华群 0595，0598，1531（fn. 66），1546（fn. 31），1621，1651（fn. 101），1708—1717，2149—2165，2442—2444

曾令良 0036—0039，2190—2198

翟雨萌 0745—0775

张金矜 0787—0812

张乃根 2135（fn. 18），2421—2424

张祥熙 2355—2363

张永彬 0030—0036，2127—2130，2132—2145

张玉卿 0318（fn. 24），0639（fn. 27），2130—2131

赵龙跃 0312（fn. 8），0319（fn. 25），2166—2176，2209—2219，2438—2439

赵云 2317—2355

征收 0034，0054（fn. 9），0589—0590，0794—0795，0872，1192—1198，1227—1233，1262—1300，1304，1342，1393，1400，1422—1423，1436，1465—1466，1473—1474，1485—1488，1501，1504，1515—1517，1533，1543—1548，1550，1552—1554，1571，1572，1580，1610—1658，1659—1671，1681，1693—1694，1701—1707，1743—1771，1772—1790，2129，2141，2159，2242—2245，2257，2311，

2328，2370—2371，2410—2411，2418—2419，2420—2422，2489

间接征收 1481，1493，1507，1521，1553，1555

征收险 1303—1390

直接征收 1553(fn.47)

中国国际法教育 2057—2065，2066—2073，2074—2080，2137—2139

中国理念 2113—2114

中国涉外仲裁体制 0950，0975，1078—1087

中国国际经济贸易仲裁委员会（CIETAC）1070—1077，1079—1085，1089—1131，1134—1182，1419，1791—1838，1883—1916，1919—1948，1950—1966，2337

中国国际经济贸易仲裁委员会仲裁规则 0940—0941，0976—0977，1002（fn.20），1073，1124，1895，1935

中国民事诉讼法 0901，0924(fn.19)，0928—0931，0932—0933，0937—0940，0943—0955，0963，0965—0973，0984—0987，1037，1039—1055，1060—1067，1071—1072，1079—1084，1123—1130，1166，1175—1176，1189—1190，1197—1198，1640—1641，1692，1873—1876，1879，1881，1895—1896，1906，1910—1916，1919—1922，1935—1936，1938—1939，1944—1948，1973(fn.2)，2334—2335

中国涉外仲裁当事人权利 1068—1077

对质权 1068—1077

申辩权 1068—1077

香港百利多投资有限公司诉香港克洛克纳东亚有限公司案 1068—1077

中国涉外仲裁监督机制 0942—0977，0978—0988，0989—1057

分轨制 0928—0939，0942—0977，0978—0988，0989—1057

中国执行外国仲裁裁决机制 1058—1067

中国仲裁法 0928—0941，0942—0977，0980，0986—0988，0993，1036—1057，1062，1065—1067，1080—1083，1123（fn.1），1144—1146，1160，1165—1167，1171—1173，1175—1176，1189—1190，1786—1787，1985，1998

"中国威胁"论 0027—0029，0038，0154—0158，0159—0197，0198—0233，0374（fn.45），0742（fn.176），0755—0756，0884，2192，2222—2224，2319—2320，2355—2363，2393—2401，2402—2407

"黄祸"论 0027—0029，0038，0141—0142，0147，0158，0159—0197，2192，2222—2224，2320，2356—2358，2395—2397

"实用主义"哲学理念 0223—0224，0347，0637，0639，0661，1169，1242，1256，1301

"天定命运"社会思潮 0221—0223

中国战略定位 0038，0234—0259，0260—0281，0282—0305，0306—0334，0335—0348，0349—0378，0890—0893，2153—2157，2166—2176，2192，2200，2273—2274，2319

中国智慧 0746—0775

对外二十八字方针 0241—0246，0260—0281，0283—0289，0354，0378，0889—0891

和平共处五项原则 0149(fn.29)，0188(fn.58)，0241—0242，0264，0336，0749—0751，0767—0768，0780，0813—0814，0888—0895，2160，2233

人类命运共同体 0155，0337，0359—0360，0746—0775，0748—0751，0767，0808—0809，2113—2114

"一带一路"倡议 0345，0357(fn.11)，0748—0751，0774，0810，0882—0883，2120，2258

中美关系 0373—0377，0616—0617，0752—0761，1119—1120，1214，1676—1678，2303—2304

钟兴国 2439—2440

朱榄叶 0609(fn.25),2145—2149,2148(fn.44)
朱学山 0015(fn.11),0019—0021,0917,2140(fn.26),2144,2145(fn.36),2147(fn.42),2483—2484
主权 0006,0029,0035,0038,0058—0061,0067,0069,0071,0081,0094,0120,0123,0160—0161,0191,0198,0230—0233,0241—0242,0256—0258,0264,0333—0034,0371—0372,0378,0379,0386,0446,0492,0547,0549—0554,0581—0583,0591,0595,0598,0615—0617,0621,0630—0676,0683—0750,0717—0719,0721—0744,0751,0756—0761,0767—0768,0778—0781,0791,0802—0804,0808—0812,0814,0823,0839,0864,0865,0870—0872,0888—0890,0905—0906,0917,0921,1221—1222,1224,1226—1234,1248—1249,1255,1274—1277,1429,1435—1441,1496,1504,1507,1523,1527—1535,1546,1550,1556,1578—1586,1590,1628—1629,1641,1644—1645,1651—1652,1658,1661—1666,1667,1671,1787,1862,1864,1872—1874,2023,2050,2053,2088,2142—2143,2158—2160,2164,2169,2192,2212—2213,2224,2232—2234,2276,2307,2309—2311,2341—2342,2367,2404,2415,2420,2422—2423,2445

经济民族主义 0251,0255—0258,2167

经济主权 0013,0020,0029—0030,0035,0059—0061,0069,0081,0099,0122—0123,0322—0334,0578—0592,0593—0598,0626—0676,0677—0682,0794—0795,0840(fn.9),0870—0872,0905—0906,1313,1661—1666,2129,2141—2143,2157—2160,2224,2447

经济主权原则 0258,0578—0592,0593—0598,0626—0676,0677—0682,2157—2160,2447

民族虚无主义 0405—0406,0448—0453,0683—0705

弱小民族国家主权学说 0379—0577,2151

 超帝国主义 0476—0481

 僧侣主义 0487—0491

 沙文主义 0492—0493,0497—0500,0522—0555,0683—0705

最惠国待遇 0111(fn.4),0211—0212,0315,0323—0327,0605,0607,0782—0783,0875—0877,1497—1498,1549—1551,1636—1658,1673—1681,1700—1701,2311

左公柳 2119—2124

 罗家伦 2119—2122

 玉门出塞曲 2119—2122

左宗棠 2120—2121,2123—2124

后　　记

一、本书第六编所辑书评荟萃数十篇，虽然并非本书作者所撰，但均是对本书作者近四十年来学术理念和学术追求的积极呼应和同气相求，形成了对国际经济法学领域"中国特色话语"的共鸣强音，在国际论坛上对共同构建"中国特色国际经济法学理论新体系"，发挥了和发挥着积极的推动作用。把国内外高端同行学者所撰数十篇书评，荟萃辑入本书，以飨读者，冀能从一个侧面，证明国际经济法学领域的"中国特色话语"，确实是"友声四起，吾道不孤"；同时，也殷切期待从更多的国内外学者和读者之中，获得对"中国特色话语"更大的共鸣强音，共同参与构建"中国特色国际经济法学理论新体系"的"理论长征"，共同推动国际经济秩序和全球治理体系与时俱进的变革和创新。

二、把"大师评论"部分放在本书的开篇，旨在表达作者对他们（其中韩、朱两师均在百岁后离世，郭师也在92岁高龄后离世）的真诚谢忱、缅怀纪念和由衷敬意。

三、本书总篇幅多达290万字。读者乍读，恐难掌握全书概貌以及其中论述主线、脉络、重点。鉴此，把几篇"学者导言"放在本书开篇，可以对许多青年读者起到"导读"作用。

四、本书各编各章虽已融为一体，但各章仍然具有相对独立性，可以各自独立成篇。同时，本书各章撰写和发表时间前后跨度近四十年，各章论述主题常有承前启后、与时俱进、互相交叉、彼此渗透之处，为便于读者理解本书各章的论证逻辑和发展思路，有的后章必须适当复述或摘引前章部分内容。这样处理，也便于日后向国外输出版权、制作单篇"数字产品"、翻译、转载等等，酌情分割、剪裁，灵活使用。

五、本书第二编"国际经济法基本理论（二）"、第三编"国际投资法"和第四编"国际贸易法"各章中，含有作者对亲身经历的二十几个典型案件的理论剖析和是非臧否。在近四十年来的法律实务中，作者秉持公正公平原则，针对这些涉外经贸争端个案的处断，依法据理，祛邪扶正，分别以法学专家、兼职律师、涉外仲裁员的不同身份，撰文从理论上伸张正义，深入探讨相关的法理问题，提出创新见解，**维护司法公正**。在这些"弘扬獬豸精神、触不直者去之"的实录中，含有大量原始附件和确凿证据,限于本书篇幅,不得不割爱从略。有心**深入研究**这些典型案件的读者,不妨前往具体办案的司法机关和仲裁机关,查阅原始案卷文档。因为,其中"独角兽"所触而去之者,既有中外不法奸商,也有外国"权威"法官和"御用大律师",还有中国"权威"仲裁机构的高级仲裁员,另外还有个别见利忘义、泯灭良知的中国律师。显然,这些枉法裁断、亵渎法律尊严的行径和人员,都有待同道学友们**追踪研究,深入质疑,口诛笔伐,彻底批判**。

陈 安

2018 年 7 月 16 日